For Bob Ghee
with warm regards —

Fred J. Hansen

MIGHTY STONEWALL

TEXAS A&M UNIVERSITY
9
MILITARY HISTORY SERIES

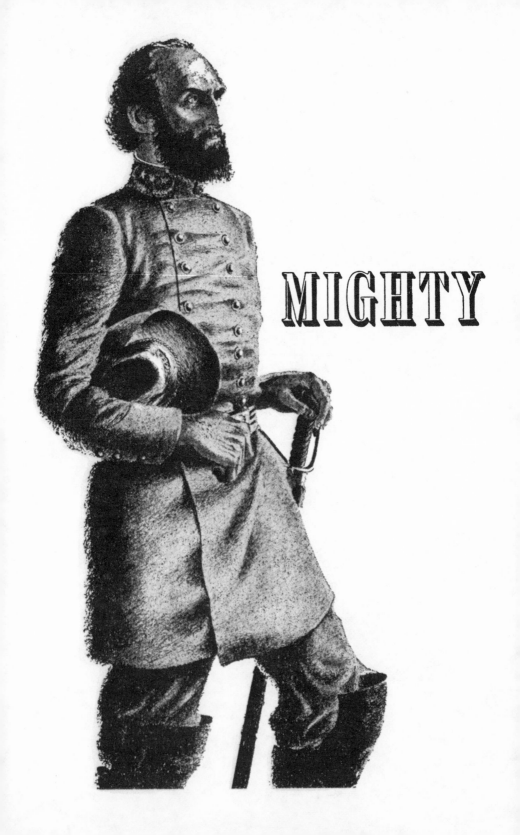

MIGHTY

FRANK E. VANDIVER

STONEWALL

TEXAS A&M UNIVERSITY PRESS
College Station

Library of Congress Cataloging-in-Publication Data

Vandiver, Frank Everson, 1925–
    Mighty Stonewall / Frank E. Vandiver.
        p.   cm. — (Texas A & M University military history series ; 9)
    Reprint. Originally published: New York : McGraw-Hill, 1957.
    Bibliography: p.
    Includes index.
    ISBN 0-89096-384-3 : $27.50. ISBN 0-89096-391-6 (pbk.) : $ 13.95
        1. Jackson, Stonewall, 1824–1863.   2. Generals — United States —
    Biography.   3. Confederate States of America. Army — Biography.
    4. United States — History — Civil War, 1861–1865 — Campaigns.
    I. Title.   II. Series.
    E467.1.J15V3   1989
    973.7′3′0924 — dc19
    [B]   88-9642
                                                                                 CIP

    Maps on pages 22 and 33 are from *The Story of the Mexican War*, by Robert S.
Henry, copyright 1950, used by special permission of the publishers, the Bobbs-
Merrill Company, Inc.
    Maps on pages 391 and 423 are adapted from *R. E. Lee*, Volume II, by Douglas
Southall Freeman, copyright 1934 by Charles Scribner's Sons; those on pages 473
and 490–491 from *Lee's Lieutenants*, Volumes II and III, by Douglas Southall Free-
man, copyright 1943 and 1944 by Charles Scribner's Sons. These and extracts from
Letters from Lee's Army, compiled by Susan Leigh Blackford, copyright 1947 by
Charles Scribner's Sons, are used by permission of the publishers.

Originally published in 1957 by McGraw-Hill Book Company, Inc.,
New York

Reprinted with the permission of McGraw-Hill Book Company in 1974
by Greenwood Press, a division of Williamhouse-Regency Inc.

Printed in the United States of America

IN MEMORY OF

DOUGLAS SOUTHALL FREEMAN

ACKNOWLEDGMENTS

LATE IN MARCH, 1953, I received a letter from the late Douglas Southall Freeman which started me on this life of Jackson. He thought it would be of some value to have a modern biography in print and so did the McGraw-Hill people. I jumped at the chance to undertake the project, and almost at the same moment suffered grave fears. What could be done to add to Henderson's splendid study and to Freeman's penetrating reappraisal of Jackson's military operations in *Lee's Lieutenants?* But I went ahead, intrigued by the enigma of Jackson. When I began research I had the idea that I would not like him at all, but this opinion suffered certain alterations in the course of work. I am indebted to Dr. Freeman not only for suggesting I do the book, but also for really introducing me to one of the most remarkable of all Civil War figures. My debt, of course, goes far beyond these things: Dr. Freeman was for years a constant source of inspiration, encouragement, and assistance. He was, to me, both hero and dear friend. In a small attempt at appreciation, I have respectfully dedicated this life of the "good soldier" to him.

No historical research could be accomplished without the untiring efforts of myriad library and archives staffs, and I wish here to express particular thanks to the following: The Rice Institute Library; Duke University Library; Southern Historical Collection, University of North Carolina Library; Division of Manuscripts, Library of Congress; Henry E. Huntington Library; the National Archives; Department of Archives, Louisiana State University; Confederate Memorial Hall; the Confederate Museum; Virginia Historical Society; Virginia Military Institute Library; Washington and Lee University Library; William and Mary College Library; Rare Books Collections, The University of Texas; Washington University Library (St. Louis); Virginia State Library; Southern Methodist University Library; Division of Rare Books and Manuscripts, University of Virginia Library; Confederate Memorial Institute.

Numbers of people gave freely of their time in finding material, putting me straight on matters of interpretation, and listening while I "talked out" the project. My especial thanks go to William H. Masterson and William H. Nelson (two long-suffering colleagues), Dr. Fannie E. Ratchford, Dr. J. Preston Moore, Dr. Edwin A. Davis, Mr. William B. Ruggles, Mr. James I. Robertson (who carefully checked a valuable manuscript collection for me), Mr. and Mrs. William D. Koons, and Mr. Charles Craig (who drew the maps).

Colonel William Couper, Lexington, Virginia, gave complete access to his prodigious collection of Jackson material, even to the point of allowing me to borrow most of it for an unconscionable period. His clear understanding of Jackson's professional life, his deep knowledge of Jackson material, and his constant encouragement were an aid beyond expression. I can only thank him for giving so freely of his time and genial hospitality.

Mr. Roy Bird Cook, Charleston, West Virginia, long a student of Jackson's early life, placed me deeply in his debt by showing me certain of his extremely valuable Jackson manuscripts and for making available his indispensable book, titled *The Family and Early Life of Stonewall Jackson.*

I cannot adequately express my gratitude to Mrs. Douglas Southall Freeman and to Mrs. Mary Wells Ashworth, both of whom sustained me through many despondent moments with their enthusiasm for the project and with their affectionate exhortations.

Two friends performed a service above and beyond the call of duty—they read the whole manuscript with critically constructive eyes. I am permanently obliged to Dr. Wendell Holmes Stephenson and Dr. T. Harry Williams, who not only surrendered a great portion of last summer to the chore of reading the rough draft but who also contributed valuable suggestions for improvement.

My wife, Susie, has long feared that she might appear in an acknowledgments section as the chief cause of some work not being finished earlier. I cannot, in this case, gratify her expectations. Susie and her mother, Mrs. Alex P. Smith of Dallas, edited, typed, and listened tirelessly during nine solid months of composition. They worked harder on styling, shaping, and typing the manuscript than I did—so all I can say is that without them the book would have probably never been finished.

This section would be woefully incomplete without an expression of deep gratitude to the John Simon Guggenheim Memorial Foundation for a fellowship which has made much of the writing possible. A great deal of the research is the result of two grants from the American Philosophical Society, and a research grant from the Special Research Fund of the Graduate School of Arts and Sciences, Washington University. Rice Institute has made extensive travel possible and, through a remarkable typing service, arranged to have the final draft made ready for the publisher.

FRANK E. VANDIVER

The Rice Institute

CONTENTS

1   "You May Be Whatever You Resolve to Be"   1
2   A Taste of Fame in Mexico   19
3   "From the Path of Eternal Death . . ."   45
4   Major Jackson's Florida Campaign   56
5   Alias Old Hickory   71
6   Ellie   83
7   A House with Golden Hinges   105
8   "An Able, Fearless Soldier"   133
9   Return of a Valley Man   165
10 "If This Valley Is Lost, Virginia Is Lost"   197
11 "God Blessed Our Arms with Victory"   221
12 "A Question of Legs"   245
13 "Jackson Is Coming"   284
14 Victory Wins an Opportunity   323
15 "Disaster and Shame Lurk in the Rear"   353
16 "The Indomitable Jackson"   372
17 The Second Corps   401
18 Headquarters, Moss Neck   433
19 "Duty Is Ours, Consequences Are God's"   455

    Notes   495
    Bibliography   532
    Index   537

ILLUSTRATIONS

PHOTOGRAPHS

Laura Jackson Arnold   *following page* 244
Mary Anna Morrison
Thomas Jonathan Jackson
Harpers Ferry
General Jubal Early
General Richard S. Ewell
Battlefield at Cedar Mountain
White Oak Swamp
Jackson's men at Manassas Junction
General Ambrose E. Burnside
The bridge at Antietam Creek
Jackson two weeks before his death

MAPS

Mexico in outline   *page* 22
Approaches to Mexico City   33
Vicinity of Harpers Ferry   135
Battle of First Manassas   157
Area of the Romney Expedition   187
Battlefield of Kernstown   206
The Shenandoah Valley   211
Vicinity of Port Republic   271
Area of the Seven Days' Battles   297
Area of Cedar Mountain   340
Campaign of Second Manassas   363
Confederate positions in the Battle of Sharpsburg   391
Confederate positions at Fredericksburg   423
Terrain and roads surrounding Chancellorsville   461
Area of Confederate attack at Chancellorsville   473
Theater of war in Virginia   490–491

xi

1

"YOU MAY BE WHATEVER

YOU RESOLVE TO BE"

—JACKSON

He became one of the Great Captains, famed not only in his own embattled Confederacy but also in the land of his enemies and far beyond foreign seas. He came to epitomize the good and the virtue of what was finally a lost cause, and people would say that had he lived the cause might have fared differently. But death struck him down at the height of a military fame enjoyed by no other Civil War figure, struck him down at the high point of Confederate success. After he passed from the stage, the Southern armies began a long retreat on a road that led downhill and inexorably toward that poignant day at Appomattox in 1865. All the bright hopes of 1861, the brilliant successes of 1862 and 1863, were tarnished then and dead. Still, the example of Stonewall Jackson, his devotion to God, to duty, and to country, burned bright, undimmed by a long succession of missed opportunities and by lost campaigns and wasted lives. The shade of Stonewall Jackson buoyed up the thin gray lines who had fought under him and fought for his side, and that same shade haunted the enemy until the last shot had echoed across the rolling hills near the courthouse where Lee and Grant had their fateful meeting.

Stonewall Jackson rose from uncomfortable obscurity to be a people's hero, a nation's shining hope. He proved a hero who never failed. As he led "that incomparable infantry" through victory after victory, Jackson's fame increased. His nobility of character, his unaffected piety, his strange personal habits—all these things became the treasured possessions of the Southern people. Finally they would become the heritage of America and the world.

Deeds he did were touched with history, but around Jackson there clung none of the traditional pose of fame. He was a mountain man, and he had the blunt honesty, the firmness, and the self-reliance of a frontiersman from the remote western parts of Virginia.

His home town was Clarksburg, a small, roughhewn frontier settlement with large hopes for the future. In the early nineteenth century the town had some claim to commercial importance because of its location in the upper Monongahela country. Settlers had gradually increased the population and a rustic sort of society had begun to flourish—not a society like that of the distant, standoffish Tidewater, but a society resting easily on friends, hard work, and a good, spare Protestant faith. Clarksburg's citizens were proud of their town, and pointed to the fact that they and their ancestors had fought for the land, had hacked down a wilderness to plant their crops, and had built a firm foundation for life west of the Alleghenies.

Thomas Jonathan Jackson's father had been one who saw something of the future written in Clarksburg's muddy streets and sprawling houses, and he had determined to settle there as soon as he gained sufficient knowledge of the law to hang out his shingle. Jonathan Jackson's winning personality and devotion to his studies gained him numbers of friends, and after he had been admitted to the Harrison County bar in 1810, he had been given the job of Federal Collector of the Internal Revenue for the district of Western Virginia. But his interest lay in practicing law, and he decided to resign the collectorship as soon as he had saved enough money for the move to Clarksburg.

Barrister Jackson had still another reason for wanting money. When, some time before, he had attended the Male Academy in nearby Parkersburg, a pretty, brown-haired, gray-eyed girl whose home was in that city had captured his undying devotion. Julia Beckwith Neale came of good family and had the uncommon advantage of education. She accepted young Jackson's proposal; the wedding took place in Parkersburg on September 28, 1817, and the newlyweds traveled to Clarksburg. Lawyer Jackson built a three-room brick cottage for his bride, began his law practice, and settled down to become a loyal citizen. People liked the sort of faith in the future that the Jacksons showed, and soon the newcomers were numbered among the most popular families in town. The law business prospered and expanded—so, too, the family.[1]

A daughter, Elizabeth, was born in 1819. She was followed in January, 1821, by brother Warren and on January 21, 1824, by a second brother, Thomas, named for his mother's father, Thomas Neale.[2] Laura Ann, last of the Jackson children, was born on March 27, 1826. Everything went well for the family in Clarksburg. Jonathan Jackson's circle of friends grew rapidly and his reputation kept pace. He served a stint in the military during the unpleasantness with the British in 1812, but the cavalry company which he and some of his friends formed did not receive a call to service.[3] Military fellowship gave way to brotherhood as soon as Herman Lodge, Ancient Free and Accepted Masons, began organizing in Clarksburg in 1814. Jackson, his family doctor James McCally, and some distant Jackson relations served as the first officers. Probably young Jackson could have had a political career had he desired it, for Clarksburg showed intense interest in Richmond politics.[4]

But Jonathan Jackson kept his eye fixed on his main goal, success in the law. Turning his full attention to the chancery courts, he soon gained local renown for winning his cases and his clientele multiplied. One personal characteristic may have aided in winning friends and increasing the number of clients—generosity. Jackson proved far too generous for his own good in a town where banks were not yet strong or trusted. Clarksburg's trade generally rested on credit, and a lawyer of good repute was sought after as an endorser of notes. Jackson could never say no; he cosigned dozens of notes. All those who asked him were friends, they were men of honor, and Jackson felt he had taken no risk. Such faith may have been justified and probably he would have made money on all these ventures had it not been for typhoid fever.[5]

Early in 1826 Clarksburg reeled under the impact of this dread disease and in March Elizabeth, the Jacksons' eldest child, came down with the fever. Her father hovered over her, frantically trying to nurse her back to health. Clearly the battle could not be won, but he kept at it until he, too, contracted the fever. Before the month had ended both father and daughter were dead.[6] Julia Jackson, anguished by the illness of her child and her husband, had been completely unable to help them because of a well-advanced pregnancy. The shock of her double loss probably brought on the birth of Laura Ann on March 27. Julia, now the Widow Jackson, found herself left with a new baby and the two boys, Warren and Thomas.

There were no family resources—Jonathan's unhappy facility for backing long-term investments had left the family without a penny. Fortunately the children were too small to comprehend the stark fact of pauperism. Had it not been for the local Masonic Lodge Julia and the children might well have been thrown out in the street. As it was, Jonathan's fellow Masons banded together to care for his family, fed them, and, since their home on Main Street had to be sold, provided a new house for the Jacksons. Small it was, a sparse little cottage, but a house soon became a home.

Julia made it a home by refusing to give up or to waste time pitying herself. Some of the stern stuff the Jacksons and the Neales had in them came to her rescue. Both sides of the family offered to help, but Julia would not rely on charity. She would hold her family together by her own endeavor, she would sew for ladies of the town, she would do anything which might bring in money and preserve independence. Some of Clarksburg's citizens remembered her as a woman of education and reminded her that the community sorely needed a new school. Julia happily became the local schoolmarm and did well in her new role, for by 1828 she had hoarded sufficient capital to buy a small cottage in Clarksburg. Whether she moved the family there is not recorded, but she did rely on it as a source of support for the children in case of further disaster to the family, and she left this bit of property in trust for Laura just before she gave up her school to marry for a second time.

Frontier communities scorned an unmarried man and consequently put a premium on marriageable ladies, who always were a scarce commodity. Widows did not usually remain so for long, and Widow Jackson, still young and pretty, had been expected to marry again. But some of her friends began to whisper that she ought not pay so much attention to Capt. Blake B. Woodson. Not that he was beneath her—he was not. Like her first husband, Woodson practiced law in Clarksburg and had a reputation as a man of "good education, and of social, popular manners." [7] It did seem unfortunate, though, that Widow Jackson should marry a man so impecunious as Captain Woodson—particularly when he seemed so "much her senior." [8]

Local gossip sold Woodson somewhat short. He had hopes of success now that a new county, Fayette, had begun organization. Friends had secured him the post of county clerk there, and shortly after he and Julia were married in early November, 1830, they moved from Clarksburg to a rude little southwestern settlement now called Ansted. Here the Woodsons found none of the metropolitan conveniences they had just left; they found few, if any, friends and realized quickly that they were stuck off in a remote backwater, far removed from everything. The isolation might have been more bearable had the family been able to stay together. But Julia's health grew delicate and her infirmity, combined with the slim financial resources of the Woodsons, forced them to farm out the children. Warren had to be packed off to his Uncle Alfred Neale in faraway Parkersburg on the Ohio River. Laura and Thomas, who had come to Fayette County after their mother found a house in Ansted, stayed on for a time,[9] but tradition has it that soon both of them were sent to the care of their grandmother, Edward Jackson's widow, who lived at Jackson's Mill, about four miles north of Weston, Virginia. Thomas resisted the separation, and left only on the pleadings of his mother.

A scant few months after the two arrived at their grandmother's word came of their mother's desperate illness. She had declined rapidly following the birth of a son, Wirt Woodson, and with little time left she wanted to see all her children. Instantly Laura and Thomas were sent back to Fayette County in the trusty care of "Uncle" Robinson, a beloved family servant, and arrived at their mother's bedside in time to receive her dying blessing and prayers. Devout, she prayed fervently for Providence to watch over her orphaned family. The six-year-old Tom never forgot the scene, and that last meeting left him with a deep and idealized love for his mother.[10]

Julia Jackson Woodson died in October, 1831,[11] and Captain Woodson could not afford to keep the children with him—and even had he been financially able to support them, his death in May, 1833, would have cast them out once again. After a brief sojourn with some acquaintances at Gauley Bridge, fortune for once smiled on Tom and Laura. They were taken into the household of Uncle Cummins Jackson, an indulgent relative with a great love for children.[12] He took them to the old home place in Lewis County, where again they came under the light, but doubtless beneficial, discipline of their grandmother.

Here they were happy and here they knew something of real home life. Laura, a pretty child with a bright, winning disposition, soon had captivated the houseful of bachelor uncles. Thomas, a rosy-cheeked six-year-old, became the particular pet of Uncle Cummins. The boy had good blue eyes, an earnest, slightly wistful little face, topped by boyish, waving brown hair. He would not be a large man when grown, but of moderate size and probably fairly sturdy. The most interesting thing about him was his quiet curiosity which reflected an inquiring mind developed far beyond his years.[13] One thing had to be watched, though, as he grew. He had a stubborn streak which seemed well-nigh unbreakable. It showed only when Tom felt some injustice had been done or when someone tried to make him do something he felt to be wrong, but it might develop into a serious defect.

Life was almost too happy at Jackson's Mill. Family misfortune struck again. Grandmother Jackson died in August, 1835, leaving behind her a desolated household, thrown into complete chaos. A maiden aunt [14] who had been at home when the children first came had married, and so a band of bachelors had to run the family and care for the children. Soon it had been decided that such an environment would not be best for the orphans, particularly for young Laura. She, at least, should be sent to the care of other relatives. Mounted behind her Aunt Rebecca White, Laura rode all the way to the little settlement of Bellsville, near Parkersburg, and there she at last found a loving, lasting home. The only bad thing about the change was that she had to leave Thomas.

Reluctantly the uncles concluded that Tom, too, should be sent to a more normal home, and his Aunt Polly—Mrs. Isaac Brake—and her husband, who lived in Harrison County, near Clarksburg, offered to take him. Somehow things did not work out. What happened is not clear—perhaps his Uncle Brake made Thomas and Cousin William work too hard, even on Sunday [15]—but whatever went wrong, it drove Thomas to an important decision. After he had seriously thought through his problem, Tom decided he must leave the Brake home. Next day, according to family tradition, he appeared at the house of some Clarksburg relatives. After he told them his troubles he was advised that he ought to go back. "Maybe I ought to, ma'am," came the firm answer, "but I am not going to." To other relations in town who heard his story he said the same thing: "No; Uncle Brake and I can't agree; I have quit, and shall not go back any more." [16] And although some thought he would soon forget his childish whim, Tom stuck by his decision. Once having made up his mind what he must do, he did it. From Clarksburg he walked to Jackson's Mill and the hospitable hearth of Uncle Cummins.[17] Whatever his uncle may have thought about Tom's running away, he joyously took his young nephew in and made a permanent place for him. Twelve of Tom's happiest years were spent at Jackson's Mill.[18]

At Uncle Cummins's, in the midst of several other jovial uncles, Thomas reveled in the only real home life he had known. Later, when he chafed under the rigors of cadet life at West Point, he would write Laura that

> times are far different from what they were when I was at my adopted home; none to give their mandates; none for me to obey but as I chose; surrounded by my playmates and relatives, all apparently eager to promote my happiness; but those were the days of my youth; they have been succeeded by days of quite a different aspect; manhood with all its cares.[19]

Under Uncle Cummins's fond eye Tom Jackson formed a firm attachment to the family and to a home place. There it was that the orphan developed a depth of feeling about home and relatives.

Cummins E. Jackson could not take the place of Tom's father, and wisely does not seem to have tried. But he loved Tom, and showed it by the kind, light rein he used in raising him. Perhaps Cummins early realized that his nephew could be reasoned with but not ordered about without reason. At any rate Uncle Cummins proved a fine influence, despite later legends about his sinful ways and about how he might easily have ruined Tom's morals.

When Tom came to live at Jackson's Mill, Cummins Jackson had already amassed considerable means and had earned a good reputation in western Virginia. A man with tolerably large landholdings, he operated a saw and gristmill and worked hard at expanding his wealth and possessions. In his early thirties, Cummins was a strongly built two-hundred-pounder, with large and piercing blue-gray eyes, and of a six-foot-two size which forced him to stoop when he went through a doorway. Like many big men, he was hardy and well-met.[20] But he understood the streak of shyness which sometimes tied Tom's tongue and confused him in conversation. Tom had to get his thoughts straight before committing himself. When he talked, he had something to say.

Cummins worried about his nephew's health as months passed and Tom did not grow as expected. At times he complained of a vague sort of dyspepsia which appeared to cut his appetite. Exercise was suggested for what seems to have been a type of nervous indigestion. There could have been no better place to carry out the prescription than at Jackson's Mill. Like most men in that part of the country, Cummins loved the outdoors and outdoor sports. He had the means to indulge an interest in horse racing, and before long he had Tom serving as a jockey in a few local races. Although this was supposedly a bad influence on the lad, Tom enjoyed the assignments, and worked hard, albeit unsuccessfully, at mastering the art of graceful riding. No matter how he tried, he never looked at home in a saddle.

Tom helped with most of the farm chores and discharged his trusts so faithfully that he worked his way into a sort of junior partnership with Uncle Cummins. Frequently he assumed charge of a small slave crew sent into the woodland to cut timber for the Jackson sawmill—and even at that early age he appeared to have no trouble managing people.

The rustic, simple life worked wonders for Thomas's health and he grew stronger with the years, although never able to throw off completely his amorphous stomach malady. He grew stronger in other ways, too. Watching his uncles in their business dealings and in their relations with employees taught Tom valuable lessons in Western morality, drilled into him the idea that when a man gave his word it was taken as his bond.[21] A man's word was as precious to him as his independence—shorn of his honor he had nothing.

Honesty was a Jackson family trait which young Tom inherited in extra measure. It had something to do with what his mother expected of him and with how he ought to represent the family, now that there were only two boys left. It also had something to do with the man in the making. Tom could not have been anything but honest, and that it surprised others surprised him. But even in an essentially honest country Tom amounted to a surprise.

Stories of how far he carried honesty grew in direct proportion to his later fame, but not all of them were fabrications. Here is one such story.

He had been fishing in the West Fork of the Monongahela, one of his favorite spots. He hauled up a striking three-foot pike, admired it, threw it over his shoulder, and started for the nearby town of Weston. At the time he was trying to make a business of fishing and he had a standing deal with Conrad Kester, the local gunsmith, to furnish fish of a certain size for a certain price. On the way to town he passed the home of Col. John Talbott, and the colonel, who knew the young fisherman well, called out: "Tom, that is a fine fish you have there; what will you take for it?"

"This fish is sold, Colonel Talbott."

"I'll give you a dollar for it, Tom."

"I can't take it, Colonel Talbott; this fish is sold to Mr. Kester."

"But, Tom," the colonel protested, "I will give you a dollar and a quarter; surely he will not give you more than that."

Earnestly Tom stuck to his point. "Colonel Talbott, I have an agreement with Mr. Kester to furnish him fish of a certain length for fifty cents each. He has taken some from me a little shorter than that; now he is going to get this big fish for fifty cents."

Kester, according to the tale, offered to give a dollar for the prize catch, but the youthful contractor would not accept a cent more than the agreed amount. Some things were matters of honor.[22]

Many people seemed to think that because of his shy manner and his exaggerated sense of fair play Thomas would be a dull, antisocial companion. On the contrary, those who knew him well enough to see behind the outward wall of courteous aloofness found him a good talker, interested in all kinds of activities, including house raisings, fiddle playing (at which he did not excel), logrollings, and all types of parties. Shyness hurt him in one important respect—it sadly retarded his progress with girls. Diffident to the freezing point in their presence, Tom became the butt of many a joke. But some girls liked him despite his silence. His courtly manners and his abject deference to every female wish and whim won the amused affection of a few local girls, who liked, too, his swift protection of feminine honor. On one occasion he attacked a huge town bully who had been pestering two of Tom's "female acquaintances," and although sadly outweighed he won the battle.[23]

Though he played a great deal and enjoyed a variety of games,[24] Tom had a more serious turn of mind than most of his young friends. His unflagging desire to learn pleased his uncles,[25] and Cummins prevailed on Robert P. Ray, a citizen with more than average education, to conduct a private school near the Jackson home. Here Thomas first attended formal classes, and later he went to a country school a little distance away at a place called McCann's Run. Once immersed in the world of knowledge he was lost. From then on his great ambition was more and more education. Learning did not come easy—Tom found he had a slow mind and that he had to go over and over the same material before he could fully understand it. One of his teachers later wrote that "he was not what is now termed brilliant, but he was one of those untiring matter-of-fact persons who never would give up an undertaking until he accomplished his object. He learned slowly, but what he got in his head he never forgot." [26]

One time only did it seem that Tom might be lured from the path of learning. The instrument was his older brother, Warren, who came to Jackson's Mill in the fall of 1836 to visit Thomas. Warren had become a glamorous, successful figure. He had obtained so much education that he had opened a school in Upshur County and had become a respected man of learning. Thomas idolized him and listened eagerly as Warren proposed that the two brothers go to Uncle Alfred Neale's, where Laura now lived. Nothing could have pleased Tom more—he had not seen Laura for far too long a time and he had missed her. Then, too, he would have a chance to travel with his big brother.

The brothers arrived at their Uncle Alfred's near Parkersburg, had a wild joyous reunion with pretty sister Laura, and heard the family gossip. Soon after they arrived they heard that numbers of people were making vast sums of money by cutting wood on the river islands for sale to passing steamboats. Off they went downriver, in search of a wood-covered island and a fortune. The Ohio offered no suitable islands and finally the boys went on to the Mississippi. Here they found wood all right, but no fortune. After what appear to have been somewhat desperate experiences the brothers returned to Parkersburg in February, 1837, each sporting a new trunk as the result of their adventure. They maintained a lofty silence about their travels into the world of business, and no amount of family joking could prod them into a recital of their troubles. Home they would go, they said, and since they had to travel on foot they parted with their trunks—Tom gave his to Laura, and Warren's went to half-brother Wirt Woodson, who lived now with the Neales.

Warren went back to his school and Tom returned to Uncle Cummins's, somewhat the worse for wear. He had contracted some type of ague during the river venture, as had Warren, and it is possible that sustained exposure on a wind-swept Mississippi island precipitated Warren's death from consumption three years later. When he died Warren was nineteen and the light of Thomas's life; after his death Thomas would stand alone as the male survivor of the Jackson family. Tom threw off the effects of ague, but found soon after he returned from the Neales' that his long-standing stomach ailment had not visibly improved.[27]

Uncle Cummins understandingly said little about the trip, received his junior partner back with pleasure, and introduced him to a new and most interesting job, that of engineering assistant with the Parkersburg and Staunton Turnpike Company, engaged in building the long-delayed main road toward far western Virginia. Tom soon became fascinated by engineering problems and instruments and proved good at his various tasks. He had to study hard to master the methods of road building, but he learned something of terrain. With the end of summer Tom resigned and went back to school.

Studies went so well that the sixteen-year-old youth was persuaded to follow in brother Warren's footsteps and teach school himself. The school was supported by the Virginia "Literary Fund," which helped families without money to send their children to private schools. Some of the pupils may not have been of the highest quality, the building may not have been the best, but Schoolmaster Jackson did a creditable job [28] during the two terms he taught. Inadequate he doubtless felt, and he struggled with his lessons twice as hard as any of the would-be scholars under his charge. The more he taught, the more he wanted to go to college, where he firmly believed a man could learn "how to work his head." [29]

Young Tom's natural curiosity expanded as he broadened his knowledge, and by 1840 his inquiries extended beyond the classroom. Religious matters caught his interest—despite the allegedly secular influence of Uncle Cummins—and soon the earnest young man became a familiar figure in church. A daughter of one of the local Methodist ministers wrote that on several Sundays "Thomas Jackson, a shy, unobtrusive boy, sat with unabated interest in a long sermon, having walked three miles in order to attend." [30] Tom's concern with spiritual affairs extended beyond formal churchgoing. Christianity he must study carefully so that he could share fully in its joys and duties. He began to read the Bible and soon became something of a Biblical scholar.

Religion opened a whole new world for young Jackson, and although careful never to force his views on anyone, he gladly would read the Scriptures or discuss theological matters if asked. In return for Tom's Scriptural instruction and the loan of his Bible, Joe Lightburn, one of Tom's best friends, gave his highly prized copy of Parson Weems's *Life of Francis Marion*. The two boys must have been vastly influenced by the Bible and by the Swamp Fox. Both rose to be generals on opposite sides during the Civil War; Lightburn became a Baptist minister after the war, and Jackson thought about going into the ministry before the war. [31] He talked of the ministry, and it appears that his deficiency in education and a fear of public speaking were all that kept him from this calling. There is little doubt that Tom's interest in religion began much earlier in life than is generally supposed.

Little time could be wasted in regret over missing the ministry, for Uncle Cummins had another task for his young nephew. A friend of Cummins—one of Tom's former teachers—suggested that his erstwhile pupil be considered for a constable's job in the Freeman Creek District of Lewis County. Some said the boy was too young for such a responsible office, but Cummins Jackson and others decided to support him. The office would do Tom good—it would give him some money, and the outdoor life which the duties required ought to stiffen the young man's constitution.

On June 11, 1841, Thomas Jackson, age seventeen, took the oath of office and was sworn in as constable.[32] Constabulary duty involved for the most part rather unpleasant efforts to collect small overdue debts, the sort of thing for which a man of more maturity would seem better suited. But Tom Jackson did his job well and soon became adept at serving processes and at finding reluctant debtors. The outdoor activity of his year-long career improved his physical condition, and the daily problems of a public servant gave him more poise and self-reliance.

Sometimes considerable ingenuity was required to force the payment of an old bill. One story has come down from this period which illustrates not only Tom's developing resourcefulness but also that dogged determination which would become one of his most famous characteristics.

A local man had been avoiding payment of a small debt to a widowed lady of Weston; exasperated, she sent the constable to collect. Jackson had trouble finding the man and more trouble extracting the money. Finally he determined to put a lien on some of the debtor's personal property. The most logical thing to mortgage would be the man's horse —without transportation he could hardly conduct his business. But it was common knowledge that a man's horse was inviolate as long as the owner occupied the saddle. The strategic objective could be easily seen: remove the owner from his saddle. How to do this would be a matter of tactics.

Tactics, sometimes, are fashioned by opportunity. Jackson was standing one day near the entrance to a Weston livery stable when he saw the lagging debtor ride up. Ducking back into the shadows, the constable waited until the rider dismounted, then reached out, grabbed the reins, and made his levy on the animal. No sooner did he see Jackson than the owner leaped back on his horse—theoretically restoring possession. But Jackson would not be stopped in the midst of doing his duty. Holding tight the reins, he led the horse toward the livery stable door. All the while the owner lashed the grimly determined constable with his whip. Straight toward the low-beamed entrance Jackson pulled the horse, and finally the rider had to dismount or be unceremoniously unhorsed. Instantly Tom seized the animal and the bill was paid. This and similar accomplishments soon earned the earnest and dutiful constable an appreciative following.

For all his hard work Tom soon realized he was underpaid, but the position did offer a fairly steady income and considerable experience. He learned something about himself during these months of collecting: he could do whatever he resolved to do. Citizens of Weston and Lewis

County learned something about Tom too—that his oath of office was a solemn obligation to be fulfilled to the letter—it was something about which he had given his word.[33]

During his last weeks in office a sudden, vastly important change occurred in his career which forced him to lay aside the duties of constable. So abruptly did Tom lay them aside that there was some dissatisfaction expressed by a few citizens. But soon his accounts were settled to everyone's satisfaction and he was free to take advantage of a rare and glittering opportunity. There might be a chance for him to obtain an advanced education. He would have to work, but he had never been a stranger to work. In addition, he needed lots of luck and all the good will he could muster.

Good will, added to his record of honesty and steady self-improvement, had qualified young Jackson as a candidate for an appointment to the United States Military Academy at West Point, New York. In the spring of 1842 Weston's local Congressman, Samuel L. Hays, had an Academy vacancy to fill from his district. Several applicants for the appointment appeared—so many, in fact, that a runoff examination became necessary. The examination eliminated Tom Jackson, whose deficiency in mathematics exceeded that of the successful candidate.

On April 19, 1842, Gibson J. Butcher was conditionally appointed to the Military Academy from Lewis County, Virginia. Weston people knew Butcher as an "orphan youth of good character and ambitious," whose family had been more or less prominent. As a student he had no reputation, and some may have suggested that his passing the examination resulted more from a close friendship with the chief examiner's daughter than from any great scholarly ability.[34] Whatever the means, he won the appointment. But life at the Military Academy came as a complete surprise to him, and as he later said: "After seeing the movements and learning the duties which I had to perform I came to the conclusion that I never could consent to live the life. I did not know as much about the institution when I applied for the appointment as I know now."[35]

The grimness of West Point appears to have so rattled Butcher that he decamped for western Virginia without even informing the superintendent. On the way back home he stopped at Cummins Jackson's and told all that had happened to him. Sad, indeed, but Butcher's retreat meant another chance, and Tom pitched in to get the vacated cadetship. He would need help.

Seeking out Matthew Edmiston, an attorney friend who had helped him prepare for the ill-fated runoff examination, Thomas asked for more coaching. Captain George Jackson, the previous chief examiner, consented to support Tom now that his future son-in-law had given up. Jonathan M. Bennett, "a talented and influential friend and connection," [36] asked the most embarrassing question when Thomas sought his aid in obtaining the appointment. Did Tom think his educational background good enough to sustain him if he received the appointment? With a chance to realize a cherished ambition, the reply came candid and determined: "I am very ignorant but I can make it up in study. I know I have the energy and I think I have the intellect." [37]

Tom's firm convictions were good enough for his friends—they wrote Congressman Hays recommending Thomas's appointment. Uncle Cummins doubtless had a prominent part in getting Hays's support, since the Congressman was partially indebted to Cummins for his Congressional seat.

Go at once to Washington, friends advised Tom—take along all the letters of recommendation and present them in person to Hays. Since the Academy entrance examinations were about to be given, it would be best if Jackson were in the vicinity of the Point in case he won the cadetship. Now that there seemed hope of success, Tom wasted no time starting his venture.

He got to Washington on June 17, 1842. Presenting himself at once to Congressman Hays, Thomas delivered his letters of recommendation and petitions in his behalf (all of which attested to his high character, firm determination, and sketchy educational background) and hoped for the best. The papers, plus a letter from Hays asking Jackson's selection, went to Secretary of War John C. Spencer. An anxious, nerve-racking wait ended on June 19, when the Secretary formally appointed Jackson a cadet.[38] Hays asked his young protégé to remain for a few days of sightseeing, but Thomas wanted to get on to West Point where the entrance examinations awaited him. He lingered in Washington just long enough to climb to the top of the unfinished capitol building for a look at the sprawling town and at the Virginia hills across the river —where, if he looked in the right direction, he could see the home of another West Pointer, Robert E. Lee. There was no time for a formal tour; he had other things to do. The most accepted route to the Military Academy from Washington was via New York City and then by boat up the Hudson. On June 20, he reached his destination.[39]

A late-comer received more than usual notice, and Jackson's solitary entrance into Academy life attracted some attention. He was, in a way, hard to miss. There was no pretense about him; he made no effort to be something he was not. So he came as he was—dressed in the best gray homespun Uncle Cummins could provide, a pair of weatherbeaten saddlebags slung over his shoulders. In keeping with his recent constabulary office, Thomas wore a large, coarse felt hat—and this gave him a somewhat ludicrous look. Casual observers noticed that the new man stood about five feet ten and that he had no particularly striking features, save a pair of grave blue eyes peering from under the absurd hat. He had a high forehead, well-cut features, a small, firm mouth, and a complexion betraying much exposure to the outdoors—all crowned by a mop of waving brown hair, revealed when the hat came off. He seemed a typical rube. His awkward, angular, ground-covering carriage, his large hands and monstrous feet, coupled with a mannerism of walking rapidly, head bent forward, made him appear the prototype of all bumpkin farmers.

Three other plebes saw him come into the barracks. They were aspiring to be officers and gentlemen, and at least one was shocked at the backwoodsy appearance of the new cadet. But all three—Birket Fry, Ambrose Powell Hill, and Dabney Herndon Maury—noticed Jackson's look of grim determination. Maury remarked: "That fellow looks as if he had come to stay," and as soon as he discovered that Jackson was a fellow Virginian, Maury introduced himself and offered help. And here he first encountered the stiff shyness of his classmate. As Maury recalled it, Jackson "received me so coldly that I regretted my friendly overture, and rejoined my companions, rebuffed and discomfited." [40] Maury probably shrugged off the slight with the thought that this new man lacked Tidewater polish, but Jackson, under the strain of his new environment, was merely more diffident than usual. The entrance examinations were hanging over his head—they might well send him home—and he could think of little else. If they were too tough he had constructed a speech which he would reel off to those around Weston who scoffed: "If *they* had been there, and found it as hard as [I] did, they would have failed too." [41]

But he passed,[42] and no sooner had that horror been put behind him than Cadet Jackson found his new life had begun in stark earnest. If he expected to be immediately introduced to higher learning, he was disappointed. The practice at the Point was to send the plebes out to summer encampment on the famous Academy plain, and there, until the end of August, Jackson spent his time attaining a "soldierly bearing" and learning the rudiments of drill and discipline. It was a crude introduction to a new life: flimsy tents, extremes of heat and rain, and sleeping on bare earth. No one had time for anything save disgust and homesickness.

That was an interesting feeling for Tom—homesickness. An orphan boy with no real homestead, Jackson had a stronger case of this common camp complaint than most others, a case that lingered for two full years.[43] He missed Laura, Uncle Cummins, and his other relatives and friends, missed them the more, perhaps, for all the years of casting about until he settled in his foster home. Home and friends had something to do with his determination to succeed at the Point. Weston had already been disappointed once by a would-be cadet; Tom Jackson would not disappoint the town a second time. Then, too, he was determined to use this opportunity to make something of himself. When he was determined, he was hard to stop.

Once academic instruction began, Thomas found it difficult to stay in school. His poor background and his slowness in learning seriously retarded him. Dogged study seemed the only answer to deficient training. When he did not absorb a day's lesson, Cadet Jackson stayed with it until he had it mastered. Consequently, he lagged behind in class recitations, and the farther behind he got the more anguished were his classroom confessions that he had come "unprepared" for that day's work. The first semester at West Point proved a hideous ordeal.

Surrounded by boys who had much more education, hampered by what he thought to be a poor memory [44] and a slow mind, tortured by the daily demand to recite, Jackson stuck out the weeks and months. The agony of going to the board and of answering questions brought the sweat out of him in such volume that his classmates were sure "the General" (a nickname in honor of Andrew Jackson) would flood the room.[45] Many things of heroic cast he later did, but none could surpass his first year at West Point as an example of sheer force of will.

Determination brought success. At the end of the first year, in a class of seventy-two, Jackson stood seventieth in French, forty-fifth in mathematics, and fifty-first in general merit and had picked up fifteen demerits for lapses in conduct.

Demerits were to decrease as Jackson's career at the Academy continued. His academic record improved, too. By the end of the second year he stood eighteenth in mathematics, fifty-second in French, sixty-eighth in drawing, fifty-fifth in engineering, was thirteenth in general merit and had incurred twenty-six demerits. By the end of the third year he was ranked eleventh in natural philosophy, twenty-fifth in chemistry, fifty-ninth in drawing, twentieth in general merit and had not a single demerit. At the end of his final year he had reached fifth in ethics (his favorite course),[46] twelfth in engineering, eleventh in artillery, twenty-first in infantry tactics, eleventh in mineralogy and geology, had seven demerits, and stood seventeenth in graduating rank. This last standing included all of his past years at the Academy, including the bad first one. Apparently his later sister-in-law was right in saying that "he did not intuitively ... take in knowledge, but his mind never lost a fact or idea once committed to its keeping." [47] A common story around the Point had it that if "the General" had stayed one more year he would have been number one in his class.

The achievement reflected by his steady rise had come at some cost. Never had he had much time for recreation. Rather than attend the frequent summer "hops" so popular with upperclassmen, Jackson contented himself with walks in the neighborhood of the Academy, with visits to old Fort Putnam,[48] and with lengthy conversations on a variety of topics with his closer friends. Spare moments were devoted to desperate study.

In spite of his aloof, cold bearing and relentless studiousness, Cadet Jackson enjoyed the respect and good will of most classmates. His associates were picked without regard to class year, which was a rare practice among the cadets, and usually became his admiring fans. Of his own class he probably liked Dabney Maury best, but there were others of whom he would learn more in later years—George McClellan, Darius N. Couch, Truman Seymour, and George Stoneman, all latter-day Yankees; David Rumple Jones, a fellow Confederate; Cadmus Marcellus Wilcox, a North Carolinian who also would go with his state; and, number fifty-nine in a class of fifty-nine, George Edward Pickett. Outside of his own class, there were others Jackson would come to know: U. S. Grant, Frank Gardner, Fitz-John Porter, Edmund Kirby Smith, Winfield Scott Hancock, William S. Rosecrans, James Longstreet, and in particular a man in the class of 1845—Barnard E. Bee.

Once a fellow cadet came to know Jackson, previous opinions frequently changed. Outwardly stolid, lethargic and gruff, the angular Virginian proved to have a nice sense of humor, to be surprisingly animated, and his kindness—especially to sick cadets—knew no bounds. When he became absorbed in a conversation or in some event, "his form became erect, his eyes flashed like steel, and a smile...would illumine his whole face." [49] The interesting thing about his personal relationships at West Point was that Jackson had so little trouble despite his rough exterior. After initial efforts to haze the country boy backfired under his calm, amused glance, he earned universal admiration. One classmate observed that he never heard an unkind word about Jackson from students or professors.[50] Only once did a fellow cadet attempt to discredit him by exchanging a dirty for a clean musket—and Jackson's un-Cavalier pursuit of exact justice cut short any similar plots in other minds.

Smooth personal relationships probably resulted as much from voluntary isolation as from anything else. Rigid study rules alone would get him through—of this he was certain—and his study habits became a West Point legend. One awed roommate in the Old South barracks commented on Thomas's incredible powers of concentration: "No one I have ever known," he wrote, "could so perfectly withdraw his mind from surrounding objects or influences, and so thoroughly involve his whole being in the subject under consideration." [51] Everyone knew that "the General" almost never went to bed when taps sounded. Piling his grate high with coal, he would stretch out on the floor in front of the fire and study his back lessons. Cadet Maury rightly noted that Jackson literally "burned" knowledge into his brain.[52] Jackson himself conceded that he "studied *very hard* for what he got at West Point." [53]

Rigid study patterns probably contributed to reviving the old stomach complaint, and Thomas had to give careful attention to diet and exercise. To sit bolt upright while reading or concentrating put less strain on the alimentary system, and this became a favorite pose. His classmates, had they not liked him so much, would have laughed loudly at seeing the thin, angular Jackson sitting stiff at a desk and staring at the wall, thinking. But he knew a regimen of this sort would improve mind and body, and his buddies, although they never could have done the same, developed an affectionate understanding of "the General's" actions. They could even restrain mirth when he tried to better his horsemanship. Ungainly, unsettled, and unhappy in the saddle, Thomas looked like nothing so much as a menace on horseback, but he determined he would improve his riding—and he did. Uncle Cummins's stable of racers had trained him better than his classmates knew.

Determination of Jackson's type required planning. While at West Point he began keeping a book in which he penned moral and ethical maxims designed for self-improvement. The maxims were not startlingly original or especially deep, but they show that the young cadet had an unswerving sense of honor, fair play, and self-discipline. One maxim earnestly scrawled in these pages became a guiding principle throughout Jackson's life: "You may be whatever you resolve to be." Some of the others, not as firm as this, reveal Thomas's developing standard of values:

Through life let your principal object be the discharge of duty.

Sacrifice your life rather than your word.

Speak but what may benefit others or yourself; avoid trifling conversation.

Resolve to perform what you ought; perform without fail what you resolve.

Use no hurtful deceit; think innocently and justly, and if you speak, speak accordingly.

Of special interest is an entry titled "Motives to action." Under this heading Jackson summed up a personal philosophy: "1. Regard to your own happiness. 2. Regard for the family to which you belong. 3. Strive to attain a very great elevation of character. 4. Fix upon a high standard of action and character." [54] These bits of wisdom sound like hundreds of others scribbled in college notebooks on myriad campuses—but what set them apart from all others was the man who wrote them. He lived by the lines he had laboriously written.

The first and second "motives to action" focused Jackson's attention on his future. To Laura he wrote in January, 1844, that he did not think he would stay in the army, preferring, he said, "to commence some professional business at home." [55] Not even a taste of local military fame when he went home on leave during the summer of 1844 could change that feeling. In August, 1845, he again wrote Laura that

> I have before me two courses, either of which I may choose. The first would be to follow in the profession of arms; the second, that of a civil pursuit, as law. If I should adopt the first I could live independently and surrounded by friends whom I have already made, have no fear of want. My pay would be fixed. . . . If I adopt the latter I presume that I would still find plenty of friends, but my exertions would have to be great in order to acquire a name. This course is most congenial to my taste, and consequently I expect to adopt it, after spending a few years in pursuing the former.[56]

With the approach of the last examinations in June, 1846, Cadet Jackson's ideas began to change. Elevation to a cadet officership might have had a little to do with it,[57] but the most decisive influence doubtless was the possibility of war. Rumors of a conflict between the United States and Mexico stirred great enthusiasm in the graduating class as early as April of 1846. Jackson now realistically told Laura that in event of war "the probability is that I will be ordered to join the army of occupation immediately, and, if so, will hardly see home until after my return," [58] and return might be years hence. He was happy to know that Laura had been safely married.[59] In case anything happened to him, the family "remnant" still would be intact.

A class excited about postgraduation furloughs and looking forward to war prepared to receive their diplomas on June 30, 1846. Now for the last time the gray uniform coatee was brushed, the brass ball buttons shined, the white drill pantaloons cleaned almost threadbare, the full-dress pompon hat spruced to its majestic best, the crossbelt whitened, and the boots blacked. The drill fields and courtyards buzzed with happy conversation as throngs of proud parents, sweethearts, and relatives gathered to see the presentation of degrees. After the usual orations had been delivered and after the scrolls had been handed out, Jackson and his classmates, more fully aware than ever that the four-year ordeal had ended, mustered for their last parade. While the band loudly rendered "Sergeant Dashing White," the group of new officers marched up to salute the commandant—the final act of graduation.[60]

High standing in the class list earned a graduate his choice of services; the best students could avoid the infantry. Brevet Second Lieutenant Thomas Jonathan Jackson requested assignment in the artillery—an honored and active arm which had also been Napoleon's choice.

2

A TASTE OF FAME IN MEXICO

THE BRAND-NEW OFFICERS, class of 1846, were going to war. United States troops had been fighting Mexico for more than a month when Jackson's class was graduated. New heroes were being made along the Rio Grande; excitement, opportunity, fame, all lay to the south. Jackson himself wanted to go home on leave, but he was more anxious to fight in Mexico.

War undoubtedly was a major topic of conversation for the small group of new officers who traveled together from West Point to New York. There Jackson, Dabney Maury, Cadmus Wilcox, Archie Botts, and others gathered for one last fraternal session at the Brown Hotel before going [1] their separate ways.

With a furlough in his pocket, Thomas went as soon as possible to visit Laura in Beverly, Virginia. A visit with his sister, her husband, and their son, Thomas Jackson Arnold, was followed by a trip down to Jackson's Mill, where Uncle Cummins and all his friends and relatives made the new officer more than welcome. Weston and surrounding communities were in an excited rush of military preparation. A West Pointer of local vintage became the man of the hour, and the Lewis County militia sought Tom's professional guidance.

No sooner had he arrived at Uncle Cummins's on Monday, July 20, 1846, than the young lieutenant received a request from the colonel of the militia to take command of a company for a muster parade. Professionalism tinged Tom's reply. "No," he told the colonel, "I would probably not understand your orders." Pressed into acceptance, he went to the parade ground, took charge of the company, and soon found himself in trouble. The colonel gave an improper command, and the strict discipline of West Point forbade any improvisation—so Jackson's company marched off the parade ground and straight through the town. The lieutenant's explanation was illuminating and characteristic: he was obeying orders.[2]

Such thorough regimentation impressed Tom's friends and apparently stimulated some volunteering. One of the militiamen who witnessed the straying of Jackson's company was a cousin, Sylvanus White, who announced his intention to join up. Pleased, Jackson told him that he too expected orders at any moment for Mexico, and added that "I want to see you at the taking of the City of Mexico. We are going to take it." White did not keep the appointment, for the Lewis County militia was not called out, but Jackson went on to prove himself a prophet.[3]

Two days after his arrival at Weston, Jackson's orders arrived. The War Department required the young lieutenant to proceed to Fort Columbus, Governor's Island, New York, there to report to Capt. Francis Taylor, commanding K Company, First Artillery. On Thursday, July 23, Jackson departed for New York.

Upon his arrival at Fort Columbus, Jackson discovered that Captain Taylor had left for Fort Hamilton, New York. Jackson followed the captain, and by mid-August had reported for his first assignment. Company K had been alerted for a move to Mexico. Jackson and Taylor took charge of thirty men and forty horses and began a march toward the war zone. Apparently the company was to join the forces of Gen. Zachary Taylor, now advancing toward Monterey. The assignment offered rich possibilities for future service, but the trek to Taylor's camps would not be easy. The little band of officers and men started their trip on land; they marched four hundred miles to Pittsburgh, then boarded a river boat and steamed down the Ohio and Mississippi Rivers to New Orleans. From the Crescent City, K Company sailed for Point Isabel, Texas, Taylor's base of operations.[4]

The thirty-six days' march had been long and wearing, but the rumor which greeted the company on arrival was exciting enough to banish fatigue—Taylor was ready for another battle! Soon came word that on September 24 (the very day Jackson's company reached Point Isabel) Taylor had captured Monterey. With this good word came the disheartening news that an eight-week armistice had been agreed upon by both sides—there would be no chance for immediate action. Point Isabel was hardly a place to find diversion. Scarcely more than a hamlet, the town now served only as a military base. In retreating from Point Isabel, the Mexicans had burned most of the scraggly buildings, and American forces had transformed what remained of the town into a huge warehouse for all kinds of army stores, with the result that the little port was a beehive of martial business but not much else.

Scarcity of entertainment did not bother Jackson. The town had other advantages. Since it was the base for Taylor's activities, a great many officers and men from the army came and went, and each had a story to relate; some had actually been in battle, others said they had. All such stories were of interest to a new officer who was fast developing an intense interest in war and all its possibilities. One officer with much to say about fighting and his part in it was Lt. Daniel Harvey Hill, a fellow West Pointer, class of 1842.

Hill chanced to visit his Regular Army friend and former West Point teacher, Capt. George Taylor, and while at Taylor's tent on a winter day in 1846, Hill met Jackson for the first time.[5] An apparently casual meeting, it nonetheless made a lasting impression on Lieutenant Hill. Taylor told Hill that "Jackson will make his mark in this war," and went on to explain why he thought so: "I was his Instructor at West Point & know him well. He kept rising there all the time & if the course had been two years longer, would have graduated head." [6] Hill recalled years later that he and Jackson, upon leaving Taylor's quarters, had taken a walk along the beach near Point Isabel. Conversation centered on fighting, with Jackson asking all sorts of questions about battles. What sort of emotions were stirred? How were the troops handled? As he talked, Hill was impressed with the fervor in Jackson's voice and with the flash of his blue eyes. Obviously Tom was spoiling for a fight. Lamenting the possibility that war was ended in the sector of Northern Mexico, he confided to Hill with a "bright & peculiar smile" that "I want to be in one battle." [7]

The remainder of the year 1846 passed without K Company's getting into any fighting. Some time was spent in installing guns in the Point Isabel defenses, which soon became more of an exercise than anything else,[8] and Jackson kept busy with an additional assignment as acting assistant commissary of the company (a job for which he could never seem to get paid).[9] Finally the monotony of garrison duty ended. President Polk and the War Department, anxious to press the war in order to intimidate the Mexican Congress which was scheduled to meet in December, terminated Taylor's armistice, and the general advanced to occupy the important town of Saltillo. There were sound strategic reasons for taking the capital of the state of Coahuila—it guarded the chief pass through the Sierra Madre range and commanded a rich granary from which the American army could take supplies. In addition, Saltillo served as a military support for Monterey.[10]

A force under Gen. William J. Worth, including a considerable artillery detachment, was ordered to take the city. At last Jackson would have a change of scene, but when the army reached Saltillo there was no chance for action, since the Mexican army had deserted the area. Only the belligerence of Saltillo's sullen populace and the fantastic prices which local merchants tried to extort for all manner of goods served as a reminder that the Americans were in hostile country.

Jackson became part of an occupation force under General Worth, and the young lieutenant could not have been too unhappy. Saltillo, beautifully situated in a rich agricultural region reminiscent of New England,[11] was certainly more of a metropolis than Point Isabel. The only trouble was that little was being accomplished in Northern Mexico.

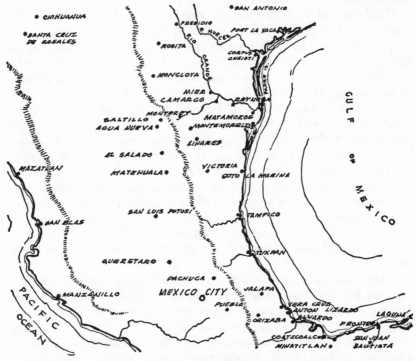

Mexico in Outline (after Henry, The Story of the Mexican War)

In December the Mexican Congress met, but instead of being intimidated by American operations in the Monterey-Saltillo area, it elected a president dedicated to resistance—Gen. Antonio López de Santa Anna. Santa Anna's election did not bode well for the future. Distance had already hopelessly complicated Taylor's plans, and disrupted a scheme to invade Chihuahua. Results would have to be achieved somewhere else. New strategy had to be evolved. No attempt would be made to march overland from the Rio Grande all the way to the Mexican capital—instead an amphibious expedition would be landed somewhere on the eastern coast of Mexico and proceed inland.

After considerable debate, President Polk had decided in November to put the combined army-navy expedition under the command of Gen. Winfield Scott, an old soldier whose experience and proficiency seemed to qualify him for the assignment even if his politics did not. Whig or no, probably no other officer could have brought the land-sea invasion to a successful conclusion.[12]

For some time Scott had been agitating for the scheme. He wanted to lead an amphibious attack against Vera Cruz, capture that fortress city, and use the famous National Road as an invasion route to Mexico City. At long last he got his wish, and in February, 1847, troops began to assemble at the island of Lobos, near Tampico. There was a ticklish problem to be faced. A good number of Scott's regular troops were to come from Taylor's army—a fact which might offend a glory-conscious soldier. Over some objections, Worth's division joined Scott, and with it went the First Artillery. Jackson and his company moved from Saltillo to Camp Palo Alto, Texas, and then back to Point Isabel.[13]

At this point the embarkation proceedings bogged down in another logistical snarl. The first combined invasion attempt to be made by the United States Army involved more than 15,000 men, boundless supplies, and careful coordination of effort by the army and navy. Naturally things went wrong—it could hardly have been otherwise, considering the newness of amphibious operations. At Point Isabel a scarcity of shipping stranded Worth's division and the artillery for a time. They were not alone. Gen. David E. Twiggs's regulars and Gen. Robert Patterson's volunteers from Tampico were also delayed. So were large amounts of supplies, including ordnance.[14]

From February 21 to March 2, 1847, Scott struggled to mobilize his expeditionary force, and finally, after mountainous frustrations, he began the move to Vera Cruz. For Lieutenant Jackson it had been a long wait. He had been sorry to leave Taylor's army,[15] but the vast fleet of transports which sailed from Lobos Island showed that Scott meant business—he was going to fight, and so were the men with him.

The immediate destination of Scott's fleet was a naval anchorage near Vera Cruz, called Anton Lizardo. Here, on March 5, Jackson saw the whole expedition come together. The little transport *Arkansas*, carrying Jackson's company, seemed an insignificant dot amid the huge armada.[16] It was quite a sight, all those ships jammed with excited soldiers, close to the enemy city and its frowning bastion, the Castle San Juan de Ulúa. Everyone wanted to go ashore and attack, but first a decision had to be made about where to establish a beachhead. Not until March 9 did the landing occur.

The site picked was a point on the beach opposite the island of Sacrificios—about two and a half miles from the city and well removed from the range of Vera Cruz's guns. The troops were put ashore in small surfboats especially constructed for the task. After watching the first and second waves go scudding toward the beach, Jackson joined the third assault group, consisting of General Twiggs's "brigade" (really a sort of demibrigade) made up of bits and pieces of regular units; Col. Persifor

F. Smith's mounted riflemen (dismounted for this occasion); the First and Fourth Artillery regiments, and the First, Second, Third, and Seventh Infantry regiments.

Reaching Mexican soil launched a new series of experiences for Jackson. Never before had he assaulted a foreign shore, participated in a real military engagement, or ridden in an assault boat—and never before had he served as an infantry officer. The First Artillery, along with the Fourth, was designated as infantry for the purpose of strengthening Twiggs's force. This was the first experience Jackson had with commanding infantry, but not the last.

Fortunately for the Americans, they met no enemy resistance. Overcoming a series of delays, Scott's forces began the formal siege of Vera Cruz in short order. The fortress city put up a stiff fight, despite Santa Anna's failure to send reinforcements. There were numerous heavy guns in the Mexican line of fortifications as well as in the huge fortress of San Juan itself. Scott soon rejected the idea of a direct assault, and a regular siege dragged on until March 27, when the superior gunnery and ordnance of the Americans, combined with lack of assistance from Santa Anna, forced the city's defenders to surrender.[17] A great American victory, the capture of Vera Cruz, and in combination with news of Taylor's victory at Buena Vista in February, it might materially shorten the war. Lieutenant Jackson had had his first exciting taste of fighting during the siege. Dividing his time between the commands of General Twiggs and General Worth, he rendered a good deal of service with advanced batteries. Although not seriously under fire during the days of his active duty, Jackson did have a fairly close singe. In a letter to sister Laura, written three days after the surrender, veteran Tom casually remarked on his brush with death: "While I was at the advanced batteries, a cannon ball came in about five steps of me."[18] A most matter-of-fact account, but he was as proud of the cannon-ball episode as he was of the part he had had in the siege. Now a hardened soldier, he felt qualified to evaluate the battle. The fighting itself he thought exhilarating, the performance of the American troops superb. Only one thing displeased him, he told Laura:

> This capitulation has thrown into our hands the stronghold of this republic, and being a regular siege, in connection with other circumstances must in my opinion excel any military operations known in the history of our country. I approve of all except allowing the enemy to retire; that I cannot approve of, inasmuch as we had them secure, and could have taken them prisoners of war unconditionally.

The sentiment here would later find expression in the familiar command "Press on! Press on!"

That March day, sitting on his improvised box chair, using his camp bed as a desk,[19] Tom revealed a lot about himself in the letter to Laura. Not only did he display intolerance for unrealistic military chivalry, but he also pulled back the veil for a brief glimpse of his own ambition. "I presume you think my name ought to appear in the papers," he wrote, explaining that there were good reasons why it did not—reasons involving army politics which had to be spelled out for his sister. Rank was the only requisite for fame.

> It is such that only those who have independent commands are as a general rule spoken of.... If an officer wishes to distinguish himself he must remain long in service until he obtains rank; then he receives praise not only for his efforts, but for the efforts of the officers and men under him. That portion of the praise which may be due to me must of course go to those above me, or be included in the praise given to the army.[20]

One other virtue there was which would aid an officer's advancement—discretion. Discretion may not have been reflected in Jackson's remarks to Laura about army politics, but he was developing this quality. At the end of the letter came a stern admonition: "You will take particular care that neither this nor any subsequent letter gets into a newspaper." Consciousness of military security would grow on him.[21]

With Vera Cruz as his base of operations, Scott wanted to move as quickly as possible against Mexico City, an important symbol to both sides. Of even more immediate concern was the *vómito*—the yellow fever season was about to descend on the lowlands, and the army would be ripe for a wholesale plague. The sooner the campaign progressed, the better for the soldiers.

Strategically Scott's problem appeared simple. Leading inland from Vera Cruz, the National Road wound snakelike through a series of mountain passes and intermediate towns and finally ended in Mexico City. The road had seen better days, but it constituted the only practical avenue to the American objective.

Tactically Scott was not sure what he faced. Santa Anna's whereabouts were uncertain. Presumably he would defend the capital, but whether he would arrive from Northern Mexico in time to contest the American advance inland was a question. The chances were that he would. Quickly the American troops must be moved to the upcountry. Distance was not as important as altitude, and fortunately the National Road climbed sharply almost as it left Vera Cruz. General Scott worked desperately to launch the invasion, but neither desperation, energy, nor will power could provide scarce horses for military transport, land supplies which had not yet arrived, or unscramble the assorted tangles of red tape which army administration inevitably produced. The general, the army, everybody waited.

While he waited, Lieutenant Jackson took time to become acquainted with Vera Cruz. Two aspects of the city impressed him. The amazing military strength of the castle and town caught his attention:

The town is of immense strength being surrounded on one side by a wall about ten feet high and forts extending around to the Gulf of Mexico, and on the gulf side is defended by the castle itself which is a large fortress of the strongest character and the works are so arranged that it is impossible for a man to approach the town on either side without being exposed to the fire of cannon.[22]

Vera Cruz interested Jackson, too, from the standpoint of health. The dread *vómito* concerned all Americans in the city, and Jackson was particularly conscious of it, since he had not been too well for some time. But Vera Cruz continued healthy through early April—and perhaps because of the ocean voyage, or possibly because of the prospects of active campaigning, Jackson found himself feeling so much better that he wrote Laura: "I am in better health than usual." [23]

While Jackson and all other occupation troops worried about the coming of hot weather and yellow fever, Scott completed a reorganization of his forces. Two divisions—Gen. William J. Worth's and Gen. David E. Twiggs's—of two brigades each were formed. And on April 8 Twiggs's division took the lead in the line of march for Mexico City.

The first town of size to be encountered would be Jalapa, about seventy-five miles west, and over four thousand feet up. Attached for a time to Twiggs's division, the First Artillery rumbled along the ancient route of Cortes with the men on the gun carriages and caissons doubtless more concerned about negotiating the grades than about the natural beauty of the scenery and the historical importance of the decaying turnpike.

To Jackson, though, the ascent from the sand hills into the "wilderness of trees and flowers" proved a continuing delight. The army passed through country decked in a riot of color, but many soldiers were unable to appreciate it—the rigors of camp diarrhea thinned the marching columns mile by mile. General Twiggs, who appeared irritatingly healthy, had set too fast a pace, and by the end of the first day over one-third of the division missed roll call. On the second day things went easier. "Old Davey" cut down the speed, allowed more frequent halts, and the road began to improve. As the troops trudged on, they learned they were crossing lands which belonged to General Santa Anna himself—the man seemed to own all the territory from Vera Cruz to Jalapa.

The column of men and guns snaked along the road until the afternoon of April 11, when suddenly Twiggs's advance elements ran into some Mexican lancers. A sharp skirmish soon drove the enemy out of sight. But the proximity of hostile cavalry stalled the American march until the next day. Twiggs wanted to throw caution aside, attack the Mexicans as soon as possible, and be on with the invasion. A day would be used in finding the enemy position; then the American division would assault on the thirteenth of April. The thirteenth boded worse luck than usual. Old Davey seemed determined to press his advance without waiting for the rest of the army. Not even scouting reports of a strong series of fortified enemy positions, crowning imposing hilltops, dampened the general's rashness. His subordinates were not happy, and a plea that the long march had tired their men won a day's postponement. Then a fortuitous series of delays held up the attack until General Scott himself could arrive with reinforcements from Vera Cruz.

The prospective battlefield did not fill Scott with the same ardent desire to attack as it did Twiggs. The ground looked well suited to defense, and Mexican engineers had selected a well-nigh impregnable position. Here Santa Anna's forces appeared determined to stop the Yankee advance. Jutting high above the village of Plan del Rio stood several imposing hills, forming a ridge which stood between the steep river canyon and the road. The road, after crossing the river, turned away from it in a northwesterly direction to surmount the mountains and return to follow the course of the river at a point about two miles farther west.

The ridge which nudged the road away from the canyon came to an end in three points, or promontories, not far west of Plan del Rio. Mexican guns looked down from each of these points. As it developed, these batteries formed the right of the Mexican position. Left of the guns, and behind them, rose an enormous conical hill called Cerro Gordo; and a half mile in front, or east of Cerro Gordo, stood another imposing hill called Atalaya, which was about the same height and had approaches almost as steep. In effect, then, the Mexican left consisted of two high hills bristling with guns; the center was open and was traversed by the National Road; the right was held by the artillery on the three commanding points of the ridge. Both right and left gun positions dominated the road. A quick glance was enough to convince Scott that a direct advance would be suicidal.

From the American positions the enemy stronghold was frightening. To men deep in Mexican territory, with retreat possibly cut off by yellow fever, the high bush-enshrouded crags with their batteries glinting ominously in the sun looked like death's dread sentinels. In the words of Capt. Robert E. Lee of the engineers, there was an "unscalable" precipice on one side and ravines which appeared "impassable" on the other.[24]

Scott was not frightened. Before he arrived at Plan del Rio (which he made his headquarters), some scouting of the Mexican position had already been done. Lieutenants Pierre G. T. Beauregard and Zealous B. Tower had concluded that the best chance for American success appeared to lie in a turning move around the Mexican left flank. But the ground on that flank was rutted with those ravines and thickets which

Captain Lee labeled "impassable," and Santa Anna himself considered the terrain so rough that not even a goat could approach from that quarter.[25] Since appearances might well be misleading, Scott continued the scouting activities.

Lee, who had already distinguished himself at Vera Cruz, was directed to try to find a route by which it would be feasible to turn the Mexican left. And at length he found one.

He found it at the cost of considerable discomfort to himself (having to remain motionless behind a log for hours, while enemy soldiers sat on the log and insects all but ate him alive), but his discovery was worth all his trouble. Reporting to Scott after dark on the fifteenth, Lee outlined the route, and the next day a group of pioneer troops hacked out a crude road for the army. On the seventeenth the advance began.

Twiggs's men were to get well behind Santa Anna's left and rear, occupy the National Road, and await an attack by the remainder of the American forces in the Mexican front. While his men toiled over the tangled trail, the Mexicans on Atalaya spotted a section of Twiggs's advancing force and opened fire. Now the hill had to be taken, lest heavy casualties thwart the flank march. After a hard fight the Americans seized the crest of Atalaya and, flushed with victory, swept on over the hill, down the other side and tried to assault Cerro Gordo. There they were stopped cold by a withering fire from enemy batteries.

Scott sent Gen. James Shields's volunteer brigade to aid the embattled Twiggs, but by the time these reinforcements arrived, the day was done and the fighting ended. Cerro Gordo was still in enemy hands, the National Road had not yet been reached by the flanking column, and the Mexicans were enjoying a celebration commemorating their great victory over the invaders.

With his men keeping the positions they held at the end of the day, Scott determined to attack again on the morning of the eighteenth. In the early hours of the day—it was a Sunday—Twiggs sent part of his force far to his right to strike the National Road at or above the main Mexican camp. The rest of his force on Atalaya poised to assault the crest of Cerro Gordo. The attack would be timed so that the storming of Cerro Gordo would not occur before Twiggs's flanking party reached the road behind the enemy. If this could be done right the enemy would be caught in a trap. That loomed as a big "if."

The men atop Atalaya attacked fiercely at about seven o'clock, and soon carried Cerro Gordo. As the Mexican defense started to crack, the American flanking column came out on the road, and swiftly then all the starch went out of the Mexican troops on the left. When the defenders of Cerro Gordo wilted, the rest of the Mexican army, which had been successfully holding the right flank against a mismanaged attack by Gen. Gideon Pillow's brigade, had to give way or be captured. Since Twiggs's flanking column came up during the Mexican retreat, not before as planned, a large part of the Mexican army escaped capture.

As soon as the enemy retreat began, Scott launched a hastily formed pursuit. Twiggs's division and Shields's brigade—both under Maj. Gen. Robert Patterson's command—were to press the enemy hard. In advance of the infantry went the two field batteries then with the army, one of them being Taylor's. Not until the pursuit did Jackson become involved in the Cerro Gordo action. When he did, he seems to have had a good time, for he wrote Laura a few days later that "we followed close on the retreating column until night and came near enough to give them a few shots from the battery." [26]

Although he did not have a really active part in the action, Jackson was an avid observer of all that was going on. This was his first real battle (Vera Cruz had been a siege), and now he knew the answers to the questions he had put to Harvey Hill not long before. The lessons of the battle he carefully noted. Scott had made good use of all available engineering talent, had found out what he could of the enemy's position, and then had flanked the enemy out of a strong series of batteries. Reduced to simple terms, Cerro Gordo had been won by sound reconnaissance, a skillful and daring flank attack, topped off with quick and hard pursuit—which might have been more effective in Jackson's eyes had the dragoons been on hand. Scout, flank, pursue—here was a formula to become familiar as Jackson's own trademark in the future.

American losses had been small—63 killed, 337 wounded. Total Mexican casualties were impossible to estimate. Numbers of Mexicans were captured at Cerro Gordo—Scott estimated the prisoners at over 3,000 [27] —although about half the Mexican army made its escape west, in the direction of Jalapa and the city of Mexico. One Mexican general was killed and five others captured. The road to Jalapa was clear. [28]

A dirty, ragged, and extremely happy American army reached the capital city of the state of Vera Cruz on April 19. The invaders were mildly surprised at the lack of hostility displayed by its citizens, and were enchanted by the beauty of the city and its surroundings. The town, which lay in a lush garden-spot area rich in flowers and fruits of all types, struck many as a Garden of Eden. If the soldiers could take their eyes away from the fabulous foliage, and away, too, from the "fair Jalapenas" who appeared not to resent them, they were doubtless stunned by the scenery outside the city. Jalapa stood surrounded by mountains, with Orizaba and the austere Cofre de Perote remotely beautiful in their snow-topped vastness. East of the city, looking over a hot, lush land, the soldiers could see the blue Gulf of Mexico. This, then, was the town which would be Lieutenant Jackson's home for some weeks. He was not altogether happy with it, but the scenery was not the cause of his dislike.

Pleased to hear that Captain Taylor had mentioned him "in very flattering terms" in a report to General Twiggs, Jackson wanted an opportunity to earn further recognition. The invasion would continue, and it seemed likely that there would be other battles before Mexico City fell. General Worth's reserve division received orders to lead off on the next leg of the march. Jackson, one of Worth's stanch admirers, wanted to go along, but Taylor's battery stayed with Twiggs. Sad, indeed, this staying behind, but at length something pleasant happened to young Tom. He was promoted, effective March 3, 1847—promotion in this case being not an unmixed blessing.

It came as no surprise to him; he had confided to Laura in late March that "I expect to be promoted in a short time to a second lieutenancy," and he had added that "this will probably occasion me to leave the light battery, but it will give me more rank, which is of the greatest importance in the army." Soon after he received word in April of his becoming a permanent second lieutenant he was, as expected, transferred to the heavy artillery.[29] The new assignment kept him in the same regiment, but shifted him from Company K to Company G. Since the heavy branch had been spending much time as infantry, the chances were good that Jackson might get into the thick of fighting somewhere.[30] And even though the change would take him from a field battery into the declining heavier branch of the service, the chance for activity—and hence distinction—was an overriding consideration. Captain Taylor tried hard to keep Jackson with his company—already the two men were good friends—but the transfer went through.

Just when it seemed he might have a chance to go forward to the advance positions of the army at Perote, the military governor of Jalapa, Brev. Col. Thomas Childs, took charge of the First Artillery as part of the garrison force, and Jackson was ordered to stay with his company.[31]

Garrison duty seemed the end of the world to a young and eager second lieutenant, yearning for the excitement of battle. Jackson was cruelly hurt—"mortified," he said to Laura—by the change in fortune. Disappointment was tempered, though, by a thoughtful bit of insight into his own character, and also by a new reliance on religion. "I throw myself into the hands of an all wise God," he wrote his sister, "and hope that it may yet be for the better. It may have been one of His means of diminishing my excessive ambition; and after having accomplished His purpose, whatever it may be, He then in His infinite wisdom may gratify my desire." Here was humility, but humility coupled with a youthful hope that the setback was only temporary. The allusions to God and His wisdom were among the first in Jackson's correspondence, but not the only ones. Possibly Captain Taylor, destined to become Jackson's unofficial spiritual adviser, had already been talking with him.[32]

Acceptance of his fate may have been made easier by diversions in Jalapa. Jackson's quarters were comfortable and he busied himself with serious study of the Spanish language. There seemed to be a very practical reason for learning Spanish—fluency in the language would enable him to carry out an "idea of making some lady acquaintances shortly." Characteristic curiosity about his surroundings led him to appreciate the local fruits, plants, and natural beauties. In Jalapa, too, he probably saw a great deal of the Catholic Church in action.

Idle days in Jalapa were interrupted by transfer in late May or early June to Tepeyahualco, a little settlement west of Perote. But still there came no chance for action. Guarding the army's line of communications was not Jackson's idea of how to win a war. After some weeks as an uncomplaining behind-the-lines soldier, a chance to get to the front came from an unexpected quarter. A general order issued on July 16, 1847, authorized the creation of some new light artillery batteries. Among the new outfits would be Company I, First Regiment, with Capt. John B. Magruder in command. Magruder had captured four guns at Cerro Gordo, and Scott had presented them to him in recognition of his gallantry.[33] The new battery commander would need at least two lieutenants to assist him, and Jackson determined to be one of the two.

Magruder's reputation had spread and Jackson knew him to be a taskmaster, quick to anger and hard to please. Consequently other junior officers did not rush to join the new battery. But Magruder was bold, had distinguished himself at Cerro Gordo, and his field battery was certain to be where hot fighting was going on. Although in many ways complete opposites, Magruder and Jackson were attracted to each other. The handsome, dashing, urbane Magruder zealously sought advancement; Jackson, though handsome, was not dashing and hardly urbane, but his desire to be in the thick of the fight equaled that of the captain. He explained his reasons for wanting the new assignment: "I wanted to see active service, to be near the enemy in the fight; and when I heard that John Magruder had got his battery I bent all my energies to be with him, for I knew if any fighting was to be done, Magruder would be 'on hand.'"[34] Young Tom was in luck, for in July he received orders to report for duty with Magruder's command.[35] Magruder was hard to find. He had joined the army's advance units somewhere around Puebla, and Jackson, with a small escort, rode hard to catch up.

Not far from Jalapa, Jackson and his escort ran into a group of Mexican guerrillas who were harassing the American lines of communications.[36] Near the "terrible pass" of La Joya, the Mexicans attacked Jackson's little band. The attacking guerrillas outnumbered Jackson's force, and soon the fighting became a desperate hand-to-hand melee. But the wild battle did not last long. The results were later reported to Laura in a laconic paragraph: "As I was coming from Jalapa I was detached with a few men in the vicinity of La Hoya [sic] and succeeded in killing four of the enemy and taking three prisoners, together with a beautiful sabre and some other equipment." Jackson had at last drawn blood in close combat, but the new lieutenant treated the experience as a routine matter. There would be other days of battle—if he could just live long enough to see them.[37]

After Jackson's little group of embattled veterans fought their way through to Puebla, they settled down to another protracted period of inaction. Stalled in the city, Scott's army awaited reinforcements. Some of Jackson's time was taken up in organizing the battery, becoming familiar with his duties, and getting acquainted with his commanding officer and with his men. He soon became second in command of Magruder's battery, a position which would put him in charge of a section of guns (usually two) in action.

Scott gathered together more than 10,500 men of all arms for his advance toward Mexico City. He picked up 2,400 regulars under Brig. Gen. Franklin Pierce, but had to leave more than 1,800 sick and a garrison of 400 men in Puebla. Some of his veteran volunteers departed as their enlistments expired. The loss of volunteers ordinarily would not have pained Scott, but a critical need of manpower gave the volunteers a certain charm. The general, who wanted more men, had to begin his march on August 7 with what a stingy administration—he was sure Washington was trying to sacrifice him—would give. Twiggs took the lead with his Cerro Gordo veterans.

After four marching days the army had crossed the mountains at 10,000 feet, and saw for the first time the valley of Mexico. It was a sight which had defied the powers of description of almost every traveler since the days of Cortes.

Twenty miles west and a half mile down lay the American objective, the capital of Mexico. Viewed from the lofty mountain vantage point, the beautiful city looked almost impregnable. Between the American army and its goal stood a pattern of lakes and marshes, a formidable natural barrier. Three lakes, Chalco, Xochimilco, and Texcoco, respectively, guarded the southeastern, eastern, and northern approaches to Mexico City. Various streams joined the lakes together, and the ground between them was marshy. Causeways raised out of the swampy land were the only roads leading into the capital. The causeways were, of course, fortified and formed an integral part of Santa Anna's plan of defense.

The network of causeways offered Scott several routes of advance. A direct road led from the base of the mountains through the village of Ayotla, on Chalco's north shore, then went between the fortified hill El Penon and Texcoco's south shore straight into the city. An alternative road ran from the settlement of Los Reyes across a marsh to the village of Mexicalcingo, then on to Churubusco, where a turn north led into the capital. It was also possible to reach the causeway leading from the south into Mexico by a long, circuitous march around the southern shores of Chalco and Xochimilco, but distance was an obvious drawback. One other possible approach would require a thirty-mile march on bad roads around the northern edge of Texcoco, then south along the lake's western banks.

Making his base at Ayotla on August 11, Scott sent his engineers out to probe the enemy defenses on all the approaches. Finally, on August 14, General Worth reported that the road south of Chalco and Xochimilco appeared rough but passable. Scott decided to flank the eastern defenses of Mexico and try to turn the whole Mexican position by moving against the city from the south.

Approaches to Mexico City (after Henry, The Story of the Mexican War)

Twiggs was left temporarily at Ayotla to give the impression that Scott contemplated an attack against the El Peñon batteries. General Worth, followed by General Pillow and Gen. John A. Quitman, took the southern road, heading for the village of San Agustin, which they reached on August 17. At San Agustin United States forces were now only nine miles from Mexico City. From this small village the road ran almost straight north, past the hacienda San Antonio, through the village of Churubusco into the capital. Beginning at San Agustin the road ran for about a mile along the edge of a huge lava field called the Pedregal—an area which seemed as forbidding as the worst possible Scottish moor.

Scouting parties soon reported that the enemy had fortified the hacienda San Antonio, about two and a half miles north of the American positions at San Agustin. Churubusco, too, was fortified. A direct advance against San Antonio offered little prospect of success, and on August 18 Capt. Robert E. Lee, who could be trusted to find the last details of ground and roads, took a small escort and set out to see if an army could get across the Pedregal and turn the right of Santa Anna's position. He found a way. It was just a sort of footpath, but hard work on the part of the pioneer troops would make it passable for wagons. On the other side of the Pedregal was what appeared to be a fair road leading toward Mexico City from the southwest, which gave promise of taking San Antonio in reverse.

Fighting began on the morning of August 19, when the Americans started doggedly digging a road across the Pedregal, aiming for the Padierna ranch, near which an enemy force was clearly observed entrenched on a hillside. The Mexicans had some well-served batteries which made road building costly, and the working parties were called back while Pillow's men went about driving General Valencia's troops from their front. Guns were brought up under Lee's direction—the light battery of Magruder included—and moved into positions close to the western edge of the lava. The American guns would be outweighed, but they were to divert the Mexicans' attention while part of the infantry tried a flanking movement. Magruder played his part well. He was to put up a large bluff, and there was nothing at which he was better. In this demonstration, which gave the light battery a chance for real separate service, Tom Jackson joyously got another taste of action. The death of a brother officer gave Jackson command of a section of guns employed in the Pedregal on the right of Magruder's main position. The situation of the light battery was anything but enviable. The Mexicans were firing on the American cannon with twenty-two heavy guns,[38] and were slowly but surely winning the duel. While the shelling went on at a range of about a thousand yards, part of Twiggs's infantry was ordered to the right to flank the Mexican lines, while a storming party was to form in the Mexican front. Something went awry. After the movement began, Gen. Persifor Smith, who was to lead the direct frontal assault, decided it would be suicidal and joined in the turning operation. The whole American force came under shattering artillery fire, which Jackson and Magruder could not stop. Scott later said that "the infantry could not advance in column without being mowed down by grape and canister, nor advance in line without being ridden down by the enemy's numerous horsemen."[39]

Fierce fighting for three hours resulted in a small American advance in the direction of Valencia's rear. It resulted, too, in the Americans' finding themselves caught between two enemy forces, each larger than the

3,500-man American force. Santa Anna had dispatched reinforcements to Valencia as soon as battle had been joined near Padierna, and the reinforcements were behind the Americans, while Valencia was in their front.

Magruder's battery had been in action during almost the whole of the battle, and Jackson had done exceptionally well. His guns blazed throughout the entire action, despite the severe Mexican fire, and when Magruder's guns moved forward a little, Jackson had come up "in handsome style, and kept up the fire with equal briskness and effect." Magruder was so pleased that he singled Jackson out in his official report to General Pillow, saying, "His conduct was equally conspicuous during the whole day, and I cannot too highly commend him to the Major-General's favorable consideration." [40]

It was nice to be praised by an exacting commander, but it would be nicer when the battle had been completely won. As things stood during the night of August 19–20, the issue still hung in the balance. Scott's main force was a good five miles away across the dismal Pedregal, and the force at Padierna was virtually cut off. Valencia thought he had put "all the Anglo-American forces... to shameful flight" and hoped to annihilate the remnants of the Yankees. [41] There was a chance he might do just that.

Rain, cold and heavy, drenched the American camps that night, adding to the gloomy atmosphere. General Smith, at his headquarters in the village of Ansaldo, received a report from one of his engineers that a route had been found which led to the rear of Valencia's line. Here might be a chance to snatch a victory from defeat. Calling a council of brigade commanders, Smith outlined a plan to attack. Captain Lee volunteered to cross the Pedregal in the dripping darkness to inform Scott that an attack would be made at 3:00 A.M. and to ask for a diversion on Scott's front. The trip must have been a nightmare, since the lava bed, abysmally dark and wet, was infested with roaming bands of Mexican pickets. But Lee accomplished the mission, which Scott labeled "the greatest feat of physical and moral courage performed by any individual, in my knowledge" during the invasion. [42]

Lee's remarkable trek made possible a secondary attack under Twiggs's direction while Smith launched his flank assault. The diversion, aided by Magruder's battery and other supporting guns, pinned down Mexican attention when fighting began after daybreak. Once Smith's flanking column arrived in position, the battle lasted a scant seventeen minutes. Then Valencia's forces broke and fled. American losses were sixty killed and wounded. The victorious Americans pursued Valencia's remnants, and soon battle was joined near San Antonio. After a brief stand, the Mexicans retreated north toward fortified positions around Churubusco, where a stubborn and bloody resistance lasted until late in the afternoon. When ammunition ran low and attacking forces had worked close to the fortifications, Santa Anna gave up the attempt to hold Churubusco. His next line of defense was much closer to Mexico's gates.

Unfortunately for Jackson, Magruder's guns saw little of the Churubusco action—they constituted the artillery reserve for most of the day. But the lieutenant was able once again to observe the advantages of a flank attack, as at Padierna (called Contreras in official reports), over a frontal assault so brutally demonstrated at Churubusco.

Fighting ceased. A temporary truce was arranged so that the American peace commissioner, Nicholas Trist, could work for an end to the war. Scott terminated the armistice on September 8; peace negotiations had broken down. In the intervening days the American army patched its wounds, rested, and longed for a final end to fighting.

Jackson, with Magruder's battery, spent most of the armistice near Pillow's camps at Mixcoac.[43] During this pleasant interlude, he probably received a notice of promotion.

Tom had been right in an earlier observation to Laura. Rank gave a chance to earn distinction, which in turn gave more rank. Word came that as of August 20, 1847, he had been promoted to the permanent rank of first lieutenant and to the brevet (temporary) rank of captain. The reasons given were highly satisfying. The first lieutenancy was for "gallant and meritorious conduct at the siege of Vera Cruz," while the brevet captaincy came for "gallant and meritorious conduct in the battles of Contreras and Churubusco." A rapid rise for an energetic young man —and yet the chance for a truly outstanding performance had not yet come.

It came when the fighting resumed. On September 8 a blundering attack against a supposed cannon foundry called Molino del Rey (at the western end of the Chapultepec park) gave Jackson only a brief chance for action—against charging Mexican cavalry [44]—but it gave him another chance to see the futility of blind assault against fortified positions.

A real opportunity for exciting action came to Jackson on the day that the American army delivered the magnificent attack on the castle of Chapultepec. This venerable structure, crowning a high hill which seemed to command the city, was more a symbol than a real fortress—a symbol that both sides regarded as highly important. Chapultepec had been since 1833 the seat of Mexico's military college, and hence had propaganda value. Also, it barred the way to two of the main gates to the city from the west and southwest—the *garitas* San Cosme and Belen.

The whole position was an elongated rectangular park, surrounded by walls. The building which the Americans persisted in calling a castle or fort—it had been in reality a summer palace for viceroyalty—stood on the hill rising from the eastern end of the park. The western end was enclosed by the battered buildings of the Molino del Rey. A large grove of cypress trees covered the ground between Molino del Rey and the base of a 200-foot hill surmounted by the palace. A small gate breached the south face of the wall, and another the southeast, both fortified. Thirteen guns defended the palace itself, assisted by a garrison of about one thousand, plus the corps of cadets of the military college. Although its defenders were few, Chapultepec's natural strength was impressive.

On the night of Saturday, September 11, guns were brought up under Captain Lee's direction and were placed in batteries facing Chapultepec's south and southwestern walls. A steady bombardment began the morning of the twelfth, and lasted for about fourteen hours. The steady shelling shattered enemy morale, and although the palace commander, Gen. Nicolas Bravo, asked Santa Anna for assistance, reinforcements were delayed so that they would not be subjected to the nerve-racking fire. While the heavy guns of the siege train did their work, a demonstration was continued against the southern approaches to Mexico, keeping Santa Anna uncertain of Scott's intentions just long enough to cause a fatal delay in his defensive troop movements toward the Chapultepec sector.

Scott was in no hurry this time. Engineers once more were put to work along with the pioneer troops—not at finding new roads, but at preparing scaling ladders, bringing up pickaxes and crowbars and other equipment for the scaling parties. Pillow's and Quitman's divisions would be the main attacking force, supported by Worth's and Persifor Smith's commands. The southern and western faces of the park walls were the first objectives of the American assault.

Jackson came into the battle on the extreme left of the attacking line. On the American left, which rested on and used the Anzures causeway running along the northern side of the Chapultepec rectangle, a fairly large and mobile force would cover the flank, would try to prevent the arrival of Mexican reinforcements from the city, and would attempt to choke off retreat from the palace and its defenses. This force, commanded by Col. William Trousdale, was made up of the Eleventh and Fourteenth Infantry and Jackson's section of Magruder's battery. When the action against Chapultepec began at eight o'clock Monday morning, September 14, Trousdale's command moved east along the causeway and took no direct part in the superb storming of Chapultepec hill. Instead, Trousdale ran into reinforcements which Santa Anna belatedly sent to the palace, and quickly the stage was set for a young man's moment of glory.

Trousdale's advance against the enemy reinforcements was delayed by a one-gun redoubt and infantry on the palace hill. Mexican marksmen poured a severe plunging fire down into Trousdale's ranks; the colonel himself was wounded and the command wavered. The redoubt must be eliminated, or the American advance might become a retreat. Racing forward with his two cannon, Jackson searched for a good battery position. In his front a shell-swept ditch barred the way to a spot from which he could fire effectively. As Jackson saw his situation, he was "in a road which was swept with grape and canister, and at the same time thousands of muskets from the Castle itself above pouring [bullets] down like hail. . . ." [45] Swiftly one of his guns was knocked out of action, most of his horses were shot dead, and almost all of his men became demoralized.

Jackson seemed oblivious to danger. While his men cowered wherever there was some protection from the dirt-flecking bullets, their mad lieutenant walked up and down in the hail of lead urging them to help him move the cannon forward. Jackson coolly told them that they had nothing to fear. "There is no danger," he cried. "See! I am not hit." This failed to inspire the men, and even Jackson admitted later that he had not convinced himself. It was, he confessed, the only lie he ever told. [46]

Deserted by everyone save a doughty sergeant, Jackson lifted a lone gun across the lead-swept ditch by hand and put it into action. General Worth, who witnessed this feat, feared for the safety of Jackson's cannon and sent him an order to retire to the cover of infantry. "I sent him back word," Jackson proudly recalled, "that, with one company of regulars as a support, I could carry the work, upon which he moved forward a whole brigade." [47] In the heat of the fight Magruder rode up, lost his horse to one of the straying bullets, picked himself up, and ran across the ditch to Jackson's gun. He found his lieutenant eager to get his other gun back into action. Magruder helped him and soon both of Jackson's fieldpieces were being loaded, fired, swabbed, loaded, and fired in answer to the roar from above.

It was quite a scene. Jackson was in front of the entire American army with his guns. Under fire from some of the biggest ordnance the enemy could bring to bear, he was holding his ground, giving almost shot for shot. And he had refused to retreat, even when ordered to do so! That refusal had turned the tide of battle on the front, since the brigade which Worth sent in reply was able to carry the Mexican redoubt—whose defenders were unnerved by the fierce combat of the American lieutenant with his two guns. Soon the whole American army knew of Jackson's heroic combat. But Jackson had not yet had his full share of that day's fighting.

Mexican resistance had not ceased, even though Chapultepec had fallen. Santa Anna himself was trying to rally the defense at the gates of Mexico, and his army remained a formidable barrier between the Americans and the occupation of the capital. There must be a quick follow-up of the Chapultepec victory—press the retreating Mexican columns rapidly toward the city, and use the enemy's confusion as a weapon to weaken the last-ditch defense. Two routes of pursuit were open. One led northeast on the Veronica causeway with its arched aqueduct to the

Tacubaya road, and thence directly east into the San Cosme gate. The other road led almost directly east from Chapultepec to the Belen gate. Scott's main effort went against the San Cosme entrance.

After the enemy redoubt was silenced, Jackson did not stop to patch up his battered section. Hitching his guns to their wagon limbers, the eager lieutenant raced along the road toward the San Cosme gate. In his headlong rush he was far ahead of the main attacking force and would have been all alone had it not been for the impetuosity of two other young lieutenants.

Daniel Harvey Hill and Barnard E. Bee, each in charge of segments of the original storming party at Chapultepec, had enthusiastically driven the Mexicans beyond the castle and along the highway to the northeast. Both American officers commanded no more than forty men, but the enemy appeared demoralized. Their pursuit continued for about a mile beyond the castle. Then the officers began to realize the spot they were in.

Far back down the road was the American army. In front lay a series of road barricades and increasing numbers of Mexican troops, including cavalry. Maybe the Americans could not get back to the army. Just as irresolution was settling on Hill and Bee, Jackson's two United States cannon thundered down the road. He promised to support the gallant forty in a continued advance, but Magruder, who rode up directly behind Jackson, was more cautious. The main army was too far back; he might lose his guns.

Here was Magruder, one of the army's most belligerent officers, being urged to audacity by three impulsive subordinates who begged him to continue the advance. Finally the captain agreed, after Hill and Bee promised that their infantry would support his guns. The little force moved on for another half mile or so before it ran into trouble.

Suddenly Gen. Pedro de Ampudia confronted the Americans with about 1,500 cavalry, formed his command, and charged. Had the causeway been wider, the charge would have finished the Americans. But the Mexican cavalry could not leave the road, could not get working room for a grand charge. As horsemen galloped down the confines of the causeway, Jackson's guns opened fire and tore huge gaps in their ranks. The attackers stopped, then retreated. But the Americans had had enough. They halted where they were and waited for the rest of the army. So ended Jackson's fighting career in Mexico.[48]

This action on the road to Mexico City was almost the end of the fighting for both armies. Worth's and Quitman's men (Quitman was attacking Belen) had some hard work during the afternoon and evening, but resistance collapsed that night, and on the next day, September 14, Scott's victorious army entered Mexico City.

Depleted, dirty, and worn, the American army occupied the enemy capital. This took nerve. Scott had barely 6,000 men left, and with them he had to police a metropolis of some 200,000 inhabitants. Rigid but fair rules for military and civilian conduct were laid down, guerrilla activities were ruthlessly punished, and soon order had been established.

American soldiers began to relax. With fighting over, the time had come to review the campaign and to pass out laurels to the heroes, among them Lieutenant Jackson. The gallant hours at Chapultepec and the exuberant pursuit toward the San Cosme gate brought more than promotion. Not only was Jackson given the brevet rank of major, but he was mentioned in General Scott's dispatches (the highest of praise!) and publicly commended by the commanding general.

The public commendation proved embarrassing. True, he basked in the meed of renown, but nonetheless he was flustered. At a levee given by Scott shortly after the capture of the capital, Jackson passed down the receiving line and was presented to the general. Scott straightened with exaggerated stiffness, put his hands behind his back, and said coldly, "I don't know that I shall shake hands with Mr. Jackson." The lieutenant reddened, and "was overwhelmed with confusion." Holding the attention of everyone in the room, Scott went on to say, "If you can forgive yourself for the way in which you slaughtered those poor Mexicans with your guns, I am not sure that I can." [49] Warmly then he shook Jackson's hand. It was the finest compliment a young officer could receive, but Scott had ample reason for taking special note of Jackson's conduct.

Most of the reports coming to the general carried some mention of what the artillerist had done. General Pillow was glowing in his remarks about Jackson at Chapultepec:

> Col. Trousdale's command consisting of the 11th and 14th regiments of Inft., and Magruder's field battery, engaged a battery and a large force in the road immediately on the [base] of Chapultepec. The advanced section of the battery, under command of the brave Lt. Jackson, was dreadfully cut up and almost disabled. . . . His brave Lieutenant Jackson, in the face of a galling fire from the enemy's positions, did invaluable service preparatory to the general assault.[50]

Worth, who went out of his division to praise Jackson, said:

> After advancing some four hundred yards, we came to a battery which had been assailed by a portion of Magruder's field guns, particularly the section under the gallant Lt. [?] Jackson, who, although he had lost most of his horses, and many of his men, continued chivalrously at his post, combatting [?] with noble courage.[51]

Magruder summed up the splendid job his fine subordinate had done. And, since it came from Magruder, Jackson must have glowed with pride [52] when he read:

I beg leave to call the attention of the Major Gen'l commanding the division to the conduct of Lt. Jackson of the 1st Arty [?]. If devotion, industry, talent, and gallantry are the highest qualities of a soldier, then he is entitled to the distinction which their possession confers. I have been ably seconded in all the operations of the battery by him; and upon this occasion, when circumstances placed him in command for a short time of an independent section, he proved himself eminently worthy of it.[53]

So General Scott not only praised him for all to hear, but also said in his official report to the government:

To the north and at the base of the mound [Chapultepec], inaccessible on that side, the 11th Infantry, under Lieut.-Colonel Hebert, and [?] the 14th under Colonel Trousdale, and Captain [?] Magruder's field-battery, 1st Artillery (one section advanced under Lieutenant Jackson [?]), all of Pillow's division, had at the same time some spirited affairs against superior. numbers, driving the enemy from a battery in the road, and capturing a gun. In these, the officers and corps named gained merited praise.[54]

Friends were quick to congratulate Jackson. They wanted to know how a hero felt. Hadn't the sight of so many men falling around him given him some anxious moments? Not exactly. His main concern had been that the action might not be spectacular enough to draw the attention of his superiors. The hotter the spot, the better he felt.

This battle feeling was a curious thing. When shot and shell were screaming around him, he felt a better control of himself and more perfect command of his faculties than at any other time. It was a valuable thing for a would-be career officer to learn—that in battle he underwent a sort of transformation, that his fighting blood came up, that he could count on himself under fire.[55]

Immodest as such remarks may have sounded to some of his comrades, Jackson's personality made him many good friends in Mexico. In daily rounds of contacts with local citizens, an innate courtesy stood him in good stead. The Castilian prides himself on inherent graciousness and native good manners, and responds to these traits in others. Consequently, Jackson became popular with several old and prominent families in the capital.

Socially he became something of a lion. His early interest in Spanish and avid study of that language gave him a great advantage over many of his brother officers. This ease with the language, plus a simple, courteous charm, won him entry into some of the best homes in Mexico. He was aware of his good luck. "I think," he wrote Laura in March of 1848, "that I pass my time more agreeably than the greater portion of the officers of the army." [56]

For one thing, his living quarters were better than most of the officers could boast—even those who patronized Mrs. Tobler's "private boarding house for officers only." [57] Located in rooms in the National Palace reserved for military units charged with police and official garrison duties,[58] Jackson's quarters were both extremely comfortable and convenient. For the first time in his life he had some leisure time—time to play, to enjoy himself, and to develop his latent social graces. Quickly he developed an extremely pleasant pattern of living.

The gracious ease of life among Mexico's wealthier families completely captivated the impressionable young soldier, and soon he borrowed certain local customs. One of the customs which he most enjoyed was morning coffee and cakes served in bed. Late dinner seemed strange to him, but afternoon tea kept him going until the evening meal. Spanish cuisine, exotic as it appeared, seemed to agree with the young lieutenant —particularly did he enjoy the plentiful tropical fruits. In fact, it was in Mexico that his enduring taste for fruit began, a taste which would contribute much to the Jackson legend in later years.

Teatime marked the beginning of Jackson's social day. After tea he went visiting. Sometimes this involved calling on friends, sometimes other activities. Taking an obvious pride in his widening activities, the formerly shy young man wrote his sister:

> Although I am usually up at six o'clock and retire to bed at ten and eleven, still the day is not long enough. The morning hours I occupy in studies and business, and the evening in a similar manner, but generally taking a walk after dinner, and sometimes a ride on the Paseo or elsewhere in the evening. The Paseo is a wide road on the southwest of the city and about half a mile in length, with a beautiful fountain in the centre, and is a place of fashionable resort. Families of wealth appear there in their carriages at sunset, partly if not entirely for show. There is also a place of morning resort between the city and the Paseo called the Almeda, which is a beautiful grove of about four hundred by six hundred yards and containing, I think, eight fountains. . . . I purpose on riding to both these places this evening hoping to see something there more attractive than at home. When not on duty I generally pay a visit after supper or tea. Among those families which I visit are some of the first in the republic, as Don Lucas Alleman [Alaman], Martinez del Rio, and I also have the acquaintance of others of some distinction.[59]

These visits seem to have brought Jackson close to the brink of matrimony. He remained characteristically secretive about his Mexico City romance but there is little doubt of his interest in some enticing *señorita*. A casual line in a letter to Laura on October 26 was the closest he came to an open confession of romantic complications: "I think that probably I shall spend many years here," he said, "and may possibly conclude (though I have not yet) to make my life more natural by sharing it with some amiable Senorita." [60]

Added evidence of his attraction for someone in Mexico may be the wholehearted warmth with which he loved the city. Everything in it appealed to him. He became a regular attendant at the Sunday night balls and was obviously a competent dancer.[61] Then, too, there was the factor of language. Jackson apparently began his study of Spanish as a means of learning more about the country. But after a time it came to mean something special to him. Spanish, he often said, was the natural language of lovers, terms of endearment in it being melodious and abundant. For some reason he became particularly familiar with the tender parts of Spanish. And in later years it was in endearing, intimate Spanish phrases that he would speak to his wife.[62]

Life in Mexico was not all a lark for Jackson. Parts of his days were spent in study. He set himself a course of reading in Spanish and English which could help him with his language study and also broaden his culture. Lord Chesterfield's letters to his son he read in Spanish and English. He did the same with Shakespeare. His main attention was directed toward history, and he wrote Laura that he was reading Humboldt's *History of Mexico*, adding that "if I can obtain good histories, I wish to devote some time to them." [63] But he had to admit, even while emphasizing his studiousness, that rain was curtailing his evening visits!

Army duty did not interfere with personal matters to any marked degree. Jackson remained in Magruder's company throughout 1847 and had developed so close a friendship with his captain that he served as the bearer of a challenge from Magruder to Gen. Franklin Pierce.[64] In December, 1847, Jackson shifted back to permanent duty with Capt. Francis Taylor's company. In May, 1848, the additional duties of company assistant commissary of subsistence and acting assistant quartermaster were given to Jackson. But the jobs were not hard, and experience in goading slothful supply agencies to action would be more valuable than Jackson realized.[65]

Reassignment to Taylor's company meant not only promotion but also reunion with an old friend. While it was sad to leave Magruder, under whom so much honor had been won, Taylor was as stanch a friend and as loyal a booster.

Captain Taylor it was, according to several accounts, who first talked seriously to Jackson about religion. During these informal discussions in Taylor's quarters, the captain found Jackson interested but uninformed. The earnest lieutenant had his own rigid code of right and wrong based on an unswerving sense of duty. The older soldier knew his man. Jackson could be guided but not pushed. Religion was a personal thing, Taylor pointed out, a serious matter which each man ought to study. Did not Jackson think he ought to give it solemn thought? Was it not a duty owed to himself? [66] Jackson thought over Taylor's questions and decided he should make a thorough study of religion.

He had little to go on. His mother, he thought, had probably been a Methodist, but he did not know for certain whether he had even been baptized. Having no denominational preference, Jackson began his study of religion by looking around him. An acquaintance with a community of Catholic monks had already introduced him to the Catholic Church—he had spent some days visiting a monastery [67]—and his friends arranged conversations with the Archbishop of Mexico. Jackson had profound respect for the primate, but he did not feel that he had found a sincere road to faith within the Catholic fold. Several things seemed to disturb him. Although impressed with the Catholic services and with Mexico's sincerely devout parishioners, he found something too ornate in the church buildings and something overly ostentatious in the homage paid the clergy. A simpler faith might appeal to him.[68]

From the time he began a serious inquiry into the importance and nature of Christian doctrine, Jackson never stopped his studies; but he was not hasty in confessing faith. Although the Bible became standard reading matter and daily prayer an established routine, Jackson later said that for some time he merely went through these motions with "no feeling stronger than having performed a duty." [69] Virtue lay in slow progress. When Jackson did profess Christianity, he did it wholeheartedly and without doubt. And the time spent in searching had taught him much. Having studied many denominations in quest of one in which he could believe, he had no bigotry in him, but appreciated all forms of Christianity. This open-mindedness would surprise people in later years and would endear Jackson to some of his soldiers. It was not the least of his virtues.

Mexico had done more than develop Jackson the person. Jackson the soldier also emerged. He left Mexico City in late June or early July, 1848, a battle-tried veteran of one of the hardest campaigns in American military history. He was healthier, less nervous than ever,[70] and he had learned a great deal. There was no doubt now that battle was his natural element. Courage was part and parcel of Jackson's nature. The young lieutenant who had studied so doggedly at West Point to learn his books had had a chance to study the things most neglected at the Military Academy—strategy and tactics. The great value of reconnaissance, flanking movements, and the necessity of careful logistical planning were all illustrated in Scott's campaigns. Probably Jackson and many of the other junior officers who were to meet again as friends and enemies in a few years missed some of the finesse of Scott's operations, but Jackson had an inquiring and observant mind. The lessons were not completely lost, and they were to give reality to a private study of war during the next fourteen years, a study which steadily would make Jackson a better soldier. There was no obvious need for continued self-improvement. The United States seemed destined for tranquillity—but there was an off chance....

3

"FROM THE PATH

OF ETERNAL DEATH..."

—JACKSON

Seven days out of Vera Cruz a United States troopship docked at New Orleans, and Jackson, with the rest of Company K, First Artillery was put ashore. Lieutenant Jackson did not have much time to enjoy the fabled Creole city, but his three days, July 17 to 20, were well spent.

The young officer looked the model of a soldier on leave. He wore a well-tailored uniform with soft collar and many brass buttons, and the man in a way fitted the uniform. The daguerreotype he had made in New Orleans reflected his growing maturity. Medium tall and slender, he had a stern set to his thin face that was softened by nice blue eyes and a shock of wavy brown hair. Young Jackson now sported a handsome, close-trimmed beard and mustache which gave him a certain dapper sophistication. The officer who looked well groomed and responsible would get ahead, and this may have been the reason for the beard, which he had not had in Mexico. There he had looked like a warrior—thinner, fiercer, in battle jacket, with flowing locks.

Jackson's three-day leave could hardly have been unpleasant. New Orleans and the country in general greeted veterans of Mexico with gusto. Good-looking veterans fared extremely well, but what Jackson did during his Crescent City sojourn cannot be determined—the picture was evidently his sole memento. Officially, he boarded the transport *Arkansas* on July 20 and arrived August 16 at Fort Columbus on Governor's Island, New York.[1]

From his new post Thomas soon wrote to Laura; he had missed her and her family, wanted very much to see them, and hoped he could

45

arrange a visit during the coming fall. But army politics had to be considered. To Laura he frankly confessed that a trip west so soon after arriving at a new station might involve "sacrifices which I ought not to make." Jackson faced a situation well known to army officers and to government workers. If he left Captain Taylor's company immediately after arriving at a new post, he feared that his position might be filled during his absence. Not because Taylor would be glad to be rid of him— the reverse seemed true. But he might be subordinated to a newcomer. "I do not believe," Thomas wrote Laura, "that Captain Taylor would give his sanction to any officer's coming to the company who would rank me so long as I remain with the company, or so long as there are officers enough with it." Trouble might arise if the number of officers present for duty dropped too low. Then a replacement might edge his way in and force Jackson either down or out. A wait until the following summer would make his stay in Beverly more secure, hence more enjoyable. Rising young officers had to keep an eye to the future.

Laura, though disappointed, would have to be content with knowing that her brother was "still getting better" and had been brevetted a captain, although, as he said, it was still not published to the army.[2]

Actually Jackson had little time to think about going home. Orders soon arrived, sending him off to Carlisle Barracks, Pennsylvania, and assigning him the thankless job of sitting on a general court-martial board.[3] Dreary and unpleasant duty it promised to be, particularly since Carlisle Barracks apparently had little to commend them to a restive young man.

Appearances were deceiving. True, the Barracks were a good hundred miles from a metropolis such as Pittsburgh, but they were close to other fairly lively towns. Then, too, social life on such an important post flourished. And although Jackson did not mention it in his correspondence at the time, his later associations at Carlisle indicate that he rapidly made friends—particularly among the ladies.

Happier than he expected to be in Pennsylvania, Thomas still felt he should visit Laura and her family. Captain Taylor, always a friend, helped him obtain leave for ninety days, effective September 14. In a way leave seemed a bit sad. Life at Carlisle had become gay, and Jackson was going to miss the almost daily "soirees." Without explaining his reasons, he told Laura that when he arrived "you must not expect me to stay with you more than a month."[4] Some of the extra time he might well spend right at Carlisle.

Delaying his arrival in Beverly until early December, Thomas pleaded haste in his flying visits to nearby relatives, and was able to persuade Laura to make only a few imperative calls in and around Beverly and Clarksburg. In the brief time Jackson spent with his sister he found Laura's health improving and discovered that in his nephew, Thomas Jackson Arnold, he had a hero-worshiping admirer. The boy and his uncle became close friends—so close that Jackson soon felt most fatherly toward his namesake.

Visiting, talking health and religion to Laura and politics to his brother-in-law, filled most of Jackson's days at home. The political discussions were interesting but hot. "Mr. Arnold," as Jackson always formally addressed Laura's husband, Jonathan, was a stanch Whig— hence fair game for a Democrat.[5] Jackson's political interests were not yet fully developed, but he was taking an active interest in elections in his home district, and he sniped at Arnold's Whiggery.[6]

The War Department expected Jackson back on duty at Fort Hamilton, New York, by December 14; and since he planned a stopover in Richmond to visit with his influential relative, the Honorable John S. Carlisle, then a member of the Virginia Assembly, he had little time in Beverly.

Ordinarily the trip to Richmond would have been no problem, but this time Jackson ran into trouble. He planned to ride to Hot Springs, Bath County, and there pick up the stage to the capital. Borrowing a horse from his brother-in-law, he started toward Hot Springs. The stage passed through Bath on Monday, Wednesday, and Friday, and Jackson wanted to catch the Wednesday run. He almost made it. Curiously enough, his mount failed him, but not in the expected way. The horse was fast enough—it was Arnold's favorite and best—and was well known throughout the Tygart Valley area.

Jackson rode about twenty miles the first afternoon. Long after nightfall he asked to stay over at the home of an elderly German, Peter Conrad. Made welcome, this moderately tall, thin and stern-looking army officer promptly announced he would arise and be on his way at three in the morning. As usual, aside from the amenities expected toward a kind host, Jackson said little and gave no indication of his connection with anyone in the vicinity of Beverly. Peter Conrad was a stolid man. He liked his friends—looked out for them, in fact. Jonathan Arnold was a friend, and this odd stranger with a fancy for early rising was obviously stealing Arnold's horse.

When Jackson arose and prepared to be on his way, he discovered that his horse was not ready, nor, from Conrad's remarks, was it likely to be. With any two other people the situation could have been easily settled, but Conrad was fearless, according to one who knew him, "and a more obstinate specimen of the genus homo never lived. Having once made up his mind . . . to change his opinion was a task about equal to a new creation." The argument which ensued was conducted by two equally firm individuals. It took much doing to convince his host that

Jackson was not a horse thief. But by then so much time had passed that Jackson missed the stage and had to spend an extra day in Hot Springs—an enforced vacation he thoroughly enjoyed.

An equally pleasant stay in Richmond, during which the eminent Representative Carlisle "allowed no opportunity to pass unimproved in which he could manifest his kindness," [7] broke the trek back to garrison duty at a new post.

Fort Hamilton stood on Long Island, about ten miles from New York City. Here the First Artillery was stationed until October, 1850. But Jackson would not be at the fort constantly—there was New York to see and still more courts-martial at Carlisle Barracks. Obviously thinking back to his sumptuous housing in the palace of Mexico City, Jackson worked hard at making his new quarters comfortable. Bachelor or not, he would have some conveniences. By February, 1849, Thomas could write Laura that "I am well fixed here, having my rooms both carpeted and decently furnished." [8]

Military duties at the fort occupied Jackson perhaps more than he had expected. Taylor's frequent absences from the company often gave Jackson the responsibility of command. Commanding the company while at the same time serving as commissary and quartermaster proved no light task. In addition, of course, Lieutenant Jackson was expected to drill his men and keep his section of guns in the best condition. No stranger to hard work, Jackson did it well and even had time to spare. Had there been more to do, he would not have been able to devote so much time to worrying. The thing that most concerned him was his health. References to health and general physical condition had frequently appeared in Jackson's correspondence before, but now he gave most of his attention to this subject.

Exactly what caused his almost constant discomfort is obscure. He believed it to be some type of "dyspepsia, not of a dangerous character," but this designation was applied to all sorts of undiagnosed diseases. [9] It was almost certainly some sort of stomach ailment, [10] but just what sort went undetermined. Not because Jackson shunned medical attention—quite the contrary. Most doctors helped him little, and he would move on to others. Finally he resorted to fads in a search for health—with some apparent success.

When Jackson reached Fort Hamilton after his visit to Beverly, he lost no time in having a physical check-up. Laura doubtless urged him to do this, and there was good reason. From a maximum of 164 pounds, he had slowly declined to a point below 140. Fears of a fundamental constitutional defect led him to the examination. There was good news—lungs and liver were all right. But the doctor had some wise and significant advice for this thin and edgy patient. Jackson must stop "confining" his mind too much; concentration, even in letter writing, disrupted digestion. It was good advice, but on this particular patient it had little effect; Jackson's existence was almost wholly regulated by his mind.

Various infirmities kept Jackson close to Fort Hamilton for a while. Gradually he thought he was better, and letters to Laura contained increasing remarks about improving health. He even fancied himself well enough in March, 1849, to contemplate a visit to New York City,[11] and the visit proved well worth the trouble. Not only did Thomas have an opportunity for some relaxation, but he consulted a new doctor, "one of the first medical men of New York City."[12] The patient improved "in both flesh and strength and ... in health also."[13] The new physician obviously did not think Jackson sufficiently infirm to confine him to quarters, and soon had him increasing his activities. Significantly, Jackson told Laura in April that "I have lately commenced visiting more frequently, and every few evenings receive an invitation to some social party."[14] But he did not intend to overstrain as he improved; delicate health could sometimes be convenient. He was able to use his health as an excuse for not doing an errand for Laura, telling her that "my strength forbids much exercise, and especially walking on the hard pavements of the city." Since this remark came in the same letter which described Thomas's increasing social life, Laura doubtless saw through the subterfuge.

Since health assumed such importance, Jackson began a study of it in relation to himself. He concluded, finally, that a rigid discipline of his system would be of real benefit, and his whole way of life changed. Schedule and regimen in habits, diet, and exercise were instituted. He was most strict about his diet—and unfortunately he was a dictatorial dieter, wanting Laura to do exactly as he did in eating. He was improving as a result of his Spartan fare, he said, and Laura might also benefit by it.

> I have so strictly adhered to my wholesome diet of stale bread and plainly dressed meat (having nothing on it but salt) that I prefer it now to almost anything else. The other evening I tasted a piece of bread with butter on it, and then the bread without it, and rather gave my preference to the unbuttered bread; and hence I may never taste any more of this once much relished seasoning.

Thomas continued his account of self-denial with apparent relish, and then exhorted Laura:

> I think if you would adopt for your breakfast a cup of moderately strong black tea, stale wheat bread (wheat bread raised, and not less than twenty-four hours old), fresh meat—broiled or roasted is best—the yolk of one or two eggs—the white is hardly worth eating as it requires digestion and affords but little nutrition. For dinner the same kind of bread and meat, one vegetable only, say peas, beans or this year's potatoes, and for

drink, plain water. For tea, the same kind of bread and drink as for breakfast, and nothing else, unless you choose a little butter. . . . Of what I have recommended, you can eat as much as your appetite craves, provided that you take regular meals and plenty of exercise, say, not less than three hours per day. I presume that your daily duties require you to be moving probably that much. . . . And I regard green tea and coffee so injurious to the nerves that you should always prefer water to either. . . . If you should conclude to adopt the foregoing, do not taste other things of which you are fond, unless it be fruits, and they should be ripe. . . . You should try and forget that you are infirm, and pay no attention to your symptoms, as most any person can, by being too attentive to every little pain.[15]

There was something odd about the last sentence coming from brother Thomas.

Weird as it may have seemed to his associates, Jackson stuck to his regimen with grim dedication. Having renounced foods which he liked, he followed his own advice to Laura: "If you commence on this diet, remember that it is like a man joining the temperance society: if he afterwards tastes liquor he is gone;"[16] and gradually his system worked. The system actually may not have been as effective as his faith in it, but whatever the cause, he was able to report real improvement in his physical condition by the end of 1849, although he still suffered severely from sore and weak eyes.

To the diet, Jackson added increased exercise, taken in more violent doses. In his spare moments at Fort Hamilton, Jackson could be seen walking, leaping, and swinging his arms furiously. This was all part of the development program—along with his single-minded dedication to regular habits and plain food. Rather marked changes took place by April of 1850. Now Jackson weighed 166 pounds, two more than he could remember ever having weighed. And he appeared inordinately proud of having hardened his muscles in addition to building up his weight.

Here was solid evidence of the soundness of his stringent program of rehabilitation. Still, Jackson realized that his rebuilding had not been accomplished without severe sacrifice. In August, 1850, he wrote Laura that if he were able to come for a visit she might not like to have him around. He thought his rules of daily conduct might be too finicky for the Arnolds' taste. "It is probable," he confessed in a burst of understatement, "that I am more particular in my rules than any person of your acquaintance."[17]

Recreation was obviously one of the basic prescriptions in the treatment of Jackson's peculiar stomach ailment. He adopted a new fad— one which was highly popular all around the nation among those with real or fancied infirmities. Droves of people were flocking to resorts where the "waters" might be taken. These waters supposedly contained a wondrous cure-all, such as sulphur or some other foul-tasting mineral. Spas and "hot springs" were not new in medical history—such places had been popular in Colonial America—but they enjoyed a popular revival in mid-century and Jackson joined the faithful. He had great hopes for what waters of various flavors might do for his particular ailment. Doubtless some of the alum liquids he consumed in the next few years damaged his delicate digestion; but he thought he was being helped, and that may have been the important thing.[18]

Much more important, he came to believe that his improvement was inevitable—the result of Divine ordinance. With this concept began the most important change in the life of Thomas Jonathan Jackson. Not an abrupt or startling transformation, or a blinding conversion, the change was rather a new emphasis, an awakening. It came slowly and almost imperceptibly. Always his letters had contained some references to Divine Providence and Almighty God, but now, coincident with his severe physical decline at Fort Hamilton, a new note of religious feeling appeared. Jackson displayed a growing tendency to mention his illness and Divine Providence together, and in time, the two subjects became inseparable. When the trend began is uncertain, but in January of 1849 Thomas wrote Laura that he was still living—a matter of mild surprise to him, apparently—"and, with the blessing of God, hope to live for some years to come." [19] Two months later, in comforting Laura about the death of several neighbors, Thomas revealed a philosophic outlook which told more of himself than perhaps he realized. "All must pay the same final debt," he wrote, "and my sincere desire and thrice daily prayer is, that when your exit comes that your previous preparation will have been made." Obviously he had been dwelling on the question of heaven and earth. He warmed to the subject:

> How *glorious* will it be in that august and heaven-ordained day to meet with mother, brother, sister and father around the shining throne of Omnipotence; there I wish and hope to meet you, with a joy that shall never be alloyed by separation.[20]

Increasing awareness of a debt to an *"All Ruling Being"* is reflected more and more in his letters throughout 1849. Conscious, now, of this debt, Jackson characteristically determined to make a formal declaration of his feelings.

The influence of Capt. Francis Taylor on Jackson's religious life has often been pointed out, and undoubtedly the captain did much to turn the mind of his earnest lieutenant to religious thought. There is no better evidence of Taylor's influence than the fact that he and a brother officer sponsored Jackson's baptism. Jackson was not sure whether he had ever been baptized, and since he now considered himself wholly a member of the Christian community, he wanted to be certain of baptism. But he did not want the sacrament to mean that he was ushered into communion in the Episcopal Church. Uncertain about which denomination he most favored, he was careful to stipulate his terms for baptism. After negotiations which faintly resembled those of Talleyrand, the sacrament was administered on Sunday, April 29, 1849, in the little St. John's Episcopal Church, across the street from Fort Hamilton, Kings County, New York.[21]

Jackson's letters to Laura throughout this period reveal an almost mystical identification in his mind between God and his own physical condition. At length he became convinced that illness was punishment meted out by Divine decree. What clearer evidence than his own case? "My afflictions," he wrote Laura, "I believe were decreed by Heaven's Sovereign, as a punishment for my offences against his Holy Laws: and have probably been the instrument of turning me from the path of eternal death, to that of everlasting life." [22]

If further confirmation were needed, his marked improvement could be cited. Diet, rigid regulation of personal habits, exercise, and all the rest were but adjuncts to Providence; they were aids to convalescence. The cure lay elsewhere. Admitting to his sister, to whom he could always confide his inner feelings, that "before the age of maturity, I ... endeavored to lead a Godly life, but obstacles so great presented themselves as to cause me to return to the world, and its own," he added that

within the past few years I have endeavored to live more nearly unto God. ... I believed that God would restore me to perfect health, and such continues to be my belief. ... yes, my dear sister, rather than wilfully violate the known will of God I would forfeit my life; it may seem strange to you, yet nevertheless such a resolution I have taken, and I will by it abide.[23]

When she realized the depth of Jackson's new faith, Laura apparently worried that her brother was becoming too ascetic. She admired him, but she could not share his new-found strength and sense of well-being. Laura became a problem. With the usual zeal of a convert, Jackson wanted to share his joy. This desire led him to a new task. He would work for Christ, and he would begin in his own family. Curiously enough, the roles of Thomas and Laura had become reversed. In earlier years, when Thomas had been at West Point and had been something less than devout, Laura had tried to serve as a spiritual guide. Now it was Thomas's task to guide his sister.

He seized upon a matter of health as a means of helping Laura. In March, 1850, he learned that his niece, Anna Grace Arnold, was seriously ill. Here was his opportunity.

I hope that my dear little niece has entirely recovered her health, but do you not think, my dear sister, that her illness has been the result of a

Divine decree. You remember that once you were a professed follower of Christ, and that subsequently you disavowed his cause. This my Dear Sister, I do not believe will go unpunished, unless you return to him. Will you not do it? You professed religion when quite young, and possibly could not at that tender age appreciate its blessings. . . . And I fear that unless you again acknowledge obedience to his Divine Laws, that some great affliction will yet be your lot. . . . I should regret to leave you unconverted, but his will and not mine be done. . . . Oh! Sister, do drop your *Infidel Books.* Come lead a happy life, and die a happy death. And indeed I hope to see that day when you will pour forth your soul in pure prayer. My daily prayers are for your salvation, and some of my prayerful petitions have been answered, and I hope that ere long this will be included.[24]

The campaign to save Laura continued for some time, but would end successfully. Work for Christ, now begun, was a task which occupied Jackson until the day of his death.

Despite his efforts to halt Laura's backsliding, Jackson was anxious to convince her that this hard daily schedule was not a type of religious penance. Spartan existence he enjoyed and found did him good. "My life," he wrote, "is not one of privation, as you sometimes see among Christians, but I enjoy the pleasures of the world, but endeavor to restrict them to the limits which Nature's God had assigned to them." There is more than casual connection, however, between his chosen way of life and the religion he later embraced.

He did enjoy himself. Visits to New York City helped. More and more he began to circulate in society, and, in addition, he became fascinated with certain other advantages of the city. Bookstores were something of a new phenomenon to him, and New York had many. A discriminating reader, he soon found the best old bookstalls, as well as the better publishing houses. Harper's and Appleton's were among his favorites, but he moved widely around town, looking, buying books, and collecting used-book catalogues which he shipped off to his brother-in-law.[25]

Walking tours of the metropolis served several useful purposes. Leisurely tramps helped Jackson's eyes, in spite of the glare,[26] and at the same time the exercise fitted in with his revitalizing scheme. The city fascinated him. It was almost too much for a country boy, even a reasonably well-traveled one; just seeing New York was a liberal education. "Yesterday, whilst walking through the city," he wrote Laura on April 7, 1849,

I thought of the pleasure which I would derive from sharing the contemplation of its beauties and wonders with you. Naturally I recalled to mind, and applied to New York, what the Frenchman asserted of Paris when he said that when a man had seen Paris, that he had seen all the world. In New York may be found almost anything which the inclination may desire but peaceful quiet. Everything is in motion, everything alive with animation. In this busy throng none feel the long and tedious hour; even the invalid for the time forgets his infirmities and with wondering admiration contemplates the surrounding scenes.[27]

The last sentence was doubtless self-descriptive.

Jackson found the city warm and friendly. His circle of acquaintances widened, and as he knew more and more people, he came to feel a part of the city and its activities. Parties, visits to friends, even such winter sports as sleighing filled his leisure hours.[28]

Other diversions there were, too, for the visits to Carlisle Barracks continued. Jackson must have impressed his superiors with his willingness to undertake the deadly chore of sitting on numerous courts-martial. Some of these proceedings lasted for several weeks, but the young lieutenant had no hesitation in accepting such assignments. The longer the trials, the longer he had with the "amiable and I might say lovely ladies" at Carlisle. Nothing was said to Laura about any special lady friend, but she probably had suspicions.[29]

Court-martial duty shuttled Jackson back and forth between Carlisle and other parts of northern New York throughout the year 1850. In May he heard trial testimony at Plattsburg Barracks "on the borders of Canada." On the way he saw Fort Ticonderoga and Crown Point and wrote Laura about their military importance; he hoped to visit Montreal and Quebec, too, but feared scarcity of money and time would prevent. In August he was ordered to Fort Ontario, "about twelve hours' travel from Niagara Falls, and consequently intend visiting there before returning home." This was not his last visit to the falls.[30]

In September official duties took Jackson to West Point. The old place looked different, somehow. One of his barracks buildings was gone, and a new one erected in its place. Some of the landmarks brought nostalgic memories of earlier good days: the Kosciusko monument, the garden, and "Old Put" stood just about the same; so did the Plain, on which he had spent some harsh summers. A few old friends greeted Jackson with joy. Gentlemanly Dabney Maury and courtly George McClellan, now instructors at the Point, were old comrades. Maury and the rest were a little older, but Maury, at least, still had his old zest for living. The young instructors were part of a happy officers' mess, presided over by a beloved Virginian, George Thomas, and Jackson doubtless enjoyed more than one convivial meal with them. To his classmates Tom Jackson had changed. He was still "cold and impassive of aspect" and still looked awkward and ungainly, but a new characteristic caught Maury's attention. As he talked with Tom he noticed that his friend kept raising an arm in the air, with rather disturbing regularity. Quizzed about this, Jackson explained that "one of his legs was bigger than the other, and that one of his arms was likewise unduly heavy." He raised the arm "so that . . . the blood would run back into his body and lighten it." [31] (The gesture was one which persisted and was to become the basis for one of the Jackson myths.) There was no doubt in Maury's mind that Tom was "the most remarkable character I have ever known."

This good visit with friends at his old school marked one of the last official court-martial assignments held by Jackson. He returned to Fort Hamilton and to the social whirl of New York. By now, though, he had decided on another phase in his campaign of self-improvement.

Not all his spare time would be given to recreation. Some of it would be used to increase his general educational background. Even during the hectic and busy days in Mexico, Jackson had prescribed a stiff course of reading and language study for himself. Never did he believe that his student days were behind him—always he was reading, thinking, studying. But now he channeled all this energy to one purpose. The studies were designed to make him a better soldier.

A wide knowledge of history would form the background for proficiency in the military arts. Not only would the campaigns of the great captains offer models to follow, but broad historical perspective would make an officer a better citizen. New York bookstores offered numbers of histories at low prices and Jackson bought them.[32] Weak eyes restricted his reading, but a careful schedule put them to minimum strain.[33] Along with ancient history, Napoleon's campaigns, and other histories, Jackson kept up with a few contemporary magazines. This may have been the reason for an increasing interest in national politics. The crisis of the Union in 1850 could hardly have failed to alarm even the most politically unconcerned. Jackson favored compromise and was vastly relieved when Webster spoke for Clay's proposals. Webster's remarks Jackson felt were "truly noble," but he pondered an ominous question: Would the Compromise of 1850 last?

The state of the Union was not all that worried Jackson. A personal loss wounded him deeply. Uncle Cummins Jackson, who had gone gold hunting in California, died on December 4, 1849. Thomas, not learning of it until the following March, wrote that the news "goes to my heart. Uncle was a father to me." [34] Briefly he hoped that the rumor of Cummins's death was untrue, but the hope was short-lived. So many relatives and old friends were going. Added reason to lean for strength on the Lord.

In October, 1850, the War Department put an abrupt end to Jackson's career at Fort Hamilton. Suddenly there would be no more society, and very little leisure time. There would not even be much time, for a while at least, to worry about eyes, health, or other personal problems. The First Artillery was ordered to duty on an Indian frontier.

4

MAJOR JACKSON'S
FLORIDA CAMPAIGN

FLORIDA IN OCTOBER promised to be a welcome relief from
the cold of New York. But Florida, a relatively new state, with about
85,000 inhabitants, already had achieved a reputation for being hard on
the army. Earlier campaigns against the Seminole Indians had cost many
lives, a great deal of money, and had left the state dotted with forts
and military posts. Social life at most of the stations was something less
than scintillating.

Theoretically, peace prevailed even in the dense swamp country of
the interior, although small numbers of Seminoles had eluded deportation
to Indian Territory in the deadly West and were lost in the woods,
palmetto thickets, and marshes. Led by the recalcitrant Billy Bowlegs,
these few holdouts were not strong enough to make sustained attacks
against army outposts, but they could make the lives of Florida settlers
fairly hazardous.

The army found itself in an odd predicament. Obviously the remaining Seminoles should be transported out of Florida. But if deportation were momentarily out of the question, they must at least be
restrained from killing citizens. State officials could not cope with the
situation alone, particularly in view of the agitation which many would-be
war profiteers stirred up in Washington. With the army ensconced in
large numbers around the state, supply contracts offered lucrative opportunities for speculators. The money motive was far more important
in garrisoning Florida than was the awesome threat of a few hundred
ragged Seminoles, skulking for their lives in some dank swamp. So the
army came.[1]

56

With other units came Company E, First Artillery, Brev. Maj. William Henry French commanding. Attached to this company was 1st Lt. and Bt. Maj. Thomas J. Jackson, who served from time to time as quartermaster and commissary. Jackson hated leaving Taylor's command, but E Company needed another subaltern, and on October 1 he received the assignment.[2] French was an old comrade in the First Artillery. With the regiment in Mexico, he had received brevets for participation in many of the same battles which had earned Jackson his own honors—captain, for gallant and meritorious conduct at Cerro Gordo; major, for similar conduct at Contreras and Churubusco. French long had commanded a company, and during 1849 had been at Fort Columbus, New York. About three weeks after Jackson joined them, French and his men embarked on the transport *Kate Hunter* for Florida, arriving at Tampa Bay on November 6, 1850, and at Fort Casey, headquarters of the troops in Florida (and Company E's nominal destination) on the tenth.[3]

On December 13 Company E moved inland to occupy Fort Meade.[4] Located on the Peace River, about thirty miles east-southeast of Tampa, Fort Meade was one of a series of small forts guarding the network of interior rivers and lakes. In December, 1850, the main part of the post consisted of a few flimsy buildings huddled on low ground, not too far from the east shore of the river. Around the fort a struggling frontier trading post had grown up,[5] but the place was isolated—department headquarters were far away, with the nearest large base at Fort Brooke in Tampa.

On December 18 French surveyed his new post.[6] His company would be the garrison—they would serve as "Red-legged Infantry," [7] keeping tabs on Indian activities in the surrounding country. Despite the rather dismal site which greeted him, French had reason to be pleased. He now had an independent command, a chance for distinction. If he did well, Fort Meade might lead to more important commands.

Captain French had ambition. A tall, bulky man, his outwardly jovial, good-humored attitude could be deceiving. A reputation for wit and excellence as an artillerist had won him his chance—if these qualities deserted him, he stood to be in trouble. Quickly French adjusted his command to routine. After guard details were organized and the fort policed to spit-and-polish gloss, Fort Meade's garrison began scouting the lake country for signs of the Seminoles.

He could count on Jackson for considerable help in making this venture a success. French knew Jackson's reputation. Not only had his lieutenant shown competence and bravery in Mexico; he had also proved able as a commissary and quartermaster officer. Good staff work would be essential at an isolated post, and Jackson seemed the man to give just that. At first the two men got along pretty well; in a way they complemented each other. Jackson, almost French's opposite, was not large of frame, was shy with those he did not know well, and was not given to raucous humor. One characteristic French and Jackson shared: both were ambitious.

Lieutenant Jackson soon could see that he would be one of the busiest men on the post. As the company's commissary and quartermaster officer, he had to take charge of all government property and issue all supplies to the garrison. Although 2d Lt. Absalom Baird, a recent transfer from the Second Artillery, would assist him, the task still loomed large. Handling of supplies was a full-time chore, but Jackson's duties were enlarged beyond supply. Since there were few commissioned officers present at Fort Meade, each was expected to participate in scouting expeditions into the Indian country. Scouting appealed to Jackson. Not only did these expeditions relieve the tedium of garrison life, but they also held out the prospect of Indian fighting.

Lieutenant Baird began the scouting missions from Fort Meade in mid-January, 1851, found no evidence of Indians, and returned without incident.[8] Shortly after Baird's venture Major French became alarmed about the possibility of Seminole depredations against settlers around Lake Tohopekaliga, which lay roughly forty miles northeast of Fort Meade. Jackson received orders to find the lake, go around it, and hunt for Indian signs.

With twelve men, two noncoms, and an ignorant guide, he left Fort Meade on January 27, heading generally east. After three days of hard marching, during which time he visited the shores of several lakes, he turned back to Fort Meade, and confessed to French that he did not think he had found the lake in question.[9] French, miffed at the failure, grumbled that a march of more than ninety miles to find an objective not more than fifty miles away displayed some sort of incompetence—although it might easily have been due to a lack of maps.[10]

The commander made quite a fetish of these scouts. Anxious that the general commanding the United States troops in Florida be aware of his good efforts to obtain intelligence of Indian movements, he announced that "all the efficient force of my command has been and will be at all seasons as well as at the times designated in readiness to keep [the general] advised of any violation on the part of the Indians, of their treaties."[11] Citizens in the country near Fort Meade, he boasted, "feel no insecurity and no apprehension of further aggression."

More scouts were sent out. French wanted to increase his garrison's reputation for vigilance. On February 17, he directed Jackson to take a detail on another hunt for the elusive lake, to strike it at its southern point, and scout along the eastern shore toward the "summit of the Lake." More specific directions were given this time, and results were expected. On the eighteenth Jackson's column moved out, equipped for a seven days' march. This time, fortunately for pathfinder Jackson, he found Lake Tohopekaliga.

Finding the lake did not make the scout a success. Rain turned the ground near the lake into an impassable quagmire, and Jackson concluded he could not take his men around to the eastern shore—he could not get past the southern end of the lake. So he altered his instructions as best the situation would permit and scouted along the western and northern edges. Unfortunately, no traces of Indians were found. There were, however, some compensations. Jackson discovered that scouting had a grand effect on his general health. Riding briskly through pine barrens, along lakes and swamps in relatively mild weather, gave him "a relish for everything." [12] The necessity of asking local residents for information helped break the monotony of routine.

While on some of these scouting trips, Jackson sampled the flavor of a society completely new to him. Most of the citizens he saw—and they were few and far between—were sugar planters. At first he was deceived into thinking that he had hit upon a large corn-producing area, so much like corn farms did the sugar plantations appear. But soon he was put right and introduced to the planters' rather fashionable homes, where he found that some Florida citizens were glad the army was on hand. Patience with the Seminoles had worn thin, and the inefficiency of government agents charged with removing the remaining Indians drove increasing numbers of people to welcome military force. [13]

Back at the fort, though, Jackson and his troopers found their reception out of keeping with the mildness of Florida temperatures. Major French, possibly prompted by reports of lavish entertaining in the interior, soon decided he would have to do his own scouting if he wanted it done right. In reporting Jackson's latest wanderings to Army Headquarters, French said:

> I propose ... to go myself and endeavor to turn the Southern & eastern point of the Lake, not that every endeavor has not been made for that purpose but that I should rather bear that responsibility myself than throw it on my subalterns should Indians be on the other side at this season which is "corn planting" time. [14]

The implication was not that his subordinates were inefficient—just that he appreciated the importance of scouting, and would personally obtain accurate information. His ambition was showing.

Everything could not be done by the commanding officer, no matter how hard he worked. Some of the scouting would still involve Jackson and Baird. Unfortunately both became sick in mid-March, and were for a time rendered *hors de combat*. And as late as March 18 French was reassuring headquarters that "as soon as practicable the detachment will make endeavor to reach the East shore of Tohopekaliga." He had not yet been able to go himself.[15]

Other duties had intervened to keep French from his scouting. Efforts were afoot to improve conditions at the fort. Part of the civilizing process involved the arrival of families of both officers and men. The post had been too small and too rough to house families at first, but Army Headquarters had given permission to expand the living quarters and to put the fort on a more permanent basis. A building program was under way.

Despite a bustling exterior, Fort Meade was a troubled station. The commanding officer concentrated much energy on keeping the appearance of good order, but appearances were most deceiving. French was aware that liquor was getting onto the post, probably through the teamsters who periodically brought in supplies. Army Headquarters, however, felt that all the blame could not be placed upon the wagoners —some men in the fort were encouraging the smuggling. Butchers in the cookhouse seemed likely candidates for the dubious honor. French, informed of these suspicions, received a curt reminder: "Of course you will take all proper means to detect & punish, as far as the law allows, such as introduce liquor into your garrison." [16] Such a situation was impossible. Nothing would do more to dim French's prospects than to have a drunken garrison lurching around the limits of Fort Meade. The whole expansion program might well be retarded, and the major's career ruined. French responded to the challenge by tightening the rein on his men—he devoted even more than the usual attention to appearances, and in due time became inordinately pleased with the looks of his command. All appeared running smoothly.

But pressures of the new discipline were felt in all quarters. Jackson in particular resented French's dictatorial manner. Compelled by the scrutiny of higher authority to keep Fort Meade calm, French assumed increasing duties unto himself—even to interfering with the business of the commissary and quartermaster officer. Such behavior Jackson felt to be intolerable. He knew his army regulations and fully understood the rights, duties, and privileges of quartermaster and supply officers in garrison service. Jackson's position, however, was a bit extreme. He felt that the quartermaster officer on a post should be virtually autonomous, under only nominal control from the commanding officer—a point of view he had been driven to by French's galling supervision. Jackson reacted by demanding an independence which was equally galling to French.

Something else added to their mutual irritation. Jackson was not just a first lieutenant—he was also a brevet major. True, French's brevet was senior in date, but still the title "Major" was being applied to Jackson by the men, a practice which Jackson, of course, did not discourage. He thought of himself as a major, and continually made it obvious to his commanding officer. Consequently the usual deference of rank for rank was not quite as much in evidence as French would have liked. The situation boiled down to a conflict of ambitions. French, anxious to command a garrison successfully, could not tolerate a subordinate who resented subordination. Jackson, at the same time, could not bear a commanding officer who so insisted on commanding. Gradually the two men came to dislike each other personally.

Personal estrangement was unfortunate, since French and Jackson had been friends for so long. Their friendship had continued even after arrival at Fort Meade. When Mrs. French and the rest of the major's family arrived on the post, Jackson was a frequent and welcome guest. The French home was an extremely pleasant place to visit. A charming hostess, Mrs. French was one of the great favorites of the officer corps throughout the army,[17] and Jackson was as captivated by her company as were the other officers.

Then, too, Major French had taken an active interest in Jackson's career. In February, 1851, Jackson sought his advice about transferring to another regiment, possibly one stationed in a less isolated spot. French said later that he had been glad to help, so willing, in fact, that he wrote Jackson's letter of application for transfer himself, "in order that it might be properly worded and most strongly expressed." Jackson did not know how to work his Mexican War commendations into the application, and French also offered advice on that point: "I pointed out to him by his wish how they could be alluded to without overstepping the bounds of modesty and propriety." [18]

Unfortunately the two men could not get along when one commanded the other—nor is there any real evidence that either tried very hard. Thrown together on an isolated post with restricted social life, dreary routine, and an unhealthy climate, they were bound to clash. The real breakup occurred over an absurd point of order, about which both felt utterly self-righteous.

Battle was joined on the question of who had the right to supervise the construction of some of the new public buildings going up at the post. Citing army regulations with the sureness of a barrister, Jackson claimed the honor for the quartermaster officer present on duty. "These rights," he complained to Department Headquarters, "Captain and Bt. Maj. Wm. H. French 1st Artillery has denied me: informing me, that I have no control whatever over the construction of the buildings. . . ." [19]

Not giving an inch, Jackson did his best to manage the building crew—consisting most of the time of one artificer. French, always on hand, continued issuing orders and telling Jackson he had no authority. The situation rapidly deteriorated. Insulted by constant interference, Jackson began to "cut" his superior dead when he passed him on the post.[20] French, for his part, grew angry. Jackson's conduct bordered on the insubordinate—and there could be little doubt that deep down he was just that. By late March, conversations between the two involved only official matters. The whole garrison could not help feeling the hostility, and it was bad for discipline. The post suffered. Something had to be done.

Jackson made the first move. Stopping French one day, he stiffly explained how aggrieved he felt. French's attitude could not be caused by anything save a deep personal dislike for him. Why was this?

Now that Jackson had broached the sore issue, French spoke in consoling terms. His junior officer had misinterpreted the whole thing. Dislike had no part in his official actions. He had been forced to hold Jackson's ambition for independence down, but only because he had to do "what I deemed right." The whole nasty mess could be officially handled, if Jackson really felt he had been unjustly treated. With a fatherly interest in his subordinates, French professed himself always ready to forward the complaints of his officers on to higher authority for decision. If Jackson felt that his rights had been infringed, French would gladly forward a letter from him to "our common superior." [21]

Jackson jumped at the chance to settle the unpleasantness via official channels. His letter, written on March 23, 1851, reviewed the army regulations which he thought gave the supervision of buildings to the quartermaster officer, and asked for a decision on whether or not his commanding officer had usurped authority. His communication contained no hint of a personal cleavage between himself and French. But French's endorsement on this letter, plus a dispatch of his own which accompanied it to headquarters of troops in Florida, painted a picture far different from Jackson's. In his endorsement French wrote that Jackson was trying to "assume to himself more importance than the Commandant of the Post." The more French thought matters over, the angrier he got. On March 26, in transmitting all of the papers to Tampa, he added this note:

> The pretensions of Brevet Major Jackson acting as Qr Master at this post to exercise an independent position as far as his duties as quarter Master are involved, are of long standing and he has continued to urge them with a pertinacity so constantly increasing that finally I informed him that any communication he might desire to forward upon the subject of what he styles his "rights" would be transmitted by me to higher authority.
>
> Hence this letter.—On account of this official misunderstanding Bt Major Jackson has for some time back carried it into his private relations with me to such an extent that I was obliged to call his attention to paragraph No. 418. Gen. Reg. 1847.—
>
> This unpleasant state of things has grown out of a mistaken view

which Bt Maj Jackson has taken in reference to his relation to his commanding officer, and as this anxiety manifested in his communication, to be relieved from subordination has manifested itself in minor ways with officers junior to him, I am impressed with the belief that the opinion and decision of the General Commanding will do much to restore a better feeling at this Post.[22]

French's letter served the purpose for which it was designed. The commanding general could hardly take a favorable stand on Jackson's request in view of a general order which appeared to cover the question.

As a result, Jackson drew a reprimand from the general. It was not too harsh, but it was a reprimand. The quartermaster officer at any post was irrevocably under the orders of the commandant, he was told; the commandant was responsible for everything done at his post—he was the one who would get the blame for failure.

"The Staff Officer, as expressed in Orders No. 13, is emphatically his [Commanding Officer's] Assistant," said the Commanding General, who proceeded to preach a little to Jackson:

It is not strange that younger officers should make claims of this kind, from the fact that older ones have asserted their independence in many matters relating to their official duties, which, if sanctioned, would reverse an established military principle, that the Senior Officer, when elligible [sic], shall command & give all necessary orders.

A difference of opinion amongst officers, may honestly occur, on points of duty.—It ought never to degenerate into personalities, or to be considered a just cause for withholding the common courtesies of life so essential in an Officer & to the happiness & quiet of garrison life.[23]

The general certainly was mistaken about one thing—garrison life was not so quiet at Fort Meade! Nor did his letter help matters. Jackson was stung by the rebuke, and in the remark about personalities he found a clue to what French had said in passing the correspondence along. The commandant had taken advantage of his position, which was hardly surprising, but nonetheless unfair.

Bad blood obviously existed between Jackson and French, but a surface quarrel about interpretation of professional rights hardly seems a sufficient basis for the events of the next few weeks. Something far more serious must have made the two men such bitter enemies. The explanation may lie in the isolation of life at Fort Meade. Indians could not be found, despite frantic searches; the scouts were uniformly uneventful, and this threw the garrison upon itself for excitement. The atmosphere grew strained and explosive. Small things loomed large— petty personal incidents took on the dimensions of mortal insults. Time for constant introspection became time for growing suspicion. The infernally damp, clammy and mild climate added to the trouble. A poisonous swamp illness came from the dampness, and with it a sinking of spirits. Dreary, deadly days stretched on until there had to be some outlet for men venomously conscious of the thereness of each other.

Jackson cracked under the strain—his weak eyes grew weaker and his general health broke. In mid-March he reported to the post physician and went on sick call.[24] Taken off the active list, Jackson had no official duties to perform, and his eyes drastically limited his reading. Frustration set in—no chance for military distinction, and the drab prospects of lengthy service under a man like French adding to his depression. He lived for distinction in his profession—for fame. In March, he summed up the feeling in a letter to Laura: "You say that I must live on it [fame] for the present. I say not only for the present, but during life." Laura, an ever-perceptive sister, sensed something of Thomas's mood, and thought he wanted to leave the army. No, he said, "it is doubtful whether I shall relinquish the military profession, as I am very partial to it." [25] But the army had its obligations.

Jackson had some obligations of his own, obligations that came with Christianity. One of these was church attendance, which was out of the question at Fort Meade, but he tried to make up for missing service by reading the Bible. Another Christian duty he had already assumed—that of spreading light in his own family. Continuing that campaign, he reminded Laura of her duty to espouse Christ again. He did not want her to do this with any reservations: "A hypocrite is, in my judgment, one of the most detestable of beings. My opinion is that every one should honestly and carefully investigate the Bible, and then if he can believe it to be the word of *God*, to follow his teachings. . . ." [26]

Another obligation which Jackson recognized was upholding Christian moral standards—an obligation closely related to professional ethics. Major French's conduct was to merge the two in Jackson's mind and to impose on him the necessity for a moral campaign.

Garrison gossip usually did not concern post officers, but Jackson's confinement to the fort put him in closer than usual touch with rumor. One particular story offended the sick major's sense of propriety involving as it did the morals of Major French. If it were true, French's conduct was not such as became an officer and a gentleman. Naturally Jackson considered his solemn duty to investigate the rumor and, if necessary, bring the facts to the attention of higher authority.

Julia, a nurse in French's employ, was the principal subject of the camp gossip. Some of the men were saying that Julia's beaus among the enlisted men had better stay away from Major French's, since the major "had taken her himself." French had apparently been indiscreet enough to be seen walking around the post in her company, sometimes far from his quarters, and once walking toward the woods.[27] Rumors of the supposed "affair" spread rapidly—reports which were certainly "prejudicial to good order and military discipline."

Conduct of the sort ascribed to French could not be tolerated. Morally reprehensible and militarily inexcusable, French's escapades brought a great many grievances to a head in Jackson's mind. Finally he took action against his commanding officer, which may have been unwise, but was certainly direct. On April 12, he called a number of enlisted men to his tent in the old cantonment area. Numbers of the men, Jackson had heard, knew something about French's frolicking with his "servant girl," and he wanted all the facts. His witnesses seemed reluctant to talk. Did one of them, who passed French's quarters and reputedly laughed as he looked in, see the major and Julia together on his bed? No, he had seen only a foot inside. If he had seen some legs, were they "bare or covered or . . . mens or womans [sic]?" Seven or eight men were so quizzed, with generally poor results.

As soon as Jackson released them, the men went to their sergeant with the story and he, in turn, went to French.[28] Immediately Jackson found himself clapped in arrest for "Conduct Unbecoming an Officer and a Gentleman." The first phase of the moral campaign against French ended in a tactical defeat.

But French himself had erred. Confinement to quarters gave Jackson more time to prepare charges. Old wounds were remembered, and attempts which French had made to restrict Jackson's authority were resurrected and put into official charges. These general charges were for unbecoming conduct and also for prejudice to good order and discipline. On reading, most of them sound trivial, but they show the depth of resentment in Jackson's mind.[29] An image of French as conceived by Jackson emerges clearly from the charges. A harsh, quick-spoken officer, with an overwhelming dedication to his own advancement, to trivia, and to appearances, French was at the same time a man who "is not to be believed as speaking the truth, when his interest in his opinion requires him to speak falsely."

Prodigious amounts of time were spent in compiling charges against French. Jackson's eyes proved unequal to the task. On April 15 he had to ask French for help in composing the charges:

> I have been on the sick report for about a month, and for some time back my eyes have been weak, and so much so since writing the accusations against you on the 13th inst as in my opinion to render it unsafe to use them either forwarding or writing. I am desirous that additional accusations against you should be forwarded by the Steamer which leaves Tampa Bay for N. Orleans on Thursday next, as in my opinion it is very important that they should accompany those already forwarded.
> About twenty specifications which are for Conduct unbecoming an

officer & a Gentleman, have been made out for some time, but owing to ill health have not been copied, and in their present condition ought not to be forwarded. . . . And as I have no other certain means of getting them copyed and soon as I deem the interest of the public service requires, I respectfully request that you will permit me to employ Corpl Bruning or such other person as you may designate for the purpose of transcribing them.[30]

The amanuensis was duly detailed to work with Jackson,[31] but French was not idle. He began piling up evidence of Jackson's "conspiracy" against him. On the defensive, he fought back hard.

Jackson's general military charges did not worry French. The implications of his moral degeneracy, though, attacked his character and could damage his reputation in the army. While drawing up charges of his own against Jackson for unbecoming conduct, French made ready to answer the moral attacks on himself.

All of Fort Meade became involved in the unwholesome quarrel. Enlisted men suffered the most, of course, for they were caught between the two camps. By reporting Jackson's questioning to French—a point which may throw some light on how they felt about Jackson—the men tried to straddle the fence but could not escape the atmosphere of suspicion. Nor could officers on the post escape. Lieutenant Baird, who had the nasty position of post adjutant, had had to strap on his saber, march to Jackson's tent, and announce him in arrest. This was the more unpleasant since Baird had been helping to collect the evidence against French. The only other officer present, Asst. Surgeon Jonathan Letterman, who appeared sympathetic to Jackson's cause, could not bring himself to attack French because of his friendship with the major's family.

Letterman was embarrassed by the fight. Should Jackson's charges concerning French's flirtations with Julia be made public, Mrs. French would suffer most. Apparently he took it upon himself to go to Jackson and ask him to drop the campaign. Arriving at Jackson's tent, he put his case: nothing could be gained, he suggested, by destroying Mrs. French's peace of mind. Only unhappiness would result if she were to learn "of her husband's unfaithfulness." Jackson sat and listened. The argument was calculated to move him deeply, since it was well known that he too shared the officers' regard for Mrs. French. When Letterman had finished, tears were running down the major's face. The thought of inflicting pain on an innocent and gracious lady was almost more than he could bear, he said, "but his conscience compelled him to prosecute the case." [32] He had to go on. Christian and military duty left him no alternative. Here was the "Stonewall" of later years—the kindly man with the iron will.[33]

With all chance of compromise gone, French earnestly set about defending himself. He composed, on April 14, a long letter to the commanding general, "in order that the truth may keep an even pace with so malicious a slander and falsehood as is borne on the face of these charges, I will give an account of the position of my family at the period of these alleged occurrences." Julia, said French, "is a respectable White woman who has lived in my family for nearly nine years. Has faithfully attended my wife and children in health and devotedly nursed them in sickness. The family is attached to her, and I know of nothing which should or shall prevent me from appearing in public as in private what I am, and ought to be, her friend and her protector." The incidents involving private strolls and meetings with Julia had been twisted out of context. French's wife, soon expecting a baby, had been moved into new quarters which had been built on a ridge, about a half mile toward Tampa from the old cantonment area. French himself had stayed for a few days in his old quarters until all housing arrangements had been completed. During these days Julia had had to come down to his quarters to get household items which had not yet gone up to the ridge. Frequently her trips were made rather late in the day, when it would have been unsafe for her to go back unescorted, and "being the only grown Male person in the family, at much inconvenience to myself I accompanied my servant once to the commissaries store for candles and once to the Beef contractors for Milk."

That, maintained French, was the whole of the story. Jackson had no real evidence pointing to anything else, but his vindictiveness had led him to rash charges. The commandant felt that most of the trouble dated back to the building incident. The reprimand had not been well received by Jackson, and

> foiled thus in his last attempt to have my official conduct reprehended, He altered his course, and descending into the purlieus of the camp he has changed his attack to a charge upon me in my family, but so blindly and upon ground so absolutely untenable that finding himself without a support in proof, he wishes to escape from the consequences of his act and be allowed to retire unscathed upon the plea of "a sense of duty." [34]

Realizing how weak his case looked upon examination, Jackson urged that a court of inquiry be called to investigate the situation at Fort Meade. Much more could be charged against the post commander, but since these charges "affect myself I feel a delicacie [sic] prefering [sic], it might be inferred that I was actuated by vindictiv[e] Motives, & consequently prefer that the[y] should result from the investigation of a Court of Inquiry." Should a court be ordered, Jackson urged that it be given wide authority to collect evidence, inasmuch as French was not above intimidating witnesses if he had the chance.[35]

Initially French seemed not to want a court of inquiry,[36] but he did favor a court-martial as possibly the only means of stopping Jackson. Jackson should be tried for unbecoming conduct in interrogating enlisted men in such a manner as to slander his commanding officer and thus lower the tone of discipline. French explained this feeling to the Acting Assistant Adjutant General of the Fifth Military Department, Capt. J. M. Brannan, on April 16:

> When Major Jackson is brought to trial for his outrageous conduct the evidence which I will bring before the court will cover him with the infamy he deserves.—Another officer who is absent from this post is becoming involved in the conspiracy against me, and notes in his hand writing I have positive proof exist from which Brevet Major Jacksons last charges were taken. It has been my duty to reprehend these officers the latter more than once, hence this thirst for revenge. I cannot yet trace the informant of Brevet Major Jackson in his charge against my moral character, the villain yet lurks undiscovered.[37]

French was firm in wanting the court to convene at Fort Meade. He had several reasons: all the evidence was there; Jackson was on the sick list and "although he walks about may plead inability to go to a distance"; the good discipline and appearance of the company and the post would show to what extent French had succeeded in his duties; the court could be housed and accommodated easily; and, finally, the weather was "cool and delightful." [38]

French himself was far from cool. By April 16, he had written Brannan that Lieutenant Baird, temporarily on leave in New Orleans, had joined Jackson's "conspiracy." French wanted him sent back to Fort Meade, to stand trial for being a co-conspirator and for helping to take testimony from the enlisted men.[39] There were other indications of French's crumbling composure. Jackson had applied for a nine months' leave of absence, with permission to leave the country. When the order granting it came through, French suspended the order "until I can receive information as to what action will be had on my charges." [40] Not only did French suspend Jackson's leave, but he also kept adding to the list of charges against his subordinate until the correspondence became fantastically voluminous.

Rumor finally reached Jackson of the paper whirlwind being stirred up at post headquarters. Now there was an added motive for a court of inquiry—he was anxious for an opportunity to "vindicate my Character, from such imputation or imputations" as French might make.[41] But he wanted a fair opportunity to clear himself. Speaking frankly, he told Brannan that French's influence at Fort Meade "is so great . . . that it would have a strong tendency to defeat the ends of justice, should the investigation be at this place." [42]

As the collection of documents bearing on these charges and

countercharges piled up at department headquarters, Maj. Gen. David E. Twiggs became increasingly displeased. He read through the reams of paper, decided that the whole thing was ridiculous, ordered French to release Jackson and Baird (who had unluckily returned to be arrested), and rejected the applications for courts of inquiry. Construing Twiggs's decision as a tacit reprimand, French appealed to higher authority. In a whining letter to Maj. Gen. Roger Jones, Adjutant General of the Army, French asked for redress, because "if the good of the service did not permit the assembling a Court in this most extraordinary case of outrage upon an officer whose reputation has hitherto stood fair before his profession, there certainly could be neither justice nor propriety, without investigation, to insinuate a censure upon him." [43] Naturally, the department commander had "misapprehended the state of things at this post."

Twiggs sent the appeal on to Washington, with an endorsement suggesting that it be denied. Jones received the packet of twenty-five lengthy documents, probably read some of them, noted Twiggs's endorsement and scrawled across the envelope: "The General-in-Chief [Winfield Scott] sees no sufficient reason why the appeal should be entertained... the decision of Brevet Major General Twiggs, is confirmed." [44]

At this point French clearly became hysterical. He refused to learn. Poor Dr. Letterman, the would-be peacemaker, was caught in the cesspool of suspicion in which French was floundering. Throughout June and July the heat of Florida was intensified by the troubles between these two men. Both preferred charges against each other, and finally Twiggs ordered French transferred to Fort Myers and placed under the command of another officer. [45]

Heartbroken at losing his command, French made one more attempt to straighten out the mess at Fort Meade. He appealed the whole case to the Secretary of War, asking for justice since he had been denied "redress in every official channel." This was a mistake. As he forwarded the appeal, Twiggs acidly penned the note which most damaged French's cause:

> I deem it necessary only to say that I have found no reason to regret the transfer of Major French to Fort Myers. Such transfer had in my judgment been rendered necessary by the fact that Maj. French had preferred charges successively against all the officers serving under his orders, and had shown himself incapable of conducting the service harmoniously at a detached post. [46]

Winfield Scott had been bothered once with the bundle of papers from Florida; Twiggs had several times tried to handle the problem; C. M. Conrad, Secretary of War, read the previous endorsements and curtly commented: "I perceive nothing in this case that calls for my interference." French lost the battle and his independence—he became a long-term subordinate himself.[47]

Jackson would have been happy at the outcome of his Florida campaign, but he was not around to hear the final decision. Released from arrest by Twiggs's orders, he was free to take his leave. Europe, however, was not to be his destination.

Back in February he had received from the superintendent of the Virginia Military Institute at Lexington a letter announcing that a Professor of Natural and Experimental Philosophy was to be elected, and asking if Jackson would be interested in the position. Jackson had thought the matter through. He had been honest in telling Laura that he liked the army and wanted to stay in it, and he told Superintendent Francis H. Smith the same thing. But, on the other hand, the offer was most flattering to a twenty-seven-year-old junior officer, and philosophy was his "favorite subject." He could not decline candidacy.[48]

Since a great many things could go wrong with his application, he did not become overly excited. The Board of Visitors would select the best man; and because the job carried much prestige as well as $1,200 and quarters, many men would be in the competition. While cautioning Laura that he was not sure of selection, he wrote her in April: "I consider the position both conspicuous and desirable. I will be in about one hundred and fifty or one hundred and sixty miles from you...."[49]

The whole matter of selection rested in the hands of VMI's Board of Visitors—a little influence with the board might help. How this could be achieved was the question. In the meantime, he must wait. Some rumors went around that he was thinking of leaving the army, which gave French the chance to say that Jackson had launched his campaign in revenge "at the time he expected to leave the post & probably the service."[50]

Although his frustrated commanding officer tried to stop his leave —and later would futilely seek to prevent his resignation from the army —Jackson happily departed Fort Meade on May 21, 1851.[51] Florida had certainly not been a happy place for him. Here he had chafed in a subordinate position. Here, too, he had faced twisted questions of morality and duty. He had met them unswervingly, but they were nonetheless unpleasant and had cast a shadow over his career in the army. Better to resign than to vegetate—and at last the chance came.

5

ALIAS OLD HICKORY

WEEKS OF ANXIETY ended with an invitation to join the faculty of the Virginia Military Institute, as Professor of Natural and Experimental Philosophy and Artillery Tactics. Quickly Jackson penned a note of acceptance. But the decision had been hard to make. One phase of his life was over; he had come to the end of one career and the beginning of another. He was leaving the army and facing civilian life. All his training, all his ambitions and efforts had been channeled into military matters. The army and its ways, good and bad, were what he knew best. Civilians lived and thought and acted differently.

His new job would be a help in the transition. As a faculty member in a military institution, he would still be closely tied to a military regimen. VMI was run on much the same order as the United States Military Academy. Military discipline, duty, academic and professional studies formed the core of life at the Institute—all of Jackson's values would remain intact. He would still be "Major" to his colleagues and to the cadet corps, and would live the life of an officer without the uncertainties of regular service. On the other hand, such a routine garrison life offered almost no excitement and no chance of military distinction.

To a man of twenty-seven there was much to be said for a VMI professorship. He would have something an officer in the peacetime army lacked—community respect! Academic status would be his, as well as an assured future. A semimilitary life, an increasing salary, good quarters, and some freedom for study—all sounded far better than staying in the army with no chance for rapid promotion, bad pay, and uncertain

71

stations. Then, too, Jackson had an added incentive for the scholarly life. Troubles with Major French had incurred the rather obvious irritation of the very high echelons of command—a situation not at all advantageous for a young career officer. Better to get out while he still had a sound reputation.

But Jackson was not running away. The French episode made it appear that way, perhaps, but he could leave with the satisfaction of knowing that in five years of service he had built up a commendable record. Promoted about as fast as possible, he had earned the plaudits of his superiors in Mexico and was recognized as a thorough, conscientious officer. The Fort Meade imbroglio had been unfortunate, but he did his duty as best he could. Too bad if higher-ups were somewhat displeased; it was not because of official frowns but in spite of them that he had decided to quit the service. Clearly the army had entered one of its long periods of quiet stagnation, and VMI offered a congenial way out,[1] if health would permit him to take it. Seriously weakened eyes and "aggravated dyspepsia" were almost incapacitating and might be a deterrent in accepting a new and arduous job. But since the appointment had come unsought, there could be no doubt that it was a gift from Providence; and if Providence had set the task, the strength to perform it would be provided.[2]

There was still another stumbling block. Since boyhood days at Uncle Cummins's, Jackson had had no experience in teaching; and Natural Philosophy, though he liked the subject, came hard to him at West Point. But the young professor recalled how determination had pulled him through the Academy and he set his mind to the new task. "I knew that what I *willed* to do, I *could* do." [3]

Providence certainly appeared to have had a hand in the VMI business. Several candidates had been mentioned for the position of Professor of Natural and Experimental Philosophy, including such later notables as William S. Rosecrans, George B. McClellan, Gustavus W. Smith, Theodore T. S. Laidley, and Alexander P. Stewart. Two of the other nominees had been offered the job and Stewart came close to accepting it. But he was temporarily committed to another school and VMI could not wait to fill the vacancy. A nasty controversy had raged among the members of the Board of Visitors over the appointment, and when Stewart failed to accept, the whole dispute appeared likely to begin again.

Almost distracted by the prospect of renewed struggle, Col. Francis H. Smith, superintendent of VMI, sought advice from many of his friends. One day late in 1850 [4] Smith's old friend Maj. Daniel H. Hill, currently a professor of mathematics at Washington College in Lexington, dropped in for a visit. He knew the story of some of the previous offers and rejections, and probably came to commiserate. Smith handed

him a copy of the *Army Register* and invited him to pick a West Point
graduate of "talent and character" who would have some knowledge of
the subjects to be taught. Surprised, but willing, Hill flipped idly through
the pages until "my eye fell upon J[ackson]'s name & the remark of
Capt Taylor flashed upon my mind [the remark made by Captain George
Taylor when Hill first met Jackson in Texas in 1846] & Jackson was
accordingly recommended." [5]

Smith then wrote the letter of inquiry which Jackson received in
Florida. When Smith read of Jackson's interest in the job, he presented
his name to a hastily called meeting of the board held in Richmond on
March 27, 1851. During the meeting John S. Carlisle, state senator from
Beverly, arose and put Tom Jackson's name in nomination, spoke in
glowing terms of his ability, told how the people in western Virginia
liked him, and urged his election. A unanimous vote followed. Distant
relative Carlisle proved once again a true friend. [6]

Two refusals of the VMI position, a name suddenly jumping out
of the long list in the *Army Register*, and a relative but recently appointed to the Board of Visitors—coincidence or Providence? Providence,
obviously.

Armed with this conviction and eager to see his new station, Thomas
first journeyed to Beverly for a visit with Laura's family,[7] then traveled
on to Lexington to have a look at the Military Institute. Discovering he
was not expected to begin duty there until August, and with a nine
months' terminal leave in his pocket, Thomas decided to go to New York
in quest of better health. For a while in Florida he had intended to use
his leave for a trip to Europe, but Colonel Smith persuaded him to
postpone it until he was firmly established at the Institute. [8]

The New York visit resulted in a chance meeting with Dr. Lowry
Barney, one of the few physicians who really helped Jackson's digestive
ailment. A visitor to New York City himself, Dr. Barney impressed
Jackson with his views on dyspepsia, and the major asked to become
Barney's patient. Since he had barely six weeks—part of July and August
—before school began in Lexington, he asked also to accompany Barney
to his home in Henderson, New York. If he remained close at hand, he
could more easily follow the doctor's orders. With slight misgivings,
Barney agreed, and the following weeks were spent in Henderson with
Jackson rigidly adhering to a buttermilk diet and improving as a result.

Dr. Barney, who became extremely fond of Jackson, gave his tense,
nervous young friend some far-reaching advice. Diet and exercise, yes,
but he needed more than that. Other physicians had rightly told him
he suffered from a nervous disorder of the digestive system. He must
avoid hard and demanding mental discipline and play more; and, said
Barney, marriage would be the best possible medication. [9]

Diet and exercise were easy prescriptions—they had been part and parcel of daily life for years—but marriage? That part of the treatment would have to be ignored at present. But advice from so good a friend and so respected a physician was kept in mind. Returning to Lexington in August, 1851, Jackson reported to the Virginia Military Institute on the thirteenth.[10] Stronger, more energetic, less nervous, he was ready to begin work.

The Corps of Cadets he found on hand preparing for summer drill and encampment. During the absence of the regular commandant of cadets, Maj. William Gilham ("Old Gil" to the boys), who was Professor of Infantry Tactics, Jackson was assigned as temporary commandant. His first view of the cadets, and theirs of him, came on the fourteenth of August. Already he was an object of much curiosity to the boys. They knew Gilham well; his quick, restless movements and high, shrill voice had become as familiar as discipline itself. Gilham could not be trifled with. Could this new man, Jackson?

As the Corps assembled for morning marching and drill on the Institute parade ground—a daily event witnessed by a fair-sized crowd from faculty quarters and from town—it was not known whether Jackson would be on hand or not, although his assignment to Corps command had been published to the young gentlemen.

The band struck up marching strains, the cadets fell in, and suddenly Tom Munford, the cadet adjutant, heard a cadet's young voice piping, "Come out of them boots, they are not allow[ed] in this Camp." Sweeping the field with a glance to see who had said this and why, Adjutant Munford saw, in horror, that the object of the remark was an officer in VMI faculty uniform who was standing among spectators at the edge of the parade. To his greater horror, he realized it was the new commandant. Munford turned over the command to the Officer of the Day, rushed over to salute Jackson and to mutter apologies for not having passed the guard in review.

As he talked with Jackson, Munford could see why the anonymous cadet had chirped about his footgear. The man's feet were enormous and they were encased in worn but well-blacked artillery boots. Later Munford recalled that he had involuntarily thought of the contrast with Gilham. "One stride of [Jackson's] would equal two of Gilham's; his foot occupied double the space. . . ." Jackson's whole appearance caused muffled and amused tittering among the boys.

To his vast relief, Munford soon saw that Jackson was paying no attention to continued cadet remarks. The major thanked the adjutant for his apology about the review and said that he was just observing, seeing how things were done. He had approached the drill field from the barracks, saw that he had not been recognized, and took refuge in the crowd while he looked at the Corps in action. He was glad, he said, that the whole thing had happened the way it did. Jackson may have been glad, but Munford was permanently shaken by the experience, in spite of his forewarning about Jackson from Gilham. Gilham had not adequately prepared him for the meeting. The major's appearance was, to say the least, uncommon. His Virginia Militia uniform of a double-breasted blue coat, white pants, and white gloves would not have been unusual had it not been so loose-fitting. Draped "*very easily*" on Jackson's fairly tall and somewhat thin frame, the uniform, the monster boots, and a brand-new cap gave a sort of ragamuffin look to the man. And Munford had to be his aide; Gilham had especially asked him to assist in getting Jackson established with the Cadet Corps.

The cadet adjutant took this assignment seriously. Escorting the new commandant to the Corps office, Munford explained that Jackson was expected to give the daily orders to the Corps, plan its doings, and establish the drill and instruction routine. In the office Jackson slowly and with obvious care examined the order book and asked for the cadet regulations. When a copy was produced, he said in his mild, pleasant tones: "This is our *chart.*" He kept the regulations and soon had a thorough knowledge of them.

After he had seen the office, Jackson sat down, turned to Munford, and said, "Adjutant, I am here amid new men, strange faces, other minds, companionless. I shall have to rely upon you for much assistance until I can familiarize myself with the routine duties, and the facilities for executing them; there is a great similarity I see to West Point, where I was educated. I trust ere long to master all difficulties." Munford was instantly sympathetic. As the weeks passed with Jackson in charge of the Corps, his adjutant became a devoted fan: "I flatter myself to have had extraordinary advantages to learn to honor & to respect and to love . . . this grand, gloomy & peculiarly *good* man." Munford was in close association with Jackson until the Corps went into barracks in September, 1851,

and during that time I was the Executive Officer & saw more of him [than] any man there [?], and as Adjutant had the best opportunity to study his disposition, and his knowledge of men—for he was *taxed* by a gay set who in those days were frequently the sons of Gentlemen able to supply more money than young men have had since the war.

Seeing Jackson in daily contact with cadet problems led Munford to understand something of his methods and ideas. It was soon clear that discipline was to be maintained, regardless of consequences. It may have been difficult to put anything over on Gilham; with Jackson it was well-nigh impossible. Excuses for failing to carry out orders were almost never accepted; punishment for infractions of the regulations was swift and hard. Jackson became a frequent user of the court-martial as a means of bracing good order. The new commandant was not quick like Gilham; his decisions were slower in coming but were irrevocable —unless proved wrong. He was "painfully exacting in details. Yet there was an earnestness in his manner and a precision in his commands that indicated unmistakably what was meant."

Munford thought Jackson was at his best in later months when he instructed the cadets in Artillery Tactics. "When he would give the command to the cannoneers to Fire! the ring of that voice was clear enough to be heard and to *burn* amid the rumbling of the wheels, giving life and nerve to the holder of the lanyard."

Close to this strange new major, Munford saw him as a man full of contradictions:

> *No two* individuals could be more unlike ... than was Major Jackson in repose when thinking of something, way off, before he was aroused and interested, the brow that had appeared inanimate and almost drooping at once elevated itself in all the consciousness of Power and the whole countenance and figure of the soldier the change [*sic*] as one who had become inspired.

But for years Munford was almost alone in his appreciation.[11]

Jackson seemed neither vastly pleased nor openly disappointed with the boys during the month he was in charge of them. The Corps took an annual trip to some of the Virginia springs, or watering places, and it fell to him to organize the summer excursion. After considerable preparation, the boys marched off for Rockbridge Alum and the Warm Springs and did not return until the barracks building was finished in September.[12] The extended march gave Jackson a chance to see what the VMI cadets were like, and they, in turn, became increasingly upset by dedication to small details. For the major, the summer trip was a success since he enjoyed the springs very much himself, took time to do a little sight-seeing, and appeared to improve considerably in health.

When the academic semester opened, late in September, Jackson was comfortably ensconced in quarters in the brand-new barracks—the east central tower room, third level.[13] Delay in finishing the building had held up academic work, but now the faculty and cadets got down to serious business.

The new professor's tasks were heavy. He taught the second-class Optics and Analytical Mechanics and the first-class Optics, Acoustics, and Astronomy. Almost wholly ignorant of these subjects, Jackson had to spend long hours preparing for his classes, in addition to conducting frequent after-class recitations in the big classroom on the western end of the barracks' second floor—the Natural and Experimental Philosophy Academy. Organizing his lessons proved a doubly hard chore to Jackson.

Not only did he have to keep the proverbial "chapter ahead of his class," but he had to do his preparing with badly weakened eyes. Optical infirmity was the main reason for the odd study habits he developed, and for which he received so much notoriety.

Ever since the first serious inroads of eye trouble back in 1848, Jackson had abandoned all reading by artificial light. Hence evening hours were lost as a time for study. Since he was busy for large portions of each day, he invented a schedule of study which made the most of limited daylight time. In the scant part of the morning which remained after his early classes Jackson hastily and mechanically read over the next day's lecture material; then, after evening mess, he devoted some two hours to standing bolt upright—or sitting rigidly erect—face to the wall, going over in his mind the lessons which he had read that morning. The hours of desperate study at West Point were paying off now, for he had developed virtually limitless powers of concentration and photographic recall of anything he read. Consequently, after he had committed the texts to memory in the morning, he could think them through at night. That practice he never abandoned, although in later years he modified it slightly.[14]

But the vagaries of higher mathematics and the whimsies of light and motion, no matter how thoroughly digested by the teacher, were not easy to explain to students. Most of the cadets displayed a healthy dislike for such abstract and hard problems. Jackson himself added to cadet dislike for he was a poor teacher. Not that he did not try—he overdid the trying at times. Basically he was too literal a man to be a successful teacher. His mind was direct, objective, and definite. Slow to solve a problem, once he grasped the solution he was committed to that one train of logic. His own method of solution was the one he presented to the class. Numerous stories tell of cadets asking for another explanation of a proof, saying they did not follow the professor, and of their being answered by a slower, more deliberate recital of the same argument. Jackson simply had no facility for drawing analogies, citing parallel examples, and developing alternate plans. Once he was committed to a line of reasoning, that was that. Single-mindedness can make a field commander a conqueror, but it ruins a teacher.

Cadets who sweated under the unbending Major Jackson never forgot their experience. Always polite in class—in his way—he did not teach. What he did was to explain how he had learned the lesson, and as a result some of the brighter students could follow the course. The weaker ones fell farther behind with each class, and some came to hate him.

Students have a shrewdness native to the breed. Any student worth his salt can spot a teacher who is struggling to keep one jump ahead of the bright ones in his class. Jackson appeared to many of the cadets a prime example of the hard-pressed teacher, and once tagged with this label—and also with the designation of a stuffed shirt—he was the object of typically brutal student humor.

He was fair game, all right. Dedicated to the rules and regulations of the Institute with what seemed to the young boys a priggish devotion, Jackson was intolerant of any breach of discipline. Failure to do an assigned duty brought sharp reprimand and possible court-martial. Justice, firm and impartial, Jackson meted out to wrongdoers, but he seldom—if the testimony of the boys can be believed—tempered it with humanity. All of which proved that "Old Hickory" Jackson was nothing more than a martinet. He even looked like one, always attired in the prescribed uniform, stalking around the parade and academic grounds in absurdly long strides, holding himself absurdly straight. He was trying too hard, thought many cadets, to act and look like a soldier. To the boys he was a prim old man. One or two in each class came to appreciate this strange apparition of a professor, but the rest, either frightened or contemptuous of him, never were able to see behind the immaculate tunic and the straight cap; they never saw the man. That was one of the reasons why Jackson failed as a teacher—he could never unbend with his students, could never share his problems and triumphs with them.

Numbers of cadet textbooks bear harsh witness to the prevailing attitude toward Jackson: "Old Jack put Frank Hannum under arest [sic] today for not obeying orders." "Old Jack skinned me to day I tell you he did." "The Major skinned me this morning by asking me extra questions on Venus. I wish he would let me and Venus be." "Dont say anything to old jack about the lesson for the day. he will skin on anything." [15] Letters from cadets to relatives and friends sometimes expressed in derisive doggerel their feelings toward the misfit major:

> I find the studies this year a great deal more interesting than they have been heretofore, with the exception of one single one, which so counterbalances the rest as to throw all the good part into the shade. . . . The study I referred to just now was Optics, which from being so very difficult and taught by such a *hell of a fool,* whose name is Jackson, has suggested the following lines,
>
> > The V.M.I., O what a spot,
> > In winter cold, in summer hot.
> > *Great Lord Al . . . ,* what a wonder
> > *Major Jackson, Hell & Thunder.* [16]

Cadet Tom Munford had said that Jackson was a "grand, gloomy & peculiarly *good* man"—and it was a perceptive description. Most of the cadets were too young, too callow, and too coddled to recognize the inherent goodness in their teacher. It was there in his almost abject humility. Some of the boys thought he knew little about his subject; he would readily admit that.

His intellectual humility was the only thing which ever breached the discipline of Jackson's classes. Jackson's scrupulous honesty in admitting that he did not know the answer to a question—he disliked people who sprinkled their conversation with "you knows" because most of the time he did not know [17]—was, of course, misunderstood by his students. They took it for weakness and for uncertainty, and their respect for their teacher faded. As respect dimmed they grew bolder. Such an ignorant bumpkin ought not to be a professor. They talked back to him, contradicted him, derided him. Once Cadet W. H. Cox, when reprimanded by Jackson, retorted that he would "dictate his own course of conduct," and refused to recite when called upon. Jackson insisted, and Cox announced that "the professor was not capable of judging." [18] This last outburst was so flagrant that it resulted in a court-martial for Cox, but other instances of insubordination occurred.

Mostly the cadets played crude practical jokes on the "hick" professor. In a way he invited them by his cold aloofness and apparently petty dedication to trivial rules. His deadly seriousness frightened the boys,[19] and in their fright they struck at his awesome dignity. They were frustrated because they could never breach that wall. Once, as Jackson passed through the Sally Port of the barracks, a couple of the boys dropped a brick from a third-story window. The brick barely missed, brushing the major's hat. If the culprits expected a reaction they were disappointed; Jackson walked straight on his course, never looking up or around.

Other pranks, less dangerous, were frequent. On one occasion there was a loud knock on the door of Jackson's quarters and when he opened the door, a cadet, neatly trussed to a chair, fell backward into the room. His cohorts, who had gleefully done the tying, had knocked and run. It was a large joke on Old Jack, but this one backfired. The head conspirators were caught and dismissed from the Institute.[20]

Perhaps the most unusual case of disrespect to Jackson, as far as consequences were concerned, involved Cadet James A. Walker, a lad who refused to stop talking in class even after ordered to do so. Walker's excuse precipitated a court-martial. The text of the excuse is preserved in the records of the trial:

> Either I did make noise, or I did not. When the noise was made Major Jackson accused Mr. Mason of making it. It is strange that he should accuse Mr. Mason of making noise if he did not think he made it; and it is stranger still that he should report me if he thought Mr. Mason made it. I suppose the amount of the matter is, I was suspected, and the report was made on suspicion. I now ask Major Jackson if [he] can qualify to my

being the author of the noise, and ask the superintendent if a report made on suspicion can hold good according to his own doctrine at his opening speech before the corps.

When the whole long trial was ended, Walker's career in the Institute ended with it. Walker was livid with rage against Jackson and made such a show of it that Superintendent Smith, in notifying Walker's father of the action, wrote: "I would advise you to come up at once and take him home as I have reason to believe he may involve himself in serious difficulty." Years later, the selfsame James A. Walker fought loyally under his former professor.[21]

Such instances as these, taken together, clearly reflected widespread cadet dissatisfaction with Jackson. Even on the parade ground, during artillery drill, they would toss taunting remarks at the major. Although they were mildly interested in his Mexican War exploits, and sometimes could be made to listen to details of some of the battles he had seen, they could not picture him as a military hero—and certain it was that he never made the slightest claim to fame. They took him at what seemed to be his own estimate, and complained loudly.

The complaints were so persistent that the Society of the Alumni had to take notice of them. In July, 1856, Prof. John B. Strange, VMI '42, was deputized to go before the Board of Visitors to present an alumni resolution concerning the mismanagement of the Department of Natural and Experimental Philosophy. The alumni, who had discussed the department in their meeting, did not object to Jackson per se, but they felt that he was not putting his subject across to best advantage. The cadets and the Institute were suffering. This was a hot issue for the board, which wanted no trouble with the Society of the Alumni. But neither did the board want to take positive action against Jackson or his department. For the moment the issue was evaded when Gen. William H. Richardson moved that the alumni resolution be laid upon the table.[22]

The matter was serious, however, and Superintendent Smith, who by now admired Jackson greatly,[23] maneuvered to take the pressure off the major and off the Institute. Smith recognized Jackson's limitations as a teacher,[24] but saw him as a "brave man, a conscientious man, and a good man. . . . His *genius* was in the Science and Art of War." [25] Such a man was worth defending.

As Smith explained it in his annual report for 1856–1857, the trouble in the scientific classes was not so much with the teacher as with the limited classroom and laboratory facilities. Experiments could not be intelligently conducted with inadequate equipment. The superintendent announced that a new room had been provided for Jackson's department, "the experimental illustrations have been commenced, and will hereafter be made more full and complete." [26]

Jackson was able to expand the scope of his classes as a result of the new equipment, and added to his required reading several more texts written by his old West Point professor, W. H. C. Bartlett. But the whispers of alumni pressure finally reached him. He was naturally concerned, for these whispers could mean only one thing—the ex-students wanted him fired.

For a brief time in 1854, it appeared the problem would be solved for the alumni and students. The University of Virginia suddenly needed a man to fill the vacant mathematics chair, and invited applications. The major jumped at the chance, made no attempt to conceal his interest from his superiors and colleagues—asking them to recommend him, in fact—and sought the assistance of all his influential friends. Since the University of Virginia had recently hired only its own graduates, he felt that there would be "strong opposition . . . to my election." Actually he mustered quite a fair list of names in his behalf, chief among them Col. Robert E. Lee (then superintendent of the United States Military Academy), Maj. D. H. Hill of Washington College, and Judge J. J. Allen of the Virginia Supreme Court.[27]

Welcome as the job would have been—he had taught math long years before and felt familiar with it—he did not get the Virginia appointment. He made no complaints; it was the way of Providence. The only comment he made was that "my friends have acted nobly in my cause."[28]

If duty dictated that he stick it out with Optics, Astronomy, and other alien topics, stick it he would. He was never very good at his teaching, but in time he overcame some of his awkwardness. He knew his limitations, however—he always knew them—and he was not surprised at alumni dissatisfaction. Even so, he had made serious efforts to improve his performance, including an attempt at writing his own text in optics![29] He would not sit idly by while his job slipped away from him. There was a matter of pride at issue here, too. He wanted to clear his name of any imputations of gross incapacity. Consequently, he addressed a letter to the Board of Visitors in July, 1857, "requesting that the communication made by the Alumni to the Board, at its annual session in '56, with reference to his Department . . . be fully inquired into." And again the board steered clear of what might easily become an alumni inquisition into the whole academic structure of the Institute. "On motion, the letter was laid upon the table."[30]

So Jackson's job was still safe, doubtless to the disgust of the alumni. One cadet, scheduled to graduate in the class of 1858, was glad that Old Jack would stay. Cadet Legh Wilber Reid was one of those rare exceptions to the class rule who saw beneath the shell of shyness and reserve enshrouding Jackson. What he saw moved him to verse, but not to the usual doggerel:

Hick, Alias Hickory, Alias Old Jack,
Alias Maj. T. J. Jackson.

Like some rough brute, that ranged the forest wild
So rude, uncouth, so purely Nature's child
Is Hickory, and yet methinks I see
The stamp of genius on his brow, and he
With his wild glance and keen but quiet eye
Draws forth from secret sources, where they lie,
Those thoughts and feelings of the human heart
Most virtuous, good and free from guilty art.
There's something in his very mode of life
So accurate, steady, void of care or strife
That fills my heart with love for him who bears
His honors meekly, and who wears
The laurels of a hero, this is fact
So here's a heart and hand of mine for 'Jack.' [31]

Cadet Reid recognized in the simplicity, piety, honesty, and humility of the inept teacher the marks of a great and good man.

6

ELLIE

A CURIOUS FELLOW, this new citizen of Lexington, Major Jackson. None of the usual social standards seemed to apply to him, nor did he seem interested in the daily doings of small-town life. Not that Lexington was like most small towns—it was not. With some thousand white residents, and a little more than six hundred colored,[1] Lexington had more than ordinary advantages.

Its location was outstanding. Resting at the southern end of the gorgeous Shenandoah Valley—that vale of rolling, rich farmland and picturesque oases of trees—the tiny county seat of Rockbridge County stood surrounded by a riotous pageant of scenery. House Mountain was a local landmark, and grandly guarding Lexington's eastern approaches stood the massive Blue Ridge, while to the south and west the lush green hills stretched away toward Roanoke and the sterner lands of Virginia west of the Alleghenies. By gift of nature, and by inclination, the people of Lexington were valley folk—they felt and lived that way.

Being valley people, they were gracious but not ostentatious, hardworking but not dull. All the glittering diversions of Richmond could not be found here, but there was much to do, nonetheless. Good Scotch-Irish stock, the Lexingtonians found much pleasure in their churches—most of them of the Presbyterian persuasion—and in the unique cultural atmosphere of the town, as well as in the recreation afforded by the Warm Springs, Rockbridge Alum Springs, Natural Bridge, and other "watering places" in or near Rockbridge County.

In the valley the "sociality, which is the atmosphere in which South-

83

ern people 'live, move, and have their being,'" centered around having and being guests. As one of Lexington's lettered ladies put it in 1850:

> If we wished for some designation that would embrace a prevailing characteristic, such as we use when we speak of the 'fox hunting English,' or the 'smoking Germans,' or the 'opium-eating Chinese,' no better could be found than the 'visiting Virginians'! [2]

At hand for invitation were many lively and unusual people. Washington College, that old and honored school endowed by the general himself, had a respected faculty who were accepted into the society of the town. Respected for his learning and loved for himself was the Reverend George Junkin, president of the college. His wife and family, especially the two elder girls, Margaret and Elinor, could be seen at many get-togethers. And among his faculty Maj. and Mrs. Daniel Harvey Hill, Major Jackson's friends and benefactors, were making quite a favorable impression. The same held true for the Misses Nottingham, who conducted the Ann-Smith Academy for girls and who were "English people of a specially intellectual turn." All of Lexington knew and appreciated the four unmarried daughters of the Reverend George Baxter (former president of Washington College, and pastor of the Presbyterian Church). These ladies took the responsibility for teaching most of the children in town, since there was no public school. The Military Institute's faculty enjoyed a growing respect on the part of the townspeople, and were included in most functions, civic or social. Colonel Smith was known and admired far beyond Lexington; Maj. William Gilham's quiet, scholarly politeness gave way to a gentle and quick wit and he never lacked for invitations; and Maj. J. T. L. Preston, Professor of Languages and English Literature, had a ready entree both because of his own winning personality and because of his family background. Major Thomas J. Jackson was new, was not a valley man, and seemed for a while out of place.

Outside the academic community Lexington's social set included ex-Governor and Mrs. James McDowell and their pretty, charming daughters. There was also the Rev. William S. White, Presbyterian clergyman, who ministered faithfully in good times and bad, and who loved his people and his town fervently. Helping him in his overseeing of the faithful was John B. Lyle, whose bookshop served the place of the usual general store as a meeting point for gentlemen—a place to browse, to talk of politics, to pass on the gossip, and to unburden the soul. And Lyle was one of the first to appreciate and befriend the lonely Major Jackson.

To the little bookshop on Main Street Jackson began to make regular visits soon after he was established in Lexington. Lyle liked him from the first, and Jackson in turn developed a warm affection for the genial, happy, and thoroughly Christian man. These visits brought Jackson contact with many of the gentlemen of Lexington, who came to Lyle's not

only to talk and confide but also to sing. Possessed of a marvelous singing voice, Lyle had a wide local reputation as leader of the Presbyterian
Church choir and as a musician of note. Jackson had no musical bent
whatever, but he enjoyed attending the sessions, meeting people.

Meeting him was not easy. Thin, sallow-looking in his loose VMI
uniform, he was impeccably courteous but exceedingly reserved, so much
so that his ingrained courtesy seemed almost grotesque. Few of Lyle's
other visitors liked the major. He did receive some invitations—matters
of courtesy—to scattered gatherings. But his high-collared correctness
and his odd way of standing at ramrod attention dampened the spirits
of hosts and guests alike. Always at social affairs he pulled around him
the shroud of stiffness of the painfully shy.[3] This shyness made him a
bad conversational partner, and when he was snared into talking, his
scrupulous honesty and attention to the smallest exaggeration soon taxed
the self-control of his auditors. A few such attempts were enough for
Lexington's socialites to vote him "eccentric" and make him fair game
for witticisms.[4]

Real friends he had, but they were few. Lyle was perhaps chief
among them, but closely following were Major Hill and his wife. These
three saw Jackson often: he turned to them in his loneliness, and through
them he slowly met others. There were so few with whom he felt at ease,
and it was uneasiness that froze him up. To the ones who knew him
well, like Lyle and the Hills, he was anything but a shy, awkward eccentric. But when they tried to tell others how interesting the major's conversation was, how nice, how fine he was, they were laughingly rebuffed.

Rumors about a local eccentric travel fast, and distortion twists them
out of perspective. All sorts of stories could be heard around Lexington
magnifying Jackson's oddities. The man had the most curious views on
health. This seemed partly to explain the awkward rigidity of his posture
when calling on people. Persuaded to take a seat, he would assume a
position of two 90-degree angles, sit bolt upright and never relax, even to
the extent of crossing his legs or reclining so that his back touched the
back of the chair. His reason, which finally was an item of amused repetition, was that he needed to keep "his 'alimentary canal' straight." No
matter the reason, the fetish added to his eccentricity in the eyes of many.

More than that, some of his hosts and hostesses who did not know
of his rules of personal health, received the distinct impression that Jackson had come calling only because of a sense of duty, and stayed a courteous, if pained, interval. A proposed visit from the staid young man must
have been a frightening prospect. What could be done with him after
he assumed the sphinxlike pose? One thing could be counted on: he was
a good listener. The trouble was, though, that he listened too carefully
and was apt to ask piercingly direct questions, particularly on subjects
about which he knew little and was, therefore, very curious. One example

of this trait served to amuse several Washington College students who either knew or had heard of Jackson.

One of these young gentlemen encountered the major one evening at the home of William Lewis. The Lewis house offered considerable attraction to Lexington's young men, since in it lived the owner's vivacious daughter Julia, and also Maggie Kerr, a close relation. Major Jackson liked the owner and the ladies, and it was during one of his visits that he encountered the Washington student. Conversation went well, the student held forth with a will, and in the course of a lively discussion, he used the word "vim." Jackson, at a suitable pause, broke in to say: "That word I often hear and it seems to be a very good word to express emphasis, what is the origin of it?"

Momentarily taken aback, the young man seized on an opportunity to display his learning. He launched into a long explanation, declined the Latin *vis,* and paraded his knowledge to the amusement of all save Jackson, who thanked him politely for an enlightening bit of information. The major, who never teased anyone, did not realize his ignorance was the butt of a joke.

Close friends recognized his admission of ignorance as the mark of a thoroughly honest man and appreciated him the more. They saw, too, that his innate modesty made him unable to assume a pose for an occasion. He explained his guilelessness as a practical handicap—"I have no genius for *seeming.*" [5]

As Jackson saw more and more of the Hills, grew close, and confided in them, Major Hill's admiration for him increased tremendously. Sincere, honest, really a good man, Jackson grew in stature. His rules of conduct, painstakingly worked out, commanded respect. He told of his poor health and of how he had to guard it at all times. He told, too, of how Providence had helped in his quest for renewed strength, and he explained his connection with the Episcopal Church at Fort Washington. Transfer to Florida had cut short any further investigations of the Church, but he had been trying to live a Christian life. As Jackson explained his theology, his complete submission to Divine will, Hill became anxious to interest him in his own Presbyterian faith.

Hill wanted Jackson to join the Presbyterian Church, but knew Jackson would make up his own mind. Would Jackson read the *Shorter Catechism?* It was concise, had comprehensive definitions, and read well. Jackson had never before seen it, and willingly took it to study. It was, he told Hill later, a grand literary composition and several of its definitions were most gratifying. Hill next loaned him the Presbyterian Confession of Faith, asked that this be studied closely and if Jackson could accept it, that he join the Church.

At the bookstore, in conversations with John Lyle, Jackson discussed his religious dilemma. Where did he belong? He had not felt completely satisfied with Episcopalianism, else he would have gone beyond baptism in that faith. Since that time, he had been living according to the light given him by the Bible. But as he read the books Hill gave him, he had become disturbed about his Christian duty. Should he formally join a church, and if so, should it be the Presbyterian?

Lyle drew him out, never preaching or arguing, letting Jackson talk. Jackson's was an old problem to Lyle; he had been advising spiritually disturbed friends for a long time; in fact, his pastor said of him that

he could speak to anyone on personal religion in a way so affable and gentle as never to give offence, and yet so pointed as to learn just what he wanted to know... he conversed and prayed with more young men when partially or deeply awakened than any man not in the ministry I ever knew.... Such cases he always reported to me, and many such he brought to my study.

Jackson could not have been in better hands.[6]

Knowing and appreciating Jackson's deep sincerity, Lyle discussed with him the whole sweep of Presbyterian theology. Hearing that Jackson had been attending services in various Lexington churches but that he felt more than a little interest now in the Presbyterian, Lyle took him to see the Reverend Dr. White.[7]

Wise in the ways of the righteous, White was unprepared for Jackson's earnest, soul-searching seriousness. There were things about Presbyterianism with which he violently disagreed—particularly the doctrine of election. How could this be reconciled? His knowledge of the Scriptures and of the doctrines at issue was frankly deeper than White's, but the minister explained that strict adherence to all doctrines was not expected of lay members, that Jackson's apparent conversion completely qualified him for membership, and invited him to become one of the congregation. Jackson hesitated. Was it right to profess faith publicly when he had strong mental reservations? Finally Hill, Lyle, and others convinced him that he could do so honorably, and on November 22, 1851, he officially joined the Presbyterian Church.[8]

Soon the whole congregation came to know Jackson, and they came to appreciate his determined rule not to "violate the known will of God." He wore well. The more they saw of him and talked with him, the more they understood this. "It was only when we came to know [him?] with the intimacy of hourly converse," one of the Reverend Dr. Junkin's daughters later wrote, "that we found that much that passed under the name of eccentricity was the result of the deepest underlying principle, and compelled a respect which we dared not withhold."[9]

Some of the new member's actions dismayed his fellow church members. Sincerity, intensity, and a will to live his religion were so marked in Jackson as to make many appear backsliders—but it was not affectation, they knew, and they admired him. Formal reception into Presbyterianism imposed on Jackson certain duties. Personal morality based on his own reading of the Bible must now give way, he concluded, to an official code of conduct. He would reappraise his way of living.

Older pleasures he gave up. In Mexico, and later in New York and at Carlisle Barracks, he went to as many "hops" as possible and he had developed a taste for the theater; now all this was put behind him. It was not because he wanted to impose an artificial asceticism upon himself, he explained, but simply because "I know it is not wrong *not to do it*, so I'm going to be on the safe side." [10] And when some intimate friends teased him about his more sinful youth, pointing to his confessed pleasure in dancing, Jackson stoutly defended his position. "Remember," he said, "I lived, then, up to all the light I had, and therefore I did not then, nor do I now, reproach myself." [11] Small satisfactions might be denied him by this stern code of Christian life, but one of his favorite Bible texts offered much compensation: "We know that all things work together for good to them that love God." [12] He would not miss smoking, drinking, or a game of cards—he had so much more.[13]

Christianity was to Jackson a great cause, and to it he gave his whole allegiance. The Church was an army defending and expanding Christianity, and, consequently, the clergy were the officers directing the Church's campaigns. Happy in this authoritarian framework, Jackson looked to the Reverend Dr. White as his superior officer. White did not at first understand the strange attitude which the major had toward him, and appeared briefly baffled at the regular reports which Jackson brought concerning his religious views and actions. Such reports would be expected by a military superior, and nothing less was due to a minister of the Gospel, charged with carrying out God's orders as revealed in the Scriptures. Naturally enough, Jackson regarded a request from his pastor as an order to be rigidly obeyed.

On one occasion Dr. White urged his congregation to attend prayer meeting with a bit more regularity, at the same time suggesting that the church officers as well as the general membership should share the duty of leading prayers. To Jackson this was an order. It must be obeyed, but it worried him. The Reverend Doctor had admonished the membership not to hide behind false modesty or shame but to come forward and do this Christian act. Jackson called on Dr. White. Was he one who should lead in prayers? Never, he said, had he had any practice in public speaking, and he feared that he knew too little about so sacred a thing as religion to be of use at such a task. "But," he said to White, "you are my pastor, and the spiritual guide of the church; and if *you* think it my duty, then I shall waive my reluctance, and make the effort to lead in prayer, however painful it may be." [14]

Finally called upon, he arose and struggled so desperately that the whole congregation was embarrassed for him. Weeks passed without a similar assignment, and finally he asked Dr. White about it. Was it because he had been so uncomfortable? When White admitted that was the reason, adding that he thought it best not to mar Jackson's pleasure at these meetings, the major firmly told him that "my comfort or discomfort is not the question; if it is my duty to lead my brethren in prayer, then I must persevere in it, until I learn to do it aright; and I wish you to discard all consideration for my feelings in the matter." [15]

Dr. White called on him after that at regular intervals. Knowing that he could do it if he willed to do so, Jackson finally became relatively proficient in leading prayers and his brethren ceased to dread the ordeal of his perspiring supplications. [16]

People could not help noticing the major in church, not only because of his shy, halting prayers, but also because he always seemed to sleep during services. Not that he allowed himself to assume an easy posture, conducive to slumber. He was conspicuous for sitting bolt upright, and for nodding in that healthy pose throughout most of Dr. White's remarks —much to the amusement of the cadets who thronged the church's gallery. Friends, and later relatives, tried to break him of the habit. He was pinched on the elbows, jabbed with shawl pins and harshly nudged, all of which he endured with somnolent calm. One of Governor McDowell's daughters, having recently seen a hypnotist's performance in Lexington, laughingly remarked about these Sunday snoozes that "no one can put Major Jackson to sleep but the Rev. Dr. White." [17] Realizing that his dozing was the object of considerable merriment and ridicule, he steadfastly refused to try to cover it by slumping in his pew. "I will do nothing," he explained, "to superinduce sleep by putting myself at ease, or making myself more comfortable; but if in spite of my resistance I yield to my infirmity, then I accept as punishment the mortification I feel, because I deserve it." [18]

Professor Jackson attracted attention for other reasons than diffidence and nodding—particularly among the young ladies of the congregation. Physically infirm or not, he was a good-looking man. Although standing about five feet ten, his military carriage and VMI uniform made him appear a six-footer. He was thin and wiry, with a complexion usually tanned by the sun (though sometimes looking "sallow"), and his high, fine forehead with its prominent brows emphasized large and expressive blue eyes. These eyes could be warm and friendly or flash fire and excitement. A finely etched Roman nose, firm, determined mouth, and chin were set off by well-trimmed brown sideburns and chin whiskers. All in all, he was pronounced "handsome." [19]

The major seemed a hard man to please. He took an interest in many of Lexington's ladies, but never showed much serious intent—probably, thought many, because of his shyness. He did overcome this drawback sufficiently to accept increasing numbers of invitations, and to participate in Lexington's "visiting" craze. These visits took him to many homes graced by lively and beautiful girls—girls whose gift for conversation, flirtation, and entertainment usually made him seem somehow staid and out of place. So, during most of his calls, Jackson engaged the men of the household in more or less serious conversation, leaving the light coquetry to younger gentlemen visitors—and all the while envying them their urbanity.

It was comfortable to visit Major and Mrs. Hill. They knew him so well, and Mrs. Hill's younger sisters—pretty and desirable—accepted him as an old friend of the family. To the Hill home on Washington College's campus Jackson came more and more often. "His conversation," wrote Major Hill in later years, "while always child-like and simple possessed great originality & I became more & more impressed with him as a man of talent." All manner of things the two friends talked about. Jackson frequently went to Hill to unburden himself of fears about his teaching and his struggle to master the subjects for which he was responsible at VMI; and with an inbred delicacy, he discussed professional questions only at Hill's office, never at his home.

Since Jackson's daily visits were anticipated, it was no surprise to Hill that his friend called at the office one evening in a pensive mood. Things had gone wrong at the Institute that day, thought Hill, or the cadets had been unusually unruly. Instead of launching into a pedagogical dissertation, Jackson, very hesitantly, began to talk of a certain young lady. This seemed rather a private matter, and Hill tried to divert the conversation to more impersonal subjects. But Jackson kept coming back to the lady. It soon developed that he was talking about Miss Elinor Junkin, daughter of the president of the college.

Hill knew Elinor well. She was charming, self-effacing, a regular at church, and present at most social gatherings. All of Lexington regarded her as a sweet girl, somewhat gifted in drawing, who was partially overshadowed by the brilliance of her sister Margaret's literary ability. Why was Jackson so upset? He had known Elinor for almost two years. Why the sudden agitation? As Hill listened to his friend's explanation he fought back loud laughter as long as he could.

Hill's advice was needed, Jackson said, because he could not analyze what had happened to him with regard to Miss Junkin. The trouble boiled down to an inexplicable change in Jackson's feelings about the young lady. "I don't know what has changed me. I used to think her plain, but her face now seems to me all sweetness." How could this be? Hill's guffaw reddened Jackson's face to his ears, but he listened carefully as Hill said, "You are in love; that's what is the matter!" Jackson thoughtfully answered that this might be the answer; he had never previously been in love, "but he certainly felt differently towards this lady from what he had ever felt before." Something would have to be done.[20]

No one else in the little town caught wind of Jackson's dilemma. Sister Laura, tuned as she was to brother Thomas's ways, may have guessed at a new interest when she received a letter in April, 1853, containing a special request:

> I am invited to a large party tonight, and among the scramble expect to come in for my share of fun. I wish that you would send me by return mail the daguerreotype which I had taken in New York after having shaved. The one with the beard on was taken at New Orleans soon after my return from Mexico. This last one I wish you to keep safely, as I prize it highly. If you remember I gave you two others, one being taken with a stern countenance, and the other with a smile. It is the smiling one which I want; and don't fail to send it well enveloped by the first mail. If you wish it to be returned, I will try and do so in a few months, or else a better one in its stead, as I think that your brother is a *better looking man* than he was when that was taken.[21]

There were other things in Tom's letters which might serve as indications of a romantic turn in his thinking: "I have for months back admired Lexington; but now, for the first time, have I truly and fully appreciated it. Of all the places which have come under my observation in the United States, this little village is the most beautiful." [22] And, in a letter dated April 1, 1853: "I derive much pleasure from morning walks, in which is to be enjoyed the pure sweetness of carolling birds. The weather is delightful at present; our peach trees are beginning to bloom, and in the course of a few more weeks the forests will be clad with verdure.... Talk to the children for me as I would were I with you." [23]

The wooing of Miss Junkin baffled Jackson. Just as new at this sort of thing as at love, he set about his campaign with deep sincerity. Seeing her more often helped—he appeared unable to stay away from the Junkins's for a great length of time.

For their part, the Junkins were surprised. Elinor ("Ellie" to the family) had had admirers before. She had spent her early years in the North, while her father had served as president first of Lafayette College and then of Miami University, and young gentlemen had been interested on several occasions. But they had made no impression on Ellie. Happy in the company of her sister Maggie, who looked the younger of the two but was not, Ellie had remained aloof. Now, in 1853, she was twenty-eight and still she showed no more than casual interest in the Virginia gentlemen attending her—until Major Jackson began regular visits.

He was an odd sort of man, most of the Junkin family thought—stiff, bashful, ill at ease, although commendably polite and courtly.

Strangely, however, Ellie did not discourage his calling at the house; nor, for that matter, did Maggie, who seemed to find in Jackson a real intellectual companion. But it was all Ellie, as far as the major was concerned; she was all he could see, though never slighting the rest of the family. What was it that Ellie saw in the awkward professor?

Certainly the rest of her family found little to appreciate. He gave ostentatious attention to too many little things, and this made him seem artificial. Peculiar stories came to the family about Jackson's almost fanatical honesty, like the time he walked a solid mile to correct a small misstatement made earlier.

Gradually, though, the Junkins realized that the major wore well. "After he became an inmate of our household," Maggie later said, "we were not long in discovering that the more rigidly and narrowly his springs of action were scrutinized, the higher arose our respect and reverence." [24]

For a long time, Ellie's parents knew very little about her regular suitor. They had heard the general information about him which had become part of Lexington gossip: that he was a fairly poor teacher, but was a deeply, honestly religious man whom many felt to be remarkably good. There was some talk of his having distinguished himself in the Mexican War, but that hardly seemed plausible—he had none of the looks of a hero.

Ellie grew more and more attached to Jackson. No amount of questioning or ridicule of him could swerve her growing affection. Beyond the ungraceful surface she saw in him a man whom she could love. For a time Jackson's suit went well.[25] But, as often happens, things went awry. What happened, why there was a sudden breakoff, is lost in the records, but certain it is that for two or three months in the spring of 1853 Jackson was heartsick about troubles with Ellie.

Ellie, sweet, merry Ellie, apparently decided against an engagement. The estrangement served, as it so often does, to add to her attractions. Jackson already knew her to be a pure, thoroughly religious girl, with an almost constantly happy disposition. At the same time, she was clear-thinking and calm, with her mother's sound judgment. She could have been paid no greater compliment than that her sister, the brilliant Maggie, depended upon her for so many things. Now that she had grown cool toward Jackson, she was lovelier, sweeter, holier, and more gracious than ever. Her disinterest was almost more than Jackson could bear.

Desolate and sorely tried, he turned with renewed zeal to his God. Never had he swerved from complete devotion, but now he unburdened himself in a private missionary zeal, aimed at sister Laura. Laura, too, was seriously troubled, and in an effort to help her, Jackson sought to ease his own pain.

Despite Thomas's previous efforts, Laura remained doubtful about

Christ and the Scriptures. Her health, possibly because of these doubts, remained poor, and Jackson's concern about her rose sharply. A sad letter from Laura in June, detailing her fading health, moved her brother to tears, but he was glad that she had told him how sick she had been. "If your health is really as you state, I would rather know it." "My Dearest Sister," he wrote,

with tears in my eyes, and a heart devoted to my *God*, I look into the future beyond the limits of this transient life of *care;* and see the dark gloom which is to exist [?] throughout infinite duration. That whilst I am "to shine like a star in the firmament for ever and for ever," you are to be assigned to *unending Misery*. What my dear sister is this life, and all its joys, compared with that which is to come? How happy would I be, did I but know that beyond this probationary life we should be together for ever more; there with those who have gone before us, to enjoy endless happiness. My Sister, do reflect upon my course of life, think and see, if I have ever erred since arriving at mature age, and then consider how I could ever have been satisfied of the truth of the Gospel; unless it is true. Have I ever erred in the affairs of this life? Remember too that strong irreligious influences have been brought to bear on me, and yet in spite of all opposing obstacles, I am one of the most devoted of Christians. Will you not have some faith in the prayers of a dying Mother & brother? My dearest Sister do thrust yourself into the hands of God; throw yourself upon his mercy, repent of your sins, and believe that the father will accept your prayers, and forgive your transgressions, for the sake of his Son's merits[?]. Remember that he hath said, that they who come unto him he will in no wise cast off.[26]

Afflictions such as Laura sustained could be traced directly to spiritual causes. If she would look back over her life, she could probably see how she had violated God's will, and once seeing this, she might be able to help herself. She had a chance, if she would but take it. "My Dear Sister," Thomas had written in January, 1852,

You are aware that I am troubled about your hopes in relation to the endless futrity [*sic*]. The best plan that I can conceive for an unbeliever in God, as presented to us in the Bible, is to first consider things in reference merely to expediency. Now considering the subject with reference to expediency only, let us examine whether it is safer to be a Christian or an Infidel. Suppose two persons, one a Christian, and the other an infidel, to be closing their earthly existences. And suppose that the Infidel is right, and the Christian wrong, they will then after death be upon an equality. But instead of the infidel being right, suppose him to be wrong, and the Christian right, then will the state of the latter after death, be inestimably superior to that of the other. And if you will examine the history of mankind, it will be plain that Christianity contributes much more to happiness in this life than that of infidelity. Now having briefly glanced at this subject, to what decision are we forced on the mere ground of expediency; certainly it is to the adoption of Christianity. Having made our selection of Christianity, the next point is to consider whether we can believe the teachings of the *Sacred* volume; if so, then its adoption should of necessity follow. I have examined the subject maturely, and the evidence is very conclusive; and if we do not receive the Bible as being authentic and credible, we must reject every other ancient work, as there is no other in favor of which so much evidence can be adduced. Oh Sister! do pray to God for his mercy, and eternal life through our Redeemer Jesus Christ.[27]

No misfortune could daunt him, Thomas wrote, for "I am cheered with an anticipated glorious and luminous tomorrow.... No earthly calamity can shake my hope in the future so long as God is my friend. And on this subject I expect to have a long conversation with you next summer." [28] Girded in the armor of his God, and thus partially protected against Ellie's coldness, Thomas went west to Beverly in early July, 1853. Still hopeful that Ellie might reconsider, he went to help Laura.

His visit was short in western Virginia—just long enough to talk seriously with Laura about her religious obligations and to assume such an obligation himself. It was probably during this visit that he undertook to give a short series of lectures in and around Beverly on the evidence of Christianity. Shocked at the lack of religious interest he found in Laura's home community, Thomas did what he could, despite his lingering lack of self-confidence in public speaking. At least he attracted fair crowds, but with unrecorded success.[29]

Glad enough to have Thomas's advice on her spiritual problems, Laura (whose husband apparently had little interest in religion) showed much interest in the source of her brother's obvious concern. Who was the young Lexington lady, and what was the matter? Thomas played the whole affair down; Ellie interested him, yes, but nothing serious had passed between them. Laura wondered.[30]

Once back in Lexington, Jackson was caught up in a gay social season. His trip, which had taken him on a business junket to New York before the swing west, had rested him, and he appeared in better health than in years. Whatever the cause—travel, or the peculiar pit-of-the-stomach sensations of lovers—he now weighed 172 pounds—six pounds more than ever before—and his face had lost some of its gaunt, sallow appearance. That was all to the good, for Major Hill had some young lady visitors in his home who needed a ready escort. And then, too, the Ellie business remained to be settled.

Gracing the Hill home were two of Isabella Hill's younger sisters— the very young and pretty Eugenia and the slightly older Mary Anna Morrison, who had recently come from Cottage Home, North Carolina, where their father, the Rev. Robert Hall Morrison, had served as the first president of Davidson College. Both of the young girls were delighted at the chance to visit Lexington. They had heard of Major Jackson, their brother-in-law's close friend, and met him with real pleasure.

Jackson had heard of the coming of the girls, greeted them with great cordiality, and, since they were strangers to the town, offered his services in squiring them wherever they might need an escort. He was an amusing man, and the two girls were amused at the formal way in which he offered his brotherly protection; and they "never looked upon him as a beau any more than we would look upon a man who was already married."

It was a nice arrangement. Since the girls had been told in Major Hill's letters of Jackson's engagement, they were at ease with him—he was ineligible for a match. Every day he would drop by to see if they were properly fitted out with young gentlemen; if not, he was available. One grand thing about him was that he was so easy to tease. And, naturally, the girls wanted to learn more of Jackson's mysterious fiancée, the Ellie that people talked about. Rarely did they see Jackson in her company, and never once during the girls' stay—they arrived in May to remain until the end of August, 1853—did he mention his engagement. Strangely enough, no one could find out whether Ellie admitted the engagement either.

The girls missed him briefly after he began his summer vacation, but there were so many parties honoring graduates of both schools that he could not be missed for long. Neither Mary Anna nor Eugenia expected to see him again, nor did they think they had made any great impression on him. But they had—particularly Mary Anna. Jackson told Major Hill often how much he liked Mary Anna and how he thought "she was more beautiful as well as more fascinating than her sister," all this in a purely academic way, of course.[31]

Jackson had to be careful in his remarks around the Hill home. Isabella was a matchmaker of the most active sort—in fact, Hill suspected that his wife had been responsible for getting Jackson interested in Ellie in the first place—and she looked out for friend Ellie's interests. She had been so concerned with the whole matter that it was to Isabella that Jackson turned in his anxiety. "One night about twelve o'clock," Hill recorded, "he roused us out of bed & insisted upon seeing Mrs H[ill] alone. He was terribly excited. I learned afterwards that the interview related to a rupture with Miss J[unkin] & Mrs H was to be the mediator. I think that he wished her to go over that night to Dr. J's, but she did not till next day." [32]

Whatever happened, whether it was Isabella's intercession or something else, Ellie and Thomas made up their quarrel. They were secretly engaged, and so well was the secret kept that their marriage came as a shock to most of Lexington. Jackson returned from his vacation, and suddenly, without warning, he and Ellie were married.

It was a quiet ceremony, performed by Ellie's father at the Junkin home on August 4, 1853.[33] The matter had been so secret, in deference to Ellie's wishes, that Jackson had not even told Laura. He had written her the day before the wedding, and the only hint he gave was the cryptic line "Tell Miss Eliza [a maiden friend of the family] that she must be on the lookout for something in relation to me, and in reference to which she called my attention."[34] This sentence was part of a letter in which he told of arriving at the Springs and of plans for a trip north, via Lexington—a trip which would begin that evening.

Jackson breathed no word of his and Ellie's plans to anyone. Mary Anna Morrison, writing years later, expressed the surprise of all Lexington:

> One August morning we were taken by surprise when our friend Major Jackson suddenly dropped in, and our many exclamations of wonder at seeing him amused him as much as his unexpected appearance astonished us. The reunion was a merry one, and he spent an hour or more, calling for his favorite songs and seeming genuinely happy; but not even a hint did he give us as to the object of his return, although we plied him with all sorts of teasing questions. We saw him no more, but were electrified the next morning at hearing that he and Miss Ellie Junkin were married, and had gone North on a bridal tour![35]

Episodes of this sort prepared Harvey Hill for the absolute secrecy of Jackson's military movements a few years later. The man was never tempted to impart a confidence—it could not be blasted out of him!

One person aside from Ellie and Thomas had been fully aware of what was going on; this was Maggie, Ellie's older sister. The two girls had been almost inseparable, dressing alike, riding together, sharing the same room, duties, and recreation. In many ways they complemented each other. Maggie, the slightly shy one, would have shunned people if Ellie would have allowed it. But Ellie, who most people said had more "pretension to beauty" than her sister—a statement which Maggie devoutly accepted—liked society and saw to it that Maggie was no stay-at-home. Ellie may have been prettier, with her dark chestnut hair, softly pink skin, straight nose, expressive eyes, smiling lips, and delicately high cheekbones, but Maggie admittedly had the brains. Although Maggie was the older, she depended on Ellie as a steadying influence, for Ellie had a firm, quiet determination about her which gave her an air of competence. Not that this detracted in the least from her sweetness—in a way it enhanced that quality, for it was born of a complete submission to God's will and the conviction that she was a child of God. She was less sensitive than Maggie, and had fewer doubts about everything. Her calm, tranquil nature much resembled that of her mother, whose utterly Christian devotion appeared to equal, at least, that of her reverend husband. Far more than an ordinary love bound the two girls together; they were closer to each other than to any of the other children.[36]

Ellie's marriage wrought a shattering change in Maggie's life. Being the girl she was, Maggie kept her personal grief at losing her sister to herself, but she poured it out on paper in her especial medium. Maggie knew and admired Jackson but could not escape heartbreak that her sister was leaving their happy home. Never able to express her deepest emotions openly, Maggie told the story of her sisterly love and sadness in a sensitive poem "To My Sister":

> A cloud is on my heart Ellie
> A shade is on my brow
> And the still current of my thought
> Glides often sadly now
> The careless smile comes seldomer
> Than once it used to come
> And when the playful jest goes round
> My lips are strangely dumb. . . .
>
> Forgive these saddened strains Ellie
> Forgive these eyes so dim!
> I must—*must* love whom *you have* loved
> So I will turn to him,—
> And clasping with a silent-touch
> Whose tenderness endears
> *Your hand and his between my own*
> I bless them with my tears [37]

Maggie was honest; she gave her heart to the good major and as time passed found him an increasingly dear companion. She was not to lose Ellie all at once. Arrangements were made for Maggie to accompany Ellie and Thomas on a honeymoon trip to the north.

The honeymoon had certain unique qualities. The major designed the trip to combine business with the occupations of the moment. He took the ladies to New York, where he hoped to see his old friend, Dr. Barney, and thence on to West Point, where he happily showed them his old school. Bridal traditions were not overlooked—Ellie obviously wanted to see Niagara Falls, and see it she did. Niagara Falls served as a base for a tour of Montreal and Quebec. The Canadian phase of the trip gave Ellie and Maggie new insights into Thomas's military nature. They knew already that he spent much time reading military history in off hours, but neither apparently had any idea how ingrained was war in his mind. When they reached Quebec, Jackson could hardly wait to visit the Plains of Abraham. Maggie best describes his reaction to the scene of the great battle:

My sister and myself stood with him, one magnificent August evening, on the Plains of Abraham, at the foot of the monument erected to General Wolf [*sic*]. As he approached the monument he took off his cap, as if he were in the presence of some sacred shrine. I never shall forget the dilating enthusiasm that seemed to take possession of the whole man; he stood a-tiptoe, his tall figure appearing much taller than usual, under the overpowering feeling of the moment; his clear blue eye flashing with such a fiery light as it used to wear on many an after battle-field; his thin, sensitive nostrils quivering with emotion, and his lips parting with a rush of excited utterance, as he turned his face towards the setting sun, swept his arm with a passionate movement around the plain, and exclaimed, quoting Wolf's [*sic*] dying words—" *'I die content!'* To die as *he* died, who would not die content!" [38]

The ladies also were to have insight into the curious mixture of God and war which formed so large a part of Jackson's character. Knowing his deep religious devotion, Ellie and Maggie received something of a shock one Sunday evening during the Canadian tour when Jackson announced he was off to witness the drill of a Highland regiment. His wife and sister-in-law reminded him that this was the Sabbath; surely he would not allow professional matters to mar the day. He had not, he maintained, regarded watching the drill as a violation of Sunday, and "if anything was right and good in itself, and circumstances were such that he could not avail himself of it any time but Sunday, it was not wrong for him to do so, inasmuch as it thus became a matter of necessity." Told by the keen ladies that his explanation was a rationalization, a practical way of "secularizing sacred time," he stopped to ponder the matter.

His willingness to examine his actions, his desire to determine if, indeed, he were giving way to rationalization convinced Maggie more than ever of Jackson's open mind. He had, she said, no stubbornness in him and stood open to conviction. It was possible, he conceded, that his premises were wrong. "When I get home I will carefully go over all this ground, and reach my own conclusions." Meanwhile, he saw the Highland drill. When he got home, though, he did as promised, decided he had been wrong, and became an earnest preserver of the Sabbath. [39]

For his own part, Jackson became increasingly proud of his wife as the honeymoon proceeded. She grew in stature the more he knew her, and he was moved to write from Boston, on the way home, to his friend Dr. Barney, that "I was married on the 4th instant to an intellectual, pure, and lovely lady.... So you observe that I continue to carry out your advice." [40] And Thomas soon learned what Dr. Barney had anticipated—that Ellie was the best of doctors in her constant concern for his health.

Back in Lexington, the newlyweds were immediately busy, Ellie in making arrangements for housekeeping, and Thomas in preparing for another school year. Ellie had the harder job. Places to live were scarce. Jackson, who had been living for a time at the Lexington Hotel,[41] had no idea of the housing shortage. At length both he and Ellie had to accept the proffered use of part of the Junkin house on the Washington College campus.

The Junkins, particularly Maggie, were happy at the decision. They all had a chance to know Jackson better, and became devoted admirers. The Reverend Dr. Junkin confessed he had never known a more devout man. The whole family found him an artless, honest soul, whose dedication was to Christianity and the broadening of his religious life. Never did he tire of theological discussions with Dr. Junkin and his brothers-in-law, some of whom were interested in the ministry.

Out of these conversations emerged the picture of a man with limitless tolerance, thorough submission to his God, and a willingness to work for his religion. None of the immediate family felt that Jackson was a fanatic or, to use the current expression, an "enthusiast." Maggie wrote of him that "in all the intimacy of our close homelife, I do not recall that he ever volunteered any expression of what is called 'religious experience.' " He had so regulated his life, though, that prayer became an integral part of everything he did. This resulted not from a desire to parade his religiosity, but simply to increase his Christian power. He explained this to the Junkins, when asked to give his definition of Saint Paul's term "instant in prayer," by offering to give an example, if he would not be thought vain in citing his own habits:

> I have so fixed the habit in my own mind, that I never raise a glass of water to my lips without a moment's asking of God's blessing. I never seal a letter without putting a word of prayer under the seal. I never take a letter from the post without a brief sending of my thoughts heavenward. I never change my classes in the section room without a minute's petition on the cadets who go out and those who come in.

Asked if, on some occasions, he forgot to do this, he answered: "I think I scarcely can say that I do; the habit has become as fixed almost as breathing." [42] Ellie served as an invaluable, unfailing ally in Jackson's attempts to lead a life closer to Christ. Her sweet religious spirit added to his own joy, made him more appreciative of God's blessings and happier than he had been.

Wife and home were new to him. Jackson, so long uprooted and adrift from a place he could call home, had a deeper yearning for family and roots than many of his friends realized. Now that he had them, he settled down to months of happy tranquillity. Home was to bring great changes in him—it made possible his giving vent to all the pent-up love and humanity so long frozen beneath the tunic of the lonesome soldier.

For the first time since he had left western Virginia for West Point,

Jackson settled down to routine home living. He thrived on it. Ellie gladly fitted herself to her husband's scheduled existence, and made no objection to his taking time for a few hours of meditation, during which he ran through the class material which he had read over in the morning. When he was not pondering pedagogical problems, Ellie interested him in family matters.

Her companionship, the gentle, happy way she had of regulating home life, was all new and wonderful to Jackson. Happier than he imagined possible, he wrote Laura that "to me my wife is a great source of happiness . . . she has those requisites of which I used to speak to you." [43] Everyone liked Ellie so much; they wanted her to come to their parties. She wanted to go, and Thomas to go with her. These affairs were no longer the frightening things they had once been: as long as he could go with Ellie, Jackson minded them not at all.

He was guided, too, into more concern about Laura and her family; Ellie wanted to know her sister-in-law, and saw to it that Thomas kept up lively correspondence with Beverly. In the letters written to Laura during the months following his marriage, Jackson inquired increasingly about the health of Laura and her family, and particularly was he interested in his nephew, Thomas Jackson Arnold. He wanted to be sure that his namesake was growing up to be a good, obedient son. Anxious about Tom's education, his uncle offered to try to get books for him. And in March, 1854, he happily wrote his sister that he congratulated himself upon being the uncle of another niece. Ellie joined him in his elation. [44]

Laura, who for a brief time had apparently thought that her brother's marriage might end their close relationship, wanted to know Ellie and to love her as Thomas did. The ladies, according to custom, exchanged locks of hair, although Ellie with her innate modesty was not anxious to do so. Thomas had to do the actual sending, telling Laura: "I send you a lock of Ellie's hair; this she reluctantly parts with because of its color, which she hopes may prove more acceptable to your taste than it has ever been to hers." Jackson added some brotherly advice: "My message to you is that you must prize it very highly as being the token of a sister's love and from a brother's wife." [45]

Ellie was so wonderful, and the Junkin family—which had closed warmly around brother Thomas—so close that it was too good to last. The Reverend Dr. Junkin, beloved president of the college, had always been a revered father and good friend to all the children. But it was mother Julia around whom the family revolved—she ran the household and upheld morale. She was the vital force in the family, and her sudden loss came as a desperate shock to the whole family. The manner in which she met death, however, inspired all whom she left behind. Jackson described it in a letter to Laura:

She without any apparent uneasy concern, passed into that unseen world, where the weary are at rest. Her life was such as to attract around her many warm friends, and if she had any enemy in this world, it was and continues to be a secret to me. Hers was a Christian life, and hers was a Christian death. She had been afflicted with rheumatism for several months previous to the close of her life, and on Saturday preceding her death she had the return of a malady which had formerly afflicted her. On the 23d of February, about three o'clock P.M., her husband told her that her end had come; she asked how long she could live; he told her that probably two or three hours, and although the physicians had the same day pronounced her symptoms favorable, she appeared perfectly reconciled. ... She asked us to kiss her and told her children to live near to Jesus and to be kind to one another. Her death was no leaping into the dark. She died in the bright hope of an unending immortality of happiness.[46]

The chance to point a moral for Laura's benefit was too good to miss:

My sister, Oh! that you could thus live; then might you thus die. Do you not remember how much you are concerned about your children when you apprehend the approach of a dying hour. Do my sister turn to *God* and cast all your care on *Jesus*. I believe that you had our Mother's and Warren's prayers, and now you have mine, and more than mine. My Dear Sister, do seek religion.[47]

With renewed strength, perhaps stimulated by Mrs. Junkin's fortitude, Jackson discussed the problem of Laura's lack of faith with Ellie's family. He must persevere—it was his Christian duty to show her the right road, and pray that she would strike out on it. If only she could be made to see the way as clearly as did Jackson. She must know that the path of righteousness was the sole road to comfort and to salvation. "Do turn to *God*," Thomas wrote her in April, 1854,

and obey the teachings of the Bible. If you do not believe the teachings, at least obey its doctrines, and I believe that *God* will give you faith. Make but the effort, and resolve to do what it teaches to the close of life, and then you may expect death to be disrobed of its terrors. Remember then you have your brother's prayers, and I hope those of several members of my wife's family, and I believe that you also received the prayers of our *Mother* and *Brother*.[48]

Ellie's example helped to rededicate Jackson's religious fervor. Her acceptance of her mother's death in her mother's own Christian spirit had helped to hold the family together. Sensitive Maggie had confessed that it now seemed, "in the intensity of my anguish ... a far harder thing *to live*." [49] Ellie, unwavering in her assurance that it was God's will that they should be left, gave them all something to lean on. Her influence on Jackson's maturing religious views—and on his character—shaped much of his later thought and action. The important thing was that Jackson not only loved her—he admired her, looked up to her, and from her honesty and piety received renewed strength in his own convictions.

Ellie often exerted her influence in humorous ways. She could joke with Thomas as no one else could, and in her jokes she often packed much wisdom, and tried thereby to temper some of her husband's rigid ideas. Duty, she told him on one occasion, was "the Goddess of his worship." He ought not allow it to consume him. Jackson scoffed, but thought about it and ever afterward he worked hard at blending duty with charity. Other things about him perturbed his wife. Ellie knew him well enough to realize the depth of his own ambition, even though usually he held it in firm check, allowing it to show at rare moments.[50]

Following Mrs. Junkin's death, all the family rallied round to help their father. For months the house was filled with brothers and sisters, and evening discussions of all sorts started again. As usual, Jackson became the center of these discussions, sternly defending his own ideas. Theologically he grew stronger. Never before had he been as sure of the strength which came with Christianity. During one of these talks, he maintained that he could suffer any combination of misfortunes if he knew they were the will of God—any Christian could do the same.

The family seized on the statement to tease him. Could he, they asked, endure blindness with equanimity? A moment's thought brought the answer: yes, "even such a misfortune could not make me doubt the love of God." The family knew his weak points, and they attacked him on one of the weakest: Would he feel the same way if he had to spend the rest of his life on a bed of wracking pain? Yes. Well, then, if in addition to all the rest, he had to accept "grudging charity from those on whom you had no claim—what then?" Silence. Then, in a low, reverent, and deliberate voice: "If it was God's will, *I think I could lie there content a hundred years!*"[51]

None of the cadets at the Institute would have recognized the cold, stern major could they have seen him at home. Relaxed, happy, and thoroughly in love with his Ellie, Jackson's naturally warm personality permeated the household. A good, honest, and often merry man he appeared to the family. Ellie was responsible for the transformation. She drew him out of his shell of shyness, played with him, joked with him, and took him places. She was there when the cares of the day were past; no longer did he face the long lonesome evenings which had been so hard to take. Ellie changed everything. Perhaps, all things considered, he loved Ellie too much.

Months went swiftly by. The Jacksons took the usual interest in the many civic and cultural gatherings of Lexington. Although Thomas did not join the Franklin Society, that jovial group of debating gentlemen from the colleges and from the town,[52] he did take an interest in public discussions. Much as he hated public addresses, attendance at several debates gave him practice in speaking, and working on his old philosophy that he could do whatever he willed to do, he forced himself into the role of an acceptable speaker—never a brilliant one, but acceptable.[53] These talks were fierce efforts; the local newspapers would sometimes comment that his speaking was "nervous," [54] but such comments never daunted him. He would become an effective speaker.

Politically, the Jacksons never made news. They shared the community's interest in affairs in Kansas and Nebraska, worried about the slave question in general, and Thomas stuck close to the Democrats. He could not bring himself to affiliate with the new "American Party" which was capturing the imagination of the valley men with its violent emphasis on nativism.[55]

Lexington's biggest excitement during 1854 was murder. One of the VMI boys, Cadet Thomas Blackburn, was slain on January 15, just outside the Presbyterian Church by one of Judge Brockenbrough's law students, curiously enough named Christian. It was a bloody business, and it concerned the Jacksons directly since Blackburn had been escorting Ellie's pretty younger sister Julia. Fortunately for her, she had already been seated inside the church and did not witness the stabbing. The affair seemed to involve some matter of honor, and all of Lexington mourned the loss of a gentleman.

The town divided over the case, and for a time relations between Colonel Smith and Judge Brockenbrough chilled. Much talk grew out of the murder and subsequent trial, and Lexington's social leaders made the most of it.[56]

All this excitement came at the time when Jackson's hopes for appointment to the University of Virginia were high. Ellie would have been happy for him had he received the position, but she was doubtless just as glad that they were to stay in Lexington. It was better to be close to home while she was ill. Nothing serious was wrong—some sort of infection of the face, apparently—and Thomas had no real worry about it.[57] Time and rest did their work. Ellie, two of her brothers, and Julia, packed up and went to the Natural Bridge in June for a vacation.[58]

Ellie needed all the rest she could get, not because of the minor face irritation, but because she was pregnant. This happy bit of news Jackson guarded with characteristic secrecy, but by summer the secret was out. He was anxious that Ellie not have to endure the heat of summer in Lexington, and since Beverly generally had much cooler weather, proposed a visit to Laura's. Nothing could have pleased Laura more, and she busied herself with preparations to greet the Jackson family.[59]

The trip, a hard stage ride over the mountains, was a great success. Ellie and Thomas stayed for several weeks, and the Arnolds grew extremely fond of their sweet little sister. For her part Ellie bore the visit well, thoroughly enjoyed Beverly, and loved Laura, her husband, and particularly the children Thomas had told her about. Sometime in August she and Thomas went back over the mountains to Lexington. Though she stoutly maintained that she had a grand time, the visit took something out of her. But it appeared to be nothing serious. She was expecting her baby in October, and had plenty of time to recuperate.

The whole thing was sudden and cruelly quick. Ellie, so full of life, so happy in the prospect of motherhood—Ellie died. And with her the baby. Cold and impersonal, the item in the paper on October 26 made it sound so minor: "Died, suddenly on Sunday the 22nd inst., at the residence of her father, Rev. Dr. Junkin, President of Washington College, Mrs. Eleanor [sic] Jackson, wife of Maj. Thos. J. Jackson, Professor in the Virginia Military Institute." [60] A short notice—died, wife of Major Jackson. . . . It was over. He had loved her—perhaps too much. The baby had been stillborn and had never had a chance.[61] But dear Ellie had had so many years before her. It was Ellie who was needed.

7

A HOUSE WITH
GOLDEN HINGES

Ellie could not be gone. "I cannot realize that . . . my wife will no more cheer the rugged and dark way of life. The thought rushes in upon me that it is insupportable—insupportable!" [1] The shield of faith was to have its test.

Stark sorrow shattered the family. Thomas's utter grief was matched by Maggie's, who cracked under the blow of Ellie's death. Her health giving way, Maggie was packed off to Philadelphia—other scenes, other people would help her over the difficult months ahead. Maggie's departure just at that time added to Jackson's woe. She had been so close both to Ellie and to him. Maybe if she had been able to remain in Lexington he could have borne the blow better. As it was, the brother and sister began and sustained a long correspondence, in a way an unfortunate correspondence, since the letters tended to concentrate on Ellie.

Maggie could not fail to notice the dismal tone of Thomas's letters— it became so marked as to cause concern about his general health. In response to consoling lines from Maggie, Thomas poured out the depth of his loss.

Those days of sweet communion are gone to me [he wrote Maggie in March, 1855], yet I rejoice in the thought, that naught disturbs her unalloyed felicity; her spirit now, and for ever, will continue to bask in the sunshine of *God's* favor. And then to think that you and I will soon join her; that she will even meet our emancipated spirits as they pass from their te[ne]ment [?] of clay, and that she will escort us to that Heaven of which Melville speaks so beautifully.[2]

Another letter, written about a week later, showed how much farther Jackson had retreated into his sorrow:

I have this morning been standing, as I delight frequently to do, over the consecrated spot where repose what was mortal of herself and Mother. What sad changes the past few months have brought in this household! The future is with God. And who would have it otherwise, certainly not I. Though the future of this life appears . . . dark; yet I feel assured that it will be illuminated by the Sun of Righteousness.[3]

As far as most of Lexington's citizens could tell, the major bore up with beautiful fortitude—his deep Christian faith was standing him in good stead. He said as much to Laura, writing her on November 14, 1854, that "religion is all that I desire it to be. I am reconciled for my loss and have joy and hope of a future reunion where the wicked cease from troubling and the weary are at rest." Laura had wanted to come to him, to be with him in case he needed her, but he assured her this was not necessary, he could bear the burden.[4]

Some of the things he wrote to Maggie, though, were most alarming. More and more he seemed to want to join Ellie in death: "I am looking forward with pleasure to that time when I shall only be seen by those who love me, as I now see *Dear Ellie*."[5] "Ah, if it only might please God to let me go now!"[6] And Maggie was not the only one who worried about Jackson's increasing concern with death. His aunt, Mrs. Alfred Neale of Parkersburg, could hardly have been pleased with his outlook when she read:

I can hardly realize yet that my dear Ellie is no more—that she will never again welcome my return—no more soothe my troubled spirit by her ever kind, sympathizing heart, words, and love. . . . She has left me such monuments of her love to God, and deep dependence upon her Saviour's merits, that were I not to believe in her happiness, neither would I believe though one were to rise from the dead and declare it. God's promises change not. She was a child of God, and as such she is enjoying Him forever. . . . If she retains her pure, human affections there, I feel that she will derive pleasure from the acquaintance of any one who in this world loves me, or whom I love. And does she not retain love there? "God is love." I believe that she retains every pure, human attribute, and in a higher state than when trammelled with flesh here. Oh, do you not long to leave the flesh and go to God, and mingle with the just made perfect? . . . I frequently go to the dearest of earth's spots, the grave of her who was so pure and lovely— but *she* is not there. When I stand over the grave, I do not fancy that she is thus confined, but I think of her as having a glorified existence.[7]

Friends close to him also worried. The Hills, in particular, realized how far Jackson had broken. In close personal conversation with Hill, Jackson confessed that often, as he made his daily visit to the grave of his wife and child,[8] he fought viciously an urge to dig up the coffin, and take one last look at Ellie's dear ashes![9] If he kept on with this line of thinking, he might do something desperate.

Maggie, obviously frightened at the tone of his letters, wrote urgently, begging him not to give way to despair but to trust in his faith. Apparently surprised at Maggie's fears for his life, Thomas consoled her as best he could:

> I regret dear Sister that I should have pained you by anything in my letter, and take this earliest moment to explain myself. I had reference to that change, which of all connected with Earth, is to me, most desirable; from a world of sorrow, to one of joy. But you must not understand me here, as being anxious, for I know that in due time if I faint [?] not, all my hopes will be realized. I have many thoughts about the future, and sometimes think that I am about entering upon its fruition; but this is human judgment; which with God, we know is foolishness.[10]

No one need worry about his deserting his faith so far as to take his own life—he would go when it was God's will. Friends and neighbors misunderstood the nature of his grief. Far from yielding to the temptation of giving up life, Jackson resolved to reconsecrate himself, rededicate his life to Christ. Ellie's death had a definite place in the pattern of Providence—there were lessons to be learned from this bereavement. Now, more than ever, did he become aware of his shortcomings and sins. In one of his notebooks he charted a course in self-improvement under the heading "Objects to be effected by Ellie's death." He would strive to eradicate ambition, resentment, to work for humility in all he did. "If you desire to be more heavenly-minded, think more of the things of heaven, and less of the things of earth."[11]

At long last Maggie came home. The family rejoiced to see her well once again, and none was happier than Thomas. He had stayed on at Dr. Junkin's, and, in a way, his agony had been good for the rest of the family. They had all concentrated on helping him through his grief, and this had diverted their own sorrow.[12]

Things were easier with Maggie around. Quickly the house settled to a routine, not like it had been before. . . . But Jackson resumed his study hours, and Maggie became his confidante. She had always been someone special; now more than ever this was true. In a way it seemed that he could talk to Maggie more easily than ever he could to anyone else, save possibly Ellie. Kind, sensitive, understanding Maggie came to share Thomas's innermost thoughts. "Knowing him as I did," she would write years after, "and having the opportunity of witnessing his daily life in my father's home, I held a key to his character, possessed, I verily believe, by none about him; because I was close enough to be allowed unguarded insight into 'the very pulse of the machine.'"

The thing that made brother and sister so close was one of the routines of the house. A custom grew up that every evening at nine o'clock, Maggie, if she had no other engagement, would go to Thomas's study for "an hour or two of relaxation and chat." Arrival a minute before the clock struck the hour would find Jackson in front of his high desk, with the light shaded and his eyes shut, silent—"not one moment before the ninth stroke had died away would he fling aside his shade, wheel round his easy chair, and give himself up to the most delightful nonchalance." They talked about all of Jackson's travels, battles, thoughts, worries, hopes, prayers. Maggie, in turn, let Thomas see something of how hard it was to be a gifted woman writer in the 1850s. She talked of her work, and of how she could do so little now that her mother and Ellie were dead. Much of what she could not write, she told Thomas. Plans for a book entitled *Silverwood*, about Ellie, mother and brother Joseph (also dead), were doubtless confided, for Jackson did not scoff at lady writers.[13] She took to heart his invitation to "come to me with every joy, and every sorrow, and let me share them with you."[14]

The two began studying Spanish together, Jackson observing often that it was a melodious language, well suited to lovers. They both found it such a pleasant study that it soon became part of their daily ritual.[15]

Maggie grew increasingly aware of the grandeur of Jackson's character. He had his little conceits, such as wanting to write a textbook in optics when he loathed the subject, and doting on punctuality to the point of complicating mealtime. But there was so much to admire. She stunned the family on one occasion by announcing that Thomas was "the very stuff out of which to make a stirring hero."[16] Dr. Junkin, vaguely amused, would admit only that Jackson was to him a "dear son," and some of Maggie's brothers conceded Thomas to be a man of "high-toned honor, deep christian humility, and remarkable conscientiousness," but hardly more than a "devout soldier."[17]

But Maggie knew better. "He was a man," she said, "*sui generis;* and none who came into close enough contact with him to see into his inner nature were willing to own that they had ever known just such another man."[18] Jackson knew how deeply Maggie cared for him; he felt the same way about her. In a sad sort of way, always under Ellie's shadow, they loved each other. But Jackson was a man of honor. Ellie remained uppermost in his affection. He still mourned.

More and more he turned his attention to religion and to his duties to the Church. So successfully did he regulate his living in accordance with Biblical command that in January, 1855, his father-in-law wrote that he was "growing heavenward faster than I ever knew any person to do. He seems only to think of E[llie] and heaven. . . ."[19]

Christian endeavor and teaching became all-absorbing. The teaching was hard enough and took up plenty of time, particularly since Jackson's eyes had gone back on him once again.[20] But in the church doings Jackson found most comfort. Reverend Dr. White, probably wanting to help Jackson as much as the church, put him to serious work collecting for the Bible Society. This society derived nothing from the weekly collections, and a special drive was needed to keep it up. Lexington and environs were divided into six districts, and a collector appointed for each of them. Jackson had a district and canvassed it thoroughly.

When he turned in his list of church members in the territory, with notations on their contributions, it was discovered that he had an additional group of names penciled at the bottom, marked as having given tiny amounts of change. The strange names brought a question: Who were they? Jackson had a ready answer: They were the militia of the Church, while the enrolled members were the regulars. These little sums had come from free Negroes in and around town. True, they did not belong to the Church, all of them, but "as the Bible Society is not a Presbyterian but a Christian cause, I deemed it best to go beyond the limits of our own church." [21]

This contact with some of Lexington's Negroes may have given Jackson the germ of an idea. It appears that for some time he had grown increasingly concerned about the lack of religious teaching for free Negroes and slaves. Doubtless he had heard of the experiment made by Richmond's St. John's Church, back in 1845, to set up a Sunday school for Negroes. Not everything had gone smoothly in setting up the school; considerable local opposition developed, but had gradually subsided. In the autumn of 1855,[22] Jackson began, on his own, a Sunday school for local Negroes.

Successful from the beginning, the school grew rapidly. He set up rules which were rigidly enforced, so that the school could be efficiently run. Instruction was given in the afternoon, and after local suspicions wore off, several citizens joined Jackson in teaching. The sessions were generally short, but they invariably started on time, and Jackson's own deep interest carried over to the other teachers and to the students.

Starting this school was peculiarly hard for Jackson. Not only did some of his acquaintances think he was violating the Virginia laws against mixed racial assemblies,[23] but he also faced the trial of conducting the first sessions alone. Never at ease in public forums, he struggled with the school. This was God's work, and he would be given the means, as well as the skill, to do it. To set the proper atmosphere at the beginning of the classes, and in spite of his total ignorance "of the science of music," Jackson would close the doors, stand at the front of the room, face the students, and begin a song. The idea was that all would join him and thus get into the proper spirit. It was quite a sight—

the tall man, ungainly-looking in his VMI uniform, keeping time with his big hands, intoning the words in an utterly unmusical voice. Almost always the words were the same:

> Amazing grace, how sweet the sound
> That saved a wretch like me.

He meant every word—something many could not appreciate.

People all over town laughed when the story of the earnest major's Sunday school made the rounds. It seemed just the sort of odd thing old Jackson would do. But some who knew the agony those first afternoon classes caused him could only admire Jackson more. Reverend White, the good pastor who knew the major well, never scoffed. In the beginning he had not been sure that the Sunday school would succeed, but he became one of its strongest friends. Jackson had persevered, had overcome his natural shyness, and finally enjoyed the work. Nothing else ever done by Jackson more impressed Dr. White with his rugged Christianity than the creation of the Negro classes. And the students seemed to like the school, despite the rules. Taking seriously the responsibility of instructing the Negroes in Christianity, Jackson personally reported each month to slave owners on the progress of his hundred pupils.[24] Finally, the Lexington Presbytery took up the campaign to give religious instruction to Negroes—after Jackson had pointed the way.[25]

To Jackson, the school had a twofold importance. Working among the Negroes helped deepen his own religion, and at the same time gave him further insight into the race problem. The more he came in contact with Negroes, the more they interested him. His opinion differed somewhat from the prevailing Southern view toward slavery. Negroes were not, to Jackson's mind, mere chattels to be sold from one master to another like items of furniture. They were human beings, children of God, with souls to be saved. They represented a virgin field for missionary work, work to which he had always been strangely drawn.[26]

Not that he opposed slavery—he did not. In fact, he acquired a couple of slaves himself in the years following Ellie's death. But having no immediate need for them, he let one hire himself out to earn money for his freedom, and he found the other, an excellent cook named Amy, a position with a Lexington family until the day he might have a home of his own.[27] Never did Jackson look upon his or any other slaves as inanimate property. The slave system had been, as he conceived it, established by Providence for reasons he could not hope to know. So it seemed to him not a question of right or wrong. He did feel, though, that Christian decency demanded that humanity be exercised by owners, and he followed that conviction scrupulously.[28] In the late 1850s he acquired several house servants and always looked out for their spiritual and material well-being; they, in turn, became devoted to him.

The piercing grief slowly eased. Thoughts of Ellie grew less painful and more precious as the months stretched out and work piled up. Not looking back, Jackson diverted his mind into various channels. Religion had been the greatest comfort, and now that his numbing loss slipped into memory, he could take an interest in current matters.

His fortune, modest but well invested, he wanted to expand. Land purchases always looked sound, and in late 1855 he looked for some likely purchases.[29] His half-brother Wirt Woodson had similar interests, but lacked capital. Jackson thought of helping Wirt; he liked him, and for the sake of the family wanted to see him do well. The trouble was that Wirt wanted to locate land in free-soil territory. And for the first time Thomas revealed his feelings on the free-soil–slavery controversy. Writing to Laura in October, 1855, he made the surprising observation that he did not want Wirt to go into free territory. Why? "He would probably become an abolitionist; and then in the event of trouble between North and South he would stand on one side, and we on the opposite." [30] Jackson had made his decision. There would be no question about whose side he would be on—if there were trouble. And he seemed to think there would be.

With his mind made up, Jackson did not spend time worrying about the future. Instead he hoped for the best and busied himself with stock transactions, hoping to realize some small profit.[31] Close to home he invested cash in a savings bank and for a few years enjoyed the status of a bank director. The venture brought a small profit, as well as some prestige.[32]

Advice from various business friends finally dissuaded him from investing in land. Sound on the surface, real estate values in Western lands—particularly Kansas—were admittedly unstable. He would do better to stick with modest dividends. With that concern off his mind, Jackson came to a lightning decision about his personal future. He had intended to use the summer of 1856 in surveying available lands in the West, but now he asked Colonel Smith to give him the leave of absence which had been postponed when he first came to VMI. Smith readily consented, and Jackson was off to Europe.

He could have gone to the Arnolds'—they expected him—but there he would have remembered things. Possibly he might never again have the time, money, and chance to go abroad. Possibly, too, a tour of some remote part of the world would lessen the loneliness a little. He had to get away—for his own peace of mind.[33]

It was the grand tour: England, Scotland, Belgium, France, Germany, Switzerland, Italy, back to Paris, then England and home.[34] Unlike other army men who took a swing around Europe, Jackson paid little or no attention to things military (with the exception of his trip to Waterloo, where he impressed certain French officers with his knowledge of the action).[35] Works of the masters, both painting and sculpture, captured his imagination. Architecture, particularly that of the great cathedrals, fascinated him. Never before had he so thoroughly appreciated art in all its forms. He came back to Virginia a changed man.

Whether Paris did it, or the permeating romance of all Europe, or simply the long trip alone, Jackson arrived back in the United States determined to remarry. Being a man of decision, he knew exactly the woman he would marry, would she but accept.

The lady he had met some years before in Lexington. They had associated under most happy circumstances when she and her younger sister had been visiting their older sister, Mrs. Hill. The girl, of course, was Mary Anna Morrison—of whom he had spoken so highly to Major Hill just before marrying Ellie.[36]

The whole matter he kept secret, as usual. For one thing, nothing immediate could be done about it, since his return voyage had taken longer than he expected. He was late for duty at the Institute and hastened to Lexington as fast as possible. Knowing him to be the most punctual of men, his friends were worried and feared an accident. When he made his appearance and his explanations, some teased him about the delay. Was he not miserable because of his tardiness? Not in the least, came the answer. "I did all in my power to be here at the appointed time; but when the steamer was delayed by Providence, my responsibility was at an end." [37]

Even casual acquaintances must have noticed a change. Jackson seemed much more robust than when he left, much happier. With relish, he plowed right into work. The old town, however, was not quite the same to him—not only because of Ellie's absence, but because the Hills had moved. Major Hill had accepted a position in the mathematics department at Davidson College in North Carolina, and their absence left a void. Maggie, so happy to have him home, helped ease the loss, as she always did.[38] She probably heard something of Jackson's newest plans. He had decided that he could, and should, make something happy out of his life—no one would have agreed more thoroughly than Maggie. What should he do about interesting Miss Morrison in his scheme?

Writing to her seemed a good opening gambit. He put his heart into the first communication, and it was one that took Anna by surprise. Never had she had a letter from Jackson, and now, suddenly, he wrote of how blissfully he remembered the summer they had been together in Lexington! She was amazed, but sister Eugenia was amused. The letter, she told Anna, was just the beginning, and she confidently predicted it would be followed by a visit from Major Jackson. Anna played the thing down, but Eugenia was right.

The Christmas holidays, 1856, gave Jackson a chance to see Anna in North Carolina.[39] Time was short, and his visit had to be cut thin. But he had to go—he must see her and conduct a whirlwind campaign.

Anna still had not taken seriously the major's letters. But one day she glanced out the window of her father's house at Cottage Home, and there, calmly striding toward the front gate, was the tall, military figure of Jackson. The Morrison family received him in some little surprise but, of course, graciously. Time pressing, the nature of his visit soon had to be made clear. Daughter Anna's hand in marriage was his objective, if she were at all interested. Reverend and Mrs. Morrison had suspected something of the sort, but the question still took them by surprise. They wanted to know Jackson better, talk with him, discover if he would be a proper son-in-law. Nothing, not even the shy but anxious requests of Anna, could persuade him to overstay his leave—they would all have to make up their minds in a few scant days.

The decision, actually, came easily. Jackson's lofty Christian principles vastly pleased Reverend Morrison; his never-failing politeness quickly captivated Mother Morrison, and his good humor won Eugenia without struggle. It was, all things considered, a remarkably successful short campaign. The best feature of it all was that Thomas and Anna already were friends. This fact gave Anna a cozy feeling; she felt safer about the whirlwind courtship. And, although nowhere is a direct statement to be found affirming it, Jackson appears to have left Cottage Home an engaged man.[40]

Still no one in Lexington, save possibly Maggie and the immediate family, had any idea of the major's romantic entanglement. Close observation, though, might have given some clues to those who knew him fairly well. Everything—his work, the climate, the town, nature—took on a special aura. Always a sensitive man, Jackson became increasingly receptive to little things: the aspen in bloom around Lexington, the weeping willow beginning to shade green. He laughed more than usual, surprising many people by his merriment upon hearing a series of comic public lectures given by an itinerant speaker.[41] There was no doubt he was a happier man. Why was not exactly clear to Lexingtonians, but it was a good sign.

Anna and Thomas grew close during the next few months, via the United States mail. Always Thomas wrote honest, strong love letters, showing no false modesty or timidity; and slowly, growing to know and trust him, Anna did the same. She learned much about her husband-to-be from his letters. Many of the peculiar stories about the strange professor she already knew to be myth, but now she caught glimpses of the real man. Devout she knew him to be, but she never ceased to be awed by the breadth and depth of his religious feeling. Right away she learned that he was a believer in keeping the Sabbath, even to the point of not writing, mailing, or reading letters which had been posted, had traveled, or arrived on Sunday—not even love letters. This was a rule he never broke until war forced him to do so.[42]

In others, such austere dedication might have been frightening to a prospective bride, but not in Jackson. Anna could see so much in his letters—a sweetness, a gentleness of character—which brushed away all fears. Thomas's letters were beautiful, tender, and they told her the one thing she most wanted to know—that he really loved her. He thought of her much of the time, he said, and never worried about her for he knew she was in the hands of "One who will not permit any evil to come nigh you." When he was alone, taking his daily walks, he wrote, "I love to . . . indulge feelings of gratitude to God for all the sources of natural beauty with which he has adorned the earth. . . . And as my mind dwells on you, I love to give it a devotional turn, by thinking of you as a gift from our Heavenly Father. How delightful it is thus to associate every pleasure and enjoyment with God the Giver!" [43] He grew strong in the conviction that their marriage was right. He said he found it "a great satisfaction to feel that our Heavenly Father has so manifestly ordered our union." [44] As he grew in this conviction, so he did in devotion: "When in prayer for you last Sabbath, the tears came to my eyes, and I realized an unusual degree of emotional tenderness. I have not yet fully analyzed my feelings to my satisfaction, so as to arrive at the cause of such emotions; but I am disposed to think that it consisted in the idea of the intimate relation existing between you, as the object of my tender affection, and God, to whom I looked up as my Heavenly Father." And, a few weeks later, he wrote: "I never remember to have felt so touchingly as last Sabbath the pleasure springing from the thought of prayers ascending for my welfare from one tenderly beloved. There is something very delightful in such spiritual communion." [45]

The engagement was not too long. Finally a secret date was set, and Jackson cast about for the groom's party. The ceremony would take place in Anna's home, and it would be better if someone close by could do the groom's honors. Major Hill was not far away, but Jackson sought someone else—perhaps the Hills called back too many old memories. At any rate they would certainly attend. Fortunately, another old friend had gone from Lexington to Davidson College—Clem Fishburne, brother of Junius Fishburne, with whom Jackson had spent so many friendly evenings at Washington College. Clem had accepted a position on the Davidson faculty in December, 1854, and seemed a convenient choice. It was a delicate matter to broach, though, since it might interfere with Fishburne's plans. Jackson, on May 25, put him the question:

> I suppose that you are looking forward to the coming vacation with all a Professor's interest in such seasons of relaxation and enjoyment. I do not

wish to interfere with your summer arrangements, but if you can without too much inconvenience officiate as a groomsman for me about the middle of July next, when I am to be married to Miss Anna Morrison I will regard it as a special favor. . . . As the time is somewhat distant I have as yet only mentioned the subject to friends.[46]

Fishburne accepted, and Jackson made arrangements to bring one other assistant with him; in addition, Anna's brother William would attend him.

For her part, Anna began a feverish preparation. Her trousseau, which had been ordered in New York, was late in coming, and she lived in deathly fear that it might not arrive before the wedding. To top it all off, her father announced that he could not possibly marry her—he could never trust himself to officiate at a daughter's wedding. Anna had to select a minister, and her choice fell on Reverend Dr. Drury Lacy, who long had befriended the family. There was another worry. Thomas had not been quite sure about the date. Would he arrive in plenty of time?[47] He did. Just as anxious as Anna, he arrived several days in advance, and, along with his second groomsman, Thomas L. Cocke, was invited to stay at the Hills'. Davidson College did not close the semester until July 15, and for this reason the ceremony was scheduled for the sixteenth—everybody could be there.

On July 16, 1857, Cottage Home, North Carolina, steamed in oppressive heat. This is how Clem Fishburne described the day:

The room into which we were put to prepare for the ceremony was upstairs and had been heated by the western sun so that dressing was hot business. The Major undertook to put on a new collar, a 'stand up,' such as were then worn and he called on me to help him adjust it. By the time I had got it buttoned it was limp. I told him it w[oul]d not do, we must try another. He produced another somewhat different in shape and by cutting the button holes before we began the adjustment we managed to get him rigged out in a dry stiff collar which stood the heat very well. He wore the uniform of the Professors at the Institute, what is known as the furlough dress of the officers, and in due time the ceremony of dressing being completed we marched down to the parlour where he was married by Dr. Lacy.[48]

Everything was fine. The trousseau and the groom had both arrived and the ceremony had been a great success, since the groom had promised to be an "indulgent husband." Immediately after the ceremony, the newlyweds departed on their honeymoon. This one differed notably from Jackson's first wedding trip—no third party went along. There were so many places that Thomas wanted to show Anna: Richmond, Baltimore, Philadelphia, New York, Saratoga, West Point, and, of course, Niagara Falls—even though Ellie had been there with him before. Anna loved the whole trip, but particularly enjoyed Saratoga and Niagara.

At Niagara she noticed with fond affection that her husband cared little for mingling with the mobs, but wanted to spend most of the time rowing her around the lake and commenting on the beauties of nature.[49]

Thomas discovered that Anna was all he could have desired—a loving, gentle person whose wit possibly was not as sharp as Ellie's, but who nonetheless had a happy sense of humor. Not only that, she was a good sport. Although she had never been a devotee of physical exercise, she was game to try hiking, boating, and sight-seeing. In some ways she was like Ellie. She looked a little like her, around the eyes. But her brown-eyed, slightly rounding face and lovely lips had their own beauty. In one way, at least, she was like her husband. Her health tended to be delicate, and on the honeymoon she began to suffer from some sort of glandular swelling in the neck.

Instantly solicitous, Jackson canceled plans for a trip to Laura's and took Anna to Philadelphia for treatment. A local physician could not decide what was wrong, but fortunately Jackson ran into a Lexington doctor who happened to be in Philadelphia, and his advice was to move Anna quickly to the Rockbridge Alum Springs, where the waters could work their wonders.[50] The Jacksons went straight to the springs and stayed there for several weeks, reading together, walking, sitting in the woods, drinking in the marvelous mountain air and the magnificent scenery—falling more in love each day.[51]

Duty finally ended the idyl; they returned to Lexington, Thomas to resume teaching at the Institute. They had to find a place to live since they could hardly go to the Junkins'. Houses were hard to find, and if found were usually beyond the present means of Professor Jackson. The temporary solution was to stay in the best of Lexington's hotels—which proved none too comfortable—until something permanent could be found.

Although she had visited Lexington before, Anna knew few people well, and she might have had a really lonesome time had it not been for Maggie. Maggie greeted Anna with open arms, saying, "You are taking the place that my sister had, and so you shall be a sister to me." [52] But Maggie could not help too much in placing Anna in Lexington society because she, too, had just been married.

Her husband, Maj. John T. L. Preston, a colleague of Jackson's at VMI, had been a widower with seven children—and was nine years her senior.[53] Why had she taken on the role of stepmother to a brood ranging in age from five to twenty-two? Age (she was thirty-seven) was probably a factor. And Preston was a grand person, well established in Lexington society, who obviously loved and needed her. Then, too, Jackson was married.

Maggie made a good wife, and the children soon came to love her. But she almost gave up writing—"because my husband did not in his heart of hearts approve of his wife's giving any part of herself to the public, even in verse!" [54] Nonetheless, all the children kept her busy, and only occasionally could she see Anna and Thomas.

Anna found that she did not have much idle time herself. Jackson's friends kept them both busy with a round of gatherings, and this sharpened their desire to find a house so that they could graciously return the invitations. Looking for one took time, and in addition Anna was adjusting to her new life and surroundings. First, she found that nothing could be allowed to interfere with Thomas's work. Work had piled up on him, and a great many hours each day he spent either at the Institute or in study at the hotel. Gradually Anna became accustomed to a routine, but it would be easier to keep the routine inviolate in a house of their own.

Jackson, too, was anxious to move into a house. He had wanted to do that when he and Ellie were living with her parents. Home had a special appeal to him, since he had never really had one of his own. It was a feeling he expressed in a letter to a friend:

> I hope in the course of time we shall be able to call some house our home, where we may have the pleasure of receiving a long visit from you. I shall never be content until I am at the head of an establishment in which my friends can feel at home in Lexington. I have taken the first important step by securing a wife capable of making a happy home, and the next thing is to give her an opportunity.[55]

Meanwhile, he and Anna tried a compromise. They moved into a private boardinghouse, which doubtless proved more comfortable and less expensive than the hotel. It had its pleasant side. In Thomas's free hours he and Anna walked around Lexington, visited, read together. He also suggested to Anna, a few months after they were married, that they might improve their Sunday afternoons by a mutual study of the *Shorter Catechism*, and they soon had it memorized. Anna knew it well from girlhood, and Jackson would not rest until he, too, could recite it correctly from beginning to end.[56]

They found their house in the winter of 1858.[57] Located on Washington Street, scarcely more than a block from the Presbyterian Church, it was not exactly the house either Anna or Thomas wanted, but it had been the only one available. Old, too large for the two of them, and sorely needing repairs, the house was intended to serve only as a temporary home. But Jackson worked on it, fixed it up, made it livable, and Anna made it homey.[58]

It was to Jackson a house with "golden hinges," with "a place for everything and everything in its place." Now real happiness came to the family. The new home became the symbol of family love and devotion, a place to relax and be happy. Inside, it was not ornate; the tastes of the owners were simple: the furniture was plain, but it was good. Amidst these comfortable surroundings, Jackson really began to live. It was as if all his life he had been waiting for this. At home he could be himself, could drop the stern mask of officer and professor. Here he could play with Anna, entertain his friends, rest after the day's work and study. Here, too, he could indulge a lifelong interest in gardening, and he succeeded in raising more vegetables than Anna could cook.

In his own study, which he planned and furnished himself, he installed his high standing desk with its constant light and his modest library.[59] His reading tastes showed wide-ranging curiosity. On his shelves were volumes on scientific, religious and historical topics, some light reading and varied titles in Spanish and French.[60]

The study served as Jackson's workroom when he came home from the Institute. Here he would retire at eleven each weekday morning and first read his Bible, then his textbooks until dinnertime. After a short while, however, he discovered that Anna missed him while he stood alone in the study, and he also discovered that she would not bother him while he was studying, no matter where he did it. So he moved into the living room where she could be with him.

Anna proved to be good at keeping routine. Jackson had a rigid schedule, and she knew his punctual nature demanded careful timing. Soon she learned to accept his rising at six in the morning for secret prayer, and she made no fuss over his cold baths. Seven was the hour for family prayers; Anna, Thomas, and their servants gathered promptly, and there was no waiting for a tardy one. After the prayers came breakfast, and then Thomas was off to the Institute for classes at eight. These lasted until eleven, then he came home for his study period.[61] Dinner was served at one and was followed by a half hour or so of leisurely talk—probably the brightest spot in the daily routine. After that Jackson went out to his garden—or out to his twenty-odd-acre farm, after he acquired it in 1859 [62]—for an afternoon's physical labor. Before supper Anna and Thomas would walk together or perhaps take a drive, and after supper they would sit in the living room relaxing and talking.

Since Jackson never broke his firm rule about not using his eyes by artificial light, he continued his habit of digesting the next day's lessons by mental concentration. And after a period of digesting his supper, he would turn his face to the living-room wall, sit bolt upright in a chair, and go over all of his morning's reading. Anna, though she did not like the hour's enforced silence, never interrupted him. When he was through, Thomas would turn to Anna "with bright and cheerful face," and they would resume conversation. This regimen marked most of the days on Washington Street. But it was never dull to either of the Jacksons, since in their times together they were very close. One of the favorite pastimes in the evening, after Thomas had finished his mental chores, was reading—Anna doing it aloud, because of the light—and they covered many volumes together.[63]

Another mutual endeavor was teaching the Negro Sunday school.[64] Anna appreciated her husband's devout nature, but only with the passage of time did she realize how remarkably fervent it was. With Jackson his church responsibilities were sacred trusts. It was a duty to aid the Church in every way, not only by working for it, but by giving it money, and he regularly gave it a tenth of his professorial salary.[65] As far as working for the Church was concerned, Jackson took his duties as deacon more seriously than most. He was honored to be elected to that office, found out the troubles that Dr. White had in persuading the Board of Deacons to meet and do things, took over the organizing of the five-man board and "made it not only a blessing to our church and congregation, but to the whole community. Indeed, it was a source of encouragement and comfort to his pastor to have the co-operation of a man who prayed and labored as he did not to be expressed in words." [66] In the works of the board, Jackson was helped by John Lyle until his friend's death in July, 1858.[67]

Duty extended to keeping fit to do more duty, and Jackson's routine included, of course, stern health rules. Anna's concern made her anxious to help. Diet and exercise formed the basis of Jackson's physical program. For some time he had been extremely careful about what he ate, and after much experimentation—plus some improvements—Jackson hit upon plain food as the key to digestive comfort: plain brown bread, almost no meat, and only cold water to drink. Water was not only good for him but it kept him from indulging what he thought an overfondness for alcohol.[68] Smoking had demonstrably bad effects on his nerves, which were generally in poor condition anyway.[69] Along with watching his eating, Jackson continued his daily exercises, walking briskly each morning, using his gymnastic equipment at home. Carefully planned exercise, he found, aided in his war on dyspepsia.[70]

Not long after he and Anna had settled in Lexington, Jackson suffered a severe inflammation of the ear and throat, to which was added the agony of neuralgia. The attack became so serious as to impair the hearing in his right ear. His eyes were bothering him still, and he tried all kinds of remedies for them—frequent cold-water soakings and a useless patent medicine which he somehow obtained. The pain in the ear and throat yielded only to a chloroform liniment and to internal doses of an ammonia preparation.[71]

Lexington's doctors were not sure what was wrong with Jackson's ear and throat. Commenting that their treating him resulted in increased loss of hearing in the right ear and the beginning of trouble with the left one, he gave up on the local physicians in disgust and sought help elsewhere.[72] In July, 1858, he went to New York City and put himself in the hands of a new doctor, but still failed to improve. By August, his doctor had decided that an inflamed tonsil was causing most of the trouble and thought that "by parting off part of the tonsil" a cure might be achieved.[73] This seemed to work, but the operation had taken time and prevented a summer visit to Laura, who was beginning to wonder if she would ever see Thomas again.

Surgery and liniments having only partly relieved him, Jackson once again turned to hydropathy as the best way to end his suffering. He thought he improved, but apparently did not. Shortly after he returned to VMI for the session beginning in September, 1858, one of the officers there wrote Colonel Smith, off to Europe, that "Major Jackson has returned not improved in health but on the contrary worsted by his *new system of treatment.*"[74] But the major refused to abandon hope. The next summer found him trying more of the waters.

Both Anna and Thomas had been ill during the summer—and part of the cause was psychological. On February 28, 1858, Anna had given birth to a girl, named Mary Graham after Anna's mother. She had been such a beautiful child that both parents had almost exploded with pride. In May, though, she had developed jaundice, and on the twenty-fifth she died. Thomas and Anna were heartbroken.[75] The loss was borne well— again the shield of faith met the test. But still it had been a tragic blow. Anna recovered slowly, for she had the added shock of Eugenia's death shortly after losing Mary Graham. A Northern tour had helped, but not as much as Anna and Thomas had hoped.

The loss worked a sort of alchemy on the family. They grew closer, and the closeness extended to the family servants, particularly now to the children among them. Amy, the good cook, was still in the Jackson household, and now there was Hetty, a chambermaid and laundress who had nursed Anna in infancy. Hetty had a twelve-year-old boy, Cyrus, and a sixteen-year-old boy, George, who were inclined to be troublesome. Jackson added one more to the family group, bringing in a little four-year-old girl, Emma, and giving her to Anna for a future maid. The children, fun that they were, also proved inclined to mischief. Things might have been unmanageable had Jackson not been the firm but fair master that he was. He saw to it that the boys learned to read, did his best to see that they received a religious education, and kept the whole clan in hand. They in turn thought he was wonderful.[76]

One thing Anna especially noticed about Thomas after the death of their baby—he grew more tender than ever toward other people's children. He had always loved children, and had a gift for getting along with them, but now his affection was greatly increased. Anna could see this in the way Thomas wrote to Laura's children.[77] She saw it, too, the night a friend and his four-year-old daughter spent the night in the Jackson house.

It was the first time the child had been separated from her mother, and my husband, fearing she might miss the watchfulness of a woman's heart, suggested that she should be committed to my care during the night, but she clung to her father. After his guests had both sunk into slumber, the father was aroused by some one leaning over his little girl and drawing the covering more closely around her. It was only his thoughtful host, who felt anxious lest his little guest should miss her mother's guardian care under his roof, and he could not go to sleep himself until he was satisfied that all was well with the child.[78]

All children—especially little ones—who came to the Jackson house loved the nice major. He enjoyed rolling around the carpet with them, playing all kinds of tricks, and chiding them with Spanish baby talk.[79]

Not that he played only with children. Most of Lexington would not have believed it, but when the cold professor came home from the Institute, nothing delighted him more than playing games with Anna, hiding behind doors, and jumping out unexpectedly at her to wave his saber above her head or give her a quick caress while muttering sweet Spanish nothings in her ear.

Without children, it was, however, a lonely house. Anna's heartbreak matched Thomas's, since she had so wanted to give him a child. His first child had been born dead, and now this. It was almost too much to watch him dote on Lexington's children. This loneliness, this need, plus Thomas's deep affection for his nephew Thomas Arnold helped bring about a new addition to the family circle.

Some sort of trouble, possibly financial, made it difficult for the Arnolds to keep their children either in school or in the hands of competent private teachers. This seemed particularly bad in the case of Thomas, who was now about twelve and at the stage where continued studies were most important to his future. His uncle proposed a way out of the Arnolds' dilemma—send Thomas to Lexington, where, for a little money, good teachers were plentiful. In addition, Jackson offered to assist in educating the boy.

Laura and her husband thought the plan excellent, and Tom made his way to Lexington in October, 1858. He remained a member of the Jackson family until June, 1859, during which time he learned a great deal about the adventurous and exciting uncle whose visits to Beverly had always been so enjoyable. Uncle Thomas had many fatherly traits. He seemed terribly intense about Tom's mastering his studies, and his views on education were not like those of most teachers. Instead of loading Tom down with many subjects, his uncle wanted him to take only two or three at a time—beginning with English and Latin—so that he might master them completely. Uncle Thomas had the idea that his nephew should not "go over anything without his understanding it thoroughly," and for this reason should not spread his studies too thin. It was explained to Laura this way:

> I regard it as a great error to require a child to study what his mind is not capable of appreciating. The tendency is to diminish his fondness for study; to give him a vague way of thinking, since he is not accustomed to see the precise point; and by overtasking the mind, his health both of body and mind are endangered. . . .[80]

It sounded as if Tom's uncle thought everyone had the same problem of comprehension that he had, with hard concentration the only guarantee of sound knowledge. There appears little doubt that both Aunt Anna and Uncle Thomas enjoyed Tom's stay. Jackson now had an opportunity to put into practice some of his long-standing ideas on educating the young. Tom seemed to want to prepare for admission to VMI, and this offered an ideal chance to give him special assistance.

Geography and history stood high on the list of subjects which a man with hopes of an education should know. Tom's geography could stand improvement, and in addition to arithmetic, which he would have to take up, like it or no, his uncle firmly insisted on aiding in his religious instruction. In the mornings, before the drums beat the call to breakfast at the Institute, Tom would go to his uncle's room to recite some Latin declensions and to repeat his catechism. The Latin business bothered Uncle Thomas, since he had little knowledge of it himself—he soon switched the recitations to English and a bit of Spanish.

Having an active young lad in the house raised some unexpected problems. For one thing, Tom seemed to be omnivorous, eating anything and everything. Jackson, always guarding his own health, worried about his nephew's diet and had to warn Laura not to send him boxes of "eatables," since the boy gorged himself and, something rare for him, complained of a stomach-ache. Similar symptoms in Jackson's own case had usually warned of a dyspeptic attack—could this be true of Tom? Such concern led to undue fussiness about the boy's gastronomic habits. What had he eaten at home? "When he first came," Laura was told, "he would use neither milk nor coffee. Since then he drinks a little coffee, but I am afraid of his doing so, as he had not been accustomed, he says, to its use. I don't wish him to change his home habits in any respect, unless there is necessity for so doing."

Aside from this problem, Tom proved to be no trouble. A good boy, he did his lessons well, stayed most of the time on fairly good behavior, and openly enjoyed going places with his soldier-professor uncle. They walked together on Saturdays and other holidays, visited the farm, sat together in church. Sometimes, encouraged by indulgent Aunt Anna, Tom would be allowed to go with Uncle Thomas to an evening entertainment of some sort or to a public lecture. Uncle was never dull. He would chat with Tom on all manner of topics, his conversation always full of interest and palatable instruction. Tom's estimate of his uncle is revealing, based upon such sustained and close daily association.

> Major Jackson took part in the usual conversation in the home, as much so as any one ordinarily would. When there was company, which was not infrequent, he talked freely, and was entertaining in conversation, and seemed perfectly at ease. I do not recall a single circumstance during my residence there, or in fact at any other time, that could be termed eccentric upon his part. I do not think he was so.

Passing the scrutiny of a bright teen-age boy was no small compliment—it tells a lot about Jackson.

When Tom left Lexington with his mother in June, 1859, the Jackson household again seemed strangely quiet, empty and a bit cheerless. But the Jacksons kept in close correspondence with Tom, who always afterward felt especially part of their family.[81]

Now that Tom had gone, the summer could be spent in further search for health. Actually Thomas had confessed improvement to Laura in May, 1859, when he wrote that he had ceased to use his old stand-by, brown bread, and that he could now eat almost anything put before him.[82] Jackson's throat continued troublesome. He convinced himself that a weird combination of liver disturbances partly accounted for the throat ailment, and determined to try the waters at White Sulphur Springs for relief. While he went there, Anna, herself unwell, was packed off to the Rockbridge Alum baths.

Hydropathy did Jackson at least fancied good, although Anna thought she became worse from the treatment. Whether the Springs did it or not, Jackson returned for the new academic year beginning in September, 1859, refreshed and "under the blessing of Providence... much improved...."[83]

The new year proved more worrisome than expected. Lexington suffered not only a smallpox epidemic but also a flurry of rumors—rumors about the state of the Union. Jackson had long been apprehensive about the question of slavery and the rights of the South; he had feared a breakup of the Union for many years. Everything pointed that way.

Fall, 1859, brought ominous news. Ever since the Compromise of 1850, the South had been winning short-term victories, while the Northern Abolitionists had been drumming on the moral wrong of slavery. The Fugitive Slave Act of 1850 had been constantly nullified by various Northern states, and although the Dred Scott decision looked like a

Southern triumph, the din of the Abolitionist crusade could be heard round the world. Fanatical old John Brown, of Kansas fame, brought matters into sudden focus.

It was a bleak October Sunday night when John Brown captured the arsenal at Harpers Ferry in northern Virginia. He had some wild scheme about freeing the slaves, and he wanted arms and ammunition to help him do it. No telling how far the old man would go—he had taken several hostages from the vicinity and seemed fully prepared to execute them. The alarm spread and brought, finally, quick action from Maryland, Washington, D.C., and Richmond. Fright and some panic were the first natural reactions. Governor Henry A. Wise, a man in an unenviable position, called out the militia in the Harpers Ferry district.

Federal troops were dispatched to assist the state of Virginia in dealing with the most dread of all horrors, a servile insurrection. Charged with the command of what United States troops could be sent immediately was Col. Robert E. Lee, Second United States Cavalry. He organized an assault on the famous engine house and recaptured it on Tuesday, at dawn.

The raid itself had been abortive, but the reaction to it, South and North, shook the whole nation. Virginia, remembering with graphic terror Nat Turner's Insurrection, loathed Brown for his effort. Northern Abolitionists found in him a providential martyr. It was the case of Virginia vs. John Brown which was important—not the pitiful stand at the engine house.

Virginia's problem was double-edged. Brown, and the three co-conspirators who had survived the siege, must be preserved to stand a fair trial—else their martyrdom would be more firmly planted. Hatred ran so high that it seemed best to take them to Charles Town for safe-keeping. On the other hand, precautions had to be taken to prevent the release of the prisoners. Open threats were being hurled in Northern papers that expeditions would be made to set Brown's party free. Spies were suspected of peering at Virginia's military preparation from behind every bush. The atmosphere in northwestern Virginia crackled with tension.

On November 2, 1859, Brown was sentenced: to be hanged by the neck until dead on December 2. The word electrified the North. Could Governor Wise be such a fool as to allow the sentence to stand? The fate of the nation appeared briefly to hang on the rope destined for Brown's dedicated neck.

Militia units of many Virginia counties congregated near Harpers Ferry and Charles Town. Preservation of the peace was the order of business. When the creaking, antiquated militia organization began to function, the state grew increasingly militant. Civil war was common gossip. Mothers wanted their sons to stand for the Old Dominion in her hour of need; old militia officers had visions of glory. Analyzed coldly, the militia system had deteriorated so far as to be almost useless. Federal troops helped prop up the lax discipline of the recruits.

From all over Virginia the Governor received offers of troops, but he still could be impressed by the tender of the Corps of Cadets of VMI. For a while he felt they would not be needed, but after he made his fateful decision for hanging old Brown, he seemed to desire the presence at the scaffold site of all the troops he could muster. The VMI boys were ordered to Charles Town.

Major William Gilham would command the Corps, while Jackson would be in charge of the artillery detachment. At 10 P.M., November 25, eighty-five cadets herded themselves and two howitzers on stagecoaches provided by Messrs. Harman & Company and rolled off to Staunton. There they entrained for Washington, and advanced units of the Corps arrived at Charles Town on November 26. The artillery detachment arrived the next evening.

Jackson had never before been away from his duty station at VMI during a school year. The expedition to Charles Town was the first real field exercise for cadets and faculty—the summer camps and marches hardly counted. This was fairly close to war. Traveling conditions, billeting, and rations had a distressing likeness to the real thing. But Jackson was happy. It was not as bad as he had expected, he wrote Anna, although he had been sleeping in a room with seven others. "Do not give yourself any concern about me. I am comfortable, for a temporary military post."

He had some reason to be relatively pleased. All the militia at Charles Town, including the commanding officer, Brig. Gen. William B. Taliaferro, looked to the VMI boys as the pace setters—all conceded their supremacy in military know-how. And Jackson's gunners easily stood out as the best drilled and best trained of the lot. The cadets joined in the pomp and ceremony of military reviews and maneuverings around Charles Town, and here they caught a glimpse of rugged old Edmund Ruffin, who joined their ranks the day Brown was hanged so that he could get a clearer view! Here, too, Jackson probably became acquainted with General Taliaferro, whom he would come to know well in the next few years.

Few had a better view of the hanging of John Brown on December 2 than Jackson. Anna received a graphic description:

John Brown was hung to-day at about half-past eleven A.M. He behaved with unflinching firmness. The arrangements were well made and well executed under the direction of Colonel Smith. The gibbet was erected in a large field, southeast of the town. Brown rode on the head of his coffin from his prison to the place of execution. The coffin was of black walnut, enclosed in a box of poplar of the same shape as the coffin. He was dressed in a black frock-coat, black pantaloons, black vest, black slouch hat, white socks, and slippers of predominating red. There was nothing around his neck but his shirt collar. The open wagon in which he rode was strongly guarded on all sides. Captain Williams (formerly assistant professor at the Institute) marched immediately in front of the wagon. The jailer, high-sheriff, and several others rode in the same wagon with the prisoner. Brown had his arms tied behind him, and ascended the scaffold with apparent cheerfulness. After reaching the top of the platform, he shook hands with several who were standing around him. The sheriff placed the rope around his neck, then threw a white cap over his head, and asked him if he wished a signal when all should be ready. He replied that it made no difference, provided he was not kept waiting too long. In this condition he stood for about ten minutes on the trap-door, which was supported on one side by hinges and on the other (the south side) by a rope. Colonel Smith then announced to the sheriff 'all ready'— which apparently was not comprehended by him, and the colonel had to repeat the order, when the rope was cut by a single blow, and Brown fell through about five inches, his knees falling on a level with the position occupied by his feet before the rope was cut. With the fall his arms, below the elbows, flew up horizontally, his hands clinched; and his arms gradually fell, but by spasmodic motions. There was very little motion of his person for several moments, and soon the wind blew his lifeless body to and fro.

Jackson's command was almost facing Brown's swaying form, with one howitzer on the left of the cadets, the other on the right. The scene struck the major as terribly solemn, and just before Brown dropped out of the world, Jackson offered up a prayer for his salvation—although he feared Brown unprepared to meet his maker since he had refused to have a minister at hand.

The wind, as it blew over that hushed assembly, ruffling the red shirts and gray trousers of the cadets and tugging on the flags of Virginia, would keep blowing until old John Brown had been moldering for years and the various truths he represented that day had marched thousands of weary, bloody miles.[84]

VMI's contingent left the day after the execution and returned to Lexington via Richmond.[85] No one really felt relieved by what had happened. The events at Charles Town did not allay fears for the Union. The more Jackson thought about things, the more qualms he had. "What do you think about the state of the country?" he asked his aunt, Mrs. Neale, in Parkersburg. "Viewing things at Washington from human appearances, I think we have great reason for alarm, but my trust is in God; and I cannot think that he will permit the madness of men to interfere so materially with the Christian labors of this country at home and abroad." [86]

Jackson acted on the sound idea that the less heated discussion of the secession–state-rights crisis, the better. He took no outspoken position, at least in public, but many others in Lexington did. All over the South the crisis deepened, and everything began to revolve around the election of 1860. Black Republicans, if they were to sweep the field, surely would lay waste to the South's rights and traditions. This feeling, less marked perhaps for a time in Virginia, could nonetheless be felt in Lexington. Business as usual went on at the Institute, but there was a bit grimmer purpose to the classes and to the fierce, ringing shout of Major Jackson as he urged his boys to "Ram home! Fire!" [87]

Still, there seemed time for the usual things of life; the election lay months in the future. While tending his classes with a military precision that was gradually winning the appreciation of the cadets, Jackson continued to worry about his health. The summer of 1860 again offered a chance to find relief from the worrisome symptoms which remained with him. All his physical ills he explained to Laura—who, incidentally, showed heart-warming indications of espousing Christianity, possibly because of her own recurrent ills [88]—so that she would understand why he and Anna might not visit Beverly in the summer of 1860.

The plan, as usual, was to go to some watering place. Thomas thought his condition stronger, but found that much exercise induced pain; and possibly a good "hydropathic establishment" would banish the symptom. Brattleboro, Vermont, boasted one of the famous baths in the East, and he determined to take Anna. [89] The Vermont spa proved useless, and the Jacksons transferred to the "Round Hill Water Cure," in Northampton, Massachusetts. This time both of them benefited from the treatment—they apparently found a doctor who really knew how to use the waters.

Some unpleasantness they encountered at Round Hill, though, because they were Southerners. Various discussions indicated a growing hostility to things Southern, and they had to suppress their anger and resentment. This discomfort could easily be forgotten when the beautiful scenery was remembered; this, plus a good doctor, made the summer's health hunt a happy one for Jackson. In addition, the doctor announced that Anna, who seemed much hobbled in getting about, could be completely restored to agility if she stayed until early October. So Jackson went back to Lexington without her; it was a painful separation, because separations had come so seldom. While they were apart he "reported" to his *esposa* regularly. [90]

Round Hill did so much for Jackson that the prospect of a hard academic year did not worry him. There could be little doubt that the year would be strained. Excitement about secession and states' rights had been building up to fevered intensity all over the South; Lexington had its own share of hotheads who wanted to plunge the state into war at once. But Jackson never joined this element. He threw his support to the

Union, without making a great thing of it. He quietly voted for John C. Breckinridge, being convinced that election of Breckinridge would do much to calm the country. If asked whether or not he thought the South ought to fight for its rights, Jackson's answer was yes, but it could make a better fight in the Union than out.[91]

Lincoln's election set off the powder kegs in the South. South Carolina had already made threats of her action, should the Republicans win, and she seemed keyed up to make good the threats. Virginia, swept by divided views, appeared to lean more toward staying with the Union, at least until the full intent of Republicanism could be discerned.

To the rising tide of hysteria and war emotions, Jackson reacted with a soldier's fear. War must be avoided, if humanly possible. He explained his feeling to nephew Tom, in a letter which did much to mold the boy's own views on the national crisis:

> I am in favor of making a thorough trial for peace, and if we fail in this, and the state is invaded, to defend it with a terrific resistance. . . . I desire to see the state use every influence she possesses in order to produce an honorable adjustment of our troubles, but if after having done so the free states, instead of permitting us to enjoy the rights guaranteed to us by the Constitution of our country, should endeavor to subjugate us, and thus excite our slaves to servile insurrection in which our families will be murdered without quarter or mercy, it becomes us to wage such a war as will bring hostilities to a speedy close. People who are anxious to bring on war don't know what they are bargaining for; they don't see all the horrors that must accompany such an event. For myself I have never as yet been induced to believe that Virginia will even have to leave the Union. I feel pretty well satisfied that the Northern people love the Union more than they do their peculiar notions of slavery, and that they will prove it to us when satisfied that we are in earnest about leaving the Confederacy unless they do us justice.[92]

With Lincoln's election causing such furor, Jackson felt it time to take some positive action himself. He joined with eleven other Lexington gentlemen in issuing a call to the people of Rockbridge County to meet in town to consider the state of the nation, and "by the expression of our opinion contribute our mite to arrest, if possible the impending calamity —and if that is impossible, then to consult together as to what is the safest course for us to pursue in the event of a dissolution of the Federal Government." The gathering was supposed to be nonpartisan, and as it convened, it appeared to be a mélange of members of all parties. The subsequent meetings took so little action and did so much committeeing that Jackson ceased to attend.[93] There was another possible cause for his flagging interest: the meetings became increasingly excited, and finally one of the committees drafted a resolution calling for a state convention to review the position of Virginia in the Union. There is no evidence that Jackson endorsed such a convention at so early a date.

There is, on the other hand, some indication that he felt the pull of opinion dragging him closer to the idea of secession.

Firm believer in the doctrine of states' rights, he could sympathize with the fire-eaters, but could not go to their extremes. He did tend toward the position held by the Cooperationists—no secession without cooperation of several Southern states. One state seceding alone would doubtless commit suicide. Basically, though, Jackson wanted more moderation than displayed even by the Cooperationists. He felt that part of the nation's troubles might be traceable to a secular trend. A call on the Reverend White gave Jackson the chance to propose united prayers for peace as a way to avert a national catastrophe. "Do you not think that all the Christian people of the land could be induced to unite in a concert of prayer, to avert so great an evil? It seems to me, that if they would unite thus in prayer, war might be prevented, and peace preserved." Dr. White thought this a grand idea, and agreed to try to arrange it; in the meantime he would so pray and direct the prayers of the Lexington congregation.[94]

Concerted prayers were, at length, arranged. The date set was January 4, 1861. Jackson relaxed. Now he felt that the people were doing all they could do—all that Christians must do—to avoid war. The outcome lay in God's hands. If He decreed peace, there would be peace. If He decreed otherwise. . . .[95]

To Laura, Thomas expressed something of his feeling, writing on December 29, 1860, that "I am looking forward with great interest to the 4th of January when the Christian people of this land will lift their united prayer as incense to the Throne of God in supplication for our unhappy country." [96]

While he relied on God's wisdom to resolve the problem, he did his best to gird for war, just in case. When in Massachusetts the previous summer he had heard about a new type of artillery piece which had gained wide attention—Capt. Robert P. Parrott's rifled gun. This gun had more accuracy, longer range, and much greater general efficiency than the old smoothbore guns. Suggested as worthy of trial by the Virginia Commission for the Public Defense in 1860, the gun was tested in July by Major Jackson's class at VMI. So impressed was he that his report led to the purchase by the commission of twelve Parrott guns.[97]

Continuing with his own personal preparations, Jackson wrote to the Hon. John T. Harris, Congressman from Virginia, to ask a special favor. He wanted a volume on heavy artillery, published some years before by the Ordnance Department of the United States Army. He had had one, but somehow had lost it, and it would be a real help if another could be sent him. "I hope," he added, "that Virginia may have no occasion to use such against the Federal Government, but personally I desire to be ready should the emergency require my services." [98]

Life went on in Lexington, tinged now with a thinly concealed excitement. Anna had to go to her father's home in North Carolina to attend the wedding of younger sister Susan, who was marrying A. C. Avery, a promising attorney. While she was gone, Thomas wrote her almost every day; but his letters were cheerful, talked of things around home and of how he missed her. Had she not found North Carolina in a wild state of secession excitement, she might have forgotten the troubles of the country—certainly her husband wrote nothing alarming.[99] Not long after Anna returned, Thomas had the pleasure of hearing from Laura that her husband, too, seemed to be turning to Christianity. He replied that "for years I have been praying for him and expect to continue doing so." [100] The letter he wrote telling of his prayers for his brother-in-law is the last one preserved in Laura's collection; it was written just a scant two weeks before Jackson marched away from Lexington on the road to war.

Lexington's calm exterior began to crumble. Those who clung to Union sentiments found they were despised by increasing numbers of citizens. The VMI cadets grew more and more restive. Saturday, April 13, 1861, marked the first serious trouble. Since it was a holiday, many cadets were in town seeking various relaxations. They witnessed the raising of a secession flag, and that of a Union standard—accompanied by much speechmaking and furor. During the afternoon one of the cadets, persistently goaded, finally became involved in a fight with a citizen of the town. This fight set the stage for a larger one. The cadets, seeing that they might be attacked by various groups of excited men, sent for help from their classmates still at VMI. Soon a wild rush toward town was on, the boys carrying their muskets with them. Some of the officers of the Institute [101] headed them off, calmed them, received assurances from town that all was quiet, and herded the cadets back to the Institute. The superintendent directed the Corps into the section room used by Major Preston—it being large enough for all of them—and made a speech designed to calm them down completely. He reminded them that they should uphold law and order, reprimanded them for their insubordinate actions. Probably Major Preston and Capt. J. W. Massie talked to them as well, and at length Jackson entered the room. The cadets, in a joking mood by now, called for "Jackson, Jackson, Old Jack." Shaking his head, he refused to speak. Smith said to him: "I have driven in the nail, but it needs clinching. Speak with them." This from the colonel was an order.

Jackson mounted the rostrum, turned to the cadets. He looked taller than usual, his eyes had a flashing, fiery light, his whole body conveyed energy.

Military men make short speeches, and as for myself I am no hand at speaking, anyhow. The time for war has not yet come, but it will come, and that soon; and when it does come, my advice is to draw the sword and throw away the scabbard.[102]

Here was Old Jack in a new light—he sounded like a fighter and he had the bearing of a fierce leader! That day he earned new respect.

Events followed in rapid order. On April 17, following Lincoln's call for 75,000 volunteers to put down insurrection, Virginia seceded from the Union. The minds of many suddenly had been made up for them. Unionist in principle or not, most Virginians felt their first loyalty was to their native state.

The Old Dominion began to feel the peculiar stress of civil war. Friends no longer were friends; family ties broke. Jackson was one of the first to feel the wrench of family disintegration.

On April 18, Dr. George Junkin, president of Washington College, resigned. He took the action as a result of what may have seemed a small event, but it had deadly serious overtones. A few days before, a group of the college students had fixed a secession flag to the statue of Washington, the highest point on the college building. Junkin had it taken down at once. Now that the state had seceded, the students put it up again, and the college faculty backed them up. Unionist to the core, Dr. Junkin could not stand the affront to Washington or to his country. He made hasty preparations, took one daughter and his niece with him, and drove in a carriage to a new home on Union soil. With him went part of Jackson's family. Maggie remained, as did Ellie's ashes, and two brothers; but the good doctor, of whom Jackson had grown so fond, was gone. Although Junkin loathed all things secessionist, he always kept a special affection for his son-in-law—even during days when he was doing dire things to the Union.[103]

Nothing could stop the rush to war now. Colonel Smith, whom Jackson had suspected of being a secessionist for some time,[104] tendered the services of the VMI cadets to Gov. John Letcher, and the Institute went on a war footing.[105] The call came in the evening of April 20, 1861. The next morning—it was, incidentally, a Sunday—the adjutant published an order of Major Preston, who had been left in charge of the Institute when Colonel Smith had gone to Richmond on the eighteenth to advise in preparing for war. The cadets would move at 12:30 for Richmond. Jackson, the senior officer present for duty, would be in charge of the marching column—it would be his first command in the war.

Everyone knew Old Jack's punctuality, and he was to show it again amidst the day's excitement. Not that he could be considered calm. He had dashed to the Institute without breakfast that Sunday morning, to get things under way. Would Dr. White come out to the barracks and offer a prayer for the boys before they left? He would. That settled, Jackson busied himself with packing and with making sure that ammunition and guns were ready.[106]

At eleven o'clock he dashed home, had a hurried breakfast and gathered a few other necessities. Then, with Anna, he went to the bedroom, took the family Bible, and began to read: "For we know that if our earthly house of this tabernacle be dissolved, we have a building of God, a house not made with hands, eternal in the heavens." They both knelt, and Major Jackson in emotion-choked words committed Anna and himself to the care of the Almighty Father, and prayed once again that peace might be granted the country. Then he clutched Anna, kissed her fervently, and walked out into the beautiful spring day.[107]

The order had been specific. It said the cadets would eat dinner at twelve noon, and at "12 ½ o'clock they will be formed to march." They ate, heard Dr. White's prayer for them, and stood in ranks, waiting. Impatient they were for the wars. "Let's go, let's go" came from up and down the line. But the exact minute had not come, so Jackson sat on his little campstool in front of the barracks and waited. He probably looked odd sitting on that stool, dressed in his VMI uniform, and encased in his huge boots. But he looked stern, too, and the cadets waited. They did not have far to march, for they were to take stagecoaches to Staunton, and the train from there to Richmond—but they wanted to be on with it.[108]

Five minutes before starting time, roll was called, and there was general sadness that several boys had been detailed to guard the Institute, so they would miss the fun.[109] Then Old Jack arose, and gave his first order: "Right face! By file, left march!" The column marched on past the barracks, the mess hall, and out of Lexington. Jackson would never see it again.

8

"AN ABLE, FEARLESS SOLDIER"

—G. T. BEAUREGARD

The boys were in a new sort of war—a war which looked as though it might be easier for the foot soldiers. True, the cadets marched away from the Institute, but not far from town was a train of stagecoaches, wagons, and other odd pieces of horse-drawn transportation waiting to take them on a thirty-mile ride to Staunton, where they were to spend the night of April 21. And next day the railroad—a new and uncertain addition to military movement—would speed them on to Richmond. It was a good beginning.[1]

Leaving Staunton late in the morning of the twenty-second, the cadets' train had its engine derailed in a tunnel passing through the Blue Ridge, and this held up the trip for a good two hours. While repairs were being made, Jackson took time out to write Anna. He did not worry her with news of the accident, but he did tell her that the war spirit everywhere was intense: "The cars had scarcely stopped before a request was made that I would leave a cadet to drill a company."[2]

A little delay hardly seemed important to the new soldiers. The VMI boys were pleased that they were in demand, happy in their sudden importance. The way to Richmond lay through many small towns, and there would be many enthusiastic crowds to cheer them on. The weather was fine, and the majestic scene from the Blue Ridge—blue hills rolling away to the east where Richmond awaited their coming—added a touch of grandeur to the glory of war.

Unfortunately the time lost could not be made up and the train did not reach Richmond until after nightfall. No fanfare greeted the cadets. In fact, Richmond had already become inured to teeming throngs of troops; the cadets were just another group of soldiers. Glamour was fleeting. They were marched off to the fairgrounds where they went into bivouac. There, the next day, Gov. John Letcher reviewed them and they were restored to some of their hoped-for prestige. Volunteer units concentrating at the fairgrounds all needed training in basic military drill, and the cadets were assigned the job. Many were parceled out to separate units as drillmasters and all were looked to as oracles of military knowledge. All but Maj. Thomas J. Jackson.

After the Corps was delivered, Jackson found himself temporarily out of things. No official duties were given him, and he volunteered his services as a drillmaster. Although he modestly did not seem to be much surprised at this, it was unusual. Virginia, particularly Richmond, had gone mad. Preparations for war all over the state resulted in confusion and wasted effort. Trained military people were desperately needed to take all these efforts in hand and direct them coherently. The Governor and his war council knew that; it was one reason they had been so relieved to hear that Col. Robert E. Lee had resigned his United States Army commission and was coming home. The whole city of Richmond rejoiced at this news. Lee was just the man to take over the disjointed doings in the Virginia capital and make sense out of them.[3]

Out at the Camp of Instruction (renamed Camp Lee in honor of Light-Horse Harry) Major Jackson heard of Lee's coming with vast relief. After Lee was appointed major general of Virginia forces and given the position of commander in chief, Jackson wrote Anna that "this I regard as of more value to us than to have General Scott as commander. ... I regard him as a better officer than General Scott."[4] Now order might come out of chaos.

Meantime, Jackson would not be idle. Having no official duties, he made himself useful by helping around the camp. He had offered his services to the state; he would now have to wait and hope.

On April 25 Jackson received notice that he had been appointed a major in the Engineering Corps of the state army. It was a galling moment. He hated engineering. Never had he been good at the business of making maps. Then, too, the rank was an insult. Virginia's officials were bestowing exalted martial titles to almost all comers—and Professor Jackson was to get the same rank he had held for years at VMI. Mexican War records counted for much these days, but nobody seemed to remember Jackson's.

The question of a title did not bother Jackson. Rank would come in the course of performance, provided, of course, there was a chance for distinction. That was the trouble: a desk job in a dingy office tracing charts scarcely gave opportunity for glory or recognition. It was not the assignment for the soldier who, some ten years earlier, had confessed to his sister that he lived for fame.[5] Good soldier that he was, though, he must obey orders—and only by luck did Jackson escape the Engineers.

News of his relegation to a useless staff job reached Jonathan M. Bennett, an old Weston, Virginia, friend then in Richmond, who immediately called on Governor Letcher. Such an assignment was a waste, he argued, and Letcher was impressed. Jackson's name was withdrawn from staff assignment and a commission as colonel of the line issued to him. The story goes that when the State Convention heard of the change in executive heart, one member, obviously bewildered, asked, "Who is this Major Jackson?" and was promptly answered by a Rockbridge County delegate: "He is one who, if you order him to hold a post, will never leave it alive to be occupied by the enemy." [6]

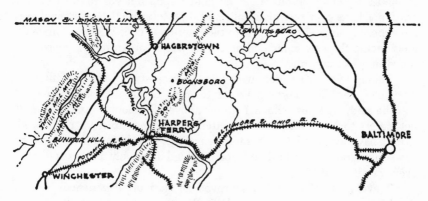

Vicinity of Harpers Ferry

Letcher, now that his attention had been focused on the odd professor, wanted him to assume an extremely difficult post. On April 27, 1861, the day that he handed Jackson his commission in the Virginia state forces, Letcher asked him to go to Harpers Ferry to take command. Always an important United States post, exposed to attack from several directions, Harpers Ferry had a symbolic value out of all proportion to its real military worth. The people in the valley of the Shenandoah looked to the old arsenal town as a key to the whole area. In addition, the arsenal and its machinery would be vital to a state trying to gird for war.

Poised at the confluence of the Potomac and Shenandoah Rivers, Harpers Ferry nestled in a great gap in the Blue Ridge, which ranged roughly south-southwest from town. North of the Potomac, in Maryland, the massive South Mountain frowned down upon Harpers Ferry, its bridges, railroad tracks, and highway. West of the town, so much less imposing that it often missed being considered, was Bolivar Heights, guarding the flank approaches. Surrounded, indeed dominated, by ranges and ridges, Harpers Ferry seemed militarily strong. But guns on any of the mountains could blow the town, the arsenal, the tracks, and bridges to bits—a point a trained soldier would instantly grasp. There were, at the moment, no professional soldiers there. The militia was coming to

Harpers Ferry in strength, and with these volunteers came untrained officers. Already the Governor could see that the militia system of the state, despite the exercise of the *affaire* John Brown, was outmoded. Jackson would have to go to Harpers Ferry, take charge of the raw volunteers, construct some sort of defense, and find out how morale stood in northwestern Virginia. General Lee would give him his instructions.

Lee's letter called attention to special problems at Harpers Ferry. There the old United States Arsenal had been making arms; the machinery would be essential to the armory in Richmond and must be shipped quickly. Guns or rifles in process of manufacture might be finished if it seemed safe, but Jackson would be held responsible for the loss of any arms, machinery, or raw materials; and if he felt that the equipment was too exposed, he ought to ship it to the interior at once.[7] The job immediately facing the new commanding officer was to organize his troops into something like an army.

Taking two VMI cadets with him, Jackson started for the valley on April 28.[8] The next morning he wrote Anna of his new assignment. It was, he said, "the post which I prefer above all others . . . and you must not expect to hear from me very often, as I expect to have more work than I have ever had in the same length of time before; but don't be concerned about your husband, for our kind Heavenly Father will give every needful aid."[9]

Traveling to Harpers Ferry proved an alarming experience. Jackson and his companions took the cars from Richmond to Gordonsville, thence to Manassas Junction, then west to Strasburg in the valley. From Strasburg, the trip north to Winchester—a major town in the Shenandoah region—had to be made by horse or stage. On April 29 the last leg, Winchester to Harpers Ferry, was made on another train. The experience prompted Colonel Jackson to telegraph Letcher on the twenty-ninth: "Recommend construction of a railroad from Strasburg to Winchester for strategic purposes."[10]

A quick survey of the situation proved depressing. Harpers Ferry had been under control of Virginia militia forces since April 18, and during that time discipline and training had been almost totally neglected. Major General Kenton Harper of the Virginia state troops had been in command, but he knew little of the realities of war. The men already there had no organization, save what little the company commanders could create. No precautions against hostile moves had been taken; little machinery had been dispatched to Richmond. About all that had been done was to occupy the town. The whole two weeks had been largely a holiday.

There was going to be trouble with the militia people. Jackson published his order taking command on April 30, and General Harper had no job—all he had was the dubious consolation of a Special Order which, while relieving him of his command, praised his patriotism in swiftly taking the field. With him, his own militia units were relieved of duty. Harper's unhappiness had been matched by that of the other militia officers, since Virginia had adopted a policy of decommissioning all militia officers above the rank of captain and appointing volunteers in their place. Jackson, consequently, inherited resentment and a shortage of officers.[11]

Taking rooms in a small hotel near the railroad bridge, Jackson and his adjutant, Maggie's husband Maj. J. T. L. Preston, got busy finding out about the men on hand. The volunteers who were willing to go into more or less regular state service would have to be mustered in officially, and then given some organization. Several anxious hours of reading muster rolls showed that numbers of men were on hand, but what they would do about joining the volunteer army remained uncertain.

During the first of Jackson's weeks as commandant at Harpers Ferry, he encountered smoldering unrest—the men had all liked their easygoing militia officers. Jackson, wisely not mixing much, had confined his activities to surveying the situation and mounting some guards. All the while he had been considering how to begin the mustering business.

The task was started for him by Capt. John D. Imboden, then in the artillery. Imboden had been to Richmond for a few days at the end of April and returned to Harpers Ferry to find many changes wrought by Jackson's presence. "I could scarcely realize the change. The militia generals were all gone, and the staff had vanished. . . . The deposed officers had nearly all left for home or for Richmond in a high state of indignation." Imboden quickly saw that someone would have to get the men started on the path of signing up in the permanent state army. He visited his own command, the Staunton Artillery, and ordered the men to fall into line.

> Then I briefly told them that we were required to muster into service either for twelve months or during the war, at our option, and urged them to go in for the full period of the war, as such action would be most creditable to them, and a good example to others. They unanimously shouted, 'For the war! For the war!' Before they were dismissed the ceremony of mustering in was completed, and I proudly took the roll down to Colonel Jackson with the remark, 'There, colonel, is the roll of your first company mustered in for the war.' He looked it over, and, rising, shook my hand, saying, 'Thank you, captain—thank you; and please thank your men for me.'

Imboden had done so well that Jackson asked him to serve as mustering officer for the other artillery companies at Harpers Ferry. Soon all the troops had signed up.

No time was wasted in creating organization; the men were assigned to companies and regiments, temporarily under charge of the senior captains. Jackson received instructions in early May to call out volunteers from counties near Harpers Ferry, to form them into regiments and prepare to defend his position.[12]

He had been right in telling Anna that he would be busy, busier than ever. The work, however, had visible results. Out of the chaos of indiscipline, rough order began to emerge. Although there was no really level spot for drilling, Jackson had put the various units to daily military exercising, and soon the 8,000 men who had come to Harpers Ferry had the outlines of an efficient force. The training had cost Jackson much concern—he had little sleep and less relaxation—but he told Anna he was healthier than he had been, and when he did get a good night's sleep he felt wonderful.[13]

To those who knew him of old, a tremendous change had come over Colonel Jackson. He still looked odd in the plain blue uniform of VMI; his gait and mannerisms still were those of the inept professor—yet he was different. Around him, and those who worked with him, a subtle air of stern military competence could be felt. In organizing and molding troops Colonel Jackson was expert. Soon the appearance of his post reflected the ability of the commander.

Conscious always of needing to know enemy plans, Jackson had his cavalry force, small though it was, doing scout, or picket, duty. To Capt. Turner Ashby, a small, vigorous man with flowing mustachios, Jackson had entrusted the command of these outposts. Ashby had already impressed observers as an active, alert partisan. In addition to Ashby's two companies of scouts, Jackson had three other cavalry companies, and all his mounted forces were under the command of Lt. Col. James Ewell Brown Stuart. Ashby and Stuart together had molded the milling horsemen into an effective force—Jackson would be warned of any Federal movement against him. He trusted Stuart, and soon he knew that he could trust Ashby.[14]

While Jackson worked at mustering and training his men, he found himself subjected to the worries of a distant government. Lee, who seems to have been echoing Letcher's concern, began a correspondence with Jackson in early May which indicated the uncertainty in Richmond. Lee was convinced of the probability of an attack on Harpers Ferry. The main threat might come via the Chesapeake and Ohio Canal or the Baltimore and Ohio Railroad, both of which Jackson must watch. As soon as news of attack came, it would be best to destroy the bridge across the Potomac and try to obstruct the canal. As a matter of insurance, Jackson "might make some confidential arrangements with persons in Maryland to destroy the Monocacy railroad bridge and draw the water out of the canal, should there be assurances of the enemy's attempt to make use of either." Lee's desire to direct military movements from a distance led

him to urge Jackson's dispersal of his force—a detachment at Martinsburg seemed a good idea.[15]

Unconcerned about worries from afar, Jackson proceeded to fortify
his position. Clearly he would have to occupy the heights dominating
Harpers Ferry. Detachments were sent to Maryland Heights and to the
northern tip of the Blue Ridge. In reporting these moves to Lee, Jackson
pointed out that he had not erected works on Maryland Heights since
this might offend the state of Maryland, but he would do so if he had to;
if Federal troops moved in his direction, he said, "I shall no longer stand
on ceremony."[16] "This place should be defended with the spirit which
actuated the defenders of Thermopylae, and, if left to myself, such is my
determination."[17]

Whether the remark about being left to himself was intended as a
gentle hint to Lee to keep hands off or not, Jackson intensified his efforts
to get ready.

Stuart and Ashby, keeping a screen flung wide around Jackson's
positions, were to give ample warning of impending attack—and so well
were they doing their job that Jackson could boast to Lee on May 11:
"Have no fear of this place being surprised."[18] Jackson possibly heard
vague rumors that Ashby squirmed under the command of Stuart; Ashby
was older than the dashing Jeb, and some of his friends agreed with him
that he should have the command himself. Nothing serious, however,
came of this minor jealousy—not for the time being.[19] Both horse soldiers
were able and devoted scouts, and Jackson counted on them with good
reason.

Cavalry was new to Jackson. About the only contact he had had with
horses came in Uncle Cummins's races, in riding lessons at the Point, and
in leading scouts during the Seminole interlude. At VMI, cavalry instruction was not pushed; Jackson's main attention had always been turned
to his favorite arm of the service, the artillery. And at Harpers Ferry artillery would prove of utmost importance.

Jackson had early decided to guard the approaches with guns on the
various mountain ranges. Unfortunately he had too few pieces of artillery
at hand to feel entirely safe—by mid-May he had been able to collect
only about sixteen guns of all sizes.[20] Although he personally directed
the emplacement of many of these, Jackson's duties kept him busy
with all branches of the command. Luckily the services of Col. Benjamin
Huger were available, and Huger, just out of the United States Ordnance
service, was particularly expert in the use of heavy guns. To him went the
task of emplacing the larger pieces as they arrived. Guns were destined
for Loudoun Heights (the Virginia side of the Potomac) and Maryland Heights; Huger would also help fortify Bolivar Heights. More guns
were needed, and Lee received a steady flow of requests.

No one at Harpers Ferry knew better than the commanding officer that in a showdown fight for the town, cavalry and artillery defenses would depend on the infantry. Control, organization, and administration of infantry units had not before been Jackson's responsibility. An artillerist by training and inclination, he had very little knowledge of the use and handling of foot soldiers and could hardly be expected to be good at it. But he was. The swift change in the appearance of infantry units around Harpers Ferry attested to that. Raw, undisciplined militia units, once sworn into Virginia and, later, Confederate service, found themselves subjected to daily drilling of the most rigid sort. Old Man Jackson —Old Jack, some called him—had a mean streak about little things. If something was important, then it ought to be done well. And to the madcap professor from VMI, all things military were important. The troops would learn their manual of arms, military courtesy, guard mounting, and all the other elements of soldiering well—even the ungentlemanly slop-carrying chores. Such menial activities ill became men of dignity, and there were many such in Jackson's command. But everyone— the Randolphs, Harrisons, Hunters, Masons, Carters, Beverleys, and Lees —did these jobs. They griped and thought Old Jack a hard man, but they soon looked and acted like good recruits.

The infantry force did not remain constant. Jackson lost some of his men as they were siphoned off to other sectors. By the middle of May he counted about 3,000 muskets (not all the men had arms in working order) and hoped to receive about 1,500 more volunteers. With this small number of troops his job would prove difficult. Not only did the Richmond authorities expect him to hold his position; he was also expected to guard possible crossing sites along the Potomac above and below Harpers Ferry, to observe the enemy, and to interrupt communication via the B&O Railroad and the C&O Canal. These were the military missions he would have to perform—but there were to be political problems too.

In later months and years division of force would be synonymous with his name, but in the early days of the war any commander who violated "the book" of tactics—be it Hardee's, or Jomini's, or anyone's— was daring almost beyond trustworthiness. Jackson's situation forced him to divide his command. All the jobs which his troops were expected to perform could not be done without splitting up the force, distributing detachments at such places as Point of Rocks, Berlin, Shepherdstown and Martinsburg—Point of Rocks, with a bridge, being to Jackson's right, the other three places to his left and apparently threatened by Federal troops. All four were vital to holding Harpers Ferry, and Point of Rocks was an ideal spot from which to harass the B&O Railroad.[21]

As far as the men at Harpers Ferry and dependent posts could see, all this business was somewhat foolish. Trains still ran, Washington remained connected with the west, and a sort of exaggerated politeness seemed to prevail between the Federal and Virginia forces facing each other at various points along the big river. The Old Man treated it all with deadly seriousness and appeared to take little, if any, notice of the high society going on in his camps. Gentlemen, even when gone to war, do not abandon all the refinements of home; and since the stint of state defense seemed little more than a glorified mustering day, the volunteers had arranged for many visitors. Ladies—wives, mothers, sweethearts— swarmed to Harpers Ferry to see "the boys." It was unfortunate, though, that some Marylanders at Shepherdstown appeared willing to shoot at their Virginia friends, and unfortunate, too, that Old Jack remained so ramrod serious. Had his men and their ladies known more of his problems, they might have been less frivolous.

Jackson had troubles. He was charged with a mission but was not given adequate authority to accomplish it. The main problem focused around Maryland. Richmond authorities seemed to live in a fog of fear that something Jackson might do would incense and insult Maryland. Here was part of the political imbroglio which Virginia and the Confederacy helped to create for themselves. Maryland might secede; she had Southern sympathies, was a slave state, and many of her citizens talked like Confederates. While she debated, no hostile act should be done to her which might induce adherence to the Union. And Jackson had occupied Maryland Heights and begun to fortify his position there.

Lee's worry was ill-concealed. "I am concerned at the feeling evinced in Maryland," he wrote to Jackson on May 12, adding that "it will be necessary, in order to allay it, that you confine yourself to a strictly defensive course." [22] Jackson had previously been chided about invading Maryland [23] but had gone ahead with his defenses. On May 10 Lee wrote what was for him a reprimand: "I fear you may have been premature in occupying the heights of Maryland with so strong a force near you. The true policy is to act on the defensive, and not to invite an attack. If not too late, you might withdraw until the proper time." [24] The invitation to retire was a direct order, coming from Lee. He did his best to palliate the sting two days later, when he reminded Jackson that the main consideration was supplies: "You know our limited resources, and must abstain from all provocation for attack as long as possible." [25]

No one could have been more acutely aware of the limited supply resources of Virginia than Harpers Ferry's harried commander. From the moment he arrived there, Richmond had been badgering him to move the remaining arsenal machinery to the capital, and at the same time complaining about having arms made at Harpers Ferry. Moving machinery proved a tough assignment. Wagon transportation could not be had since local merchants were paying double for it. For this reason Jackson, in early May, was introduced to the need for impressing private property— commandeering wagons to move machinery rapidly.

No food for his troops came from Richmond. Not only that, but his commissary officers had no money, and Richmond proved extremely slow in meeting their requisitions for funds. Valley farmers and merchants would not honor the credit of the state, and had it not been for the fact that Jackson's supply officers had local standing and personal credit, his troops would have gone hungry much earlier than they did.[26] One of the local officers, John A. Harman, reluctant quartermaster, would do more to make Jackson's operations possible than anyone save Jackson himself. Jackson saw Harman's natural talent for the post of quartermaster and urged Lee to make him a permanent fixture with his command. At the same time he persuaded Harman to stay, despite Harman's anxiety to get back to his business and, later, to go to the field.[27] While the negotiations for Harman's services were under way in mid-May, Jackson developed some theories of his own about supply.

Lee had made it clear that the troops at Harpers Ferry would have to rely largely on local markets for their needs. Without money, local procurement would be impossible unless impressment were allowed. Lee frowned on impressment, and possibly for this reason successfully arranged the assignment of Harman to Jackson's staff.[28] With Harman in charge, local dealers would advance supplies. Where should they be concentrated? Jackson thought Harpers Ferry ought to be designated supply depot for the whole of northwestern Virginia—an opinion which the exposed nature of the town doubtless soon altered.[29]

A temporary depot in mind, Jackson engaged in direct methods of procuring what was needed to feed, clothe, and arm his men. Richmond's red tape already had made itself obnoxious—Jackson knew that little could be expected from there. Impressment was the only answer. He felt about impressment much as he did about the silly coddling of Maryland. In war hard things had to be done in order to spare future hard things. Lee's objection to impressing supplies was that it would "embarrass the legitimate commerce of our citizens." [30] Military necessity overrode all such ideas. Harman and commissary officers said that horses were needed, not only for supply wagons, but for artillery. Nothing should be allowed to immobilize the artillery. Harman received authority to go into the neighboring counties and buy or impress what was needed. Such directness surprised Harman—and others. Jackson might be a hard man.[31] Never, though, did he impress anything for his personal use, even from captured Federal property. On one occasion, after a B&O train fell to his men, Jackson spotted a small sorrel horse which struck his fancy. Thinking it would be a nice present for Anna, he took the animal, but scrupulously paid his quartermaster a fair evaluation. (Unfortunately for Anna, he became so fond of the sturdy mount that he kept it for his war horse—the famous "Little Sorrel.")

When it came to equipping troops, it seemed the commanding officer had to do everything. Lee and the ordnance people in Richmond could not send enough of what was needed at Harpers Ferry, and troops coming there frequently had no arms. Jackson soon found himself involved in a long correspondence with Lee in an effort to pry arms from Richmond. Reminded that the call was urgent from all quarters, he had to do his best to obtain arms locally by offering five dollars per musket.[32] Meanwhile, the troops would have to drill without them—there would be no shirking training on an excuse of no guns!

There was also the question of politics. Lee had confessed concern about northwestern Virginia—disaffection seemed to be growing there. What did Jackson think ought to be done? [33] Since the center of trouble appeared to be Beverly, Jackson's personal concern was immediately piqued. Laura, of course, was there, and some news of how badly Southern sympathizers were being treated had come to him. He had a plan, he wrote Lee on May 21, which might be feasible now that things were steadier in and around Harpers Ferry:

> I would suggest that a force destined for the northwest be assembled, ostensibly for the defense of this part of the State, at Winchester, or some point near here, and that the moment that the governor's proclamation announces the ratification by the people of the ordinance of secession, such troops be put in the cars, as though they were coming to this place, but that they be immediately thrown into the northwest, and at once crush out opposition. This force need remain there only for a short time, until the local ones could be armed. You will pardon me for urging promptness in what is to be done for that section of the State. Any want of this may be disastrous.[34]

He might even be able to offer some troops for the expedition—he would like to go himself, but this he confessed only to Anna.[35] Nothing could, at the moment, be done. His plan could not be tried, but it was nice to be consulted. After all, he was a man from beyond the mountains; he seemed a logical choice if an expedition should be sent at some future time. Meanwhile, he had his hands full.

His hands became fuller on May 24, when three officers of the new Confederate States Army arrived at Harpers Ferry. One, sporting the then highest Confederate rank of brigadier general, was an acquaintance —Joseph E. Johnston. The smallish, iron-gray-bewhiskered, ramrod-straight general, looking like the prototype of his rank, sent Jackson a note shortly after he arrived. Would Jackson have an order published and circulated announcing that Johnston assumed command of the post? The order would also specify that quartermaster and engineering operations would henceforth be conducted by men of Johnston's staff.[36]

If this came as a shock, it must not show. There remained an important duty to perform. Johnston had no proof that he had been assigned the command by Virginia—no order from Lee had been sent.

And until the Governor or General Lee made the change official, Jackson would be happy to show Johnston and his staff around the post, help them get familiar with things, but he would remain in charge. Johnston was not offended—the VMI professor was being eminently correct, most military. Among his papers Johnston found a letter from Lee, with an endorsement to this effect: "Referred to General J. E. Johnston, commanding officer at Harpers Ferry. By order of Major-General Lee: John A. Washington." When Jackson saw it, he immediately transferred the post and now had no command.[37]

There was no question of justice. There was no question of any kind. An order was to be obeyed without question, without remorse. Still, Anna might worry about the change, thinking that Johnston's coming reflected on her husband's performance. She must be told not to worry,[38] and Col. John T. L. Preston, who had served so loyally with Jackson at Harpers Ferry, could explain it all to Anna when he arrived back at VMI. As for himself, he must not worry either.

Still, it was hard to fight back a question: Was the sudden appearance of Johnston an indication of failure on Jackson's part? Viewed broadly, his administration of affairs at Harpers Ferry showed commendable thoroughness, decision, and ingenuity. With a minimum of debate, the missions assigned to his force had been carried out; his troops had been introduced to basic training; his post had been well policed and preparations for its defense advanced. Movements along possible main arteries of enemy traffic had been observed, interrupted, and some rolling stock of the B&O purloined. Efforts had been made to stiffen the sagging morale of counties west of Harpers Ferry.

In doing these things, the professor had shown himself to be extremely energetic and determined. Willing to assume authority, he had done some things—such as putting troops into Maryland—which irked and worried his superiors in far-off Richmond. He had been chastised, but those who scolded him were too remote from Harpers Ferry to know what ought to be done. It was a Napoleonic maxim that the officer present on the scene had the right and duty to make final decisions on matters of tactics, and in certain cases, on matters of strategy. He was at Harpers Ferry, exposed and vulnerable from several sides. Swift measures had to be taken if the town was to be held, and Richmond wanted it held. Surveying the whole situation, Jackson had nothing for which to blame himself.

From the standpoint of his superiors in Richmond, Jackson's activities might have seemed unpredictable. Some of his earlier letters to Lee contained wild-eyed phrases vaguely reminiscent of certain communications President Davis would soon receive from General Beauregard. The staid, dull schoolman had talked of "throwing" troops here and there, spoke of holding Harpers Ferry like Thermopylae, and wanted to put a depot of supplies at an advanced and overexposed place. Such things made him sound inexperienced and overanxious. Harpers Ferry was too touchy a post to have an excitable and edgy officer in charge.

For these reasons, then, Lee may have assumed greater control of Jackson's operations than the colonel liked. But Lee doubtless felt reassured of Old Jack's ability when he received a letter, dated May 15, from one of Virginia's most prominent men, the distinguished James M. Mason. Mason's concern for the safety of citizens in the northwestern part of the state took him to Harpers Ferry during the first two weeks of May. "I spent the evening and night at Colonel Jackson's headquarters," wrote Mason, "and even my limited observation there confirmed the general tone of all around him, that all were in good hands under his command." [39]

One such testimonial did much to offset criticism of the impressing of supplies in the face of Lee's reluctance. There was no hint of official dissatisfaction with Jackson's performance—everyone seemed pleased. Johnston's coming on the scene appeared to be the result of Virginia's adherence to the Confederacy, the taking over of all state military affairs by the Confederate government.

Very soon Johnston made clear his own feelings about the job Jackson had been doing: he appointed Jackson commander of one of the brigades into which he reorganized the Harpers Ferry forces. The brigade was made up mostly of Virginians, largely men from the valley counties who had come out in response to militia calls. These were the men Jackson had been drilling hardest, the ones he had counted on most in case of an attack on Harpers Ferry.[40]

The new command, although small and not independent, was one which seemed peculiarly suited to Jackson's taste. The men he already knew, and before much time passed he had become convinced that his brigade numbered among the best in Confederate service. "I am very thankful to our Heavenly Father for having given me such a fine brigade," [41] he wrote Anna. In the next few months the whole country would know the unit by its honored title: the "Stonewall Brigade."

General Johnston created three brigades out of the force at Harpers Ferry, and in addition had a small unbrigaded infantry force. To the infantry were added the cavalry—some 334 men by the end of June— and the artillery, numbering about 270 men. His total strength in and around Harpers Ferry in May amounted to about 5,200, and by the end of June had climbed to 10,500 men.[42] As soon as organization took shape and the new commander became familiar with the post and assignments, changes began to appear. Johnston knew that he would have to keep on with the work started by Jackson, but he had plans of his own. Much about Harpers Ferry disquieted him. While he pondered his problems, his brigade commanders were given assignments to patrol along the extended observation line above and below the Ferry, and to put up as good a front as possible in order to delay any Federal advances. The First Brigade, Colonel Jackson commanding, took position on Bolivar Heights, to be within cooperating distance of any of Johnston's troops.[43]

With his own headquarters near Harpers Ferry, Jackson settled down to a brief spell of routine duty—organizing, drilling, and disciplining his troops, getting to know the company and regimental commanders. Routine might have been boring, but much purpose lay behind the daily exercises. Well situated in a nice house—with a yard which Anna heard about in some detail—the colonel confessed himself personally comfortable.

One result of the coming of Johnston was that Thomas now had more time to write to Anna. Before, with the heavy troubles of command on his shoulders, he had had to content himself with brief notes, letting her know that he was all right. She had been unhappy at the shortage of letters; she did not understand, either, why other officers brought their wives up to Harpers Ferry and she could not see Thomas. Not that he did not want her to come—lonesome and homesick, he wrote her that her "sweet, little sunny face is what I want to see most of all."[44] But home was one thing, war another. If she had been closer, in Winchester perhaps, she could have come, but from such a distance as Lexington it seemed imprudent. She almost persuaded him, but finally they both decided she should go to her father's home in North Carolina. There she would be safer. The sad thing was that the Lexington house would have to be closed or rented—their home, the one they had waited for so long.

Little Anna seemed to have trouble getting used to being a soldier's wife. She wrote long, chatty letters, full of news. And she seemed disappointed that Thomas's loving replies contained almost nothing about the war. Surely he must be doing important and exciting things. He had to explain:

> You say that your husband never writes you any news. I suppose you meant military news, for I have written you a great deal about your *esposo* and how much he loves you. What do you want with military news? Don't you know that it is unmilitary and unlike an officer to write news respecting one's post? You wouldn't wish your husband to do an unofficer-like thing, would you?

Women found it hard to understand the whys of army secrecy, and Anna was not unique. Unfortunately too many other men did not share Jackson's own sense of military security.[45]

With his division—soon to be called the Army of the Shenandoah—busily learning more of the lessons of soldiering, Johnston set about a private campaign of his own, one which depended on strict secrecy. He wanted to abandon Harpers Ferry. Good, sound reasons he had to justify this desire, reasons which he submitted to Lee:

Considered as a position, I regard Harper's Ferry as untenable by us at present against a strong enemy. We have outposts at the Point of Rocks, near the ferry at Williamsport, and the bridge at Shepherdstown, the extreme points being at least thirty miles apart. Our effective force, including those detachments and two others on the opposite heights, is about five thousand men, with one hundred and forty thousand cartridges and seventy-five thousand percussion caps. The only way in which this force can be made useful, I think, is by rendering it movable, and employing it to prevent or retard the enemy's passage of the Potomac, and, should he effect the crossing, in opposing his advance into the country. This I shall endeavor to do, unless instructed to the contrary.[46]

A shortage of ammunition, too few men, and too much exposed ground surely constituted good reasons, reasons which Johnston repeated in letters to Richmond through late May and early June. The import of these could hardly be missed by Lee and President Davis. Lee tried to reassure the general that all efforts were being made to send him men and supplies. Harpers Ferry, its commander was reminded, had more than military value, and its loss would be a blow to the morale of the whole South. Johnston should hang on.

Johnston had other ideas. He wanted out right away. As he saw it, he could be cut off easily from the rear, and he was not going to sit still and let that happen. At the same time, he hated to take full responsibility for giving up a position of so much importance. Finally, on June 13, the Adjutant and Inspector General, Samuel Cooper, wrote Johnston that "as you seem to desire ... that the responsibility of your retirement should be assumed here ... you will consider yourself authorized" to abandon Harpers Ferry—making sure to destroy everything of military value.[47]

On the fourteenth Jackson could confide to Anna that Johnston had blown up and burned the railroad bridge across the Potomac and was about to put the public buildings to the torch.[48] The whole command received orders to quit the town on the fifteenth and retire along the road leading to Winchester, a highway hub of the northern valley, some forty miles to the southwest. Federal troops under Gen. Robert Patterson were threatening the lower valley, and Johnston saw that if he stayed at the Ferry he would be outpositioned by the enemy. On the other hand, if he marched quickly he could cut across country to Bunker Hill, about twelve miles north of Winchester, well ahead of the enemy.[49] He marched quickly.

Elated, Jackson hoped for a quick battle. The sooner the invaders were turned back, the sooner would they understand the determination of the Confederates. The First Brigade ready for anything, Jackson prepared for an advance against Patterson. There seemed every chance the fight would be on by the evening of June 17 but such a possibility did not fit in with Johnston's plans. Recent intelligence indicated that Patterson's force numbered about 18,000 men while the Confederate force totaled only 6,500, and in addition the Confederates were short on ammunition, a fact which made Johnston "overcautious." [50] Outnumbered and with scant ammunition, there would be no attacking done by Johnston's troops—a real disappointment to the commander, First Brigade.

Johnston would fight if Patterson advanced on the Confederate positions—and in order to be ready, the Army of the Shenandoah was deployed in a line of defense near Bunker Hill. After remaining in that situation several hours, Johnston ordered a march south, toward Winchester. This march the troops made at a "snail-like pace" according to Jackson, who, in a rare mood of exasperation, wrote Anna on the eighteenth that "I hope the general will do something soon. . . . I trust that through the blessing of God we shall soon be given an opportunity of driving the invaders from this region." [51]

Quickly a chance for action—and independent action at that—came to the First Brigade. It received orders to march to Martinsburg, establish a base of operations, and destroy all the rolling stock of the B&O Railroad which could be found. A line of scouts and couriers would keep Jackson informed of enemy activity, and he could act accordingly. [52]

Throwing engines into the Opequon River, tearing up track and wrecking cars might be interesting work, but it was depressing too. [53] What excited Colonel Jackson most was the chance that his brigade might run into Federal opposition. As his troops moved north from Bunker Hill, unmistakable signs of Federal troops in the vicinity were reported, but the enemy dropped back as the First Brigade moved forward.

Wrecking B&O property expertly, Jackson kept an eye turned toward General Patterson, whose troops kept crossing and recrossing the Potomac. Cavalry scouts brought word on June 22 that some of Patterson's men were once again venturing into Virginia at Williamsport; characteristically Jackson wrote Anna that "I am making the necessary arrangements for advancing to meet them." [54]

A little help from the main body of the army would be welcome. Johnston, after considering Jackson's scheme for attacking, counseled against it. Apparently his unpredictable colonel wanted to pursue the enemy, once routed, across the river into Maryland—a course which might jeopardize political maneuvers. "It is not time," he said, "for us to invade." [55] More words of caution from the commanding general: Stand on the defensive, and take care about being outflanked.

Jackson could not help feeling restive. Standing on the defensive would not repel invasion, it would not win smashing and telling victories. In fact, with the enemy afraid to fight, defense would provide no victories at all! [56] Attack, carry the war to the enemy, let him know its horrors—this was the true strategy. But orders required patience; there were, of course, many factors to be considered which Jackson could not know.

News from other parts of Johnston's command brought joy to the army. Colonel A. P. Hill had conducted a small, but apparently brilliant, bridge-burning raid into Romney in far western Virginia. This little success, and it could hardly be listed as anything decisive, inspired the troops—Jackson's men were spoiling for a fight. So was the colonel, and he could not keep his desire secret from Anna.

As June passed he dropped more and more bits of information about the army to his wife in his frequent letters. She learned a good deal about the life of a soldier—it was hard, exposed, and not comfortable. But with her keen, observing eye she must have been happy to see evidence that Thomas's health improved under his new living conditions. Sleeping out had not been one of Thomas's habits, but now he seemed to be on the ground or in a bedroll every night. According to him, he thrived on the outdoor routine.

Men of the First Brigade grew to know their commanding officer much better during June. They found him to be fair, careful, and a strict disciplinarian. Tolerating no foolishness, he looked out for their comfort as well as supplies would allow. Constantly he worked to improve brigade organization. When toward the end of the month the enemy showed signs of inching again toward Martinsburg, Jackson had his brigade well in hand. His staff, including Edwin Lee as aide and Alexander ("Sandie") Pendleton as ordnance officer, consisted of men he trusted to do promptly what they were told—and he felt that the whole brigade would do the same.

Something of the efficiency of Jackson's command was known to the enemy, and they respected him. To General Patterson, Jackson appeared as an oppressor who held the people of Berkeley County in thralldom with an effective, if small, force. The force was annoying, and Patterson decided to move against Jackson.[57]

A courier dashed to Jackson's headquarters at 7:30 A.M. July 2, carrying a note from Jeb Stuart. Federal troops, reported Jeb, were four and a half miles away, advancing. The First Brigade did not have to get ready—after all, 7:30 was a comparatively late hour. Jackson did not have to concern himself with alerting his men, but with ordering them under arms and finding out how strong a force moved against him. Johnston's instructions had been specific—do not fall back unless the enemy advances in force, but if he comes in strength, retire under cover of Stuart's cavalry. Avoid a general engagement. A reconnaissance in force seemed in order.

Colonel Kenton Harper's regiment of Virginia volunteers, supported by Capt. W. N. Pendleton's battery, would go ahead of the brigade and Jackson would go with them. The other regiments, alerted, would support Harper should the opportunity appear. Baggage and other impedimenta went to the rear under guard.

Skirmishers out, advancing column closed and in hand, Jackson moved up the road. Stuart had reported that the enemy's position centered around Falling Waters. Jackson had determined to attack, or to provoke one in order to determine enemy strength. Having left three of Pendleton's guns on the route of march, possibly as cover in case of retreat, Jackson could count on only one gun in the forthcoming action.[58]

With the enemy in sight, Jackson ordered Harper to deploy two companies in support of his skirmishers. This maneuver appeared to goad the enemy into action. Advancing in line of battle, with a wispy line of blue skirmishers ahead, Patterson's men came on. Soon the Yankees walked into a withering fire from Jackson's skirmish line—a fire which temporarily drove the advanced Federal line back on its reserves.

Taking cover in a house and barn which dominated the battlefield, some of Jackson's men were able to stall the Yankees' attack for a time. Soon, though, the house and part of Harper's line were threatened by a flanking movement on the right,[59] which could cut them off. Seeing this, Jackson quickly ordered Harper to get his men together and fall back slowly, watching for further turning attempts by the enemy.

With the beginning of Patterson's turning movement Jackson's plan of battle changed. No longer did he hope to capture the enemy or to drive the Yankees back. Clearly the Confederates stood outnumbered— Patterson was advancing in force. This automatically put the second part of Johnston's instructions into effect. Retreat, contesting the ground, was the order. Johnston had been willing to support Jackson with Gen. Barnard E. Bee's regiment—Bee, an old West Point classmate, would have been glad to help—but the strength of the enemy at Falling Waters made it seem the better part of valor to find more suitable ground before making a determined stand.

The battle changed, in Jackson's mind, from a reconnaissance in force to a rear-guard action. And as a rear-guard action, Jackson fought it well.

As Harper's men pulled back from the house and barn, through an orchard scattered with Union dead, Jackson put Pendleton's gun to effective use. The enemy's pursuit concentrated along the road; and when it was sufficiently congested, Pendleton fired on them with solid shot. Confused, they stopped, sending their own shells after Jackson's men.

No sooner had he decided on a change in plan than Jackson sent Major Harman to the rear with wagons and with instructions to send the brigade baggage train farther south, since the enemy was present in force. Knowing that he had no wagons to worry about, Jackson managed the rear-guard fighting himself. Rather than concentrating and marching down the road in column, Harper's men were kept deployed in line. They fell back stubbornly, through fields and woods, keeping their formation, halting, firing, falling back. All the while Pendleton's obnoxious gun supported them—throwing shot and shell into enemy units trying for another flank movement. The professor blended the use of artillery and infantry with surprising skill.

Orders went to Colonels Allen and Preston to bring up their regiments in Harper's support. They were not needed, however, for Harper's men and Pendleton's gun proved equal to the job of slowing the advance. Jackson planned to make a stand a mile or so north of Martinsburg and sent orders to Stuart—who had tried a flanking move of his own against the Yankees—to meet the brigade there. With Stuart at hand, Jackson decided against a stand, left a cavalry screen in front of Martinsburg and took the infantry back to Big Spring, two and a half miles south of the town. There he camped until the morning of July 3, when Johnston ordered him to join the main army at Darksville.

In the spirited skirmish at Falling Waters Jackson could report much bravery on the part of his own men, and fortunately few casualties. Of 380 infantry engaged, only 12 were wounded and 13 killed and missing. Stuart came in for special praise in Jackson's report to Johnston. Not only did the cavalry capture 49 Yankees, but Stuart had "exhibited those qualities which are calculated to make him eminent in his arm of the service." Jackson was happy with his first taste of a fight—so happy that he told Anna more than seemed prudent. He even confided that one of Johnston's staff officers had told him that the general had recommended him for a brigadier general's commission. "I am very thankful that an ever-kind Providence made me an instrument in carrying out General Johnston's orders so successfully." [60]

Probably while the army waited in line of battle at Darksville, not far from Martinsburg, and hoped to provoke Patterson into an attack,[61] Jackson received official notification of his promotion, which dated from June 17, 1861. Right away he sat down at his field desk and scrawled a happy letter to Anna.

My promotion was beyond what I anticipated, as I only expected it to be in the volunteer forces of the State. One of my greatest desires for advancement is the gratification it will give my darling, and [the opportunity] of serving my country more efficiently. I have had all that I ought to desire in the line of promotion. I should be very ungrateful if I were not contented, and exceedingly thankful to our kind Heavenly Father.[62]

Actually news of the promotion could not have been unexpected. Jackson had been "politicking" for a brigadier generalcy since early

June, and his Weston friend, Jonathan M. Bennett, had been working for him in Richmond. For a time Jackson's hope was to get the promotion and a transfer to northwestern Virginia, but by late June he hoped for the promotion alone.[63]

The surprise for Jackson lay in the fact that promotion came in the Confederate Army and that the announcement had been accompanied by complimentary letters from Johnston and Lee. Johnston's read most pleasantly. Writing on July 4, Johnston told Adjutant General Cooper that Jackson's conduct at Falling Waters "gives most satisfactory evidence of the skill" which Jackson could show in battle, and recommended his advancement.[64] Lee's letter, tardily forwarding the commission, had been perfunctory but nice: "I have the pleasure of sending you a commission as Brigadier General in the Provisional Army; and to feel that you merit it. May your advancement increase your usefulness to the state."[65]

The new general received orders dated July 4, 1861, assigning him to the Army of the Shenandoah. So he was not going to the northwest, but he would keep his "promising brigade."[66]

Johnston's army, waiting in battle array and expecting a Yankee thrust, was disappointed. No Federal attack came. Johnston waited for four days—nothing. Patterson stayed at Martinsburg, a strong town with good defensive possibilities. Johnston did not feel strong enough to attack there. Stalemate. Johnston fell back, finally, on Winchester and began constructing earthworks.[67]

With Johnston entrenching and worrying about Patterson's intentions, Thomas could tell Anna much more of how he was getting along. His health, she would be glad to know, continued fine—sleeping outdoors had not yet produced any bad results. Army rations were not the best, but at least corn bread could always be had. And although she would like to receive a daily letter from him, Anna would understand why he stuck to his practice of not mailing a letter if it would have to travel on Sunday. "I feel well assured," he wrote of this subject, "that in following our rule, which is Biblical, I am in the path of duty, and that no evil can come nigh me. All things work together for my good." "Look how our kind Heavenly Father has prospered us!"[68] Letters could cease and be things of the past as soon as the war was over. In none of these letters, though, was there a hint of Johnston's activities.

Throughout early July Richmond watched with concern the increasing threat of a Federal advance against Centreville and Manassas Junction—an advance against the Confederate army under Beauregard's command. Convinced of the situation's seriousness, Beauregard called for reinforcements; he wanted 10,000 more men.[69] Obviously, if Beauregard were attacked Johnston would have to help him—or vice versa. Both generals had agreed on that.[70]

About one o'clock on the morning of July 18 Johnston was rudely awakened by a telegram from the Adjutant General's office in Richmond. Electrifying news. General Cooper tersely reported that "General Beauregard is attacked." Johnston's army was needed at Manassas:

> To strike the enemy a decisive blow a junction of all your effective force will be needed. If practicable, make the movement, sending your sick and baggage to Culpeper Court-House either by railroad or by Warrenton. In all the arrangements exercise your discretion.[71]

Johnston's decision was already made. The Army of the Shenandoah would march east, if it could escape General Patterson long enough to beat him to the battle. That might be a nasty problem. Patterson had to be eluded, bluffed somehow, so that he could not reinforce Gen. Irvin McDowell's main army in front of Manassas.

Strategically the situation facing Johnston during the first two weeks of July had been touchy. General Patterson's forces, erroneously estimated by the Confederates at some 30,000,[72] doubtless were aimed at either fighting and beating Johnston or at pinning his army firmly in the valley. The question was: Would Patterson be aggressive—would he energetically push Johnston's command, fixing it possibly in the Winchester entrenchments? Jackson's brush with the enemy advance had indicated that the Yankees would fight, but Patterson had displayed noticeable lack of anxiety to attack while the Confederates had awaited him in line of battle at Darksville. Until July 17 Johnston remained unsure of Patterson's intentions.

On that day the Union general displayed a fatal weakness. Instead of moving straight down on Winchester from Bunker Hill, which he occupied on the sixteenth, he sidled to his left, aiming for Charles Town on the Winchester–Harpers Ferry road. He had elaborate reasons for this move, the most valid of which was that he feared the restiveness of his ninety-day volunteers, many of whom were about at the end of their enlistment period. Whatever the cause, Johnston immediately saw his chance to sneak away unobserved. Patterson had put himself out of contact with Johnston's doings; in fact, the Pennsylvania general was working on the theory that Johnston had been receiving a steady stream of reinforcements from Beauregard.[73]

Acting quickly, Johnston arranged for the care of his sick in Winchester, and left a militia guard to garrison the town. Jeb Stuart's cavalry, serving as a screen, also stayed behind until nightfall of the eighteenth. Tight, airtight, the screen was, and the whole day passed with Patterson blissfully unaware that his quarry had departed.[74]

Speed and secrecy were the two elements which would make the movement of the Army of the Shenandoah decisive. The troops, unaware of where they were going or why, moved grudgingly out of their camps about noon of the eighteenth. The road through Winchester to the east seemed an odd one to take. It led to Millwood, then through Ashby's Gap in the Blue Ridge. Where were they going?

Leading the way for the army was the First Brigade, Jackson's men. Hot, dusty, and dispirited, the column snaked out of Winchester, marching hard, Jackson goading them on for about an hour and a half. Suddenly, Old Jack called a halt.

General Joe Johnston had an order he wanted read to all the troops. Jackson's adjutant read it, very loud: "Our gallant army under General Beauregard is now attacked by overwhelming numbers. The commanding general hopes that his troops will step out like men, and make a forced march to save the country." Wild shouts went along the line. Firm, determined steps now—everyone wanted to keep up. Old Joe said he wanted no straggling, and Old Jack kept that fresh in the minds of the men.[75]

Eating dust for eleven miles, the infantry, interspersed with artillery pieces and caissons, halted for lunch and a rest at Millwood. Canteens filled, Jackson's men, still proudly setting the pace for Johnston's army, started toward the Blue Ridge. Just about dark[76] the column came to the Shenandoah. Through the waist-deep water the infantry waded. Some of the artillerymen were luckier and were able to hitch rides on horses and caissons.

On the eastern side of the river, Ashby Gap stared the army in the face. A hard climb, particularly for men who had been marching through the heat of a July afternoon, but the prospects of a big battle drove them on. Not until two in the morning of July 19 did Jackson's advance halt for the night at the little settlement of Paris, on the southeastern side of the Blue Ridge. Weary, bone-tired, the men filed into a grove of dimly seen trees and collapsed on the ground, with no thought of food or of anything else but sleep. They were becoming aware of war's basic necessities.

Some men were lucky enough to find rooms in the few houses and the tavern of the town. A local tradition in Paris has it that Jackson and Johnston rested together on the porch of a house across the road from Ashby Tavern. Tired as he was, Jackson doubtless found time for evening prayers—the Lord's blessing might be desperately needed on the morrow.[77]

For Gen. Joseph E. Johnston, July 18 had been a day of incredible frustration. Never in his life had he seen so much go wrong with a marching column. Never had he seen such delays. His men of the Army of the Shenandoah were not regulars, accustomed by hard training to

cadenced marching. They were individuals, walking to a battle. They
would get there, and they would fight, but they would do all this in
their own way. Old Joe became excited about time. He grew so worked
up that by nightfall, when it had become clear that at the current
glacierlike pace none of his men would arrive at Manassas before
Beauregard had fought McDowell, Johnston had hit on a scheme to
speed his army. He would mechanize it, put it on the railroad, and give
it what modern logisticians call "strategic mobility." It was a good plan,
and it saved the "Napoleon in gray," blustering around at Manassas.

The Manassas Gap Railroad offered Johnston the quickest approach
to the scene of battle. From Paris a short, six-mile march would bring
his infantry to Piedmont, a small depot town on the railroad. It was
thirty-four miles from Piedmont to Manassas, and without the advantage
of a railroad on inner lines of communication, these would have been
fatal miles.

With the first gray streaks of dawn Jackson's men were on the move
—quick marching, for Old Jack wanted to reach the railroad. Early
morning made the fast pace easier and by seven o'clock the van of First
Brigade had swung into Piedmont.[78]

People packed the tiny town. From the surrounding country they
came in droves to cheer Johnston's men on. Nothing was too good for
the boys; "eatables of all kinds" were offered to the men, and as one
dazed Confederate recalled, "We fared sumptuously." [79] Breakfast for
once proved to be no problem.

Fortunately, another problem appeared to have been solved. The
Manassas Gap road had gathered together sufficient cars to move most
of a brigade of infantry—the trains stood smoking, awaiting passengers.
Only the infantry would ride; artillery, the wagon trains, and Stuart's
cavalry, which had already passed through Ashby's Gap, would go by
road. Most of the First Brigade boarded the trains within a couple of
hours and reached Manassas Junction by four in the afternoon.[80]

During the twentieth more of Johnston's men reached Manassas, but
not all of them. Promises by Manassas Gap officials that all the nine
thousand infantry would be on the field near Manassas before sunrise,
July 20, meant nothing. Johnston's last brigade—that of Gen. E. K. Smith
—did not reach the field until near midday of the twenty-first. Jackson's
brigade, arriving almost in one piece, picked up its artillery and cavalry
during the twentieth, and found itself assigned a camping area behind
the center of Beauregard's proposed line of battle.

All around Jackson's men fantastic confusion reigned. Manassas
Junction itself already had that look of "desolation . . . such as as [sic]
marks a place where soldiers have been encamped and where they get
supplies." [81] Stretching off to right and left lay Beauregard's army.
Gradually some of the men got an idea of what was going on.

Turning and twisting, the Confederate line roughly paralleled the course of Bull Run, "a small stream," as Beauregard described it,

running in this locality nearly from west to east to its confluence with the Occoquan River, about twelve miles from the Potomac, and draining a considerable scope of country from its source in Bull Run Mountain to a short distance of the Potomac at Occoquan. At this season habitually low and sluggish, it is, however, rapidly and frequently swollen by the summer rains until unfordable. The banks for the most part are rocky and steep, but abound in long-used fords. The country on either side, much broken and thickly wooded, becomes gently rolling and open as it recedes from the stream. On the northern side the ground is much the highest, and commands the other bank completely. Roads traverse and intersect the surrounding country in almost every direction.[82]

Selecting the southern side of the Run, with its lower level, as the line to hold, Beauregard had stretched his 25,000 men along an eight-mile length of the stream. With some exceptions, most of his line faced north toward the town of Centreville, and his dispositions had been designed to cover seven major crossings of Bull Run, plus the railhead and base at Manassas Junction.

Pierre Gustave Toutant Beauregard did not like the defensive. Sitting quietly behind the stream, inadequately guarded with thin and incomplete intrenchments, was not his idea of war. Attack, imitating the great Corsican's maxim of *audace, audace*—this was the true strategy. And while fighting a defensive skirmish at Blackburn's Ford on July 18, he had been planning—planning in grandiose terms.[83] Be it said in Beauregard's favor that he thought he would get more men from Johnston's army than he did, but still the plan he proposed exceeded the bounds of reality.

Whatever plan Beauregard had, Johnston would probably be stuck with it. Although he outranked the Great Creole, a point about which he had punctiliously sought confirmation from President Davis, Johnston did not arrive at Manassas until about noon of July 20. Beauregard wanted to attack on the twenty-first; consequently, Johnston had no time to study the ground, or to familiarize himself with the location of Beauregard's men. He had to accept whatever it was that his co-commander called a Battle Plan.

Briefly, Beauregard wanted to throw most of his force, including that of Johnston, around the left of General McDowell's line, which was supposed to be located north of Bull Run with its center at or near Centreville. Firmly determined on the idea of attack, Beauregard appeared to have given little or no thought to defensive deployment of his troops. Most of his men were posted to the right (east) of the Manassas-Centreville road, which meant that one-half of his army was bunched along three miles of his right center. His main strength centered on

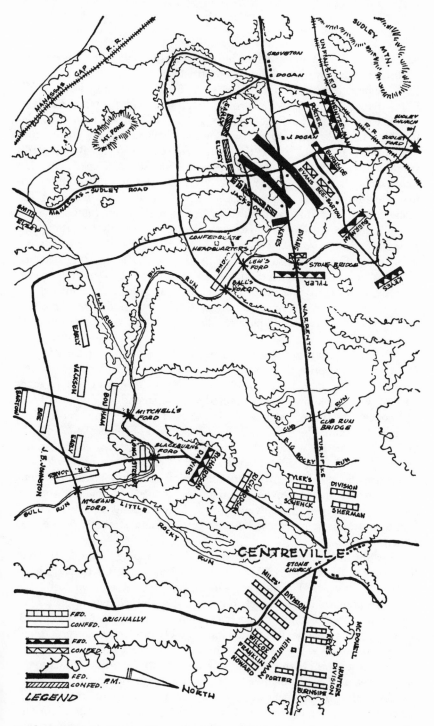

Battle of First Manassas (Courtesy National Park Service)   157

his right, along the most defensible crossings of Bull Run: Blackburn's Ford, defended by Gen. James Longstreet's Fourth Brigade; McLean's Ford, defended by Gen. D. R. Jones's Third Brigade; and Union Mills Ford, defended by Gen. Richard S. Ewell's Second Brigade. To these troops were added the First Brigade of Gen. Milledge L. Bonham, defending Mitchell's Ford, to the west of Blackburn's. Further upstream to the west (far away from the main concentration of Beauregard's strength) was the Fifth Brigade, Col. Philip St. G. Cocke, covering Lewis's and Ball's Fords; and stuck off at the extreme left of the Confederate line was the small, 1,100-man Seventh Brigade, watching the Stone Bridge over Bull Run, on the Warrenton Pike—a "quiet sector."

Johnston could hardly have been pleased to hear that Beauregard's strength had been so badly weighted to the right. Even the slim reserve of his army, Col. Jubal Early's Sixth Brigade, lay in supporting distance of Jones or Longstreet. And to this same overcrowded portion of geography Beauregard had directed Jackson's brigade as it came on the field. First Brigade, Army of the Shenandoah, was guided to a position near Early and constituted part of the fluid reserve on the morning of July 21, 1861.

Very early that morning things started to go wrong for Beauregard. Johnston had approved, perforce, the scheme to turn McDowell's left flank with the Confederate main body. Unfortunately, McDowell's exact position was not known to the Confederate commanders. Supposedly he had concentrated the majority of his reported 54,000 men [84] on his left, at about the same place Col. I. B. Richardson had been checked at Blackburn's Ford on the eighteenth. The Confederate attack, going around behind the left end of McDowell's line, wherever it was, would aim at Centreville and at cutting off the Union general's communications with Washington. McDowell, though, had conceived much the same scheme. And it was McDowell's move to get around and behind the Confederate left that wrecked Beauregard's grand strategy. There was something else, too.

Beauregard contributed a good deal to undoing himself. He had been slow in issuing his battle order for July 21, and after he had finally drafted it, received Johnston's approval, and sent it out, he lost track of it. Beauregard had a knack for writing grandiloquent appeals, but he was an incredibly bad composer of military orders. Most orders which he hatched were vague, incoherent, and subject to several interpretations. Things got worse as he became excited.

About 5 A.M. on the morning of the twenty-first, flushed with the bright dream of a Napoleonic sweep of the field, Beauregard received the disquieting news that McDowell's men were seen in strength near Mitchell's Ford, far to the left. With the news came the sound of firing from that direction—could it be as far left as the Stone Bridge? Should the enemy be attacking in real force on the left, the Confederate advance would have to be canceled. McDowell had jumped off first. This forced one of the many changes of heart which Beauregard underwent during that hectic day. Now he began issuing a rash of orders and counter-orders. Brigades and regiments marched and countermarched. Longstreet's crossings and recrossings of Bull Run were almost frantic. He was looking for someone to attack and also for someone to assist in the hunt for the enemy. The reserve of the army, small as it was, must go in—although no one knew quite where.

Jackson, with his brigade and nine guns, received orders to leave his position in general support of Longstreet and D. R. Jones, to move west and support General Bonham. Such a switch in the position of the First Brigade imposed some hardship on Longstreet, who had already called on Jackson for two regiments. But Jackson had to move, and did so.[85] In the flood of orders coming from army headquarters Jackson received further instructions: continue moving to the left and support General Cocke. Next he was told, in vague, but at least discretionary terms, to go to a position which would enable him to aid either Cocke or Bonham. The change in his orders had been urgent—more troops had to be sent to the left.

By nine o'clock fateful news had come from Capt. Edward Porter Alexander, chief signal officer. From his high vantage point near the Confederate center, Alexander had seen the gleam of bayonets and cannon crossing Bull Run two miles above and beyond the Stone Bridge at Sudley Springs Ford. The Confederate line had been outflanked. Nothing to do now but to change front, put as many men as possible over from the right to left, and hope for the best.

The immediate question facing Beauregard and Johnston was how soon could the full strength of the Federal attack be brought into action? Would there be time to reinforce the left after wasting so much time on abortive efforts to begin an attack on the right?

Beauregard was managing the battle. Johnston, doubtless keeping in mind the President's comment that he counted on "harmonious action," [86] had magnanimously left Beauregard in charge of the fight. Finally, with the sound of artillery and musketry growing louder to the west, Johnston could stand it no longer—he determined to go to the sound of the firing. Calling to Old Borey that "the battle is there, I am going!" he rode off at about 11:30, with Beauregard soon trailing along behind.

The two were tardy. By the time they left Field Headquarters near Mitchell's Ford the die had been cast. The drama had begun and neither Beauregard nor Johnston were directors of the play.

It was Jackson and the First Brigade who dominated the crucial fight on the left. Not that Jackson was on the scene when McDowell began to cross Bull Run at Sudley Springs and to threaten the Confederate rear—he was not. The first Confederate unit to receive the brunt of the Yankee advance was the small half-brigade under Gen. N. G. Evans. Evans had soon discerned that a threatening advance against the Stone Bridge by Gen. Daniel Tyler's regulars was a false alarm, a feint. Then a wigwag from Signal Hill alerted him to the real danger: "Look out for your left; you are turned." Without waiting for orders, Evans left a few companies to play a game with Tyler and marched the main part of his force some three-quarters of a mile west and took position on Matthew's Hill. Deploying at 9:15 A.M., Evans opened fire on Burnside's brigade as it came into view. So began the action on the left. It built up from there. More Federal troops were coming to the support of Burnside. Commanded by McDowell himself, the Second and Third Federal Divisions of Generals Hunter and Heintzelman constituted the attacking force—altogether about 13,000 men.

Evans, with his pitiful numbers, could not hope to do more than delay the advance awhile. He fought desperately, and, fortuitously for him, he received help. Beauregard had, around 7 A.M., made a small effort to reinforce the left by sending Gen. Barnard E. Bee's brigade of Johnston's army, plus a Georgia unit under Col. Francis S. Bartow, to the Stone Bridge—about 2,800 men. With these added muskets, Evans wrecked Burnside and immobilized his brigade for the day. Increasing pressure—Porter's, Franklin's, Willcox's brigades extended the Union line right and Sherman's and Keyes's extended it left—drove the small Confederate force back. Not even the addition of Wade Hampton's gallant Legion of 600 could stem the advance. About noon, with Federals threatening to turn both ends of their line, the Confederates broke. In confusion and disorder they fell back across the little stream called Young's Branch and finally reached the Henry House hill. While they were retreating, Jackson was preparing to aid them.

Jackson had no orders to take position on the Henry House hill—but there he was. Like the other Confederate commanders on the left, he did what seemed necessary. As he took his brigade toward the left to aid either Cocke or Bonham, Jackson heard that Bee and other units with him were hard pressed. Without hesitation, and apparently without telling any superiors of his action, Jackson notified Bee that he was coming and set off toward the sound of Bee's battle.

On the way to the fight Jackson and the First Brigade encountered some of Bee's, Bartow's, and Evans's men falling back in disorder. A position must be found on which to rally the beaten troops. Some commanders might have found it hard to resist the temptation to continue advancing until contact was made with the enemy—or at least moving up to support the main bodies of demoralized Confederate troops. Jackson thought of neither possibility. With an unerring eye for ground he selected the "first favorable position for meeting the enemy"—the Henry House hill. Halting his men there about 11:30 A.M., Jackson noticed the peculiar configurations of the ground as he glanced across the two hundred yards of plateau which crowned the hill. On the western edge of the plateau stood the small frame house of widow Judith Henry and six hundred yards northeast of her house was the home of free Negro James Robinson. The southeastern edge of the hill, slightly higher than the opposite edge, obviously formed the military crest—behind this Jackson drew his line of battle. Some cover could be had by his men, for the line had formed right along the rim of the pine thickets which ringed the brow of the hill, and the men could lie down in safety.

Artillerist always, Jackson emplaced his batteries with great care. On the way to his position he had encountered Capt. John D. Imboden's battery, of Bee's brigade, retiring in some despair. No urging was needed to get Imboden to join in Jackson's advance, and his three guns were added to Jackson's total. The guns were placed on the plateau, in front of the infantry, but not far in front. As the battle joined and raged through the rest of the morning and early afternoon, Jackson moved up more guns. By bringing up batteries not directly under his command he achieved a heavy concentration of fire, which proved vital in the course of the battle. Actually, the very fact of his forming line of battle on the Henry House hill had a significant effect on the action.

As Bee rode to the rear, trying to rally his men behind the Henry Hill, he met Jackson coming up and bringing along Imboden's guns. Sweating heavily in the heat of one of the hottest of days and battles, Bee waved his sword and moaned, "General, they are beating us back." A steady, hard look from flashing blue eyes, then: "Sir, we'll give them the bayonet." Rallying his men behind Jackson's rapidly forming line, Bee saw that his troops were unsteady, nervous. Pointing to Jackson's men on the edge of the plateau, Bee shouted an immortal battle cry: "There is Jackson standing like a stone wall. Let us determine to die here, and we will conquer. Follow me."

Urged by Beauregard, a recent arrival on the scene, the men rallied, formed, and moved to Jackson's support behind Bee, who recklessly exposed himself during the whole battle and soon was killed. But the rallying cry which came to him in the midst of the fight struck the fancy of the army—and the Southern people.[87] "Stonewall" Jackson became to the Confederates a name synonymous with victory, and to the Yankees a name which had the ring of doom.

By one o'clock in the afternoon Jackson had established his men securely along the ridge. He rode up and down in front of his men, supremely unconcerned about the whistling Minié balls and shells—a grand and steadying sight. Old Jack was a real commander. His example of bravery as he carelessly held up a wounded hand inspired his men.[88]

Colonel Harper's Fifth Virginia held the right of his line; next left stood J. F. Preston's Fourth Virginia; then Lt. Col. John Echols's Twenty-seventh Virginia; Col. James W. Allen, Second Virginia; and on the left was Col. A. C. Cummings's Thirty-third Virginia. Out in front of the infantry the artillery was in battery: Brockenbrough's four guns in front of the Second Virginia, Stannard's four guns in front of the Fourth Virginia, Imboden's three guns in front of the Twenty-seventh Virginia. Alburtis's battery of four guns was placed to the right of the Fifth Virginia. More guns were needed to strengthen the position, for Mc-Dowell's artillery, mostly regular batteries, had shown itself to be extremely good, and its guns outranged and outweighed the Confederate metal. There could not be too many Southern guns in Jackson's front.

This seemed particularly true when, after one o'clock, two splendid Federal batteries of eleven rifled guns came careening up the Henry House hill, took position south of the house and went into action—range 330 yards.[89]

By sheer good luck, Johnston, on his way to see what was happening on the left flank, found Capt. W. N. Pendleton's Rockbridge Artillery battery of Jackson's brigade. It had lost contact with the battle, but the Reverend Captain was awaiting orders. Johnston peremptorily ordered Pendleton forward and the battery soon found itself engaged in front of Jackson's line. Clem Fishburne, best man in Jackson's wedding, was in the Rockbridge Artillery and described the situation as the battery went into action:

> As we went through this woods, rising toward the final fighting ground, the shells & minnie [sic] balls from the enemy made a terrible racket over our heads and near us; and we passed some of the Washington College boys, who belonged to the 4th Va. Infantry in our Brigade, taking care of a wounded comrade. . . . We reached the top of the hill & turned to our right in an old field and unlimbered our guns and commenced firing to the left of the direction in which we entered the field. Just in rear of the Battery we found the Infantry lying on the ground, the Colonels & field officers at the head of each and Gen Jackson riding backwards & forwards in front of them. When we approached he gave orders where each gun should take position—just in front of his infantry, except one gun which was sent a little to the right of his line. . . .[90]

An artillery duel between Jackson's guns—some accounts say he had twenty-six working in his front [91]—and the two courageous Yankee batteries must be forestalled, since Ricketts and Griffen had moved their rifled guns so close to the Confederate line that they could cut Jackson's men to pieces. They had to go. As yet Union infantry had not come up in full support of the guns, and the opportunity was not lost.

While the bluecoats were filing in to stabilize the position of the guns, Stuart, whose cavalry had been drifting around the left of Jackson's line, delivered a short, sharp charge, demoralizing the infantry support. At almost the same time [92] three Yankee guns were moved to the right, trying for a small rise in the ground which would give them a flank, or enfilade, fire on Jackson's artillery. The move also took the guns closer to the Confederate line, and without waiting for instructions Col. A. C. Cummings shouted to his men, "Attention! Forward march! Charge bayonets! Double quick!" The Thirty-third Virginia rushed forward, fired a volley which mowed the gunners down, and took the pieces. They could not hang on. Soon a Union countercharge drove them back to their original positions, but the guns were unmanned and silent, standing in a sort of no man's land.

The adventure of the Thirty-third Virginia apparently encouraged Beauregard. He had taken personal command of the battle on the left, sending Johnston to the rear—after all, the senior commander should not recklessly expose himself! Seeing what the Virginians did excited the general and at about 2 P.M. he ordered an attack along the right of the Confederate line on the Henry hill. By then Jackson's line had been strengthened on the right and left. Many scattered units had reformed or come up from the rear, and a strong front faced the enemy from the vicinity of the Robinson house on the right to the edge of the woods circling the southern and western rim of the hill. Johnston, who could see something of the situation from his vantage point at the "Portici" house, was sending reinforcements to the left of Beauregard's line: that was the danger point, since McDowell was trying to turn the Confederate position by prolonging his front beyond the Manassas–Sudley Springs road to some high ground near the Chinn farm, southwest of Jackson's main position.

Concerned for the safety of his left, Beauregard hoped to relieve some of the pressure with his advance. When the attack started around the Robinson house, succeeding units took it up along the line and Jackson ordered his whole brigade to charge bayonets. Quickly the plateau was crossed and the enemy pushed from it—but a counterattack, supported by heavy shelling, regained the ground for the Union. The need for diverting Yankee attention from the threatened left increased. Hoping desperately for more men there, Beauregard ordered another assault along the front on the plateau. Jackson's brigade took the brunt of the charge, and again it succeeded, but the casualties were staggering. Brigade and regimental officers fell rapidly. The attackers stuck like glue this time, and the Yankees finally lost their grip on the plateau.

Suddenly the whole trend of the battle shifted. For six hours McDowell had been winning in his venture to turn the Confederate flank, but at last the Manassas Gap railroad brought in Johnston's stray brigade. Johnston sent Kirby Smith's men into position on the left of Beauregard's line. Now one more brigade on that flank would reach beyond the Yankee line—the flanker would be flanked. Long, anxious moments crept by. A dust column to the southwest brought field glasses to Beauregard's eyes. He made out a flag, but it drooped around the standard and could signal either friend or foe. If foe, the game on the left was lost. The Confederates would have to concentrate to the rear and hope to save something of the battle later. The hero of Sumter could not bear to retreat. In agonized dread he waited—a puff of breeze spread the flag. Confederate! Early's brigade it was, moving to the far left. The news spread along the line. There was a brief pause while Early and everyone else got set. Then over the field floated a weird sort of chant—like thousands of Southern foxhunters chasing their quarry—and with it the crashing of muskets, as all along the Rebel line, from right to left, Beauregard's men attacked. Jackson gave his men the word: "Reserve your fire till they come within fifty yards, then fire and give them the bayonet; and when you charge, yell like furies!" [93]

The First Brigade knew how Old Jack liked the cold steel—they "charged bayonets," struck the Federal center, and sent it reeling back. McDowell's men lost the impetus of attack; the concerted Rebel advance, brilliantly supported by Stuart's cavalry and a fresh battery on the far left, broke the Federal line. The Yankees ran for Bull Run. It was over. First Brigade did not pursue the enemy far; there was disorganization to repair and many wounded to patch up.[94] But Stonewall worried about pressing the retreating Federals. Hardly would the victory be complete if McDowell were allowed to escape with anything like an army.

Jackson had had a rough day. The middle finger of his left hand had been broken by flying shrapnel, but he had wrapped a hasty bandage around it and continued to command. His uniform coat had been gouged by a whistling fragment of death, and his horse had taken a piece of iron in the thigh. But Stonewall was happy—on the whole it had been a grand day. Never had a brigade behaved so well, or, indeed, done such decisive deeds. "Whilst great credit is due to other parts of our gallant army," he wrote Anna the next day, "God made my brigade more instrumental than any other in repulsing the main attack. This is for your information only—say nothing about it. Let others speak praise, not myself." [95] Beauregard voiced that praise in his report of the battle: Jackson was "an able, fearless soldier," worthy to command "his efficient brigade." [96]

9

RETURN OF A VALLEY MAN

Heroes abounded in the Confederacy. Beauregard added new laurels to his already bulging supply and Joseph E. Johnston leaped into prominence. Every state with men at Manassas had its own particular hero for the local press to enshrine. Virginia had vast numbers of daring doers and the state's newspapers poured out volumes of copy about each and every son of the Old Dominion who had been brave at Manassas. But mostly it was the important generals who received credit for the success.

All the publicity given to Beauregard, Johnston, and a few others crowded a great many lesser officers out of the public light, including Jackson. It was the failure of the papers to give adequate recognition to Thomas which most irked Anna. Down in North Carolina she had been reading all she could about the battle and waiting anxiously for news about Thomas. The story about Bee and the "Stonewall" episode received wide circulation in the South Carolina papers, interested in touting the heroism of Bee and his Palmetto State boys. From the South Carolina journals the story was copied far and wide, and Anna doubtless read of how her husband's presence steadied the course of the battle. Soon, too, she received his letter written the day after the fighting reporting that, aside from breaking his middle finger, left hand, he was fine.

Possibly it was this letter which tended to upset Anna. Thomas had been his usual modest self in reporting the part he and his men had played in the battle, but he had hinted at the importance of their achievements. It was only right that the world should be told of the great things Thomas and his men had done. Anna thought that there ought to be more space given to Thomas in the newspapers, and she indignantly told him so.

"And so you think the papers ought to say more about your husband! My brigade is not a brigade of newspaper correspondents," he wrote on August 5.

> I know that the First Brigade was the first to meet and pass our re-treating forces—to push on with no other aid than the smiles of God; to boldly take its position with the artillery that was under my command—to arrest the victorious foe in his onward progress—to hold him in check until reinforcements arrived—and finally to charge bayonets, and, thus advancing, pierce the enemy's centre. I am well satisfied with what it did, and so are my generals, Johnston and Beauregard. It is not to be expected that I should receive the credit that Generals Beauregard and Johnston would, because I was under them; but I am thankful to my ever-kind Heavenly Father that He makes me content to await His own good time and pleasure for commendation—knowing that all things work together for my good.[1]

And to Jonathan Bennett, Jackson imparted a bit more of his personal satisfaction with what his brigade had done. Bennett, after all, had helped get him the command and doubtless would be interested: "You will find, when my report shall be published, that the First Brigade was to our army what the Imperial Guard was to the First Napoleon—that, through the blessing of God, it met the thus far victorious enemy and turned the fortunes of the day." [2]

Battle was for some a time for glory and for others a time for dying. More than 480 of Jackson's 3,000 men had been killed or wounded —among the heaviest casualties in the army. The whole brigade had been steady and gallant; they had convinced their general that they could be counted on for the roughest service. The tragedy in the sacrifice of so many good men lay in not gaining a really decisive victory.[3]

Watching opportunity slip by galled Jackson. McDowell had been thoroughly beaten—Jackson knew that as soon as the Union retreat began on the afternoon of the twenty-first. The story of his impatience spread. Rumor later had it that even while he was having his finger attended to at a field hospital, right after the battle, Jackson had told the doctor that he wondered if Generals Johnston and Beauregard knew how badly the enemy were whipped. "If they will let me," he said, "I'll march my Brigade into Washington tonight!" [4] But they would not let him.

Elaborate reasons were piled up in later years as to why the Confederates did not chase the Yankees into Washington after the rout along Bull Run. At the time President Davis, who came to Manassas just as the battle drew to a close, agreed with his top generals that the army's disorganization, lack of transport and other supplies made such an advance hazardous. So reorganization and rebuilding were begun. If Jackson chafed at this careful war, no official hint of it reached his superiors or his friends at home.

Lexington had been waiting anxiously for authentic news of the battle. The local papers printed all the copy which came to hand about the part the VMI and Washington College boys had had in the fighting, but real information could be expected to come in letters from Lexington's men at the front. A day or two after the battle, according to Anna, a large crowd gathered around the little post office in town. Everyone hoped for tidbits about the battle. The Reverend Dr. White, handed a letter in a well-known hand, shouted to the crowd that Deacon Jackson had written and that "now we shall know all the facts." He would read it to all, he said, and began: "My dear pastor, in my tent last night, after a fatiguing day's service, I remembered that I had failed to send you my contribution for our colored Sunday-school. Enclosed you will find my check for that object, which please acknowledge at your earliest convenience, and oblige yours faithfully, T. J. Jackson." [5]

Duty, in a way, was indivisible. When Deacon Jackson made his contribution to his Negro Sunday school he was doing part of his Christian work, just as he was doing another part in war. Duty was living for God. And living for God might require various things—praying, giving, fighting, and very possibly dying.

Part of duty, too, lay in subordination to authority—ecclesiastical, civil, or military. Subordination at times might be hard, but it came easier as it was recognized as God's way of working for the good of a Christian. Obedience tempered ambition, and, in turn, the tempering of ambition made obedience less difficult.

In the days and weeks immediately following the battle of Manassas, Jackson and his men were occupied with routine camp duty; the days of glorious opportunity had passed. The army, now combining both Johnston's and Beauregard's forces, was being reinforced and resupplied. The duty of camp life lay in daily routines, the most important of which was drilling and artillery practice. The men must not be allowed to get rusty with inactivity. Jackson became much concerned about the health and welfare of his brigade. Sickness laid many of the valley men low in late July, which was oppressively hot and humid.

The campsite of the First Brigade left much to be desired: the water was bad and the location in general depressing. Explaining to General Johnston that a change of camps would increase the efficiency of his command (and also reduce the sick list), Jackson moved on August 2 to a new site near Centreville, on the road to Fairfax Court House. Quartermaster Harman had found the new site, had persuaded farmer Utterbach to permit the use of part of his land, and ushered the brigade to "a beautiful place where we had good water." The men liked it, so did Jackson, and they named it Camp Harman in honor of the finder.

The general and his quartermaster worked hard to better the condition of the troops. New tents were obtained—not enough, but some —and the men received their first pay. Food could be had aplenty, and with a little money it was possible to buy a few luxuries: chicken, butter, and even eggs.[6] Old Stonewall kept hard at the ordnance and supply people for more arms and clothes.[7] He had an eye for the little things that make a soldier less uncomfortable, and a general with an eye for the welfare of his men was apt to become immensely popular.

About one thing Old Jack proved to be particularly harsh—furloughs. Duty required everyone to stay with the army, and this included the general himself. Many of the officers and men wanted to go on leave, see their families, and tend to things around home. No leaves were permitted, unless emergencies demanded. When Anna complained that it seemed a shame Thomas could not come to North Carolina for a visit, her soldier wrote in reply:

> My darling, I can't be absent from my command, as my attention is necessary in preparing my troops for hard fighting should it be required; and as my officers and soldiers are not permitted to go and see their wives and families, I ought to not see my *esposita*, as it might make the troops feel that they were badly treated, and that I consult my own pleasure and comfort regardless of theirs.[8]

Fairness in dealing with officers and men alike characterized Jackson's handling of this problem. A story which soon gained wide circulation had it that an officer serving under Jackson received word that one of his family had just died and another lay on the brink of death. Such a desperate situation called for emergency leave, and Jackson received the application. The reply read:

> My Dear Major,—I have received your sad letter, and wish I could relieve your sorrowing heart; but human aid cannot heal the wound. From me you have a friend's sympathy, and I wish the suffering condition of our country permitted me to show it. But we must think of the living and of those who are to come after us, and see that, with God's blessing, we transmit to them the freedom we have enjoyed. What is life without honor? Degradation is worse than death. It is necessary that you should be at your post immediately. Join me tomorrow morning.
>
> Your sympathizing friend,
> T. J. Jackson.[9]

Hard, unfeeling—cruel even? Not really. Jackson's letter revealed clearly the mixture of compassion and duty which formed so large a part of his character.

A soldier's duty, at times, appeared more than Anna could fathom.

She seemed particularly upset that her sister Susan's husband obtained sick leave and had come home to convalesce. Envy of Sue had crept into Anna's letters, and Thomas wrote her on August 22 that

> sickness may compel me for a time to retire from camp, but, through the blessing of God, I have been able to continue in command of my brigade. . . . Still much remains undone that I desire to see effected. But in a short time I hope to be more instrumental in serving my country. Every officer and soldier who is able to do duty ought to be busily engaged in military preparation by hard drilling, in order that, through the blessing of God, we may be victorious in the battles which in His all-wise providence may await us.[10]

Camp life with its dreary, daily routine wore down many of the men. Jackson could not help being lonely. Perhaps he might see Anna without shirking the tasks of command. She might come to visit him. He tried to fight down the urge to invite her to Centreville, writing her happy letters about all the old army friends and classmates he saw and about the excitement of alarms when a Federal advance was rumored, dwelling on the beauties of the country near his camping ground, and finally writing—probably as much to convince himself as Anna—that their separation had been caused by patriotism, "a sense of duty." [11]

Anna kept after him. Could she come, even if for a brief moment? There were numbers of reasons why she ought not; camp living was crude and inconvenient, and traveling in troop trains was dangerous. Still, Thomas wrote, he thought he could find quarters for her with the family of his host, farmer Utterbach. She could come, he grudgingly said, provided a suitable escort were found.

Anna found one, and after a trip which proved at least venturesome, she arrived in September. Met at the Manassas railhead by her husband —driving an ambulance with *élan*—Anna found herself whisked off to church services for the First Brigade. Afterward the general's lady became the center of admiring attention. Anna loved it. The Utterbachs had made charming accommodations ready for her, and Thomas stayed close at hand since his headquarters tent was right outside in the farmyard.

Finding herself something of the belle of the ball, Anna reveled in army life. She watched the campfires of Jackson's men at night—a "grand spectacle"—and extended her field of callers. General Joseph E. Johnston and staff impressed her as "fine specimens of the Southern gentleman." [12] Not even a visit to the recent scene of death could dim Anna's pleasure with the trip. True, the faint stench of dead horses and the drying bones of soldiers along Bull Run lent a touch of the macabre to camp life,[13] but she was too overjoyed at seeing Thomas and enjoying the role of his wife to have her spirits much damped.

One thing that made life pleasant was that the Utterbachs' farm seemed so homey. Anna usually ate with Thomas and his staff at their mess table, and she particularly noticed that although the food was not fancy, it was good. George, Thomas's cook, obviously looked out for his master; in fact, he had an inordinate interest in doing so, since he wanted to keep his job. He boasted loudly to all comers that "I outranks all de niggers in dis army," because he served a general.

It proved a happy visit, but at length it ended. Anna hoped it could go on, but the grim business of war soon made it necessary for her to return to North Carolina, carrying with her joyful memories. Left a bachelor once again, Jackson threw himself into affairs of his brigade with great zeal; work might help fill the void left by Anna's departure.

The months after the battle of Manassas were hard on Jackson, hard on all real soldiers. Southern spirits soared—it was easy to beat the Yankees! Too easy. As he watched complacency settle over the army and the people, Jackson felt that it would have been much better had the South lost the battle. Later he would recall the weeks after Manassas as the darkest period in the Confederacy's history.[14]

Demoralization can easily develop in a time of complacency, and this Jackson fought hard to prevent. His men drilled, practiced, drilled, practiced without respite. They griped, resented Jackson's dedication to hard work, but continued to be soldiers. Not all the brigades did as well. Johnston and Beauregard worried a good deal about the mass furloughing and general apathy which pervaded the army. But the First Brigade remained ready.

For a brief time in September and October, things looked particularly bleak to Jackson. Just as he saw his brigade rounding into top shape, just as the troops were beginning to know and appreciate their hard-driving general, he received word that he might have to return to VMI. Short of faculty, the Institute's Board of Visitors cast about for some means of bringing back at least a few of the men lost to the army. A circular to each faculty member inquired whether he wished to return to VMI, and implied, at the same time, that a failure to return would result in being dropped from the Institute.

True, in sending the circular, Virginia's Adjutant General William H. Richardson had made the friendly observation that if Jackson wanted to stay in the field "I think the Board . . . will feel it due to you to make such temporary arrangements, as will leave it at your option to do so" and still remain on the staff.[15] But the matter remained uncertain.

It would be hard indeed to lose the chair of Natural and Experimental Philosophy and the instructorship in Artillery Tactics as a result of joining the army. Jackson loved VMI, his job, Lexington and its people —he wanted to stay with the Institute. Still, duty and honor had called him to the field, and Virginia's and the Confederacy's need for defenders was greater now than before. In a showdown he would have to stay with the army. But it would be worthwhile trying to arrange a leave of absence for the war. He explained his problem to Richardson and to the board:

> I only took the field from a sense of duty; and . . . the obligation that brought me into active service still retains me in it; and will probably continue to do so, as long as the war shall last. At the close of hostilities, I desire to resume the duties of my chair, and accordingly respectfully request that if consistent with the interests of the Institute, that the action of the Board of Visitors may be such as to admit of my return upon the restoration of peace.[16]

Anna doubtless would have been happy to have Thomas go back to teaching, where he would be safer, but he never seriously thought of it and she knew it.[17] She rejoiced with him when the news came that he had been granted leave from VMI for the duration of the war.[18] The board could not have done anything else. Lexington's citizenry would have revolted at any action restricting the usefulness of Jackson and his famous Stonewall Brigade. His exploits and those of his command were the subject of admiring comment in the town's press and parlors. So famous a product of the town must be encouraged to greater glory.[19]

Many of Jackson's Lexington friends, as well as total strangers, sent boxes of food, sweets, and other presents. Embarrassed by this unusual flattery, Jackson played it down when reporting to Anna and confessed that "what I need is a more grateful heart to the 'Giver of every good and perfect gift.' "[20] With all the attention given a new hero, Jackson probably found it difficult at times to get on with the serious business of command.

Certainly it seemed as though the whole country wanted to see the heroes of Manassas. Such special attention made it hard to keep the men at their work. But Jackson must have been pleased to find that not all his effort had been wasted, even when the proof proved discomforting. Late one night, with rain pelting around brigade headquarters, Jackson approached his tent. Out of the dripping darkness came a loud challenge—give the countersign! Soaked to the skin, Jackson nonetheless grew deliberate; this was a matter which had to be properly handled. He would not give the countersign. Where was the Lieutenant of the Guard? Disgruntled at having to brave the rain, Lt. Henry Kyd Douglas walked to the first of countless interviews with Stonewall Jackson.

When Douglas arrived, Jackson asked him in clipped and quiet tones what his authority was for asking the countersign at that hour, when Jackson's orders did not require it until after taps? "I replied," said Douglas, "I did not know of his order, but my authority was

Gilham's *Manual*. He told me quietly and apparently without any annoyance to reinstruct the sentinel and bring Gilham to his tent next morning. I did both and he was very cordial in the morning reception, admitted Gilham's authority, but had a copy of his order given me." [21] The men were learning to stick by some authority, at any rate.

Actually, the whole brigade had developed into an efficient and effective outfit. At the end of October Jackson had a chance to show them off. A grand review of the Virginia troops was held for Governor Letcher on October 30, and amid much "pomp & circumstance" he presented each regiment with a state flag. The next day, wrote one observer,

> there was a still grander pageant presented in a review of some 10,000 of the troops. The column was nearly a mile in length, and with the martial music, floating banners, and the usual display of such occasions, the scene presented was quite grand & imposing. There has not probably been collected so many Generals at a single spot during the war as this evening were assembled around the Governor. Generals Johnston, Beauregard, G. W. Smith, E. Kirby Smith, Jackson, Longstreet, Van Dorn, Steuart [*sic*], Sam. Jones, Clark, Early, Toombs, and several others attended by their staffs were all there and you can well imagine what interest and éclat their presence gave the occasion.[22]

There, viewed by an imposing array of civil and military leaders, the First Brigade showed how well trained it was. Jackson was very proud.

While things like reviews offered diversion to the men, Jackson found them time-consuming and probably felt that the energy of the men could have been more wisely spent. As for himself he missed Anna more than ever and had asked her in mid-October: "If I get into winter-quarters, will little ex-Anna Morrison come and keep house for me, and stay with me till the opening of the campaign of 1862? Now remember, I don't want to change housekeepers. I want the same one all the time." [23] Continuing study of religion helped him overcome the loneliness. To his great joy he was visited late in October by his pastor, the Reverend Dr. White, and his friend the Reverend Dr. Francis McFarland. He entertained them with pleasure and readily consented to join Dr. White in evening prayers each day. One such occasion White never forgot:

> Never while life lasts, can I forget that prayer. He thanked God for sending me to visit the army, and prayed that He would own and bless my ministrations, both to officers and privates, so that many souls might be saved. He gave thanks for what it had pleased God to do for the church in Lexington, "to which both of us belong"—specially for the revivals He had mercifully granted to that church, and for the many preachers of the Gospel sent forth from it. He then prayed for the pastor, and every member of his family, for the ruling elders, the deacons, and the private members of the church, such as were at home, and especially such as then belonged

to the army. He then pleaded with such tenderness and fervor that God would baptize the whole army with His holy spirit, that my own hard heart was melted into penitence, gratitude, and praise.[24]

Rising from his knees, Jackson stood by the campfire, the flame lighting one line, then another, of his expressive face. Looking at Dr. White, he said: "Doctor, I would be glad to learn more fully than I have yet done what your views are of the prayer of faith?" The two talked for hours, with the man of God listening and learning from the soldier.

While Dr. White was still with the army, seeking to spread the Gospel, Jackson received exciting news. He was to return to the Shenandoah Valley and take charge of preparations for its defense. It was a great opportunity and it showed something of how his superiors felt about him, but he hated the assignment. It meant he would have to leave the Stonewall Brigade behind.[25]

He already had the rank to go with an important geographical command, for he had been promoted to major general in the Provisional Army of the Confederate States on October 7, 1861. There could be no denying, either, that Jackson had hoped for something like this new assignment. By promoting him and by giving him wider responsibility, the Secretary of War and the President were recognizing the ability of one of the best brigade commanders in Johnston's army. Jackson knew, however, that the recognition was providential. He wrote Anna that "I am very thankful to that God who withholds no good thing from me (though I am so utterly unworthy and ungrateful) for making me a major-general." [26]

Promotion had been earned. A review of Jackson's part in the campaign of First Manassas clearly revealed him as a superior leader of men. Quick marching had characterized the move of his brigade from the valley to the scene of battle, and the swiftness of movement had gained for his men a day's rest before the battle—rest which proved almost decisive during the long hours of fighting on July 21. Although his men were the volunteers which so many professional soldiers despised, they had showed a steadiness under fire which had given them a strength beyond their numbers. Their general could take credit for having instilled soldierly quality in a minimum of time with his grinding attention to the fine points of discipline. Then, too, his brigade had been as well prepared for action as a general with a sense of logistics could make it; the men had arms, ammunition, rations, and such clothing as could be provided. In battle, Jackson had been unique on the confused field of Manassas. Most who saw him that day acknowledged that he had a fire in his eye and an aura of power which made men stand and die. Whether it was the iron faith which his men were coming to respect or something else, the quality of an outstanding leader in battle had been displayed by his complete lack of concern for the hail of lead. Dauntless himself, Jackson inspired something of the same courage in all who followed him. For these reasons he deserved a chance at bigger things.

Some of the higher officers, who felt Jackson had no peer as a brigade commander, were not sure he would do well in a larger role. One of them expressed the feeling in strong terms: "I fear the Government is exchanging our best Brigade Commander for a second or third class Major General." [27] Davis and Benjamin, neither of them any too sure about his ability to command more men, had given him the new assignment for a variety of reasons.

The people in the Shenandoah Valley had called loudly for someone to take charge of military defense in that part of the state. They wanted someone who knew the valley and who knew them. Too much attention was apparently given to Richmond and to the army charged with the protection of the capital; after all, there were other portions of the state open to Federal devastation. Appeals of this type, coming from all over the Confederacy to the President and his harassed Secretary of War, had to receive attention. It seemed that the question of aiding the western parts of northern Virginia might be included in the larger one of how to settle a lingering argument about who commanded the Confederate Army of the Potomac, Johnston or Beauregard. A geographical department made up of three separate districts, each with its own commanding general, appeared to be the way out. Johnston could command the big department. Beauregard, Theophilus H. Holmes, and Jackson could command the districts. Jackson's would be the valley district, taking in the "section of country between the Blue Ridge and the Allegheny Mountains." [28] Secretary Benjamin's letter of instructions showed that much was expected of Jackson and that he would have to do whatever was done by himself, for he was not going to get much help. "In selecting an officer for this command," wrote Benjamin on October 21,

the choice of the Government has fallen on you—This choice has been dictated not only by a just appreciation of your qualities as a Commander, but by other weighty considerations—Your intimate knowledge of the country, of its population and resources rendered you peculiarly fitted to assume this command—Nor is this all—The people of that District with one voice have made constant and urgent appeals that to you, in whom they have confidence, should their defense be assigned.

The administration shares the regret which you will no doubt feel at being separated from your present Command, when there is a probability of early engagement between the opposing armies, but it feels confident that you will cheerfully yield your private wishes to your country's service in the sphere where you can be rendered most available.

In assuming the command to which you have been assigned by general orders, altho' your forces will for the present be small, they will be in-

creased as rapidly as our means will possibly admit, whilst the people
will themselves rally eagerly to your standard as soon as it is known that
you are to command—In a few days, detailed instructions will be sent you,
through the Adjutant General, and I will be glad to receive any suggestions
you may make to render effective your measures of defense.[29]

Enough of the situation in the valley was known to convince Jackson
that while the new assignment meant opportunity, it also meant back-
breaking work. The valley stood almost without troops, save a few thousand widely scattered and partially disorganized militia units,[30] and the
defense of the new military district would have to be organized from
the ground up. So hopeless did the task appear that General Johnston
delayed obeying General Orders No. 192, Adjutant and Inspector General's Office, October 28, 1861, directing Jackson to take charge of the
Valley District and establish his headquarters at Winchester. Johnston
wanted him close at hand, still commanding the Stonewall Brigade, in
what seemed like an imminent battle.[31] But the battle did not materialize
and events in the valley changed Johnston's mind.

Since what happened in Jackson's new command also concerned
Johnston, who retained over-all command of the whole department of
Northern Virginia, the plaints of the people there about the safety of
the district and about the pitifully small number of militia in the field
struck home. Johnston decided Jackson had better go. No troops could
go with him—they were all needed to stem the threatening advance of
the Federals. Johnston prepared a travel order for the new major general
on November 4, directing him to proceed to Winchester and take command of the Valley District.[32]

During the two weeks intervening between the original assignment
to the valley and the issuance of Johnston's order, Jackson had been
preparing to go. News of his coming departure could not be kept from
his brigade. They knew they were going to lose him and they grieved—
but they were proud, too. Some of the bigger generals might not think
Stonewall competent for district command, but the First Brigade knew
better. General Jackson could handle any assignment. The Old Man did
not want to leave the brigade behind, the men all knew that. But there
was nothing he or they could do about it. They were needed at Centreville, he was needed in Winchester. The whole brigade wanted to go
with him. Most of the men came from the valley and they very much
wanted to "be again in the limestone region and among a people whom
we know." [33]

Jackson worked at having troops assigned to his district. Enemy
activity in the northwestern part of the state threatened Confederate
control of the northern end of the valley. But no troops were available,
at least at the moment. He would have to make do with the few men
already out there. One story was certain to impress the people he was

going to defend, a tale carried back to the valley by one of its worried citizens, cavalryman Col. Angus W. McDonald. McDonald rode across the mountains for a visit with General Johnston; he hoped to persuade the general to send more troops to the valley. Also, he wanted to meet Jackson, the man soon to be his superior and to have charge of hanging onto the land between the mountains. Johnston offered no help. But Jackson did.

It was not really the sort of help which McDonald sought, but it might do. In a conversation with Jackson, McDonald outlined the plight of his part of the state, and finished the recital with a question as to the force Jackson would take with him. Jackson, looking at him with that peculiar intensity he showed in moments of great earnestness, replied quietly, "No physical force, Col. except my Staff." [34]

While he waited for final clearance Jackson thought of the brigade. Did any officers wish to call on him before he left? Delegations from each regiment were sent. The general, pleasant and cordial, said a brief farewell to all of them. Out of one such group a young officer advanced to shake hands and to say that, since he had recently been in the ranks, he wanted Jackson to know that the men grieved at the general's departure. As Jackson listened, and perhaps recognized the young lieutenant of the guard who had quoted Gilham's manual to him on the duties of a sentinel, Kyd Douglas told him that the men wished him success and they

hoped he would not forget that the old brigade he left behind would be ready to march at a moment's notice to his assistance when he needed them. As I said this [Douglas wrote later] a strange brightness came into his eyes and his mouth closed with more than its usual tightness. But he held my hand to the door and then said in his quick way, 'I am much obliged to you, Mr. Douglas, for what you say of the soldiers; and I believe it. I want to take the brigade with me, but cannot. I shall never forget them. In battle I shall always want them. I will not be satisfied until I get them. Good-by.' [35]

After receiving Johnston's order to go west, Jackson thought once again of the men who had earned so much just fame at First Manassas (including the thanks of Congress) and had done so much for him. Once again he would see them—and try to tell them how he felt.

On the morning of November 4, the First Brigade was summoned to attention in column of regiments, shredded colors waving in the wind. They formed, spit-and-polish, waiting for Old Jack's farewell. The brigade parade was quite a sight, standing at arms. He came, then, riding Little Sorrel, sitting in the saddle bent forward as he always seemed to do.[36]

Not a sound greeted his coming. Old Stonewall was leaving and was telling the men good-by. He looked at them, five regiments of them, standing rigid in a clearing surrounded by reddening autumn forest. For a long moment he could not speak. His eye roamed the line seeming to look into each face. At last, speaking with difficulty and in partially choked words, he said:

> Officers and men of the First Brigade, I am not here to make a speech but simply to say farewell. I first met you at Harper's Ferry in the commencement of the war, and I cannot take leave of you without giving expression to my admiration of your conduct from that day to this, whether on the march, in the bivouac, the tented field, or on the bloody plains of Manassas, where you gained the well-deserved reputation of having decided the fate of the battle. Throughout the broad extent of country over which you have marched, by your respect for the rights and property of citizens, you have shown that you were soldiers not only to defend, but able and willing both to defend and protect. You have already gained a brilliant and deservedly high reputation, throughout the army and the whole Confederacy, and I trust in the future by your own deeds on the field, and by the assistance of the same Kind Providence who has heretofore favored our cause, that you will gain more victories, and add additional lustre to the reputation you now enjoy. You have already gained a proud position in the history of this our second War of Independence. I shall look with great anxiety to your future movements, and I trust whenever I shall hear of the First Brigade on the field of battle it will be of still nobler deeds achieved and higher reputation won.

He stopped for an instant, and it seemed that he might be finished. But something more had to be said, something less formal, something that would show those men how much he cherished and admired them. All reserve forgotten in the emotion of the moment, Jackson threw the reins on Little Sorrel's neck, stood in the stirrups, and stretching out his right hand, shouted now with fire in his eye and in his voice:

> In the army of the Shenandoah you were the First Brigade; in the army of the Potomac you were the First Brigade; in the second corps of this army you are the First Brigade; you are the First Brigade in the affections of your General; and I hope by your future deeds and bearing you will be handed down to posterity as the First Brigade in our second War of Independence. Farewell!

Slowly Jackson settled in his saddle, took up the reins, pulled Little Sorrel's head into a turn and started to ride away.

The wild, discordant yell that shook the forest as he turned showed they understood. He slowed, listened, and told his staff that the shout was the "sweetest music I have ever heard." Then, unable to hold back his own feelings he waved his forage cap to the men and galloped off—but for a long distance along the road that yell echoed in his ears.[37]

There was time for a quick note to Anna, telling her that he was on his way and also that he hoped "to have my little dove with me this winter." Maybe, if things were arranged swiftly, he could send for her, but much had to be done before he and Anna could think of being together: "My trust is in God for the defence of that country. I shall have great labor to perform, but, through the blessing of our ever-kind Heavenly Father, I trust that He will enable me to accomplish it."

Last-minute preparation made, Jackson, Colonel Preston and Sandie Pendleton took the cars for Strasburg—the railroad from there to Winchester had not been built, despite Jackson's suggestion of the previous spring. The trip took time, and proved wearing, for Jackson wanted to reach his destination as fast as possible. Nothing could induce him to stop over. He had determined to travel all night if necessary in order to arrive at Winchester before dawn on the fifth.[38] The three travelers reached their goal late at night on November 4. The next morning they officially established Headquarters, Valley District.[39]

First, the new commanding general had to find out exactly what he commanded. The whole valley came under his jurisdiction, and large parts of it were under direct threat from the enemy. Federal troops had recently occupied Romney, across North Mountain, and almost 6,000 of them could soon be ready to make trouble near Winchester and at other places in the lower valley. To meet the large enemy force, Jackson had parts of three widely dispersed militia brigades "to a greater or less degree in service," some ragged cavalry units, and a few guns without gunners. Altogether there were about 1,651 men available in the valley.

Wasting no time, Jackson issued a call for all the militia in the Valley District not yet in the field, and the response was surprisingly good. But militia, raw and untrained, could not hope to stem the advance of well-equipped and trained Yankee troops. No sooner had the militia summons been issued than Jackson wrote Benjamin, explained the exposed condition of the valley area, and urged the need for "disciplined troops of not only infantry, but also of artillery and cavalry." Could he have reinforcements possibly from the Army of the Northwest, strung out in the passes of the Alleghenies? Could he have also a trained artillerist to supervise the emplacement of heavy guns for the protection of Winchester?[40]

Desperate appeals for more men were too numerous to excite the War Department any longer, but Jackson's plea happened to strike a responsive chord. Benjamin had been worried for some time about affairs in Jackson's district and had tentatively decided to send more men. Some were to come from Gen. William W. Loring's Army of the Northwest, but they might be quite a time en route. Other troops would have to be sent quickly, since Winchester appeared to be threatened from the direction of Romney. On November 5 the Adjutant General issued an order which would gladden the hearts of the Stonewall Brigade.

Jackson's old brigade was to be detached for duty with him. Since Johnston prized the First Brigade beyond most others and protested the transfer, Benjamin tried to compensate for its reassignment by sending Johnston double the number of men he was losing to Jackson.[41] So upset did Johnston become over this episode that President Davis personally tried to explain the whole matter to him. All of Johnston's objections had been considered and rejected because of the time factor—troops had to reach the valley almost immediately. Then, too, Jackson could best work with troops known to him and who had confidence in his leadership. So his old brigade drew the assignment—men who had "served in the valley, and had acquired a reputation which would give confidence to the people of that region, upon whom the general had to rely for his future success." [42] Reluctantly Johnston ordered his prize brigade sent speedily by rail to Jackson.[43]

With his own men now on hand, under charge of Brig. Gen. Richard B. Garnett, Jackson prepared for hard work. Daily drilling was nothing new to the Stonewall Brigade, although it came as a rude shock to many of the militiamen. Jackson now began to construct an army. The camps around Winchester soon had a military air despite bitter weather through November and December. The men found it difficult to get passes, and visitors found it harder to see friends in the ranks. Disorganization began to fade; discipline set in. General Jackson's attention to details once again brought results.[44]

As Jackson thought hard about his situation at Winchester, he grew restless. Sitting in camp, waiting for something to happen, went against his better judgment. The war should be carried to the enemy.

So far the Confederates had been having much the worst of the fighting in northwestern Virginia. Even General Lee, from whom Jackson expected great things across the Alleghenies, had failed to drive the enemy out of the mountains. As affairs stood in November, Federal troops dominated most of western Virginia from the Ohio River to the Shenandoah Valley. Numerous troops under Gen. William S. Rosecrans served as the army of occupation. On the other side of the Potomac the Federals were concentrating still more troops. Once these were brought together, Jackson's puny force would be blown out of the valley. One way to throw the enemy off balance and delay concentration would be to attack first.

Other considerations pointed to attack as the best policy. Jackson had a deep personal interest in the country west of the Alleghenies and along the valley of the South Branch of the Potomac. Here was land not far from Beverly and other boyhood playgrounds. Here was mountain ground, which he understood. Here, too, were mountain people, for whose safety he was most worried. Enemy depredations, enforced oath-takings, and many other hostile irritations were bringing piteous requests for help—requests which he found it hard to ignore.[45] These personal reasons had some influence on Jackson's anxiety to carry the war to the northwest, but sound strategy proved the decisive factor.

A great deal more could be accomplished by a campaign west of the

Alleghenies than just the relief of oppressed citizens. By November 20 the new commanding general of the Valley District had conceived a scheme which might achieve highly important results. This, his first attempt at strategic planning, he explained to the Secretary of War in a letter written that day. In itself the plan was important, but it was important too for what it revealed of Jackson's broad outlook on the war.

He had been worried about the masses of raw troops which General McClellan had drilling near Washington. Though green in late 1861, the passage of the winter would find them trained, equipped, and probably fit for a hard fight. Little Mac ought to be tempted into an attack on Johnston's army before his men were beyond the stage of recruits.[46] An expedition to the northwest might deceive McClellan into thinking Johnston's army weak enough to suffer easy defeat. Occupation of the town of Romney, in the South Branch Valley, would give the Confederates control of a road hub dominating the whole area, for here crossed the road from Winchester to Grafton on the B&O and the road from Monterey, Virginia, to Cumberland, Maryland, on the Potomac. With this town went control of the northwest valley. So, even if McClellan did not take the bait, a large area would be cleared of the enemy and Confederate forces would hold the key to the northwest. And, if McClellan did attack Johnston, Jackson's men could join him, repeating the Manassas moves.

With the small force which had been built up by the time he wrote Benjamin, Jackson knew he could not undertake any sort of expedition. Reinforcements were urgently needed, and he had an idea where he might get them. West and south of Winchester, strung along the crest of the Allegheny Mountains guarding the Staunton-Parkersburg road, Gen. William W. Loring's Army of the Northwest numbered about 6,000 men. With the advent of winter it seemed improbable that further hard fighting would take place in the mountains—Loring's army would give Jackson the numbers to make his expedition. Since Federal strength in Romney, according to Confederate calculation, stood at about 5,000 men, Jackson would be able, aided by Loring's army, to attack the town with superior force. Once the South Branch area had been cleared of Federal Gen. Benjamin F. Kelley's troops, Jackson felt that a minimum garrison disposed at strategic points could hold that sector of the state.

Logistics also dictated attack. "I deem it of very great importance that Northwestern Virginia be occupied by Confederate troops this winter," Jackson wrote the Secretary.

At present it is to be presumed that the enemy are not expecting an attack there, and the resources of that region necessary for the subsistence of our troops are in greater abundance than in almost any other season of the year. Postpone the occupation of that section until spring, and we may expect to find the enemy prepared for us and the resources to which I have referred greatly exhausted. I know that what I have proposed will be an arduous undertaking and cannot be accomplished without the sacrifice of much personal comfort; but I feel that the troops will be prepared to make this sacrifice when animated by the prospects of important results to our cause and distinction to themselves.

General Jackson had thought the matter out carefully. There were, he saw, certain points which might be criticized in what he suggested, but he had answers.

It may be urged against this plan that the enemy will advance on Staunton or Huntersville. I am well satisfied that such a step would but make their destruction more certain. Again, it may be said that General Floyd will be cut off. To avoid this, if necessary the general had only to fall back towards the Virginia and Tennessee Railroad. When Northwestern Virginia is occupied in force, the Kanawha Valley, unless it be the lower part of it, must be evacuated by the Federal forces, or otherwise their safety will be endangered by forcing a column across from the Little Kanawha between them and the Ohio River.

Admitting that the season is too far advanced, or that from other causes all cannot be accomplished that has been named, yet through the blessing of God, who had thus far so wonderfully prospered our cause, much more may be expected from General Loring's troops, according to this programme, than can be expected from them where they are. If you decide to order them here, I trust that for the purpose of saving time all the infantry, cavalry, and artillery will be directed to move immediately upon the reception of the order. The enemy, about 5,000 strong, have been for some time slightly fortifying at Romney, and have completed their telegraph from that place to Green Spring Depot. Their forces at and near Williamsport are estimated as high as 5,000, but as yet I have no reliable information of their strength beyond the Potomac.[47]

Jackson forwarded his businesslike and carefully considered scheme to Benjamin, via Johnston's headquarters. The department commander read it with interest; here was a man, this Jackson, whose energy ought to be infectious. But it was a bad time of year, and his plan probably was too ambitious. Still, it would be worth a try. Jackson's idea had good foundation. Napoleon had acted on the theory that "an active winter's campaign is less liable to produce disease than a sedentary life by campfires in winter-quarters."[48] If Jackson could not accomplish all that he hoped, he might yet achieve important objectives in preventing the rebuilding of the B&O and in checking marauding bands of the enemy in South Branch Valley. And in addition to keeping his army relatively healthy, these projects would be worth an increase of his force. Johnston thought Loring ought to be attached to the Army of the Valley.

Benjamin liked Jackson's proposal, but certain problems forced him to move cautiously. General Loring had already made clear his conviction that his men should remain where they were through the winter, guarding the passes in the mountains. General Lee seemed in agreement with

Loring on this point. Faced with this situation, Benjamin wrote Loring on November 24 his own approval of Jackson's proposition and sent a copy of it along. The War Department would not order Loring to join the expedition to Romney. Whether or not he wished to go was left to Loring's discretion.[49]

Loring decided to cooperate, but he could not move as quickly as both Benjamin and Jackson had hoped.[50] When Jackson's plan was approved by the War Department and by Loring, the Adjutant General issued orders to Gen. John Floyd on December 2 to fall back with his command to Dublin Station on the Virginia and Tennessee Railroad, thus acting on a suggestion which had been contained in Jackson's initial letter to Benjamin.[51] While Loring and the quartermasters worked to get his army on the march to Staunton, Jackson took his small force to do mischief to the Chesapeake and Ohio.

On December 6 part of his force struck Dam No. 5 on this important artery of communication between Washington and the West. The idea was to cut the dam and drain the water from a large section of the canal. Recognizing the importance of the canal, Federal authorities had stationed troops at vital points along the waterway—there were some at Dam No. 5. In their first attempt to break the canal, Jackson's men failed. Two companies of the Stonewall Brigade volunteered to brave Union bullets, wade waist-deep in the canal's chilly water, and do as much damage as they could. Sniping stopped the work before it had been completed, and Jackson retired to Winchester. But he determined to try again. Taking a large force with him this time, he started on December 17, pushed the work hard, and by the twenty-first felt that sufficient damage had been done to immobilize the canal for a while. The good thing was that he had lost only one man. He lost something else, though, on the way back to district headquarters at Winchester—dignity.

"Returning home from one of these expeditions," recorded Kyd Douglas,

> after riding along some distance, the General spied a tree hanging heavy with persimmons, a peculiar fruit of which he was very fond. Dismounting, he was in a short time seated aloft among the branches, in the midst of abundance. He ate in silence and when satisfied started to descend, but found that it was not so easy as the ascent had been. Attempting to swing himself from a limb to the main fork of the tree, he got so completely entangled that he could move neither up nor down and was compelled to call for help.

Little wonder that the staff could hardly calm down enough to find some fence rails to make a skid for their general to use in returning to earth.[52] Funny or not, they doubtless were sternly commanded to put the fence rails back in place.

Memories of hard service and mild mortification were forgotten almost as soon as the troops reached Winchester. Anna was coming to visit "Mr. Jackson."

She had been anxious to come for some time. Proud of Jackson's promotion to major general, she wanted to see him presiding over his new domain. Something of her pleasure had crept into her letters, and she had been duly chided: "I trust that my darling little wife feels more gratitude to our kind Heavenly Father than pride or elation at my promotion." [53] Nonetheless, Thomas had painted such a handsome picture of his valley command, of his quarters, and of the people of Winchester that Anna had to see for herself. And he had already hinted on November 16 that he hoped she could come:

> You can have plenty of society of charming ladies here, and the Rev. Mr. Graham, our Presbyterian minister, lives in the second house from [headquarters], his door being only about thirty yards from our gate. ...I have much work to perform, and wouldn't have much time to talk to my darling except at night; but then there is so much pleasant society among the ladies here that you could pass your time very agreeably. I hope to send for you just as soon as I can do so, with the assurance that I am in winter-quarters.[54]

Anna needed no further encouragement. Without waiting for an aide to be sent for her, she found friends traveling to Richmond and from there traveled in the company of an "absent-minded old clergyman" until she reached Winchester. After a rough stage trip from Strasburg, Anna arrived hopeful of being met. On the way, though, she heard a rumor that Thomas was off on some sort of raid against the Chesapeake and Ohio Canal. The news topped off a bad day. Her trunk had been lost somewhere en route, and she was thoroughly worn out and lonesome.

The stagecoach deposited Anna in front of Taylor's Hotel about midnight. Still attended by her enfeebled escort, she started in, but noticed a group of soldiers standing on the walk outside. One of them seemed familiar. Anna turned to look and saw him, entrenched in a heavy military coat, with his cap pulled far down, hurriedly following her. She went on, reached the veranda of the hotel and suddenly found herself caught in the arms of a greatcoat. Strong arms bent her head backward and she was kissed hard, then kissed again. It was Thomas. Gasping for breath, Anna wanted to know why he had not met her at the door of the stagecoach. Laughing, the amorous general said that he wanted to be sure he was not going to kiss "anybody else's *esposa.*" [55]

He had been lucky, since he had returned from the Dam No. 5 raid only a few hours before Anna arrived. Happily she turned all her baggage troubles over to Thomas and settled down to enjoy her stay.

Ensconced comfortably in Jackson's quarters, Anna attended services with him in Dr. Graham's church and soon became acquainted with numerous Winchester citizens. As he had predicted, Thomas had to leave her on her own, for he seemed most preoccupied with a plan to lead an expedition to fight the enemy. Anna did not learn too much about this plan, for Thomas kept the whole thing under wraps. She discovered she had company in her ignorance.

Even the members of Jackson's staff seemed unaware of what Old Jack had up his sleeve. Colonel John Preston, Maggie's husband, might have been a bit wiser than some of the others, but if so, he was sufficiently wise to keep all to himself. The rest of the uninformed staff proved to be young and merry men whom Anna liked immediately. Alfred Jackson, a relative of more or less distance, had recently joined; and with him served the irrepressible Sandie Pendleton, whose love of good fun never flagged. George Junkin, one of Ellie's relatives, also had been appointed to the staff, and all these, together with Jackson, formed the general's mess. Eating, talking, and joking together, they had grown close. The young men, too, were obviously coming to appreciate Old Stonewall.

He took little part in the raillery of the after-dinner period, usually sitting "grave as a signpost, till something chances to overcome him, and then he breaks out into a laugh so awkward that it is manifest he had never laughed enough to learn how."[56] Simplehearted Stonewall was, but so good that the boys soon ceased to laugh at him. They saw him go often to his room during the day, and soon they were convinced that when there he prayed fervently. And while they themselves prayed appreciably less, they respected their Old Man immensely. He grew on them, as he did on most people.

The staff finally caught wind of a large project. Colonel William B. Taliaferro's brigade of the Army of the Northwest had marched into Winchester on December 8,[57] and surely this addition to Jackson's force meant something.

Major Harman, the indefatigable quartermaster, learned sooner than others that Loring's whole army would be attached to the Army of the Valley. One of his close relatives who served as depot quartermaster at Staunton (soon to be one of Jackson's principal bases of supplies) had been working for weeks to arrange the transportation of reinforcements to Jackson's army.[58] By December 21 more units of Loring's troops had arrived, although that officer had not as yet reached Jackson's headquarters.

There were increasing signs of Jackson's preoccupation. He became touchy about any attempt to change his staff organization, even telling the Commissary General in Richmond on December 13 that he had no objection to having another commissary officer sent to the valley, but that he wanted his own chief commissary, Maj. W. J. Hawks, kept in that position. "I respectfully request that he may not be superseded, as I am satisfied that no good would result to the Public Service, and much injury might." [59]

Jackson's staff officers began to understand why he had been so inquisitive about their personal habits before attaching them to his headquarters. He had wanted to know if they were intelligent, faithful, and industrious, and most important, he asked each if he got up early in the morning! Deficiency in any of these canceled their chances of serving with him.[60] But by late December they all realized that he had had good reason for asking these questions. With more troops pouring into Winchester, each of them had larger duties to perform. The days did not last long enough. The general had launched a harsh tightening-up of the army.

Stricter attention to picket duty was demanded; [61] more men were turned out to learn the use of the heavy 24-pounder guns which had recently been mounted on carriages; [62] orders were issued to collect the arms left on the Allegheny Mountain by the Third Arkansas, Taliaferro's brigade, and have them sent to Winchester.[63] Lieutenant Colonel Turner Ashby, commanding the small cavalry forces in the Valley District, felt the increasing sternness of Jackson's administration.

Discipline in Ashby's companies had grown lax, and Jackson sharply complained to the commander, detailing measures which should be taken to keep the mounted troops in hand.[64] Discipline in the cavalry was all-important, since Ashby was expected to render peculiarly valuable service. On December 25 Jackson directed him to learn all he could about the movements of the enemy in Morgan County and on the B&O railroad, the information to be sent swiftly to district headquarters. On the twenty-seventh Jackson wrote more pointedly, saying that he had to have accurate information about Federal movements to reoccupy Bath. Reports of Ashby's scouts should be sent immediately, because, Jackson reminded his cavalry leader, he could make no move without accurate intelligence.[65]

At Christmastime, when everyone expected a rest, Jackson continued his strange activity. Preston, who doubtless wanted to be home with Maggie, drew an assignment taking him to Richmond. What he was to do there remains a mystery, but he recorded that "Jackson sent me down on a forlorn hope. . . . The Secretary of War received me very kindly, and so did President Davis." Apparently Jackson had hoped to extend the scope of his proposed advance into northwestern Virginia. Perhaps he sent Preston to ask for the addition to his army of the troops serving under Col. Edward ("Allegheny") Johnson, still in the mountains west of Staunton.[66]

Whatever his mission, Preston returned to Jackson's headquarters, vowing to stay with him "if he makes the movement he contemplates."

Loring finally arrived, just before Christmas. Jackson now had all the men he was going to get. Without hesitation he decided to attack at once.[67]

First must be settled the question of Loring's position in the Army of the Valley. Jackson had originally thought the Army of the Northwest should be listed as the First Division, Army of the Valley. But a conversation with Loring drew the information that, as Loring understood matters, the War Department expected him to continue as commander of his army—that the two armies would be cooperating, with Loring willingly leaving the over-all command to Jackson. Jackson agreed, and withdrew his former recommendation.[68]

A rash of orders from district headquarters on December 31 signaled the beginning of Jackson's expedition. Every officer and man was directed to keep ready a white badge, three inches wide and long enough to go around his hat or cap, and not to wear it until ordered.[69] The artillery batteries were directed to load their limber chests and be ready to move at six o'clock in the morning.[70] All the troops in Winchester were ordered to draw five days' rations, and until further orders, to keep on hand one day's cooked rations and to keep their canteens full.[71] All commands were to be ready to march, but nobody knew where. One thing was certain: the happy days of Winchester, its many diversions and hospitable citizens, were over.[72] Jackson seemed determined on this winter campaign.

One detail remained. Anna had to be made safe and comfortable during the time Jackson would be gone. Early in the morning of New Year's Day, 1862, Jackson strode up the front walk of the Graham residence, seeking an audience with the Reverend Doctor. Hesitatingly, with great diffidence, the general wondered if he might ask the Grahams a great favor? Would they take Mrs. Jackson into their home for a few days while he was out of town? Quickly he added that he would not impose on them were it not an emergency. Anna was a stranger in Winchester, she was the daughter of a minister, and he would feel content about her safety if the Grahams would do him this great favor.

Graham found it impossible to refuse a request so delicately put, and within the hour Anna had been deposited with the family. Jackson embraced her, kissed her good-by, and rode off on Little Sorrel, trailed by his staff.[73]

Very early that New Year's morning, Jackson's army filed out of Winchester, taking the road leading northwest toward Pughtown, Unger's Store, and Bath (or Berkeley Springs). A campaign could hardly have started more auspiciously. Spring seemed to be in the January air. Balmy, sunny weather made a number of the troops throw away the burden of heavy overcoats, and others stored their winter covering in the regimental baggage wagons. This proved to be a great mistake. A cold wind began to whistle along the marching column, and the temperature fell steadily. Spitting snow, mixed with sleet, flailed the toiling army. Men without coats soon were shivering, huddling together with their heads bent down, trudging onward. Orders were to press on; the weather was not to alter the general's plans. Not until the troops reached the vicinity of Pughtown did he permit the columns to halt for the night. That night froze into the memory of many men. Cold—bitter, penetrating cold—settled over Jackson's camps. To make matters worse, the wagons had been unable to keep up as roads grew icy, so the men went into bivouac with no rations. Obviously the orders, so carefully given, for each man to take with him a day's cooked rations had either been ignored, or the rations had already been eaten.

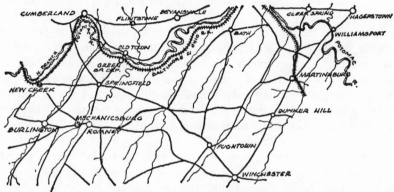

Area of the Romney Expedition

As evening approached, Jackson himself had begun to feel the cold. That morning, just as his army had left Winchester, one of the citizens had presented him with a bottle of good aged whisky—a bottle which Jackson believed contained wine of some sort. He remembered it as the day grew more frigid, retrieved it from the staff member who had lovingly cared for it during the day, and took a long pull. It was a big drink, even for wine. With growing admiration, the staff watched as the general drank the whisky down without bothering to taste it. Finished, he passed the bottle around, and, prompted by the example of their intrepid leader, the staff took equally stern doses.

None of the young men knew Jackson well enough to realize that they had witnessed a rare event. But soon Old Jack complained of getting warm, unbuttoned his coat and then part of his tunic. The warmer he got, the more he talked, until finally he even delivered a discourse on the sudden temperature changes which occurred in the valley.[74] The general was half drunk!

By the end of the second day's march some of the men were beginning to think a great deal more than a hangover was wrong with Jackson. There were still no wagons. Many of the men were without coats, and almost all without food. Nothing could be accomplished in the midst of such brutal cold. Still the Old Man pushed on. In the evening of January

2, he picked up reinforcements—part of a brigade of militia and segments of two cavalry companies—bringing his whole force to about 8,500 men.[75]

If the march seemed madness to many, Jackson had sound reasons for making it. He hoped to attack Bath, to clear the enemy from that vicinity and from Hancock, Maryland, not far north of Bath, to destroy communication between Federal Generals Banks and Kelley, and to threaten Kelley's rear. Cut off, without news of what was happening around him, Kelley might be driven to evacuate Romney without fighting, or he might be goaded into fighting alone. If he fought alone, Jackson would outnumber him—a tactic which Jackson always sought to employ.[76]

Organization held up fairly well the first two days. The Stonewall Brigade, under Brig. Gen. Richard B. Garnett, took the punishment of the elements in good spirits. Loring's three brigades did not bear up quite as well. By nightfall of January 3, the advance of Loring's command went into camp about four miles from Bath; the army had marched about thirty-six miles in three days—not good enough for Jackson. Pushing on, the general sent his militia units around toward the rear of Bath, hoping to take it in a pincers attack.

The next day proved to be one long, cold frustration. Nothing went right. All the men appeared to be moving in slow motion. Hoping to attack quickly, Jackson soon found that he could not get Loring to drive his men steadily. But the Federals, after skirmishing for some hours, evacuated Bath and fell back on Hancock. Again delay hampered Jackson's plans—he could not organize an effective pursuit. The only compensation was that Confederate troops spent the night of the fourth right across the Potomac from Hancock, Maryland. Unfortunately for the men, they were just as exposed as ever.

A demand by Jackson for the surrender of Hancock drew a swift rejection, and on the fifth he shelled the town as retaliation for the random shelling of Confederate Shepherdstown.

On January 7 Jackson marched his men back down the road toward Unger's Store, where a highway led southwest toward Romney. That day many were to remember as the most hideous of a ghastly campaign. Snow and sleet had been falling for several days and the mixture made the roads a glazed toboggan race. Things were bad for the infantry, but almost impossible for the artillery and wagons. An unfortunate oversight had left the horses without winter shoes, with the result that they slipped, fell, and slid all over the roads. Gunners, wagoners, officers, and infantrymen had to help hold back the vehicles at the top of each hill, so that they would not run down the poor stumbling animals. Reluctantly Jackson halted at Unger's Store while the animals were roughshod.

Not until the thirteenth could he resume the march toward Romney, but, once on the road, he pressed on relentlessly. Suffering could be seen on all sides, and as he rode along, Jackson heard the mock *sotto voce* comments which only a cold, starving foot soldier can make. The troops called him crazy, blamed him for the cold and every other hardship, and dubbed him "Fool Tom Jackson." [77] Not even the unusual sight of the general climbing down from Little Sorrel and putting his shoulder to a wagon wheel in an effort to prevent backsliding helped. It was bad, and when officers joined in, it was worse.[78]

After a march tragically like Napoleon's retreat from Moscow, Jackson reached Romney with the van of his army on the night of January 14. The main body of troops came up the next day. No resistance had been encountered; the enemy had fled just as he had done at Bath, leaving behind some valuable stores and equipment.

The men who shuffled stiffly into Romney were sadly in need of a rest, as were the animals, whose condition wrung the hearts of men almost as wretched. Many of the horses, said one soldier in the Rockbridge Artillery, "had been bruised by their falls—all were covered with dried sweat and from one horses knees there were icicles of blood which reached nearly to the ground." [79]

Too much time had been wasted at Unger's Store for Jackson to give serious thought to another prolonged halt. Eager to capitalize on the retreat of the enemy, he wanted to move farther west, to press the enemy back and demolish several of the B&O's bridges across the Potomac and Patterson's Creek. He would take the Stonewall Brigade and Taliaferro's with him, destroy the bridges near Cumberland if possible and disrupt Federal communications over a wide area.

This time he could not do what he planned. Taliaferro's brigade, fatigued, marched-out, and worn by disease, had become all but demoralized. None of Loring's troops seemed in a condition to march anywhere. More than that, they were becoming surly and insubordinate. Such troops could not be trusted, and the Stonewall Brigade, willing though it was, could not advance alone. The project had to be canceled.

Disappointed, Jackson reported his situation to Secretary Benjamin, and added that with some rest, Loring's men could probably hold Romney while camped in winter quarters.[80] A new plan for the defense of the lower valley was proposed to General Johnston, a plan designed to take advantage of the food supplies in the South Branch Valley. Jackson's force would be split into several parts, each within supporting distance of the others. He would take Garnett's brigade back to Winchester, where these thoroughly tested and reliable men could watch the approaches into the valley from the vicinity of Harpers Ferry and Williamsport; General Carson's militia brigade would be kept at Bath to hold that point and to threaten Hancock; General Meem's brigade would go on to Martinsburg, to observe that avenue of approach from Maryland and to retire toward Winchester or advance to the assistance of the troops west of the Alleghenies; General Boggs's militia brigade would be broken into observatory groups at various points in their native South Branch Valley and his pickets would join with those of Gen. Edward Johnson on the Allegheny Mountain; Loring's three brigades with thirteen guns would be in winter quarters at or near Romney, where they could cooperate with Boggs and Johnson. Cavàlry units would be kept well forward, feeling out the enemy's positions, and all the units would be tied together with a courier system.

As for Jackson, he would go back to Winchester, which would continue to be district headquarters. From there he planned to construct a telegraph line to Romney so as to keep in close touch with his far-flung troops.[81] Taking his old brigade—now referred to by Loring's men as "Jackson's pet lambs" [82]—Jackson reached Winchester on January 24, 1862.

For the most part Jackson felt satisfied with his campaign. True, he had not achieved all that he had hoped, but he had already expressed his fear that he might miss the full objective. In his official report of the operations in the northwest, written about a month after returning to Winchester, Jackson had summed up the value of the trek. "On January 2," he wrote Johnston's Adjutant General,

> there was not, from the information I could gather, a single loyal man of Morgan County who could remain at home with safety. Within less than four days the enemy had been defeated, their baggage captured, and, by teaching the Federal authorities a lesson that a town claiming allegiance to the United States lay under our guns, Sheperdstown protected, which had repeatedly before, though not since, been shelled; the country east of the Big Cacapon recovered; Romney and a large portion of Hampshire County evacuated by the enemy without the firing of a gun; the enemy had fled from the western part of Hardy; had been forced from the offensive to the defensive.[83]

In reporting the initial success of the expedition to the Secretary of War on January 14, Jackson characteristically said that what had been done resulted "through the blessing of God." [84]

Unfortunately there had been some unpleasantness during the campaign—in addition to the insolence of Loring's men. Reluctantly, Jackson preferred charges against his VMI colleague, Col. William Gilham. "Neglect of duty" was alleged, a serious accusation and one which might easily offend a gentleman's honor. Nothing came of the charges, but Gilham soon went back to VMI.[85]

Hoping for a breathing space to rebuild and refit his army, Jackson went to work bringing up supplies and straightening out petty problems of authority, such as deciding who was the medical director of the Army of the Valley, his own personal friend and physician Hunter H. McGuire or one of Loring's doctors.[86] While rebuilding, Jackson thought seriously of breaking the B&O Railroad in order to embarrass his opponent, Gen. Frederick W. Lander. But he needed more cavalry and had to abandon the idea.[87]

At last there appeared to be time for him to relax and to visit with Anna. As soon as he returned to Winchester he had gone to her, found her so pleasantly a part of the Graham family that he could not bear to take her away, and had asked Mrs. Graham to let him move in too.

Thus began one of the happiest interludes in the life of Anna and Thomas. The Reverend Doctor's house was soon almost as dear to them as their own in Lexington, and they, in turn, came to be part and parcel of the Graham household. Two rooms, one upstairs, one down, formed the Jackson apartment. They ate with the Grahams, joined in their family devotions, and shared their daily hopes and fears.[88]

Anna soon became part of the happy and gracious social whirl of Winchester. She loved the ladies who entertained her and who formed the circle of her friends. But above all she loved the Grahams and their home, where, she later wrote, "we spent as happy a winter as ever falls to the lot of mortals on this earth." [89]

That winter, Anna confessed, she saw everything under "rose-colored light." It was wonderful being with Thomas, having him home every night, having him at hand for breakfast—even though he had already been to headquarters to issue his General Orders for the day. Tom, too, was happier than ever. He loved the Graham children, and they loved him; to them he was no stern soldier but the merry man who carried them downstairs on his big shoulders and frolicked with them on the floor.

The older Grahams loved him, too. Reverend Graham found his boarder to be one of the most devout, humble Christians he ever met. And in later years the Reverend Doctor would protest violently the assertion that there was anything peculiar about Jackson. He had no idiosyncrasies, as far as Graham could see. "Whatever peculiarities he had were just those individual characteristics which we all in a greater or less degree possess. . . . He was just a simple gentleman, such as we meet in large numbers every day upon our streets, and whom we salute without once thinking whether there is anything peculiar about them or not." True, he sometimes appeared solemn to the family, but they saw underneath the cloak of shyness and reserve to find in him the character of an humble soldier, loving husband, and dedicated Christian. They found, too, that Jackson possessed the true nobility of simplicity. When they discerned that, they came to understand him—and that was something rare.[90]

At the Grahams', Jackson's troubles over the Romney expedition began. All the problems came to a head early on the morning of January

31, 1862. He had gone to district headquarters before breakfast as usual. But the morning mail that day contained a real shock: a telegram from the Secretary of War, dated January 30, which said curtly, "Our news indicates that a movement is being made to cut off General Loring's command. Order him back to Winchester immediately." [91]

Astonished but obedient, Jackson dispatched the necessary instructions to Loring and then wrote Benjamin:

> *Headquarters Valley District,*
> *Winchester, Va., January 31, 1862.*

Hon. J. P. Benjamin, Secretary of War:

> Sir: Your order requiring me to direct General Loring to return with his command to Winchester immediately has been received and promptly complied with.
> With such interference in my command I cannot expect to be of much service in the field, and accordingly respectfully request to be ordered to report for duty to the superintendent of the Virginia Military Institute at Lexington, as has been done in the case of other professors. Should this application not be granted, I respectfully request that the President will accept my resignation from the Army.
> I am, sir, very respectfully, your obedient servant,
>
> *T. J. Jackson,*
> MAJOR-GENERAL, P.A.C.S.[92]

That letter dispatched through Johnston's headquarters, Jackson then composed one to his friend and old Lexington neighbor, Governor Letcher. He explained that he had received Benjamin's order and had promptly complied with it,

> but as the order was given without consulting me, and is abandoning to the enemy what has cost much preparation, expense and exposure to secure, and is in direct conflict with my military plans, and implies a want of confidence in my capacity to judge when General Loring's troops should fall back, and is an attempt to control military operations in detail from the Secretary's desk at a distance, I have . . . requested to be ordered back to the Institute . . . [or] to have my resignation accepted. I ask as a special favor that you will have me ordered back to the Institute.

Jackson then went on to tell the Governor that if the Secretary of War continued to interfere with military operations, considerable chaos might result. His campaign to Romney he defended as worth the trouble, and closed by saying that he did not wish to attack the Secretary of War, since "I take it for granted that he has done what he believed to be best, but I regard such a policy as ruinous." [93]

Once these letters had been written, Jackson ceased to worry about them. Back at the house during breakfast he calmly mentioned that he and Anna expected to be in Lexington soon. That touched off a rash of questions and soon he explained what had happened. Now that the matter seemed finished, Jackson did not hesitate to discuss it. This in itself was unusual, for he almost never talked over army matters with the family.[94]

In the hot discussion which soon raged, the only calm one present was the general himself. He had done what had to be done, now he would not worry about it. Nor would he permit criticism of the government, saying only that "the department has indeed made a serious mistake, but, no doubt, they made it through inadvertence and with the best intentions. They have to consider the interests of the whole Confederacy, and no man should be allowed to stand in the way of its safety." Both he and Anna looked forward to the return to Lexington and their own happy house. There matters rested.

Something of why Benjamin's peremptory order had been issued was known in Winchester, and many of the citizens were irate about the episode. The town was almost heartbroken; everyone felt that to lose Jackson would be a brutal waste, particularly in view of the circumstances. Some of Jackson's staff offered to go to Richmond to present his case. But permission was denied. He would say nothing. Let Loring and his malcontents do all the agitating.

Loring's men were behind the Secretary's actions. But there was more to the affair than just the disaffection of the Army of the Northwest. Eleven officers of Loring's command had signed a petition asking for the withdrawal of the army to Winchester. One of them had written directly to a Richmond politician to protest the isolation of Romney and the probability of being cut off. The whole implication was that Jackson's dispositions were inept and dangerous and that he had failed to take into consideration basic lessons of tactics.[95]

General Loring had forwarded the rebellious petition without disapproving it; in fact, he said it reflected the "true condition of this army." But not only did Loring forward the document through channels, he also asked General Taliaferro, just granted leave, to take a copy of it to Richmond and personally hand it to the President. Davis made the inexcusable mistake of accepting the paper from Taliaferro and even went so far as to ask for a detailed explanation by the general of what things were like in Romney. Handing Taliaferro a map, Davis asked him to point out where Jackson's troops were located. "He did not hesitate to say at once that Jackson had made a mistake," Taliaferro later recalled, "and he ordered the concentration of the troops at Winchester by telegraph that same morning." [96]

All the agitating behind the scenes disgusted Jackson and he would not be part of it. Content to await the outcome of his letter of resignation, he went on drilling his men and building up the defenses of his district. While he remained unconcerned, his letter had produced some interesting ramifications.

General Johnston had had no knowledge whatever of Benjamin's orders until he read Jackson's letter. Shocked, he wrote Jackson a friendly note asking that he reconsider.

Under ordinary circumstances a due sense of one's own dignity, as well as care for professional character and official rights, would demand such a course as yours, but the character of this war, the great energy exhibited by the Government of the United States, the danger in which our very existence as an independent people lies, requires sacrifices from us all who have been educated as soldiers. I receive my information of the order of which you have such cause to complain from your letter. Is not that as great an official wrong to me as the order itself to you?

He suggested that both he and Jackson should "reason with the Government on this subject of command, and if we fail to influence its practice, then ask to be relieved from positions the authority of which is exercised by the War Department, while the responsibilities are left to us." He had, he said, held up Jackson's resignation until he could get a reply, held it up "not merely from warm feelings of personal regard, but from the official opinion which makes me regard you as necessary to the service of the country in your present position." [97]

Privately Johnston seethed, because he had received no official copy of the order to Jackson until February 4 or 5. Johnston wrote his friend Samuel Cooper, the Adjutant General, asking him to give the President a letter requesting that the Valley District be separated from his department since "a collision of the authority of the honorable Secretary of War with mine might occur at a critical moment." [98]

No reply came from Jackson, and sadly Johnston sent his resignation on to Richmond with the endorsement: "Respectfully forwarded, with great regret. I don't know how the loss of this officer can be supplied. General officers are much wanted in this department." [99]

In the meantime Letcher was busy. He received Jackson's request for reassignment to VMI and rushed over to Benjamin's office. The Secretary was on something of a spot and was glad to listen. Perhaps a way out could be found. Too many people were anxious that Jackson's resignation should not be accepted. Letcher wanted to communicate with Jackson; would Benjamin hold off acting until a reply could be received? Benjamin was happy to agree.[100]

Letcher sent a letter to Jackson by the hand of Col. A. R. Boteler, Confederate congressman and the general's close friend. Boteler wrote before he left Richmond, urging Jackson to reconsider his action. Right away the firm reply came: "I hold to the opinion that a man should be in that position where he can be most useful. And I don't see how I can be of any service in the field, so long as that principle which has been applied to me—of undoing at the War Department what is done in the field—is adhered to." [101]

Nothing daunted, Boteler went to Winchester, where he had a long talk with Jackson. The general had made up his mind; the best thing he could do was to resign. Boteler talked fast. Finally the right words came to him: in this great war Virginia needed all her sons, and Jackson had no right to go home in the middle of the fight. Jackson cracked—a little. Boteler's words reinforced the multitudes of letters coming to Jackson from all over Virginia and the South. Chief among the correspondents had been clergymen, who feared the army of the Lord would lose a Christian soldier. To the powerful clerical appeal, Boteler added a clincher: Governor Letcher felt that Jackson's resignation would have a depressing effect on the country.

On February 6 Jackson wrote the Governor that

> if my retiring from the Army would produce that effect upon our country that you have named . . . I of course would not desire to leave the service, and if, upon receipt of this note, your opinion remains unchanged, you are authorized to withdraw my resignation, unless the Secretary of War desires that it should be accepted. My reasons for resigning were set forth in my letter . . . and my views remain unchanged, and if the Secretary persists in the ruinous policy complained of, I feel that no officer can serve his country better than by making his strongest possible protest against it . . . rather than be a willful instrument in prosecuting the war upon a ruinous principle.[102]

Letcher saw to it that this letter reached the War Department.

The crisis ended with Jackson's letter of resignation going back to him. Loring was shifted out of the Valley District, but not until Jackson had preferred charges of neglect of duty and of "conduct subversive of good order and discipline." Although Johnston thought the charges ought to be aired before a court-martial, nothing came of them. Loring was asked to answer them, which he did—more or less—and soon he was promoted to major general. Jackson felt that Loring ought to be cashiered from the army, but getting him out of the district was something to be grateful for, at any rate.[103] Many officers serving with Jackson were happy to see "Loring's . . . terribly disorganized band" quit the valley.[104]

With no more mention of the Loring affair, Jackson settled down to drilling and training his men, building fortifications, and trying to bring up supplies. He had only about 4,500 men to cover Johnston's left flank, but a bold front might accomplish a great deal. He could have done more with a bold front had he been able to keep men out in the South Branch Valley.

Viewed from the standpoint of over-all strategy, Jackson's dispositions in the Romney area had appeared precarious, too strung out for safety. Violating the principle of concentration had inherent dangers which everyone could see. But Jackson saw other things. Once he had driven the enemy back from Romney, he had a psychological advantage, an advantage which might be maintained by a show of strength all along the line in northwestern Virginia. Since the enemy had fallen back in the face of a prospective attack, he might be bluffed further by the same troops, at least until he built up an overwhelming superiority of numbers.

Although Loring and his subordinates had wailed that they were subject to being cut off, Jackson had taken precautions to forestall such a possibility. The communications network he had in mind would have reduced the danger of surprise, and he knew that Ashby could be counted on to reduce the danger still further. His troops looked badly scattered, but a glance at the map would show they could be easily brought together for unified action. Daring use of a small force Jackson hoped would bring the same results as careful use of a large one. From this standpoint, the strategy as well as the tactics of the Romney campaign reflect the growth of Jackson as a commander—he was willing to take what appeared to be carefully calculated risks.

Watching the growth of Federal forces north of the Potomac, Jackson began to prepare for action. Knowing he did not have enough men to hold off Lander and Banks, should they cooperate in an attack on the lower valley, he prepared to show them as much strength as he could. He could not show much. Enlistment terms of many volunteers ended about this time, and the practice of granting furloughs had been instituted to encourage reenlistments, thus reducing Jackson's force still further.

As he feared, the enemy began to draw together for an advance. February—a disastrous month for the Confederacy—dragged on. Late in the month Gen. Nathaniel P. Banks crossed the Potomac, collected James Shields's (formerly Lander's) division and moved south, occupying Bunker Hill and Smithfield on March 6. It would not be long before Jackson would be forced to move—somewhere.

By the time Banks had reached Bunker Hill, Jackson's sick and wounded, baggage, and all other impedimenta had been sent toward Woodstock, where a hospital had been established.[105] Winchester's towns-people could not mistake the signs; their general had to leave them. Anna, of course, would have to go too. It was hard to leave the Grahams and harder still to leave each other. Thomas was particularly upset, for Anna had been sick, violently sick. Mrs. Graham had her suspicions about the nature of the illness, but delicacy forbade her confiding them to the general.[106] He took Anna to the railroad and put her aboard the train which carried his wounded south. Ill herself and surrounded by such suffering, she looked lonely and forlorn—just the way he felt.

To make matters more dismal, for two days Jackson had not heard from Gen. D. H. Hill, who was stationed east of the Blue Ridge and who would cooperate in case of trouble. Since he wrote regularly to Jackson, the sudden failure looked ominous.[107]

10

"IF THIS VALLEY IS LOST, VIRGINIA IS LOST"

— JACKSON

Gloom had settled over Winchester much as it had over the whole Confederacy in recent weeks. Nothing seemed to be going right for the South. Disasters followed one another with startling speed in the west, where Forts Henry and Donelson, guarding the Tennessee and Cumberland Rivers, had fallen. General Albert Sidney Johnston's army had been compelled to retreat, and by the end of February southern Kentucky and middle Tennessee were in enemy hands.

Even more depressing to the Confederate people along the Eastern Seaboard had been the loss of Roanoke Island, North Carolina, early in the same month. As the country looked for a scapegoat, and as despondency shook the patriotism of many, Gen. Joseph E. Johnston pushed preparations to retreat the main Confederate army in northern Virginia. Facing him and extending detachments east and west was a rejuvenated Federal army which had been cajoled out of the Bull Run doldrums by a new commanding general, George B. McClellan, alias Little Mac.

Anywhere they looked, the Confederacy's citizens could see masses of Yankees poised, ready to follow the retreating Southern soldiers. Nowhere was there even a ray of success, save in remote New Mexico, and that ray would soon be blotted out.

In Winchester, faced with an overwhelming enemy force inching toward his little band of volunteers and militia, Stonewall Jackson worried not about retreat, but about attack. With scarcely more than 4,600 men he could not do serious injury to the 38,000 Federals concentrating against him,[1] but Jackson had an idea. If he could build up formidable-

197

looking works ringing the northern crescent of Winchester, he might conceivably hold the town until reinforcements arrived.

Such a scheme had the virtue of boldness, but it also had drawbacks. For one thing, Johnston had already instructed the commander of the Valley District to fall back when the main Confederate army at Centreville retreated. Jackson's little flank guard in the valley must conform to the general movement in the department, else it stood to be cut off. Sound as this strategy was, Jackson balked—not to the point of stubbornness, but to the extent of explaining his problems to Johnston, who always had been willing to give wide discretion to his subordinates in remote theaters.

Johnston expected the valley army to perform several functions: keep between the main army and the enemy, oppose the Federal advance up the valley, and delay that advance "as long as you can."[2] In some ways, these tasks were mutually exclusive. "If you will examine the roads leading from the valley across the Blue Ridge," Jackson wrote his superior on March 3, "you will see the difficulty of keeping between you and the enemy and at the same time opposing his advance along the valley." There were too many ways by which Banks might get between Jackson and Johnston, or cut Jackson off, once the little Confederate force started to retire.

If more troops could be sent to the Army of the Valley, the situation might be altered. And although troops were needed everywhere, Jackson wondered if the force commanded by brother-in-law Daniel Harvey Hill might be sent. After spending some time in observation near Leesburg, Hill's force had retired southward, conforming to Johnston's movement. Could Johnston spare Hill's 3,000 men? "The very idea of re-enforcements coming to Winchester would, I think, be a damper to the enemy, in addition to the fine effect that would be produced on our own troops, who are already in fine spirits."[3] More men would give him greater freedom of movement and enable him to take advantage of opportunities to attack.[4] More than that, Jackson explained, "if we cannot be successful in defeating the enemy should he advance, a kind Providence may enable us to inflict a terrible wound and effect a safe retreat in the event of having to fall back."[5]

There, succinctly put, was the essence of all that Jackson was to do in the succeeding turbulent weeks. While he would have to stand on the defensive, protecting his own army and the left flank of Johnston, he would attack where and when he could—he would employ a fluid offensive-defensive strategy, suited to his compact and mobile force.[6] Although he probably did not work out the whole plan for some time, this is the strategy he developed almost to perfection.

While Old Jack plotted the means for checking Banks, his staff continued preparations to unclutter the army. Orders to move all baggage, heavy ordnance, and impedimenta, including railroad rolling stock, to the rear were carried out through the last days of February and early March. "Old John" Harman, Jackson's chief quartermaster, had sent all his stores south toward Strasburg on March 6, had portioned out wagons, and had even removed the few remaining heavy guns.[7]

No less efficient had been the activities of Maj. Wells J. Hawks, chief commissary of the army. After distinguishing himself by keeping up the rations—with a short lapse—during the Romney expedition, Hawks had won the added admiration of his general by providing abundant quantities of bread and meat. The valley, bulging with wheat, was a granary not only for the Army of the Valley but also for the Commissary Department. Vast amounts of food had been procured from the lower valley and from the South Branch area during the Romney campaign. Much of what had been gathered was in Winchester warehouses. Hawks was to get it out.

By February 23 he had directed that further shipments of food to Jackson's army would be held at Strasburg, the railhead for army supplies. Hawks thought far ahead, decided that Strasburg might not be safe, and ordered a commissary depot to be established at Mount Jackson on the Valley Turnpike closer to the army. So well did he do his work that the Commissary General praised him for leaving nothing behind—a rare achievement.[8]

Jackson expected the staff officers to do their work well; he consulted with them every morning and told them what he wanted. He had picked his chiefs of staff departments with care, and their subsequent success showed he knew his men. Unfortunately confused logistics were to mar Jackson's next move.

At last came the sad word that no more men could come to the valley. Jackson would have to do what he could with what he had. The Richmond authorities, of course, had many fronts to worry about, but reinforcements for the vital Shenandoah area would have done so much. To his friend in Congress, Alex R. Boteler, Jackson disclosed his feelings. Not discouraged by the odds against him, he wrote on March 3 that one thing had to be kept in mind: "If this Valley is lost, Virginia is lost."

Surely it would be folly to stay longer at Winchester, threatened by an overwhelming force. But for Jackson, giving up Winchester was hard —not only because of its kind people but also because of its military value. Could he make a last effort to turn on the enemy? Since such a move would involve the safety of the army, he would talk it over with his subordinate commanders—call a council of war, despite Napoleon's admonition against these vacillating bodies. Meantime, while the council was assembling, he went to the Graham house to assure them that Winchester still might remain Confederate. After they joined in prayer, the general, in full war regalia—boots, spurs, saber—talked hopefully of what might be done. In fact, he was so cheerful that sadness began to lift from the Graham house. Obviously he planned at least a delaying action.

Returning to headquarters, already denuded of papers and of most of the furniture, Jackson conferred seriously with his brigade commanders and probably with Ashby.[9] What he heard infuriated him. During the morning of March 11 his infantry had been following the army wagon trains south toward Strasburg; it was the evacuation of Winchester by the army that had thrown the town into deep despair. But the evacuation was not exactly what the general had been planning. What he had hoped for, even when talking to the Grahams (who had shared the general fear as they heard the rumble of Jackson's wagons and the cadenced tread of his infantry), was to move only a short distance out of town, and after dark, turn swiftly to attack Banks and the Federals as they were milling into Winchester.

During the council of war Jackson apparently learned for the first time that his army had continued to march south until it had reached the vicinity of Kernstown and Newtown. Most of the infantry had marched at least five miles. They had literally been marched out of any possible night attack.[10]

He must return to the Grahams to put right the false impression they had received from him. Again the familiar figure in the VMI uniform stalked up the front walk, measuring his steps in those monstrous boots. But this was a different Jackson. He was sad and depressed. The council, he explained, had resulted in the cancellation of his proposed surprise attack that night. Had he been accustomed to explain his military movements, he might have added the obvious—that without the advantage of surprise and the cover of night his little band would be unable to attack, possibly unable to avoid annihilation.

As he talked he was grim. His idea had been sound. After his first flush of embarrassment, he grew calm. Musing aloud, he said: "But— let me think—can I not yet carry my plan into execution?" Suddenly grabbing the hilt of his sword, he turned to the family with the most determined look they had ever seen; his eyes burned with a fierce light— that light which became famous on many a later battlefield—as he thought of reviving his attack. The moment passed, the light faded, and his head drooped. "No; I must not do it; it may cost the lives of too many brave men. I must retreat, and wait for a better time." Sadly he bade farewell to the Grahams, mounted his sturdy little sorrel, and followed his army south.

Jackson did not quit the town personally until after dark, and then, in company with the Medical Director of his army, Dr. Hunter H. McGuire, he rode out. As the two horsemen reached a hill on the Valley Pike overlooking Winchester, Jackson halted for a long look. McGuire was at the point of tears as he gazed at his home town, left now to the mercy of the Yankees. Caught in the nostalgic moment, he looked at his companion and forgot his sorrow. Jackson's face was almost on fire; he was in a burning, towering rage. The awed doctor watched as Stonewall Jackson came to a decision which Napoleon had made before him. In a savage, hoarse shout, he cried, "That is the last council of war I will ever hold!" So it was.[11]

Resolute now, Jackson took his army back to Strasburg, collected his advanced supplies, then withdrew further south to Mount Jackson, some forty-two miles from Winchester. Here he stopped and the army went into camp.

Problems abounded. Of first importance was the army. It had to be built up, militia units brought in from the valley counties, and arms provided. Recruiting and drilling occupied the general's attention. And despite the near presence of enemy forces, routine soon had good effect on Jackson's men. The wagon train had been parked close enough for some baggage to be brought into camp, and the staff officers worked long hours to procure arms, tents, and other equipment. For months the troops had gone without pay, particularly the militia, and Jackson fought to end this irritation. The Quartermaster General was urged to send funds, not only for payrolls, but also to provide bounty money for those reenlisting for the war. Everything must be done to increase morale.[12]

Dreary, daily army administration tested the morale of the commanding general. Most of an army commander's time was taken up with administration—all preparatory to a brief moment on the battlefield. If the preparation were badly done, the battle might go wrong. Despite his efficient command of his brigade, Jackson had not shown himself to be a good administrator at the army command level. During the Romney expedition the men had been exposed to terrible weather without proper food or clothing, and the animals had not been properly shod. The men had begun to lose faith in their general. A lingering suspicion about him still persisted.[13]

But Romney had taught Jackson a good many lessons and he remembered them. The weeks spent at Mount Jackson did much to restore him in the esteem of his men. Again it was the little things that meant so much to the individual soldier, as they had to the Stonewall Brigade before and after Manassas. Better rations, good campsites, and rigid discipline—all these things impressed and encouraged the men. Old Jack was not so bad, after all.

One thing was certain: the men saw much more of him around the Mount Jackson encampment than before, and at closer range. A concern for details took him round the camps frequently, and the fading blue coat, slouched-over kepi cap, dusty boots, and Little Sorrel became familiar sights.

The Old Man put on no airs. A plain man, he lived plainly, eating what the men ate, occasionally having corn bread instead of wheat with his milk and butter.[14] Businesslike and hard-working, the general arose early and had tended to most of his letter writing before breakfast—a habit which seriously discomfited the young men of his staff, who were expected to be equally early risers. The security and good order of his camps he inquired into personally, requiring frequent reports from outpost officers and cavalry scouts.

Furloughs had to clear through Army Headquarters, and soon the men realized that Old Jack himself would never be absent. Neither would any other officer, without an ironclad reason. To be at the post of duty was the primary function of a soldier.

Although military to the heart of his being, the general did not go in for unnecessary spit and polish. His army thus presented an odd sight to the casual eye. Costumes of all sorts could be seen—Confederate gray uniforms of older volunteer units, spectacular collections of garments in the cavalry, and militia outfits ranging from broadcloth to homespun. What mattered was the men—would they make good soldiers?

The general's personal habits naturally formed the topic of much camp gossip. It was common knowledge that he prayed frequently— the men often saw him going into his tent during the day, obviously for that purpose. Some said he had been a deacon in a Lexington church, and his manifest concern for the spiritual well-being of the men pointed up this fact. As the word spread around and was embroidered, Jackson became a fanatic, a sort of Cromwell. The men began to call him "Old Blue Light." But they were not ready to laugh; something about Jackson stifled ridicule. Those who saw him up close, or spoke to him, felt the strength of his personality. A big man, standing close to six feet, he looked angular but strong. His deep blue eyes, with their steady gaze, conveyed an inner determination which could be frightening or encouraging, depending on circumstances. He was not a man to laugh at—or to trifle with.

Some said he never laughed himself. Certainly his narrow lips enshrouded in a wavy brown beard conveyed that impression; but it was not true. His staff knew better. Being a lively crew, these young men led by Kyd Douglas and Sandie Pendleton had a merry time around the headquarters tent, especially at dinnertime. Usually Jackson tolerated the pranks with an amused twinkle; on occasion he took part in them himself.

One evening after dinner, Sandie Pendleton began reading an article in the New York *Mercury*. Since Jackson viewed newspapers with suspicion, particularly when they contained embarrassingly flattering stories about him, he showed little interest. Sandie explained that this particular issue had an article about Jackson which would help him digest his dinner.

"Go on, Captain—let's hear it, if it will make us laugh." Sandie read aloud: "The life and character of the rebel General, Stonewall Jackson." Jackson jerked to his feet and remarked that he did not want to hear any more.

"Hold on, General," Sandie urged, "it is only a parody on the 'Lives' which fill the Northern papers; it is entirely unobjectionable and you will enjoy it."

Uncertainly Jackson sat down. With mock seriousness Pendleton read on. The general's pedigree was traced back to Jack the Giant Killer, and from there the story progressed to an absurd account of his boyhood, "followed up the development of his peculiar mental and moral traits, and laid special stress upon his force of will and that wonderful abstemiousness which enabled him to live for a fortnight on two crackers and a barrel of whiskey."

All through the "Life" Jackson listened, sitting bolt upright, as usual. As Pendleton read along, the serious expression relaxed, a smile played around the corners of the thin mouth, and finally "he broke into the heartiest and loudest burst of laughter." [15]

It was good to have the boys around. John Preston, Maggie's husband, still remained with the staff, adding dignity and age, but even he became infected occasionally with the young men's gaiety. After a day of army business, the mess table needed all the humor it could get.

By the middle of March Jackson's army had not materially grown in size, but it began to look and act like a cohesive force. There had been some troubles with the Dunkards of Rockingham County, whose religious scruples interfered with their militia obligations. Although showing little sympathy, Jackson finally agreed to use the conscientious objectors in supply and staff work. They would have to drill in their spare time, "so that in case circumstances should justify it arms may be given them." [16] No desertion would be tolerated; Jackson promised to deal with the Dunkards in good faith and he expected the same from them. Every man ought to be ready to do his duty in repelling the invaders of Virginia, if not in a shooting capacity, then in some other quasi-military job. The Dunkards proved most useful as teamsters and as guides, for they knew the valley well.

On Friday, March 21, the routine of life at Mount Jackson came to an abrupt end. That evening Jackson bent over a dispatch from the trusted Colonel Ashby. The enemy force at Strasburg, consisting of General Shields's division,[17] had pulled out of town and taken the road north. Ashby, with only one rested company of horse and Robert Chew's battery, was in pursuit.

Federal withdrawal could mean only one thing. McClellan had decided to reduce force in the valley, leaving possibly one division to tease Jackson, and bringing most of Banks's army east of the Blue Ridge to cooperate in the great pincers movement—by land and sea—against Richmond. Such a reduction of Federal forces in the valley was exactly what General Johnston wanted Jackson to prevent.[18]

Johnston had reminded Jackson of this objective several times and on March 19 had written expressing concern at the distance between Jackson and the town of Winchester. He had asked, in characteristically discreet terms, whether Jackson's presence closer to that point might not prevent the detachment which was now taking place.[19]

Jackson gave orders to break camp. He had to stop the Federal move. It was risky in the extreme, pressing them, especially since reports of their strength ranged from 10,000 to 20,000 men in the vicinity of Strasburg.[20] But swiftly the army moved. Forced marching would be necessary. All day Saturday, the twenty-second, Jackson's infantry pushed north. It was hard work, for Old Jack permitted no relaxing—"Press on, press on." Infantry could move fast, for the trains were left behind, the men carrying with them three days' cooked rations. The column had been stripped of extras and was headed for something big.

Saturday's stint proved more than some of the men could take, and scores of stragglers fell far behind. That day some units made twenty-one miles and the rear regiments did better, covering about twenty-seven.[21] Jackson could be seen straining forward close to the van of the army, nervously urging the men on.

That night Jackson's headquarters were at Strasburg,[22] not far behind the advance brigades. Quietly Jackson kept his own council. Much depended on further news from Ashby. While he waited, he would pray. The next day was the Lord's, set aside for Him. Would Ashby's news force the breaking of the Sabbath? Devoutly Jackson hoped not, but resolutely he made ready. Marching orders were already issued and the army took the road early—at the crack of day—heading still toward Winchester.[23]

By about two in the afternoon of a raw, cold day [24] Garnett's Stonewall Brigade, leading the march, approached the hamlet of Kernstown, followed closely by the brigades of Colonels Fulkerson (one of "Loring's men") and Burks, in all about 3,000 men. Artillery firing could be heard before the men saw Ashby's cavalry near the little settlement. The cavalry was involved in an artillery brush with the Federals, but Ashby rode quickly to report exciting intelligence. The night before, he had pushed very close to Winchester, fighting along the way, and had learned from Confederate friends that Federal strength in the town amounted only to four regiments of infantry with some cavalry and artillery. These troops were, according to Ashby's informer, under orders to move toward Harpers Ferry. The enemy troops which Jackson could see halted east of the Valley Pike were the rear guard.

The odds were in Jackson's favor. Enemy forces were not too large, they had been retiring, and his rapid advance pinned them down when they did not want to be pinned down. A rear guard might be cut off from Banks's main force. But it was Sunday.

Here was a terrible dilemma. For years, Jackson had ardently respected the sanctity of the Sabbath—not even reading a letter which arrived that day. Surely fighting on the Lord's day would be a hideous desecration.

Where lay the duty of a true Christian who was at the same time a general, responsible for his army? If this were a war of the Lord's, then the Lord would give the answer—and it might be given through military considerations. Still, the matter required thought. Jackson shunned the battle, gave orders for his men to bivouac. He studied the ground, considered carefully Ashby's news. As he saw it, he must answer a primary question: Could the battle be postponed to the next day without jeopardizing the army or its objective? For a time he believed so, but finally the enemy took a position which gave them a view of Jackson's army—that settled it; if he waited, more men would be brought up and he would be outnumbered when he did attack. Several weeks later, in explaining to Anna why he fought on Sunday, Jackson restated his thinking that afternoon:

> I felt it my duty to do it, in consideration of the ruinous effects that might result from postponing the battle until the morning. So far as I can see, my course was a wise one; the best that I could do under the circumstances, though very distasteful to my feelings; and I hope and pray to our Heavenly Father that I may never again be circumstanced as on that day. I believed that so far as our troops were concerned, necessity and mercy both called for the battle. . . . Arms is a profession that, if its principles are adhered to for success, requires an officer to do what he fears may be wrong . . . if success is to be attained.[25]

The Lord would be the ultimate judge; if He forgave the sinning soldier, He would grant victory. The issue was, as always, in God's hands.

Bivouac orders canceled, the brigades formed line of battle. Old Jack had made up his mind that an attack on his own right would be foolhardy. There the ground was open and dominated by Union guns. But on the left, west of the Valley Pike, wooded hills overlooked the enemy's positions. Ashby received orders quickly—hold the Valley Pike, cover the Confederate right, and threaten the enemy's left flank. He could count on Col. Jes Burks's little brigade for infantry support if needed, since it would be the army's general reserve. Some of Ashby's men must go to the left, to forestall any turning operation by Shields's troops. Artillery— Jackson had about twenty-seven guns on the field—would stay near the center of the Confederate line until the attack opened, when it could be fed in where needed. The big effort was to be made on Jackson's left.

The Stonewall Brigade would be part of the attack; already some of its men were thinking that they had to pay dearly for their reputation, since Stonewall seemed always to hand them the dirtiest jobs. This time they would be assisted by Fulkerson's Third Brigade. The two of them would turn the Federal right.

No serious tactical problems were presented by the ground. The front, narrow and confined by topography, gave opportunity for fewer men to do much more damage than usual. Most of the units were on the field and in position. As soon as the men were ready, Jackson ordered the attack. Fulkerson's men led out, supported by the Stonewall Brigade; artillery followed as needed. Everything went well. Ashby held his ground, beating back an enemy feint on the right.

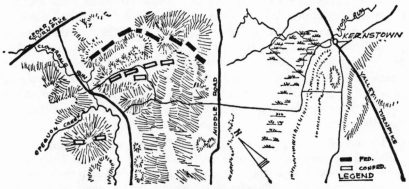

Battlefield of Kernstown

From a hill on the left Jackson watched his battle. Two of his regiments advanced smoothly, breaking up two enemy attacks, and pushing on. Fulkerson, spying an advancing line in blue, posted his men along a stone fence, from where they leveled a withering fire at the onrushing Yankees. Back went the bluejackets. Garnett brought in his men; the battle raged all along the Union right. Jackson looked on confidently as his own boys pushed forward, aiding Fulkerson. Advancing steadily, holding where need be, Jackson's infantry seemed on the point of turning the Union flank.

But the fighting was desperate. Firing grew more and more rapid, men borrowed cartridges from one another. A weird stand-up, almost toe-to-toe fight grew in anger. In the center, suddenly, the enemy's fire grew in volume—the Confederates' diminished. In front of Jackson's eyes some of his men began to move toward the rear—the ammunition supply was running out.

Immediately the general rode to the spot where he had seen some of the deserters. Soon he ran into a man from F Company, Twenty-first Virginia. "Where are you going?" the fierce-looking man on Little Sorrel asked. He had run out of cartridges, explained the hapless private, and was on his way to find some more but did not know where to look. Icy-blue eyes bored into the man, and in a clipped voice Jackson said, "Then go back and give them the bayonet." Abruptly he whirled the sorrel's head and dashed toward the front.

By the time he reached the battle line he saw that things had gone radically wrong. Garnett's men, the Stonewall Brigade, were in retreat. On the left of the line hordes of Yankees bore down on the retiring Confederates. Obviously Jackson was fighting much more than a rear guard. But Garnett should stand his ground, give the enemy cold steel. Why had he given the order to retire? Stonewall rode to find out.

As often happens, the order to retreat panicked some men, and they bolted headlong from the field. With Garnett's troops pulling back, Fulkerson's right was unprotected and he had to fall back. All along the line, then, Jackson's army backed up. As the men reeled rearward, they met Jackson. Riding along the line furiously, he sought to stem the retreat, to rally his men.

There still might be a chance—two regiments were in reserve and the rearguard had not yet arrived on the field. Possibly a new line could be formed and behind it the broken companies could reform. After writing for his reserves, Jackson rode to General Garnett. Why had he ordered a retreat? It must be stopped. Spying a drummer boy, Jackson grabbed him and demanded he beat the rally. Standing resolutely on a little knoll, the boy beat away furiously, but nobody seemed to hear. The ebbing flow of men continued. Jackson still hoped for help from the reserves, but they did not come up.

Soon he heard why. Garnett had ordered them to form line of battle to the rear and cover the retreat. That ended that; the field had to be given up. Jackson would yield slowly, covering the withdrawal of supplies, equipment, and wounded.

Dr. McGuire protested that much time would be consumed in gathering up the wounded who could safely be moved, perhaps more time than the army had. "Can you stay to protect us?" "Make yourself easy about that," came the grim reply; "this army stays here until the last wounded man is removed." Looking full into McGuire's eye, the general added, with emotion, "Before I will leave them to the enemy I will lose many more men."

Fortunately the enemy did not pursue closely and Jackson's army fell back grudgingly to the trains, parked near Newtown, about four and a half miles south of the battlesite. Stung at having been wrong in his information about enemy numbers, Ashby stuck close to Shields, passing the night of the twenty-third near Bartonsville, a scant mile or so from Kernstown. Next time he would be certain of his information, but actually he had little to reproach himself about. Shields had ably hidden most of his 9,000 men, and had contrived to keep his secret well.[26] Still, it was a lesson Ashby would remember.

The major general commanding the Valley District followed his dispirited infantry part way toward Newtown but finally turned back toward Bartonsville, as if to wrest something from the enemy out of sheer personal presence. He toasted awhile by a fence-rail fire, and then curled up in a corner of the damaged fence to sleep soundly. If the army could not quite understand what had happened,[27] the general, at least, seemed unperturbed.

He had said as much to a young trooper before bedding down for the night. The brash lad had found the general standing by the fire, approached him and said, "The Yankees don't seem willing to quit Winchester, General!"

"Winchester is a very pleasant place to stay in, sir!"

The boy went on: "It was reported that they were retreating, but I guess they're retreating after us."

Still staring moodily at the fire, Jackson shot back, "I think I may say I am satisfied, sir!"[28]

He echoed this idea in a short report to Johnston, sent on March 24. He had reported the previous day that "with the blessing of an ever-kind Providence I hope to be in the vicinity of Winchester this evening."[29] The expectation had been realized, but now he had to report what had happened. Honestly and without excuse he told Johnston that he had fought and lost and that he had left a gun and three caissons on the field. Yet there was another consideration which ought to be mentioned: "This fight will probably delay, if not prevent, their [the Federals'] leaving, and I hope will retain others." After all, then the strategic objectives of the battle might be achieved—Banks might not leave the valley. Those Federal troops already on the march east might be returned to Winchester. If so, the battle had been worth the loss of over 700 killed, wounded, and captured.[30] Jackson believed that the Federal loss greatly exceeded his own.

A reduction of his force of any size, though, imposed added difficulties. Prospects of filling the ranks might be good, if the militia kept turning out. Still, he had the problem of using what men he had on hand to continue stinging Banks and fixing him in the valley.

Large questions of strategy were involved. How could a small division—really a corps of observation—continue to neutralize a huge Yankee force? It would have to give the appearance of greater than actual size. And this might be done by swift movement, careful hoarding of resources, and judicious use of geography.

Geography offered peculiar opportunities. Jackson had retired from the lower valley, would probably have to retire still further, and consequently could make use of the peculiar mountain formations of the middle Shenandoah region. He soon began a serious study of topography, putting the able engineer Jed Hotchkiss to work on a map of the valley from Harpers Ferry to Lexington.[31] As he looked at a map it was immediately apparent that his front would be circumscribed by the Blue Ridge on the east and the Alleghenies on the west. For a good distance along the valley these ranges were about twenty to thirty miles apart.

From the town of Strasburg on the north to Harrisonburg on the south, the Shenandoah Valley became two valleys, divided by an eerie, low range called Massanutton Mountain. The wooded vale resting between this odd formation and the Blue Ridge was called the Luray Valley, and the country west, stretching to the Alleghenies, kept the name Shenandoah. On both sides of Massanutton flowed branches of the Shenandoah River: the North Fork on the western side, the South Fork on the eastern. At Front Royal, near the head of the Luray Valley, the branches united and the main stream rolled northward to the Potomac.

A rough parallelogram of roads encased the Massanutton. The Valley Pike, macadamized (or metaled, in the idiom of the time), flanked the western slopes of the mountain from Strasburg south, some forty-five miles to Harrisonburg. A poorer road ran the length of Luray Valley from Front Royal south to Conrad's Store. From Conrad's Store a dirt road led west to Harrisonburg. Strasburg and Front Royal were connected by a road and by the Manassas Gap railroad.

Most important in a study of the valley ground were the passes through the Blue Ridge and the vital Luray Gap in the Massanutton which led from New Market on the Valley Pike east to the town of Luray. Passes in the Blue Ridge which might be of strategical value were: Manassas Gap, east of Front Royal, leading to Manassas Junction; Thornton's Gap, east of Luray, leading to Sperryville; Fisher's Gap, between Luray and Conrad's Store (especially important because a branch of the New Market road passed through it), leading to Madison Courthouse and thence to the rail center of Gordonsville; Swift Run Gap, almost opposite Conrad's Store, leading to the Virginia Central Railroad at Mechum River Station. Passes in the Alleghenies were few, roads in those mountains bad, and there seemed small likelihood of important operations in that area.

If all the facets of valley geography could be fixed in the mind of an able strategist, almost limitless opportunities leaped from the map. It might be possible to induce an enemy with less knowledge of the ground to join in an elaborate game of blindman's buff. Much caution would have to be used, for the valley's contours presented as many pitfalls as opportunities. Jackson pondered these questions, and meanwhile had to fall back. The enemy began to move against him, up the valley, inching closer to the Massanutton. How could this situation be turned to advantage? A good beginning might be to construct several tables of mileage between the various towns of importance.[32]

Throughout the remainder of March and early April Jackson fell back slowly. Finally able to stabilize his lines near Mount Jackson, he kept Ashby, with infantry support, in front of his camps and had the army settled down for rest and refitting.[33]

Jackson needed rest himself, but he had no time for it. An interlude in camp seemed an ideal time to apply some of the lessons learned at Kernstown. Taking stock of himself, he had reason to be pleased. By most standards he had done well. The decision to march toward the enemy had been swift and carried out with determination. Once on the field, Jackson had been quick to evolve a good plan, and his orders had been crisp, clear, and decisive with no vacillating to confuse his subordinates. Deployment had been accomplished easily and with minimum confusion. If personal leadership could have saved the day, as it sometimes could, his own example ought to have won the battle. Most important, he had most of his men in action and had well blended the working of all three arms.[34] As soon as he conceded further resistance useless, he had ably directed the withdrawal of his troops and had stayed close to the rear guard. All through the afternoon he had been close to the front—something he expected of his commanders—and never did he lose contact with the battle. On the credit side, then, he had proved himself cool, decisive, of sound judgment, and personally courageous. His plan showed him to be a good tactician, and his recognition of the value of the battle showed his strategic sense.

One thing might be said against Jackson's performance. He had greatly reduced the number of men available for battle by overtaxing his infantry. Most of the men had marched between thirty-five and forty miles in less than two days; stragglers dotted the road and pointed up the poor marching order.

Jackson paid little attention to what had been done well—it was part of duty. What had not been done well was another matter. Rest camps gave time to concentrate on weaknesses; the army would drill and become efficient marchers, with no straggling. Nothing could be more important, for in swiftness lay the one hope of the Army of the Valley.

One way to avoid lax discipline was to tighten the high command of the army. First on the list of reorganization was a new commander for the Stonewall Brigade. Garnett was through. The excuse which had been circulating that his men had run out of ammunition made no impression on Jackson.[35] Garnett had given an unauthorized order, had disorganized Jackson's line of battle, and he was, on April 1, relieved of his command and put in arrest.[36]

A storm of indignation broke out in the Stonewall Brigade. Unanimously came the opinion that Jackson had been too hard on Garnett. Every one of Garnett's subordinates declared him to have been absolutely right in retreating his brigade. He had probably saved it from disaster. Jackson could not be mollified. Charges and specifications were drawn up against Garnett and sent to Johnston's headquarters. Thus began a

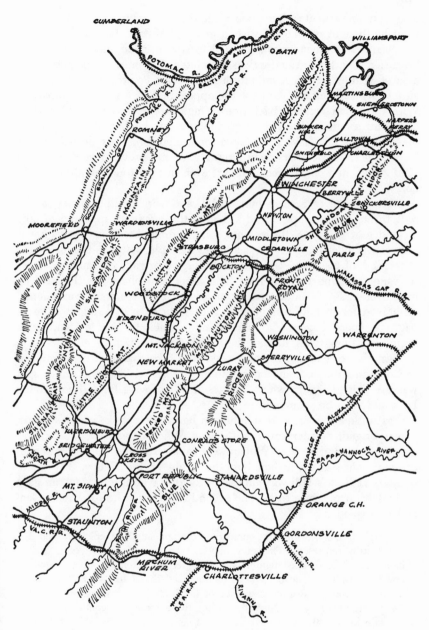

The Shenandoah Valley

long and unfortunate altercation with Garnett, who remained, despite what he thought was an injustice, a great admirer of Jackson.[37]

Another commander was needed for the brigade and finally a new brigadier, Charles S. Winder, was appointed. It would not be easy for a man of Winder's type. A military-looking West Pointer, always sporting an immaculate uniform, he gave the appearance of a firm disciplinarian. With wavy hair combed back from a high forehead, deep-set disturbed eyes, and a curling beard that accentuated his intelligent, sensitive expression, he might have been taken for a mere dress-parade officer, but he was not. Those that knew anything of his previous record in the "Old Army" had confidence in him.[38] Men in the Stonewall Brigade did not.

They chose to receive him coldly, and with audible hisses, as he rode through the camps.[39] And although the brigadier appeared to take no notice at the time, the colonel commanding the offending regiment soon felt Winder's anger. It was another example, as far as the men were concerned, of his "airs." Unfortunately for the brigade commander, Jackson's new scheme for marching light went into effect shortly after he took over and the sudden reduction of the baggage train was blamed on him. After that he was greeted with *sotto voce* pleadings for "more baggage, more baggage." [40] But Winder stuck to the job and gave promise of doing well, despite the brigade's ill feeling.

Another brigadier was badly needed to take charge of the command of Col. Jesse Burks, home on indefinite sick leave. The one bright spot was the Third Brigade, where Fulkerson was proving himself constantly. He could soon be promoted.

Meantime it seemed that Johnston had anticipated Jackson's needs. A new brigadier general was on the way. When he arrived, Jackson was dismayed to find it was William B. Taliaferro, one of Loring's malcontents, once again assigned to the Army of the Valley. The headquarters at Rude's Hill was almost too small for both men. Jackson gave no hint of displeasure to anyone around him, but to the Adjutant General he exploded.

> Through God's blessing my command, though small, is efficient, and I respectfully request its efficiency may not be injured by assigning to it inefficient Officers. Last winter Gen. Taliaferro had charge of a Brigade and he permitted it to become so demoralized that I had to abandon an important enterprise in consequence of the inefficient condition in which ꝫ reported his Brigade. Notwithstanding the demoralized condition of his ꞵgade he left and visited Richmond, thus making a second visit there within two months. His brigade since he left it, has, under other hands, become efficient, and it, as well as the others bids fair to render good service if not placed under incompetent Officers. I attach so much importance to this matter as to induce me to send this communication direct. The same statement will be forwarded through Gen. Johnston.[41]

Probably, as he penned his exasperation to General Cooper, he thought back to a remark he had made not so long before in a letter to the Hon. William Porcher Miles of the Confederate Congress. He had been complaining about the political generals who were ruining the efficiency of the army, aided by the destructive election system, and had written:

> I know one general officer who is so incompetent for his position, as to be unable to take proper care of his command in ordinary campaign duty. —What can be expected of such an officer in battle? The trouble in the case that I refer to, results from want of Military information, judgement, nerve and force of character. Merit should be the only basis of promotion.

An unintentionally self-revealing postscript had closed the letter: "Whilst I highly prize Military education, yet something more is required to make a general." [42]

Taliaferro reported on Sunday, the thirteenth of April, which offered some consolation. Taking solace in the Lord's work, which reminded a humble Christian of the path of duty, Jackson left headquarters for the camps to pass out religious tracts. Even if he could not have the "privilege of hearing the word of life," there was satisfaction in doing Christian labor. It was hard, sometimes, to remember humility, but all things worked for the good of a true Christian.

Taliaferro, for his part, shared Jackson's dismay at his reassignment to the Valley District. To Johnston he had expressed his fear that Jackson's animosity remained strong against him and that surely it would reduce his chances to succeed as a brigade commander. Since he had so recently won his promotion, it seemed hard to begin service under such a handicap. Johnston had been sympathetic, but Jackson needed general officers and Taliaferro had to go. He had been right, Jackson had not forgotten. Nothing was said openly to wound the new brigadier's feelings, but he felt the chill at headquarters.

Taliaferro reacted in a Jacksonesque way. He got mad. "I determined to do my duty," he recalled later, "the best way I could and satisfy [myself] if I did not satisfy Gen. Jackson. I determined to disabuse his mind by my conduct of any personal feelings against him, and try to let him judge of me by my subsequent actions." An additional irritation increased the difficulty of Taliaferro's position: he had been sent to command Fulkerson's brigade, not Burks's. He was not needed for Fulkerson's brigade, but he took over. Having expressed his displeasure officially, Jackson let matters stand and gave Taliaferro a chance. He would not be sorry. [43]

Petty irritations ruffled the feelings of some regimental officers. Garnett's dismissal still rankled, and Jackson's cool manner toward several colonels who came to headquarters tended to produce personal recriminations against the general. One colonel, curtly shut off in conversation with Jackson, vowed never to go into his headquarters again, unless ordered. Another, the able A. C. Cummings of the Thirty-third Virginia, became disgusted with Jackson and quietly refused to run for reelection. Losing a man like Cummings showed something was seriously wrong. The election system, considered downright subversive by Jackson, tended to disorganize the brigades rather than to improve conditions. None of these things outwardly disturbed Jackson, although he felt most of them deeply. Only one command problem disturbed his exterior calm. It was a matter involving Ashby.

A mass move had begun in the infantry units during the army's reorganization to shift to the cavalry. Regulations prevented that, but the attempts brought to a head some unpleasant matters of discipline in Ashby's command. Ashby claimed, for one thing, that special orders from the Secretary of War authorized him to recruit cavalry, infantry, and artillery into a sort of legion. Consequently, while Jackson might forbid men already enlisted to change service, he could not stop Ashby's securing new men for his command.[44]

Ordinarily there would have been no real problem, but since Ashby had no brigade or regimental organization—the cavalry remained divided into twenty-one companies—the larger his force grew, the more demoralized it would become. The issue had to be handled carefully and cautiously, for Ashby's popularity with his men transcended all bounds. Jackson himself liked and vastly admired him and in time would say that "as a partisan officer I never knew his superior."[45] True, inexperience had led Ashby to give an erroneous estimate of enemy numbers at Kernstown, but he had made up for that by conspicuous gallantry during the battle and ever since. Clinging like a leech to the Federal advance, he had perfected his intelligence-gathering capacity to almost fantastic accuracy. Jackson could trust him now without question.[46]

Nothing dented the bond of loyalty Ashby's men felt for him, and it was understandable. He was a rare sort of man, a man with a mission. Ashby, said his troopers, lived to kill Yankees. He was revenging the murder—for that was what it amounted to—of his brother Richard. Implacable, deadly, he hunted the enemy. All around him hung an aura of glamour, for he was the handsome pride of an ancient clan of Fauquier County. Ashby's grandfather had been the renowned "Captain Jack" Ashby of the Revolution and the well-esteemed and comfortable Ashby family knew and was known by most of the gentry. To serve with him was to serve in a cavalier outfit.

As befitted gentlemen hunters, Turner Ashby's men were not burdened with discipline—other than that imposed by the desire to emulate the feats of their leader. Emulation of his deeds of daring became increasingly hard. For one thing, he so completely looked the part of a hero that men cast in rougher molds could hardly compete. A soldier has perhaps best described him:

He will quit a meal at anytime for a chance at a Yankee . . . perhaps killed more of them with his own hand than any one man in the State. He is the *bravest* man except for Old Jack that I ever saw. I'll describe him. Imagine a man with thick coal black hair, heavy black beard, dark skin, large black eyes, sleepey [*sic*] looking except when the Yankees are in sight —Then they *do* flash fire, so much for his face. His [?] person is small & slight. Say 5 feet 8", weight about 130 ¹, shape elegant—the best & most graceful rider in the Confederacy—He suits Old Jack to a T.⁴⁷

Everything Ashby did was a feat of some kind. Sheer physical courage transformed his activities into daily brushes with death, and his men loved him for it. The whole army talked of how he had waited on a bridge on April 17 while Jackson's rear guard crossed. He sat his white charger calmly, preparing to blow up the span. The enemy pushed close to the rear guard, and Ashby's explosives ignited slowly. The Federal cavalry rode fast toward the bridge. Still that magnificent figure stayed motionless on his storybook horse. On came the blue horsemen. The fuses burned bright, Jackson's men were across now, and Ashby was almost in the hands of the Yankee troopers. He whirled suddenly and rode furiously toward Rude's Hill and away from North River. The splendid horse soon outdistanced the pursuing Federals, but they gave him a mortal wound. He carried Ashby to the safety of his own lines and then collapsed. Brokenhearted, Ashby held the horse's head, stroked his mane, and watched him die. Kyd Douglas, who saw it all, put the feeling of the witnesses into moving words: "Thus the most splendid horseman I ever knew lost the most beautiful war-horse I ever saw." ⁴⁸

Such heroics gave to Ashby an importance far beyond his thirty-eight years and his capacities. For, despite his daring, he was a bad disciplinarian. Later, after missing a marvelous chance to break up Banks's army in retreat at Winchester on the Valley Pike, Ashby was to cry out: "Oh, that my cavalry were in place," and that anguished wish would tell much about him as administrator.

Things began to get out of hand when, on April 16, one of Lee's staff wrote inquiring whether or not the cavalry had been regimented and if the lawful number of field officers had been elected. If not, why? Only one colonel and one major for at least 1,200 sabers was ridiculous. Jackson's "prompt attention" was asked.⁴⁹ Though it implied a lack of diligence, the inquiry from Richmond provided a way out of the Ashby dilemma. Jackson now had to act, and he began by ordering the cavalry organized into two regiments and parceled out to Winder's and Taliaferro's brigades for disciplining.⁵⁰ If he felt like it, Ashby could take some consolation from the general order which gave him command of the advance and authority to apply for the troops he needed.⁵¹ But Ashby took no comfort from this order; instead he sent in his resignation.⁵² Major Funsten let it be known that he would not remain under the circumstances. Wild rumors raced around the cavalry camps. Out of a serious situation an impossible quandary had emerged. Jackson had to do something—something that would save the cavalry and at the same time not completely vitiate his authority as army commander. He needed to talk to Ashby, but the time was not propitious. Here General Winder appeared in the picture. Winder had made friends with Ashby, and as soon as he heard rumors of resignations he sought out the cavalryman, talked with him, and then rode to talk with Jackson. As a result, a personal meeting between Jackson and Ashby took place the night of the twenty-fourth.[53]

What was said became a matter of wild speculation, but the results soon became clear. The next day a general order detailed all the cavalry units recently assigned to the First and Third Brigades to Ashby. This proved a neat compromise. Ashby was not given direct command over the units, but they were detailed to his use. Ashby seemed mollified; Jackson made the best of an awkward situation. The army, depending on who liked whom, speculated that either Jackson had given Ashby back his men only after he had promised to discipline them, or that (and this version Major Harman circulated) the trouble had been settled "by Genl. Jackson backing square down," which tended to reinforce an opinion Harman had expressed only the day before that "we are in great danger from our cracked-brained Genl. . . ."[54]

Those who thought that Old Jack seemed to be slipping by letting Ashby "get away" with bucking authority would have been interested in a letter written to Alex. R. Boteler on May 6. In it Jackson said:

> With regard to Col. Ashby's promotion I would gladly favor it, if he were a good disciplinarian, but he has such bad discipline and attaches so little importance to drill, that I would regard it as a calamity to see him promoted. I desire so soon as he gives proper attention to these matters (which are so essential to success in operating with large masses of troops) to see him promoted. I recommended him for a colonelcy, and will always take pleasure in doing all I can for his advancement consistent with the interest of the Public Service.[55]

Old Stonewall's memory was long, and simply because he had to face the fact of a possible loss of his cavalry through the wounded feelings of one officer did not mean that he forgave the breach of "good order and discipline." Ashby would either learn or stay where he was.[56] In the meantime Jackson hoped to resolve the conflict of authority created by the special recruiting permit to Ashby.[57]

Reorganization problems were not confined to the brass prima donnas. The militia always seemed to be in a state of incipient disorder, a condition much aggravated in early April by the new conscription law passed by Congress. There was something terribly permanent about being put into the army for the duration of the war. Most of the men, if they were not conscientious objectors, would answer a call to militia service, but they expected to go home fairly soon. Now that was over—they would be in permanently. A great deal of grumbling could be heard about the law, but some of the militiamen from Rockingham County decided to do more than grumble—they took to the hills, holing up somewhere around Swift Run Gap.

Although the general had a healthy respect for the militia which was coming to his army daily, he acted quickly to quell the "Rockingham Rebellion" by sending out four companies of infantry and two guns to round up the deserters. An old lady living near the deserters' resort later explained that they "had mortified in the Blue Ridge, but that General Jackson sent a foot company and a critter company to ramshag the Blue Ridge and capture them." [58]

They were "ramshagged" all right. The officer in charge of rounding up the skulkers found their hiding place and literally blew them out of the mountains: one killed, twenty-four captured.[59] Similar treatment was meted out to men AWOL. The quartermaster at Staunton, which might be an attractive place to a runaway, was instructed on April 21 to "arrest every man whom you possibly can find absent from this District, unless he produces proper permission to be absent and send all such delinquents to their posts *in irons as deserters*." [60]

Such cold examples of ruthless justice helped infuse order into chaos created by the renewed rash of elections which marred the reorganization period. Had it not been for the Conscription Act many of Jackson's men would have gone home, having served their enlistment terms. Now they were mustered out and mustered right back in.[61] About all they had left was the right to elect officers, and that unfortunately included field officers. Jackson hated this provision, arguing time and again in his correspondence that merit should be the basis for commissioning and promoting officers,[62] but he scrupulously saw to it that elections took place in his army.

After reenlisting, the men supposedly were entitled to a ninety-day leave, and this practice helped to riddle the ranks. Despite the stiffening effect of hard application of the Articles of War, Jackson was not encouraged by conditions in mid-April. Arms were hard to obtain for the militia units—so scarce, in fact, that he was forced to ask for pikes! [63] Richmond seemed to take almost no interest in helping the valley area, despite a brief moment in early April. It had taken time for the full import of the battle of Kernstown to sink in at Richmond, but on April 9 Congress had passed resolutions of thanks to Maj. Gen. Thomas J. Jackson and "the officers and men under his command for their gallant and meritorious service" in the battle of Kernstown. The resolutions had been sent to the Army of the Valley by General Johnston, who issued a congratulatory order of his own.[64]

On only one other front did Jackson now have to complete reorganization—his staff. Kernstown had showed that much improvement could be made in the work of Jackson's personal aides. In late March he wrote his old Lexington friend, the Reverend Robert L. Dabney, about his joining the army's official family.

> If you come as a Chaplain, I will take special pains to see that neither you nor your family shall have cause for regret. But if you desire strictly Military duty, and you can secure a commission, I will give you a corresponding position.[65]

It was the general rather than the deacon who wrote again on April 8, enclosing an application for Dabney's services to the Secretary of War, and urging Dabney to take the enclosure to Richmond,

> get the appointment and join me at once; provided you can make your arrangements to remain with me during the remainder of the war. Your rank will be that of Major, your duties will require early rising and industry. . . . [P.S.] Your duties would be such that you would not have an opportunity for preaching except on the Sabbath.[66]

There were numerous reasons now for having only the most diligent men for staff duties. With the militia reinforcements coming to the valley army, increasingly difficult problems of supply and logistics had to be handled by the staff. Although Dabney's profession was the clergy, he was known to Jackson as a man of great general competence.[67] It would be a comfort to have him close to hand, even though he could preach only occasionally. His presence might stimulate the Lord's work in the army. Possibly, as Jackson wrote Anna, "it may be an army of the living God as well as of its country." [68] To Dabney, Jackson added a fervent prayer: "I am thankful to God for sending so many of His children into this army and my prayer is, that He will continue to send them, and that He will bless them and those with whom they cast in their lot." [69]

Other members of Stonewall's staff would be glad to have Dabney around. The men, most of them, were young, but they were pious, and felt that army life had greased the backslides. If Dabney had any sense of humor at all, he would fit in happily. Sandie Pendleton, only twenty-two, impressed at least one of his colleagues as a "man of fine sense & acquirements," while Dr. McGuire, a professional twenty-six, was "one of the Bro. George sort of men, blunt, good humor & full of honest life." Lieutenant Boswell, the Chief of Engineers, "is an excellent good natured honest Presbyterian of Ala. formerly of Fauquier Co. . . . has a sweetheart in Fauquier . . . and he talks much about her . . . is one of your wide awake smart young men." The energetic topographical engineer, who thus characterized his fellows, cheerfully bore the nickname "Mr. Lipkiss" while the army was near Rude's Hill—one of the Dutch girls gave it to him because she could not pronounce Hotchkiss.[70] Likable, energetic, jovial they all were, but they were also able or the general would not have appointed them.

From all indications, the army's work would start soon. Digesting his daily reports from Ashby and his rotating infantry supports,[71] Jackson realized that the enemy had at last piled up enough troops to justify an advance toward the Confederate Army. He had been hoping for some time to get sufficient reinforcements to justify an advance himself, but the only help Johnston could offer—and that tentatively—was the division under Gen. Richard S. Ewell, numbering some 6,500 infantry and 500 cavalry.

Johnston had his own problems. For some time he had been holding the line of the Rapidan River, but as McClellan's scheme for approaching the Confederate capital from the Virginia peninsula began to develop, Johnston abandoned the Rapidan line and pulled his army south to cover Richmond. When he left the river he uncovered Jackson's little army. Johnston knew it, and sent Jackson new instructions. Banks must be kept away from the depot town of Staunton, where he would be much too close to the main Richmond supply line and would completely dominate the rich Shenandoah farm land. Far better if he could be driven entirely out of the valley, but that was probably too much to expect from Jackson's army.[72]

Aware of Jackson's exposed condition, Johnston suggested the possible attachment of Ewell's division in the upper valley and a joint attack on Banks. The harder the blow, the greater the number of men it might pin down in the valley. These new instructions opened up several possibilities.

Now that Jackson no longer had to worry about keeping between Banks and Johnston, he had more freedom to maneuver.[73] Fortunately Ewell seemed eager to cooperate in any proposed attack; the problem was where would the two forces meet? The answer depended on what Jackson thought could be done to Banks. Johnston had apparently considered Swift Run Gap the best junction point. There the combined divisions would be on the flank of any Federal advance up the valley toward Staunton and could pick a place to attack. If Banks chose to move against Jackson's force, it would be well protected in the mountains and could easily beat off an assault. But Jackson had not yet made up his mind about how to use the Massanutton. He might wish to get behind Banks by using the New Market–Luray road, or he might wish to meet Ewell farther north.

Banks took a hand in the proceedings by advancing from Strasburg and pushing Jackson along the Valley Pike. Much to the irritation of Major Harman, Jackson insisted on moving his large wagon train well ahead of the army, leaving nothing behind. Harman would not have objected had he been told what Jackson intended doing, but he was not. Consequently he grew alarmed for the safety of his base, fearing that Jackson would leave Staunton to the scavengers of Banks.[74]

As his column marched south, Jackson mulled over possible courses of action. On April 18 he and his staff rode to Harrisonburg, where Stonewall showed peculiar interest in making arrangements for dividing his wagon train, sending part south toward Staunton and keeping part with the army. On the nineteenth camps were established near Conrad's Store.[75]

On the twentieth a strange visitor came to see Jackson—Brig. Gen. Edward Johnson, better known as "Allegheny" Johnson because he had so long held the top of the Allegheny Mountains west of Staunton against all comers. He and Old Jack conferred for long hours.[76] Then the tough-looking Johnson rode off to his little band of men on the mountain. General Jackson was reaching an important decision. Lee suggested to him on April 30 that since no other troops could be sent to the valley, he try a union not only with Ewell, but also with Johnson, who had probably close to 2,000 men.[77] With the combined forces something serious might be done to Banks.

Jackson accepted the over-all suggestion—he doubtless had thought of it for some time—but considered long how to bring about the junction of the three forces while preventing Banks from receiving reinforcement in exactly the same way. The big problem was how to join Edward Johnson's little army without permitting Johnson's opponent, Gen. R. H. Milroy, to reach Banks.

11

"GOD BLESSED OUR ARMS

WITH VICTORY"

—JACKSON

GENERAL, I will start at once if I can get a horse." With this promise began one of the roughest adventures in the young life of Kyd Douglas. The summons from Jackson had come suddenly on the road to Harrisonburg—Douglas rode quickly through the rain to the general,[1] touched his cap, and waited for orders. From the folds of his dripping rubber cape Jackson took a paper and handed it to Douglas with the request that he take it to General Ewell on the other side of the Blue Ridge. A vital message, Old Jack could not trust it to a regular courier, especially since it had to be delivered by daylight the next day.

"For a moment I was stampeded, paralyzed," recalled Douglas later. He had no idea of the country, the roads or exact information as to Ewell's location. But Old Jack was offering him a matchless opportunity: "I was being weighed in the balance right there."

With a horse provided by a friend, Jackson's youngest staff officer prepared for his desperate ride. All he had to go on was that Ewell seemed to be "somewhere near Culpeper Court House," and someone told him to start in the direction of Stanardsville. As he mounted to ride for the Blue Ridge, Douglas heard the general's voice calling after him, "Good night. . . . A successful and pleasant ride!" Just at that moment the remark sounded peculiarly sarcastic, kindly meant or not![2]

Round the base of Massanutton, through tiny McGaheysville, across the South Fork of Shenandoah, the rider sped to Conrad's Store. With each mile the rain-sheathed Blue Ridge grew more ominous, and the soaked young lieutenant stopped long enough at Conrad's to get a "small bottle of whiskey for an emergency"; on, then, up Swift Run Gap.

Darkness and rain blotted out the road, and horse and rider traveled by instinct. "At times I heard the water rush under us and across the road and tumble in torrents so far down below that I knew we were traveling on perilous edges." Never had Douglas felt so alone.

At the summit a fellow rider was encountered—a courier going from Ewell to Jackson. He traded directions for Douglas's bottle, and Stonewall's messenger rode on. At Stanardsville time was wasted in a fruitless effort to get another horse, a wrong fork in the road took more time, and finally Douglas roused a farmer and asked him for a mount. Awakened by a muddy, wilted rider on a spent horse, the farmer declined, but invited Douglas in.

But daylight would soon break. Douglas called to the farmer: "My dear friend, I am an officer of Stonewall Jackson's staff, carrying an important message, and I must have a fresh horse." "The devil!" Bang went the upstairs window. Soon Douglas heard him shouting, "Saul! Saul! Drat that sleepy nigger! There you are—run you woolly head, bring out the big black mare and be quick about it!" Farmer, Saul, and horse soon appeared, and in the light of a lantern Douglas exchanged bridle and saddle and mounted up. The farmer threw the light of his lantern on Douglas's face, and said tenderly, "Good luck. I have a boy, maybe your age, with Stonewall Jackson."

Again riding hard, Douglas drove the black mare into Madison Court House and picked up another mount at the courier station. Accidents continued to plague the ride. Not far from Madison, the new horse dropped dead, leaving Douglas stranded in the pitch dark. Fortunately a Negro, sent by his mistress to fetch a doctor, took word of Douglas's trouble to a nearby settlement. Soon, mounted on another horse, he again raced for Ewell's headquarters. One more change of horses brought him to Culpeper Court House just at the crack of light on the horizon.

Culpeper seemed exceedingly martial. Reveille could be heard in all directions, and soon Douglas ran into a group of officers sitting their horses. He dashed up, found he was addressing Gen. Richard Taylor, and explained his mission. Taylor's orders from Ewell were to march, but to Douglas's discomfort, he was to march "evidently in the wrong direction." Suggesting that nothing be done until further orders from Ewell, Douglas borrowed a fresh mount and rode for Brandy Station and Ewell. Six interminable miles later, he reached Old Baldy's quarters.

Ewell, just up, greeted the young messenger with his usual popeyed interest, listened to Douglas's explanation of his orders, and read the soaked dispatch. As the exhausted young staff officer collapsed on the general's cot, Ewell pondered the message he brought. Jackson wanted help quickly—the enemy appeared to be moving against him. Ewell had to come at once.

Exactly where his division would join Jackson seemed to be an open question. Jackson's correspondence throughout most of April had indicated possible cooperation between his little Army of the Valley and Ewell's force. But the odd VMI professor's changes of mind were proving disturbing to Dick Ewell's dyspepsia. Jackson talked of Fisher's Gap, then Swift Run Gap, then seemed unable to decide between them.[3] Now, according to the dispatch, Jackson had decided on Swift Run Gap and wanted Ewell to march quickly toward Harrisonburg. Patiently, Ewell changed his plans, sent a copy of Jackson's orders to the Adjutant General of the army and took the road for Gordonsville and Stanardsville.[4] Then a refreshed Douglas was sent back across the Blue Ridge to tell his general that orders would be obeyed.

Jackson greeted the news with his characteristic "Very good." Still, there were many problems to consider. Some of these the commander of the Army of the Valley discussed in dispatches to General Lee, who had fortunately assumed charge of military operations outside of the Richmond theater.[5]

Lee had made it plain that he favored a joint attack by Jackson and Ewell on Banks, either directly or by getting behind him. If that appeared impossible, then Ewell might be used near Fredericksburg, where Federal pressure mounted. One thing was certain: "The blow, wherever struck, must, to be successful, be sudden and heavy."[6] With this Jackson fully agreed.

Jackson's position at Conrad's Store in Elk Run Valley had advantages; situated on the flank of the Valley Pike, his army threatened any Union advance toward Staunton, and at the same time was protected by the Blue Ridge from direct assault. Elk Run Valley led up to Swift Run Gap, and consequently Jackson could join with Ewell easily, or if necessary he could safely leave the Shenandoah. Elk Run Valley had some disadvantages; if the bridge over the South Fork at Conrad's Store were taken by the enemy, Jackson's force would be neatly bottled up. A bold enemy commander would see this weakness and take advantage of it, but Jackson had sized up his adversary and felt that Banks could not be lured near the Blue Ridge.[7]

Moving slowly and without apparent concern about Jackson's doings, Banks had advanced part of his army to Harrisonburg on April 26 and established his headquarters at New Market. With his columns spread out between those towns, his army offered a "golden opportunity for striking a blow," and Jackson looked for ways of attacking. If Lee could only spare another 5,000 men, the task would be simple; if not, "I will watch an opportunity for attacking some exposed point."[8]

By April 29, when Banks had moved the bulk of his forces south to Harrisonburg, Jackson had decided on three possible plans of attack. They were the result of much thought and no little prayer. Unsure of what to do about Banks, he had slowly withdrawn to Elk Run to evolve the proper strategy. There were several uncertainties which complicated the situation, but "unless you send me large reinforcements," Old Jack wrote Lee on the twenty-ninth,

> I am disposed . . . to adopt one of three plans, viz, either to leave General Ewell here to threaten Banks' rear in the event of his advancing on Staunton, and move with my command rapidly on the force in front of General Edward Johnson, or else co-operating with General Ewell, to attack the enemy's detached force between New Market and the Shenandoah, and, if successful in this, then to press forward and get in Banks' rear at New Market, and thus induce him to fall back; the third is to pass down the Shenandoah to Sperryville, and thus threaten Winchester via Front Royal. I believe that this would cause the enemy to fall back. From Sperryville I could move either in the direction of Front Royal, Warrenton, or, if my command should be opposed by too large a Federal force, it could turn off toward Culpeper Court-House. To get in Banks' rear with my present force would be rather a dangerous undertaking, as I would have to cross the river and immediately cross the Massanutten Mountain, during which the enemy would have decidedly the advantage of position. Of the three plans I give the preference to attacking the force west of Staunton, for, if successful, I would afterward only have Banks to contend with, and in doing this would be re-enforced by General Edward Johnson, and by that time you might be able to give me re-enforcements, which, united with the troops now under my control, would enable me to defeat Banks; and if he should be routed and his command destroyed, nearly all our own forces here could, if necessary, cross the Blue Ridge to Warrenton, Fredericksburg, or any other threatened point. I have written to General Edward Johnson to know what force, in addition to his command, would be required for a successful blow in his vicinity. If I receive an answer justifying a move in that direction I may leave here to-morrow via Port Republic.[9]

Of these plans no one in Jackson's army knew a whisper. Ewell, who had ridden over the Ridge for a long conference on April 28,[10] had some idea of what was in the wind, but the part his troops were to play remained vague. He knew that his division was to cross the mountains via Swift Run Gap, and to occupy the camps of Jackson's men in Elk Run. Quietly and quickly this was done on the morning of the thirtieth. Apparently Ewell was to stay at Conrad's Store and threaten Banks's flank.

News from Johnson had been good.[11] Without waiting for a reply from Lee concerning his three plans of action, Jackson adopted his favorite. Early that rainy day Jackson's trains took the road toward Port Republic, followed in the afternoon by the infantry.[12] Nobody knew why or where they were going. All of Old Jack's actions for the last several weeks had been clothed in such secrecy that Major Harman, the harried quartermaster, concluded that "as sure as . . . I live Jackson is

a cracked man...." With the roads turning to quagmires in the tor-
rential rain, the general insisted that a long wagon train precede the
army. Harman could not understand why this concern for the wagons
when Jackson had admonished all infantry commanders to pare down
the baggage of their men. There was no sense in what was going on.

Jackson had issued a series of orders for the morning of April 30
which, had anyone been able to see them all together, made extremely
good sense. Ashby's men were ordered to push forward toward the
enemy positions near Harrisonburg in what seemed designed as a reconnaissance in force. Orders to the infantry, artillery, and staff officers indicated plans for a march across the Blue Ridge, via Brown's Gap, possibly the first leg of a quick dash to Richmond. Ashby's advance toward
Banks was in reality a screening move for the march of the main army
toward Port Republic. The infantry, guns, and trains were indeed leaving the valley, but only for a brief moment. Jackson planned to strike
the Virginia Central Railroad at Mechum Station, entrain his troops,
and head west for Staunton. The Army of the Valley was marching to
help Allegheny Johnson.

The march was a horror. Not only did the wagons and guns sink
axle-deep in mire, but the infantry had to fight to keep out of the frequent quicksands. Jackson and his personal staff left the old camp-
ground late in the afternoon of the thirtieth and rode hard to bypass
the crawling column. When the general and his entourage detoured
across a sandy field to get to the head of the marching men, they were
greeted with lusty cheers. Old Jack kept his head down and drove
Little Sorrel splashing through the mud. Finally, by nightfall, headquarters was established at "Lewiston," the hospitable home of General
Lewis, a good thirteen miles from Conrad's; but the main army camped
a scant five miles from where the march began.

May 1 proved another drenching day. The general and his staff
"spent the day with large details of soldiers, making and repairing roads
and helping the wagons and artillery along through the mud and quicksands." [13] Again five miles was all the distance covered, and Jackson
kept his headquarters at "Lewiston." [14] The next day, after hard, sweating labor by most of the army including the commanding general, the
trains and wagons reached the entrance to Brown's Gap. Fortunately
the sun came out and things began to dry off.

The warmth of a balmy spring day descending, the mud-spattered
army crossed Brown's Gap on the third, heading for the Virginia Central station at Mechum River. As Old Jack came down the eastern side
of the Blue Ridge in the afternoon, he stopped long enough at the foot
of the grade to watch some of the Stonewall Brigade wash away the
remains of three days' sloshing through the mud. The men looked happy,
splashing around in the clear mountain brook; they seemed little the

worse for a three-day trail which reminded some of the march to Romney. Sitting the sorrel for a while, Stonewall looked at his boys, then galloped off toward the railroad.[15] He arrived at Mechum River Station to find the van of his army there and received word that the rest of the men would be up the next day.

As the line of gray infantry swung along the road leading out of the valley at Brown's Gap, the morale of the men probably sagged a little.[16] It was hard leaving the valley to the kind attentions of Banks and possibly of Milroy. True, Ewell stood at Conrad's watching the Federals, but if Old Jack was on the way to Richmond it was certain that a general concentration of Confederate troops around the capital was under way. No one could be surprised at the move; it was common gossip that Joe Johnston needed all the men he could get to hold McClellan in check on the peninsula.

Some distance away, Maj. Gen. Nathaniel P. Banks, U.S.A., was doing some worrying himself. Until sometime on the first of May he had been sure that a demoralized Jackson had left the valley, but on the second he began to have grave doubts. To the Adjutant General in Washington he even suggested that it might be Stonewall's intention to go to the aid of Johnson, west of Staunton. And on May 3 he was writing Secretary Stanton that "I do not think it possible to divide our force at this time with safety." What bothered Banks most by this time was Ewell's force, which he came to think had been sent to replace Jackson's army.[17] Actually Jackson had so carefully screened his movements that by the end of the first week in May the Union high command conceived it possible that he was advancing against Milroy on the one hand, and on the other, moving against General McDowell at Fredericksburg.[18]

Jackson's madcap maneuvers also baffled the citizens of the loyal Confederate town of Staunton. The daily lives of the people there had for several weeks revolved around rumors of Jackson's movements. They had been panicked by a reckless letter from Major Harman, prophesying doom, which stampeded the town into an evacuation of most stores and vehicles and the removal of bank capital and official archives—only to hear several days later that the information had not come from the general but from his quartermaster! Harman had suffered for that and other instances of indiscretion. Chastising him severely, Jackson provoked him into threats of resignation; at the same time, the major's letters grew less informative.[19]

Old Allegheny Johnson's movements, west of the town, mystified some of the residents. In late April his small force had fallen back from the Shenandoah Mountain toward West View, and seemed on the point of retreating right into the town. Johnson had apparently ridden east of Staunton for a conference with Jackson but had come back tight-lipped. Rumors of Jackson's movements flew rapidly at the end of April, and on

May 1 four distinct stories were around town: (1) Old Jack was on the way to Winchester; (2) he was marching toward McGaheysville, to engage Banks; (3) he was at Port Republic the night before and Ewell was at Swift Run Gap; and (4) Jackson was at Harrisonburg. When the express rider came to town in the afternoon he told anxious listeners that the general was at Swift Run Gap when he left that morning and that there had been no signs of a move. All these conflicting stories added to the melancholy of a rainy day.

On the second the news seemed confirmed that Jackson's men were at Port Republic and that Allegheny Johnson had orders to move, probably down the valley. A new rumor had it that the VMI cadets were ordered to Staunton. They were to arrive on the third. By the time the nattily clad boys moved into the large brick building next to the Central Bank, the whole populace had been shattered by word that the Army of the Valley had left them to their fate. Across the Blue Ridge via Brown's Gap had gone Jackson and his men. A few people, trying hard to boost their flagging spirits, said that the story was too ridiculous to be true; others said it was a strategic move and that Stonewall would come back via Rockfish Gap. Strategy or whatever, most townspeople were sick. One observer noted with interest that a half-dozen ambulances went down to Jackson that day—"Strange if he is moving across Blue R."

A frightened, rattled Staunton settled down for the night. But not for long. At 2 A.M. Sunday, May 4, General Johnson, spending the night in town, received a hurry-up call to his army: The enemy was advancing in huge numbers against him. Through a long numb morning various stories of what was happening to Old Allegheny filtered back from the west. Over 10,000 Yankees were advancing on him; his pickets had been driven in; he was fighting desperate skirmishes at North Mountain and Buffalo Gap; various enemy forces were said to be threatening his flank.

Citizens with an appetite ate hasty lunches and waited for more news. Shortly after dinnertime came the sharp alarm of an engine whistle. Crowds rushed to the depot—was it Johnson's army retreating, or was he receiving aid? The freight train due the day before puffed into the station, and a disgusted throng went home. But shortly after three o'clock the ominous wail of another engine chilled the people. This time no disappointment was in store. A long, long train, pulled by no less than two locomotives, rumbled in from the east.

As the citizens looked on in amazement, car after car moved into town, filled with soldiers. Stonewall Jackson had come to save Staunton! [20]

Had Jackson known of the confusion his movements created in all directions he would have been pleased, but hardly surprised, for security measures were worked out to a fine point. Ashby's cavalry had succeeded in keeping Banks uneasy about Ewell's and Jackson's doings for days, and the practice of sealing off the army as it passed through the countryside kept word of its exact location from leaking out. When he reached Mechum River Station on May 4, Jackson had been careful to picket all roads leading to the settlement. On the way to Staunton he had been careful not to divulge too much information even in his dispatches to Ewell, and that officer shared the general bewilderment at what Stonewall was doing. Sitting at Swift Run Gap, Dick Ewell had bemused himself with thoughts of attacking Banks via Luray Gap, a possibility which he had talked over with General Jackson. On May 3, from Brown's Gap, Old Jack had vetoed the scheme as "too hazardous so long as Banks keeps a strong force near New Market," [21] but beyond suggesting Ewell might learn more of Yankee movements by the use of spies, Jackson offered no constructive ideas. Ewell fumed. During the next several days a weird assortment of orders and counterorders came from "Fool Tom Jackson," as one of his ex-cadets called him in conversation with Ewell.

On May 4, writing in his hasty sprawling hand from White Hall, Jackson told his nervous subordinate that "General Edward Johnson informs me that yesterday evening a regiment of the enemy from the west advanced within 16 miles of him, and he requests me to 'come up as soon as possible!'" While Jackson pressed ahead, Ewell was asked to "do what you can consistently with the safety of your command to prevent Banks giving assistance to the forces in front of Johnson." [22] Another dispatch the next day reported that the Yankees supposedly had left Harrisonburg, and "if the enemy has advanced in the direction of the Warm Springs it must be for the purpose of effecting a junction with Milroy, and if you can do anything to call him back I hope that you will do so." [23]

To these continued orders were added others coming from General Lee, and under the avalanche Ewell became increasingly edgy. Jackson specifically enjoined him not to leave the valley "so long as Banks is in it and I am on the expedition of which I spoke to you." At the same time Lee wondered if Ewell could cut off a body of union troops at Culpeper Court House. [24]

All this was too much for the unruly stomach of Old Baldy. Frustrated and uncertain, he poured out his troubles to his niece:

I have spent two weeks of the most unhappy I ever remember. . . . I have been keeping one eye on Banks, one on Jackson, all the time jogged up from Richmond, until I am sick and worn down. Jackson wants me to watch Banks. At Richmond, they want me elsewhere and call me off, when, at the same time, I am compelled to remain until that enthusiastic fanatic comes to some conclusion. Now I ought to be en route to Gordonsville, at this place, and going to Jackson, all at the same time. . . . I have a bad headache, what with the bother and folly of things. I never suffered as much from dyspepsia in my life. As an Irishman would say, 'I'm kilt entirely.' [25]

Had Jackson known of Ewell's state of mind he doubtless would have moved west from Mechum with much misgiving. But he need not have worried. Though Ewell fussed and fulminated, he would stand like a rock.

When Jackson and his staff rode into Staunton Sunday afternoon, May 4, the general found that his advanced troops had placed the town in wraps. Pickets on all roads had kept a lot of country people in the confines of the city, but no leak had occurred. His troops were in grand spirits, despite their tattered appearance—the subject of much comment in Staunton—and were anxious to be on with whatever business Old Jack had cooked up. The army rested during part of May 5 and all of the sixth. Plans depended on Johnson's situation.

West of Staunton affairs appeared critical. Out beyond Buffalo Gap Johnson's brigade of some 2,800 men was taking up a line of march toward the force under Gen. R. H. Milroy, which constituted the advance element of Maj. Gen. John C. Fremont's army. The Yankee plan appeared to be for Milroy to join Banks on the Harrisonburg–Warm Springs road, and then for the joint force to take Staunton.[26] Johnson would have to be reinforced, since Milroy, supported by Gen. Robert C. Schenck, could count on having about 6,000 men in case he had to fight.[27]

Johnson's men were well on their way west when the three brigades under Jackson marched after them early on the morning of May 7. Taking his own men into account, along with those of Johnson, Jackson was going toward the enemy with no less than 10,000 men. If all went well, he would be able to hurl superior numbers at the enemy—a favorite bit of strategy.

Skirmishing began on May 7, but the real fighting took place on the eighth, near the village of McDowell, some twenty-five miles west of Staunton. McDowell was not much of a battle although it raged hot and angry for some time and casualties were high. Jackson's army beat off a determined attack by Milroy on Sitlington's Hill, which dominated the field, and which formed the objective of both forces. Jackson's plan was to flank Milroy's position during the night of the eighth but Milroy tried a direct assault on the hill before the flank move against him could take shape.

The rugged nature of the ground restricted the number of men Jackson could get into action, which helped keep something of a balance for Milroy. The Union attack was determined, well led and well sustained, but it was repulsed. The repulse was achieved by Jackson's men without the use of artillery; again the ground worked against them and no guns could safely be brought up the hill.[28]

The Confederates could hardly brag about what they had done. Milroy had been beaten back, had been forced to abandon the battlefield and to retreat during the night of May 8–9. But he had inflicted 498 casualties, while sustaining only 256. A great deal might be said by faultfinders about the way the battle had shaped up. Still, Milroy had been repulsed, and Jackson knew he would retreat.

Jackson showed no disappointment; Milroy would not reach Banks. As for himself, Stonewall was thoroughly exhausted, having spent most of the day close to the fighting. Reaching his temporary quarters about one o'clock on the morning of May 9, he told Jim Lewis, his personal servant, that he was too tired to eat supper, threw himself on the bed, and was soon fast asleep.

In the morning Jackson saw he had been right; Milroy was gone. He had left his campfires burning during the night and had slipped away while they covered his withdrawal. Damage to the Confederates was high. As Jackson surveyed the field he was grieved to recall that Allegheny Johnson had been incapacitated by a bad leg wound. Several other field officers were killed or wounded. But there could be no time wasted on the killed and maimed. Victory came only to the thankful and to the enterprising.

"God blessed our arms with victory at McDowell yesterday." With this humble telegram, Jackson gave his preliminary report of the battle to the authorities in Richmond. That done, he joined in the pursuit. Milroy and Schenck must be pressed hard in their northward rush to meet Fremont. Much was to be gained by keeping the pressure on— panic might lead to rout, which in turn could infect all of Fremont's army. The farther the Federals could be shoved back, the less chance they would have to join with Banks.

Nothing went right with the pursuit. Jackson's infantry could not start as rapidly as he desired; they had to wait for rations. By the time the gray column took the road toward Franklin behind the small force of cavalry, the Yankees had a commanding head start. Forced marches on the tenth and eleventh brought the van of Jackson's army closer to the enemy, but the Yankee rear guard set fire to the forests lining the road, and Jackson's infantry was enveloped in dense smoke, sniped at from every bend in the road and shelled intermittently. In this foggy game of hide-and-seek Jackson's men spent Sunday, the second Sabbath in a row they had been kept at hard work. Jackson was much disturbed by thus violating the Lord's Day, particularly since He had so blessed their cause at McDowell. But again the general yielded to military considerations.[29] Better to pursue the enemy while there remained a chance to wreck him than permit him to escape unscathed to ravage the valley.

After making sure that everything possible had been done to block all roads leading east [30]—ensuring against Milroy's and Fremont's racing to Banks—Jackson concluded to halt the pursuit. The Yankee smoke screen had been so effective, Jackson admitted to his Adjutant General, that it made an advance during daylight as dangerous as at night. The smoke, plus the proximity of Fremont's reinforced main army, dictated a halt. Since the major objective had been accomplished—the prevention of Milroy's joining Banks—and the enemy was retreating in some disorder, Jackson felt he could safely turn back to the Shenandoah Valley. In fact, the sooner he rejoined Ewell the better. The time had come when serious attention could be given to destroying General Banks.

During the morning of Monday, May 12, Jackson issued one of his rare congratulatory orders to the army. Characteristic of Old Blue Light, the order read:

> *Headquarters, Valley District,*
> *Near Franklin, Va., May 12, 1862*
>
> *Soldiers of the Army of the Valley and the N. West:*
>
> I congratulate you on your victory at McDowell. I request you to unite with me, this morning, in thanksgiving to Almighty God, for thus having crowned your arms with success, and in prayer that He will continue to lead you on, from victory to victory, until our independence shall be established, and make you that people whose God is the Lord. The Chaplains will hold Divine service at 10 o'clock, A.M., this day, in their respective Regiments.
>
> *[T. J. Jackson]* [31]

A gentle sun warmed the valley of the South Branch as the different units knelt in prayer. Doubtless on this particular occasion the Reverend Dr. Dabney took the opportunity to desert his military duties for a session in the pulpit. The general himself rode through the camps, seeing that the services were under way.

As the sorrel jogged stolidly along, Jackson spied a young captain standing in the road, meditatively smoking his pipe. When Jackson drew near, the young man whirled, jerked off his cap, and stammered, "Good morning, General." Off came the little kepi cap, and then, in mildly quizzical tones: "Captain, is divine service going on in your camp?" A moment's awkward silence. "I don't know, sir," came the honest reply. "Where is your Colonel's quarters?" Extremely embarrassed, the captain pointed. "Shall I take you to them, sir?" For an agonizing moment the ungainly figure sat his little sorrel, looking at the hapless truant. "Yes," came the reply.

Following the captain's lead, the general reined up his horse, and said, "I see service is going on." Looking down at his guide with deep blue eyes, Jackson chided him: "Captain, the next time I order divine service to be held won't you promise me to attend?" A muffled "Yes, sir," ended the interview. As the young man watched, Jackson rode on to the assembly of men, tied Little Sorrel to a tree, took off his hat, and walked in among the reverent throng.

The captain followed him, still keeping an eye on Old Jack. The sermon was almost over and a light rain was beginning to fall. When the last hymn ended, rain was coming down in earnest, and by the time the minister had pronounced benediction, the men were drenched. Stonewall Jackson, the captain recorded, "stood with his head uncovered, his arms crossed on his chest, and his form bowed. As he stood thus I thought it, and have always thought it since, a sublime exhibition of his noble religious character." Deacon Jackson had not forgotten how to work for the Lord.[32]

After the troops had eaten, Jackson's infantry filed into the road for a return to the Shenandoah Valley. There would be no dawdling. The trip from Swift Run Gap to McDowell, with its agonizing delays, had pointed up anew the need for better marching discipline. On May 13 Jackson put into effect a whole new marching regime, designed to obtain maximum speed with minimum trouble. This regime, carefully considered and based on close observation, was to transform the veterans under Old Jack from infantry into "foot cavalry" and to make them the fastest and hardest-hitting force the country had ever seen:

> Canteens must be filled before marching and during halts only. Upon leaving Camp when not in the vicinity of the enemy the troops will march with unfurled colors and music until the command 'route step' is given by the Regtl. commander. Upon leaving Camp and after each subsequent rest, the men will carry their arms and march as though they were on drill, until they have advanced two or three Hundred yards when the command 'route step' will be given, when the company commanders will fall to the rear of their companies & the men will carry their arms at will until the command 'attention' is given by brigade Commanders which will precede every halt & be repeated by each of the Regimental Commanders. At this command Captains will return to the front of their Companies which will march and carry their arms as they were previous to the command 'route step.' Every hour the Infantry must be halted, arms stacked on one side of the road, ranks broken and men rested for ten minutes.
>
> About 12 or 1 oclock the halt will be an hour that the men may take their lunch. The sick of each Regt. will be in charge of a Regimental Officer, who will accompany his ambulances immediately in the rear of his Regt. If the Regimental Qr.Mr. has any empty wagons they move with the Ambulances for the purpose of carrying the sick, their arms accoutrements, & Knapsacks. The men will carry their Knapsacks.
>
> Nothing will be carried in the baggage wagons except entrenching tools, cooking untensils [sic] and officers baggage. Officers baggage must be in separate wagons.
>
> No man unless he is too unwell to keep up with his company, will be

permitted to leave ranks, except in case of Necessity and then only for a few minutes, and during this time he will not be permitted to take his Musket with him, but it will be carried by another man whom the Company Commander will detail for that purpose. If a man is too unwell to keep up with his Company, his Comp. Commander will see that he is examined by the Regimental Medical Officer in charge of the Ambulances and if excused by him from marching he will be carried with the sick. Rolls will be called immediately before leaving Camp & also immediately after arriving in Camp and at such other times as Brigade or Regimental Commanders may indicate for the purpose of verifying the presence of their men, and delinquents will be duly punished. During marches men will be required not only to keep in ranks but the proper distance will be preserved as far as practicable, and thus convert a march, as it should be, into an important drill, that of habituating the men to keep in ranks. Each Brigade Commander will see that the foregoing orders are strictly adhered to, and for this purpose will from time to time allow his command to move by him, so as to verify its condition, he will also designate one of his staff officers to do the same at such times as he may deem necessary.[33]

Quickly the men learned these regulations as the army headed back toward McDowell. Old Jack was pushing the vanguard as hard as he could. By Wednesday the column was passing over the recent battle-site, and turned east toward Staunton. Several administrative details had to be cleaned up before Jackson could leave McDowell. The VMI cadets, under General Smith and Colonel Preston, were there, having done hard and valuable duty guarding prisoners and picking up castoff equipment. General Smith explained that he now had to take his boys back to Lexington; the state would not permit them to stay longer away from their studies. Professor Jackson readily consented, and issued a flattering order, thanking the Corps for its great service in a moment of crisis.[34]

News which had been coming from Ewell in recent days made Jackson anxious for the safety of the Army of the Valley. Conflicting instructions had continued to pour into Ewell's headquarters. Lee still seemed to want him somewhere to the east, and Banks, who had begun to retire toward New Market, gave indications of quitting the Shenandoah area. If Banks were actually leaving the valley, Ewell's task would be to strike him on the way out, if possible. What did Jackson want him to do? Inaction at Swift Run Gap had almost completely unraveled Ewell's nerves.

Jackson, on May 13, wrote his peripatetic subordinate that he was on the road back and did not think Banks intended to leave the valley.

My belief is that he is aiming not to form a junction with the Fredericksburg troops, but with Fremont, and if practicable to move on Staunton before Fremont arrives. If he leaves the valley at this time, not only Winchester, but the Baltimore and Ohio Railroad would be exposed, both of which it is important to the enemy to hold. . . . If Banks goes down the valley I wish you to follow him, so that he may feel that if he leaves the valley, not only will we reoccupy it, but that he will also be liable to be attacked so soon as he shall have sufficiently weakened his forces on this side the Shenandoah.[35]

As the strategic situation was thought through, and as Hotchkiss's maps of the valley were studied, Jackson came to a decision. He would direct his army toward Harrisonburg, where a swift union with Ewell's division might make a strong attack on Banks possible. When the army halted at Lebanon Springs, Jackson had matured his plan sufficiently to tell Ewell something of it—without giving too much away. "I am now about 30 miles from Harrisonburg. I will probably remain to-morrow in my present position. What news have you from Banks? I am on my way to join you at Harrisonburg, if necessary." [36] Everything depended on Ewell. If he were suddenly ordered elsewhere, Jackson could hardly think of attacking Banks, even though he had Johnson's men with him. Ewell must stay. Fortunately General Lee seemed willing to let Jackson keep him—for a while—providing something damaging were done to Banks. Lee summed up the matter by telling Jackson what he already knew: Banks must be detained in the valley. He had to be kept away from either Fredericksburg or Richmond. On the other hand, Jackson must remember that "it may become necessary for you to come to the support of General Johnston, and hold yourself in readiness to do so if required." With that point in mind, "whatever movement you make against Banks do it speedily, and if successful drive him back toward the Potomac, and create the impression, as far as practicable, that you design threatening that line." [37]

Lee had, in essence, outlined a campaign for Jackson. It was exactly the sort of thing Old Jack enjoyed. Attack, push the defeated enemy, and wring every possible advantage—military and psychological—out of victory. A swift thrust at Banks, should it prove successful, offered exciting prospects. A victorious Confederate Army, rushing down the valley, might change the whole strategic situation in Virginia, might even relieve the pressure on Richmond. So thought Jackson, and so thought Lee.

Resolute in his mind about what he would do, Jackson kept his men at Lebanon Springs during the sixteenth, a day decreed by the President for national fasting and prayer. He attended divine services and spent part of the day in private meditation. There were "manifold sins" to be confessed, and the Lord's "favour and blessing" must be sought for the army in future battles for "all that a Christian people holds dear." [38]

While the Army of the Valley gave thanks to God and besought Him to stretch forth His arm again in this war against evil, Richard Stoddert

Ewell was being weighed in the balance—and with him Stonewall Jackson.

A crisis of command broke over Ewell's distracted headquarters. General Johnston, still commanding the Department of Northern Virginia, sent Ewell a dispatch on May 13, which altered the valley situation: "Should [Banks] cross the Blue Ridge to join General McDowell at Fredericksburg, General Jackson and yourself should move eastward rapidly. . . ." [39] This order assumed critical importance on May 17, when Ewell obtained definite intelligence that General Shields, with some 6,000 of Banks's men, had crossed the Blue Ridge.[40] No discretion was left to Ewell now. Johnston's orders made it imperative to follow Shields but still Ewell hesitated. He had received word not long before from Jackson which whetted his curiosity. Old Jack had pulled back the curtain of secrecy just enough to let Ewell glimpse a novel piece of strategy. Nothing would come of it if Johnston's orders were obeyed, but what else could be done?

"About daylight" on Sunday, May 18, Jackson and his staff, having spent the night at Mount Solon, were surprised at the sudden appearance of Old Baldy. Riding up in his nervous way, Ewell brought all his cares for discussion with Jackson. A "long consultation" concluded, Jackson, his unexpected guest, and the staff rode out to the camp of one of the brigades to attend divine service. The Reverend Dr. Dabney took the pulpit. His text was, "Come unto me, all ye that labor and are heavy laden, and I will give you rest" [41]—one that seemed peculiarly apt that day. When Ewell left, he rode away happier than when he had come.

Jackson, too, was happier. Their conversation had resulted in new hope for the move against Banks. All the orders coming from Richmond had been reviewed, and as the two talked, Ewell grew to understand better the strange man who had told him days before that through the aid of Providence he had captured Milroy's wagon train. At that time the peppery Ewell had exclaimed, "What has Providence to do with Milroy's wagon train? Mark my words, if this old fool keeps this thing up, and Shields joins McDowell, we will go up at Richmond!" But the longer he talked with the "old fool," the more he trusted him. Underneath the surface, Jackson burned with one desire—to attack. That was something Dick Ewell could appreciate.

The news from the east obviously disappointed Stonewall. Naturally Ewell would have to obey orders, though there might never again be a chance like the present one to get at Banks. With Shields gone, Banks was weak and had fallen back to Strasburg, where reports had him throwing up dirt and hiding behind trenches. Something of Jackson's anxiety to strike proved contagious. Ewell suddenly grew bold and offered to stay with Jackson if his immediate commander would let him, at least until Jackson could get further orders from Johnston.[42] To cover his subordinate in case of later trouble, Jackson wrote Ewell, reminding him he still operated within the Valley District and was still part of Jackson's army. "You will please move your command so as to encamp between New Market and Mount Jackson on next Wednesday night, unless you receive orders from a superior officer and of a date subsequent to the 16th instant." [43]

With Ewell ready to cooperate in the attack, Jackson rushed his own preparations. He ended the incipient rebellion in Taliaferro's brigade by swiftly threatening the mutineers with execution; then he suggested Harman ought to speed up his supplying of the troops, commenting that he had not been as efficient as before.[44] Again this almost resulted in Harman's resignation, but again it produced renewed efforts. Wagons, forage, grain—all manner of quartermaster stores were ordered from Staunton toward Harrisonburg. Harman was not sure where Jackson was headed, but he was collecting supplies at a central point so as not to be caught out of position. He was, in short, beginning to act like Harman again.

The long lines of gray infantry swung down the valley, heading for Harrisonburg. The men were not sure what was happening, or when they would meet Ewell's troops. But something big was up, because they were ordered to leave their knapsacks in the courthouse at Harrisonburg, and "when General Jackson ordered knapsacks to be left behind he meant business." [45]

Ewell meanwhile issued orders to strike camp and be ready to march down the Luray Valley. He had already called the force under Gen. Lawrence O'B. Branch to him from across the Blue Ridge, with the admonition that "the road to glory cannot be followed with much baggage." The natty 3,000-man Louisiana brigade under Gen. Richard Taylor, Ewell sent west of the Massanutton to join with Jackson's force near New Market in accordance with Old Jack's wishes. Ewell felt better. Action was in sight: The Confederates were sweeping down both sides of the Massanutton, and Banks still heaved up his dirt. That maniac Stonewall Jackson was about to put some of his madness into practice.

On May 20 Taylor's brigade marched swiftly down the valley to New Market.[46] A beautiful day, a fair road, and good spirits plus some little curiosity about Stonewall Jackson and his army spurred the Louisianians along.

Taylor, proud of his men, watched as they strode easily toward New Market. Finally they began to pass crowds of soldiers lining both sides of the Pike; Jackson's veterans were gawking like tourists at their reinforcements:

Neat in fresh clothing of gray with white gaiters, bands playing at the head of their regiments, not a straggler, but every man in his place, stepping jauntily as on parade . . . in open column with arms at "right shoulder shift," and rays of the declining sun flaming on polished bayonets, the brigade moved down the broad, smooth pike and wheeled on to its camping ground.[47]

But there was little time for admiration as Taylor rode off to report to the man who impressed Ewell as both genius and lunatic.[48] Stonewall Jackson was only a name to Taylor, and at that a name somewhat beclouded by Romney, Kernstown, and the apparently fruitless pursuit of Milroy. So it was without awe that he followed a staff officer's pointing finger to spy a man sitting on a rail fence hard by the road. That, he said, was Stonewall Jackson.

Approaching, I saluted and declared my name and rank, then waited for a response. Before this came I had time to see a pair of cavalry boots covering feet of gigantic size, a mangy cap with visor drawn low, a heavy, dark beard, and weary eyes—eyes I afterward saw filled with intense but never brilliant light. A low gentle voice inquired the road and distance marched that day.

"Keazletown road, six and twenty miles."

"You seem to have no stragglers," the hunched figure said.

"Never allow straggling," Taylor said proudly.

"You must teach my people; they straggle badly." Obviously Jackson meant it. Taylor bowed, acknowledging the compliment.

One of Taylor's Creole bands struck up a waltz just as Jackson spoke. For a long moment Old Jack listened, sucking meditatively on a lemon. Finally, after thinking it over, he said, "Thoughtless fellows for serious work." Taylor retorted that he hoped "the work would not be less well done because of the gayety." Jackson took another drag on the lemon, still brooding, and Taylor made a hasty withdrawal. That there was something odd about Jackson was beyond debate: Taylor's first encounter with the general made a lasting impression—so did the lemon.[49]

Unprepossessing as Jackson appeared,[50] he was on the point of making one of the most important decisions of the war, a decision which stamped him a soldier of great potential.

Sometime during May 20 a courier from Ewell dashed into Jackson's camp with sickening news. Johnston had ordered Branch back toward Richmond and, in a letter just received by Ewell, vetoed an attack on an entrenched Banks, saying that Jackson should stay in the valley watching the enemy while Ewell moved east. Here was the contingency which Jackson had passionately hoped would not arise—"orders from a superior officer" directing Ewell's movements. As he read Johnston's letter, which Ewell sent him, Jackson surveyed his situation. Fremont and Banks had not joined; Shields had been detached from Banks's force. The time was now. An immediate attack might wreck Banks and "drive him . . . toward the Potomac," as Lee desired.[51]

Quickly, across the bottom of Johnston's letter, Jackson scrawled a note to Ewell: "Suspend the execution of the order for returning to the east until I receive an answer to my telegram." An appeal to higher authority, asking for permission to attack, had to be made; a telegram to Lee must go at once.

> Camp near New Market, Va.,
> May 20, 1862
>
> General R. E. Lee:
>
> I am of the opinion that an attempt should be made to defeat Banks, but under instructions just received from General Johnston I do not feel at liberty to make an attack. Please answer by telegraph at once.
>
> T. J. Jackson,
> MAJOR-GENERAL.[52]

Outwardly calm, Jackson gave no hint of the anguished waiting after he sent the telegram. His attack now rested in the capable hands of the man he most trusted in Richmond. Lee wanted Banks smashed; if the authority could be procured, Lee would procure it.

What happened in Richmond when his electrifying message reached Lee, Jackson did not know. What Lee did still remains a mystery, but he probably consulted with President Davis to save time. By nightfall Jackson's dilemma had been resolved. His troops would march in the morning. Faith in Lee had been fully justified.[53]

In the dawn of what was to be a fine warm day, Jackson's infantry formed in the road near New Market. Old Jack's marching instructions had been meager: the troops would move north. The jaunty Louisianians took the lead and set a rapid pace. After a short march, Jackson turned the head of his column east, pointing across the Massanutton through Luray Gap. Somewhere over there Dick Ewell waited nervously for the valley army's appearance. "Fool Tom" Jackson's cherished offensive had begun.

Back on the Valley Pike near Strasburg, Ashby's pickets pressed close to Banks's lines, sealing off the enemy from knowledge of Jackson's movements. Ashby, leaving a covering force, would follow the main army on the twenty-second; very special work was in store for the cavalry. As the men toiled on over the mountain, Jackson rode silently, lost in meditation. The steady progress of the march was interrupted now and then by a courier riding to Jackson, handing him a dispatch, and spurring off again. No interruption seemed to disturb the commanding general's meditative mood. By evening the army had crossed the Shenandoah's South Fork, and went into camp not far from the village of Luray.[54] The

Louisianians speculated long in their camps that night about the strange man who marched them all around Massanutton only to bring them almost back to Conrad's Store. Dick Taylor explained it this way: "I began to think that Jackson was an unconscious poet, and, as an ardent lover of nature, desired to give strangers an opportunity to admire the beauties of his Valley." [55]

As for the general, he had reason to be pleased that night. At last his whole force had been concentrated. With Johnson's men and Ewell's, he now commanded a good 16,000 and could bring 48 guns to bear on a field of battle. With Ashby protecting the rear, Jackson's position offered clear advantages. Between Banks and the Blue Ridge passes, he could intercept any sudden eastward dash; in the Luray Valley his army's movements were completely screened and he could move secretly toward his objective, Front Royal; and if he were successful in taking that objective he would have an opportunity to flank Banks's fortifications at Strasburg and get behind him. This might compel a hasty retreat—which would offer further opportunities. So plotted the man who had a short time before told Anna that "it appears to me that I would appreciate home more than I have ever done before." [56]

Situated near Luray, the army had a choice of routes: east across the Blue Ridge, or north to Front Royal. Few had certain knowledge of Old Jack's intentions. The Reverend Chief of Staff probably had been told, and Major Harman, still worried about forage. [57] The rank and file had no further doubt when early the next morning they followed the South Fork northward. Taylor's men still led the way, the rest of Ewell's men and Jackson's hardened marchers following along behind. Some delay was caused by soft roads, but the men stepped along confidently.

Strict adherence to the new marching orders had become almost ingrained by now, and the richly wooded spurs of the Blue Ridge sped past the long gray line. Nightfall found the army bivouacked within ten miles of its objective.

If all went as the general planned, there would be little trouble tomorrow. Front Royal, resting in a small valley near the confluence of the Shenandoah River's two branches, had no natural strength. Circled by high ground, the village could be swept by artillery. What Jackson wanted was to take the settlement swiftly, surprising and isolating its small Union garrison so that no news could leak to Strasburg. At the same time, precautions must be taken to prevent any aid from reaching Front Royal from Banks.

A direct advance along the main road into the town was possible but might be costly; the road doubtless was well covered by Yankee guns. Was there another way to reach the high ground near Front Royal? Yes, the alternate road was smaller and probably less solid than the main Luray Pike, and it bore a piquant name which the men doubtless would enjoy—Gooney Manor. This road, then, would serve to divert the attention of the garrison, and would add to the surprise.

Nothing was to be left to chance. Front Royal must be isolated: the telegraph line and the railroad cut by Ashby's cavalry. The troopers could cross the South Fork before the main advance began, move across country northwestward, and strike the rail and telegraph lines between Front Royal and Strasburg. That done, the Yankee garrison could not retreat to the protection of Banks, nor could he send aid to his detachment. No need to worry about the Federals' retreating eastward through the Blue Ridge—the position of Jackson's attacking army would rule out that possibility. Northward, across bridges on each fork of the Shenandoah, was the only route left open to the Unionists when they were routed. The complex bridge pattern had engaged Jackson's attention some time before, and he undoubtedly anticipated that crossing the two streams might retard not only the enemy's retreat but also the Confederate pursuit.[58] The Federal garrison at Front Royal had two bridges available across the South Fork, but only one across the North.

All these factors considered, a swift, well-coordinated attack by the valley army might result in the defeat and capture of the garrison, or at worst, drive the enemy north along a predetermined route of retreat. If all went well, Jackson's strategic planning would predestine the fate of his foe. Such, of course, should always be the goal of strategy, but rarely can a general so skillfully plan as to dictate an opponent's every move. The commander who coldly calculated the ruin of the garrison at Front Royal bore little resemblance to the man who led his frozen columns to Romney a scant four months before.

Battle orders were clear and concise: The cavalry was to execute the cutoff maneuver west of Front Royal, capture any stray force along the road, and prevent reinforcements' reaching the garrison. The infantry would take the Gooney Manor road, and advance on the town from the south. Carefully Jackson made sure that Ewell's division would lead the attack—his men were far fresher than Jackson's own marchers. The attack was to be pushed, the enemy driven and pursued.[59]

Swiftly now the advance started. For a time the troops stayed on the main road to Front Royal with the First Maryland Regiment leading the way, in the van by request. They wanted to meet the First Maryland Federal Regiment, and they snapped along in their rapid Zouave step, singing cadence:

> Baltimore, ain't you happy,
> We'll anchor by and by;
> Baltimore, ain't you happy,
> We'll anchor by and by.
> We'll stand the storm, it won't be long,
> We'll anchor by and by.[60]

The going got rougher after turning into the Gooney Manor road, with its slight grade. Old Jack, who stayed with the advance, pushed on, paying no attention to the mudholes or the woods. On he went, intent on his battle. An officer rode to catch him, and took him off toward the rear. In Jackson's absence, Dick Taylor had charge of the advance. With Taylor rode young Kyd Douglas, eager to be with the first attackers. Soon skirmish firing began and Douglas's quick eye, sweeping the scene toward Front Royal, caught sight of a woman in white moving swiftly out of the town and coming toward the Confederate positions. She did her best to keep a hill between herself and the Federals, and as she ran, she kept waving a bonnet. As Douglas recalled the incident, he was sent to meet the intrepid figure and to find out what she was doing.

> That was just to my taste and it took only a few minutes for my horse to carry me to meet the romantic maiden whose tall, supple, and graceful figure struck me as soon as I came in sight of her. As I drew near, her speed slackened, and I was startled, momentarily, at hearing her call my name. But I was not much astonished when I saw that the visitor was the well-known Belle Boyd whom I had known from her earliest girlhood. She was just the girl to dare to do this thing.
>
> Nearly exhausted, and with her hand pressed against her heart, she said in gasps, 'I knew it must be Stonewall, when I heard the first gun. Go back quick and tell him that the Yankee force is very small—one regiment of Maryland infantry, several pieces of artillery and several companies of cavalry. Tell him I know, for I went through the camps and got it out of an officer. Tell him to charge right down and he will catch them all. I must hurry back. . . .'[61]

Douglas quickly reported the information to Taylor. Impressed by the precision of the report, Taylor acted on it. Double-quick, he ordered, and led his men forward. Almost instantly Jackson, followed by a troop of cavalry, came riding out of the woods, and, seeing Taylor's men going forward at the double-quick, rode fast to take command of the advance. Taylor had been so eager to attack that he had moved without deploying skirmishers. Jackson's curt order to fan them out on either side of the road served as a sharp reminder that rashness can be foolhardy. The general rode on toward the front. His attack was developing.

Down in the town sudden pandemonium broke. "There was . . . the quick, sharp report of a rifle," a girl noted in her diary,

> and another and another in rapid succession. Going to the door we saw the Yankees scampering over the meadow below our house and [we] were at a loss to account for such evident excitement on their part until presently Miss B. White rushed in with purple face and dishevelled hair crying, 'Oh, my God! The Hill above the town is black with our boys. . . .' Ma and I did not wait . . . but started for home in double quick time, all the [while] hearing the firing exchanged more and more rapidly. Found all

the family upstairs at the windows. Nellie, spy-glass in hand, clapping her hand exclaiming, 'Oh, there they are. I see our dear brave fellows just in the edge of the woods on the hill over the town! There they are, Bless them!' I looked in the same direction and surely enough some of our cavalry emerged from the little skirt of woods above the court house. As long as I live, I think I cannot forget that sight, the first glimpse caught of a grey figure upon horseback seemingly in command, until then I could not believe our deliverers had really come, but seeing was believing and I could only sink on my knees with my face in my hands and sob for joy.[62]

The battle for Front Royal began about a mile and a half from town, at about two o'clock in the afternoon, May 23, when Taylor's men drove in the Federal pickets. Jackson ordered the advance pushed; the pickets must be unceremoniously ushered into the village. The First Maryland, supported by the fierce and outlandish Louisiana Tigers commanded by their beloved Rob Wheat, moved quickly ahead, giving the retreating Federals no time to stand. Taylor brought the rest of his brigade swiftly into action, and the men soon were in the town, driving a careening mass of confused Yankees before them.

But the Federal commander, the gallant Col. John R. Kenly, First Maryland Regiment, though badly surprised and hopelessly outnumbered, determined to make as much of a stand as his thousand men and two guns would permit. Realizing that he had no chance in the town, Kenly got out of Front Royal to take position on a hill north of the town and on the right of the Winchester turnpike. Here his guns were in position to do damage.

Colonel Stapleton Crutchfield, whom Jackson had recently put in charge of his artillery, sent back for Ewell's ordnance. What Crutchfield wanted were some rifled pieces, but Ewell had no more than three in all his batteries—so valuable time passed while Jackson's infantry advance went on without artillery support. The Marylanders attacked the Federal front; the Louisianians attacked the flanks. While the infantry pressed the attack, some Confederate cavalry streaked for the bridges on the west side of the South Fork, across from Front Royal. If the troopers could reach the important Pike Bridge over the North Fork ahead of the Yankees, the Union retreat would be cut off. Kenly saw the threat, ordered his guns limbered up, and moved his infantry out, heading for the bridges. Confederate troops ran in pursuit, on through the blazing Union campsite down toward the South Fork bridge. Jackson, staying close to his battle, raced to the head of the pursuing troops, urging them on to cut off the enemy's chance to escape. Rushing across the South Fork, Old Jack did his best to get a sufficient force over the bridge to break up the retreating column, but at last he sat his Little Sorrel and watched the bluecoats marching away toward Winchester.

The long line of men was a magnificent target—where were the guns? As he watched, eyes burning with battle light, Jackson shouted, "Oh, what an opportunity for artillery! Oh, that my guns were here!" and to the nearest staff officer he yelled, "Hurry to the rear, order up every rifled gun and every brigade in the army." [63]

Impatient, Jackson watched his chance to shatter Kenly's little band slipping away. These people must be caught and cut up. A blazing heat rising in him, Jackson may have recalled a similar day on the road to Mexico City when he had been pursuing a retreating foe. He had felt the mouth-drying exhilaration of fighting on that faraway day and he felt it stronger now than ever. Crutchfield's unfamiliarity with Ewell's artillery had caused some of the delay; bad staff work had done the rest. Since guns were not brought up—a sad blunder for the professor of artillery tactics—Jackson would have to improvise. Casting about for something to hurl at the bluecoats, who had disappeared by now over a ridge, he seized on Col. Thomas Flournoy's cavalry—part of Ewell's command— which had come back from the wire-cutting mission west of Front Royal. Ashby had ridden on to take Buckton on the railroad, but Flournoy rejoined the battle. Jackson waved toward the vital Pike Bridge, partially afire, and urged the horsemen across. Carefully avoiding the burned patches, Flournoy soon had four companies on the other side, and Jackson ordered him to ride hard—no time to wait for more men.

Flournoy ordered the advance, his bugler sounded the call, and the men thundered forward over the ridge and after the line in blue. On they pressed. Jackson, riding with a young officer, followed. As he galloped along, a shout from the rear brought him up with a start: "Get out of the way of my men!" Turning, Jackson saw a line of men in column of fours trotting toward him. They were part of Flournoy's force and were hastening to catch up with him. The general's young companion pointed at Jackson and yelled, "This is General Jackson." Surprised, the nimble-witted Capt. George Baxter called for three cheers. Old Jack seemed not to hear, wheeled around and rode on.

Two and a half miles north of the Pike Bridge, near the hamlet of Cedarville, the Yankees had been forced to make a stand. Flournoy's men had caught them and forced them to deploy a line of battle. They were forming as Jackson galloped on the field. No time to lose—instantly Flournoy must attack. The general himself gave orders to the thin force of some 250 troopers. They deployed for a charge. Over the field rang the chilling notes of a bugle. A moment's hesitation as the horses braced, then a wild cheering rush forward, right at the enemy's center. A volley from the blue infantry cut some of the horsemen down, but the charge rolled on unwavering. The Union center broke, the men running madly for cover in a nearby orchard. A few rallied here, but again the inexorable Jackson ordered a charge. Once more Flournoy's men smashed at the infantry and the guns, once again the line broke, and this time there was no rallying anywhere. It was a complete rout. Only a few enemy troopers escaped, their guns remained on the field, and the shattered infantry soon was rounded up by the gleeful First Maryland (Confederate) Regiment.[64]

Jackson, obviously excited, told some of his staff who had joined him that never had he seen so gallant or efficient a cavalry charge. High praise indeed from the guarded general—but he had reason to be satisfied. The attack on Front Royal had been almost all he anticipated.

*Stonewall Jackson's sister,
Laura Jackson Arnold*

*Thomas Jonathan Jackson, a copy made
by Mathew Brady from picture taken
by unknown photographer (uniform,
apparently painted on later, is fake)*

*Mary Anna Morrison, Jackson's
beloved second wife, a photograph taken around 1880*

A contemporary photograph of Harpers Ferry. Jackson's first command in the war was to organize the defenses of the town

*Top, right,
General Jubal Early; below,
General Richard S. Ewell,
one of Jackson's favorite
and most reliable lieutenants*

The battlefield at Cedar Mountain

*White Oak Swamp, the scene of one of Jackson's
rare bad showings as a field commander*

*Debris at Manassas Junction
after Jackson's attack*

The bridge at Antietam Creek

General Ambrose E. Burnside, who faced Jackson's forces at Antietam and Fredericksburg

*Jackson in a photograph taken about two weeks before
his death following the Battle of Chancellorsville*

12

"A QUESTION OF LEGS"

—A. LINCOLN

IN CONSEQUENCE of Gen. Banks' critical position I have been compelled to suspend Gen. McDowell's movement to join you. The enemy are making a desperate push upon Harper's Ferry, and we are trying to throw Fremont's force & part of McDowell's in their rear." [1] With this message to General McClellan, Lincoln began a campaign of his own in the Shenandoah Valley. He would meet offense with offense. But Mc-Clellan would have to do without McDowell for a while; one Confederate objective had been achieved.

Information coming to Washington from Banks showed that officer's confusion. No one had a clear idea of how critical his position was—not even he. By nightfall on May 23, 1862, Banks reported that the Front Royal garrison had been stampeded into retreat toward Middletown by a force of some 5,000 Rebels. Beyond that he knew nothing. But that dispatch alone sufficiently alarmed the President and Secretary of War. During the night the harried general sent more dispatches, and a pattern of disaster began to take shape.

Something had gone wrong. Banks, who tried to be realistic in his estimate of events, labored under the disadvantage of having suspected himself threatened with attack for several days, but he had expected the attack to come from south of Strasburg, not on his outpost at Front Royal.[2] War Department officials sought to stiffen his resistance by rushing reinforcements and exhorting him by telegraph not to "give up the ship before succor can arrive." [3] Early in the morning of May 24, the Federal commander had decided that Ewell's men were the attacking

245

force at Front Royal—and by then the numbers had climbed to between 6,000 and 10,000—while Jackson remained in front of Strasburg.[4] At the same time, despite what seemed an enemy move to attack him in front and rear simultaneously, he bravely announced, "We shall stand firm."[5]

By the end of that harrowing day the firm general had retreated to Winchester, and was writing President Lincoln that "I was satisfied by the affair at Front Royal yesterday that I could not hold Strasburg with my force against Jackson's and Ewell's armies, who I believed intended immediate attack."[6] During the twenty-fourth information had reached him that Ewell intended to get behind him, cutting off retreat to Winchester. Since he had "vast stores and extensive trains," he elected to run for it, trying to outdistance Ewell.

His mind made up, Banks had done well. His trains and garrison—about 5,000 men—were put on the road to Winchester, and the march was pressed. Rebel forces struck his retreating column at Middletown, but he reached the supposed protection of Winchester in relative safety.[7] Still aggressive, he announced that having saved his trains he would return to Strasburg—an idea which Lincoln viewed with a jaundiced eye, as it seemed to leave the precious wagons without protection.[8]

At the same time, Lincoln and Secretary Stanton breathed more easily, believing that Banks's army had escaped. They told him: "Your movement is regarded by the President as wise and prudent. We have felt deeply concerned for your safety, and have used every exertion to send you re-enforcements." Now that some idea could be formed of where Jackson and Ewell were, Lincoln confidently planned to catch them between Banks, who was being strengthened, and Fremont, who was ordered to move toward Harrisonburg. The two Federal armies ought to be able to trap the Rebels—if they coordinated their operations.[9]

Unfortunately for the first phase of Lincoln's offensive, Jackson gave Banks no time to rest or to coordinate with anybody.

After the action at Front Royal, Jackson had spent a night in deep thought. Sitting in the warm glow of Dick Taylor's campfire, he pondered a difficult problem in strategy. What occupied him Taylor could not tell, and beyond saying that the Louisianian would march with him in the morning, the general said nothing. As the two men sat silently, Taylor studied his commander. "I fancied he looked at me kindly," Taylor recalled later, "and interpreted it into an approval of the conduct of the brigade. . . . For hours he sat silent and motionless, with eyes fixed on the fire. I took up the idea that he was inwardly praying, and he remained throughout the night."[10]

Prayer might have helped form the solution of a problem in plane geometry, a solution which Jackson worked out sometime in the morning.[11] What he had to do was reduce Banks's freedom of choice to a minimum. Banks could do three things: stay where he was; dash past Jackson's flank over the Blue Ridge; retreat on Winchester. Road conditions in the Alleghenies almost ruled out a march west, but the Army of the Valley must be prepared to anticipate any other move, while keeping its own movements shrouded in a cloak of secrecy and surprise.

Since almost all the Federal force at Front Royal had been killed, wounded, or captured,[12] there would be little danger of any accurate information reaching Banks from there. The victory had other immediate advantages: large amounts of stores and equipment, including two locomotives, had come into Confederate hands and would lighten supply problems for Harman and Hawks. Banks had already earned a small reputation as Jackson's "commissary."

Still, the problem of meeting his next move had to be handled. The cavalry would have hard work on the twenty-fourth. Ewell's troopers, now under charge of veteran Gen. "Maryland" Steuart, would move for the Valley Pike somewhere north of Middletown. Ashby, headed for Middletown, would keep a sharp eye south for any hint of a flight east across the Blue Ridge via Front Royal. Minus Taylor's impressive brigade, Ewell would stick to the road leading northwestward from Front Royal and march toward Winchester. Jackson himself would go with the van and the rest of the army on a road which led from Cedarville diagonally over to the Valley Pike five miles north of Strasburg—here they might move south to attack Banks if still he hugged his trenches, or they might crash into his retreating column. If Banks boldly struck east for the Blue Ridge, Ewell could countermarch to take him in rear, aided by the force from Middletown.

On the surface, the strategy left something to be desired, particularly if Banks moved east. But in light of the evening's recent action, Jackson's plan appeared sound. Banks had already retreated, without goading, from Harrisonburg; he seemed addicted to falling back. An unexpected shove would probably find him reacting the same way. The calculated risk proved successful.

When the cavalry and artillery advance reached the environs of Middletown around 1 P.M., a long column of dust could be seen north and south of the village. Here was Banks's army, retreating fast. Although Taylor's infantry had not arrived in strength, Jackson directed the Louisiana Tigers, supporting the guns on hand, to go into action. Instantly the road became a wild, milling slaughterhouse. "The road," said Jackson, "was literally obstructed with the mingled and confused mass of struggling and dying horses and riders."[13] Some force of the enemy was still south of Middletown, and Taylor's men, coming up in strength, were dispatched to deal with whatever Yankees could be found. Taylor moved swiftly through the chaos of Middletown, taking prisoners right and left. Soon he had scattered to the four winds a small segment of Banks's army seeking to cut through the Confederates. By now it was four o'clock. Banks had abandoned fantastic amounts of stores, to the grim satisfaction of the "wagon hunter," but he was still on the road to Winchester. Taylor's brush with the small Union force had been illuminating; it showed that Banks had already passed Middletown with most of his men. He had thirteen miles to go to reach the protection of the hills around Winchester, and those miles offered glittering opportunities to take more wagons and to break up the Federal army.

Ashby had already been urged to press on after the wagons—capture them, halt the madly whipping drivers, stop them. More infantry might be needed on the Valley Pike, and at 4:30 Jackson sent to Ewell for Arnold Elzey's brigade. Taylor's successful fight south of Middletown canceled worries about needing more men, but Elzey could come on.

The Stonewall Brigade, Winder leading, took the head of the pursuit. Prospects were bright, and Jackson could hardly suppress elation: "From the attack upon Front Royal up to the present moment every opposition had been borne down, and there was reason to believe, if Banks reached Winchester, it would be without a train, if not without an army." [14] Taking the road north himself, Jackson soon came upon two of his guns on the fringes of Newtown, slugging it out with some Yankee ordnance and standing almost completely unsupported by either infantry or cavalry. Shameful conduct on the part of some of Ashby's and Taylor's men, Colonel Crutchfield explained, had retarded the Confederate pursuit of Banks's column. Crutchfield had been careening forward on the road north when he discovered that no troops were keeping up as support. He had been delayed a good two hours looking for aid, but the men melted away, looting abandoned Yankee wagons. Pillaging had served as a better rear guard for the enemy than they could have imagined!

Not even the enterprising Ashby, who had ridden to assist Crutchfield, could collect more than fifty troopers to throw at the Federals. Lack of discipline in the cavalry stood clearly revealed; if Ashby had not before appreciated what it could lead to, the wrath in his general's eye suddenly brought it home to him. The men, Jackson said, were "forgetful of their high trust as the advance of a pursuing army," and they "deserted their colors, and abandoned themselves to pillage to such an extent as to make it necessary . . . to discontinue farther pursuit." [15] But not for long would Old Jack be content with waiting. As soon as he found some infantry units coming along the road, he gathered his staff around him and led the way.

All along the Pike burning Union wagons testified to the fatal delay. Much later, when he thought back to that evening, Jackson still seethed: "As we advanced beyond Newtown the same profusion of abandoned Federal wagons loaded with stores met the eye; but we derived no benefit from this property, as the time lost during the disorder and pillage . . .

and the consequent delay of our advance at Newtown, enabled the enemy to make arrangements for burning them." [16]

In the growing darkness the little cluster of horsemen rode through Newtown. During the ride Old Jack had been as silent as ever, head down, plodding along at Little Sorrel's walking gait. Taking cue from the general, the whole staff rode without much conversation, conserving their breath for whatever nocturnal devilment the Old Man had been hatching. Kyd Douglas had lapsed into happy contemplation of certain romantic maneuvers he might execute if the army got into Winchester. Suddenly, from across the road, came the low voice of the general: "Mr. Douglas, what do you think of the ladies of Winchester?" Trapped in his thoughts, Douglas stammered and blushed, glad that the darkness hid him from sight. The young officer fancied he saw Jackson smile at his guilty discomfort before continuing: "I mean the ladies generally. Don't you think they are a noble set, worth fighting for? I do. They are the truest people in the South." Down lower came the dirty little cap, and Little Sorrel jogged ahead a bit faster. Douglas noticed with relief that the general appeared to expect no reply.[17]

Long after dark Jackson was still urging the men along. Almost everyone staggered from bone-weary fatigue. Many of the veterans were to remember the night of May 24–25 as one of the hardest nights they had ever spent. The Old Man gave them no rest, and the enemy made frequent attempts to organize some kind of rear guard. In the darkness a sudden streak of fire along a wall would identify a Yankee position. From behind assorted trees separate flashes showed where one or two Federals had halted to deliver a parting shot. These ambushes almost picked off the general and his staff on a few occasions, and finally, against his desire, Jackson sent a line of skirmishers ahead to clean out the bushwhackers.[18]

Since there seemed to be no organized rear-guard line, Winder deployed a skirmish line only, which did the job while the main columns shuffled forward, doing their best to stick to Jackson's marching orders. Moving so slowly that some of the men almost fell asleep in ranks, the column covered an imperceptible distance on that hideous march.

Concerned only with pressing on, Jackson appeared to need no sleep at all. Soon his sublime unconcern at the hissing bullets proved contagious. "I quite remember thinking at the time," wrote Taylor of the night's ride, "that Jackson was invulnerable, and that persons near him shared that quality." [19] A succession of couriers interrupted the anxiety of Jackson's thoughts, and finally Major Harman caught up with the little entourage. Road-weary and out of breath, the quartermaster brought disquieting news: The muddy roads in Luray Valley had held up the army's commissary trains and they were far behind. Looking at him hard, the general snapped, "The ammunition wagons?" Harman was ready with his answer: "All right, sir. They were in advance, and I doubled teams on them and brought them through."

"Ah!" No other comment, but the tone of relief amounted to a commendation for Harman.

Kind Dick Taylor thought something more ought to be said, and remarked jocularly: "Never mind the wagons. There are quantities of stores in Winchester, and the general has invited me to breakfast there to-morrow." [20]

Startled, Jackson reached out to touch Taylor's arm—jokes could be damaging to secrecy. The gay Louisianian began to wonder if his general lacked a sense of humor as well as a normal appetite. "Without physical wants himself," Taylor concluded, "he forgot that others were differently constituted, and paid little heed to commissariat; but woe to the man who failed to bring up ammunition!" [21]

Such an estimate of his invincible digestion would have amused Jackson—although even he was forced to admit that active campaigning had vastly improved his health.[22]

One further observation Taylor made about his commander as a result of Banks's retreat had the ring of honest admiration: "In advance, his trains were left far behind. In retreat, he would fight for a wheelbarrow." [23]

After midnight Col. Sam Fulkerson approached the general and respectfully suggested that the troops be allowed to rest for an hour or so: "My men are falling by the roadside from fatigue and loss of sleep. Unless they are rested, I shall be able to present but a thin line tomorrow." A reasonable request, certainly, but Jackson had reasons for the forced march.

Quietly he replied, "Colonel, I yield to no man in sympathy for the gallant men under my command; but I am obliged to sweat them tonight, that I may save their blood tomorrow. The line of hills southwest of Winchester must not be occupied by the enemy's artillery. My own must be there and in position by daylight." Then, thinking of the hard miles, the many days: "You shall, however, have two hours' rest." Amazed, the men found that the column had halted; they fell by the road and slept. Weariness blotted out war. No battle could be as important as sleep.[24]

Jackson had no time for sleep. Close to his advance units he stayed, going forward with the weary skirmishers. Everything hinged on whether or not Banks had been able to lay firm hold of the hills near Winchester, and on Ewell, who should be in position southeast of town. Straining his eyes to catch sight of the enemy, Jackson had the men aroused and marching at 4 A.M. Again he would have to fight on a Sabbath—as he had explained to Fulkerson earlier, the whole purpose of the march was to save blood by swift fighting.

Soon word came that a line of blue skirmishers had been spotted on the commanding ridge of hills, skirting Winchester on the south and southwest. If the enemy were there in strength. . . .

Swiftly Jackson went forward; he would reconnoiter personally. So far it looked as though the occupants of the strategic ridge were a thin line—skirmishers only.

Winder rode up to report that his skirmishers were in contact with those of the enemy on the ridge. Confident and showing not the slightest sign of fatigue, Jackson had surveyed the field and had determined what had to be done. "You must occupy that hill." [25] As Winder disappeared to the front, Jackson sent some artillery up to support the line and to fire on the enemy's batteries. In company with the Second Brigade's commander, Col. John A. Campbell, the general followed the infantry up the ridge. The men were moving swiftly; the little rest he had been able to allow seemed to have been enough. Soon the crest was in Confederate hands, but Banks was holding a lesser ridge nearer town and had his guns raking the occupied hills along the top, doing their best to make it impossible for the Confederates to mount an attack.

Winder's line of battle spread from a bit east of the Pike westward in a slightly concave crescent, and soon his left received galling fire from well-placed Union guns and infantry supports. Although the Confederates held their ridge position, they were paying dearly for the privilege. More metal must be sent up to help balance the unequal duel, and the artillery would need strong infantry assistance in case the enemy tried an assault. As he wheeled toward the rear, preparing to send up more men and guns, Old Jack saw a Yankee regiment moving toward his left in the direction of a stone wall which stood almost at right angles to Winder's battle line.

An extension of the line left had to be made; the Union regiment would be in position to pour deadly fire into Winder's men, and it must be dislodged. Down the hill went Jackson, seeking more troops. On the way he spotted Winder and told him that reinforcements for a flank move would be sent. Taylor's men could handle the assignment; Winder would attend to ordering up more guns. [26] Soon W. T. Poague's Parrotts were smashing down the stone wall on the Confederate left with solid shot. An attack over that ground now would spill less blood.

Riding toward Taylor's vanguard, Jackson ran across the famous Thirty-third Virginia Regiment posted on the lee edge of the blazing ridge. Colonel John Neff pointed out his positions to Old Jack.

"What are your orders?" asked the general.

"To support that battery," came the firm reply, as Neff pointed toward two of Cutshaw's guns just going into position.

Fist clenched and blue eyes fixing Neff, Jackson said fiercely: "I expect the enemy to bring artillery to this hill, and they must not do it! Do you understand me, sir? They must not do it! Keep a good lookout, and your men well in hand; and if they attempt to come, charge them with the bayonet, and seize their guns. Clamp them, sir, on the spot!" [27]

On down the hillside, then, to find Taylor's brigade, which had been designated the reserve of the army. Off to the right came the sound of firing; no need to worry about Ewell, he was in position and fighting hard. It was still very early—about 6 A.M.—but the battle had developed fast. At the moment it showed signs of going sour. His own metal outweighed, and the left of his line of battle threatened with a turning movement, Jackson had to act quickly. Did Kyd Douglas know where Taylor was? Yes, he would lead the way. Swiftly the two horsemen covered ground, passing by some of the Virginia regiments who had long been part of the Army of the Valley. Strict orders were not to make noise, so they could not cheer Stonewall as he galloped along by them. Instead, they took off their hats in an affectionate salute. The stiff and ungainly man on Little Sorrel raised his battered cap in reply. The Old Man did some strange things still, but he was winning. That counted for a lot, especially when casualties were light.

At last there was Taylor, riding on ahead of his splendid troops.

"General, can your brigade charge a battery?"

"It can try."

"Very good; it must do it then. Move it forward." [28]

Taylor took his men to the left. He had scanned the ground after speaking to Jackson and realized that his attack would have to flank the enemy's right. Round toward the far end of the Confederate battle line he marched. Riding on the flank of the brigade, between his men and the enemy, Taylor suddenly noticed that the taciturn Jackson kept pace with him. The line could be seen by the enemy—did not the general think he should leave such an exposed position? Apparently Jackson did not hear the question—he was lost in thought.

When Taylor's men came within effective range of Union guns on the ridge they were to assault, a brutal fire poured down on them. Gaps were torn in the ranks, shot and shell shrieked up and down the line, and some of his men began to duck their heads. Incensed, Taylor whirled and yelled: "What the hell are you dodging for? If there is any more of it, you will be halted under this fire for an hour!" Magically, the men snapped to attention. Then Taylor felt a hand on his shoulder, turned, and looked into the face of Jackson, whose expression of "reproachful surprise" the chagrined brigadier never forgot. "I am afraid you are a wicked fellow," [29] Jackson said gently and, leaving a mortified subordinate behind, rode away to find a vantage point and watch his battle. [30]

The "wicked fellow" set about earning another reputation. Shortly Jackson thrilled to one of the finest of all martial sights—a gallant and well-led charge. "Steadily, and in fine order," he noted, Taylor's men advanced, "mounting the hill, and there fronting the enemy, where he stood in greatest strength, the whole line magnificently swept down the declivity and across the field, driving back the Federal troops and bearing down all opposition before it." [31] Winder's men joined in the attack, and Ewell had launched one of his own against the Union left. Banks's positions folded all along the line. Back into Winchester streamed the beaten troops. Victory—sharp, decisive victory—had proved the virtue of the early bird. "Order forward the whole line, the battle's won," shouted Jackson as Taylor's men rushed over the Yankee positions. "Very good! Now let's holler!" Sitting Little Sorrel, he waved his cap in the air, and while his astounded staff gaped, Old Jack cheered at the top of his lungs. [32]

Enemy troops spilled back through Winchester, at first in "remarkably" good order, [33] then gradually losing their organization. By the time they escaped the town and were on the road north to Martinsburg, Banks's men stumbled and jostled together in a large amorphous mass of humanity. Relentlessly the Confederates pushed them on. As Jackson's men advanced into Winchester they were met with wild scenes of joy. The dusty figure on Little Sorrel thought "our entrance into Winchester ... one of the most stirring scenes of my life." People seemed unaware that the tail end of a battle blazed around them; citizens poured out of homes and shops to line the streets.

Veteran infantrymen were greeted with screams of delight by tearful women crying with happiness and by some odd souls simply standing on the streets singing at the top of their voices. [34] Most welcome were those carrying baskets of food who ran up to the men and urged them to eat their fill. No army of liberation had been met with greater gratitude. Everybody wanted a glimpse of Old Stonewall, but he raced through the happy town, pressing the enemy.

From Jackson's point of view, Banks had done just the right thing. He had not taken the road toward Harpers Ferry, but instead had directed his retreat toward Martinsburg on the Pike from Winchester to the Potomac crossing at Williamsport. As a result he was separating himself from the relatively small garrison at Harpers Ferry, which was all to the good. He must be pursued hard; his demoralized retreat must be turned into a rout.

When Jackson reached the northern outskirts of Winchester and caught sight of Banks's ruined army, his face flamed with excitement. Defenseless and scattered, the Union force could be cut to pieces, decimated. Swift and effective measures could capture or destroy what was left of Banks. Quickly the cavalry must be brought into the fight; a repeat of Flournoy's efforts of two days before would finish the Yankees. But where were Ashby's and Steuart's men? Impatiently Jackson scanned the fields around town; "Never was there such a chance for cavalry," Old Jack shouted to Dabney. "Oh that my cavalry were in place!" [35] "Never," he later said, "have I seen an opportunity when it was in the power of cavalry to reap a richer harvest of the fruits of victory." [36]

No trace of troopers could be seen. Jackson had not spotted any of Ashby's men since early the night before and saw none now. Steuart presumably was aiding Ewell—at any rate he was not at hand to join in the pursuit. Jackson did all that could be done. Infantry and artillery units were urged forward, firing into the confused mass of Union troops. Pressure must be kept on until the cavalry could finish the job. Ashby's men probably had not yet regained their composure after hours of pillaging, but Steuart could still wring the last vantage from victory.

Sandie Pendleton must go to find him and order him to the Martinsburg Pike where he could attack at will. Pendleton rode off and Old Jack ordered up more guns to pound the Yankees. "Order every battery and every brigade forward to the Potomac," he shouted at one of his staff. But it was too late. Steuart did not come; Ashby could not be found. The infantry, willing as ever, had marched too far, fought too hard. After a grueling six-mile pursuit, the tired foot soldiers went into bivouac. [37]

Soon Dick Taylor was on the scene. Old Jack had bestowed the supreme accolade on him by wringing his hand when the Union rout began. Now the young brigadier made an unfortunate blunder. Surveying the field, he turned to his superior and asked, "Where is the cavalry?" The glowering glance ended further questions. [38]

An hour or so later, at about 10:30 or 11 A.M., [39] Steuart's 600 or 700 troopers [40] reached the Martinsburg Pike and galloped on after the Federals. Too late—strong rear guards were established and all "Maryland" and his tardy squadrons could do was pick up Yankee stragglers. Jackson was disgusted: "There is good reason for believing," he wrote in his report, "that, had the cavalry played its part in this pursuit as well as the four companies had done under Colonel Flournoy two days before in the pursuit from Front Royal, but a small portion of Banks' army would have made its escape to the Potomac." [41] More than ever it was clear that poor discipline in the mounted arm could ruin the best of plans.

When Jackson learned the facts behind the cavalry's delay, he discovered that in one sense there had been too much discipline. According to his story, Ashby had simply taken off around the Federal left, aiming to cut off a segment of Banks's troops heading for Harpers Ferry. A laudable ambition, but he had made the move without orders or without reporting his intention. Still, much could be forgiven an officer with the proper spirit of attack. "Maryland" Steuart's reasons were different, the result of being too long laced in Old Army discipline and red tape.

When Sandie Pendleton found Steuart's men dismounted about two and a half miles east of Winchester, he had looked vainly for the general. Another half mile's ride overtook Steuart, and Pendleton delivered Jackson's urgent order to join him instantly on the Martinsburg Pike. No,

Steuart would not go. He was, he said, part of General Ewell's command and could obey no orders that did not come from his own superior. Pendleton, amazed, explained that Jackson's order "was peremptory and immediate, and that I would go forward and inform General Ewell that the cavalry was sent off." As soon as Old Baldy heard Pendleton's orders, he readily consented to Steuart's departure and expressed some surprise at the cavalryman's devotion to etiquette. Riding back toward Jackson, Pendleton ran into General Steuart riding slowly toward General Ewell's headquarters. Appalled that the cavalry were not already well on their way, Pendleton quickly told the errant general that his superior consented to the move; satisfied at last, Steuart got his men into action. Jackson admitted that when they finally joined the pursuit they did very well, but nothing could forgive Steuart's strange conduct. He would have to be shifted to some less sensitive position where a dedication to "regulations" could not hamstring an army.[42]

Although Banks had been allowed to escape with some of his troops, Jackson's sudden attack and stern direction of the initial pursuit had all but wrecked the Federal remnants at a cost of only 400 casualties. In two days the Army of the Valley had driven Banks's force almost sixty miles and for a good portion of that time the distance had been in fairly close contact, pressing, attacking, and demoralizing. There was not much of an army left for Banks to save. Over 3,000 of his men were prisoners,[43] and he had abandoned a great many wagons, two guns, warehouses full of precious medical supplies and commissary stores, over 9,300 small arms, and much ammunition. Federal efforts to burn stores before leaving Winchester failed. "We have 'busted' Banks," wrote the gleeful John Harman as he surveyed the fantastic amounts of supplies captured. "Commissary" Banks had resupplied Jackson's army with almost everything, and had also contributed staggering amounts of excess supplies—wagons and other transportation would have to be impressed from all over the upper valley in order to remove the material from Winchester.

As soon as he had called off the infantry pursuit, Jackson had returned to Winchester, leaving the problems of prisoners and captured supplies to his staff officers. The general was going to visit old friends in one of his favorite towns. Once more the familiar big boots strode up the Graham walk. The whole family greeted him with joy and a shower of questions. How had he contrived the brilliant scheme which turned Winchester's tormentors into running cowards? Where was he going? Did he know of his reputation as the liberator of Winchester, the "Champion of the Valley"?[44]

Gently Jackson turned the questions, played down his part in the victories and, as usual, ascribed success to Divine Providence. There seemed little about him of the great hero: he played with the Graham children; he sat humbly at the dinner table while the blessing was asked; he was happy at the chance to "come *home* on Sunday." Mrs. Graham, with a practiced wifely eye, observed in a letter to Anna that she had never seen him "look so fat & hearty," and that he "was as bright & happy as possible." [45] But no matter how they tried, not a word of hopes or fears or plans could the Grahams extract from him.

By the time he made his second visit to the Graham house the family doubtless knew that he had rested the army during Monday, the twenty-sixth, and had ordered religious services to be held throughout his camps. God had richly blessed the army; thanks must be given along with prayers for "His continued favor." [46] The order had another purpose: it contained a curious apology from the general to his men.

General Order Number 53   *May 26, 1862*

> Within four weeks this army has made long and rapid marches, fought six combats and two battles, signally defeating the enemy in each one; captured several stands of colours and pieces of artillery, with numerous prisoners and vast medical, ordnance and army stores, and finally driven the boastful host which was ravaging our beautiful country into utter rout. The General Commanding would warmly express to the officers and men under his command his joy in their achievements and his thanks for their brilliant gallantry in action and their patient obedience under the hardship of forced marches, often more painful to the brave soldiers than the dangers of battle. The explanation of the severe exertions to which the Commanding General called the army, which were endured by them with such cheerful confidence, is now given in the victory of yesterday. He receives this proof of their confidence in the past with pride and gratitude, and asks only a similar confidence in the future. But his chief duty today, and that of the army, is to recognize devoutly the hand of a Protecting Providence in the brilliant successes of the past three days which have given us the results of a great victory without great losses; and to make the oblation of our thanks to God for his mercies to us and our country in heartfelt acts of religious worship. For this purpose the troops will remain in camp today, suspending, as far as practicable, all military exercises, and the chaplains of regiments will hold Divine service in their several charges at 4 o'clock p.m. today.

> > R. L. *Dabney,* A.A.G.[47]

Certain problems had to be resolved during the army's brief rest at Winchester. Pillaging and its offspring, "the evil of straggling," had to be stopped, else the efficiency of the army might be fatally reduced. Although Jackson felt that "the battle at Winchester was on our part a battle without a straggler," he worried considerably about the men who had stopped to scavenge during the march from Middletown. A severe General Order, issued on May 27, pointed out that "all captured property belongs to the government and for individuals to appropriate it is theft."[48] Permits to visit Winchester were curtailed and the provost guard ordered to arrest any soldier there without written authority.[49] Shabby as the Confederate uniforms had become, no soldier would be allowed to wear any items of the Yankee uniform; all captured Federal clothing must be turned in to the quartermaster.[50] And, of course, while administration was being strengthened, the troops were not to remain idle. All commands were to spend four hours a day in good hard drilling.[51]

As the Army of the Valley enjoyed a short sojourn at the expense of General Banks, its position, and the causes therefor, worked curious changes in the military thinking of high Union officials. With Banks's precipitate retreat from Winchester President Lincoln's scheme for bagging Jackson began to go awry. Banks appeared to be in no condition to coordinate his operations with Fremont—or anyone else. True, his dispatches indicated that he had saved most of his property and his army, but could his reports be trusted?

Around midafternoon of May 25, Banks sent word of the debacle at Winchester. Outnumbered, he said, 15,000 to 4,000, he never had a chance. Some demoralization set in while the men dashed through the town, but once on the Martinsburg road, he had reestablished order. Army trains were in front of his retreating column, and he assured Secretary Stanton that they "will cross the river in safety." Since he had earlier estimated his strength at Strasburg as around 6,000 men, the new and shrunken figure meant either incredible losses or distortion. In reality Banks's strength on the days of Front Royal and Winchester stood at about 8,500 and his losses at about 3,000. As John Harman said, Banks was "busted."[52]

Banks had demonstrated one interesting quality during the hectic hours after Front Royal: When the unexpected began to happen, he became a victim of rumor. All the stories filtering in about enemy movements he had promptly passed on to Washington; after all, he had a duty to keep his superiors informed. Now that he was on the road to Maryland, conflicting intelligence reached him from all directions. Immediately he passed on every Rebel scheme and plot that reached his ears, and the Rebels were dreadfully active. They were advancing in all directions, some of them coming after him at Martinsburg, others careening toward Harpers Ferry. Banks even knew their intentions—they were going to cross into Maryland. So was Banks.

Even before the news of defeat at Winchester had reached President Lincoln, he had begun to react to Jackson's strategy. At five o'clock in the afternoon of May 24 he ordered General McDowell, at Fredericksburg, to halt "the movement on Richmond, to put 20,000 men in motion at once for the Shenandoah." Even though the first phase of Lincoln's own Valley Campaign had been thwarted, he was far from through. Quick to improvise, he decided to take advantage of mass manpower and concentrate a horde of bluecoats in Jackson's rear. Once the Confederate Army of the Valley had been disposed of, McDowell could resume the movement to join McClellan and take Richmond.

McDowell's troops, moving swiftly west, were to cooperate with Fremont's men, directed to move from Franklin across the Alleghenies to Harrisonburg. Even if Fremont failed, McDowell was assumed to be of sufficient strength to destroy Jackson singlehanded. But speed held the key to success.

General McDowell and General McClellan both felt that the valley situation did not call for such a disruption of plans. While announcing compliance with the order, McDowell added that "this is a crushing blow to us." Lincoln sympathized, and replied that "the change was as painful to me as it can possibly be to you or to any one." [53] Everything, said the President, depended on the "celerity and vigor" of McDowell's movements. This exhortation spurred McDowell into an explanation of some basic military science. In a restrained letter, the general told the President that

> co-operation between General Fremont and myself to cut Jackson and Ewell there is not to be counted upon, even if it is not a practical impossibility. . . . I am entirely beyond helping distance of General Banks; no celerity or vigor will avail so far as he is concerned. . . . By a glance at the map it will be seen that the line of retreat of the enemy's forces up the valley is shorter than mine to go against him. It will take a week or ten days for the force to get to the valley by the route which will give it food and forage, and by that time the enemy will have retired. I shall gain nothing for you there, and shall lose much for you here. It is therefore not only on personal grounds that I have a heavy heart in the matter, but that I feel it throws us all back, and from Richmond north we shall have all our large masses paralyzed, and shall have to repeat what we have just accomplished. I have ordered General Shields to commence the movement by to-morrow morning [May 25].[54]

McDowell believed that the sudden crisis in the valley rested largely in the exaggerated imagination of a frightened General Banks.[55]

On the other side of the Alleghenies, Maj. Gen. John C. Fremont entered into Lincoln's strategy. Ordered to move against Harrisonburg on May 24, Fremont replied that he would instantly comply, and thus drew the thanks of a worried President, who told him that "much—perhaps all—depends upon the celerity with which you can execute it. . . . Do not lose a minute." [56] Stanton, showing that he knew Fremont, cautioned him not to stop anywhere to collect supplies: "Seize what you need and push rapidly forward." [57]

Instead of going across the Alleghenies and moving on Harrisonburg well behind Jackson's force, Fremont had by May 27 moved his army north to Moorefield, much to the surprise of Lincoln, who asked, "What does this mean?" [58] The explanation did considerable unconscious credit to Jed Hotchkiss's hard work in blocking the roads from the South Branch Valley. Fremont found that most of the roads leading east were sealed off, and a move north, looking for unobstructed routes, was his only alternative. Jackson's planning had been well done—engineering operations had effectively protected the rear of his army.[59]

With Fremont out of position and moving north, Lincoln had to juggle his plans. For a time he had the idea that Jackson's advance amounted to a break-through in a ring of Union positions and that if the hole were closed, Jackson would be caught within the Federal lines. Fremont and McDowell were to close the gap.[60] McDowell's obvious lack of faith in the whole enterprise did not discourage the President; he remained the only one who thought of taking the offensive against Jackson. Still, if his field commanders failed to move swiftly, the offense would fizzle out. And there was something to McDowell's contention that cooperation between his force and Fremont's had to be considered problematical. Napoleon's maxim that the combination of two armies in the face of the enemy was one of the most difficult of military maneuvers could not be ignored.

Lincoln had made his choice. He had decided that Jackson's army must be dealt with, even at the expense of weakening McClellan. On May 25, in a dispatch to his general in front of Richmond, the Union President revealed how deeply concerned he was for the safety of Washington:

> The enemy is moving North in sufficient force to drive Banks before him in precisely what force we can not tell. He is also threatening Leesburgh and Geary on the Manassas Gap Rail Road from north and south in precisely what force we can not tell. I think the movement is a general and concerted one, such as could not be if he was acting upon the purpose of a very desperate defense of Richmond. I think the time is near when you must either attack Richmond or give up the job and come to the defense of Washington.[61]

McClellan tried hard not to let Lincoln throw everything into a desperate defense of Washington, but did not wholly succeed. The President, in almost apologetic tones, explained the reasons for halting McDowell's movement toward Richmond by giving McClellan a hasty résumé of the situation as known by the evening of May 25 and pointing out that an effort was being made to trap Jackson's army.

> If McDowell's force was now beyond our reach, we should be utterly helpless. Apprehension of something like this, and no unwillingness to sustain you, has always been my reason for withholding McDowell's force from you. Please understand this, and do the best you can with the force you have.[62]

Now it was clear to all Federal commanders that all else was to be subordinated to the protection of Washington. Jackson's quick marches proved the point to both Yankees and Confederates.

Several anxious days passed while General Banks retired ungracefully to the Potomac and finally crossed it on May 26. Reinforcements and artillery were sent to the Harpers Ferry garrison in a move to prevent Jackson's crossing the Potomac there. Banks's force, demoralized as it was, would have to prevent a crossing at or near Williamsport.

Jackson advanced quickly from Winchester, having pressed Banks hard. Immense stores of all kinds were picked up at Martinsburg, where the Federals had built up a depot and left it virtually untouched.[63]

News reached Jackson on the morning of May 28 that McDowell had been ordered to march against him, and General Shields's advance of about 10,000 men was already on the way toward Strasburg. Listening to the report, Jackson decided to press his advantage. Instead of directing a retreat up the valley, he ordered the army to march toward Harpers Ferry, and sent reconnaissance parties out toward Martinsburg and Williamsport to cover the withdrawal of captured stores. Winder's infantry skirmished briefly with a small enemy force near Charles Town, drove them back, and pushed on toward Halltown.[64]

Old Jack seemed to have an attack on Harpers Ferry in mind. Knowing the weaknesses of the town from his days of command there, Jackson sent a regiment to the Loudoun Heights on May 29, "with the hope of being able to drive the enemy from Harper's Ferry, across the Potomac." [65] General Rufus Saxton, the nervous Harpers Ferry commander, felt unsafe. The town, obviously indefensible if any of the heights overlooking it fell into enemy hands, was inadequately garrisoned with some 7,000 men and 18 guns. Rumors undermined Saxton's determination. Jackson, he heard, was sending a division across the Potomac above the Ferry and had already occupied Loudoun Heights. Now he might be threatened from the flank and rear. He shortened his lines, sending infantry over to Maryland Heights to support some of his guns. What was Jackson planning? [66]

It was a question also being asked by some of Old Jack's subordinates. News of Shields's movement toward the valley had leaked out at Winchester. Many officers had expected an order to retreat long before May 30, and still the Old Man kept his headquarters at Charles Town and his men picketing the Potomac and skirmishing at Harpers Ferry. He had already more than obeyed Lee's order to drive Banks to the Potomac. What was he waiting for? Stapleton Crutchfield, trusted chief of artillery, summed up the feelings of many when he gloomily quoted to Kyd Douglas, "quem Deus vult perdere, prius dementat." [67]

On the morning of the thirtieth couriers brought Jackson confirmation of the news about Shields's move toward Front Royal and additional tidings that McDowell marched on Berryville. Banks also was reported as reorganizing his army at Williamsport. Unruffled that such masses were concentrating against him, Jackson received a delegation of

Charles Town's ladies who called to "pay their respects." Then he went to the front, watched some skirmishing exchanges. When rain began to fall, the general took cover under a tree, stretched out, and was soon asleep.[68]

When he awoke, Jackson found one of the volunteer staff members, his old friend Col. Alex R. Boteler, nearby making a sketch of him.[69] Studying it for a time, Jackson said, "My hardest tasks at West Point were the drawing lessons, and I never could do anything in that line to satisfy myself, or indeed, anybody else." Then, shortly: "But, Colonel, I have some harder work than this for you to do, and, if you'll sit down here, now, I'll tell you what it is." Jackson then outlined Boteler's mission: "I want you to go to Richmond for me. I must have reinforcements. You can explain to them down there what the situation is here. Get as many as can be spared, and I'd like you if you please, to go as soon as you can."

Boteler would go immediately, but what exactly was the situation Jackson faced? The colonel had the privileges not only of an old friend but also of a politician whose words would command high audience in Richmond. Speaking frankly, Jackson outlined the combinations building up against him. Banks and Saxton, with a total of possibly 12,000 men, would push south, and now he knew, he said, that McDowell and Shields were coming to the valley. Obviously Fremont with 15,000 men would join in the attempt to trap his force:

> McDowell and Fremont are probably aiming to effect a junction at Strasburg, so as to cut us off from the upper valley, and are both nearer to it now than we are; consequently, no time is to be lost. You can say to them in Richmond that I'll send on the prisoners, secure most, if not all of the captured property, and with God's blessing will be able to baffle the enemy's plans here with my present force, but that it will have to be increased as soon thereafter as possible.

One final thing might be confided to the President—a plan which probably had been brewing in Old Jack's mind for some time and became increasingly attractive as Banks continued to race northward. "You may tell them, too, that if my command can be gotten up to 40,000 men a movement may be made beyond the Potomac, which will soon raise the siege of Richmond and transfer this campaign from the banks of the James to those of the Susquehanna." [70] Boteler left at once to board a train at Charles Town for Winchester.

The man who revealed this scheme to the anxious colonel had come a long way from the swamps of Florida and the sheet ice of Romney. Decisive now, sure of himself and of his army, Stonewall Jackson's will had made him a formidable field commander.

Apt as usual, Lincoln had sized up the situation in the Shenandoah Valley as of May 28 as essentially "a question of legs." [71] Basically the question was, whose were best—Confederate or Federal? Jackson's estimate of affairs in the valley coincided exactly with Lincoln's. Not a minute could be wasted, now that panic had subsided in Washington and the Union high command had begun to get a grip on itself.[72] A reasonably correct estimate of his purposes and numbers had been formed by Yankee commanders, which meant that further demonstration against Harpers Ferry and the Potomac would serve no useful purpose. Now the army must be extracted from the prongs of President Lincoln's pincers movement.

Winder made a last feint at the Ferry; Jackson headed back for Charles Town while the infantry once again took to the road, heading south. As Jackson rode toward the town with Hotchkiss and Col. Abner Smead (his Inspector General), a young lieutenant of cavalry dashed up to ask: "General, are the troops going back?"

Jackson said coldly, "Don't you see them going?"

Nothing daunted, the officer blundered on: "Are they all going?"

Jackson took a long look at him, turned to Colonel Smead and snapped, "Colonel, arrest that man as a spy." Only the timely arrival of Ashby—and his explanation that the lieutenant was simply stupid—saved the poor lad.[73]

Dinner at the home of Major Hawks was the last leisure Jackson could afford. While there he had received a dispatch from General Johnston dated May 27, mixing congratulations with suggestions: Could he threaten Baltimore or Washington? All that could be achieved along this line had been done, and Johnston soon would learn the story. Now was the time for prudence and fast moving. While the army marched swiftly, Jackson took the cars from Charles Town to Winchester—the train which Boteler had ridden to catch still awaited the general. Boarding Boteler's car, Jackson settled in a seat, rested an arm on the seat in front, leaned over and fell asleep as the train rattled away toward Winchester.

Soon Boteler saw in the distance a horseman riding wildly, waving to stop the train. He was wearing a Confederate uniform, and Boteler waked Jackson, who ordered the train halted. Quickly the courier galloped to a window and handed Jackson a dispatch. He read it without comment, tore it up, and requested the conductor, "Go on, sir, if you please." Then he went back to sleep.

What news the courier brought the other passengers learned soon after the train reached Winchester. It had been sent by trustworthy Jed Hotchkiss, who had ridden his horse from Charles Town and had arrived ahead of the cars. He had, in fact, arrived just in time to meet a worn messenger from Col. Z. T. Conner, in charge of the Twelfth Georgia Regiment of Edward Johnson's old force, which had been left as guard and garrison of Front Royal. Conner had been abjectly surprised by Shields, moving west toward Strasburg, and had decamped hastily for Winchester, leaving his regiment to fend for itself. Despite the wails of their colonel, the regiment thought escape possible and, under the command of a somewhat antiquated captain, maintained order and retired on Winchester. Conner's panicked news had been the reason for Hotchkiss's messenger to Jackson.

Staff rumor had it that in the evening the general sent for Colonel Conner. "Colonel, how many men did you have killed, Sir?"

"None," came the miserable reply.

"How many wounded?"

"None, sir."

"Do you call that much of a fight?" With that Conner was ordered in arrest.[74]

Jackson had ample reason to be angry. Conner's men, in getting out of Front Royal, had destroyed some three hundred thousand dollars' worth of captured supplies, and the thrifty John Harman confessed himself "mortified" at the fact that "we had to burn all that was left in the town and abandon those wagons on the road that had been loaded." [75] Then too, Conner's hysteria had immeasurably restricted Jackson's field of maneuver. With Shields firmly planted at Front Royal, the Luray Valley had to be ruled out as a possible line of retreat. And, at Front Royal, Shields stood a scant eleven miles from Strasburg and probable junction with "Pathfinder" Fremont. Jackson's men were about forty-four miles from the same point. The disparity in distance probably accounted to some extent for the summary handling of Conner's case. The general had much to do in Winchester on the night of May 30.

Certain important papers would have to go to Richmond with Colonel Boteler. When the colonel went to headquarters to pick up the dispatches, he had two whisky toddies sent to the general's room, and offered one to his superior. "No, no, colonel, you must excuse me; I never drink intoxicating liquors." "I know that, general, but though you habitually abstain, as I do myself, from everything of the sort, there are occasions, and this is one of them, when a stimulant will do us both good, otherwise I would neither take it myself nor offer it to you. So you must make an exception to your general rule and join me in a toddy to-night."

A little more coaxing finally got the glass in Jackson's hand for a few tentative sips. Then he asked: "Colonel, do you know why I habitually abstain from intoxicating drinks?" Boteler did not. "Why, sir, because I like the taste of them, and when I discovered that to be the case I made up my mind at once to do without them altogether." [76]

At 3 A.M. Saturday, May 31, Jackson interrupted Jed Hotchkiss's slumber with an assignment: "I want you to go to Charlestown and bring up the First Brigade. I will stay in Winchester until you get here if I can, but if I cannot, and the enemy gets here first, you must bring it around through the mountains." [77]

Winder's brigade still skirmished near Harpers Ferry and he had
large numbers of rich wagons with him. His men would have to be res-
cued, and so would the wagons. Hotchkiss noted that Old Jack was in
"fine spirits," despite the fix his army seemed to be in.

Wagons were a problem in Winchester. Harman worked feverishly
to save all the stores and did an excellent job. Large numbers of temporarily impressed wagons had come to him from all parts of the upper
valley and for once he had more than he could use—a quartermaster's
idea of paradise.[78] Jackson, too, still the wagon hunter, supervised evacuation of captured property and the 2,300 Union prisoners who had been
kept at Winchester. They would march toward Staunton under guard. If
they could be taken past Strasburg, they might be retained. Shields,
however, was doubtless beyond Front Royal, and Fremont was coming
from Moorefield via Wardensville toward Strasburg. If they had already
joined forces, there would be trouble.

Meanwhile the Yankees were having trouble of their own. Fremont
was bogged down in a morass of bad roads and a shortage of supplies.
He had promised Lincoln that his troops would be at Strasburg on Saturday, May 31,[79] but the tone of his dispatches lacked conviction. Still, if
he showed moderate diligence and Shields continued his rapid advance,
Lincoln had every reason to believe that his geometrical résumé of the
situation in a message to McClellan on the night of May 31 would be
correct:

A circle whose circumference shall pass through Harper's Ferry, Front-
Royal, and Strasburg, and whose center shall be a little North East of
Winchester, almost certainly has within it this morning, the forces of Jackson, Ewell, and Edward Johnson. Quite certainly they were within it
two days ago. Some part of these forces attacked Harper's Ferry at dark
last evening, and are still in sight this morning. Shields—with McDowell's
advance, retook Front Royal at 11 a.m. yesterday. . . . and saved the
bridge. Fremont, from the direction of Moorefield, promises to be at or
near Strasburg at 5 p.m. to-day. Banks, at Williamsport, with his old force,
and his new force at Harper's Ferry, is directed to co-operate.[80]

If all went well, it would be a simple matter to link up Fremont and
Shields, who could then hold Jackson back while Banks and Saxton attacked him from behind. The circle Lincoln had been constructing for
days was almost complete.

Straight toward the remaining break in the circumference Jackson
drove his columns. Leaving as little captured property behind as possible,[81] Jackson put his wagons on the Valley Pike first, followed by the
large horde of Yankee prisoners under guard, then the infantry. Hotchkiss
he counted on to alert Winder and the First Brigade as quickly as possible; it would take time to get all the army through Winchester and
maybe the van of the Stonewall Brigade could arrive before all the other

troops had gone. If not, they would have to fend for themselves—time was running out. At very "early dawn" the long gray line began unwinding through Winchester. Townspeople watched "anxious and troubled." [82] Not even a whole week had passed since liberation, and now the liberators were leaving. By 2:30 P.M.[83] all Jackson's infantry save Winder's had departed, leaving behind some of Ashby's troopers who would try to keep the town clear of Yankees long enough to get the Stonewall Brigade safely through.

Marching steadily, resting ten minutes every hour, the men trudged south. Stragglers were discouraged, but the steady pace proved too much for many. Jackson mounted the sorrel, took a final look at Winchester, and left with the last of his infantry. He rode forward to the van, as usual, and as the head of the column drew close to Strasburg, his concern increased. No sound of firing could be heard, but rumor had the town in enemy hands at different times during the day. Steadily the advance continued, skirmishers out. No contact—the enemy had not entered Strasburg! Jackson had won the race; the army was safe, so far.[84]

Old Jack knew what had to be done. The trains, a double line of wagons eight miles long,[85] would stay on the Pike heading south toward Woodstock. Infantry camps would be as close to Strasburg as possible, with Ewell's division and Taliaferro's brigade almost in town. Ewell got orders for the next day's work before he went to bed: "Move your command forward promptly at daylight tomorrow morning. When you reach Strasburg, let the troops take the road leading to Wardensville." Old Baldy directed his brigade commanders to move at "earliest dawn," knowing that Jackson expected his troops to stand off Fremont, who doubtless lurked somewhere west of town.[86] The army was going to stay in Strasburg until Winder's brigade safely caught up. Stonewall would save his trains all right, but he was also saving his old brigade.[87]

Scarcely a man in the army could help knowing that they were in danger. Jackson's army—15,000 men when Winder came up—was squarely between McDowell's force of probably 20,000 and Fremont's of probably 17,000.[88] The Old Man, though, seemed unconcerned.

After dark Jackson appeared at Dick Taylor's campfire, sat down and became "more communicative" than the Louisianian ever remembered him, before or after.

> He said Fremont, with a large force, was three miles west of our present camp, and must be defeated in the morning. Shields was moving up Luray Valley, and might cross Massanutten to Newmarket, or continue south until he turned the mountain to fall on our trains near Harrisonburg. The importance of preserving the immense trains, filled with captured stores, was great, and would engage much of his personal attention; while he relied on the army, under Ewell's direction, to deal promptly with Fremont. This he told in a low, gentle voice, and with many interruptions to

afford time, as I thought and believe, for inward prayer. The men said that his anxiety about the wagons was because of the lemons among the stores.[89]

It had been a hard day—most of the army had marched eighteen miles, and Winder's men covered at least twenty-eight, one of the regiments completing thirty-five.[90] This meant that Jackson's heavy concentration was at Strasburg and Winder was at Newtown, about ten miles north of the main army.

Ewell's men made contact with Fremont early on what gave promise of being a pleasant, warm Sabbath.[91] Jackson rode west on the Wardensville road to supervise deployment of part of Ewell's line. Maneuver would be the prudent thing—maneuver to avoid a general engagement. Light contact, sufficient to hold back the enemy advance, would make possible breaking off the fight as soon as Winder cleared Strasburg. But from the dense woods crowning the hills west of town, thick musket smoke and puffs of cannon looked ominous. Fremont seemed to be coming on in dead earnest. Ewell formed line of battle while Jackson watched anxiously.[92] Soon realizing that the field could be in no more capable hands, Jackson headed back for town where his long trains still rolled south. On the way back, he spied Dick Taylor's personal body servant, the "tall, powerful, black as ebony" Tom Strother. He stood firm on a hill which was suddenly churned by concentrated Yankee artillery fire. The general rode up to him and suggested he move to a less exposed point. Strother replied that "if the General pleased, his master told him to stay there and would know where to find him, and he did not believe shells would trouble him"—a sentiment Old Jack would long remember.[93]

Behind him the battle petered out into a game of tag. Ewell could not goad Fremont into an advance, even though he tried driving in the blue skirmish line. Taylor then ventured a successful flank movement around the Federal left. His men "walked down" the Federal line of battle, which melted away before them. Old Baldy had visions of driving Fremont all the way back into the mountains, but stuck to Jackson's instruction not to stray too far from the Pike. "Wagon-hunter" Jackson had to save his precious lemons! And although Ewell and Taylor wanted badly to wreck Fremont, they recognized the prudence in Jackson's orders.[94] Finally Fremont began to back up and all threat to the Army of the Valley ended. Firing died out around noon. Lincoln's circle would never close.[95]

Back down the Pike, Winder's wearied men marched grimly toward Strasburg. Jackson's stock stood at a low ebb with his old brigade. Always he gave them the dirty jobs, and this time he had done too much—they were to be sacrificed to the mad gyrations of "Tom Fool" Jackson. They were cut off, and as they drew near Strasburg, the sound of cannon seemed to confirm every suspicion. But the men soon found they were wrong. Stonewall was fighting to hold the road for them. "Old Jack knows what he's about! He'll take care of us, you bet!" From that moment on, the army never doubted.[96]

There was no more reason to stay at Strasburg. Taylor would place his brigade on a line of hills west of the Pike; the cavalry under the indefatigable Ashby would cover the flanks and rear; the rest of the army would follow the trains south. Still it was a "question of legs." Should Shields get to New Market or Harrisonburg ahead of Jackson, the shadows of death might yet gather over the valley. Weary men and bone-tired animals must press on.[97]

Even though enemy cavalry exerted only occasional pressure on Taylor's rear guard, the men suffered from huge hailstones flailing them during a vicious evening storm. But they toiled forward toward Woodstock. Here Jackson and his staff spent the night, after the general had made sure that a cavalry force would ride swiftly to burn the White House and Columbia bridges over the South Fork of the Shenandoah and prevent Shields's crossing the Massanutton in his rear.[98] A short night's rest at Woodstock ended with the retreating trains falling into wild confusion, getting mixed up with the infantry and the whole mass all but stopping. Jackson, who had risen ahead of his staff, ordered Hotchkiss to straighten out the tangle. Riding into the melee himself, he reproached an infantry commander sternly: "Colonel, why do you not get your brigade together, keep it together, and move on?"

"It's impossible, General; I can't do it."

"Don't say it's impossible. Turn your command over to the next officer. If he can't do it, I'll find someone who can, if I have to take him from the ranks."[99] Up and down the heaving, pitching mass of men, vehicles, and animals Jackson rode, shouting his stern orders. In a remarkably short time order began to appear, and the trains resumed their progress. Hotchkiss stuck with the head of the column and led it into New Market.

Taylor's rear guard, after a severe night's work, was relieved during the day by Winder and by Ashby; the enemy stood checked north of Mount Jackson. Once certain that pursuit had been halted, the general spent the night at Israel Allen's, near Hawkinsville.[100] Usually Jackson refused to impose on private citizens, but the rain and wretched night made solid shelter extremely appealing, and when Sandie Pendleton announced he had found a hospitable house, Old Jack consented to go. When the staff reached the house, and entered a sort of closed porch, they found "an athletic specimen of an infantry soldier" resting on a bench. Taking an instant dislike to intruders who looked suspiciously like cavalrymen, the barefoot, tattered and weary man looked at Jackson's gum cape and boots. "I say, Mister," he asked, "what *cavalry* do you belong to?"

"I don't belong to the cavalry," Jackson replied.

"Don't, eh! Must be couriers for some general or other."

Jackson smiled. One of the staff quickly presented him to the astounded soldier. As Old Jack went on into the house, the soldier fled down the road muttering: "Well! If I didn't put my foot into it that time, may I be d_____!" [101]

At Allen's, Jackson received a report of rear-guard fighting from Col. J. M. Patton. Federal troopers, the colonel said, had been especially daring and had broken through the rear screen briefly, only to have all save one of the attacking force killed or captured. Patton was sorry to see the Yankees shot down. "Why do you say that you saw those Federal soldiers fall with regret?" Jackson asked when Patton's report was finished. The colonel explained that they had displayed more bravery and valor than the enemy usually did, and he thought they deserved a better fate. "No," came the dry comment, "shoot them all: I do not wish them to be brave." [102]

Rain continued to fall. The Shenandoah began to rise. As it rose, it added to Fremont's troubles. Jackson would cross the river at Meem's Bottom, south of Mount Jackson, and if the bridge there were destroyed, Fremont might not be able to cross for some time, even though he had a pontoon train with him. [103] On Tuesday, the third, after his columns had crossed the bridge, Jackson ordered Ashby to burn it. For a while, at least, the Army of the Valley had eluded its pursuers. The general let the army rest, pitching his own tent in a field below New Market. During the night he was all but floated away by a devastating deluge—which was all to the good since the river rose apace.

After moving to higher ground the next morning, Jackson received the unpleasant news that Fremont's pontoons were being used to get him across the North Fork. Swiftly then the army must prepare for further retreat and the rear guard would have to make ready for hard work. Rumors flew thick. Fremont had not crossed at Mount Jackson, but was trying to turn Jackson's flank; so the troops formed in line of battle a bit farther south on a range of hills near Williamson's. [104] The rain still pelted down, and this time it trained its full wrath on Fremont, causing the North Fork to rise twelve feet in four hours. To save his pontoons, Fremont had to cut them loose from the south side of the river and swing them to the north. Once again Jackson had gained a day.

A plan began to take shape in Jackson's mind, and Hotchkiss, without knowing it, had an important part in formulating it. Twice during Wednesday, the fourth, he had been summoned to Jackson's quarters. The general, studying maps, had been curious about certain topography to the south. What, he asked Hotchkiss, was the country like in the vicinity of Port Republic, a little village resting in the angle formed by the North and South Rivers where they met to become the South Fork of the Shenandoah. Two important roads led into the town: one from Harrisonburg, crossing the Shenandoah's South Fork over a good bridge; the other coming southwest, hugging the south shore of the river from Conrad's Store and the Luray Valley. Actually Port Republic represented the apex of a triangle whose base ran from Harrisonburg across the tip of Massanutton to Conrad's Store. A force holding the town could, if certain river crossings were blocked, control the whole upper valley.

Jackson knew something of the ground. When his campaign started in late April, his trains and troops had traversed some of the area which now attracted his notice. How could Port Republic be put to best use? First, a cavalry detachment must burn the Shenandoah bridge at Conrad's, thus leaving only the Port Republic crossing.

God's blessing was manifested in many ways, but particularly in the weather. Deluge after deluge had swelled all valley streams higher than in many years; fording became impossible and bridge repairs were stalled. Marching up Luray, Shields had been frustrated when he reached the ruins of the Columbia and White House bridges. Across Massanutton he heard the roar of cannon, knew that Fremont pressed the enemy, but was powerless to aid. Once again the accursed Massanutton protected the Army of the Valley. When his column camped near Conrad's at about 4 P.M. on June 5, his chance to turn and move to Harrisonburg in front of Jackson had vanished.[105]

Early marching on June 5 soon had Jackson's men in Harrisonburg,[106] but the columns continued and soon turned left, onto a road leading toward Port Republic. Mud replaced the macadamized surface of the Pike, and the wagons stalled badly, despite efforts of special pioneer troops to keep them going.[107] Infantry units found the marching relatively easy, but Major Harman's problems became confounded beyond his wildest imaginings. Jackson's solicitude for the wounded had led him to order the ambulances sent on to Staunton, a course which would reduce the army's trains and spare the maimed the dangers of poor roads and possible enemy raids. Harman approved, but found himself involved in desperate efforts to pass the wounded across the North River at Mount Crawford while tending to the other wagons at the same time.[108] An additional irritation was that the hard-working quartermaster had no real idea of where the wagons were going. For a time it seemed that Old Jack aimed for Waynesboro, then that he intended to leave the valley altogether, and finally that he was seeking ways and means of fighting Fremont and Shields.[109]

The task almost overtaxed even the Gargantuan energies of thirty-eight-year-old John Harman. He confided to a brother that "if I get through this safely Gen. Jackson must either relieve me or reduce the train. I will not be worked so _____ [sic] any longer through this trip. ...Oh for a few days rest!"[110] As long as Harman complained, and protested that the tasks assigned could not possibly be accomplished, Jackson had no worries. He knew his graying quartermaster well by now. Harman, touchy and proud, insisted on being treated as a favored member of the staff and sulked at fancied slights, but he worked harder than most, and in many ways stood unique. "Maj. Harman was a rough man in his manners," recalled one of his clerks,

and made no concealment of the fact that he knew nothing of any duties connected with his department except the active duties. . . . He was . . . kind and generous toward everyone in whom he took any personal interest and I had occasion to recognize his goodness frequently. . . . I always found him cordial and pleasant. He was greatly criticized by his enemies & he was a man to have many, and vague hints were thrown out that he had made use of his position as Q. M. to accumulate money for himself. All such intimations & insinuations I believe to be entirely without foundation. He was the busiest man in the Corps, excepting the Genl. himself & his Adjutant Genl. and gave his mind entirely to the active duties of his office and discharged them to the entire satisfaction of his Chief . . . who would not tolerate any negligence.[111]

As time passed, Harman developed great respect and affection for his superior. But in June, 1862, he believed him somewhat mad. As frequently as Jackson's plans changed, Harman changed direction of the army trains. Finally, after he reached Port Republic on June 6, the supply officer felt the wagons at least temporarily safe, depending on Jackson's whimsy.[112]

When Jackson himself camped near Harrisonburg on the evening of June 5, his trains and his prisoners were close to Port Republic and his infantry strung out between Harrisonburg and the sparse settlement of Cross Keys. Late that night Hotchkiss, who had been on Peaked Mountain observing Shields's movements, brought the general the happy intelligence that the enemy's advance had stopped short of Conrad's Store. Considering the quagmires which Shields had to use for roads, he could not now beat Jackson to the bridge at Port Republic. Once the valley army reached that strategic little hamlet, it would stand neatly between Fremont and Shields. Should fighting become necessary, Jackson now could look forward to throwing his whole force against one or the other Federal army, and if he could fight them one at a time he might be able to indulge in a favorite piece of strategy—hitting a portion of the enemy's force with superior numbers.

When Hotchkiss sought the general that night, he found him sharing Taylor's fire. Ewell's division trailed the army, and Taylor had camped near Harrisonburg. The evening had been pleasant. Tom Strother, whose famous Creole coffee had always frightened the dyspeptic Ewell, poured for his master and distinguished guest. Much to Taylor's surprise, Jackson arose and "gravely shook him by the hand." Seated again, he told Taylor about Strother's steadfast conduct on the Strasburg hill four days before.

Later, Taylor wrote that "I used to fancy that there was a mute sympathy between General Jackson and Tom, as they sat silent by a camp fire, the latter respectfully withdrawn; and the ... incident ... at Strasburg cemented this friendship." [113]

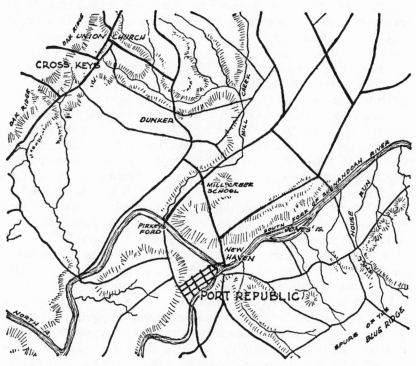

Vicinity of Port Republic

June 6 found the Army of the Valley concentrating near Port Republic, with Ashby's men fanned out guarding the flanks and rear. When Jackson established headquarters at the hospitable Kemper house, he had reason to be satisfied. Shields and Fremont could not join without running into the Confederates, since Jackson held the all-important Shenandoah bridge; his position at Port Republic limited Shields's field of maneuver to the narrow strip of ground between the Blue Ridge and the river, and put the Confederates on the flank of any move Fremont might make toward Staunton. Safely at Jackson's back loomed Brown's Gap in the Blue Ridge, which offered easy access to the Virginia Central Railroad in case his army was needed at Richmond and also gave him a chance to move swiftly east of the mountains to intercept Shields, should he attempt a flanking march. Briefly stated, Jackson's position gave him strategic and tactical superiority—his army could either intercept or immobilize any moves the enemy could make. [114]

While he waited on June 6 for the Federal plans to develop, Jackson probably received a letter from President Davis, written on the fourth. Although he praised Jackson's "brilliant campaign," the President could not spare reinforcements to the valley. Boteler had done all he could, but Jackson, as usual, would have to get along with what he had.[115]

Bad news it was, but Stonewall had grown used to bad news. It did make necessary certain changes in plan. No longer could he think of renewing the offensive, driving Shields on Front Royal and isolating Fremont.[116]

Without reinforcements, Jackson's men had accomplished about all even he could expect. During the afternoon of the sixth he penned a dispatch to Johnston, who he thought remained in command of the forces defending Richmond in spite of a wound received during the recent action at Seven Pines. "Should my command be required at Richmond," he wrote, "I can be at Mechum's River Depot, on the Central Railroad, the second day's march, and part of the command can reach there the first day, as the distance is 25 miles. At present I do not see that I can do much more than rest my command and devote its time to drilling." [117]

While Old Jack had been thinking out the problems posed by lack of reinforcements, Ashby—newly commissioned a brigadier general—had been engaged with Fremont's advance, which had pushed ahead with vigor. A Federal column was feeling its way southeast of Harrisonburg on the Port Republic road. Spotting Ashby's men mounting for a fight, the bluecoats quickly deployed and charged, only to be met with one of Ashby's wild and reckless countercharges. After a smashing moment of impact, the lines recoiled and the Yankees left over sixty prisoners behind.

One of the dismounted Yankee horsemen ambled into the Confederate lines without visible concern. He was a colonel, a big man with "huge mustaches, cavalry boots adorned with spurs worthy of a *caballero*, slouched hat, and plume." As the prisoner passed, Rob Wheat of the famous Louisiana Tigers leaped off his horse with a shout: "Percy! Old boy!" "Why, Bob!" came the reply, and there in the shadow of Massanutton two of Garibaldi's old soldiers were reunited—Sir Percy Wyndham, of many of the world's armies and navies, and Rob Wheat, who had also had his day as a soldier of fortune.[118] After the reunion, Kyd Douglas escorted the distinguished prisoner to Jackson's headquarters. Although the Britisher's appearance and reputation were glamorous, Douglas managed to work up a dislike for him: "He was not an attractive-looking warrior and looked like what he was, a soldier of fortune." [119]

Jackson greeted Wyndham pleasantly enough and the two settled down for a talk. By then the general knew that Ashby expected the Federals to continue advancing and that he had called for infantry support. No need to worry, though—Ashby and Ewell could handle the field.

While the two were talking—it was about 9 P.M.—an officer tapped on Jackson's door and asked to speak privately. Excusing himself, Jackson went into the hall. The messenger's news was impossible—Ashby was dead! After repelling the early Union cavalry attack, Ashby had called for infantry support, and when it arrived he had decided with Ewell to try to flank an advancing Pennsylvania infantry regiment called the "Bucktails" and drive it into the open, where it would be ripe for his men to ride it down. Something went wrong when Ashby, leading two infantry regiments, got into dense woods to the right of his original position. Ewell had to send him reinforcements and a hot fight raged for a while. At length the enemy retired. But Ashby had been hit. First his horse was shot from under him, then, while leading the infantry on foot, waving his saber —"Charge, men; for God's sake, charge"—suddenly he was down, a bullet through his chest.[120]

Jackson, heartsick, had Wyndham dismissed, locked himself in his room and paced. The Lord giveth and the Lord taketh away.... Ashby was so close to him. No model disciplinarian, he had been much more— brave, courageous, a gentleman and a soldier. "As a partisan officer I never knew his superior," Jackson would record. "His daring was proverbial; his powers of endurance almost incredible; his tone of character heroic, and his sagacity almost intuitive in divining the purposes and movements of the enemy." [121] War was not the place for emotion. Killing and dying were everyday affairs. But sometimes the killing and dying struck close to the heart. Jackson would agree with the trooper who spoke the eulogy of Ashby's men: "We shall miss you mightily, General, we shall miss you in camp; we shall miss you as we go out to scout. But we shall miss you most of all when we go out to—" and here a sob choked off the words.[122] Maggie, with her gift for beauty, would help express the void left by Ashby's going:

> Saw ye the veterans—
> Hearts that had known
> Never a quail of fear,
> Never a groan—
> Sob mid the fight they win,
> Tears their stern eyes within
> Ashby, our Paladin,
> Ashby is gone! [123]

News of Ashby's death soon reached Richmond, then the country, and mourning was widespread. General Lee, preoccupied as he was with McClellan's operations against the capital, took time on June 7 to write the Secretary of War that "I grieve at the death of General Ashby." The question of his successor bothered not only Jackson but the Richmond authorities. While the attention of the War Department focused on the bereaved Army of the Valley, Lee took occasion to urge reinforcements to Jackson. He had instructed Jackson to rest his army and to be ready to march toward Richmond, but to miss no opportunity of striking a telling blow. Any blow he struck would be harder had he a few more men, and Lee admonished the Secretary that "we must aid a gallant man if we perish." [124]

Saturday, June 7, dawned clear and sunny. Roads were still miry, but they would be drying soon. By then Jackson had formed a good idea of the ground near Port Republic and had faithful Jed Hotchkiss hard at work on a detailed map of the surrounding country. The important points of terrain which had to be considered were the two rivers which flowed on either side of Port Republic, the lower ground on the southeast shores of both South River and the South Fork of the Shenandoah, and the high, commanding ridge which looked down on Port Republic from the left bank of North River, near the point at which it merged into the Shenandoah. From this ridge all the ground east and southeast rolled away in a gentle, open meadow. One or two miles away a line of heavy woods swathed the spurs of the Blue Ridge. The whole area could be plastered by well-placed guns on the high ground. Of further importance was the one bridge at Port Republic, a long wooden affair, spanning North River at the northeast end of town. South River, running along the village's eastern side, could be crossed by two fords a little more than half a mile apart, the "upper ford" being slightly southeast of Port Republic and the "lower ford" opposite the town proper.

A quick glance would show that if Jackson held the high ground north and slightly west of the village, he could dominate the field over which Shields would have to come from Conrad's Store. At the same time, he would be in a good position to hold up Fremont's advance and prevent his joining Shields. If, on the other hand, Jackson lost control of the high ridge while engaged with Shields on the eastern side of the Shenandoah, his army could be mauled by Fremont's guns placed on the ridge. Geography, then, dictated that Jackson stay north of North River, keeping hold of Port Republic with his artillery. He could put the long wagon train on a road leading south, out of Port Republic toward Mount Meridian and Brown's Gap, and have it largely out of danger.[125]

Tactically there were some objections to fighting Fremont first, while Shields remained safe on the other side of the river. But on June 7 Jackson reasoned that if he could goad Fremont into a fight, he still could hold the ridge near Port Republic and keep Shields at arm's length. He wanted very much to avoid burning the North River bridge, as this would limit his field of movement. The only movement he wanted to limit was the enemy's.

Intelligence reports indicated that Fremont approached slowly from Harrisonburg and that Shields still hung about the outskirts of Conrad's Store. About four miles northwest of Port Republic, on the Harrisonburg road, Ewell's division held a position near the settlement of Cross Keys. There Ewell's men would be in line to receive Fremont's advance, and Jackson rode back up the road to supervise personally the attempt to entice the "Pathfinder" into a misstep. Nothing seemed inviting to Fremont's vanguard—they refused to attack. Finally, concluding that there remained no hope of contact, Jackson rode with his staff to Port Republic and pitched the headquarters tent near Dr. Kemper's house, just outside town on the Mount Meridian road.[126]

For a change it seemed that Sunday, June 8, might be a day of rest and relaxation; the troops and the general's staff could enjoy a fine, cool day. Jackson seriously wondered if either Fremont or Shields intended to fight. So far everything they had done indicated that so long as they were separated they would not be daring. Late in the night a rumor that Shields had at last begun to move south seemed worth checking, and Jackson had sent a cavalry scout across the Shenandoah, and later sent another under one of Ashby's most trusted captains, G. W. Myers.[127]

Early in the morning the captain of the first scouting party sent word that he had contacted a Federal scout of twenty men near the North River bridge at Port Republic, and that he had pursued them without result for more than two miles east of the town. When he reached the Lewis mansion, he turned north for another two miles toward Conrad's Store. Suddenly he ran smack into a Yankee cavalry regiment, and while he wrote, the enemy were just below General Lewis's.[128] Jackson read the dispatch carefully, but did not become alarmed. Nothing had changed, unless Shields and Fremont both decided to move vigorously at the same time. Should that be the case, things might become nasty. As yet there was little to worry about. Deciding to check on the situation personally, Jackson sent a copy of the cavalry report to Ewell and suggested that for the time being he confine his operations against Fremont to picket quarreling alone.[129] The general did not hurry his own activities. Dabney reported to him, requesting orders, and was told that there would be no military operations that day: "You know I always try to keep the Sabbath if the enemy will let me." [130]

So beautiful was the day that Jackson, with some of the staff, lingered in the front yard of Dr. Kemper's, watching horses graze and enjoying a rare moment of leisure. Sometime around 9 A.M.[131] a trooper galloped up to Jackson. Gasping, he blurted the news that Yankees had crossed the South River with artillery and guns and were already in the town. "Go back and fight them," the general replied. Firing broke out not far off, and Jackson, whose horse was not handy, strode briskly toward the sound. Soon others of the staff joined him and someone brought his horse. Down one of the streets Jackson had seen a Union cavalry force. Whether they had seen him and the cluster of staff officers he did not wait to discover.

Mounting hastily, Old Jack dashed for the bridge. Not all his staff made their escape—Col. Stapleton Crutchfield and Lt. Edward Willis, bringing up the rear, were captured.[132]

Unexpectedly the situation in and around Port Republic had become critical. Jackson gained the safety of the north bank of North River and rode directly to some of his batteries, ordering them to fire on any Federals they could see. A defense of the bridge must be organized. If the Federals succeeded in destroying it, the army would be cut off from its ordnance and other wagons. Jackson quickly ordered Winder and Taliaferro to hold the span. While the infantry formed, movements of some Union artillery disturbed Jackson. Two guns crossed South River into Port Republic and disappeared. From below town the sharp rattle of musketry and bark of guns indicated an attack on the wagon train, strung out on the Mount Meridian road. Where were the two Union guns headed? They had tried some long shots at the bridge with no effect—were they moving up for closer work or joining the attack on the wagons?

Soon a single gun rumbled up a street toward the bridge. Looking at the gunners closely, Jackson gave the order to Poague to "fire on that gun!" Poague hesitated, and his gunners shouted, "General, those are our men!" "Fire on that gun!" Poague broke in to say, "General, I know those are our men." When Jackson hesitated, Poague explained that a new battery, recently sent to the army, had uniforms which much resembled the Union garb. Quickly Jackson rode a bit closer to the ridge overlooking the span. In a loud, commanding voice he ordered: "Bring that gun up here." There was no response. Again, louder this time and angry: "Bring that gun up here, I say!" The gun began to swing around so that it pointed toward Jackson and the battery on the ridge. No doubt now—a Federal gun. "Let 'em have it," commanded Jackson in quick, sharp tones. An exchange of shots resulted in a few casualties among the infantry coming up toward the bridge, but Jackson sat his horse unruffled. Wheeling, he rode to the head of the infantry, directed the men to go down to the bridge, fire a volley, and rush across with fixed bayonets. When he gave the order to use cold steel, Jackson dropped his reins, viewed the unfolding charge with excited gaze, and raised both his hands high in the air. A roar from his men was lost in a ripping volley which drove the gunners from the bridge, and in an instant it was in Confederate hands.[133]

Providentially a patched-up defense of the wagon trains had discouraged the Union cavalry regiment by now. Enemy horsemen and artillerymen raced north, out of range of the guns on the ridge—so that both the wagons and the bridge were safe. Jackson soon learned that the shameful conduct of some of his cavalry in Port Republic had allowed the sudden attack. Their negligence could have been costly indeed.[134]

While the threat to the wagons and bridge had been at its peak, Jackson had sent an urgent order to Taylor's brigade—double-quick to

Port Republic. Not waiting to quibble about getting an order from Ewell, à la "Maryland" Steuart, Taylor moved instantly, sending word of his action to Old Baldy. Actually, his prompt obedience posed some troublesome problems, because Ewell's division had been skirmishing with Fremont since early in the morning, and Taylor's skirmishers were engaged. Slipping Arnold Elzey's brigade into line where his own men had been, Taylor soon had his infantry striding rapidly toward Port Republic. Two miles glided by in quick time, when another officer brought word from Old Jack. Taylor must halt where he was and await further orders.[135]

Just as the danger at the bridge subsided, Jackson had heard sounds of battle from the direction of Cross Keys. At that moment he had ordered Taylor to halt and had started to ride toward the fighting. About half an hour after sending orders to stop Taylor, Jackson found him waiting on the Cross Keys road. Succinctly explaining to the capable brigadier why he had been summoned and then stopped, Jackson sketched the trouble at Port Republic, leaving out all mention of his close escape. That done, he rode on to find Ewell, trailed by Taylor, whose brigade went into reserve behind the battle line.

When Jackson found Old Baldy enjoying his fight with Fremont, he knew that the battle had gone well. It had begun early in the morning and for a long time sputtered between opposing skirmish lines. Shortly before noon Fremont opened an artillery duel and then ventured something like an advance on the Confederate right, which was brutally repulsed by sixty-year-old Isaac R. Trimble and his brigade. Trimble then took the offensive and drove the Union right a good mile before Dick Ewell reluctantly called a halt. Jackson and Ewell consulted and agreed that the attack should not be pushed too far. With the Cross Keys field under Ewell's capable charge, Jackson went back to Port Republic, where he found Taliaferro, as per orders, in the town, and Winder posted down the Shenandoah, observing the Federals around the Lewis house. He had guessed correctly; Shields had not advanced. Replying to a staff officer's suggestion that Shields would surely move to cooperate with Fremont's battle, then clearly audible, Jackson had said, "No sir!" and pointed to his artillery on the high ridge overlooking the east side of the river. "No! He cannot do it; I should tear him to pieces."[136]

As the afternoon wore on, Old Jack appeared lost in thought. Once he roused long enough to address his Reverend Chief of Staff: "Major, wouldn't it be a blessed thing if God would give us a glorious victory today?" His tone was low, but his glance fervent. While he hoped for the aid of Providence, he planned carefully. By late afternoon he knew that Ewell had stalled Fremont cold, and had done it at minimum cost—288 casualties.[137] The time had come to attack.

As he thought out his plan, Jackson decided to attack Shields the next morning. There were several reasons for picking Shields as the target: "First I was nearer to him, second he had the smallest army, then I was nearer my base of supplies, had a good way of retreat if beaten— and Fremont had a good way to retreat if I had beaten him, while I knew Shields had a bad road to go over." [138] With a narrow front, Shields's freedom of maneuver would be restricted and Jackson might be able to use fewer troops than usual in attacking. If Shields were attacked quickly and driven decisively, Jackson might be able to whirl his attacking force, cross the rivers at Port Republic, and join Ewell for a joint thrust on Fremont. There was a chance for a magnificent battle which could result in the defeat of two separate enemy armies on the same day. And if something went wrong, the bridge could be burned after Ewell got across—neatly canceling Fremont out of further operations.

Such, then, was the plan which formed in Jackson's mind during the afternoon of June 8. Orders were issued in quick succession. Ewell would have the hardest job, since some of his division had to hold back Fremont while the rest of the army dealt with Shields. Old Baldy was summoned to headquarters. Jackson outlined the plan; it called for daring and cool-ness and suited Ewell thoroughly. That night, Jackson said, Ewell should move his trains over North River to his division so that rations could be issued. That done, the wagons were to be sent back and put on the road for Brown's Gap in the Blue Ridge, headed out of danger. At Jackson's favorite marching hour—"earliest dawn"—Ewell would start toward Port Republic, leaving Trimble's brigade supported by a regiment and the Irish battalion in front of Fremont with orders to delay him as long as possible, and if hard pressed, to fall back across the North River, burn-ing the bridge behind them. While Ewell moved toward Port Republic, Winder would cross North River via the bridge, then South River via a temporary wagon span, and go into action against Shields. Ewell would follow and support Winder's attack.

Leaving nothing to chance, Jackson summoned Col. J. M. Patton, who would be in charge of Ewell's rear guard. There had to be a heavy show of strength in Fremont's front the next morning. "I wish you to throw out all your men, if necessary, as skirmishers," Jackson told Patton earnestly, "and to make a great show, so as to cause the enemy to think the whole army are behind you. Hold your position as well as you can; then fall back, when obliged; take a new position; hold it in the same way; and *I will be back to join you in the morning.*" Patton understood, but reminded the general that his unit was small and that the ground over which he might have to withdraw offered few natural strongholds. With this in mind, how long would Jackson be absent? A time schedule had already been formed in the general's mind: "By the blessing of Providence, I hope to be back by ten o'clock." [139]

One final personal touch was needed. The vital temporary wagon bridge over South River must be constructed in time for use at dawn.

Jackson would supervise the construction himself. Shortly after midnight he collected a group of pioneers and directed their work at the ford. The bridge when completed left much to be desired, but in the moonlight it looked serviceable.[140]

Now Old Jack could permit himself to rest until time for the men to be moving out. Back to headquarters, up to his room, and then without bothering to take off his saber, boots, or anything else, Jackson fell face down on the bed and slept.

Not long after he heard someone enter his room, remain briefly, and then start to leave. Turning over, Jackson sat up and called out: "Who is that?" In the light of the sputtering candle Col. John D. Imboden moved closer and started to apologize for the intrusion. He had been looking for Sandie Pendleton. "That is all right. It's time to be up. I am glad to see you. Were the men all up as you came through camp?"

"Yes, General, and cooking."

"That's right. We move at daybreak. Sit down. I want to talk to you." Imboden knew better than to prod the conversation and waited. Finally Old Jack talked of Ashby's death—an irreparable loss, he said. Seizing the opportunity of a break in Jackson's discourse, Imboden changed the subject: "General, you made a glorious winding-up of your four weeks' work yesterday."

"Yes, God blessed our army again yesterday, and I hope with his protection and blessing we shall do still better to-day." [141]

Then, speaking of the impending battle, Jackson told Imboden that he expected the new guns which he had brought to be used in breaking up any stand Shields might make in the wooded country near the Lewis house.

Soon Jackson was outside, mounting up. His confused staff joined him; they were well trained by now not to be late. "Early dawn," in the General's parlance, meant exactly that. What had confused them was all the crossing and recrossing of the river by the wagons during the night. John Harman had been hard pressed to get the moving done, and doubtless he kept up a constant stream of his impressive epithets. It seemed foolhardy to jeopardize the wagons by shuttling them back and forth, but Sandie Pendleton explained it in a well-used phrase—Old Jack was "crazy again." [142]

Oblivious to the professional criticism of his staff, Jackson looked anxiously for signs that his plans were working. They were. Before 5 A.M. Winder was encountered with the head of his brigade. He was crossing North River, leaving the ridge in charge of part of Taliaferro's brigade. Jackson noted that Winder, as usual, was prompt. He had ordered the brigadier to be in Port Republic at 4:45 A.M., and Winder was there. As to orders, Jackson would ride with the brigade. All that need be divulged at the moment was that Winder should cross South River via the temporary bridge. After that the baffled brigadier received instructions from his taciturn commander to follow the road leading northeast toward the Lewis house. With an advance guard out, Winder moved through the morning haze. Sometime around 7 A.M. the news came from up front: a Yankee picket line had been found. What were Jackson's orders? [143] Drive in the pickets, attack the enemy—quickly now. The enemy's position had strength, but the time factor pressed. A determined assault might break the Yankee line suddenly, and then the army could be about the business of dealing with Fremont.

His own failure to reconnoiter worked against Jackson's attack. From the Shenandoah eastward toward the Blue Ridge the ground rose gently, broke sharply upward about a mile from the river, then fell away in a slope for a short distance before it rose again. On the second tier of table-land stood the country house of the Lewis family, Lewiston, and behind it, east, was a fairly large "coaling" yard, where charcoal was made. The coaling was the left of the Federal line and was anchored by six guns not visible to the advancing Confederates. General E. B. Tyler, the Union commander in charge of Shields's vanguard, had his center near the Port Republic road and his right extended toward the Shenandoah. Altogether he held strong ground and had deployed his 3,000 men advantageously. But he was surprised by the swiftness of Jackson's attack.

Winder began the attack efficiently. His skirmishers bounded rapidly through ripening wheat toward the Union lines. Two guns opening in support of the advance drove in Tyler's pickets.[144] Winder deployed in line of battle and followed his skirmishers across the wheat field toward what seemed to be the enemy's line, strung out behind a double fence along a lane running perpendicular to the road.

No sooner did the advance begin than a cloud of shells thundered down from the Lewiston coaling ground; the fire was accurate and fast and it killed men. Jackson saw instantly that the Federal guns high up and to the right of his line would decimate Winder's brigade, stall and finally repulse his advance. A force must be sent at once to take those guns. Some of his own artillery would move to the right and endeavor to find a position above the enemy's battery.

Things began to go wrong. Winder had expected support from the Thirty-third Virginia of his own brigade and Jackson expected Taylor's Louisianians on the field momentarily. But they did not come. Spying the liberated Crutchfield on the field, Jackson ordered him to hurry to the rear and urge Taylor to speed up his advance. In the meantime Jackson waited anxiously for his flanking regiments to get hold of the coalyard, and for the comforting sound of Carpenter's guns opening from above the Yankee position. While he waited he watched the Stonewall Brigade cut to pieces by a cross fire of shells and musketry.

From his vantage point just behind the center of Winder's thinning and wavering line, Jackson saw that the battle had gone awry. Swiftly he made a decision. No chance now to gain a swift victory over Shields's advance and turn on Fremont—the Army of the Valley would do well to beat Shields. Two couriers were hurried in succession to Trimble: give up the delaying action and march instantly for the battlefield, burning the bridge across the North River.[145] Every man available must be thrown at Tyler; Winder's line had to be strengthened and the death-dealing guns on the right had to be eliminated. How?

Reliable Dick Taylor brought the answer with him—his brigade. Hearing the sound of firing, he had marched quickly from his night's bivouac not far east of Port Republic.[146] Jackson saw him coming, and greeted him in normal tones: "Delightful excitement." Taylor replied that he was glad to hear the general was enjoying himself "but thought he might have an indigestion of such fun if the six-gun battery was not silenced." Turning to Jed Hotchkiss, who fortunately appeared just at that moment, Jackson commanded him to "take General Taylor around and take those batteries." [147] Off into the laurel underbrush went Hotchkiss, Taylor, and the leading elements of the Louisiana Brigade.

Riding out a little ahead of Winder's line,[148] Jackson observed Union skirmishers moving forward—the enemy was getting set. Any minute now they might launch a general assault which assuredly would blow the then thin Confederate infantry units right off the field. But there was a touch of Jackson in Winder. He would not wait for an attack, he delivered one. It was, of course, just the thing to do, weak as he was. Well and gallantly delivered and supported by the few guns he had been able to keep in action on the exposed wheat field, Winder's sudden advance shocked the Federals into caution. When the outnumbered attackers reached a fence which offered some protection, they had to use it. They could go no farther. Desperately Winder kept them where they were until numbers of men had used up all their cartridges.[149] At length, the hard-pressed commander of the Stonewall Brigade called for reinforcements. It was his second call, and again he got no help.

Jackson understood the situation clearly. If Taylor did not open up on the Federal battery soon, Winder would have to retreat. Precious now, time passed. Still the guns on the right pumped shell into Winder's ranks. Jackson saw his line gradually start to go to pieces. The few guns which had been able to stay in action against the Lewiston battery had done no good, and now the infantry had stayed beyond the limit of endurance. A break in the line! Men running to the rear, losing organization in a headlong flight from the battle. Winder and the regimental commanders tried to halt them, to re-form them, but the men were beyond stopping for the moment.

Fortunately Dick Ewell had at last come on the field, and seeing the plight of Winder, he directed an attack on the Federal flank with part of his Second Brigade. Surprised by the attack, the Federal line faltered, but changed front and drove Ewell into the band of woods on the right of the Confederate line. The scene greeting Jackson's gaze was one of Confederate retreat and confusion everywhere.

Just at the moment which Jackson felt most critical,[150] the guns on the coaling ground stopped firing. Taylor had made his thrust! Unknown to Jackson at the time Taylor had made three thrusts, and had paid a high price for the guns, but he had taken them. Grandly and with precision, the Union army changed front and moved toward Lewiston and Taylor's little force. Unsupported, he could not hold out.

Winder, now much relieved as the Federals concentrated on Taylor, re-formed and pressed forward, directing a heavy artillery fire on the exposed flank of the Union line moving east up the Lewiston hill. Coordinated as if by previous signal, Taylor—aided by Dick Ewell himself and two regiments—jumped off in an attack at the very moment that Winder began his artillery pounding and advance. That did it: the Federal line wavered, fell back and began a retreat hastened by the guns Taylor had captured and by a volley from Taliaferro's newly arrived brigade. No rout, this, but an ordered withdrawal. Still, it marked the end of Yankee resistance—the battle was won by 11 A.M.

Finding Ewell and touching him gently on the arm, Jackson summed up the significance of the battle: "General, he who does not see the hand of God in this is blind, sir, blind!" [151] Then, with a fierce battle light in his eyes, Jackson rode up to Taylor, grasped his hand as he had done at Winchester, and promised that the captured guns would belong to the Louisiana Brigade. Wild cheers from Taylor's men drowned out the parting shots of Shields's retreating regiments.[152]

Pursuit was pushed, since Jackson wanted every possible advantage wrung from victory. Old Jack himself led the forces pressing on Shields's heels but after some four miles, increasingly dense woods made further advance risky. Reluctantly Jackson called a halt for the infantry, and let the cavalry stay with the enemy for another four miles.[153]

Back toward Port Republic Jackson rode, to discover that Trimble had done his work well. He had crossed North River and succeeded in burning the bridge just ahead of Fremont. Now the high ridge overlooking the recent scene of slaughter was lined with Fremont's men and guns, but he could not get at Jackson's army. He contented himself with shelling some of the ambulances scudding about the battlefield.[154]

Port Republic had been a bloody battle. Jackson lost more men here than in any other valley combat—over 800. Tyler, who fought the battle with a force of about 3,000, had few casualties in the fight but during the retreat many of his men were captured. Total Federal losses were around 1,018.[155]

Now that Tyler had been disposed of, Jackson determined not to leave his army open to any possible combination of Fremont and Shields. As soon as the men could be rounded up, the booty of victory amassed and put into wagons,[156] the infantry started on the road for Brown's Gap. By June 10 the Army of the Valley was perched in a mountain eyrie, safe from attack. Stonewall Jackson still looked down on his valley —and now, as a result of his dazzling maneuvers during May and June, his mere presence was a guarantee of protection.

13

"JACKSON IS COMING"

— J. GORGAS

Y ESTERDAY," announced the telegram from Jackson, "God crowned our arms with success by repulsing the attacks of Fremont & Shields at Port Republic." Lee read the terse notice with elation; this might be the time for Jackson—"gallant Jackson"—to put his plan for invading Yankeeland into effect. When Boteler, in early June,[1] had first explained Jackson's idea for a Northern offensive, Richmond authorities had agreed with the scheme in principle but had confessed themselves unable to see where they could lay their hands on the men Jackson needed.

Lee had felt even more pessimistic after he received Jackson's dispatch to Johnston, written two days before the action at Cross Keys. That letter, in which Jackson seemed to contemplate nothing more than resting and drilling his little band,[2] indicated that even replacements for his losses would be useless and ought not to be sent.[3] With the Army of the Valley idle for the moment, Lee had again considered the expedient of bringing it east to assist in an attack on McClellan.[4]

Abruptly the situation changed. The amazing Jackson, hurling his small army first at one and then another of his enemies, had gained a double victory to top off his lightning Valley Campaign. Not only had he pinned down some 60,000 Yankees in his district (at least 40,000 of whom should have been aiding Little Mac in his glacierlike advance on Richmond) but he had also crippled both Fremont and Shields to such an extent that they were retiring down both sides of the Massanutton.[5] A weakened, frightened, and demoralized foe offered rich opportunities. With sizable support, Jackson might now be able to sweep down the valley and launch a profitable crossing of the Potomac. Could troops be

284

sped to the valley? [6] The question, put to the Chief Executive on June 10, brought swift approval. Davis, aware that a Georgia brigade under Gen. Alexander R. Lawton and a North Carolina battalion had already been ordered to Jackson, supported Lee's proposal to send two of Lee's own brigades west.[7] The brilliant West Pointer, William H. C. Whiting, would command the two brigades and he would leave on June 11.[8] These reinforcements (or replacements) totaled no more than 7,000 men and would bring Jackson's strength up to about 18,500.

News did not travel fast, and Jackson, poised strategically in Brown's Gap, hatched another plot, much like the one already proposed. He wanted Boteler to go again to Richmond with an appeal for men. If strengthened, Jackson would move rapidly north on the eastern side of the Blue Ridge, cross behind Banks, who had retired on Winchester, destroy him, and cross into Maryland and Pennsylvania.

Before the trusted aide left for the capital, Jackson read a letter from Lee suggesting that he might be needed in Richmond. Written on June 8, it had been penned before Lee had learned of the victories of June 8 and 9. But the possibility of moving to Richmond had never been out of Jackson's mind. His army's main function had always been to defend Richmond, one way or another; now, apparently, it would defend the capital at close quarters. Still, Boteler should go with Jackson's plan; its purpose, too, was the defense of Richmond. A strong thrust, suddenly delivered at the heart of the Union, would doubtless draw McClellan back or at least drain off large numbers of his army. Richmond's relief could be achieved while the North was made to feel some of the ravages of war.

At the same time, in a dispatch written on the thirteenth, and carried by Boteler, Jackson told Lee that "you can halt the reinforcements coming here if you so desire, without interfering with my plans provided the movement to Richmond takes place. So far as I am concerned my opinion is that we should not attempt another march down the valley to Winchester until we are in a condition under the blessing of Providence to hold the country."[9] That changed Lee's mind; if Jackson doubted the wisdom of a diversionary advance and advised only a strong, serious offensive, then McClellan ought to be disposed of first, leaving to the valley army only a mopping-up operation. Lee had already explained the situation to Jackson:

Headquarters,
Near Richmond, Va. June 11, 1862.

General: Your recent successes have been the cause of the liveliest joy in this army as well as in the country. The admiration excited by your skill and boldness has been constantly mingled with solicitude for your situation. The practicability of re-enforcing you has been the subject of earnest consideration. It has been determined to do so at the expense of weakening this army. Brigadier-General Lawton with six regiments from Georgia is on the way to you, and Brigadier-General Whiting with eight veteran regiments leaves here to-day. The object is to enable you to crush the forces opposed to you. Leave your enfeebled troops to watch the country and guard the passes covered by your cavalry and artillery, and with your main body, including Ewell's division and Lawton's and Whiting's commands, move rapidly to Ashland by rail or otherwise, as you may find most advantageous, and sweep down between the Chickahominy and Pamunkey, cutting up the enemy's communications &c., while this army attacks General McClellan in front. He will thus, I think, be forced to come out of his intrenchments, where he is strongly posted on the Chickahominy, and apparently preparing to move by gradual approaches on Richmond. Keep me advised of your movements, and, if practicable, precede your troops, that we may confer and arrange for simultaneous attack.

I am, with great respect, your obedient servant,

R. E. Lee,
GENERAL.[10]

While Lee's letter and the reinforcements were on the way to Jackson, he had begun the job of refurbishing his army. Down from their perch in the mountains came the weary infantry to find camps in the fertile rolling ground south and east of Port Republic. South River was to be used for bathing, followed by a general washing of clothes and other equipment.[11] The wagon train could now be replenished from Staunton, and regular rations issued.

Old Jack relaxed. Within a few days of the battle of Port Republic he was unwinding from the long strain of marching, meeting time schedules, and fighting. The physical features of the region helped: all around the area from Massanutton south through Port Republic and on to the Blue Ridge, fascinating caves and grottoes abounded, many of them well known to local residents and vacationing tourists of happier days. Not far from Port Republic, on a road leading ultimately to Staunton,[12] was famous Weyer's Cave, and near here Jackson established army headquarters for a few days.

Now there was time to tell Anna something of what had been happening. She knew already that Thomas and the army had come through the last two battles safely, and that God had once again protected His faithful. Thomas wrote her on June 14 that there had been something special in God's protecting grace for the past several weeks—he had "thrown his shield over me in the various apparent dangers to which I have been exposed." Perhaps Dick Taylor had been right when he felt that around Jackson and those close to him was a circle of invulnerability. One thing was certain: The Army of the Valley had been delivered from evil by Providence and there would be a time of thanksgiving.

On Saturday, June 14, after cavalry and infantry units had effectively threatened an advance against the retreating Yankees, the general called his men to prayer.[13] The next day, the Reverend Chief of Staff preached in the camp of Winder's brigade, and in the afternoon communion was taken by the Third Brigade in their hushed wooded camps. Reverend Dr. Dabney made "some excellent remarks," admitted the critical Hotchkiss, and drew the earnest attention of Jackson, who was sitting "humbly devout" among the men.[14] Over the whole assembly a solemn spirit prevailed, with at least one man thinking of home and peace. "How I do wish for peace," Thomas confided to Anna, later asking, "Wouldn't you like to get home again?"[15]

At Mount Meridian on June 16, news reached the war-weary general that reinforcements were arriving. Jackson's pleasure spilled over to his staff and they basked in his reflected good humor. Forgotten for the moment were the long miles of marching and pent-up fatigue. New men, new blood, new battles—every indication was that Old Jack would attack somewhere soon.

With the men Jackson also received important instructions from Richmond. Lee had read Jackson's dispatch carried by Boteler, and after noting the positions of Fremont and Shields as well as Jackson's opinion that no move should be made down the valley lest it be decisive, had made a decision. Jackson should come to Richmond as soon as possible— if he concurred in Lee's views. He did. Lee had correctly surmised that the divided position of Fremont and Shields would make attack on both difficult and would complicate the problem of breaking off pursuit for quick transfer to Richmond when that became imperative. Obviously the thing to do was make that transfer now.

Deception and mystery—these must be practiced to the fullest possible degree. "To be efficacious, the movement must be secret," wrote Lee, adding, "be careful to guard from friends and foes your purpose and your intention of personally leaving the valley. The country is full of spies, and our plans are immediately carried to the enemy." While leaving the final arrangements in Jackson's hands, Lee mentioned one compelling consideration:

> Unless McClellan can be driven out of his intrenchments he will move by positions under cover of his heavy guns within shelling distance of Richmond. I know of no surer way of thwarting him than that proposed. I should like to have the advantage of your views and be able to confer with you. Will meet you at some point on your approach to the Chickahominy.[16]

Actually Lee need not have taken pains to explain so fully the reasons for ruling out the offensive. Jackson could see by the limits placed on the reinforcements that a decisive advance down the valley and across the Potomac would be impossible. He and Lee were thinking alike. Concentration at the threatened point became essential when nothing more of value could be achieved by diversion. The sooner Jackson moved the better, since the enemy probably would begin a move to send McDowell back to the Fredericksburg line where he might again work toward co-operation with McClellan. Because Jackson was closer to Richmond than was McDowell, the Confederates could make use of two important elements in the art of war as preached by Napoleon and Jomini: concentration and inner lines of communication.

Jackson had already anticipated Lee on one point—deception. His movements since Port Republic had been so clouded in secrecy that John Harman had once again been distracted into offering his resignation because "Jacksons [sic] misterious [sic] ways are unbearable" and also because no amount of badgering could persuade the Old Man to reduce his precious wagon train.[17] The quartermaster was not the only one baffled by the general's doings. Fremont, who was carrying on negotiations with Jackson concerning Federal wounded at the recent battlefields, was treated to choice bits of misinformation transmitted by his flag-of-truce emissaries. Each time they were received in the Confederate lines they managed to overhear odds and ends of military gossip about new troops coming to Jackson. As a result Fremont continued his retreat down the valley and Jackson ordered his cavalry to keep the screen tight around his army, allowing only doctored information to leak through.[18]

Jackson's personal movements were shrouded in mystery. Lee had cautioned that word of Jackson's absence from the valley should not spread, and it did not. Some of the commanders of the reinforcements found it difficult to keep up with the commanding general. General Whiting, a slightly overstuffed makebate, found Jackson's reticence discourteous, not to say rude. Summoned to the presence of Old Jack on June 17, not long after his arrival in the valley, Whiting expected to have future plans and strategy outlined for him—an expectation heightened by Old Jack's wording: "Let me see you at my headquarters upon important business." [19] He returned that night to the home of his host, Col. John Imboden, in a towering rage, announcing that Jackson had treated him shamefully.

"How is that possible, General?" Imboden asked in amusement. "He is very polite to every one."

"Oh! hang him, he was polite enough. But he didn't say one word about his plans. I finally asked him for orders, telling him what troops I had. He simply told me to go back to Staunton, and he would send me orders to-morrow. I haven't the slightest idea what they will be. I believe he hasn't any more sense than my horse."

The next morning a dispatch arrived. Whiting was to put his troops on the cars for Gordonsville at once. At Gordonsville he would receive further orders. This was too much. Whiting erupted: "Didn't I tell you he was a fool, and doesn't this prove it? Why, I just came through Gordonsville day before yesterday." [20]

If Whiting thought his frustration unique, he would have been wrong. Even the trusted Ewell knew almost nothing of Jackson's plans. John Hood's and Law's brigades were under Whiting at Staunton, and some of Lawton's Georgia boys had joined the main army near Weyer's Cave, a place which many of the men shunned with a soldier's horror of too early an introduction to the underground.[21] The new troops heard rumors of Old Jack's puzzling movements, but had no notion of what plans he had in mind. Even Jed Hotchkiss, whose maps had been such a vital factor in the Valley Campaign, knew nothing beyond the fact that the general wanted him to continue mapping the valley.[22]

Something certainly was about to happen. The Old Man had been more than usually touchy for several days. Harman's trouble served as one example, and the favored commander of the Stonewall Brigade also felt Jackson's temper. A few days after the battle of Port Republic Winder had made the mistake of asking for leave to go to Richmond. With his usual belief that the place for all officers was at the post of duty, Jackson had denied the request. Charles Winder, gentleman, resigned instantly, took his departure, and rode over to Dick Taylor's quarters where he told his story. There were many reasons why he had resigned, Taylor discerned, and the refusal of leave only topped them off. Winder, a cherished friend of Taylor's, had proved himself too competent an officer to be lost so easily. Taylor listened and sympathized, then, after his visitor left, rode over to Jackson's headquarters and gained an interview. Appealing to Jackson's "magnanimity," Taylor "dwelt on the rich harvest of glory he had reaped in his brilliant campaign." Surely enough had been gleaned to relax canons of duty in favor of so fine and proficient a lieutenant. As he spoke, Taylor was treated to a rare insight into Jackson's character. "Observing him closely, I caught a glimpse of the man's inner nature. It was but a glimpse. The curtain closed, and he was absorbed in prayer. Yet in that moment I saw an ambition boundless as Cromwell's, and as merciless." [23] Old Jack listened attentively but made no reply. Finally, when the brigadier rose to leave, Jackson said he would ride with him. Silently the two rode toward Taylor's camp, where they parted. Apparently the mission had failed. But it had not: "That night a few lines came from Winder, to inform me that Jackson had called on him, and his resignation was withdrawn." [24] That brief look beyond Jackson's outer shell explained many things to Dick Taylor. Always an admirer of the strange, silent soldier, he now had an even greater appreciation of the man's virtues. He realized that Jackson warred constantly with himself:

> I have written that he was ambitious; and his ambition was vast, all-absorbing. Like the unhappy wretch from whose shoulders sprang the foul serpent, he loathed it, perhaps feared it; but he could not escape it—it was

himself—nor rend it—it was his own flesh. He fought it with prayer, constant and earnest—Apollyon and Christian in ceaseless combat. What limit to set to his ability, I know not, for he was ever superior to occasion. Under ordinary circumstances it was difficult to estimate him because of his peculiarities—peculiarities that would have made a lesser man absurd, but that served to enhance his martial fame, as those of Samuel Johnson did his literary eminence.[25]

The perceptive brigadier would not have been surprised by the lines in a bygone letter to Laura: "You say that I must live on it [fame] for the present. I say not only for the present, but during life." [26]

Fame had come in boundless abundance—Jackson now ranked as the hope of the Confederacy. No other star burned so brightly in the firmament, no other general dared so much. Jackson alone carried the war to the enemy, and as the press extolled his brilliance it also told the people of his dedication to a great maxim: "Attack at once and furiously." [27] Everywhere in the South, and in many parts of the North, the name "Stonewall" was magic. Now the discretionary order from General Lee offered a chance for renown on a larger stage. Jeb Stuart's audacious "ride around McClellan" had set that stage.[28]

What lurked in the Old Man's mind none of the staff dared guess, but they all knew by June 17 that he had come to some decision. That night he and one of his aides, Col. William L. Jackson, left the camps of the army and rode to Staunton. After midnight the men were routed out, tents were struck, and once again the Army of the Valley marched—this time southeast toward Waynesboro, resting at the base of Rockfish Gap.[29] For some hours the general eluded his staff, who wandered around hunting for him.

In Staunton he had tended to routine administrative matters and set out on the morning of the eighteenth for Waynesboro. Late in the afternoon he caught sight of the army, sprawled on the western slope of Rockfish Gap,[30] with campfires winking on both sides of the highway leading east across the Blue Ridge. Some of the men had already crossed the ridge and reached Mechum River Depot that day, but the bulk of the army rested quietly, waiting.

Hotchkiss greeted the general soon after he reached Waynesboro, and fell in with him on the way up the mountain.

We saw General Whiting [Hotchkiss recorded] at the foot of the mountain and then rode on, in the darkness, looking for our Hd. Qrs. camp by inquiring at every camp fire, but could not find it. I saw Gen. C. S. Winder at the Mountain Top House, Rockfish Gap, where I went to look for our Hd. Qrs. On my return I said, "General, I fear we will not find our wagons tonight." He [Jackson] replied, earnestly, "Never take counsel of your fears."

Hotchkiss drew the assignment of finding some sort of lodging and rations for the night, a task he performed with typical efficiency, taking the general and a few aides to a home at the eastern foot of the gap.

It had been a long, hot day. The riders were weary, dust-covered, and worn, but still Hotchkiss noticed that

> the General was long at his devotions after we retired to our chamber, he, Col. Jackson and myself, having each a bed in the same large room. After we had retired I amused him by telling of the various opinions I had heard during the day from the citizens in reference to our destination. When I was through he asked, in his own quick, sharp way, "Do any of them say I am going to Washington?" [31]

Where they were going, the men camping on the side of the Blue Ridge could not tell, but they had suspicions. Wherever it was, there was no doubt that Old Jack would press hard toward victory. A current joke summed up the army's feeling about their hard-driving general: While they were resting astride the Blue Ridge, waiting for orders to go somewhere, two Irish infantrymen fell into conversation. One sighed, "I wish all the Yankees was in Hell!"

"And faith," said the other, "and I don't wish anything of the sort."

"The divvel you don't, and why don't you?"

"Because Old Jack would have us standing picket at the gate before night and in there before morning—and it's too hot where we is to suit me!" [32]

The man who variously impressed as one who would order a charge on the gates of hell or an advance to the North Pole roused his staff early on the nineteenth in great good humor, mounted up and rode for Mechum River. All the way he chatted easily with Hotchkiss, commenting on a great variety of things, among them the nature of the soldiers he led. He had found, he told Hotchkiss, "that our men would rather fight and march than dig"—an opinion which coincided exactly with a discovery made by General Lee as he tried to get his men to throw up dirt in front of McClellan. [33]

March they would but they would ride too, as limited rolling stock could be shuttled back and forth between the army and Fredericks Hall, fifty miles from Richmond. [34] Jackson would himself take the train for Charlottesville, but first he must give some idea of his destination to the Reverend Chief of Staff. No one, not even poor Harman, knew the route of march beyond Charlottesville, though he guessed at the ultimate objective. [35] Unhappy at divulging a whisper of his plan even to Dabney, Jackson called him to a hotel room, locked the door, and revealed that he was going ahead of the army to Richmond for a conference with General Lee; the army would join the main force at Richmond. Before the troops reached Richmond he would be back from his visit, but in the meantime Dabney would be in charge of the march along the Virginia Central right-of-way. Special precautions to ensure secrecy were outlined to Dabney, then Jackson climbed aboard the postal car of an eastbound troop train and disappeared.[36]

A considerable strain was put on Dabney's silence when later that day he dined with Dick Ewell, who appeared to be in a bitter mood. Jackson, Ewell opined, was too reserved and closemouthed. "Here, now," he piped to Dabney, "the general has gone off on the railroad without intrusting to me, his senior major-general, any order, or any hint whither we are going; but Harman, his quartermaster, enjoys his full confidence, I suppose, for I hear that he is telling the troops that we are going to Richmond to fight McClellan." Here was a doubly dangerous situation. Harman's gossip could destroy the urgent secrecy of the move and also alienate the finest of subordinates. Dabney grew confidential and persuasive: "You may be certain, General Ewell, that you stand higher in General Jackson's confidence than any one else, as your rank and services entitle you. As for Major Harman, he has not heard a word more than others. If he thinks that we are going to Richmond, it is only his surmise, which I suppose every intelligent private is now making." [37]

Down the railroad the troops toiled, with the tail of the column anxiously looking for the next shuttle train. It proved to be slow going. Roads were none too good, and the wagons, artillery, and what limited cavalry Jackson detached from the valley struggled forward with difficulty. There seemed to be a general letdown of vigilance. The troops detailed to protect the trains paid little heed to their tasks, and all through the day the staff officers rode past crawling lines of vehicles and animals urging greater speed and care. The oppressive heat and dust turned a bad dream into a nightmare of sweating, cursing, stumbling men, vehicles, and horses.[38]

Some of Jackson's troops reached Gordonsville early on the twenty-first, and by noon most of the army had arrived. A much surprised Major Dabney found General Jackson there. Instead of going on to Richmond, he had stopped at Gordonsville to investigate a rumored advance of an enemy force from the Rapidan front. Holding Ewell and his own division near Gordonsville, Jackson late in the day sent Whiting's division and Lawton's Georgians on east. Once the troops had arrived at Gordonsville they were more puzzled than ever. A strategic rail center, the town offered train connections northward toward the Rapidan and to Manassas, or southeast toward Richmond. Which way were they going?

Richmond might be a good guess, but if so, why had all the reinforcements been sent from there only to go back? Fredericksburg looked like the best bet. There the Army of the Valley could unite with another Confederate force and possibly advance on Washington before McDowell extricated himself from the snare of Massanutton. The more and wilder the rumors, the more confused grew the reports going to the Federals. Although Lee did not intend Whiting's and Lawton's movement as a ruse—as has often been recounted—he was not averse to confounding the enemy.[39] Jackson cooperated in building the ruse. Orders went to the cavalry to screen the army as tightly as ever it had been in the valley, and the added veil of mystery intensified the rumors.

Jackson had to move swiftly now. He had lost time checking on the false alarm, and he must be on with his visit to Richmond; General Lee wanted to see him. Near suppertime on the twenty-first he summoned Major Dabney and asked him, "Will you take a railroad ride with me? We will leave our horses and so forth, with the staff." Dabney, already fascinated with Old Jack's masterly use of the railroad in logistics, readily consented. A mail car and an engine composed their special train, and soon after the engine whistled out of Gordonsville, Jackson threw himself on the mail clerk's bunk and fell sound asleep. Rattling rapidly on the Virginia Central track, the general's train had him in Fredericks Hall by Sunday morning, June 22.

Here he found comfortable quarters in the house of Nathaniel Harris. It was a warm, pleasant Sabbath, and Jackson joined in attendance at some camp meetings in Hood's brigade, which had arrived and gone into bivouac near the little railroad settlement. Since it was Sunday, Major Dabney, who impressed the younger members of Jackson's staff as "too old, and too reverend, and too unelastic" [40] to be good company, doffed his martial manner and took the pulpit. Jackson forgot his pressing military problems for the rest of the day.

After services had ended and the Harrises' distinguished aggregation of military guests had returned to the house for dinner, Mrs. Harris asked Jackson when he wished breakfast in the morning. Courteous as usual, Jackson wanted no break in the routine simply for his sake—whenever breakfast was ready would suit him fine.

Morning and breakfast time came, and Mrs. Harris sent for the general. Jim Lewis, Jackson's proud and faithful servant, responded for him: "Sh! you don't 'spec' to find the general here at this hour, do you? He left here 'bout midnight, and I 'spec' by this time he's whippin' Banks in the Valley." [41]

During Sunday, John Harman had ridden hard toward Fredericks Hall, bringing Jackson's horse with him. Arriving at the Harris house, Harman found Jackson "at his devotions," waited until he was finished, and reported.

Probably about 1 A.M.[42] on Monday, the twenty-third, Jackson mounted and began his ride to Richmond, accompanied by Harman, Mr. Harris,[43] and a local guide familiar with the roads. Armed with a pass signed by General Whiting authorizing him to impress horses,[44] Jackson instructed his companions to call him "Colonel," and determined to do his best to avoid recognition. Even barring delay, the trip would take a considerable time since Lee's headquarters were located at High Meadows, some fifty-two miles from Fredericks Hall.

The General's penchant for mystery slowed the trip a bit. Whiting's pass had been designed to get the party past any sentinels on the way, but when a wary outpost guard halted the riders and demanded their passes, Jackson requested permission to speed on as a colonel on an important mission. The soldier had his orders. Even if he were President Davis, came the acid reply, he could not go farther without a pass. Here Whiting's paper apparently worked.

Still farther, however, Jackson received a dose of his own medicine. Challenged by an alert guard, Old Jack demanded, "What company is this?"

"Company D, Southern Army," came the baffling reply.

Jackson pressed his quizzing, but had no better luck. Finally the guard took the offensive: "What company do *you* belong to?"

"Don't ask me any questions," Jackson snapped, curtly.

"Then why the devil do you ask so many yourself?" the soldier shot back. A corporal stepped to the guard and whispered, "That's Old Jack." Apparently not hearing the *sotto voce* identification, Jackson, now somewhat irked, brushed past the sentry, asking, "Is it necessary to know who I am?"

"Not more than I already know," was the answer that followed the spurring horsemen.[45]

Fourteen hours after leaving Fredericks Hall, four weary and mud-spattered riders entered the yard of the little Dabb House, behind Lee's lines on the Nine Mile Road at High Meadows. Quickly the rumpled "colonel" strode into the house and reported to the commanding general. Courteous and gracious as always, Lee bade him welcome and asked him to wait briefly while urgent business was concluded. Jackson went outside and leaned on a fence, lost in his own meditations. Soon a rider approached, and Jackson recognized his brother-in-law, Gen. D. H. Hill. Hill had noticed a "dusty, travel-worn, and apparently very tired" soldier resting on the fence and when he realized the man was Jackson, had been both warmly pleased and dumfounded. By last accounts the professor had been badgering Fremont and Shields in the valley, and now here he was near Richmond. Details of the frantic relay ride were related, and the two old friends walked into General Headquarters, where Lee met them and offered the fatigued Jackson refreshments. A glass of milk would do nicely.

Soon other ranking officers began to arrive—James Longstreet, A. P. Hill. Lee closed the door on the conference room. The men to whom would be intrusted the great attack on McClellan had assembled. Together they were an interesting group, a study in contrasts. Most of them Jackson knew, some very well. He surveyed his colleagues with interest. Lee, a commanding and distinguished figure in immaculate gray uniform, had the looks and manner of a Virginia gentleman. Handsome he was, with high forehead, even brows, and gentle, steady eyes. Curling gray hair and full beard made him look older than his fifty-five years. On first glance his countenance and graceful carriage seemed out of place in a military uniform. Closer study showed the firmness and audacity of a Great Captain.

Longstreet, rather heavy-set, not tall, with full-flowing beard partially covering a somewhat stolid face, looked to be a dogged sort of man. He was much younger than Lee, although his whiskers disguised his forty-one years with remarkable success. Around the man who would soon be called Lee's "war horse" hung an air of languor. He would be steady in battle, but never quick.

Thirty-seven-year-old A. P. Hill looked melancholy—perpetually so. Thin and frail, his auburn brown hair and waving locks exaggerated his long face, giving a mournful aspect to deep-set eyes. Hill, a West Point classmate, Jackson knew well: they had served in the valley the previous summer. He looked nervous, high-strung, and appeared to wear his well-earned major general's rank a trifle self-consciously.

Harvey Hill had not changed much since Lexington days. If anything, army life had given an even more calculating cant to the eye, which his scraggly beard accentuated into a baleful gaze. By now he was forty, and had earned much distinction in Presbyterian circles. Capable and open, Harvey still had strong likes and dislikes and a long-standing belligerency. In a fight he would stick it out to the last.

Most of the men in the room looked with renewed interest at Jackson. His lightning Valley Campaign had been a prime topic of comment for weeks, and his reputation had preceded him. So had accounts of certain peculiarities. Strange that the former artilleryman—now a tired and dirty man in faded uniform and Gargantuan boots—had so marvelously confounded a large Yankee aggregation. His small blue eyes looked calmly into those of his curious associates, and his thin, pale lips and sharp nose had a distinctly unmartial look. Nor was he a tall, arresting figure. Sitting in on that conference, Jackson had a shabby, nondescript air. But when stirred to sudden interest, his eyes flashed, his body tensed, his sweet expression disappeared—and there, for a brief moment, "Stonewall" was revealed.

Lee outlined the reason for the conference. Jackson's force, he said, would join the main Confederate Army for an attack on McClellan. Strong reinforcements had been sent to the Army of the Valley, and they had been duly publicized in Richmond papers which he felt sure McClellan read diligently. A possibility existed that the move of the reinforcements had confused the enemy into fearing an attack by the intrepid Jackson on Washington—at least he had been able to slip away from the valley undetected. And now his strong force marched toward Richmond to take part in a concerted effort.

Little Mac had so arranged his troops as to have part of his army north of the Chickahominy River while retaining the bulk of it on the south side. His line, running roughly northwest to southeast, had its right resting on nothing in particular, and here it stood exposed to a turning movement. If the right (north) end of McClellan's position could be turned, rail communications with his base at White House on the Pamunkey River might be cut. The York River Railroad, the Union main artery, crossed the Chickahominy only twelve miles behind his sensitive right flank. A serious threat aimed at the railroad north of the river might force McClellan to cross his whole army to that side to defend his base, or to abandon White House and all his positions to the north side while he scrambled to establish another base. No matter what the Union general decided to do, he would be compelled to get out of his trenches in front of Richmond and defend himself. Once out of his works, McClellan would lose the advantage of siege artillery and his army would be on even terms with the Confederates.

Obvious problems were presented by the plan. The President had already pointed out one of them: Suppose McClellan left his right wing to fend for itself and seized the initiative while Lee attacked him north of the Chickahominy? What was to prevent his advancing straight against Richmond on the south side? Lee said that he doubted McClellan would try such a bold venture and even if he did there would be time to shift some Confederate troops from north to south before the capital fell. Generals Benjamin Huger and John B. Magruder could hold the Richmond front on the south well enough while Lee took McClellan in flank and rear.

Ground might serve as another formidable obstacle. The positions held by the enemy north of the river were naturally strong, and they dominated certain vital bridges which would have to be cleared before Lee's full attack could develop. Jackson's army would eliminate this danger by moving on Ashland, sixteen miles north of Lee's army, and from there advancing toward the southeast. Jackson would be completely clear of the Chickahominy above formidable Beaver Dam Creek, where rumor placed the extreme right of the Union forces. Jackson's route of march, then, would take his army around McClellan's flank, forcing the Yankees to abandon their entrenchments at Beaver Dam Creek and to fall back along their whole line north of the river in order to cover the York River Railroad. The Yankee retreat would clear critical bridges on the upper Chickahominy and open the way for Lee's full attacking force to go into action.

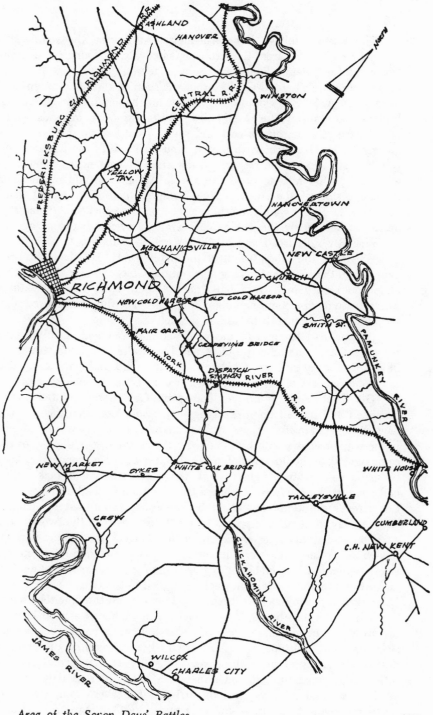

Area of the Seven Days' Battles

The attack itself—a huge wheeling turn toward the southeast—would be en échelon from the left. Stuart's cavalry, forming the extreme left of the Confederate line, would screen Jackson's flank while his army pressed its march toward Cold Harbor. As soon as the Meadow bridges were open, A. P. Hill would cross, attack Mechanicsville, and clear the bridges near that town for D. H. Hill's and Longstreet's commands, which would then join the attack east and south. Complex the plan was, requiring D. H. Hill's troops to pass behind A. P. Hill's division on their way to join Jackson, and requiring Longstreet's command to connect up with A. P. Hill's men to press the attack. All units would move along the north side of the river to New Bridge, where they would make contact with Huger's and Magruder's men on the other side. Once that union had been made, the whole Confederate Army could advance against the York River Railroad and McClellan's flushed forces.

What did the others think of the plan? D. H. Hill had not been happy with the idea of attacking north of the Chickahominy, feeling that more could be gained by a blow on the south side. Lee knew there would be some objections and many questions. Tactfully he excused himself and left the generals to discuss the details.

Jackson had listened to the plan without comment. Doubtless he recognized that one other problem had been raised by Lee's strategy—timing. His army still struggled toward Richmond and on it depended the whole success of the battle. Speed would count in lives saved.

Details of roads and bridges, enemy and Confederate positions, were discussed and agreed upon. Turning to Jackson, Longstreet said: "You have distance to overcome, and in all probability obstacles will be thrown in the way of your march by the enemy. As your move is the key of the campaign, you should appoint the hour at which the connection may be made co-operative." Through all the conversation Old Jack's mind had been working. He would hurry the men, and he had an answer for Longstreet's questions. He could be in position southeast of Ashland the next day, June 24, and would be ready for battle on the twenty-fifth.

Longstreet, knowing much more about local roads and perhaps remembering his name for Jackson's army—"the second-raters in the valley"—thought Jackson ought to give himself more time, at least another day. After a moment's thought, Jackson agreed to the twenty-sixth. When Lee returned to the room he accepted the details and the time schedule.[46]

The conference broke up, and Jackson immediately started back to his army. As he mounted, darkness was falling; it would be another sleepless night. No time could be wasted—Lee counted on the promptness of the Army of the Valley. Miles sped by as the general and his little group raced through the rain which fell harder as dawn broke. Well after breakfast time Jackson arrived at Beaver Dam, where he found the head of his army—but only the head. Ominously his infantry stretched as far back along the road as Jackson could see, sprawling fifteen miles along a road growing soggier by the minute.[47]

Dabney had had a very bad day during Jackson's absence. Lax marching discipline replaced Old Jack's stern valley regimen. Commissary wagons fell hopelessly behind, and hungry men moved more slowly as a new and oppressively damp heat bore down upon them. The farther from the valley, the less was known of the ground or the roads, so Dabney had been almost obliged to stick to the route paralleling the Virginia Central as Jackson had told him to do. As lassitude settled over the army, Dabney also succumbed, but to a different malady. Seized with a violent intestinal upset, he had been forced to take to his bed and leave marching problems to others of the staff even less equipped to handle such things.

A quick glance at the troops was enough to convince Jackson that he would have to halt the head of the army at Beaver Dam long enough to close up the columns. Whether all the units could be closed during the twenty-fourth seemed problematical; certainly much time would be lost. Even John Harman, whose logistical sixth sense had turned other delays into miracles, could not be counted on now; he had to recover from the exhausting circuit to Richmond. For that matter, so did Jackson.

Giving orders to his staff to hurry on the men and wagons as fast as possible, Jackson sought a room for rest. Taking time to remove his wet, mud-caked uniform and put it before a fireplace to dry, Jackson fell into bed and—surprisingly enough—read a novel until sufficiently relaxed to sleep.[48] Dead-tired and benumbed by over a hundred hard miles in the saddle, Jackson lost something of his usual quickness of perception. Curiously, he appears not to have impressed on anyone during the twenty-fourth the need for desperate haste. Instead of ranging up and down his column shouting his familiar "press on, men, press on," Jackson rested, content with halting the van of the army to wait for the rear. It was not like him; nor was the incipient disorganization like the Army of the Valley. Something was wrong. From Beaver Dam the distance to Ashland was easily twenty miles, and Jackson had promised to be in position six miles beyond that point by the end of June 25. Many times before the troops had done much better than twenty-six miles in a day, but then they were swinging along the macadamized Valley Pike.

Late in the night [49] a courier brought Lee's detailed battle order to Jackson's headquarters. Preparations were going ahead at Richmond, based on Jackson's keeping to his time schedule. He had to do it, since the attack would begin with his advance at 3 A.M. on June 26. If he were in position with his 18,500 men,[50] Lee's numbers north of the Chickahominy would be somewhere near 56,000 and the whole of Lee's army would total almost 85,500. While Little Mac probably had 150,000 men at his command by some Confederate estimates, only a fraction were north of the river and that fraction could be wrecked, shattered, and possibly eliminated by the strategy Lee had devised if Jackson were on time, and if the Federals remained blissfully unaware that doom bore down upon them from the Shenandoah Valley.

There were too many if's. Superlative as had been Old Jack's devices to keep secret his march toward the capital, word began to circulate in Richmond that something big was about to happen. Most people dared not speculate or hope that the Confederacy's newly elevated hero had been called to assist Lee, but some thought it likely. The able Chief of Ordnance, Col. Josiah Gorgas, had been vastly relieved when he could confide to his diary on the twenty-second that "Jackson . . . is coming."[51] On Tuesday, the twenty-fourth, he noted that "a train leaves to-morrow morning for Hanover, where Gen. Jackson *may* be. It will carry ammunition which he needs, and therefore, he will not be ready tomorrow morning."

Jackson was coming, but he was late. Shaking off some of the stupor brought on by fatigue, he returned to normal on the twenty-fifth and all through the dreadful humidity of that day he worked desperately to get the men and trains moved. On the railroad most of his baggage and heavy equipment had been transported with relative dispatch, but the leapfrog method of spurring on the "foot cavalry" had ended at Fredericks Hall where the Virginia Central track had been torn up by Federal raiding parties. From Beaver Dam on, the familiar rider in faded tunic and slouched kepi moved constantly along the marching columns, urging the men forward. Men moved listlessly, field officers were not diligent in starting them at an early hour, and time was consumed in cooking rations. Roads were sticky, streams became raging torrents, and missing bridges stalled the march again and again. When the sun went down on that dismal day Jackson's veteran pacers were five miles short of their goal. The army went into camp near Ashland, the men caked with mud and utterly spent after sloshing twenty miles.[52] Jackson's distress had grown with every dragging hour, and had been heightened by news of cavalry skirmishing below Ashland, followed by word that the telegraph lines had been cut near there.

Nerves wore thin, tempers grew short. Jackson, finding Winder with the Stonewall Brigade, directed him to have his men fed and ready to march at dawn. "That is impossible," Winder replied, "because of the position of my baggage-train." "General Winder, it must be done." The tone, almost a snarl, seemed peculiarly discourteous to the listening Major Dabney.[53] Humiliating as it might be, word of the delay must be sent to General Lee, along with assurance that the march would resume before 3 A.M. The commanding general must also be told of the cavalry action near Ashland and the break in the telegraph, two incidents with ominous portent: McClellan apparently had discovered the approach of Jackson's army.

Unfortunately Jackson's suspicion proved correct. A deserter from his ranks had carried word to the Federals on the twenty-fourth—the element of surprise had been lost.⁵⁴ Now more than ever, the battle rested in the hands of God.

Whiting and Ewell, visiting Jackson's quarters after midnight with a question about roads, were convinced that the general planned a night of prayer. He put off their question with a promise to think it over and they left. Ewell understood Jackson's reticence: "Don't you know why 'Old Jack' would not decide at once?" he queried the brigadier. "He is going to pray over it first!" And Old Baldy was not surprised, upon returning to Jackson's quarters for his forgotten saber, to find his superior kneeling in fervent supplication.⁵⁵

The army was ordered to march at 2:30 A.M., led now by a general who had all of ten hours' sleep during the past four nerve-rending days. Though a man of "iron fortitude," in Dabney's apt phrase, Jackson could not long remain clear-thinking and vigorous, could not function at his best.⁵⁶

By 8 A.M. on Thursday, June 26, Jackson's men began the march on McClellan.⁵⁷ It started inauspiciously. Eight o'clock was far too late; Jackson grew increasingly irritated. Lee counted on the Army of the Valley. What was the matter with such pacers as the Stonewall Brigade, Taylor's stalwarts from Louisiana, and Lawton's impressive Georgians?

In a way the answer rose from the ground. A vague, unhealthy aura seeped from the dank swampland. Alien, repelling, bafflingly flat, the river bottoms stretched endlessly ahead of the valley troops. Heat, aggressive and wilting, beat down on the men as they shuffled along sticky and badly rutted roads. The heat offered a kind of resistance to troops conditioned to fighting in the bracing air and varied terrain of Massanutton country. Other resistance came after they left Ashland in the form of Yankee cavalry. Not until 9 A.M. did Jackson's vanguard reach the crossing of the highway and the Virginia Central Railroad—and by then he was six hours behind Lee's time schedule.

From that point, at which he sent notice of his position to General Branch so that the sweeping turn could begin north of the Chickahominy, Jackson moved farther and farther from anything familiar.

Skillful Yankee delaying tactics slowed progress to a crawl. Cavalry hung close to the skirmishers of Hood's brigade which Whiting had thrown out; the sharp report of an irritating gun now and then caused a halt. Trees and logs thrown across the road at intervals added to delay.

Uncertain of enemy intentions, and bereft of Hotchkiss's unerring knowledge of topography,⁵⁸ Jackson grew cautious. Not even the presence of an extremely capable guide, who joined the staff at Ashland, could remove the feeling of strangeness. Still as aggressive as ever in his manner and in his orders,[59] Old Jack nonetheless groped his way forward. Gone now was the solid certainty of those rapid marches in the valley —marches timed to a hair's breadth and founded on absolute knowledge of distance and geography. Here, in the steaming peninsula, Jackson moved without good maps, without his topographical engineer, and without Turner Ashby. Stuart's men ranged widely along his left, guarding it and bringing in some information, but as yet Jackson had not learned how best to use the splendid eyes of the daring cavalryman whose recent ride around McClellan gave him some knowledge of the lay of the land ahead. Now the Army of the Valley crept along behind a cloud of skirmishers, shelling ominous-looking woods and stopping to repair bridges. The daring Jackson fell increasingly behind time. Weary and grimy, Jackson's infantry reached Hundley's Corner at about 5 P.M., and here Ewell's men, coming up by another road, joined the main army. Now all the valley forces were where they should have been so much sooner; but the divisions of A. P. Hill and Harvey Hill were not there, a disturbing absence because Lee had said they would be on Jackson's right in support at this point.

Heavy firing and artillery dueling during the late afternoon indicated sharp fighting south, but what this meant Jackson did not know. Ewell had established contact with Branch during the afternoon, but Branch had not contacted A. P. Hill. No news or orders had come to Jackson from Lee. As far as Jackson could tell an engagement had begun, but not according to plan, and he decided to bivouac until more information could be obtained. Further advance without help might jeopardize the whole battle. While his men gladly made camp, he could hear quite distinctly the sound of fierce combat to the south.

It had been a strange and hostile day. Riding hard and chafing at his slow advance, Jackson had made no effort to send progress reports to Lee or to the several commanders on his right whose attack would be contingent on his position. On the other hand, Lee, curious about why Jackson did not come into action as planned, made no effort to find out —no courier or staff officer was sent to locate the Army of the Valley. And while Jackson went his way, A. P. Hill, supported by D. H. Hill, had impatiently launched an attack of his own against the Federals holding along Beaver Dam Creek. A bloody, gallant, and sickeningly futile charge cost some 1,400 casualties. The charge should not have been delivered, true, but had Jackson been where he was supposed to be, the charge would probably have been against empty works—the enemy would have been flanked.

Caution, growing uncertainty, no attempt to move toward the sound of fighting, lethargy both in movement and in thinking—was this typical of Stonewall Jackson? Would Longstreet's mocking description of Jackson's worn followers prove true: Were they, after all, the "second-raters of the valley"? [60]

The troops stirred early on the morning of June 27. Jim Lewis hastily made breakfast for the general and the staff and learned that he would go no farther; the headquarters wagon could catch up later.[61] Men were restless, anxious to be on with the job. Old Isaac Trimble, routing out his soldiers, still brooded because Jackson had not marched toward the sound of firing the previous evening when enough daylight remained to do something.[62] Renewed cannonading south and to the right of Jackson's army promised fighting during another steaming day. Rations were cooked, men ate, joked, and thought. In the camp of the fierce Louisiana Tigers, the swashbuckling Maj. Roberdeau Cheatham Wheat summoned his *enfants* to a daily devotion. "Boys," he thundered fondly, "now for the day's rations." He opened the well-worn Bible his mother had pressed into his hand when he rode off to this war, and his powerful voice floated over his battalion as he read the lesson for the day: "Fear not your enemies, though they be ten thousand strong"—a stirring text, and dreadfully prophetic.[63]

To Jackson the all-important objective would be the turning of McClellan's right flank. Although a hot combat raged not far away —probably A. P. Hill engaging the enemy—Lee's over-all strategy had to be considered. No time could be wasted in indulging a taste for fighting. If the physical presence of the Army of the Valley in the Yankee rear could induce a retreat or a meeting in the open, so much the better. Resolutely, then, the divisions of Whiting, Ewell, and Jackson must grope farther to the southeast and stoutly ignore all chances for a fight until the time proved propitious.

Ewell's men took the lead, marching south to flank the enemy out of the Beaver Dam Creek positions. Soon, near where the road crossed the east-west artery from Mechanicsville to Bethesda Church, a Federal force came in sight. Ewell made ready to drive them, but D. H. Hill's division suddenly came swinging along the road from Mechanicsville, heading for a junction with Jackson. The Yankees fled, and Old Jack directed Hill to continue east toward Bethesda, keeping in touch and in supporting distance. From then on, Hill's division formed a part of Jackson's growing command.[64]

Mounted, for a change, on a large, gaunt, and incongruous sorrel, Jackson rode earnestly ahead, pointing his column almost straight south toward Walnut Grove Church. Sounds of battle to the right shifted finally; A. P. Hill seemed to be pushing the enemy now that Jackson had passed the head of Beaver Dam Creek. Nothing save the alien ground and an inexcusable scarcity of good maps slowed this march. Federal resistance melted away, leaving in its wake the silence of a waiting battlefield. Ranging ahead of the van as usual, showing typical unconcern for lurking snipers, Jackson spied the tiny crossroads marked by Walnut Grove Church. A. P. Hill seemed to be fighting nearby, although the boom of cannon and rattle of small arms had waned.

Quickly Jackson surveyed the scene, and seeing the tall, thin figure of A. P. Hill near the church, rode up and asked for news. Hill pointed toward the south and east in the direction of Gaines' Mill, and explained that soon he hoped to force the retreating Yankees to a stand—his pursuit of their rear guard had been swift and gratifying. They doubtless feared for the safety of their line of communication with the White House and would defend the York River Railroad. As the two major generals talked, the jingle of horses caught their attention and they saw coming along the road from Mechanicsville a large and magnificent staff. The commanding general, restless and anxious about the course of the battle, had ridden from Mechanicsville seeking word of his division commanders. Hill, touching cap, rode off, leaving Lee and Jackson to confer.

Removing the "mangy little cadet cap" [65] and swinging down from the dreary sorrel, Jackson walked with Lee until the commanding general settled himself on a stump and began to speak in muffled words. Nobody heard what the two said. The members of each staff were too busy looking, respectively, at the man who had planned Little Mac's discomfiture and at the wizard of the Shenandoah Valley. Old Jack's staff—those who had kept up—were frankly impressed. Handsome and immaculate was General Lee, earnest and competent. But Jackson's aides were impressed, too, by something in the manner of Lee's staff: the commanding general's aides were desperately curious about Old Jack, and gazed at him in rapt attention. A few skeptics on the valley staff took away from the meeting at Walnut Grove a new respect for their dirty and bedraggled Professor of Artillery Tactics.

Talking hastily, the two generals concluded their conference at 11 A.M., when Jackson mounted and led his men sharply eastward toward Cold Harbor. Lee's ideas had been absorbed and Old Jack hastened to put them into effect. The commanding general had outlined the presumed position of the opposing forces. Under Jackson now was the bulk of Confederate strength north of the Chickahominy, particularly since D. H. Hill would stay with him. Swift marching toward Cold Harbor would turn the enemy out of what seemed like a strong north-south line just east of Powhite Creek. Flanked, the Federals would be flushed from their works into a retreat, and if they failed to retreat, Jackson could cut their line of communication on the York River Railroad. He could take a position on the flank and rear of the Yankees and mow them down when Longstreet and A. P. Hill drove them eastward into his line of fire. A good and simple plan—it required only hard walking on the part of the infantry.[66]

Once more on the road, Jackson spied a company of cavalry and asked if any local boys served in it. Yes, from scattered troopers. Instantly appointing these boys guides, Jackson confided to one an inkling of his objective. He wanted, he said, to go to Cold Harbor. A choice of roads could be had from Walnut Grove Church to Cold Harbor, and since Jackson had been matter-of-fact in his request, the guide led his columns down the larger, better, and more direct route.

Through dense brush country, dotted with masses of trees, Jackson's men pushed on for over a mile. Suddenly Old Jack stiffened in the saddle, listening intently to the reverberation of a thunderous cannonade. "Where is that firing?" he asked his nearest guide, sharply. It sounded, came the answer, as though it were from the direction of Gaines' Mill. "Does this road lead there?" Yes, said the guide, it went through Gaines' Mill and on to Cold Harbor. "But," Jackson said in his clipped, almost fierce tones, "I do not wish to go to Gaines' Mill. I wish to go to Cold Harbor, leaving that place to the right." "Then," said the guide, acidly, "the left-hand road was the one which should have been taken; and had you let me know what you desired, I could have directed you aright at first."

Reverse the column—nothing else could be done. Back to the road D. H. Hill had taken, and then on to Cold Harbor. Much good time would be lost, time which, considering the murderous sound of battle, might be fatal. Many of the staff grew nervous, but they noted Jackson's continued calm. When one of them asked him if he feared the delay might lose the battle, Old Blue Light answered: "No, let us trust that the providence of our God will so overrule it, that no mischief shall result." [67]

Confusing as was the ground, the reversal of infantry units proved even worse. Once back on the road followed by D. H. Hill, some of Jackson's men mistook the rear of Hill's division for the enemy and almost precipitated a disaster. Whiting seemed to be responsible for the overzealous identification and received a frigid snub from Jackson. Whiting smoldered—he would have an opportunity to vent his anger later. Meantime the men must be shoved along.

Winding and muddy, the road led Jackson's troops farther into the swamp bottoms. Visibility grew limited as a tangled forest of bramble and trees surrounded the men. It seemed to many in the ranks that one of the hottest battles ever fought raged nearby and that Jackson was marching away from it.[68] But he increased the pace until the column sped along in quick time. No one knew what would happen, or where they were. All kinds of rumors circulated, but there could scarcely be any doubt of an imminent fight.

Around three o'clock Jackson reached the vicinity of Old Cold Harbor and found D. H. Hill (who had taken the Bethesda road) in contact with the Federals, waiting for him. Did Hill know anything of the enemy's general position? No more than Jackson, which was nothing. Apparently Hill had struck part of a Federal flank guard, but he could not be sure. At all events, the Yankees held strong ground, well protected by rugged terrain and by hastily constructed works. Hill had not felt like rushing to the attack unsupported. Jackson, agreeing that attack without further information would be foolish, gazed at the Union lines, listened to the rolling sound of artillery and musketry from the west around Gaines' Mill, and made a decision. Longstreet and A. P. Hill must be driving the enemy toward him, as Lee had anticipated. If Hill stayed where he was, facing almost south, he might not be able to get at the retreating enemy, and lost in the tangle of bush his men could easily be mistaken for Yankees.

To prevent any mix-up, Jackson directed Hill to back up and take a position along a strip of woodland facing west. In front of this new position was some relatively open ground, and Hill's men could see whom they were shooting.

A change in the sound of battle fixed Jackson's attention. He had been wrong. Powell Hill's men were not advancing—they were falling back! Receiving word that Ewell's division, which had been behind him on the road, was in action supporting A. P. Hill, Jackson began to understand what had happened. Not only had he been wrong, but so had Lee. Major General Fitz-John Porter, fighting McClellan's battle north of the Chickahominy, had not fortified the north-south line behind Powhite Creek. He had posted his men in a vast convex east-west line, stretching from that creek on the left to the vicinity of Cold Harbor. His center, protected by a sluggish stream, Boatswain's Swamp (not shown on Confederate maps), had an impregnable look.

If A. P. Hill were retreating, and if Lee had ordered Ewell in to support the right and center, there must be a gap between D. H. Hill's men and the rest of the Confederate Army. Winder and Whiting must fill that gap, and fill it quickly.[69]

Poor staff work, combined with Whiting's unwillingness to take any orders from the insulting Jackson, slowed the movement of the rest of Jackson's command into position. All along the Confederate front desperate efforts were being made to construct a continuous line of battle so that a general assault on the Union positions could be delivered, but petty and unexpected delays of the sort Jackson encountered hampered the work. Deployment went awry, with some of Jackson's men arriving behind Confederate units already engaged and with others taking positions in isolation.[70] Most of the brigade commanders found it all but impossible to maintain order in the rough terrain, and when advancing through woods and dense underbrush many commands lost all semblance of formation.

Over the whole area around Gaines' Mill and Cold Harbor hung a pall of smoke,[71] and the ground literally shook with the most fearsome din of battle that many participants could recollect then or thereafter.[72] Stubborn and stalwart, Fitz-John Porter's men were holding, counterattacking, and raking the Confederate lines. Altogether the situation by late afternoon looked uncertain. A. P. Hill's men were worn out; Ewell could fight with help and was about to receive the aid of Lawton's Georgians; Winder had wandered around and had found A. P. Hill, who directed him to a place in the line. Off to the far right Longstreet calmly prepared to advance. A general attack, pressed home along the whole line, just might carry the Union positions—that seemed the only hope. The burden of victory lay on the Confederates. All Porter had to do in order to save his 35,000 men [73] was to hang on until dark—merely hold those imposing lines for three more hours. If Lee hoped to gain anything from the costly slaughter at Ellerson's Mills, Beaver Dam, and Gaines' Mill, he would have to gain it swiftly. After dark, Porter could slip over the Chickahominy, burn his bridges, and join in Little Mac's new plan to change his base from the White House to the James River.

Down the road from Old Cold Harbor galloped a begrimed and weary horseman. Covered with dust, little cap pulled far down over his eyes to repel the summer glare, he showed fatigue in the way he sat his saddle, in his frugality of gesture, and in the way he sucked his lemon. Lee saw him, rode swiftly to meet him. "Ah, General," he said to Jackson, "I am very glad to see you. I had hoped to be with you before." A jerky nod of the head, an unintelligible word greeted Lee's genteel rebuke for tardiness.[74]

Around the two horsemen roared the shrieking din of close infantry and artillery combat. Lee shouted: "That fire is very heavy. Do you think your men can stand it?" Jackson listened a moment: "They can stand almost anything! They can stand that." [75] Jackson, then, must take his remaining troops in rapidly. Lee would see to the rest of the line.

Finally, after more than five hours of marching and countermarching the reserve units, Lee's line took shape. He had one hour of working daylight left. Now was the time, now or never. Near A. P. Hill on the Confederate right center, Lee spied General Hood, detached from Jackson's command to reinforce the other flank. The enemy, explained Lee to Hood, remained unshaken and had not been driven from his works. "Can you break his line?" Hood would try,[76] and as he turned to ride away, Lee raised his hat and said, "May God be with you." [77]

A dreadfully long half hour crept by. Louder grew the sounds of conflict. From here and there along the Confederate line a telltale skulker slipped to the rear; some units were being withdrawn. If the attack stalled longer, the game would be lost. From the right side of his line Lee suddenly heard a high, shrill cry—the Rebel yell! It had started.

Whiting went forward, with Hood's Texans carrying the brunt of the charge. That day they earned the deathless admiration of the whole South—and also a place in the heart of General Lee never occupied by another unit.[78] Farther left, Ewell could be dimly seen down in the swamp, urging his own men on. Old Isaac Trimble, in his black plumed hat, raged up and down his line yelling, "Charge, men; charge!"[79] Lawton's Georgians, 3,500 magnificent men, went forward in splendid order. Winder, leading the Stonewall and other brigades of Jackson's division, rushed forward as at Winchester.

The rolling scream of the charge reached the left. Jackson, worrying his lemon still, forgot weariness, forgot the confusion of terrain, forgot the necessity of strictly obeying orders—he caught fire. Every one of his division commanders received a message, a message that told them Old Jack had come out of the swamp doldrums. In a "voice which rang with the deadly clang of the rifle," he shouted to his staff officers: "Tell them this affair must hang in suspense no longer; sweep the field with the bayonet!" D. H. Hill want in on the left, and all along the line now Rebels yelled to the charge.

Face blazing with that peculiar battle light, eyes flashing fire, Jackson rode up and down the line, watching, exhorting, urging. Forgotten in the heat of action was a promise made just before the battle started, a promise to Rob Wheat of the Louisiana Tigers. "General," Wheat had said, "we are about to get into a hot fight and it is likely many of us may be killed. I want to ask you for myself and my Louisianians not to expose yourself so unnecessarily as you often do. What will become of us, down here in these swamps, if anything happens to you, and what will become of the country! General, let us do the fighting. Just let me tell them [the Tigers] that you promised me not to expose yourself and then they'll fight like—er—ah—Tigers!" Jackson had listened carefully, knowing how the Tigers revered him in their own peculiar way, and he had been touched. "Major," he had said, "I will try not to go into danger, unnecessarily. But Major, you will be in greater danger than I, and I hope you will not get hurt. Each of us has his duty to perform, without regard to consequences; we must perform it and trust in Providence." At the time Jackson had remarked to Kyd Douglas that the request was so like Wheat—always thinking of others. Wheat had happily gone back to the Tigers, told them of their general's promise, and taken them into battle against their "enemies 10,000 strong." They fought at the hottest spot near the center of the Federal positions, and there Rob Wheat fell. His last request was to hear of Jackson—was the general all right?[80]

While Wheat, Sam Fulkerson, and thousands of others were dying in the sunset charge, Jackson grimly sat his horse, sucked his lemon, and urged more of his batteries into action.[81] The charge succeeded.

The Federal line broke, and bluecoats scattered toward the Chickahominy. McClellan's army north of the river had been routed. Prisoners,
guns, and wounded fell into Confederate hands. Lee announced the
victory to the President, and Richmond went wild. But 8,000 Confederates were dead, maimed, and missing—a hard-bought victory, a battle
won in spite of itself.

Orders, deployment, everything had gone wrong. Lee had misjudged
the Federal position. A. P. Hill had injudiciously attacked at Beaver
Dam. And strangest of all, Stonewall Jackson—the man all Richmond
now idolized—had been perpetually late. But there was no time to seek
the cause of these deficiencies now; McClellan must be pressed. There
would have to be a reconcentration of Confederate forces, and definite
information must be obtained about McClellan's intentions.

No "distant thunder drum" of cannon roused men the next morning,
no petulant rattle of a skirmish clash. Silence reigned over the dismal
swamplands, and the dead mutely held the battlefield. Early in the morning Longstreet and Jackson pushed out skirmishers to find the enemy
but found no one. Jackson's scouts had gone to the Grapevine Bridge
and found it wrecked; Porter must have crossed the Chickahominy. Still
Lee could not be sure that Little Mac might not recross the river farther
downstream and retire on his base at White House. Just in case that
scheme lurked in the Federal general's mind, Ewell received orders to
take his division with cavalry escort along the north bank as far as
Dispatch Station on the York River Railroad, destroy the station, and
tear up some track. And until reliable intelligence regarding Yankee
movements arrived, the army could take a well-earned rest.

A vast sort of wanderlust settled over the troops. Singly and in
bunches they roamed the scenes of carnage, looking for a lost friend,
a relative, some helping the ambulance and burial details with their
somber labor. Those who did not wander slept—almost anywhere—or
wrote letters telling that they still lived.

Stonewall made an early appearance on the field, after spending
part of the night sleeping on the ground in company with General Stuart.
He had remarked to Jeb before they both went to sleep that from Gaines'
Mill he had heard "the *most terrific fire* of musketry I ever heard," and
was curious to see the ground so desperately disputed.[82] When he looked
on the slope carried by Hood's Texans, Old Jack's emotion overcame
him and he exclaimed to one of his staff: "The men who carried this
position were soldiers indeed!"[83]

Eager to apply pressure to McClellan, whatever he might be doing,
Lee directed that the Grapevine Bridge be repaired, a task which occupied a group of dilatory workers from Jackson's command throughout
most of the twenty-eighth. The men would not be hurried, despite Old
Jack's efforts, and he devoted some of his time to details of clearing his

front of dead and wounded. There was no great rush; Lee yet lacked reliable information on Little Mac's plans.

Early morning of the twenty-ninth brought decision—the enemy had abandoned his line of communication and moved to change his base. South of the Chickahominy McClellan would concentrate his army, guard his flank and rear, and move toward the James River and the protection of his gunboats. Was there still a chance to head him off in the jumbled skein of roads and swollen streams below the river? Lee determined to make the effort, and had new orders for his generals.

Grapevine Bridge should be repaired as quickly as possible and used by Jackson's command as it pushed south and east into comparatively passable ground between the Chickahominy and the oozing, boggy area called White Oak Swamp—a ten-mile half circle of marshy land through which a brackish stream meandered. Jackson would approach White Oak Swamp from the north, where there were several usable roads leading to a maze of fords and bridges. As his men descended from higher, firmer ground they would be forced to move into the swamp, but care and the experience of the famous Port Republic mud march should take them through. The mission of Jackson's command would be to cooperate with the division under John Magruder, ordered to press the Yankee rear down the Williamsburg road and try to bring the Federals to battle ere they lost themselves in White Oak Swamp.

South of Magruder, connecting with his movement, the troops of Benjamin Huger would strike the Federal flank via the Charles City road, a route which might lead them into combat in the swamp or just above it. Ewell for the moment would be out of things. His division had to remain at Bottom's Bridge, holding the crossing of the Chickahominy; the dyspeptic and bellicose Ewell would chafe at inactivity, but his assignment was essential.

In the blunt hands of "Old Pete" Longstreet rested the success of Lee's new scheme for trapping McClellan. Longstreet received orders to take his own division plus that of Powell Hill and to cross the Chickahominy at New Bridge, upriver from the Grapevine span, march south past the rear of Huger's and Magruder's men to the Darbytown road, turn east and strike for the Longbridge road. Lee hoped that Old Pete's route would bring him into position in front of McClellan, cutting off his retreat to the James. As Lee visualized his plan, McClellan would be trapped in a sack, whose sole open end faced east. And if he moved east, down the same road he had taken on his way up the Peninsula, the damage to Northern morale would be tremendous. He would fight hard to reach the James, and one other force could be thrown forward along the northern banks of the James as insurance against his reaching that river. For this purpose the command of antiquated and picturesque Theophilus H. Holmes had crossed from the south side and would march southeast on the right of A. P. Hill and Longstreet. McClellan's rear would be threatened by Jackson and Magruder, his right flank open to the general attack of Huger, Longstreet, A. P. Hill, and Holmes. If coordination of effort could be achieved—and this was a big "if," considering the experience of the past two days—there seemed a good chance that the Grand Army of the Little Napoleon would be smashed to bits in the swamps. Move at once, Lee ordered his subordinates.

How had Major Dabney progressed with repairing the Grapevine Bridge? Not well at all. He had been given a detail of soldiers to help him and they proved to be "the usual shilly-shally sort." The warm Sunday slipped by, and still remarkably little had been done. Jackson's temper sharpened at the added delay, but there was not much he could do. Finally he saw to it that Capt. C. R. Mason with his group of Negro laborers went to the bridge in the forenoon, relieving the Reverend Major of an unpleasant and unnatural task. Speedily, then, work went ahead.[84]

Magruder, through a staff officer, requested word from Jackson about his position, and Old Jack replied that he would probably be across the bridge and moving along the south side of the river in two hours; more than that he did not say, revealing to Magruder no hint of his orders from Lee.[85] His brigades were ordered to close toward the bridge, and as soon as Mason opened it, they were to cross. But Jackson's expectations had outdistanced the realities of bridge repairing; when his units approached the river they found Mason's workers still hard at it. Jackson watched without comment, but his restlessness led him to cross over to the south side as soon as the span had been partly fixed. He must find out what Magruder and the rest were doing. South he rode into unfamiliar territory, scanning the land, fixing as much of it as he could in his mind. He missed Hotchkiss. Jackson had no real facility for grasping the lay of land. Hotchkiss could drill it into him, and once ground had been envisioned, Jackson always interpreted it strategically. But to learn it by himself—that was hard.

As he rode, firing broke out to the south, but of its significance Jackson knew nothing. Should he take his men in that direction as soon as the bridge was ready? Lee had instructed him to move eastward by the Savage Station road, "parallel to and not far distant from the Chickahominy; to guard all the northward, so as to prevent any Yankee attack from that quarter, thus forming a line of protection on that side of the movements of Lee's other columns south of him; and not to leave that eastbound road until he had passed the extreme northern flank of McClellan's forces and gotten in his rear." [86] Explicit as were these instructions, battle necessity changed many things and might readily change orders. Just after 3 P.M., as he listened to the conflict and debated moving to aid Magruder, Jackson received curious intelligence.

A courier raced desperately along the road, and reining up, handed him a note from General Stuart. It was a dispatch to Stuart from Lee's Adjutant General, directing the cavalry to watch the Chickahominy as far as Forge Bridge and to look for any Federal attempts to recross the river in that direction. Advise General Jackson of this order, Lee said, as he was expected to resist the enemy passage of the river until reinforced. Something unexpected had happened. Lee, certain that morning of McClellan's intention to forget his communications with the White House, must have new information which made him wary of leaving the Chickahominy bridges unguarded. All forward motion of Jackson's men must cease; they had to stay where they were until Lee released them.

Briskly Jackson scrawled an endorsement to Stuart's message: "3ʰ 5ᵐ P.M. Genl. Ewell will remain near Dispatch Station & myself near my present position." [87] Riding back toward his command, Jackson was overtaken by a messenger from the doughty Gen. D. R. Jones, of Magruder's division. Where was Jackson, asked Jones, and could he be counted on in support of Jones's imminent battle with the enemy? Back went the messenger—Old Jack could not come, he had "other important duty to perform." [88]

Through the afternoon the bridge repairers struggled at their task, but now the urgency of crossing had passed and Jackson ceased to worry about haste. He must get some sleep; already the strain of too many hours in the saddle and the maze of a strange country were having their effect. He had roused himself for the climax at Gaines' Mill, but he could not hope to stay fresh much longer. The night before, when he had stretched out by Stuart on the recent battlefield, the two had talked and planned for hours, and much good sleeping time slipped by. With the popping of Magruder's infantry fire dying away in the distance, Jackson lay down in the open and slept. About 1 A.M. a drenching rain roused him and drove him to the cover of a wagon; but too wet and excited to sleep any more, he waked Dabney with orders to start the infantry across the bridge at "earliest dawn," mounted his horse, and rode in search of General Magruder. [89] By now it seemed obvious that no enemy attempt would be made to cross the Chickahominy—but the false alarm had cost the Confederates a serious delay.

Through the wet darkness Jackson rode, and at about 3:30 A.M. finally found Magruder, wide awake and highly nervous. "Prince John" was caught in his own imagination; enemies were lurking everywhere, about to pounce. He must have reinforcements; when would Jackson come? Old Jack's answer reassured Magruder: his men would be up "probably by daylight." [90] Relieved, Magruder relaxed for an hour's sleep —"the first in forty-eight." [91]

Remaining at Magruder's position, Jackson awaited the arrival of his own men. When the sun was up, and before Magruder began a weird adventure of his own on the thirtieth, Lee arrived for a last conference with the excitable "Prince John." Finding Jackson, Lee reviewed with him what would have to be done in McClellan's rear that day. If Lee had any doubts about Jackson's alertness, they must have been quickly dispelled—Old Jack showed more than usual energy and drive. Swiftly he absorbed Lee's plans, elaborated on them, saluted, and joined his troops as they arrived. [92] Soon the head of his column reached Savage Station on the York River Railroad, the place where Magruder had fought the previous afternoon. Signs of a hasty Yankee retreat abounded; abandoned equipment lay in all directions. A lavish summer hospital had been left behind, containing 2,500 sick and wounded Federals; blankets, clothing, and staggering numbers of small arms had been thrown by the wayside. Hastily Jackson made sure that D. H. Hill, in charge of the advance, detailed two regiments to pick up the booty and to take charge of prisoners coming in from the woods.

Such scavenging took time, but Jackson would not miss a wagon even if it meant slowing his progress. While Hill's men went about the business of collecting, Jackson stopped to write a letter. Many days had passed since Anna had heard from him. Sitting down, he wrote in his hasty battlefield scrawl: "Near White Oak Swamp Bridge. . . . An ever-kind Providence has greatly blessed our efforts and given us great reason for thankfulness in having defended Richmond." He could impart small bits of military information in this letter, for Anna would read it later.

To-day the enemy is retreating down the Chickahominy towards the James River. Many prisoners are falling into our hands. General D. H. Hill and I are together. I had a wet bed last night, as the rain fell in torrents. I got up about midnight, and haven't seen much rest since. I do trust that our God will soon bless us with an honorable peace, and permit us to be altogether at home again in the enjoyment of domestic happiness.

You must give fifty dollars for church purposes, and more should you be disposed. Keep an account of the amount, as we must give at least one tenth of our income. I would like very much to see my darling, but hope that God will enable me to remain at the post of duty until, in His own good time, He blesses us with independence. This going home has injured the army immensely. [93]

None who watched him writing his letter could guess that he was homesick, hopeful that he could soon quit the field and return to Lexington and Anna. But the post of duty allowed little time for sentiment. On his men marched, heading now for the bridge across White Oak Swamp, the stream that could cause much trouble.

While some of his men moved ahead, Jackson followed along the narrow road, which twisted now through small, bramble-covered hills and gradually sloped toward White Oak Swamp. About noon he reached the edge of the swamp and found Stapleton Crutchfield searching for a good position in which to emplace guns. Crutchfield, who had arrived near the bridge at about 9:30 A.M., found that the retreating Federals had fired the span and had posted guns to contest any crossing. The stream itself lay hidden beneath a dense cover of trees and undergrowth, and the approaches to it from the north confused and depressed the valley soldiers. No sylvan glade, this, scented and alive with flowers and outdoor creatures. What lay ahead was a bog, made worse by the night's hard rain, mud-splashed and repelling—a bog with higher ground on each side and Yankee guns frowning from the southern heights.

Instantly the Professor of Artillery Tactics grasped the situation. Federal infantry and artillery could be seen on the Confederate left, but directly in front and to the right tall timber obscured the view. What was important to Jackson was that the enemy guns had been put in battery. He would meet metal with metal. Crutchfield had found an admirable spot for his guns, but it stood exposed. How could Jackson's batteries be brought into action before they were blasted to bits by Federal ordnance? Fortunately a hidden approach to the proposed battery site could be used. Jackson called up twenty-eight guns, told Crutchfield to load them under cover, and at 1:45 P.M. they were rushed to the dominating ridge and opened fire.[94]

The thunderous barrage caught the Federals utterly unprepared. Jackson watched with pleasure. He had been working toward a new use of artillery, and he had just been vindicated. Rarely had the concept of mass firepower been tried; he had tried it on Henry House hill, and at Gaines' Mill when he put thirty guns in action.[95] Now, as he watched, Union cannoneers limbered up and pulled out of their batteries. Three shattered guns they left behind. Could massed artillery clear the way for the infantry?[96] As the deafening explosions continued, Jackson waited for an answer to that question. Some of the Union infantry, commanded by Maj. Gen. William B. Franklin, leaped up and ran to the rear pursued by the screaming shells. But the main body stood unshaken. Something else would have to be thrown at them.

Time assumed increasing importance. Two o'clock now, and off to the right and south Longstreet's men waited for sounds of Jackson's and Huger's advance, while Magruder crossed behind Huger to aid on the right. Huger, busily engaged in chopping trees and clearing a way for his artillery, forgot about time. Jackson did not—for a while.

Ordering a battery slipped close to the bridge, Jackson directed that it should drive off sharpshooters. Then, seeking out Col. Tom Munford, whose Second Virginia Cavalry had come on from the valley,

Jackson asked for a reconnaissance across the swamp and an attempt to pick up the abandoned Yankee guns. He would ride with the troopers. In column, ready, Munford gave the word—forward. Galloping down the hill, through the slough, and up on the hostile side, Munford swiftly deployed, just in time to receive a hot fire from sharpshooters and a blast from a well-hidden field battery. Scanning the field, Jackson saw what had happened after his opening barrage had driven off the Unionists on his left; they had moved across their own rear and taken position on a hill dominating the Confederate right and center and barring passage of the swamp road. For the slight Confederate mounted force to engage would be suicide—instantly they must retire! Munford headed his column east to elude the fierce fire and Old Jack recrossed the swamp.

That little excursion had been a lesson in futility. Union infantry and artillery were deployed in great numbers and their positions were naturally strong. Back came the gun sent to drive away the sharpshooters; under cover of woods went Jackson's infantry. As Jackson reasoned, the "marshy character of the soil, the destruction of the bridge over the marsh and creek, and the strong position of the enemy for defending the passage prevented my advancing." [97] This was Jackson's later explanation in his official report, but at the moment he thought an attempt to repair the bridge ought to be made. If successful, it might lead to a general advance of all arms. [98] Meanwhile Crutchfield's guns could change their aim, and harass the new and well-concealed enemy positions. [99]

Once these measures were ordered, Stonewall Jackson went to sleep. Weary and worn beyond endurance, he gave his instructions and then lost interest in the situation. Dabney, with much the best chance to observe his chief's actions, later speculated on the reasons for his lassitude that day:

> Nobody could blame Jackson for being done out. . . . Remember he had had a hard time since leaving Beaver Dam; not a wink of sleep the night at Ashland; not a regular meal after leaving Hundley's Corner Friday morning. Our head-quarter wagon and servants all in the rear; no mess chest; no cook; no regular rations drawn; no mess tables set, Friday, Saturday, Sunday, Monday, nor Tuesday. Very little sleep Sunday night, which from one o'clock was spent on horseback. I suppose he had neither breakfast nor dinner Monday. I know I had none, and I suppose he was no better off, and next to no meals for three days before. [100]

D. H. Hill could not bear the inactivity. While Jackson slept, Hill threw some skirmishers across the swamp and at the same time struggled to get a working party busy on the bridge. Nobody could be persuaded to action that weird afternoon. The troops were as tired as the general, and finally gave up trying to patch the bridge. The heat steamed the sweating men, they swatted at battalions of flies and mosquitoes, and stayed under cover. A fierce cannonade continued between Jackson's and Franklin's guns, but with little effect. When the firing faded now and then, the sound of a terrific infantry and artillery battle to the southwest was clearly audible; Longstreet's men were fighting hard.

When Jackson finally awoke, he seated himself on a tree trunk, staring wordlessly at the ground. Not even the appearance of a new and unattached brigadier seeking orders stirred him. He merely suggested that the brigade cross the swamp back upstream and rejoin its division.[101] Nothing could be done at White Oak.[102]

By mid-afternoon Jackson had failed to send orders to Tom Munford, who had reported finding a feasible crossing east of the bridge, and had failed to detach any troops to aid Longstreet, who was engaged in a raging fight at Frayser's Farm.[103] Although giving the appearance of energy,[104] Jackson could not seem to focus his mind on what had to be done.

When, at length, one of his new brigadiers, Gen. Wade Hampton, reported that he had found a way to cross the swamp just behind the enemy's right flank, Jackson asked quickly if the South Carolinian could build a bridge at the spot he described. Yes, Hampton replied, for infantry, but if he felled timber for an artillery road, the Federals would discover the movement. Build the bridge, Jackson ordered. In a short time and without difficulty the span took shape, and Hampton returned to tell Jackson. The general showed no emotion, no evidence of reaction. When the long silence became embarrassing, Jackson stood up and without a word walked away.[105]

Throughout the rest of the day, while Longstreet fought out the hearts of his men in a desperate action almost within cannon shot of Jackson, the "Champion of the Valley" did nothing. His staff, noticing that he did not seem to be himself at times,[106] caught a glimpse of how worn out Stonewall was that night. As they sat together having supper, Old Jack's head lolled forward—he was sound asleep, with a biscuit between his teeth! Roused, he looked blankly around and then said: "Now, gentlemen, let us at once to bed, and rise with the dawn, and see if to-morrow we cannot *do something!*" [107]

Had Jackson known the identity of one of the Federal units disputing the White Oak Bridge, he doubtless would have exerted fiercer efforts that day. Across the swamp stood the brigade of an old antagonist, William H. French, who this time had the better of the argument.[108]

What happened to Jackson in the White Oak Swamp that he failed to do two important things? Why did he not go to the aid of Longstreet at Frayser's Farm? Once and once only did his staff hear him answer this question. Some two weeks afterward, listening to his aides discussing whether or not he should have moved to support Longstreet, he sharply cut off the debate by saying: "If General Lee had wanted me he could have sent for me." [109] Orders from Lee pinned him to the road leading across White Oak Swamp, and he did not feel he should ignore Lee's desires.

Why did he not attack or turn Franklin's position? Physical exhaustion appears the only sensible explanation of Jackson's apathy. Worked beyond the limit of even his iron endurance, Jackson did not realize that he had lost contact with reality. By nightfall it had become obvious to his staff, at least, that he was in a stupor possibly caused by pent-up fatigue, unhealthy and unfamiliar climate, and the confusion of foreign geography. He had wasted the better part of a day, and his remark to his messmates on the evening of the thirtieth indicates he knew it and would try to atone for his lapse on the morrow.[110]

When darkness blotted out all action that Monday, it ended one of the most frustrating days of the whole Seven Days' Campaign. All along the line errors of omission had snarled Lee's plan for reconcentration and coordinated attack. Only at Frayser's Farm had any of his troops come to effective grips with McClellan's fleeing bluecoats, and there Longstreet and A. P. Hill had fought alone, without any of the support which lay close at hand on either flank. There was much to be regretted about the failures of that day, but time permitted only swift measures to insure a continued advance.

Early in the morning of July 1, Jackson sent Whiting's men to test the crossing, and quickly came the report: the enemy had gone! Repairs swiftly completed, Jackson's mud-spattered columns moved south over ground their artillery had raked the day before. If the infantrymen felt unhappy that they had not been called upon to carry those hills, they made no audible complaints.[111] Soon Jackson's lead elements made out a gray line of battle formed on the right of the road, screened by a curtain of skirmishers on the left. Straight between the two lines marched Jackson's divisions, greeted by lusty cheers from Magruder's boys, who had relieved the battle-weary veterans of Longstreet at Frayser's Farm.[112]

Close to the head of the column—always his post of duty—Jackson soon spied a knot of officers near Willis Church. Lee had arrived and established field headquarters. Here, too, A. P. Hill and Longstreet could be seen, along with D. H. Hill. Lee seemed in a slightly testy mood, although obviously clear in his thinking. Jackson impressed those present as being exceedingly alert and ready. Sleep had refreshed him. D. H. Hill appeared worried; if McClellan could reach Malvern Hill, an eminence of which Hill had just heard, the Young Napoleon might succeed in saving his army. So strong was the position that the usually bellicose Hill had words of caution: "If General McClellan is there in force, we had better let him alone." Bluff Pete Longstreet laughed loudly, and exhorted his friend: "Don't get scared, now that we have got him whipped." Only he was not whipped—and Hill soon had ghastly proof that his fears were well grounded.

All units were ordered to follow McClellan. His wagon trains might be hit or his army brought to bay before he completed his change of base, but the orders lacked conviction. The motions, however, had to be gone through, despite abysmal ignorance of the ground ahead. Not even Lee had a clear idea of what terrain would be encountered, and McClellan gained the advantage of being able to pick his battlefield.

Jackson's men, on his request, drew the lead in the march from the north, followed by Magruder. Huger would be put into pursuit when he arrived—a doubtful point, since he had undergone almost complete demoralization the previous day. A. P. Hill and Longstreet would hold their battered battalions in reserve for a hard-won rest.[113]

Down the Willis Church road Jackson led his column for about a mile and a half,[114] when suddenly his van received a volley from Federal outposts, who fell back as the Confederates came on. The enemy had concentrated on Malvern Hill and held strong positions. Another mile brought the infantry close to the northern foot of Malvern Hill, and here they stopped to deploy.[115] To the left of the road into the fields of the Poindexter farm, where good open ground had the protection of shallow woodland, Jackson sent Whiting's division. D. H. Hill took a position to the right of Whiting athwart the Willis Church road, and later the gap between them was plugged by Trimble's brigade from Ewell's division.[116] As his gaze swept the field, Jackson saw that Whiting's division would be the left element of Lee's line.

The ground worked as an active ally of McClellan. With a few patches of farm land the exception, the Confederate line of battle would be drawn in an incredibly dense forest and thick underbrush. In front of the Poindexter farm and across the road ran a small stream constituting a lesser White Oak Swamp. This stream could be crossed only at certain points, which would further confuse deployment in the woods. Formation in the jungle appeared impossible, and even if a line of battle were constructed, organization would disappear as soon as the line advanced.

Above the maze into which the Confederates moved stood Malvern Hill, mocking and serene. Not high as hills go, and consequently deceiving, McClellan's new position had all the elements of a Gibraltar. The Union left rested on a bluff crowned with guns, and as the line curved toward the center a gentle decline dropped away toward the Confederates. Facing Jackson's men, the center and right of McClellan's line rested on the same rise of open ground, offering magnificent opportunities for killing to his formidable batteries on the crest of the hill.

Not all the defensive virtues of Malvern Hill could be seen by Jackson as he made an initial reconnaissance. But the number of guns, supported by several lines of infantry, were enough to convince him that an immediate attack on the Union right would be impossible. Whiting's ground on the Poindexter farm offered some possibilities for artillery, and again Jackson called for his guns. It was almost ten o'clock before he developed his full front and had much of his ordnance in action. His infantry were in position, supporting what few guns could be found by 11 A.M.[117]

Bringing up guns proved a maddening problem. Stapleton Crutch-field had gone on sick call that day, and no temporary chief of artillery had been designated since Jackson acted in that capacity. Bad logistics —possibly Lee's fault—had put too many brigades, wagons, and guns on the small Willis Church road, and as a result batteries lagged far behind. Riding back himself, Jackson sought any guns he could locate. When he reached the point at which the Poindexters' road joined the choked highway, Jackson told Dabney to take position there and direct guns and reserves to the east where his men were forming. Finding a reliable battery on the road, he personally directed its emplacement, helping to shove the pieces into position.[118] But despite herculean personal efforts, Old Jack could never bring more than eighteen guns to bear on the Federals, and these fought piecemeal. Each gun could hardly send off a round before shells from McClellan's massed metal knocked it to pieces. Vainly Jackson sought General Pendleton's reserve artillery batteries; they did not come up. D. H. Hill's guns had gone to the rear for refitting; he had none at all. Jackson could not put to use his massed-fire concept, and at length most of his guns either retired from the unequal battle or kept up a wild, ineffective contest.[119]

Lee, who watched the battle for a time from a vantage point back of Jackson's lines, became alarmed at Old Jack's personal concern for his guns. While the two had been talking, Jackson received word of damage to some of his batteries and galloped off to see for himself. Lee had called after him not to go, but Jackson's bad hearing doubtless obscured his chief's words. Riding along the line, Jackson, Sandie Pendleton, and Kyd Douglas drew the especial attention of some Federal ordnance, one shell exploding directly in front of Jackson's horse. Pulling his quailing mount to its feet, Jackson rode on until one of Lee's staff officers caught up and yelled: "General, General Lee presents his compliments and directs that you return at once." Meekly Jackson retraced his course.[120]

Still Jackson worked to give more power to his line. He hoped, in spite of the incredibly strong position held by the enemy, that Lee's plan to crush McClellan would succeed that day. In the heat of battle, with shot and shell screaming around him, Jackson became exhilarated and increasingly optimistic. On a ragged bit of paper, he scribbled a note to friend Jeb Stuart, whose cavalry had been guarding his left flank:

11^h 20^m A M Near Dr Poindexters
[July 1, 1862]

General Stuart:

I am engaged with the enemy. I trust that God will give our army a glorious victory. . . .

T. J. Jackson.[121]

While he wrote, sitting against a tree by the road, the sudden shriek and explosion of a heavy shell killed some passing infantry and showered dirt on him. Shaking the paper he was writing on, Old Jack calmly finished his note.[122]

Through the morning Lee's commanders fought to get their men in position around the northern approaches to Malvern Hill preparatory to a general assault. Lee had given orders that at a designated signal the whole Confederate line, from Jackson on the left to Magruder on the right, would leap forward and carry the enemy line. Such an attack could succeed only if the Union guns on the crest were subdued and the Confederate brigades attacked in unison.

The battle of Malvern Hill, like so many of the engagements of that week, went to pieces. No coordination of orders or efforts could be achieved. Magruder became confused, took a wrong road, and after he arrived on the battlefield found himself confronted with what appeared peremptory orders from Lee to attack without delay. Many hours had been wasted while Magruder and others groped their way through the tangled underbrush toward the front, and in the meantime most of the guns which Lee's men had brought into action had been silenced or were running out of ammunition.

Lee and Longstreet had ridden to the left of Jackson's positions looking for a way to flank the Union lines. There seemed a chance. Reserves must be brought round quickly. But, like everything else that day, this hope died a-borning. While Lee worked on the flank plan, a series of messages indicated that the enemy might be leaving his bastion, and that limited success on the Confederate right gave cause for hope. Cancel the plans for the flank move, concentrate on the right. At six o'clock Magruder, thinking he was obeying orders, launched an attack on the strong left side of McClellan's line.

The sound of infantry fire filtered through the heavy booming of Yankee cannon. D. H. Hill, holding Jackson's right, took the sound to be the signal for a general advance, and according to outdated orders he was right. Forward, he cried, and took his men into a slaughter pen which bathed the slopes of Malvern Hill in Southern blood. No general attack had begun—Hill was alone. "Fractions against masses" was Dick Taylor's phrase to describe the futile and magnificently heroic charge of Hill's men. Small elements of other divisions got into the attack.

Magruder fought unaided on the right, but nowhere did the Confederates have a chance. Mowed down steadily by the deliberate, sickeningly effective cannon they sought to storm and raked by sheets of infantry fire, Hill's gallant men fell back in one of the bloodiest repulses of the campaign.

Jackson had watched his men start, had seen quickly that Hill had been wrong, and had ordered Ewell's and his own divisions to double-time to the front. But it was too late.[123] The clogged road, bramble, and forest slowed the reserves, and they arrived after Hill's bleeding men were through.

Five thousand dead and wounded grayclads lay on the field. Still, old Isaac Trimble would make a try, undaunted by darkness and the belching flames atop Malvern. Old Jack spotted Trimble, doggedly deploying for battle in the dark. "What are you going to do, General Trimble?" "I," said the rugged old soldier, "am going to charge those batteries, sir."

A silence; then: "I guess you had better not try it. General D. H. Hill has just tried it with his whole Division and been repulsed; I guess you had better not try it, sir." So even Jackson, who many hours earlier dared hope for a great victory at God's hands, had given up. Brutal and costly had been the attack. Jackson's command alone lost a total of 2,162 killed, wounded, and missing,[124] and McClellan still stood intact.

The restless guns continued a relentless pounding of the infantry until about 10 P.M., when all firing gradually died away.[125] Young Kyd Douglas, who had been hard pressed to keep up with Old Jack's energetic efforts to strengthen his lines during the day, watched the battlefield as darkness hid its horrors. The scene made an indelible impression:

Night, dark and dismal, settled upon the battlefield of Malvern Hill, its thousands dead and wounded. The rain began to fall on the cruel scene and beat out the torches of brave fellows hunting their wounded companions in the dark. The howling of the storm, the cry of the wounded and groans of the dying, the glare of the torch upon the faces of the dead or into the shining eyes of the speechless wounded, looking up in the hope of relief, the ground slippery with a mixture of mud and blood, all in the dark, hopeless, starless night; surely it was a gruesome picture of war in its most horrid shape.[126]

Dreadful had been that day, the final climax to a long series of errors and blunders pointing to the need of much-improved staff work. As Jackson rode back in search of his headquarters wagon, a vast fatigue overcame him. Jim Lewis had laboriously brought the wagon from Ashland, and at last the general could have a reasonably good supper. Jim made a bed for him in a farmyard, and after eating he stretched out and slept. Nothing more could be done—he refused to worry.

About 1 A.M. Ewell and D. H. Hill awoke him to report. All three squatted in a circle, resembling in Dabney's sleepy eyes a triumvirate of frogs conversing. Old Jack asked quick questions: In what condition were the divisions? Where were the various units? The answers were all discouraging. Ewell finally said, with great weariness: "If McClellan knows what he is about he will take the aggressive in the morning; and I tell you we are in no condition to meet it." Jackson's reply, in flat, calm tones, surprised Dabney and the others, but obviously he was serious: "Oh no, McClellan will clear out in the morning." [127]

As the apprehensive Confederates stared into the mist of dawn on July 2, they saw some Federals still on the hill—but the main army was leaving! Where would McClellan go? Could he be pursued? Jackson thought so.

14

VICTORY WINS AN

OPPORTUNITY

GENERAL LEE presided over the conference at the Poindexter farmhouse. Assembled there that rain-lashed morning of July 2 were the commanding general, Jackson, and numbers of their respective staffs. Lee studied maps, heard reports of McClellan's supposed movements, and talked with Jackson, Maj. Walter H. Taylor, and Dr. McGuire. Everyone present understood the problem Lee faced: Where had Little Mac gone, and could the Confederate Army get at him? Over the room hung an air of anxiety.

Major Dabney arrived a little after 11 A.M., reporting that Jackson's orders to have his command put in three lines of battle, stack arms, build fires, and cook rations had been carried out. Ushered into the presence of Jackson and the commanding general, the Reverend Chief of Staff made his report and sought a warm corner where he could see and hear what went on. What he saw proved most interesting. Lee questioned Jackson about the condition of his command, routes, and possible plans. Making quick and deferential answers, Old Jack grew pensive and worried.

Longstreet arrived in a brusque mood, and in reply to a query from Lee about the outcome of the battle of Malvern Hill snapped: "I think you hurt them about as much as they hurt you." Soon Old Pete sloshed out to see if his men were ready to march. Not long after, two soaked riders entered, shaking off the rain. Lee quickly went to greet the President and his brother, Col. Joseph Davis. While Lee and Davis were shaking hands, the President's glance took in the room and fastened on

323

Jackson. Jackson stood stiffly at attention, obviously standoffish—he still remembered Davis's attitude at the time of the Romney controversy.

Lee attempted to thaw the atmosphere: "Why, President, don't you know General Jackson? This is our Stonewall Jackson." Davis, ever perceptive to personal slights himself, instantly sensed Jackson's mood and merely bowed. Old Jack saluted and said nothing.

The commanding general led Davis to a table and began to show him the situation as he knew it. Describing the impossible condition of the roads, the bottomless mud, the conflicting reports on enemy activity, Lee also detailed the disposition of Confederate troops and plans for pursuing the retreating Federals. Davis listened, shot an occasional question, and studied the maps. What ought to be done, he asked. The uncertainty of enemy movements, conditions in Confederate camps, and the weather led to a decision: no pursuit would be made that day. Sitting modestly in a corner, withdrawn and increasingly morose, Old Jack was not consulted. But Dabney fancied he could tell what went on in Jackson's mind. He was, in Dabney's estimation, "uttering a mournful protest against their conclusions." Old Jack's face

expressed first surprise, then dissent, mortification, sorrow, anguish. As a true soldier he was too subordinate to say a word to his superiors, to anybody, but I believed then I knew his thoughts. . . . He had the true instinct of genius. He knew McClellan was beaten, was retreating, not manoeuvring [sic]. . . . He heard Lee and Davis arguing that the scouts reported fearful mud in McClellan's rear, that not much artillery could be dragged along; our men wet, tired, etc. . But Jackson's mind reasoned; if these invaders can trudge through mud and mire, to save their bacon, surely patriot heroes could do it to save their country and to reap the fruits of a great victory bought for us with so much precious blood.[1]

Accepting without question the final conclusions of his superiors, Jackson made ready to push his troops forward the next day. Lee gave orders that the army would march after McClellan as soon as possible—and as soon as his position became known. Stuart reported on July 3 that the Federal army had taken shelter under its gunboats at Harrison's Landing, eight miles below Malvern Hill. Harrison's, then, would be the point of Confederate concentration. But concentration proved dismally slow. Longstreet had the lead—because the Army of the Valley had moved so slowly during the Seven Days—and Jackson followed along in the hideous ruts and chuckholes. Three miles only could his columns move on the third, possibly indicating to Old Jack that rapid pursuit on the second would have been impossible.[2]

The added delay, crowning a series of delays, was almost the last straw. Jackson's temper gave way under the strain; he became testy and irritable. By nightfall his staff had selected a house "a mile or two east of Willis Church" as headquarters for the general and his entourage.

Hardly speaking to anyone, Old Jack accepted the hospitality of the home, and sought out a poor, hapless private, assigned him as a guide. He wanted some important data on the roads of the vicinity. The soldier gave a reply—"stupid and childish" in Dabney's words—which showed he knew nothing about them. "Jackson broke out on him fiercely, and ordered him from his presence with threats of extremest military punishment." Just before going to bed, the general addressed his cowed staff: "Now gentlemen," he said, "Jim will have breakfast for you punctually at dawn. I expect you to be up, to eat immediately and be in the saddle with me. We must burn no more daylight."

At "earliest dawn" Old Jack appeared dressed and ready to eat. Jim, an old hand at getting up ahead of the general, had breakfast steaming. The Reverend Maj. Dabney, sleepy and disarrayed, put in an appearance—but no one else. "Major, how is it that this staff will never be punctual?" Dabney had an answer for that one. "I am on time," he acidly replied, "I cannot control the others." Jackson exploded in a blind, towering rage. Whirling on Jim, he roared, "Jim, put back that food into the chest, lock it, have the chest in the wagon and that wagon moving in two minutes. Do you hear?"

Swiftly, with an eye to the warm food, Dabney ventured a suggestion: The General ought at least to take some food with him, oughtn't he? Too angry to eat and too angry to think of the poor major, Jackson repeated his instructions and hurled himself in the saddle, to ride swiftly out of sight. Jim, with a low whistle for emphasis, shook his head: "My stars! But the General is mad dis time; most like lighten [sic] strike him." While the famished Dabney watched, Jim deliberately scattered the breakfast and doused the coffee on the ground—he had already had his! [3]

When at last Jackson's men reached position near Harrison's Landing on the fourth, Longstreet, the senior general present, made preparations to attack the Federals, who held a strong eminence from which they had just driven Stuart's cavalry. Jackson did not want to attack; his men were worn out from rough marching. Would Longstreet hold up the battle until Lee's views could be had? Doubtless convinced by this that his opinion of the "second-raters" was correct, Longstreet sent a courier for Lee.

Lee arrived on the field, and he and Jackson went forward on foot to scout the strength of the Federal lines. McClellan had again selected a minor Gibraltar—Evelington Heights. Cannon bristled from the crest in familiar abundance. Jackson had been right; an attack here would probably result in another gory repulse and in casualties which the army could ill afford. The attack plan was canceled. [4]

So ended the campaign against McClellan. True, the Little Napoleon had not been destroyed, nor had he been driven from the Peninsula as all Richmonders devoutly wished, but he had been forced into a fast and costly retreat and ignominiously pushed to the protection of the United States Navy. He showed no immediate signs of leaving that comforting protection, and Richmond no longer lay besieged. Much in the Confederate campaign could be criticized—and was—but one thing stood out clearly: the object of the campaign, the relief of the capital, had been achieved.

For several days the army lay in line near McClellan's men, but there were no more battles. The time had come for a rest and for reorganization. The time had come, too, to deal with a new threat to Virginia.

In late June, following Jackson's move toward Richmond, Federal authorities had created a new field force, the Army of Virginia, made up of the troops in the Shenandoah, McDowell's ill-starred army, and the units designated to defend Washington. To command this hodgepodge came Maj. Gen. John Pope, fresh from the Middle West, where he had looked promising. Vigorously he had taken command, had sized up his army, and had decided it lacked spirit. He could remedy that. Operating with his headquarters in the saddle—where, in Lincoln's fabled opinion, his hindquarters ought to be—Pope on July 14 issued a contemptuous address to his new command.

> I have [he declaimed] spent two weeks in learning your whereabouts, your condition, and your wants, in preparing you for active operations, and in placing you in positions from which you can act promptly and to the purpose. These labors are nearly completed, and I am about to join you in the field.

Then he got down to business:

> Let us understand each other. I have come to you from the West, where we have always seen the backs of our enemies; from an army whose business it has been to seek the adversary and to beat him when he was found; whose policy has been attack and not defense. . . . I presume that I have been called here to pursue the same system and to lead you against the enemy. It is my purpose to do so, and that speedily. I am sure you long for an opportunity to win the distinction you are capable of achieving. That opportunity I shall endeavor to give you. Meantime I desire you to dismiss from your minds certain phrases, which I am sorry to find so much in vogue amongst you. I hear constantly of "taking strong positions and holding them," of "lines of retreat," and of "bases of supplies." Let us discard such ideas. The strongest position a soldier should desire to occupy is one from which he can most easily advance against the enemy. Let us study the probable lines of retreat of our opponents, and leave our own to take care of themselves. Let us look before us, and not behind. Success and glory are in the advance, disaster and shame lurk in the rear.[5]

Had Pope's activities been confined entirely to bombast, the Confederacy could have enjoyed a good laugh at the Yankee general's expense, but he added brutality to vainglory. In a series of General Orders published to his army during middle and late July, Pope set up his own rules of war—rules which were not in accord with those currently in use on either side at that comparatively early stage of the fighting. His troops, announced the bold commander, were expected to live off the enemy's country.

> Vouchers will be given to the owners [of confiscated supplies], stating on their face that they will be payable at the conclusion of the war, upon sufficient testimony being furnished that such owners have been loyal citizens of the United States since the date of the vouchers.

Sabotage or guerrilla activities would be dealt with in an exceedingly modern manner:

> Wherever a railroad, wagon road, or telegraph is injured by parties of guerrillas the citizens living within 5 miles of the spot shall be turned out in mass to repair the damage. . . . If a soldier or legitimate follower of the army be fired upon from any house the house shall be razed to the ground, and the inhabitants sent prisoners to the headquarters of this army. . . . Any persons detected in such outrages . . . shall be shot, without awaiting civil process.[6]

By the time these orders became known to the people of Virginia and the South, Lee's army had drawn back from Harrison's Landing toward its old encampments near Richmond. Jackson's men, after being ordered to wash off the Chickahominy mud,[7] moved into camps two or three miles from the city. The general himself began to emerge from his swamp melancholia. While the army rested and recruited, Jackson took time to bring Anna up to date on what had happened to her *esposo*. He confessed that during the week of the Seven Days' Battles he had "not been well, have suffered from fever and debility, but through the blessing of an ever-kind Providence I am much better to-day. . . . It would be delightful to see my darling, but we know that all things are ordered for the best." [8]

Had Anna been able to talk with any of Thomas's staff, particularly with Kyd Douglas, she would have learned that he continued in excellent health, although the kind attentions of some local ladies taxed him slightly. Now that he had become the lion of Virginia, the savior of the capital, streams of people brought him all kinds of presents, ranging from baskets of exotic foods (which would have wrecked his simple diet had not his voracious young staff relieved him of the unhealthy gifts) to abominable straw hats designed to frighten away the Yankees Stonewall did not kill.[9] Anna would have been amused to hear that Thomas had gone blackberry picking with Kyd Douglas near Harrison's Landing.

But she would have been frightened beyond words to hear that the berry picking went on between Confederate and Yankee picket lines, while the Minié balls, in Douglas's phrase, were "as plentiful as blackberries." [10]

The news that Thomas wanted very much to leave the swampland of the area below Richmond would not have surprised Anna; she knew how much he loved the highlands and his valley. But she would have been scared had she heard where he wanted to go.

The idea had been growing ever since Jackson sat in the corner listening, while Davis and Lee "took counsel of their fears" and decided against striking a final blow at McClellan. It had been growing since he had irritatedly told his staff they must "burn no more daylight." While his command rested in arms after McClellan had been driven to his gunboats, Old Jack decided to do something with his plan. To his tent he summoned friend Alex Boteler.

"Do you know," began the general excitedly, "that we are losing valuable time here?"

"How so?" asked the colonel.

"Why, by repeating the blunder we made after the battle of Manassas, in allowing the enemy leisure to recover from his defeat and ourselves to suffer by inaction. Yes," continued the clipped voice, rising now in excitement, "we are wasting precious time and energies in this malarious region that can be much better employed elsewhere, and I want to talk with you about it." McClellan, he assured Boteler, had been thoroughly whipped; his army would have to be reorganized and reinforced before it could resume the attack, and consequently the safety of Richmond had been assured. Jackson came to the point. His plan for an invasion of Maryland, which Boteler had outlined to Davis weeks before, ought to be put into operation—the time was at hand for a northward thrust by the Confederates. Would Boteler once again broach the idea to the President, and make it clear that Jackson sought nothing in the plan for himself? He would gladly follow any general named to head the expedition.

Cautiously Boteler asked: "What is the use of my going to Mr. Davis, as he'll probably refer me again to General Lee? So why don't you yourself speak to General Lee upon the subject?"

The secret came out. "I have already done so," said Jackson.

"Well, what does he say?"

"He says nothing," Jackson answered. After a moment's pause he continued quietly: "Don't think I complain of his silence; he doubtless has good reasons for it."

"Then you don't think that General Lee is slow in making up his mind?"

"Slow!" came the exclamation. "By no means, Colonel; on the contrary, his perception is as quick and unerring as his judgment is infallible. But with the vast responsibilities now resting on him, he is perfectly right in withholding a hasty expression of his opinions and purposes."

Another pause, then with emphasis Old Jack added: "So great is my confidence in General Lee that I am willing to follow him blindfolded. But I fear he is unable to give me a definite answer now because of influences at Richmond, where, perhaps, the matter has been mentioned by him and may be under consideration. I, therefore, want you to see the President and urge the importance of prompt action." [11]

Once again Davis listened to Jackson's plan for an invasion of the enemy's country, and once again he could not authorize it; the important thing at the moment was to do something about the obnoxious General Pope. Jackson might be just the man for the job.

The problem of dealing with Pope became complicated by a question of mathematics. Confederate losses during the Seven Days' campaign had totaled over 20,000 killed, wounded, and missing. If Jackson's command went to deal with the Federal Army of Virginia, Lee's forces facing McClellan would be drastically reduced. Counting the command of Holmes, now ordered south of the James, Lee would face the Federals below Richmond with about 69,000 men. [12] But the gamble must be made; if Jackson could come to grips with Pope at a reasonable distance from Richmond, he might be able to defeat him and send back some of his men.

Thinking over the record of the Seven Days, Lee could hardly have been enthusiastic about the performance of Jackson and the Army of the Valley. During the course of those battles, Jackson had fallen far short of the reputation earned in the valley. Should the important expedition against Pope be entrusted to Old Jack? Yes, Lee decided. In his official report of the Seven Days' campaign Lee did not praise Jackson, but he studiously avoided censure. Of the delay at Grapevine Bridge, Lee merely noted that Jackson had been held up by the necessity of reconstructing the span, ignoring (if he knew of them) the orders from Army Headquarters. Of the baffling day's halt on June 30, Lee wrote: "His [Jackson's] progress was arrested at White Oak Swamp. The enemy occupied the opposite side and obstinately resisted the reconstruction of the bridge." [13] Nowhere did the commanding general hint at any loss of confidence in Old Jack. But undoubtedly he asked himself if Jackson's nature would permit him to function at his best under someone else's direction. Was he the type who chafed under subordination?

Orders were issued on July 13, directing Jackson to take his own and Ewell's division toward Gordonsville and "there to oppose the reported advance of the enemy from the direction of Orange Court-House." [14] Already Lee had shifted troops around to keep Jackson's numbers at something like normal. Taylor's superb brigade had been detached, but another took its place. Even so, the total force which would be entrusted to Jackson could not have been much more than 10,000 men.[15] With this scant army, Jackson must find Pope and, if Pope erred, as seemed possible, beat portions of his army in detail. Speed would be vital—the valley army, once out of the swamps, might regain some of its lost mobility.

For the first stages of the move, Jackson's men would take the cars. Railroad officials worked furiously to hurry the transfer of troops, but the broken bridges between Richmond and Gordonsville posed formidable obstacles. Still, Stonewall Jackson's name appeared to work magic on repair crews; if he wanted to move fast, they would see to it that he did. After superhuman efforts, the road opened, and Jackson's eighteen trains of fifteen cars each rolled northwestward, taking troops, guns, and supplies.[16]

A final conference with the commanding general and with the President would work out the details of cooperating strategy. Reluctant as ever to draw attention to himself, Jackson had to ride into the capital for the conference on July 13. He had been in Richmond on rare occasions during the rest period after the Seven Days, and each time his presence, once detected, had resulted in embarrassing adulation. If only the people would give "all the glory to God, and regard his creatures as but unworthy instruments. . . ." There was too much adoration for mortal heroes.[17] Since a top-level conference involving the President had been called, there was no way to avoid the Richmond trek this time.

Reverend Dr. Dabney, ill and much enfeebled by the lowlands, had regrettably resigned.[18] With his new Adjutant General Sandie Pendleton, plus other members of his staff, Jackson rode from his camp on the morning of the thirteenth. Riding almost grimly, not looking right or left, Old Jack made for the Governor's mansion where he met General Lee. What went on at the conference men of the respective generals' staffs did not know, but the meeting took little time. Soon the two came out, bade good-by to Governor Letcher, and mounted for a ride to the White House.

The White House conference took longer. Enviously one of the new additions to Jackson's official family recorded what he saw of this meeting:

I suppose they had a council of war—certainly a lunch. . . . When the lunch was over . . . I found the staff officers assembling in front [of the White House]. We still had to wait awhile, but soon the different generals, Longstreet and others, came out, but the particular two were kept to the last and then Lee, Jackson and President Davis came out together, a very distinguished trio, and stood talking on the steps. Lee was elegantly dressed in full uniform, sword and sash, spotless boots, beautiful spurs and by far the most magnificent man I ever saw. The highest type of the Cavalier class to which by blood and rearing he belongs. Jackson, on the other hand was a typical Roundhead. He was poorly dressed, that is, he looked so though his clothes were made of good material. His cap was very indifferent and pulled down over one eye, much stained by weather and without insignia. His coat was closely buttoned up to his chin and had upon the collar the stars and wreath of a general. His shoulders were stooped and one shoulder was lower than the other, and his coat showed signs of much exposure to the weather.

The observer, Capt. Charles Minor Blackford, then went on to give his impression of Jackson—whom he most erroneously judged as a reincarnation of one of Cromwell's minions in the Model Army:

His face, in repose, is not handsome or agreeable and he would be passed by anyone without a second look, though anyone could see determination and will in his face by the most casual glance—much I would say to fear but not to love. I of course speak only from a casual observation and from no acquaintance, but that of a line officer who, in the course of his military duties, has been introduced to his commanding general. A means of observation and acquaintanceship that might be likened to that of a glow-worm with the moon.[19]

Farewells said, Jackson mounted "his old sorrel horse" and rode rapidly away, without a word to his staff. Getting back to his quarters in a hurry seemed to be his aim, and the staff galloped to keep up. Reaching the Mechanicsville Pike, the general found it choked with wagons and grimly set about weaving in and out among them. Too slow, far too slow. Abruptly, and in direct violation of his own orders, he reined the sorrel off the road, calling to Pendleton to form the staff in single file. Then they all launched out into a large oat field, pushing through it speedily. Suddenly looming in front of them stood a formidable figure seething with righteous indignation. Old Jack, in front, slowed and seemed about to retreat, but before he could draw rein, the fat little bundle of anger screamed, "What in Hell are you riding over my oats for? Don't you know it's against orders?"

Confused, Jackson fumbled with his bridle and looked terribly abashed. While he fought for something to say, the little man resumed his attack.

"Damnit! Don't you know it's against orders? I intend to have every damned one of you arrested! What's your name anyhow?"

"My name is Jackson," came the miserable response.

"Jackson! Jackson!" the squire spat in Gargantuan contempt. "Jackson, I intend to report every one of you and have you every one arrested. Yes, I'd report you if you were old Stonewall himself instead of a set of damned quartermasters and commissaries riding through my oats! Yes, I'll report you to Stonewall Jackson myself, that's what I'll do!"

"They call me that name sometimes," came the subdued and half-affrighted voice.

"What name."

"Stonewall."

"You don't mean to say you are Stonewall Jackson, do you?"

"Yes, sir, I am."

Before the eyes of an almost hilarious staff, the fat man changed from a fury to a fan. Tears running down his chubby cheeks, he stood briefly speechless, then made the only amends he could think of. Waving a big bandanna, he yelled: "Hurrah for Stonewall Jackson! By God, General, please do me the honor to ride all over my damned old oats!" [20]

One more awkward encounter with civilians awaited him before he could devote his energies to discommoding General Pope, this one fortunately more lighthearted than the skirmish in the oat field. On the way to Louisa Court House and Gordonsville, Jackson and company stopped for the night at a private home near Ashland and the next morning received several invitations to breakfast from local citizens. Jackson's staff, ever on the lookout for a good meal, accepted one of these offers for their general and he dutifully consented.[21] That morning things were going better: the army appeared to be moving well, the swampland lay behind at last, and prospects for a profitable independent command lay ahead. Old Jack, in fine humor, chatted easily with a little girl in his host's household. A young lady of the family rushed to play the piano and sing for him, and he listened with rapt attention, although he had, of course, no ear at all for music. During a lull in the solo, Jackson, seeking to show interest, said, "Miss, won't you play a piece of music they call 'Dixie'? I heard it a few days ago and it was, I thought, very beautiful."

There was a long silence. Then the young virtuoso, baffled and upset, said: "Why, General, I just sang it a few minutes ago—it is about our oldest war song."

"Ah, indeed, I didn't know it," Jackson said in all innocence. Kyd Douglas, fighting back laughter, had a disrespectful thought—since Old Jack had heard "Dixie" a thousand times, "perhaps he thought he would startle the young lady with his knowledge of music: if so, he succeeded." [22]

"Headquarters, Valley District," were finally established at Gordonsville on July 19, and here, much to Jackson's satisfaction, Jed Hotchkiss once more joined the staff and soon drew an assignment to work hard on maps of northern Virginia. Overjoyed to see Jackson, Hotchkiss noticed that his chief and troops looked the worse for their trip to the Chickahominy bottoms. Although acting alert and refreshed, the general looked "weary" to his old friend.[23] And unfortunately hard work piled up at once on Army Headquarters.

Determined that discipline be reestablished, Jackson put his men into camps around Gordonsville and Louisa Court House, set up guards for the Virginia Central Railroad [24] and set the men who had arrived to hard drilling.[25] Respect for military authority must be restored not only to the file but also to the rank. Now that the army had halted for a time, with the prospect of immediate action dim, courts-martial could be convened to deal with a variety of large and small breaches of discipline. Particularly important loomed the case of Gen. Richard B. Garnett, still under a cloud because of Jackson's charges against him following the battle of Kernstown. The services of that useful officer had been largely lost to the army since Old Jack's stern sense of duty compelled him to press his charges. A court-martial had convened near Richmond the very day Jackson received orders to move, and consequently nothing had been done. Now a traveling court had been ordered which could sit and take testimony as Jackson's command moved around. Jackson readily consented to give evidence as soon as the court opened session.

Meanwhile Old Jack found that he could not escape public attention. People flocked to his headquarters at Gordonsville. He had accepted the hospitality of the Ewing family, with whom he had stayed on the way to Richmond. In the yard he pitched his headquarters tent, and had been most pleased with his situation. "My tent," he wrote Anna, "opens upon the Blue Ridge in the distance," and he obviously gloried in the sight of his familiar mountains. In a way the Ewings reminded him of the Grahams in Winchester. Taken into the family, Jackson enjoyed the Ewings' children and soon became the object of the particular affection of one little girl who delighted in playing with him. He promised her one of his uniform buttons when his coat wore out—a promise he kept months later. Especially did Lexington's itinerant deacon enjoy taking part in family worship as the Reverend D. B. Ewing conducted the services. As at Winchester, he impressed the whole family with his piety and theological knowledge.[26]

Reverend Ewing, as stirred by the general's faith as Graham had been, gloried in Jackson's prayers.

> He did not pray to men, but to God. His tones were deep, solemn, tremulous. He seemed to realize that he was speaking to Heaven's King. I never heard any one pray who seemed to be pervaded more fully by a spirit of self-abnegation. He seemed to feel more than any man I ever knew the danger of robbing God of the glory due for our success.[27]

Once again Jackson could devote much attention to religious matters, and he did so with evident pleasure. For several weeks he made a

334

point of being a regular attendant at church,[28] and he took pains to see that his Christian responsibilities at home were executed. In a letter to Maggie's husband, Colonel Preston, he asked a favor:

> Please say to Dr. White that I wish him to pay my stipends last due, from the money I sent him by you. I think he acknowledged the receipt of the funds, but said nothing about the stipends, and I fear that he did not feel authorized to pay himself from the funds placed in his hands.[29]

Even after he had shifted his headquarters into Louisa County, not far from Gordonsville, to escape the crush of visitors, Old Blue Light continued with a personal revival. On July 28 he wrote Anna:

> My darling wife, I am just overburdened with work, and I hope you will not think hard at receiving only very short letters from your loving husband. A number of officers are with me, but people keep coming to my tent—though let me say no more. A Christian should never complain. The apostle Paul said, "I glory in tribulations!" What a bright example for others![30]

During the weeks spent near Gordonsville Jackson's entire religious spirit seemed to center on glorifying God for the successes of men. He confided to a reverend friend that "without God's blessing I look for no success, and for every success my prayer is, that all the glory may be given unto *Him* to whom it is properly due."[31] The Christian fought desperately against the sin of ambition, and through fortitude, deep faith, and the type of asceticism which army life allowed, the Christian seemed to be winning.

Although delighting in his catharsis through vitalized religious thought, Jackson remained ever the commanding general. Slowly the army revived. Brigade commanders, by now well trained to Old Jack's form of discipline, applied the rod harshly. Charles Winder—whose men thought him a martinet and calculatingly cruel—resorted to "bucking" as a means of stopping straggling. This was too much and resentment mounted to such heights that a delegation of officers called on Jackson to report that such harsh treatment would result not only in straggling but in desertion.

Ordinarily Jackson's reaction to this protest would have been to arrest the officers who made it, but this time he listened and agreed. Too sudden and too harsh a return to strict discipline had to be ruled out. Not only should bucking and "gagging" be eliminated as punishment but also flogging. The realities of desertion had to be considered: if sterner punishments would deplete the ranks, then the policing of the army would have to be done on a more gentle basis. Those who branded Jackson as a fanatical disciplinarian would have been surprised at his practical adjustment of a thorny problem.[32]

Discipline troubles continued in the cavalry. Since Ashby's death the troopers had resented any attempts to force them into the mold of regulations. Munford had done reasonably well with those under his charge, but he had not been given Ashby's command. Jackson had asked for a replacement, and Davis consulted Lee for a nomination. The final choice appears to have been the President's, and he selected Beverley H. Robertson, who was promoted brigadier general and sent to Jackson. There seemed no reason why he would not succeed, unless personality worked against him. Balding, with unsmiling eyes and flowing mustachios, Robertson had a good deal of Indian service behind him and he had the advantage—some would say—of being a West Pointer, class of 1849. But he lacked spark, and what was worse, he lacked Jackson's confidence. Why is not clear, but the important fact is that Old Jack never quite trusted Robertson, despite that officer's almost incredible devotion to discipline. Jackson wanted a change of commanders for his cavalry, but Lee could think of no one else at the moment, and had a suspicion that part of Jackson's trouble with the cavalryman lay in expecting too much. For the time, then, Robertson would stay.[33]

Enforcement of the new discipline rested on the several brigade commanders, and also on the courts-martial grinding away at their work in Jackson's camps. At one point Jackson had to confess to Lee that he had so many courts in operation that he had been forced to put all his general officers on that duty [34]—not a particularly good recommendation for Jackson as an army administrator.

Worry about that very question may have been the basis for a letter from Lee to Jackson. For some days in middle and late July the two had been exchanging correspondence regarding Pope's movements and the question of reinforcements for Jackson. At last, convinced by the reports of some of Jackson's scouts that Pope had begun to move forward, Lee decided to send additional men to the valley command. A. P. Hill's well-known Light Division would go, but first a delicate point would have to be made to Jackson. On July 27 Lee wrote him, saying: "A. P. Hill you will, I think, find a good officer, with whom you can consult, and by advising with your division commanders as to your movements much trouble will be saved you in arranging details, as they can act more intelligently." Then, possibly to take the sting out of the thinly veiled rebuke, Lee added: "I wish to save you trouble from my increasing your command."

Consideration of personalities doubtless made Lee's remarks imperative. A. P. Hill had a sensitive streak, and might resent the close-mouthed Jackson. In the same letter Lee sent other instructions on army administration which might have rankled more had they come from anyone else. "Do not let your troops run down if it can possibly be avoided by attention to their wants, comforts, &c., by their respective commanders. This will require your personal attention; also consideration and preparation in your movements." By far the most significant line in the letter said, "I want Pope to be suppressed." Hill would take with him more than 18,000 men, and these combined with Jackson's present numbers ought to be enough for the suppression.

The Light Division, plus the reconstituted Louisiana Brigade, to be commanded by Harry Hays, arrived at Gordonsville by the end of July.[35] Now Jackson had a more adequate force for his task, and he was also well supplied with intelligence of enemy movements. He had already developed a fairly efficient spy system by that time, doubtless drawing on the experience of the famous John S. Mosby, who had been recommended to him by Jeb Stuart.[36]

Meanwhile on August 6, 1862, the traveling court-martial for General Garnett assembled at Ewell's headquarters near Liberty Mills and began to amass evidence.[37] Clearly Old Jack still believed himself entirely right in clinging to the charges of neglect of duty against Garnett for retreating at Kernstown without orders. The testimony Jackson gave jibed not at all with Garnett's memory of several events. Garnett cross-examined, drew direct and relentless answers. In his own behalf Garnett repeated that Jackson had never confided anything of his plans or intentions, even though Garnett might have had to take command of the field at Kernstown in case anything happened to Jackson. "Had he conferred freely with me on that occasion," Garnett said, "I am confident all cause of complaint, as far as this specification is concerned, would have been avoided." Categorically Garnett denied the charges, and concluded that "General Jackson not content with arresting me and depriving me of my command, was determined that I should not be restored to active duty as far as it was in his power to prevent it.... Such covert attacks are inconsistent with honor and justice, and should arouse grave doubts as to the motives and truthfulness of these secret allegations." [38] As Jackson sat and listened to the proceedings he might have been reminded of many days at Carlisle Barracks, where he got his first introduction to the court-martial process, and perhaps of many hot and endless days in Florida, where the excitement of a court-martial would have relieved the tedium of routine. There was a preciseness about him which responded always to the legality of military courts— he might have been a successful barrister.

But in the midst of the Garnett trial sterner things intruded. Scouts reported that part of Pope's army had occupied Culpeper. Pope had split his forces, had made the error which had seemed likely. Now he must be hit, and hit decisively. Droning speeches stopped abruptly. Jackson's orders to move soon made the rounds, men stirred in the camps, wagons began to move out.

Charles Winder, gravely ill, sent an aide to Old Jack with an awkward question. If there was to be no battle immediately, Winder would obey his surgeon's advice and stay quiet; but if an immediate battle loomed, he would be up and in command of his division. The aide delivered the query in a panic of fear—Old Jack never tolerated such direct probing for military secrets. Jackson noted the young shavetail's fright, and answered him kindly: "Say to General Winder I am truly sorry he is sick." A pause, and then: "There will be a battle, but not tomorrow, and I hope he will be up; tell him the army will march to Barnett's Ford, and he can learn its further direction there." Overcome with gratitude, the lieutenant rushed to deliver the message to Winder, who would follow the army.[39]

Long lines of infantry filed into the roads leading north toward Orange Court House—country roads, this time, secretly scouted by Hotchkiss and not patrolled by the enemy.[40] For a while it seemed as though the old marching zest of the "foot cavalry" had returned, and the day's objective was easily reached. Jackson slept part of the night in the street, but finally accepted an invitation to stretch out on a bed in the home of one of the residents of Orange Court House. The army slumbered close by.

No one save General Lee knew what plan the Old Man had in mind, and even Lee lacked precise information. Jackson had confided to him some time before that "I would like to advance before he [Pope] concentrates much more," and wondered if that would fit into the overall plan for Virginia. On the day that Jackson struck his camps and marched, Lee had come to a decision—or rather had decided not to come to a decision. Faced with as yet unexplained moves by several Federal forces in Virginia, including McClellan's growing truculence at Malvern Hill, the commanding general gave Jackson carte blanche. Not able to promise further reinforcements, though wishing he could, he wrote: "I must now leave the matter [of Pope] to your reflection and good judgment. Make up your mind what is best to be done under all the circumstances which surround us, and let me hear the result at which you arrive."[41]

While Lee penned his letter, Jackson had anticipated its contents and had elected to attack, hoping "through the blessing of Providence, to be able to defeat [the part of Pope's army at Culpeper] before reinforcements should arrive there."[42] So began a model relationship between Lee and his lieutenant. Tuned to each other with rare sympathy, they acted not as superior and subordinate, but as equals with a single purpose.

During the night of August 7-8, Jackson changed his marching orders. Ewell's division would take a road to the left of the Orange-Culpeper road and rejoin the main column near Barnett's Ford on the

Rapidan River. For some inexplicable reason A. P. Hill received no notice of the change of marching arrangements. Still moving according to previous instructions, his supposedly swift Light Division dawdled badly during the early hours of August 8. As Hill understood it, his troops would follow those of Ewell on the main road, and he waited for Ewell's brigades to pass through Orange Court House. Finally a division he first assumed to be Ewell's approached the town and moved through, Hill discovering at length that it was Jackson's own division. No sooner did the infantry clear the town than division wagon trains poured in, and Hill felt he should wait until they moved past his own infantry. At length he took the road, but made almost no progress due to a traffic jam at the Rapidan ford. Late in the afternoon Jackson ordered Hill's men back to Orange Court House, and since the head of the column had advanced only about a mile, Hill bivouacked where he was.[43]

The whole army appeared to wilt in the dust and heat.[44] Never had the veterans of the valley done so poorly on the march, not even in the muggy swamps. While Hill covered a scant mile, Ewell could boast of only eight. Deeply chagrined and unhappy, Jackson realized that Federal cavalry—which had been skirmishing with Robertson's men through the eighth—would warn Pope. The element of surprise had evaporated. In this mood of despair Jackson had spent a good part of the day at the head of Ewell's columns, urging men on. He had had time, however, to think of things other than "burning daylight."

During the afternoon, as he ranged well ahead of his troops, he noticed a cavalryman riding rapidly and heading for his command. The lad, very young, looked familiar, and as he silently saluted, Jackson called him to a halt. When the young soldier drew close, Jackson began to talk about the Lexington Sunday school, for the boy had once been a teacher in Jackson's pet church project. Did the lad know that the school had been kept up, despite the war? Briefly they chatted, then Old Jack touched the sorrel's flank and rode off, leaving an extremely confused trooper behind.[45]

Nothing could be done about the miserable marching. It did, however, pose a question: Should the advance be canceled, now that surprise was gone? Jackson decided to continue. If his men could reach Culpeper ahead of Pope, they would hold a strategic hub of roads. Pope had ordered the three separate segments of his army to converge on Culpeper by roads which centered there, and if Jackson held the hub he might prevent the concentration of the Federal units. He must press on, despite the sneaking fear, expressed to Lee in a dispatch early on the ninth, that "the expedition will, in consequence of my tardy movements, be productive of but little good."[46]

If Jim Lewis watched the signs as usual during the evening of the eighth, doubtless he had the general's gear and breakfast ready early the next morning and had made preparation for a fight: the Old Man prayed long that night.[47]

About noon on the ninth,[48] with the army still some eight miles from Culpeper,[49] Jackson received exciting news from Old Baldy: Yankee cavalry "in strong force in our front." Jackson hurried forward and found that Ewell had reconnoitered, had brought up some guns, and begun shelling the blue horsemen, who withdrew over a hill out of the line of fire. Almost immediately unseen Federal cannon sent shells screaming over the hill, intended for the Confederate battery. Apparently Federals were present in considerable strength.

Ewell and Jackson surveyed the situation. Topographically the important feature of ground was Slaughter's, or Cedar, Mountain, a little more than a mile east of the Culpeper-Orange road. High and commanding, this eminence dominated the surrounding terrain—it must be seized by the Confederates. Immediately in front of Ewell's infantry lay a fork in the road, the right branch leading to Culpeper, the left to Madison Court House. In the angle of the fork, dense woods obscured the view, and to the west, on both sides of the Madison road, forests stretched greenly almost as far as the eye could see. East of the Culpeper road low ridges rolled northeastward, and there the land was cleared and some of it under cultivation; certainly it lay cleared between the road and Cedar Mountain, save for isolated clumps of woods. Several small streams, the most important being Cedar Run, traversed the valleys between the ridges, but they appeared on closer look to have no tactical significance.

As soon as he saw the ground and looked at his map with Ewell, Jackson hatched a plan of battle. He would take Cedar Mountain and deploy part of Ewell's infantry in front of it, while Jubal Early's brigade went into line just north of a country road leading eastward to the Crittenden house. Here Early would occupy the crest of a ridge and might dominate a portion of the field. Left of the Culpeper road Winder's men would form in support of Early, and extend the Confederate line so that it could turn the right flank of the Federal force—commanded by an old friend, Gen. Nathaniel P. Banks, who, as Jackson observed, "is always ready to fight . . . and . . . generally gets whipped."

As at Port Republic Jackson went into battle too quickly. There is no evidence that he directed a reconnaissance be made of the wooded ground to the left of the Culpeper road, ground which was impassable to horses and guns but might be opened to a flanking column. The battle, Jackson decided, would be on the right side of the road, with some of his own men sweeping forward on the left, turning in behind the right end of Banks's line and rolling it up toward Trimble's and Henry Forno's brigades of Ewell's division, which would be attacking from Cedar Mountain on the extreme Confederate right. A good plan, considering the time taken preparing it, but it had one deadly flaw—the assumption that the enemy's entire strength lay to the east, or right, of the Culpeper road.

It took time to bring up all the Confederate infantry—20,000 men and fifteen batteries stretched out over more than seven miles of road.[50] With the enemy already in position, the two hours required for deployment was simply not available. As Kyd Douglas later recorded, Jackson "marched into the battle by the flank and commenced the fight with the first file of fours." Ewell's men began to form first, a little after 1 P.M.,[51] then Winder, while A. P. Hill's hardened veterans grimly trudged toward the battlefield.

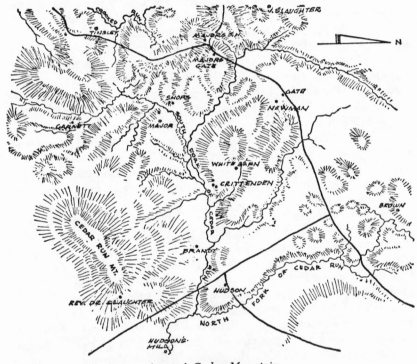

Area of Cedar Mountain

Foolhardy, some said, but all things considered Jackson seemed to be taking little risk. Although he had no exact knowledge of Banks's strength, he guessed that even without Hill the Army of the Valley outnumbered the foe. It did, but not by much. Banks's force, including cavalry, numbered probably 9,000 men, while Jackson's total force came to a little over 23,000, of which slightly less than half made up Hill's Light Division. So, when the battle began, opposing infantry forces were about even.

Eager to see the enemy's positions, Jackson rode forward, took the country road to the Crittenden house and perched himself on a hill near the dwelling. He and Captain Blackford drew a few Federal shells, and soon they rode back toward the main highway. At the gate to Mrs. Crittenden's farm, Jackson posted Blackford with instructions to direct Hill's men forward in support of Early and Ewell. With no backward glance Old Jack galloped toward Early's lines.

For a time all seemed to go well, save for the fact that Jackson could not establish a connected line of battle in the Federal front. Ewell's main force stood far removed on the right; Early, with the support of the Twelfth Georgia and some guns, held what passed for the center; Winder had his men forming parallel to the highway in the woods on the left. Professor Jackson probably noted with satisfaction that his artillery when in position did good execution—guns to the right and left and guns in the center directed an effective cross fire on the Federals, in line on the ridge opposite Early. Twenty-six fine 3-inch rifles and 12-pounder Napoleons blasted the Yankee lines but took considerable punishment in return.

There was something about the woodland on the left. . . . Reining the sorrel in that direction, Jackson rode over to have a close look and found that Winder's Second Brigade, commanded by Lt. Col. T. S. Garnett, constituted the flank element, aligned along the southern edge of a large wheat field. To the right of Garnett, Winder had posted Taliaferro so that his line formed almost a right angle to Early's front. Considering that Winder anticipated an attack across the field ahead of Early, his dispositions were wise, but they were dangerous should Banks try a turning movement.

Jackson's battle disintegrated suddenly. Not long after he had completed his dispositions at 4 P.M. Charles Winder fell, horribly mangled by a shell. Instantly command of the left passed to William Taliaferro, who was, as he later reported, "ignorant of the plans of the general, except so far as I could form an opinion from my observation." [52]

Word of Winder's mortal wound reached Old Jack, who for the moment showed little or no emotion. Riding at once to Garnett's position he told the colonel to look well to his left and call on Taliaferro for reinforcements. About 5 P.M. Banks ordered an attack on Early's right and front,[53] and timely arrival of some of A. P. Hill's men helped beat off the advance. As anxiety hung over Jackson's center, an ominous rolling roar of musketry on the left caught the general's ear. Banks had started a turning movement; Jackson had been outflanked!

Regiments, brigades, companies—a wild mélange of broken troops began falling back in front of the assault. Various units were surrounded, the guns on the left were exposed, and disaster stared the Army of the Valley squarely in the face. Toward the center of the rout rode Stonewall. Face burning fiercely, he rode into the mass of running, shooting, bayoneting men. Yankees and Confederates were hopelessly mixed, but

Jackson paid no heed. Waving a sword in one hand and a battle flag in the other, he shouted, "Rally, men! Remember Winder! Where's my Stonewall Brigade? Forward, men, forward!" [54]

Instantly men turned and followed. Captain Blackford, who saw the whole episode, felt that "the men would have followed him into the jaws of death itself; nothing could have stopped them and nothing did. Even the old sorrel horse seemed endowed with the style and form of an Arabian." A Yankee officer, hatless and carrying a broken sword, watched Jackson's rally in rapt admiration and asked Blackford: "What officer is that, Captain?" "Stonewall Jackson," was the reply. "Hurrah for General Jackson!" yelled the Federal, "follow your General, boys!" Touched beyond expression, Blackford let the Yankee escape. [55]

Gallant as was Jackson's effort, it was foolish. General Taliaferro rushed to him and urged him to go to the rear—this was no place for the army commander. Surprised and suddenly subdued, Old Jack retired, saying, "Good, good!" But he continued to urge Hill's arriving troops forward to stop the rout. Finding Lawrence O'B. Branch's North Carolina Brigade making ready to advance, he galloped to its commander, cutting short an inspiring speech by that proficient politician with an order to "Push forward, General, push forward!" [56] Everywhere on the left the rally continued, fresh units went in, broken ones steadied. The Federal attack stalled, rolled back. Banks's chance had passed. Jackson moved to the attack.

Following Branch's advancing men, Jackson urged his troops to keep up the pressure; now that the Yankees were retreating they must be pushed hard. A reckless, gallant, and bloody Federal cavalry charge against Taliaferro's brigade failed, and took all the starch out of the Union right.

Old Baldy, dyspeptic and mortified at not having done more in the battle because of Confederate artillery fire across his line of advance, finally cleared an annoying millpond and launched an attack on the Federal left. Broken on his right and bending on his left, Banks gave up the field and was in full retreat when the sun went down. [57]

All energy, now that his men were attacking, Jackson ordered his brigades to pursue Banks's retreating army. Late though it was, the objective for the day must be reached—Banks must be driven beyond Culpeper if possible. Hill's men, less battered than the rest of Jackson's troops, took the lead, but the advance moved cautiously. As heavy woods were approached, Hill shelled them, threw his skirmishers far ahead and crept forward. Prisoners, demoralized and dazed, were taken all along the route of march. [58]

As Jackson watched the skirmish line, a scout rode up to him, reporting that a few hundred yards in front of Jackson's men stood an enemy line of battle. Halting the advance, Jackson posted a battery to feel out the Federal position. Almost immediately a shattering return fire silenced the Confederate guns and showed that Banks had prepared to make a stand. This sudden belligerence, plus word from quaint "Grumble" Jones of the Seventh Virginia Cavalry that prisoners he had taken reported heavy Yankee reinforcements, caused Jackson to call a halt. A night battle against unknown odds might be too risky.

Exhausted and spent, the troops slept where they were. Jackson rode back toward the battlefield, seeking shelter at various farmhouses. At each one he received a welcome but was told that wounded filled the rooms. Fearing to deprive one of the wounded of a refuge, he decided to camp out, found a grassy plot, dismounted and told his staff that here he would sleep. Would he have something to eat? "No, I want *rest, nothing but rest!"* [59]

Heat made the morning of August 10 a horror for the wounded. Hundreds of them, Yankee and Confederate, lay exposed to a baking sun. Moans, cries for water, piteous shrieks came from all parts of the battlefield. Jackson's surgeons and burial details moved among the fallen, carrying the maimed to the shade of a tree, carting off the dead; scavenger parties gathered up arms and accouterments—Old Jack wanted every bit of public property put in his wagons. [60]

Jackson next considered what ought to be done about Banks. Fairly sure that Pope had brought up large masses to Banks's support, Jackson ruled out an attack, but stood ready to receive one, putting his men in positions which would enable him to hold the former battlesite.

More information about enemy doings was badly needed. The cavalry should provide it. Where Ashby would have been hanging onto Banks's coattails, sending back detailed information, Beverley Robertson had contributed almost nothing thus far; reconnaissance seemed not to be a strong point with him. Jackson had partially anticipated his failure and had, on August 7, dispatched a note to Jeb Stuart, now a warm and trusted friend. Revealing far more than usual, Jackson wrote: "This evening I leave for Orange C. H. en route for Culpeper C. H. I wish you could bring your command up . . . and make the Inspection that has been assigned to you. I desire you to make it during active operations; as I may thereby secure your services for the time being." [61]

Stuart came, loud, jingly, friendly as ever. True, he arrived a day late to help in the battle, but his services were even more necessary on the tenth. After a happy greeting, Jackson posed a question: Would Stuart take some of the cavalry, scout the enemy positions, and bring intelligence which could be relied on? Nothing could have intrigued Stuart more. Off he rode, coming back at length with confirmation of Old Jack's suspicions. Banks had been heavily reinforced and an attack by the Confederates in their present condition would be foolish. [62] Jackson would stay where he was until attacked or until he could scrape the battlefield of men and equipment. The two armies looked at each other across a respectful distance throughout most of the morning. When it began raining hard in the afternoon, chances of a fight appeared washed away.[63] Again that night Jackson held his ground, waiting.

Next morning enemy horsemen galloped toward the Confederate lines. It was a deputation, bringing a request for a truce; the Yankees wished to succor the wounded, bury the dead. Jackson jumped at the chance—it would help in getting his trains out.

As the eleventh wore peacefully on, Jackson took stock of his operations for the past four days. To Lee he sent news of the battle: "On the evening of the 9th instant, God blessed our arms with another victory. ...Whilst our list of killed is less than that of the enemy, we have to mourn the loss of some of our best officers and men. Brigadier-General Charles S. Winder was mortally wounded whilst ably discharging his duty at the head of his command." [64] Winder's loss hurt deeply. He had often been at odds with Jackson and the two never were friends, but still he had been a fine leader and had impressed Jackson as a man with a bright future. When, months later, he wrote his official report of Cedar Mountain, Jackson resorted to rare adjectives in paying tribute to the commander of the Stonewall Brigade: "Richly endowed with those qualities of mind and person which fit an officer for command and which attract the admiration and excite the enthusiasm of troops, he was rapidly rising to the front rank of his profession. His loss has been severely felt." [65]

Other losses hurt too. In the fiercely contested fight, which dragged on for several hours, 1,276 of Jackson's men had been killed or wounded, the only consolation being that Federal casualties amounted to some 2,381. But statistics told a false story of the battle.

Although absorbing fewer losses than the enemy, Jackson had not managed his fight well. Apparently the Seven Days' experience had done something to him; he had lost his touch. With almost 20,000 men close at hand, he did not get his maximum strength on the field; he failed to coordinate the several battles going on at once, leaving Ewell off on the right, Early hotly contending by himself in the center, and Winder arranging a third segment of his force on the left. When the fighting began, Jackson apparently—and typically—thought of little else than preparing an attack and getting at the enemy. But was this prudent, when the enemy had been on the field for some time before Jackson deployed? Was it prudent to plan the battle and fight it without making a thorough scout of the densely wooded left? Tactically Jackson badly botched Cedar Mountain.

On the other hand, it was Jackson, and Jackson almost alone, who saved the battle when it disintegrated. Riding straight to the crumbling left wing, he displayed qualities of personal leadership which showed him to be far more than a brilliant strategist; he was a natural field commander, a leader of men. Once he had restored his line, he got control of the whole field. His pursuit was quickly organized and pressed hard with minimum confusion, and he knew when to call a halt. The crisis on his left seemed to work a strange alchemy on Jackson: suddenly he returned to normal—the normal of the valley campaign—thinking quickly, surely, and adjusting to changing situations with his old pliability. To the extent that the battle of Cedar Mountain restored Jackson's confidence in himself, it stands as perhaps his most important battle.

Amid the praise of the Confederacy came the special approval of General Lee, who wrote: "I congratulate you most heartily on the victory which God has granted you over our enemies at Cedar Run. The country owes you and your brave officers and soldiers a deep debt of gratitude." [66] But even though he had whipped Banks, Jackson broke up his camps and began falling back during the evening and night of the eleventh. Vast numbers of Federals posed too serious a threat to his little Army of the Valley. On the other hand, Jackson sought to use his retreat as an offensive weapon, as he had done in the valley. He hoped, he reported to Lee, "that by thus falling back General Pope would be induced to follow me until I should be re-enforced." He might draw Pope farther from his base, while the valley troops drew nearer to theirs —but Pope could not be lured into Jackson's lair. Taking refuge behind swollen streams, Pope waited to see what Jackson would do. It was like waiting for a cobra to strike, but Pope had not yet been initiated into the snake-bitten club, presided over by General Banks.

If the army had any suspicions that Jackson had abandoned the offensive, they would have been dispelled by an order given to Hotchkiss at Gordonsville on August 12, to make as many maps of Virginia from Gordonsville to the Potomac as possible: "Do not be afraid of making too many." [67] The Old Man had some scheme in mind. None could tell what it was, but big things were happening. On August 13, General Longstreet arrived at Gordonsville, bringing heavy reinforcements for the Army of the Valley.[68]

Old Pete now became the senior general present, but declined to assume command, asserting that Jackson knew the situation and that Lee would soon command in person.[69] If Longstreet felt any dislike for Jackson, no one knew it. Relations between Lee's chief lieutenants seemed cordial, but deep down Longstreet harbored a creeping envy and resentment. His jealousy burst forth many months later, but already some of his men gossiped openly about how rude, arrogant, and beastly Jackson was, and said that "a month uncontrolled and he would destroy himself and all under him." [70] Longstreet himself had begun to think that "Jackson was a very skillful man against such men as Shields, Banks, and Fremont, but when pitted against the best of the Federal commanders he did not appear so well." [71]

Bad feeling existed elsewhere in Jackson's camps, and seemed to be growing—bad feeling between Old Jack and Powell Hill, apparently stemming from the misunderstanding about marching orders on the night of August 7–8. If it developed further, there would be real unpleasantness.

The outward spirit of cooperation continued during Divine service held throughout Jackson's camps in gratitude for the victory at Cedar Mountain.[72] With that perception native to veteran troops, Jackson's men needed no prompting to realize the prayers they offered that Thursday afternoon had a special significance. Jed Hotchkiss summed up the feeling of the valley soldiers: "Gen. Jackson has been to Richmond and aided in driving McClellan off and now the whole army comes to help Gen. Jackson in his long cherished move towards Maryland." [73] There would be hard marching and hot fighting soon—every peaceful, prayerful moment was savored.

Almost as soon as he arrived on the fifteenth,[74] Lee called a conference; he had decided on a plan to "suppress" Pope. Speed and secrecy, the two ingredients most likely to please Jackson, held the key to success. As Lee explained the situation, Jackson grew excited. Information received in Richmond indicated that the Union high command had decided to shift the remainder of McClellan's army to northern Virginia and use it to strengthen Pope for his attack on Confederate supply and communication lines. While McClellan hung suspended between the James and Pope's army, the Army of Northern Virginia would strike.

Could the Army of the Valley move at once? Yes, the infantry was ready, rations cooked, haversacks packed; transportation, carefully collected by the tireless John Harman, stood available in greater amounts than ever.[75] A stir ran through the camps; Old Jack had ordered another march. This time he meant march, swiftly and without dawdling. No more would he tolerate Longstreet's men taking the lead. The new order must have seemed hard to men still recovering from Cedar Mountain, but the veterans of Front Royal, Winchester, and other lightning battles slung their haversacks over their shoulders and moved out with no more than the usual grumbling. "I can't tell where they are aiming to go," ran a typical comment, "but I think Jackson is determin[ed] to go in Maraland [sic]. . . . Jackson travels too much for me I cant stand this kind of a life." [76]

Jackson set a fast pace. Speed, Lee had said, would mean the difference between success and failure. A time schedule had been worked out which could conceivably demolish John Pope's army. Pope had committed tactical suicide: he had collected his estimated 65,000 to 70,000 men [77] hardly more than twenty miles away, between the Rappahannock and Rapidan, camping on the sliver of ground formed by the confluence of the rivers. A bridge at Rappahannock Station had been used to get the men into the cul-de-sac; it would have to be used to get them out. Jackson had advised attacking Pope in his camps on August 17, but the commanding general had set the eighteenth for the assault, thus giving Stuart time to get behind Pope and burn the Rappahannock bridge.[78]

By nightfall of the fifteenth, Jackson's columns camped near Mount Pisgah Church, five miles northeast of Orange Court House; they had stepped along in something like their old form. Here Old Jack ordered a bivouac, since closer approaches to the enemy's position might alert Pope to the concentration against him. He must be kept calmly unaware of gathering doom. Rolling, productive farmland, a succession of ridges to the west, and here and there a copse—such was the terrain of north central Virginia, and it offered little cover to the movements of large masses of men. Hidden behind Clark's Mountain and protected by undulating ground, Jackson's men would wait for Lee's strategy to develop. Intelligence came to Old Jack from a signal station he had established on Clark's Mountain: The enemy still lay in camp, drilling, marching, and countermarching, unconcerned. Something of Stuart's mission Jackson doubtless knew—that he would move to the attack on the eighteenth, and his advance would trigger Lee's general crossing of the Rapidan and the attack on Pope's main army. Stuart, however, had troubles. Fitz Lee's brigade lazed along on its way to the proposed point of attack, blissfully unaware that upon the shoulders of each trooper hung the fate of the Confederacy.[79] But Fitz Lee's delay and Stuart's minor discomfiture at the hands of a Federal cavalry raiding party were not decisive factors in General Lee's postponing the move against the Army of Virginia. Throughout the night of the seventeenth the feverish preparations to get the whole Confederate Army in position simply could not be completed. Failure of logistics, faulty coordination, bad staff work— the bugaboos of all armies—laid fateful hold of Lee's men. Nothing to do but set the attack for the nineteenth.

Old Jack chafed as the daylight burned. There must be a way to get at the enemy—never had there been such a golden opportunity. On the other side of the Rapidan sat a whole army, utterly unprepared. A sudden stroke, desperately delivered and stoutly pressed, would butcher the Federals, exterminate thousands and drive thousands more wildly into the Rappahannock. It must be done. Sandie Pendleton, almost the only member of the staff not on the sick list, was summoned: Get Blackford, a few troopers, and prepare for a long ride. With the small entourage assembled, Old Jack mounted and led the way. It seemed darker than usual that night of August 19,[80] and the darkness complicated the problem of the riders. Old Jack instantly left the main roads and trotted off into byroads and trails. The men fought to keep up, faces lashed by branches, bodies lacerated by underbrush. Hours passed. There seemed no pattern to what the Old Man did—wandering here and there, up one track, down another. Finally Blackford concluded that "it was one of those freaks which sometimes seize him and which make many people think he is somewhat deranged." The horsemen, fatigued and badly punished, fell asleep as they rode. Whether Old Jack did or not no one could say: he rode firmly ahead. After an endless span of time, Blackford awoke in the saddle and sleepily asked his companion: "Sandie, where is the old fool taking us?" "What?" came a puzzled query from the figure nearby. Blackford reined his horse and fell back in horror—he had been talking to Old Jack!

Apparently the aim of the ride had been to scout roads, but about dawn the riders found themselves—after a half-hour's nap on the ground —atop Clark's Mountain, gazing at the spreading Union tents in the early morning sunlight. Had they been thoroughly awake, they doubtless would have appreciated the sight more—tired as he was, Blackford thought it "a magnificent view." [81] For about half an hour Old Jack studied the Union position, suddenly mounted and rode back to his camps.

The next day Lee started his army across the Rapidan, but he knew already he had lost his chance. Pope had taken alarm and fled. Now all that could be done was to follow and try to assist him into another position of equal potentialities. As the troops started north on the twentieth, a new organization had unofficially developed: Jackson commanded the Left Wing of the army, Longstreet the Right. The Army of the Valley was no more. [82]

The Left Wing's commander had made preparations to move promptly "at moonrise," and had arisen at 3 A.M. He and the staff found Jim with breakfast ready—he had been reading the signs again—ate, and mounted to ride. Jim would stay behind with the headquarters wagons until some idea could be formed of where to send them. Little Sorrel trotted along in the cool morning air toward what Jackson supposed would be the empty camps of his infantry. But the camps remained occupied; the men had not yet moved.

Careful attention had been given to the issuance of marching orders, particularly since A. P. Hill's men were to lead, [83] but the Light Division still sat in its camps. Jackson raged into the camp, found one of the brigades almost ready to move, and ordered it forward instantly. Calling to the staff, he detailed a man to ride with each division—he would have personal assurance that the marching orders were being obeyed. Hill simply could not be trusted to move promptly; he bore watching. [84] Should the delay prove important, Hill might be guilty of disobedience of orders, and there would be a chance to convene another court.

Such dereliction might be encountered among the generals, but Old Jack had reason to doubt that desertion or straggling would be a serious threat to his command. His courts-martial had been dealing out summary justice, and just the afternoon before, several men convicted of desertion had been shot in front of their comrades. A grim and impressive sight, it pointed a sound moral lesson.[85]

Jackson understood clearly the problem in strategy now faced by General Lee. Before the plan to strike on the Rapidan had been scrapped, Lee had intended to drive at Pope's left to get between him and his potential reinforcements. Now things had changed. McClellan's men, plus others destined for Pope, were closer, and there would be less time available to deal with the arrogant commander of the Army of Virginia. A thrust between Pope and Washington, now that he was above the Rappahannock, would expose Lee's right to attack from Fredericksburg; the only thing to do was to sidle up the Rappahannock, seeking a point at which to cross and turn Pope's right flank: a difficult problem, made worse by the fact that the northern banks of the Rappahannock were higher and more commanding than the southern. Consequently Pope could line his side of the river with guns and batter any Confederate attempt at crossing. Time, too, added to the complexity of the strategical situation—whatever the Confederates did, they would have to do soon.

The two wings of the army—they were now called, unofficially, corps [86]—moved toward the Rappahannock, and on the twenty-second, when his men approached Beverly Ford, Jackson saw the Federals. They held the opposite bank, in a position of great strength. Quickly Old Jack ordered up a battery and opened fire. The ford was cleared long enough for Stuart to cross, reconnoiter, and bring back word that the Yankees were thick and were coming back to the crossing. The rest of the day guns of both armies spat at each other from opposite banks.

While Stuart made ready for a rash adventure behind Pope's lines (which he may have told Jackson about at breakfast on the twenty-first), [87] Jackson's orders led him up the south bank of the Rappahannock, probing for a crossing. As his troops passed over the tributary Hazel Run, he ordered Isaac Trimble—who had told him joshingly a few days before that "before this war is over I intend to be a Major General or a corpse" [88]—to halt his brigade and guard the right flank of the wagon train against any sudden dash from the other side of the river. It was unpromising duty, but Trimble pulled out of line and began to select his positions. His orders enjoined him to hold his ground—and the Wagon Hunter's wagons—until the vanguard of Longstreet arrived and took over the assignment.[89]

Not long after he set up his lines, Trimble had trouble. Federal troops—perhaps as many as two brigades—had come over to the southern bank and cut some ambulances out of the Confederate wagon train.

Swiftly Trimble dealt with that move, but worried about the numbers he might have to face. He concluded to wait for Hood's Texans to support him, and when they came up, Trimble delivered a hard, sure attack that broke the Federal front. Having learned much from Old Jack, he ordered the rout encouraged with cold steel.[90] The wagon train had been preserved and a star added to the record of the venerable Trimble. Jackson did not forget.

While Trimble had been enjoying his independent war, Jackson had had a bad day. Still noting that the enemy's troops paralleled his line of advance, Jackson reached a point opposite Warrenton Springs [91] where he found the bridge broken.

No Federal troops were seen guarding the other side. Could the bridge be rebuilt? If so, Lee's army might get over here and get at Pope. As he looked at the river and the ground beyond the opposite bank, Jackson decided to send a force over to scout the position, and if it looked good, to throw his whole corps over. Some of Lawton's Georgians were ordered to begin crossing at the Springs, while Jubal Early's brigade of Ewell's division crossed about a mile below on a dilapidated dam. A violent, lashing rainstorm had turned the approaches to the dam into mush, but Old Jube pushed his men ahead as the rain slackened. No sooner had he started than the rain fell once again, heavier this time.

Ewell, fidgeting and upset about Early's dispositions, went over with him and helped place his regiments. Forno, with the Louisianians, had been instructed to follow Early, but darkness fell before his men could start. Early was alone, except for Lawton's men upstream. Soon he discovered that Lawton had not come over in strength—only one regiment and two batteries. Pope had been presented with a grand chance to beat a segment of Lee's army, if he could do it quickly. Already high, the river rose rapidly during the night and its roaring drowned out sounds from the friendly Confederate shore. Early made ready to die hard.

Dawn, which usually brightens all prospects, failed to brighten Early's. Soon, though, he received a message from Old Jack, called across the river to one of his men. Move upriver, take command of Lawton's regiment, and hold a good defensive position, which Jackson had seen, until the bridge could be rebuilt. If Early's situation became desperate, he should move upstream farther to Waterloo Bridge, which could be used. His march along the north bank would be covered by Jackson, who would move along the south side with his corps, protecting Early's command with artillery.[92]

All during the night Jackson had grown increasingly concerned about Early. As daylight broke, he rode to a hill overlooking the position held by Ewell's isolated brigade. The men held on, with enemy cavalry showing some interest in them, but thanks to an ever-kind Providence, no blue infantry had made an appearance. The Rappahannock still roared and boomed, although the rain had stopped. As the general gazed at the other side, an officer rode up with a dispatch. Finally tearing his eyes away, Jackson noticed that Captain Blackford was the courier, and took from him a letter from Lee, the contents of which were apparently irritating, for Blackford noted the frown and rough manner in which Old Jack tore up the paper. Blackford fancied Lee had penned a reprimand to Old Jack for leaving his marching line exposed to sneak attack. Whatever the contents, it produced only momentary irritation, for Jackson's whole attention had settled on the tiny patch of Confederate ground on the Yankee shore. Those were his boys over there, and his responsibility bore down just as hard as did Early's that morning. Spurring the sorrel viciously and curtly ordering Blackford to follow him, Old Jack rode for the river, and then into it, finally forcing the sorrel to swim. When he reached the solid ground of the still standing abutment to the fallen bridge, he stopped and remained for a solid hour, saying nothing to Blackford. The two of them stood out in the river, staring helplessly at Early's *tête-de-pont*. At length A. P. Hill swam his horse out, but could not rouse Jackson from his concern, and returned to shore without orders and with scarcely a civil word from the general.

In the afternoon, as the river fell swiftly, a number of others came out to Jackson's vantage point. Finally he organized a volunteer bridge-repair crew to fall to at the span. Work progressed rapidly. By late afternoon a makeshift bridge had been completed, but still Early held his position against weak Federal advances, as the span, narrow and flimsy, could not yet be trusted. Jackson spent the whole afternoon on the bridge pier, watching and praying. During the night, Ewell went across to confer with his exposed brigade commander. Hearing of the large numbers of Federals lurking around Early's lines, Ewell ordered his command back across the rickety bridge, and Early felt that he had been delivered from the jaws of death.[93] Old Jack's comment on Early's conduct, the brigadier could count as the highest accolade: "In this critical situation the skill and presence of mind of General Early was favorably displayed."

While Old Jube certainly merited praise for preventing panic and standing firm, General Pope had actually saved the Confederate detachment. Had he displayed even moderate energy, he could have crushed Early without much of a fight. Possibly Old Jack, as he kept his prayerful vigil in the river, noted the reluctance of the Federal commander to come to grips with the Confederates—and if so, doubtless came to a decision about Pope.

Had he known of the boundless capacity of Pope to delude himself, Jackson's opinion would have been even more marked. In a daring raid around the Federal right, Stuart had struck the enemy communications at Catlett's Station on the Orange and Alexandria Railroad, captured some important dispatches and General Pope's coat, destroyed some wagons and vanished as mysteriously as he had come. Pope, seeing some mystical connection between Stuart's retreat and Early's evacuation of his exposed position, convinced himself that Jackson—who he thought had been on the Union side of the river in great strength—had given up hope of turning the Federal flank. Once having come to a conclusion, Pope clung to it with a tenacity that would have done credit to a bulldog but not to a general in the field.

To the little village of Jeffersonton, where Jackson had established his headquarters, rode the commanding general. It was early in the afternoon of Sunday, August 24; the day was bright, warm, the grass and foliage green with the peculiar luster of a recent rain. Lee sought out Old Jack, and the two entered into a brief conversation. There might be a way to wreck Pope before all of McClellan's men could reach him, a way which could put the Confederates between the Federal Army and Washington. As Lee outlined his scheme, Jackson forgot his ill humor at slow quartermasters, commissaries, and infantrymen. Lee had hatched a daring plot, and he wanted Jackson to put it into effect. He would take his command far around Pope's right, circle behind him, and cut his communications with Washington. Should the Yankees react as they had in the Shenandoah, Pope would reverse himself, and march hastily to prevent the capture of the capital—and as he did so would be moving farther away from the reinforcements coming from Fredericksburg sector. Never had such a chance for decisive achievement been offered to any Southern general. While Jackson held Pope's attention, Lee would bring up the rest of the army for a crushing blow at the enemy; but it would be Jackson and his veterans who would set the stage, who would take the largest chance, and who would win or lose. If the plan worked ... The admiring gaze of the world would sorely test a Christian's humility.

Details were left to Jackson. He should select the point at which to hit the railroad behind the enemy, he should decide where to wait for Lee. These discretionary orders understood, Lee asked the obvious question. Jackson replied quietly that he would move at once.[94]

15

"DISASTER AND SHAME

LURK IN THE REAR"

— J . POPE

Dawn, and more than 20,000 sun-baked, weatherworn soldiers formed for a march. Stonewall's orders had called for "the utmost promptitude," and the men would move with light equipment, leaving their knapsacks behind.[1] Ewell's lean veterans were the pace setters, followed by Hill's and Taliaferro's men. It was cool that morning of August 25, just bracing enough to hasten the step. Everyone in Jackson's command knew the general had something big planned, and though they had no idea what it was, they wanted to be at it. Excitement crackled in the half-light of morning.

Northwestward the Old Man led his army, heading straight toward Front Royal. Was the Army of the Valley returning to the scene of its greatest triumphs? Was Jackson striking for Maryland through that "rifle barrel pointed at the heart of the Union"? Or was he off on some other mission? From Old Jack, of course, nothing could be learned: the objective would be made clear when the time came. At first, the men thought of little things. They had been ordered to cook three days' rations, but had moved out so swiftly that the cooking remained ununfinished. Some thought about where to cadge a few roasting ears or possibly an apple. Some thought about home. Jackson thought about Anna.

Just before he mounted to ride, he penned a short note to tell her of his doings. "The enemy," said the scrawl, "has taken a position, or rather several positions, on the Fauquier side of the Rappahannock. I have only time to tell you how much I love my little pet dove."[2] Jackson told Jim to keep things in order and started for the head of his army.

Peacefully, swiftly the miles jogged by with the infantry keeping at something like the valley pace. As the sun rose, the day grew warm, then hot, and dust rose in clouds over the shuffling men. Still northward the Old Man led them, their progress punctuated by the rumble of guns, caissons, ordnance wagons, and a few ambulances, by the casual talk of men who know they are heading toward death, and by Jackson's repeated "Close up, men, close up."

From Jeffersonton to Amissville, then a bit east of north to Orlean—still the men moved fast, resting their ten minutes in every hour, but sticking hard at the job. Here and there along the line a man would dart from ranks to raid a passing cornfield or orchard, but he returned—straggling would not be tolerated. Apparently much thought had been given to the route. Short cuts were found by Capt. J. K. Boswell, the engineer on Jackson's staff who rode ahead and directed the advance. Nothing interfered with speed as the army swung along the Rappahannock's south bank. Far behind could be heard the angry argument of Longstreet's artillery, which had slipped into place where Jackson's guns had recently been. Pope faced Longstreet still, covering the crossings of the river and watching warily. If the rolling clap of Longstreet's salvos bothered Jackson, he gave no sign. Calmly looking ahead, he rode easily, occasionally dropping back to check the spacing of his marchers and close the column. He was leaving almost half of the Army of Northern Virginia behind him, and marching away from the sound of firing. Surely it was not like him; nor was it like Lee to allow such detachment in the face of overwhelming enemy concentration.

In reality, of course, nothing more completely typified the military temperaments of Jackson and Lee than the march which so mystified the men making it and so mystified General Pope. Lee had determined to do something which the rules of war ruled out: he was dividing his army in the face of the enemy, detaching part of his force to flank Pope's masses, get behind the Union army and cut its communications with Washington. Jackson, who seemed always to do better on his own, was the logical man to "lurk" in Pope's rear—if anyone could bring disaster to the Yankees, Stonewall could. The boldness of the plan excited Jackson. There seemed hardly a chance that he could get behind Pope without detection, but the opportunity would be worth any risk. He recognized the odds against him and knew that his segment of the army might be cut off and possibly annihilated. But he knew, too, that smaller armies have to resort to daring deeds, that the battle is not always to the strong. He would have to be quick, hit hard, and play for time. If all went well, Pope would retreat to save his communications and leave Longstreet free to help Jackson—but time would pass before that could happen, and Pope would have to be kept at bay.

At Orlean the point of the column angled slightly east of north again, and the men thought that maybe the Old Man meant to strike the Potomac a little above Washington. The afternoon wore on; men talked less, conserving their wind. Route step kept the troops striding, and they covered ground well.

Ranging ahead of his men, Jackson rode on toward Salem, a small village on the Manassas Gap Railroad. Well to the right of Pope's main army and behind the Federal flank, Salem would be a good place to bivouac for the night. Before he reached the town, the evening's beauty arrested Jackson's attention. Dipping low on the Blue Ridge, the dying sun cast a special glow over the restless country between the purple-hued peaks and the Bull Run Mountains. Jackson dismounted, climbed to the top of a giant rock alongside the road, and, cap in hand, gazed steadily toward the west. Up the road came a column—the men saw Old Jack standing grandly on his perch. Caught in the twilight's brilliance, he looked the prototype of all conquering captains, despite the mangy cap and road-colored uniform. He was theirs—they loved him—they cheered. A swift motion to silence the shouts, then Jackson dispatched a staff officer to tell them that undue noise might alarm the enemy. "No cheering, boys," was Old Jack's order; but they could wave, smile at him, raise their tattered old hats in quiet adoration. He watched them proudly. Rarely had he been so moved. Beaming, he turned to some of his staff and said: "Who could not conquer, with such troops as these?" [3]

Old Baldy's infantry reached the vicinity of Salem, and then came the order to halt for the night. The rest of the column must be closed on Ewell, so Hill's and Taliaferro's boys had to march a bit longer. Ewell had done the tradition of the Army of the Valley proud; twenty-five miles had been covered that day—very commendable indeed, when the shortage of rations was remembered. Many of the men slept without supper, but there seemed to be little grumbling.

Dawn again found the men in ranks, marching. Jackson had to push them; they would have to march as far on the twenty-sixth as they had the day before, perhaps farther. Ewell had led out once again, heading his men east now, climbing toward White Plains. Some of the men may have begun to suspect what Old Jack had in mind: if they stuck to the present route, they would come to Thoroughfare Gap in the Bull Run Mountains and would be on the direct path toward Pope's main artery of supplies, the Orange and Alexandria Railroad. There would probably be hot fighting at Thoroughfare. Although not as formidable a pass as others, it could be held by a fair-sized force with ease. But the Old Man seemed unconcerned. No sign of enemy activity came from the south. All roads leading in that direction had been covered by the cavalry; Jackson's men marched on. Dust, thick clouds of it, floated above the fast-striding infantry—surely Pope could see it, and had moved to intercept the threat to the rear he despised.

Word came back from cavalry patrols that Thoroughfare was un-defended—not a Yankee in sight! Good news, but no time could be lost in gloating. The men moved more silently this day; marching was hard work on short rations. Through the gap they went, on to Hay Market. There the cavalry had skirmished with a few straggling bluecoated troop-ers, picked up some prisoners and learned that the enemy had no idea of a large flanking movement by Jackson.[4] Good, good. Close up.

All fears of Federal threats to the Confederate right flank ended when Jeb Stuart and his men were met at Gainesville. Stuart had fought the Federals along the Rappahannock until early the morning of the twenty-sixth, then slipped across the river and caught up with Jackson via parallel roads.[5] At Gainesville Jackson had reached the main highway from Washington to Warrenton and Pope's army, but resolutely push-ing on, Jackson aimed his vanguard at Bristoe Station on the Orange and Alexandria Railroad, about four miles southwest of Manassas Junction. A good road led toward the objective and the men, although hungry and tired, kept up the pace. Jackson wanted to hit Bristoe especially, for that station was on Broad Run and destruction of the bridge there would paralyze the railroad for some time.

Dick Ewell had placed Hays's Louisiana Brigade, with some of the old units under Taylor, in the van of the army. They were directed to support Col. Tom Munford's cavalry in a dash on the station, and as they drew near their goal the fading puff of a locomotive's smoke whetted their appetites for spoils. Reports had it that few Union troops guarded the station—the resistance would be light. Munford's men crept to within a hundred yards of the depot before they were discovered, and as soon as the alarm sounded they charged, scattering the small Federal cavalry force and demoralizing the company of Union infantry. While Munford mopped up, Ewell's infantry came in.

A train sounded, coming from the direction of Warrenton. Swiftly Confederates piled up wooden rails, worked feverishly to tear up track—anything to stop the train. On it came, screaming through the station, hitting and scattering the wooden barrier without slowing. Men fired into it, at the engine, at its crew, but on it went. The alarm would be given now in Washington—there could no longer be any doubt. More trains were coming, though, and the men determined not to ·be balked again. A derail switch was opened, some North Carolina infantry lined up along the right-of-way and leveled their muskets; this time nothing would be left to chance. Soon came the sound of another train, the sudden rattle of the cars as they roared into the hamlet, the clap of a volley, then a horrendous crash as the train hit the open switch. Debris, spinning wheels, hissing steam gave vivid testimony to the proficiency of Jackson's men in wrecking United States property. The prize disappointed them, though, for it was an "empty" going back toward Alexandria for more supplies. While the happy wreckers looked on their handiwork, a third train puffed into Bristoe and rammed into the jumble of wood and metal already crowding the track. Again, as the men rummaged in the swirling dust, the sound of an engine alerted them to a further prize. But this time the engineer saw the danger, braked, and reversed. He would carry the alarm to Pope just as the first train had carried it to Washington. Now Jackson's little army stood squarely between Pope and the defenders of the United States capital—and his enemies were alerted.

As Jackson thought about it, his situation had possibilities. He could force Pope to abandon the line of the Rappahannock; in fact, he had probably already accomplished that objective. He could, if he desired, move on Washington, but the defenses of the city would probably prevent a capture. He could stay where he was, and draw Pope toward him, fight him from behind while Lee came up from the other direction. As long as Jackson's men held the communication line with Washington, Pope would have to deal with them. On the other hand, the situation, though appetizing, was dangerous in the extreme. Jackson probably knew that McClellan's army had been moving to reinforce Pope for some time, and that most of Little Mac's men were coming up from the Aquia Creek–Fredericksburg district instead of from Washington. They were, consequently, south and east of Jackson's position at Bristoe. If they moved swiftly, they could threaten his flank. At the same time, Pope's position put him five miles closer to Thoroughfare Gap than Jackson's— and through that gap Longstreet would have to come to join Jackson's corps.[6]

All these considerations Stonewall appreciated, but at the moment his interest centered on reports from local residents that seven miles away, at Manassas Junction, stood Pope's main base of supplies. Instantly Jackson determined to capture Manassas. "I deemed it important," he later wrote, that "no time should be lost in securing" the supplies. Reports of what riches lay in depot at Manassas were the sort to arouse the Wagon Hunter's acquisitive blood. Rations, quartermaster stores, sutler reserves (all manner of expensive delicacies)—everything— had been stored there by the supply services of the Union Army. If this almost limitless warehouse could be captured or destroyed, Pope's men would find themselves reduced to the same penury as the ragamuffins under Jackson.

While military necessity demanded that Manassas be taken, the human element in war appeared to make it impossible. The gray infantry had marched over fifty miles in two days,[7] and Jackson knew that the seven miles to Manassas would make the day's mileage well over thirty. Who could go? Isaac Trimble reported. He had heard that Jackson needed men for a forced march—he offered his. Always Jackson had urged the last full measure of effort to gain the most from victory; now he had a chance to make that effort. The "gallant offer" Jackson gratefully accepted, and directed Trimble to take two regiments totaling about 500 men and, supported by Stuart's cavalry, capture the Junction.[8]

Smartly Trimble carried out his assignment, his men rushing and capturing two Federal batteries about midnight and scattering defending infantry. As a culmination to a historic march, Manassas Junction was in Jackson's hands.[9]

Spread before Trimble's weary but victorious regiments was a sight to beggar the imagination. Acres, literally acres, of army stores and supplies jammed Manassas Junction. Warehouses, piles, and freight trains stood ready for picking. Fatigue was forgotten instantly and the men chafed to dig in. Trimble, however, growing in military stature daily, feared for the safety of his command and kept the men under arms all night. His men watched in an agony of impatience as Stuart's cavalrymen helped themselves to whatever struck their fancy.

Shortly after daybreak—a day remembered long by Jackson's scrawny veterans—Old Jack pushed the Stonewall Brigade to Trimble's support and saw to it that the men went through the paradise of temptation to good defensible ground. They were to guard the plunder while others enjoyed it: hard orders, but they were the Stonewall Brigade. Still some of the men contrived to break into the sutler stores before they moved on to form line of battle. Those who cracked the wall of guards did themselves proud. As Pvt. John Casler recalled the debauch years later:

When we had appropriated all we could carry [of sutler stores] we found a barrel of whiskey, which we soon tapped; but as we had our canteens full of molasses, and our tin cups full of sugar, we had nothing to drink out of. We soon found an old funnel, however, and while one would hold his hand over the bottom of it another would draw it full. In this way it was passed around. But the officers soon found us out and broke up that game.

We then sallied forth in quest of more plunder, and went to the captured trains of cars. They were loaded with everything belonging to an army—such as ammunition for infantry and artillery, harness, tents, blankets, clothing, hospital stores, and several loads of coffins for officers to be sent home in (we didn't want them), and one car was loaded with medical stores in boxes. Here we found something we did want, for each box had stored away in it from four to eight bottles of fine brandy and whiskey. We soon commenced taking them to pieces, throwing the medicine around in every direction in search of bottles. I squeezed into the car among a number of others and got a box opened and found eight bottles of brandy in it. . . . Our surgeons, seeing that it was a medical car, came up and begged us to save the morphine and chloroform, as they were scarce articles in our army and they would greatly need them in the coming battle. But we paid no heed to their entreaties, telling them that we had no use for medicine. They then rode off and informed General Jackson how affairs stood. He then ordered the guard to disperse us and save the medicines.[10]

There would be no repetition of the ruinous plundering which had marred the march on Winchester. Ruthlessly the guard broke up the frenzied treasure hunt. A sudden crash, then another, then another—an angry Federal battery, emplaced a good distance away, was shelling the wild melee of men. Jackson sent Poague's guns out to silence the protesting battery and supported Poague with most of Hill's division. Jackson rode with the artillerymen and soon saw a line of bayonets advancing from the direction of Bull Run. As Hill's men looked on, a fine brigade of New Jersey men—under Gen. George W. Taylor it turned out—marched against them, obviously determined to brush aside the raiding party which had hit Pope's supply base. They were new to war—their uniforms, equipment, and bearing showed that—but they were coming on gallantly, bayonets fixed and fire in their eyes. They were heading straight into the heart of a large Confederate division and had no chance at all, but they had no inkling of their danger. Poague's guns began raking the line; Carpenter's took up the grisly execution—gaps were blown in the blue ranks. Still on came the Federals. Hill's men cocked their muskets, took aim, and made ready to obliterate the Union left elements.

Old Jack watched the enemy attack with growing admiration, observing that "the advance was made with great spirit and determination and under a leader worthy of a better cause." Finally, observing the slaughter his artillery had wrought, Jackson called a cease-fire. Waving a white handkerchief, he rode out ahead of his line and asked the bold New Jersey boys to surrender before they were exterminated. A rifle volley was the answer. Riding quickly back to his men, Jackson ordered the fire reopened as the Yankees pushed on. Ragged gaps were widened in the blue line, the men lost organization, halted, and broke. Hill's furies chased them from the Bull Run bridge, on to the train which had brought them from the direction of Alexandria. About 300 prisoners were taken and 135 casualties inflicted on the Federals, but the main units were allowed to escape. Some Confederates thought that Old Jack deliberately spared the foe—curiously unlike the man who usually wanted to "shoot the brave ones." But enough had been done. The train burned and the bridge destroyed, Jackson had secured his front while he attended to Pope's vast depot at Manassas.

By noon most of Hill's men had returned to the Junction and found that they were almost too late. Jackson's own division under Taliaferro had come up and taken charge of the depot. Some sort of order had to be brought from the chaotic press of men. Taliaferro set up a loose apportioning system, issuing some of everything to the various units while at the same time stuffing the medical and ordnance wagons with critically needed items. The Wagon Hunter still hoped to carry off most of the material, or at least to hold on to it until Lee could bring up the reserve army wagons. In the meantime Hill's and Taliaferro's men were skewered on a horn of plenty. While Ewell's troops guarded the rear at Bristoe Station,[11] the rest of the army gorged outrageously. John Worsham, F Company, Twenty-first Virginia, Second Brigade, Jackson's division, explained how sudden gustatory riches demoralized his messmates:

A guard was placed over everything in the early part of the day, rations were issued to the men, but not by weight and measure to each man. ... These are some of the articles issued to F. Company. The first thing brought us was a barrel of cakes, next, a bag of hams. We secured a camp kettle, made a fire, and put a ham on to boil; and we had hardly gotten it underway before a barrel of sugar and coffee, the Yanks had it mixed, and a bag of beans were sent to us. After a consultation, we decided to empty the ham out of the kettle, as we could take that along raw, and in its place put the beans on the fire, as they were something we were fond of and had not had for a long time. About the time they commenced to get warm, a bag of potatoes was brought us;—over the kettle goes, and the potatoes take the place of the beans. We now think our kettle is all right, as potatoes cook in a short time, but here comes a package of desiccated vegetables, and the kettle is again emptied, and the vegetables are placed on the fire, as soup is so good.[12]

General Taliaferro, keeping the issuing process well in hand, found the Federal post commissary, a major, and demanded to know where the main supply of liquor was located; Old Jack, much to the army's dismay, had given orders to destroy all the firewater not needed by the surgeons. The major, willing enough to point out the cache, had a piteously bureaucratic request: Would the general spare him his account books so that he might settle with his superiors? He seemed inordinately upset when Taliaferro offered to audit the accounts and certify them "destroyed by the enemy." While they talked, the major took the general to the liquor reserves, but the gourmet in the major led him to suggest a special bottle of cognac be kept for Taliaferro's private stock. Taking his vintage liquor back to temporary headquarters, Taliaferro encountered General Jackson and Jeb Stuart and proudly displayed his spoils, inviting his two guests to "test at once the commissary's judgment." Jackson pleasantly declined and Stuart, doubtless with some regret, followed Old Jack's lead.[13]

While Taliaferro sampled his beverage alone, Jackson received interesting intelligence from doughty Dick Ewell. He reported himself hard pressed and falling back toward Manassas, but falling back fighting. In fact, Ewell's rear-guard action the afternoon of the twenty-seventh showed him to be one of the most competent of Stonewall's subordinates. He fought, broke off the fighting, fell back, fought, fell back, all in good order and without great loss. He crossed Broad Run, destroyed the railroad bridge, and the enemy halted their pursuit near Bristoe Station.[14] News of a Federal advance forced Jackson to a strategic decision. "Heavy columns" of the enemy had pressed Ewell; apparently Pope had abandoned the line of the Rappahannock. Phase one of Jackson's "raid" had been completed. What next? He concluded not to remain at Manassas; he would seek better ground.

Before he moved, the stores at the Junction had to be destroyed, since they could not be taken with the army. Before such wealth was wasted, however, the men would be allowed to take what they could carry. Instantly Manassas Junction became a scene of Gargantuan plundering. Men milled in the fabulous wealth of clothing, shoes, tents, food, "segars," beer, canned goods.

> It was hard to decide what to take [recalled Worsham, the caldron of soup forgotten in the sudden rush], some filled their haversacks with cakes, some with candy, others oranges, lemons, canned goods, etc. I know one who took nothing but French mustard, filled his haversack and was so greedy that he put one more bottle in his pocket. This was his four days' rations, and it turned out to be the best thing taken, because he traded it for meat and bread, and it lasted him until we reached Frederick City.[15]

One dust-brown scarecrow was seen eating canned lobster and drinking Rhine wine! [16] Altogether it was a day to be remembered—a day when the army ate "high on the hog." But it was a day to appall the sensibilities of a quartermaster or a Wagon Hunter. Jackson would not have allowed such wanton pillage had he been able to save the stores; since this obviously could not be done, he let his starving followers go ahead. The army loved him for it, and doubtless conceded Pope a better commissary than the hapless Banks.[17]

Ewell's men began to arrive at Manassas—too late to share in the plunder—and now Jackson concentrated on saving his army from the wrath of the enemy. Arrangements were made to burn all that the troops could not carry of the 50,000 pounds of bacon, 1,000 barrels of corned beef, 2,000 barrels of salt pork, 2,000 barrels of flour, and ordnance, quartermaster, and sutler stores filling two trains, each fully half a mile in length.[18] As his men moved out, Jackson watched the beginning of a huge conflagration—fiery evidence of disaster in Pope's rear. Soon the countryside rocked to the explosion of the ammunition trains, the sound resembling that of a large battle.[19]

Already Jackson had selected his ground. Not in vain had he made a careful study of the terrain near Manassas a year before. He knew that he would need to take a position within reach of Lee and one which, at the same time, might offer maximum protection against attack and maximum opportunity to strike at Pope. Near the old battlefield of Manassas an ideal position suggested itself—a low ridge north of the Warrenton-Alexandria Pike, about a mile west of the now-famous Henry house. There Jackson would be on Pope's flank, would be in position to cut the main highway, and would have the right of his line extended west, toward Thoroughfare Gap. In case something went wrong and General Lee could not join him, the ridge near the settlement of Groveton offered a good route for retreat through Aldie Gap in the Bull Run Mountains. In brief, the position selected near Groveton had three possible advantages: it was good for defense, for offense, and had a covered escape route. Quickly, then, the divisions must concentrate there.

Things did not go well on the night of August 27–28. Through a complicated mix-up in orders, caused partly by Jackson's ingrained secrecy, his divisions became dispersed. Taliaferro moved northward on the southern side of Bull Run and got into position without trouble; Hill marched on to Centreville, almost ten miles east of the Groveton heights; and Ewell, stumbling around in the hands of a hopelessly confused guide, ended the day encamped south of Blackburn's Ford on Bull Run.

Morning of the twenty-eighth brought conflicting reports to Jackson's headquarters near Groveton. The Federals appeared to be in a state of confusion as great as that of Jackson's wayward division commanders. Captured dispatches indicated that Pope's main concentration was directed at Manassas and that he had yet to learn of Jackson's present position. Some evidence probably reached Jackson to the effect that Pope's army had been strengthened by more of McClellan's command.[20]

Intelligence from cavalry patrols about midday indicated that a Union force approached from the direction of Gainesville, on the Warrenton Pike, apparently heading for a crossing of Bull Run at the Stone Bridge or Sudley's Ford. Since this force appeared unsupported and isolated from Pope's main army, Jackson determined to attack it. The attack would have two purposes. First, Jackson's 20,000 men at Groveton might destroy the Union force by operating on the well-used principle of fighting segments of the enemy's army. Second, the attack would unclog Pope's mind; he would at last know where Jackson had taken a stand. Hence the attack would fix the enemy's attention on Jackson's corps, bring about a concentration against him and prevent the escape of the Union Army to McClellan's reinforcements before Lee could join in a decisive attack. All preparations for an advance had to be canceled, though, for the Federal column turned off toward Manassas before Jackson's men could strike.

The afternoon passed. Jackson waited. That seemed the larger part of war—being separated from home and waiting. As the sun began to

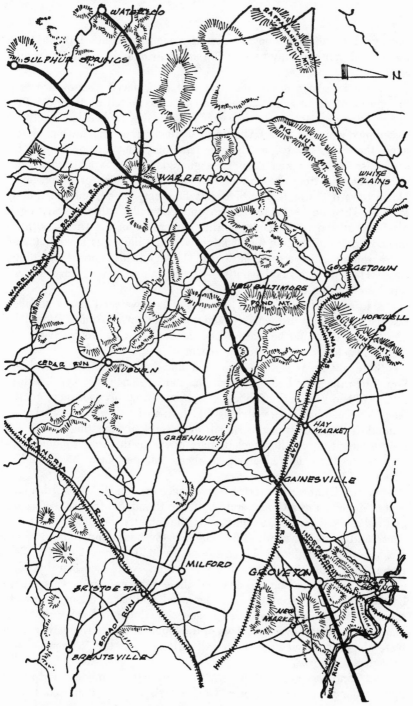

Campaign of Second Manassas

sink over the rolling hills near Groveton, a compact, tightly formed Union force strode purposefully toward the Stone Bridge along the Warrenton road.

Taliaferro's men, supported by Ewell, had moved west of Groveton to a position not far from Gainesville and were posted north of the Pike in the edge of a woods.[21] They could assail the Yankee left easily by sweeping down on the road. Should they attack? True, the day had almost gone, there was not too much light remaining, but an opportunity for a surprise flank attack could not be ignored. Jackson would reconnoiter personally. Out from the protecting woods rode a lone gray horseman. Down toward the marching bluecoats he went, halted, and sat quietly looking. Then he began to trot up and down the column, scanning it carefully, all the while staying within easy range of the Union skirmish line covering the striding file of infantry. Some bluecoats looked at him, but a solitary rider created little stir. The Federals ignored the dingy Rebel. He kept up his odd scouting—trotting along, halting, reveising his direction, trotting back, halting again.

A scant quarter mile away Jackson's officers watched him in horrified fascination, feeling instinctively what went on in his mind. Would he attack now, or would he wait? None doubted that he would strike, but he would select the time and the place.

Suddenly he reined up, wheeled and galloped toward his lines. Straight to the little knot of officers he rode, serenely touched his dirty little cap, and said in the calmest of voices: "Bring up your men, gentlemen." The men had been watching Old Jack anxiously and knew what he wanted. Taliaferro gave the signal, and, suddenly bursting out of the ring of woods, a line of grayclads bore down on the arm-swinging Federals, while there floated ahead of them that peculiarly blood-chilling Rebel yell.[22]

As old Trimble's stentorian battle voice screamed, "Forward, guide center, march!" three Confederate batteries thundered forward, wheeled, and unlimbered for action. On rushed the infantry, heading for a farmhouse and orchard near the Pike. Gaining the house and a piece of the orchard, the Confederate charge stopped cold. They ran into Maj. Gen. Rufus King's division, Burnside's corps, and were met first by John Gibbon's brigade of one Indiana and three Wisconsin regiments. These hard fighters turned from the road, deployed, and began a long, desperate stand-up combat which exceeded in sheer unadulterated nerve any fight many of the officers ever saw. Two of the toughest brigades in either army were slugging it out: the Stonewall Brigade and the Wisconsin Iron Brigade.

As Confederates piled up in numbers near the farmhouse and in the open ground east of it, Abner Doubleday's brigade deployed to aid

Gibbon—six regiments held the Union front. Against this array, Taliaferro put in most of his division, and received considerable help from Ewell. For well over two hours the hostile lines stood facing each other, firing volley after volley at almost point-blank range. Men fell, others filled their places. Neither side advanced or gave an inch. Artillery seared the lines, blasted opposing batteries, but still the men faced each other, firmly rooted to their little plots of ground. It was, said General Taliaferro, "one of the most terrific conflicts that can be conceived of." [23]

Finally, at about 9 P.M. the Federals broke off the fight, but not because they were drubbed. Although Jackson's men held the field, they had bought it at the highest of prices. The action had a higher percentage of casualties than almost any Jackson had fought—the Stonewall Brigade now numbered about 425 men. Losses among the officer corps were ghastly. The irreplaceable Dick Ewell had, as usual, personally led a charge and had been cut down with a badly shattered knee. His leg would have to be amputated; he would be lost to Jackson for an uncertain time, but it would surely be too long. Taliaferro, too, who had struggled so hard to make up for his lapse at Romney and had done well enough to get Jackson's own division, had been wounded severely. He kept his command through the action, but then had to turn it over to a new brigadier general, William E. Starke. There seemed to be a jinx connected with command of the Stonewall Brigade and Jackson's division—Winder and now Taliaferro. How long would Starke last? Ewell's division went to the conscientious but plodding Alexander R. Lawton. Casualties among the lesser officers were, perhaps, even more significant. Many men of bright promise had fallen that day—John F. Neff, colonel of the Thirty-third Virginia, killed; Col. A. J. Grigsby, Twenty-seventh Virginia, wounded; Lt. Col. Lawson Botts, commanding Second Virginia, mortally wounded. Far too terrible a butcher's bill for so indecisive a battle.[24]

Actually Jackson had not distinguished himself by pitching into a fight where he did. The action had not been well planned, and although it seemed that he had sufficient strength present to brush King's division aside, the grayclads had been checked. Instead of resorting to maneuver when the advance stalled, Jackson had been content to await the outcome of sheer bravery. This seemed strangely unlike the crafty tactician of the Valley Campaign whose reliance on maneuver almost invariably spared the lives of his men.

If Jackson had fumbled the tactics of the sharp engagement near Groveton, he had managed the strategy with consummate skill. In a way the action resembled Kernstown, although with less far-reaching strategic consequences. Jackson wanted to bring Pope's full attention on him, and the Groveton action did just that. At last Pope understood where his adversary was; no longer could he enshroud himself in an unwillingness to see. He must concentrate and he must attack. He might be able to crush Jackson before Lee could reach him.

The idea had merit, but Pope had already helped to undo his own plan by failing to lay firm hold on Thoroughfare Gap; once again he permitted his enemy to get through that defensible gorge without a serious effort to hold it. But in Jackson's immediate front, Pope acted quickly and with decision. East and west of Jackson's position Pope sought to concentrate a total of 50,000 men. Between the jaws of two equal forces he would grind Jackson to pieces, then turn and deal with Lee and Longstreet.

To meet this threat Jackson occupied an interesting position. Almost due north of tiny Groveton, situated at the crossing of the Sudley Springs road and the Warrenton Pike, the graded cut of an unfinished railroad ran close along the top of a ridge in a northeast-southwest direction. Behind the cut the wooded ridge had patches of open ground, and near the western side of the Sudley road a woody knoll dominated the ridge. In front of the cut the ground fell away in a gradual decline toward the Dogan house, at the intersection of the two roads about 3,500 yards away. The cut itself was occasionally shrouded in dense growth, but for the most part it looked down on cleared land dotted here and there with clumps of trees.

Resting his left on the knoll near the Sudley road, Jackson deployed his line of battle along a front of about 3,000 yards with A. P. Hill's division formed in two lines holding the left, Lawton's men holding the center, and Starke's men, badly worn, holding the stronger ground on the right. Facing toward the scene of earlier triumph at the Henry house, Jackson had some 18,000 men in line, supported by as many of his forty guns as he could put in position.[25]

Puffs of smoke near the Warrenton Pike at about 10 A.M. on the twenty-ninth marked Pope's battery positions in front of Jackson's right—the battle had begun. Jackson's guns returned fire, and a lengthy artillery duel rolled along the line from right to left. The morning dragged by with shells churning the ground in and around the cut, spraying the infantry with flying dirt and rock. Still Pope's masses formed without making a move to advance.

After a half hour of shelling, Jackson's men on the right spied a column of dust to the west, then saw a brigade deploying on the continuation of the Confederate ridge to the right and slightly south of Starke's position. Friend or foe? Starke sent to find out, and soon the shout "It is Longstreet!" ran down the line. Jackson's right flank had been covered, and he shifted Early's two brigades to the left to see how Hill's men were deployed.

Some light contact on Hill's front in the morning resulted in the

Confederates' throwing back a few enterprising Union regiments, and after that a short lull settled over the field as Pope built up his attack on Hill's front. Wave after wave of blue infantry advanced up the grade in front of the cut, plowed into the dense growth, poured their fire across the railroad into Hill's ranks, took galling volleys in return, and stumbled back down.

More Federals assembled for the assault. They headed now for a dense clump of underbrush which penetrated the Confederate line and offered the best cover. As they charged, an interval in the line of Confederate musket smoke indicated a break in the front. Covered by brush, Federal troops crowded into the railroad cut in front of the gap in Hill's ranks, then charged toward it with a rush, splitting two of Hill's brigades apart. A critical moment. Would the Federals roll up Jackson's lines, push straight on toward his rear where the wagons were parked, and demolish his wing of the army?

Swiftly reserves were thrown at the breaching Union force, men fired into one another's faces at ten paces, and the Yankee break-through was contained.[26] But back to the attack came more bluecoats. Hill's line appeared on the point of being engulfed by sheer weight of numbers. Yankees were everywhere, firing, falling, retreating, attacking again. The railroad cut and the ground behind it became obscured in a dense cloud of musket smoke as two lines of sweating, bleeding, struggling men fought it out almost toe to toe.

Fighting was so continuous on Hill's front that his men ran out of cartridges and threw rocks at the advancing clouds in blue, bayoneted them, clubbed them with musket stocks—fought with anything to hold the line. So desperate had been the contest that finally Hill knew he had to tell Jackson he doubted the ability of his men to repulse another assault. To Kyd Douglas, who arrived with some word from Field Headquarters, Hill gave his message. Ride to General Jackson, Douglas was told, and explain to him the critical situation on the left; tell him that Hill's men would do the best they could to beat back another thrust, but they would probably fail.

As Jackson anxiously scanned his front from a vantage point behind the line, Douglas galloped up, dismounted, and breathlessly told of Hill's plight. Hill might not beat back the next wave. It meant the ruin of the army. The little group clustering at Field Headquarters noted the dark shadow gathering on Stonewall's face. His men must again stand like a stone wall. Sharply he spoke to Douglas: Go back to General Hill, "tell him if they attack him again he must beat them." Off started Douglas.

The danger to the left had become so serious that Old Jack decided to go there himself and he followed Douglas's racing mount. Shortly Hill could be seen riding toward Field Headquarters. As Hill outlined the desperate straits of his division, Jackson listened quietly; then, with great calm, he said, "General, your men have done nobly; if you are attacked again you will beat the enemy back." [27]

As he spoke Jackson heard the ripping sound of musketry in the direction of Hill's command. "Here it comes," Hill said, and touching his hat, galloped to the battle. "I'll expect you to beat them," Jackson's voice floated after him.

More desperate than ever, the Federals' charge raged. At about 3:30 P.M. Hill called for reserves. Early and Forno went to help him, but still hordes of bluecoats stormed the hill, apparently determined to win by shining bravery what their generals could not win by brains. At last the strength of Early and Forno, added to Maxey Gregg's spent South Carolinians, broke the back of the enemy offense. Fiercely now the Confederates pushed forward, taking back the ground that heroic Northern blood had so dearly earned. On past the railroad cut went the counterattack, down to the point from which the Federals had launched their charge.[28] The Rebel yell faded away and the jubilant Hill sent word to Jackson.

At Field Headquarters a staff officer rode up, saluted, and reported: "General Hill presents his compliments and says the attack of the enemy was repulsed." Smiling broadly—a rare thing indeed—Old Jack replied: "Tell him I knew he would do it." [29]

Six separate and grimly determined assaults had been beaten back that afternoon. Would there be another? Artillery boomed from the Union lines; serried masses of men still stood to arms. But at long last the day drew toward an end. The whole army watched in thankful relief. As Kyd Douglas said:

> For the first time in my life I understood what was meant by "Joshua's sun standing still on Gideon," for it would not go down. No one knows how long sixty seconds are, nor how much time can be crowded into an hour, nor what is meant by 'leaden wings' unless he has been under the fire of a desperate battle, holding on ... hour after hour, minute after minute, waiting for a turning or praying that the great red sun, blazing and motionless overhead, would go down.[30]

That August 29 struck many men as one of the longest days in their lives. Ham Chamberlayne, the brilliant young lieutenant on A. P. Hill's staff, summed up the feelings of the whole army when he wrote his mother that "the sun went down so slowly." [31]

Later in the evening, as the men were filing past the ammunition wagons, replenishing for the next day's work, Jackson stood by his camp-fire, finishing the supper Jim (who had found his way to the army) had cooked. A coffee pot was nearly boiling as Dr. McGuire walked up to report on casualties. Again it had been a gruesome day. Old Trimble had been wounded, along with many field officers. Hill's division alone had lost over 1,500 killed and wounded.[32] As McGuire tolled off the list,

Jackson listened. Wearied lines of his face, highlighted in the fire glow, showed no change in expression. Among the dead, said McGuire, was young Will Preston—Col. John Preston's boy. Jim, who knew and loved Willy as his own, "rolled on the ground groaning, in his agony of grief, but the General's face was a study. The muscles in his face were twitching convulsively," McGuire noted, "and his eyes were all aglow. He gripped me by the shoulder till it hurt me, and in a savage, threatening manner asked why I had left the boy. In a few seconds he recovered himself, and turned and walked off into the woods alone." [33] Little Willy —who had been one of the first in Jackson's Sunday-school class "where I became attached to him when he was a little boy"—was to have been an aide, "but God in His providence has ordered otherwise." [34] Death striking so close to Maggie and John brought back once again the dear memory of Ellie and all that she and her family had meant to him— memories that could not be forgotten, even if he wanted to forget. He might soon join Ellie where he knew so certainly she awaited him.

Getting control of himself, he came back from the seclusion of the woods and joined the group drinking coffee at the fire. Dr. McGuire tactfully went on with his report; the list of wounded and dead grew longer in each battle. At length, finishing his statistics, the doctor observed: "We have won this battle by the hardest kind of fighting." A gentle expression softened the blue eyes, and Jackson replied quietly, "No, no, we have won it by the blessing of Almighty God." [35]

Dawn, August 30, was strangely silent. Hot dry air gave warning of a blistering day. Jackson rode to his right and noted that Longstreet's men were in position, bending a little south and west of his line, forming a concave angle, with its apex where a hill divided Jackson's and Longstreet's commands. With his staff Old Jack watched the marching and countermarching of Union troops, as they appeared to prepare for another fight. This time it looked as though they would aim their spearhead at Jackson's right, but there could be no certainty. In fact, Jackson remained unconvinced that there would be a fight at all. Curious about what was happening with the rest of the army, he rode over to Army Headquarters and conferred for a while with Lee, Longstreet, and Stuart. Lee discussed ways of goading Pope into another attack. Soon Jackson rode back to his lines.

Silence hung heavy over the field. After high noon passed quietly, Federal guns could be heard rumbling into position, but still no actual evidence of an attack could be seen. Jackson rode to his front anyway, inspecting the lines and observing the Union guns. About 2 P.M. he ordered the Rockbridge Artillery to fire on some new Yankee batteries facing Starke's lines. Swiftly and with precision the Rockbridge men opened fire and drove off the enemy pieces. "That was handsomely done, very handsomely done"—high praise from Professor Jackson.[36]

Back behind the lines Old Jack rode, selected a comfortable spot, dismounted, and waited. It was a drowsy afternoon. Flies buzzed around the men living and dead; horses stood on one foot, then another. As the afternoon lazed on Jackson grew more certain that Pope would not attack.

Late in the day—Jackson said it was 4 P.M.[37]—a tearing sheet of musket fire on the right announced a major attack. Swiftly and silently Jackson mounted a little bay horse and rode toward the sound of firing. Strong Federal lines of battle pressed up the hill against Starke's men. Other formations of Yankees were preparing to move against Jackson's center and left; a general assault it was, delivered in larger numbers than on the previous day and so constructed as to prevent any shifting of reserves from one part of the line to another.

Soon the right had become desperately engaged, with the Stonewall Brigade losing Col. W. S. H. Baylor. Jackson exhorted his old command to hold firm, to maintain its reputation,[38] and watched anxiously as the attack spread along his whole line. Sterner than ever the Federals came on. They held their ground longer, pushed ahead farther. This time they would prove the *élan* of misled Union boys. There would be so many brave Yankees today, that not all of them could be shot.

Once again Jackson's men were locked in combat under a pall of musket and cannon smoke. Hand-to-hand fighting raged at different parts of the line. Ammunition again gave out, men again threw rocks, again clubbed their foes with muskets, rammers, anything. All the while, clouds of bluecoats stalked up the slope, bayonets fixed, ready to crack the embattled Rebel line. Jackson could not do it alone. Reinforcements were needed, and instantly. Stonewall called for help from Longstreet.

Old Pete had been observing the attack from the hill between his lines and Jackson's. Swiftly he saw that it would take time to send infantry support to Jackson, but that from the hill he occupied, artillery could smash and wither away the Union left flank. Without bothering to order a transfer of troops, Longstreet directed Col. Stephen D. Lee's batteries to begin firing. Lee's field of fire spread before him. His muzzles faced east and he would be sending shell and canister straight across Jackson's front into the helpless Yankee left flank. Fire! Lee's whole battalion sent sheets of iron tearing into the Yankee troops. Bewildered, the attackers slowed; the second and third lines crumbled and recoiled. When the first line found itself in contact with Jackson's men without support, it fell back in disorder. As Longstreet saw it, his artillery counterblast had halted the Federal attack in less than ten minutes. In half an hour the Federals were in full retreat.[39]

Now was the moment. As the Yankees stumbled back over the sheaves of dead in blue, the Confederates must attack! Longstreet, anticipating an order from Lee, waved his men forward. Jackson's men, sensing the turning point in the battle, leaped ahead to join in the charge. Wild scenes of slaughter followed. Relentlessly the Rebel yell wafted across the field as the long line in gray pushed the huddled, disorganized Federals toward the Stone Bridge on Bull Run. Rarely in the history of attacks had one been so well delivered, so thorough and so completely coordinated. The grayclads were irresistible; as one Northern observer said, "they came on like demons emerging from the earth." [40]

There was some confusion in the advance, some drifting, and pockets of resistance held back the rush, but the attack that afternoon of August 30 was the sort of attack Lee had been trying to deliver all through the Seven Days' Campaign. For more than a mile and a half, well into the old battlefield of First Manassas, Lee's screeching hellions drove the Yankees back. They did not do everything that could have been done to Pope. They halted short of the Henry house, and called off the chase as darkness and a threatening storm made visibility uncertain; they did not destroy the Federal army completely or cut off retreat across Bull Run, but they did do this: They completely wrecked Pope's organization and shoved him demoralized into Bull Run, across the Stone Bridge. They proved, too, that Pope had been a prophet when he wrote about disaster and shame lurking in the rear.

One further thing the grayclads did—they convinced their general they could do almost anything.

Old Jack watched his boys advance with pride, and joined the pursuit until it halted. Then he made his way back to camp. On the way he spied a young soldier trying to climb up the railroad embankment, near the spot where the fighting had raged most fiercely. Riding quickly to the boy, Jackson asked if he was wounded. "Yes, General, but have we whipped 'em?" "Yes," replied Old Jack, dismounting and going to help him. What was the lad's regiment? "I belong to the Fourth Virginia, your old brigade, General. I have been wounded four times but never before as bad as this. I hope I will soon be able to follow you again."

An examination relieved Jackson—the wound was deep, but in the flesh of the thigh. Touched by the boy's devotion, he put his hand on the hot forehead, and in husky, half-choked tones told him: "You are worthy of the old brigade and I hope with God's blessing, you will soon be well enough to return to it."

Ordering several of his staff to carry the wounded man to a comfortable spot, Jackson sent for an ambulance and directed Dr. McGuire to take special care of him. The ragged private tried to thank the general, but tears shut off the words. Silently he looked at Jackson, and Stonewall understood. [41]

16

"THE INDOMITABLE JACKSON"

—R. E. LEE

I TELL YOU a soldier in Jackson's Army has got no time to write. . . . If he can only address his wife he is Satisfied to close and retire to bed immediately." With Pvt. Noah Shealy's bit of philosophy General Jackson would have been in complete agreement.[1] Anxious to make the victory over Pope still more decisive, Lee, on the afternoon of August 31, ordered Jackson's command to move across Sudley's Ford on Bull Run and intercept the Yankee retreat. It was hard on the men under Stonewall —after all, they had taken the brunt of the fighting—but the position of Jackson's corps put it closer to Pope's line of retreat. It was Sunday, it rained in the afternoon, nobody got any rations, and the troops had to be content with sodden roasting ears. A sad denouement to a great victory.[2] But as Jackson sat at his field headquarters near Pleasant Valley next day, snatching a moment to pen a note to Anna, his mood was not sad but grateful:

> We were engaged with the enemy at and near Manassas Junction Tuesday and Wednesday, and again near the battle-field of Manassas on Thursday, Friday, and Saturday; in all of which God gave us the victory. May he ever be with us, and we ever be His devoted people, is my earnest prayer. It greatly encourages me to feel that so many of God's people are praying for that part of our force under my command. The Lord has answered their prayers; He has again placed us across Bull Run; and I pray that He will make our arms entirely successful, and that all the glory will be given to His holy name, and none of it to man. God has blessed and preserved me through His great mercy. On Saturday, Colonel Baylor and Hugh White were both killed, and Willie Preston was mortally wounded.[3]

372

Letters of like sentiment he had written to Dr. White and other Lexington friends, and by now the deacon general was famed not only for military prowess but also for selfless devotion to God. So often had he asked the prayers of his old congregation, and those of all patriotic Christians, that in early September the Lexington Presbytery passed a special resolution concerning Jackson and his army.

> As it is known to us that the General . . . greatly desires and highly prizes the prayers of his Christian friends, offered in behalf of himself & the army under his command, we hereby pledge ourselves to him & them that we will pray to the Lord of Hosts that he may protect them & grant them abundant success in the defence of our country. It is also, Resolved, that it be recommended to all our Ministers, that in their public prayers, this General & his army shall be frequently remembered. The same also is recommended to our Christian friends in their more private devotions.[4]

Prayers for the general and his tattered remnants were sorely needed. During the afternoon of September 1, while the heavens poured down a blinding, raging rain—as if to wash away the horrors of Second Manassas—Jackson's men ran headlong into a strong Federal force near the mansion of Chantilly. While thunder and lightning drowned out the roar and flash of cannon and musketry, Hill's, Lawton's, and Starke's men fought a desperate, confused, and bloody fight with troops under Generals Phil Kearny and I. I. Stevens. Outnumbered, the Federals almost won the day, but retired when their generals were killed.[5]

Weary, hungry, and buffeted by the storm, Jackson and his men had not taken the action at Chantilly seriously until almost too late; consequently the Federals had achieved their objective of covering Pope's withdrawal toward the Washington defenses. With the escape of Pope's shattered divisions, Lee faced new problems in strategy.[6]

Pursuit of the enemy to the capital's forts would accomplish little since there were not enough Confederates to storm the works. The Army of Northern Virginia could not long remain in the vicinity of Manassas and Centreville because that part of the state had been stripped of food and forage and the lines of communication with Richmond stood exposed to Federal raiding parties. Lee reasoned that he could fall back toward the less ravaged country around Warrenton, could move to the Shenandoah Valley, or could invade the North. When the political considerations were weighed with the military, Lee concluded to carry the war to the enemy.[7]

Maryland's citizens were presumed loyal to the Confederacy, and Lee felt that his ranks might be filled by a vast influx of volunteers. At the same time a new star might be added to the Confederate flag—the army could cross the Potomac in the role of liberator. Diplomatic results might be important, too, since an offensive move would be viewed with intense interest in England and France. President Davis agreed with the invasion plan and removed the possibility of political objections.

But what of military objections? Could the army undertake a northward campaign in hostile country? For almost a solid month the troops had been engaged in marching and fighting. Casualties had cut down over 9,000 Southern men, and all but canceled the value of reinforcements coming to the army in the divisions of D. H. Hill, Lafayette McLaws, and John G. Walker.[8] Ammunition reserves were low, and Lee worried a great deal about building up the supply from Richmond. Although enough shells and cartridges were in the ordnance wagons for a short campaign, the army's commissary had collapsed. Many wagons had been left behind, but even had they been with the army, the commissaries could not find enough food in northern Virginia to sustain the troops.

Wagons, all kinds, were badly battered by the long campaign, and the commanding general wondered if the groaning, creaking splinter collections which passed for transportation in his army would stand the strain of an offensive.

But the fundamental question was: Could the men stand the strain? As he surveyed his camps near Leesburg on September 3, Lee must have had serious misgivings. Lean his men were, and wiry—so lean that Confederate corpses resisted the ravages of decomposition much longer than the more sleek enemy on the fields of Manasses. The graycoats were hardened to severe marching, were accustomed to traveling on light rations and with little baggage. But September would be cool, especially at night, and most of the gray uniforms were crazy quilts of patches, mends, and tatters. Many of the men were without shoes and could not stand long marches on rough roads.[9]

But never had morale been so high as now. Lee's gallant tatterdemalions were equal to any task, and he counted far more on them than on anything else.

What of his wing, or corps, commanders; how did they feel about invasion of the enemy's country? Sensing Lee's desires, Longstreet reminisced about his Mexican War experiences, and remembered that for two days at least General Worth's division had lived on roasting ears and green oranges. Surely Maryland would offer at least that frugal a diet. Old Pete wanted to go.[10] Jackson? No need to worry about Stonewall's views—at last the time had come to put into effect his long-cherished dream of letting the Yankees feel something of the war. If the move meant striking a blow, Jackson could be counted on without question. Lee issued his orders; the columns were put in motion.

Jackson's men, coming toward Leesburg from the direction of Centreville, camped near Dranesville during the night of September 3-4. Old Jack was not happy. As his command had marched during the last few days, he had seen many stragglers. Uneven pacing by some of the divisions—particularly A. P. Hill's—had caused part of it, but straggling must be curbed. During Wednesday evening, September 3, the division commanders received careful marching instructions from Jackson's headquarters. They were to be on the road toward the Potomac at specified times in the morning.

At "earliest dawn" on the fourth, Old Jack, mounted on a cream-colored claybank, since Little Sorrel had been missing for several days,[11] rode to the highway, seeking his men. Where were they? Hill's troops were in camp. Each brigade appeared to be shifting for itself with no supervision from division headquarters. Riding up to Gen. Maxey Gregg, who had so gallantly fought on the left of the railroad cut, Jackson demanded to know why his brigade had not marched. His men were filling canteens, explained the brigadier. Raising his voice so that the slightly deaf Gregg could not mistake his words, Jackson sternly announced: "There are but few commanders who properly appreciate the value of celerity." [12]

Gregg was ordered to move as soon as his men were supplied with water, and Jackson waited to make sure. After the column formed and began to swing along the road Old Jack looked in vain for Hill. Surely he would obey the long-standing order to ride back along his command and make sure it was well closed? No, Hill kept to the head of his division and so did his staff officers. Straggling began and grew as the march continued. Hill ignored the injunction to halt his men for a rest. All this Old Jack noticed; he lost his temper and, riding to the leading brigade, ordered a halt. That brought Hill back, wrathful. Why had the brigade halted? On orders from General Jackson, he was told. Now Hill lost his temper. Turning to Jackson, who was quietly observing the exchange between the division and the brigade commanders, Hill exploded that if Jackson intended to give orders to the division, he should command it. He took off his saber and held it out to Jackson. "Consider yourself under arrest for neglect of duty," snapped Stonewall. The division passed to the command of General Branch.[13]

For some time Hill had displayed laxity and negligence on the march; he must be disciplined. In the meantime he could ride behind his division. The humiliation might teach a valuable lesson.

The old Army of the Valley covered comparatively little ground on the fourth, bivouacking for the night not far from Ball's Bluff.[14] The whole army grew excited—by now every man in the ranks knew where they were going. They were carrying the war beyond the borders of the beleaguered Confederacy!

It was a grand day for invasion, bright, clear, and balmy.[15] About 10 A.M. Jackson's corps reached the Potomac River at White's Ford. The Tenth Virginia led the van, and to the left of the column, a little ahead of it, Jackson rode, erect and energetic. Gaily the men plunged into the river, carrying the Virginia flag. Jackson watched. The long line of dusty brown troops splashed in the current, the sun danced on the water, and abundant autumn flowers added to the color of the scene. A band began to play "Maryland, My Maryland." Wild cheers broke out, men began to sing. Jackson touched the claybank's side and headed for the Potomac.[16]

At midstream, he reined up, caught the spirit of the moment, pulled off his cap and stood posing for his troops. His men cheered him wildly. The moment passed; he rode on into Maryland.[17]

As the general and his staff pulled up on the northern shore of the Potomac, they were greeted with a present—"a noble melon"—and also with the sight of Federal pickets departing hastily from a position near the river. As the troops snaked along the road toward Frederick, flocks of people crowded to see them, talk to them, cheer them on. Many local citizens were anxious to profess long-standing sympathy with the Southern cause—and to protect their property. Of genuine friendship there was much. Multitudes wanted to see Stonewall Jackson, to invite him into their homes and give him gifts. One gift was to prove unexpectedly troublesome. On the road that afternoon Jackson, with some embarrassment but also with innate courtesy, accepted a new mount. A strong, muscular gray mare, the gift horse threw Old Jack when he spurred her the next day and badly shook him up—so much so, in fact, that he lay on the ground for some time, stunned. Finally gaining his feet, he still felt so unsteady that he turned the command over to D. H. Hill and spent the rest of the afternoon sullenly riding in a rickety army ambulance.[18]

Sad as was this event, it had a ludicrous side which Jackson could not, for the moment, appreciate. A few days before, General Lee while grabbing for the reins of his horse Traveller, which had been startled by a sudden noise, fell and badly bruised one hand and broke a bone or two in the other.[19] Unable to hold the reins, he also was riding in a medical wagon: two of the Confederacy's conquering heroes were rolling into the enemy's country in ambulances.

Army and corps headquarters were established on September 6 not far from the city of Frederick. Cornfields were plentiful, and neighboring farmers were philosophical about selling or donating fence rails for the roasting process. Lee issued strict orders that no pillaging would be permitted and directed that all food supplies must be obtained by purchase.[20] Old Jack, himself, late in the afternoon delighted his watching soldiers by pulling a big roasting ear out of his haversack and deliberately munching away.[21]

To the camps of Lee, Jackson, and Longstreet—all fairly close together in Best's Grove, near Frederick—numerous visitors came during the afternoon and evening of September 6. Some were disappointed not to see Lee, whose bruises and business kept him close to his tent. Nor did Jackson seem to be on display. Longstreet, making a real social effort, although he too was suffering from a heel blister, saw as many of the visitors as possible.[22] But it was Jeb Stuart of the flowing beard and plumed hat who did the army command proud. He readily consented to see any and all of the good-looking women.[23]

While Jackson, still smarting from his fall, was attending to corps business in his tent, Kyd Douglas hesitantly brought him a visitor. From the Douglas homestead not far from Sharpsburg his mother had come to see him. She wanted so much to meet the general her son served— would he mind, just for a few moments? Instantly Jackson was affability itself. Saying little—"but that little was of his kind"—he spoke well of Mrs. Douglas's boy, and urged her to spend the whole day with her son. Pleased and flattered, the happy mother took her leave. She stopped for proud moments with Lee, Longstreet, and the ubiquitous Stuart. It was a visit "long to be remembered." [24]

All the visitors were full of praise for the assembled generals, and they embarrassed Jackson. His defense was the self-imposed exile in his tent, but this device failed him in the late afternoon when General Lee sent for him. He walked, since the commanding general's tent stood not far away and he could not yet bear the thought of mounting. As he passed a carriage adorned with two pretty Baltimore belles, he found himself suddenly attacked without warning. The girls had hurled themselves from their conveyance and rushed upon him. One took a hand, the other embraced him, and both chattered excitedly and so fast that the general caught none of it. He could not get away, and seemed, to Kyd Douglas, "simply miserable." After a few minutes the girls ran out of breath, and "jumping into their carriage, they were driven away happy and delighted; Jackson stood for a moment cap in hand, bowing, speechless, paralyzed, and then went to General Lee's." As soon as he could he went back to the comparative safety of his tent and "did not venture out again." [25]

September 7 was a Sunday, but Jackson did not go to church in the morning. Routine army matters had to be attended to, and even though it was the Sabbath, Jed Hotchkiss must be put to work on some good maps of Maryland. Assistant Adjutant General Elisha Paxton was called to Old Jack's tent. A rule would have to be violated this Sunday. Adjutant Paxton must write a letter. Directed to Gen. A. P. Hill, it said that Hill's request for a copy of the charges against him had been received and that "should the interests of the service require your case to be brought before a Court Martial a copy of the charges and specifications will be furnished. . . ." Hill would remain with his division until further orders.[26] Old Jack had not relented.

Sunday night Kyd Douglas and Joseph Morrison were called in. Would the two staff members care to accompany the general to an evening church service? And would Douglas procure a proper pass for the party, so that they could get through the city guards? Douglas thought the latter request a trifle absurd, and said to Jackson that it hardly seemed necessary for him to have a pass to go through his own army. Possibly not, but General Lee had ordered that everyone going into Frederick display a pass. Paxton wrote it out:

> Hd. Qrs. Valley District
> Sept. 7. 1862

Guards and Pickets
    Pass Maj. Genl. T. J. Jackson and two staff officers and attendants to Frederick to church, to return tonight.

> By Command of
> Major Genl. Jackson
> E. F. Paxton
> A. A. GENL.[27]

As the little group rode toward town, Jackson asked Douglas to recommend a church, since the Presbyterians were not holding evening service. The Reformed Church seemed to Douglas the next best thing, and there they went. The Reverend Dr. Zacharias, a Union man, noted that his congregation included no less a personage than Stonewall Jackson, but he stuck to the prayer for the President of the United States. He was credited with considerable bravery later, but he had been in no danger. Jackson sat well back in the church and had, as usual, gone to sleep. Douglas and Morrison knew, but the rest of the congregation did not. Nonetheless, Jackson returned to his tent much pleased with the service, and next day wrote Anna:

> Last evening I attended a German Reformed church in Frederick City. I was not quite near enough to hear àll the sermon, and I regret to say fell asleep; but had I been near enough to hear, would probably not have been so unfortunate. The minister is a gifted one, and the building beautiful. The pews are arranged in a circular form, so that every person faces the pulpit.... The ladies and gentlemen were sitting in front of the doors, and all looked so comfortable, and I may say elegant, according to my ideas, and their enjoyment looked so genuine, that my heart was in sympathy with the surroundings. If such scenes could only surround me in Lexington, how my heart would, under a smiling Providence, rejoice! [28]

General Lee got down to business on the eighth. He knew by now that Little Mac had been restored to command of the Union Army in the field against him, and that radical reorganization was afoot in the Federal camps. While McClellan took his time refurbishing Pope's tarnished troops, the Confederates would do their best to realize positive results from the Maryland excursion. To the people of that state Lee issued a proclamation outlining the reasons for the Confederate Army's being in their midst, and assuring them that political repressions would be avoided, and explaining that the sole desire of the Confederacy was to assist in throwing the despot's heel from Maryland's shore. "It is for you to decide your destiny freely and without constraint. This army will respect your choice, whatever it may be; and while the Southern people will rejoice to welcome you to your natural position among them, they will only welcome you when you come of your own free will." [29]

Already Lee had been disappointed in one expectation; Marylanders did not come of their own free will to join the Confederate ranks. Some few hundred men signed up around Frederick, but there had been no vast outpouring of Southern patriots. [30] The army could not wait indefinitely; not only would the enemy move soon, but also the problem of food had to be considered. Diligent scavenging of the country around Frederick had produced fair rations, but 53,000 men consumed incredible quantities of food, and the supply was approaching exhaustion. Logistics, then, would force Lee to move the army. Where? [31] When he had first thought of a northward strike, Lee considered the possibility of going from Maryland into Pennsylvania, and he had not abandoned the scheme. To do this, though, he would have to move west, beyond South Mountain, possibly basing his army at Hagerstown. From there he could run his line of supply through the Shenandoah Valley to Richmond. The valley would offer excellent cover for Confederate communications—if the whole valley were in Confederate hands. It was not. A Federal force still held out at Harpers Ferry. Lee had supposed that all Union troops along the Potomac would be withdrawn north of the river as soon as the Confederates crossed. The unanticipated garrison at Harpers Ferry threatened the Southern line of communications through the valley and would have to be eliminated.

Harpers Ferry might be captured by part of the army as it moved west toward the proposed point of concentration at Hagerstown. Jackson's men were the logical choice for detachment on the Harpers Ferry mission. Many long months before, Old Jack had commanded the town and plotted ways and means of defending it—he would know better than most its weak spots. A further point in Jackson's favor: he could be relied on. Sometime on the eighth or ninth Lee asked Jackson to come to headquarters.

When Jackson reached Lee's tent he found Gen. John G. Walker, whose division had just reinforced the army, already in conversation with the commanding general. Joining the two, Jackson soon learned that Lee desired to talk about Harpers Ferry and about ways to get at it. Pleased at the prospect of a return to the valley, Jackson observed that he had been neglecting his friends there. Lee replied that those "friends," he feared, would not be glad to see Stonewall. [32] Then, as it appeared Lee wanted to confer privately with Jackson, Walker found a pretext to leave. Lee closed the flap of the tent.

Harpers Ferry, Jackson was told, must be taken quickly. Celerity being of utmost importance, the capture might be accomplished most efficiently by sending a force large enough to do the job without faltering. The attack must be made from several sides at once to ensure no relief of the garrison and no retreat. What were Jackson's views? Recalling vividly the months he had worked on the defenses of the Ferry, Jackson doubtless mentioned the absolute necessity of taking the dominating mountains and heights. If Loudoun Heights and the Maryland Heights were in Confederate hands, well-placed guns could reduce the garrison in short order. Lee agreed. The attack would be made by Jackson's three divisions, which would seal off the Ferry's defenders from the land side; two other divisions would cooperate with Jackson: McLaw's would take Maryland Heights, north of the Potomac, and Walker's would seize Loudoun Heights, on the eastern side of the Shenandoah. Pinned between the converging fire of guns on three sides, the Yankees at Harpers Ferry would be forced into swift capitulation.

General Lee was offering an opportunity for more semi-independent action, action of the sort which best suited Old Jack. Never was he better than when making a fast, daring thrust from an unexpected direction—a fact which had induced General McClellan not long before to wail that "I don't like Jackson's movements. He will suddenly appear when least expected." [33] The valley army, a sentimental fiction to which Jackson clung stubbornly, could return to its protective role in the Shenandoah.

While Jackson and Lee discussed details, a familiar voice was heard outside. Longstreet had asked one of the staff if he could see General Lee and, told the General was busy, was starting to leave when Lee opened the flaps and urged him to come in. The Harpers Ferry plan had been under discussion—what did Longstreet think? Unenthusiastic, Old Pete expressed concern at the division of the army in the enemy's country. As he understood the scheme, it envisioned sending five divisions under Jackson south of the Potomac, sending Longstreet's command to Boonsboro, and assigning D. H. Hill's division as the army's rear guard. In the mountainous country through which Lee's troops would pass, Longstreet feared for the consequences. If the move against Harpers Ferry were deemed imperative, then the whole army should go, certainly enough of the army to brush aside all resistance in time for quick reconcentration. Beyond that, Old Pete had nothing to say.

Obviously he disapproved, and he apparently did not like Jackson's receiving the independent assignment. Here was one more point to be held against "Tom Fool" Jackson. Soon Longstreet's troops would be saying that Jackson "is the rudest and most arrogant pious man alive. ... His army they say is a rabble." [34]

But this time Longstreet had to sulk in vain; Lee had made up his mind. On September 9 he issued Special Orders No. 191, which carefully assigned the routes to be followed by the five infantry segments of the army and designated portions of Stuart's cavalry to cover Jackson's, Longstreet's, and McLaw's operations. A rigid time schedule called for the capture of Harpers Ferry on Friday, September 12, and a reconcentration with Lee at Hagerstown or Boonsboro.[35]

Back at his own quarters, Jackson painfully copied out Lee's order and sent it by hand to brother-in-law D. H. Hill—a courteous way of letting Hill know that Jackson understood he had been detached from service with the Army of the Valley. Hill received another copy from Army Headquarters—a copy destined to cause the Army of Northern Virginia some exceedingly uncomfortable days. Orders went to Jackson's men: prepare to march. The infantry would move early on the morning of the tenth.

At 3 A.M. the staff was routed out and joined the general on the road. No dawdling would be permitted; Lee's schedule must be maintained. As Jackson ranked the other generals assisting in the Harpers Ferry venture, his orders governed the pace. Urging on his sleepy staff, Old Jack rode into Frederick just as the sun began to appear. No one should have been stirring in the town at that uncivilized hour, but streets were crowded with the curious. Ostentatiously Jackson asked for a map of Chambersburg, Pennsylvania, inquired the distances to various places in different directions, and left the citizens in a daze as to his destination.

Pointing his column toward Hagerstown, Jackson rode ahead of his troops, but he was screened this time by a small cavalry escort a mile or so in front. As the infantry settled down to serious walking, Jackson took Kyd Douglas off to the side of the road and did something he had never before done—at least to Douglas. He told the young lieutenant where he was going. Although such a revelation represented a breach in security, there were good reasons for it: Douglas had been born not far from Sharpsburg and he knew intimately the country through which Jackson's men were to pass. What roads were the best, and which fords on the Potomac would be in good order at this time of year?

Well ahead of the infantry now, Jackson and his staff rode into Middletown, where they were soon treated to the sight of two pretty girls—Kyd Douglas thought they were pretty—wearing red, white, and blue ribbons in their hair and waving Union flags almost in the general's face. Bowing from the saddle, Jackson doffed his cap and smilingly said to his staff: "We evidently have no friends in this town." That brought down the miniature battle flags, and drove the Unionist girls away much abashed.

Still slightly north of west Jackson led his men, heading up toward Turner's Gap in South Mountain. After the troops had crossed to the western slope of the mountain and had come to within a mile of Boons-boro, he called a halt for the night. The headquarters tent was pitched, and Jim set about preparing supper. Kyd Douglas sought permission to ride on into Boonsboro, where he thought he might obtain accurate information about fords and roads. Old Jack felt he ought not to go, but the young man obviously had things other than roads on his mind. Cautioned to proceed carefully, Douglas took a courier with him and departed.

After a while Jackson grew restless. Leading his horse, he began to walk along the road toward town. The evening was clear, but too warm for his cap. Swinging it idly in his free hand, Jackson ambled along slowly, enjoying the twilight. As he approached a rise in the road he heard the clatter of galloping horses and suddenly Douglas and his courier companion came flying over the hill, pistols smoking. Not waiting to see more, Jackson hurled himself in the saddle and dashed toward his camps. Behind him, Douglas, the courier, and a third cavalryman—a providential volunteer who happened to be near at hand—whirled, yelled orders to fictional reinforcements, and charged toward the company of Yankee cavalry which had been in hot pursuit. The ruse worked; the Yankees halted, then fled. Jackson was saved.

When Douglas and his bodyguard arrived at headquarters, Old Jack congratulated him on his narrow escape and complimented the speed of his horse. Douglas refused to be the goat. Wordlessly, but with mock politeness, he presented the gloves which Jackson had dropped during his hasty retreat. *Touché!* Jackson smiled and retired to his tent. It would be better not to pursue the matter further.

Two other good moments there were that day. First, from far behind the enemy lines, where he had escaped from a Federal prison, came young George Junkin, Ellie's kinsman who had been captured at Kernstown. There was time for a reunion, and possibly some old memories. Second, Powell Hill's request to command his division in the forthcoming fight had been granted with pleasure.[36]

Early Thursday morning the men were put in motion, and soon Stonewall himself rode into Boonsboro. People again lined the curbstones to catch a glimpse of the famous Confederate. Bursting through the crowd, a "tall, straight, graceful" girl brandished one of Kyd Douglas's pistols in mock salute and cried "a Maryland girl's welcome to Stonewall Jackson." Off came the scraggly cap, the whole staff saluted, and Jackson had an opportunity to return Douglas's favor. He saw his young staff officer not far from the girl, realized why he had gone into town so early that morning, and sent back an order for him to remain behind and close up the regiments, a process which would leave him ample time to find out a great deal about roads and fords from his charming guide. But

Douglas, realizing that the general wanted him at hand to advise on directions, ignored the order and rode to the head of the column.

Anxious to catch the Federal garrison at Martinsburg, Jackson departed from his orders and changed direction on the morning of the eleventh. Instead of striking for the Potomac via Sharpsburg, he headed west for Williamsport, where his command crossed the river in the afternoon.[37] On the Virginia side, Jackson may have had a moment's nostalgia as he passed by the battlefield of Falling Waters—that little skirmish, which had seemed so big at the time, had been his first combat command. He had come a long way since then, from an unknown colonel of Virginia infantry to a hero of his country. "The race is not to them that's got the longest legs to run."[38]

A. P. Hill would move straight on Martinsburg, while Lawton's and Starke's divisions would swing west and cut off the garrison should they flee in that direction. The Federals took warning and raced eastward to join forces with the defenders of Harpers Ferry, and Jackson's troops entered Martinsburg on the twelfth without resistance.

Martinsburg went wild. The "Champion of the Valley" once again had liberated the town; eager crowds gathered to cheer Old Jack and the army. Private larders were thrown open along with Federal food depots, and the hungry marchers ate hearty.[39] The frenzied welcome which he received reminded Jackson of his entrance into Winchester on Banks's heels, and he smilingly uncovered as he rode through the happy throngs. Again it was a moment to test the fortitude of a humble Christian warrior.

Headquarters were established in the Everett house, where Jackson attempted to write dispatches for a while. People gathered, all feverishly trying to see him. Men, women, boys, girls, everyone wanted Stonewall. Ensconced in the parlor, he had the door locked and the windows shuttered. All such defenses were of no avail. Shouts came through the shutters, which rattled fiercely as admirers sought to break them down. While they called for him, the mob pulled handfuls of hair out of his horse's mane and tail—erroneously thinking it was Little Sorrel. Finally the shutters gave way. Kyd Douglas described the scene which followed:

Then with a rush little maiden noses and cherry lips were pressed against the clouded panes of glass, and little twinkling-stars of eyes tried to pierce the gloom of that forbidden room in search of their hero. They called out 'Dear, dear General,' and managing to force up the window a little way they threw red and white roses all about him. Soon a smile broke over his face, for there is a point beyond which to resist the pleadings of woman is not a virtue. At any rate his dispatch was finished and, giving it to me with very definite instructions for a courier, he said, 'Now admit the ladies.'

They came and swarmed about him. They all tried to get his hands at once. . . . They all talked at once with the disjointed eloquence of a devotion that scorned all coherent language. Blushing, bowing, almost speechless, he stood in the midst of this remarkable scene, saying, 'Thank you, thank you, you're very kind.'

Would the general give his autograph? He did, great numbers of times scratching out that labored T. J. Jackson. One darling little girl—would Mary Graham have looked like that?—reached her chubby little hands up and caught a button on his coat. Could she have it? Quickly he cut it off—but that was a fatal error, for almost at once he lost half of the total supply on his coat. For once in his life he apparently had given himself up entirely to the joy of adulation. But when a lady asked for a lock of his hair, that was too much. He terminated the interview.[40]

He had no time for further public relations; he had fallen behind General Lee's time schedule. Hill's infantry went on toward Harpers Ferry.

Rapidly eastward strode Jackson's columns on the morning of the thirteenth. Marching was better since a little rain during previous days had laid the dust, and although it was warm the men moved well.[41] By 11 A.M. Jackson caught his first glimpse of the Federal lines on Bolivar Heights. Closing his men to within two miles of the enemy works, Jackson deployed so as to cut off any escape on the land side of Harpers Ferry. Before he could do more, he must find out if the cooperating divisions of McLaws and Walker were on hand. They had been ordered by General Lee to be in position by the twelfth, but Jackson himself had been delayed and he could not count on the others' keeping to time.[42]

Sweeping the hills surrounding the Ferry with his glasses, Old Jack could not be certain whether they were in Confederate possession. Here was just the situation where he could employ the semaphore signal system in which he had so much confidence. Hotchkiss received instructions to set up a line of signals with Walker's division as soon as possible.[43] Captain Joseph L. Bartlett, Jackson's signal officer, must open a signal station and try to make flag contact with McLaws and Walker immediately. He worked hard at the task, but received no response. The only indication of activity on Maryland Heights was the sound of firing drifting south. What it meant none could say. Couriers were sent to Loudoun Heights and to Maryland Heights—Jackson had to know where his supports were.

During the afternoon he received word that McLaws had reached the formidable peak on the other side of the Potomac and was emplacing his batteries.[44] Late in the night the courier to Loudoun Heights returned with word that Walker had arrived and had taken position. The detachment had concentrated. The Federals were pinned from three sides.

How best to capture the town? Tactics must be devised which would ensure coordination of the huge force under Jackson's control. Since McLaws and Walker were separated from Jackson's men by two rivers, Old Jack decided that his troops would have to bear the brunt of any direct fighting. He would count on the isolated divisions for artillery support and to cut off the possible escape routes from the Ferry.

If all went well, there might be no need for close combat. Professor Jackson had never before had such an opportunity to use his guns. When he commanded at Harpers Ferry he had surveyed the heights all around the town, and he knew that guns placed where Walker's and McLaws's were would blow the town's defenses to pieces, provided the guns were rifled and of good range. There was the rub. The distance from the hovering heights to the Federal line of battle along the Bolivar ridge appeared too great for effective firing. But if all the batteries ringing the Federal stronghold could be brought to bear at once, enemy resistance ought to fade rapidly.

During the morning of the fourteenth Jackson established a signal contact with Walker and heard, about 10 A.M., that he had six guns ready and wanted to know if he should begin firing. Jackson signaled: "Wait." He wanted McLaws to join in the bombardment when he got his pieces in position. Unfortunately, though, no contact could be made with McLaws's signal station during the morning. Finally Jackson rode to his own signal officer and had him send an order to both heights. McLaws and Walker were to do as much damage as possible, but "I do not desire any of the batteries to open," Jackson said, "until all are ready on both sides of the river, except you should find it necessary, of which you must judge for yourself. I will let you know when to open all the batteries." [45]

The day dragged on as Jackson continued his efforts to signal Mc-Laws. By courier that morning Old Jack had sent a letter to Maryland Heights, explaining the current situation to McLaws, and urging him to move swiftly, get his guns in position, and report. Jackson would send a flag of truce to the Federal commander with a message suggesting the removal of noncombatants, and if the Yankees refused to surrender, all Confederate guns would blast away.

> Should we have to attack [wrote Jackson], let the work be done thoroughly; fire on the houses when necessary. The citizens can keep out of harm's way from your artillery. Demolish the place if it is occupied by the enemy, and does not surrender. . . . The position in front of me is a strong one, and I desire to remain quiet, and let you and Walker draw attention from Furnace Hill, so that I may have an opportunity of getting possession of the hill without much loss. [46]

Sometime during the morning of the fourteenth Jackson developed his plan of battle, which he wrote out carefully and had signaled to Walker and, he hoped, to McLaws. A copy was sent by courier to the troops under his immediate command. The order set up a pattern for an artillery battle. McLaws and Walker were to take as many Federal positions in reverse as possible, thus relieving the pressure in Jackson's front. A. P. Hill's men were to move along the bank of the Shenandoah, turn the Yankee left flank, "and enter Harper's Ferry." While Hill advanced, Gen. J. R. Jones, again commanding Jackson's division, would make a vigorous demonstration in front of the Federal right. Lawton would press the center.[47] Exposed to a shattering fire from the hills behind and attacked by infantry in front at the same time, the Federals would have no chance at all. It should be all over quickly.

But an incredible amount of time elapsed while Jackson's battle order was wigwagged to his subordinates. Walker became confused by some of the wording and more signaling took up more time. So many frustrating hours were consumed in exchanging messages—with McLaws still silent—that Jackson could do nothing until late afternoon on the fourteenth. At length he established a line of battle all across the spit of land between the Potomac and the Shenandoah, with Hill on the right and Jones on the left. Obeying his part of the battle order, Jones sent the Stonewall Brigade forward, supported by a battery. A slight demonstration soon gained commanding ground. On the Federal left a hill dominated part of the Union line—it was held by infantry alone. A dashing attack by Dorsey Pender's brigade cleared the hill, and during the night Confederate guns rumbled into position. Guns also rolled into battery on the ground taken by the Stonewall Brigade.

Everything appeared to be ready. At 8:15 P.M. Jackson wrote General Lee's Adjutant:

> *Near Halltown*
> *September 14, 1862—8.15 P.M.*

> Colonel: Through God's blessing, the advance, which commenced this evening, has been successful thus far, and I look to Him for complete success tomorrow. The advance has been directed to be resumed at dawn to-morrow morning. . . . Your dispatch respecting the movements of the enemy and the importance of concentration has been received. . . .[48]

From information sent by Lee, Jackson knew that McClellan's army had pushed ahead far too rapidly and had attacked Confederate positions on South Mountain. Unless Harpers Ferry surrendered immediately, Lee might have to retreat into Virginia or be badly beaten.

The trap must close tighter around the Yankee defenders. During the night Jackson ordered ten guns sent across the Shenandoah and emplaced at the base of Loudoun Heights in a position behind the Union left flank. They would wreck the Union works in front of A. P. Hill's men. At the same time the remainder of Lawton's guns were stationed on high ground near the center of Old Jack's lines. The general had done all he could, and when dawn broke on the fifteenth a grim ring of iron encased Harpers Ferry. The professor was about to have his day.

Heavy morning mist blotted out the target for a while, but as soon as the gunners could see anything, the ten cannons at the base of Loudoun Heights rocked and jumped from battery. As soon as the flashes could be seen from above, Walker's gunners began firing. The bombardment was taken up by the batteries of Poague and Carpenter far away on Jackson's left, and soon all Confederate guns belched fire. McLaws, who apparently had not received the order to begin firing, took his cue from the others. For a while the Federal guns tried to make a fight of it, but Professor Jackson had prepared his firing pattern too carefully. Shells tore into Federal gun emplacements, ripped into infantry ranks, shattered wagons, killed men and horses. Shells came from all directions—there was no use to resist further. As the Yankee fire slowed and grew increasingly wild, Jackson ordered Hill's guns—those on the little knoll Pender had so handsomely captured—to cease fire. It was the signal for the infantry attack. Hill's men made ready to go forward. As they moved toward the deadly-looking works in front and as many of them made ready to die, a white flag appeared on the Union entrenchments. They were saved! Professor Jackson had won the battle with his guns. A few stray shells came from batteries which had not recognized the white flag, but soon all firing ceased.

Out from the Federal lines rode an officer whose numerous staff betrayed his rank. A. P. Hill met the Union general and the little group rode to Jackson's command post. General Julius White had been sent by Col. Dixon Miles to seek terms of surrender, and although representing a defeated garrison he looked the model of a brigadier general. As he sat his handsome black mount, White's spotless blue uniform, gleaming braid, and burnished saber contrasted ludicrously with Jackson's dusty, dingy-looking clothes, almost without rank markings. The staffs of the two also contrasted much to the detriment of Jackson's, and forced Kyd Douglas to concede that he and his colleagues were "not much for looks or equipment." [49]

Now that the siege had ended, Jackson turned his whole attention toward Maryland and reunion with Lee. Beyond telling White that there would be no terms save unconditional surrender, Old Jack took no part in the negotiations. Since Hill's men had borne the brunt of the little fighting at Harpers Ferry, Hill would be the Confederate commissioner appointed to accept the surrender. Concessions, Hill was told, should be liberal: officers to retain sidearms and baggage, all officers and men not Confederate deserters to be paroled and allowed to return home. Two days' rations would be issued to the prisoners—an amount which must have pained Major Hawks, since it all but emptied the Federal food depots. One of the most liberal provisions was an unofficial one, worked out between Hill and White: the enlisted men were permitted to keep their overcoats and blankets, and two wagons per regiment could be used for the transportation of Federal baggage.[50]

Jackson could afford to be generous. Not only had he eliminated the Union force on Lee's line of supply, but he had also captured 73 guns, some 200 wagons, 13,000 small arms, and about 11,000 men, not to mention the depots of quartermaster and commissary stores. Before he went into the captured town to survey the booty, he must write General Lee:

> Near 8 A.M., September 15, 1862.
>
> General: Through God's blessing, Harper's Ferry and its garrison are to be surrendered. As Hill's troops have borne the heaviest part in the engagement, he will be left in command until the prisoners and public property shall be disposed of, unless you direct otherwise. The other forces can move off this evening so soon as they get their rations. To what point shall they move? I write at this time in order that you may be apprised of the condition of things. You may expect to hear from me again to-day after I get more information respecting the number of prisoners, &c.
>
> Respectfully,
>
> T. J. Jackson,
> MAJOR-GENERAL.[51]

One more note must be written ere he could get on with the business of moving out of Harpers Ferry. Although there had been more time on Sunday, he could not write then—but his *esposita* had not long been out of his thoughts. Anna should be reassured.

> It is my grateful privilege to write that our God has given us a brilliant victory at Harper's Ferry to-day. Probably nearly eleven thousand prisoners, a great number of small-arms, and over sixty pieces of artillery are, through God's blessing, in our possession. The action commenced yesterday, and ended this morning in the capitulation. Our Heavenly Father blesses us exceedingly. I am thankful to say that our loss was small, and Joseph Morrison and myself were mercifully protected from harm.[52]

And while Hill arranged final details, there might be time for one further matter. George Junkin, happily returned from a Yankee dungeon, apparently brought news of Ellie's family in the North. He brought also a request from his father that Jackson meet him somewhere between the lines. Hoping for a chance to see Thomas, Reverend David X. Junkin had come south with George and had finally caught up with the army. Would the general see him? Certainly, he would always be glad to see any of Ellie's family. David Junkin he knew well, from the long evenings of happy conversation in Dr. Junkin's house. The conversation today was to be private; Jackson and George rode away from headquarters, and soon the elder Junkin met them.

A warm handclasp, affectionate greetings—it seemed almost as though the brothers-in-law had never left that happy house in Lexington. Pleasantries disposed of, Junkin began a lengthy monologue. Did not Jackson realize the error of his ways—that "the rebellion was inexcusable"? Could he not see he was on the side of the godless in an evil war against righteousness? Jackson listened attentively, considered it, entered objections, and Junkin renewed his discourse. For two hours the three talked, while the silent crags of Maryland Heights loomed above, lending a grandeur to the scene which Junkin would remember the rest of his life.

Finally Thomas gathered his reins and grasped Junkin's hand. Doubtless Junkin firmly believed all he had said, but others had their convictions. Jackson must return to the war. "Farewell, General," Junkin said, "may we meet under happier circumstances; if not in this troubled world, may we meet in . . ." Tears choked off the words. Tears stained the general's face, too, as he pointed a gauntleted hand upward and finished the sentence—"in heaven." Wheeling suddenly, he spurred off toward his army. It was useless to look back.[53]

By 11 A.M. Old Jack had reached the lines which the Federals had evacuated and was on his way into Harpers Ferry. His guns had done well. Hill reported that all organization had disappeared in the enemy's camps; artillery fire had demoralized the whole garrison. A well-directed pattern of fire had destroyed morale but little valuable property—most of the booty could be salvaged for the Confederacy.

Down the road from Bolivar Heights rode Jackson and his staff. "The road," observed Kyd Douglas, "was lined with Union soldiers curious to see Stonewall Jackson. Many of them saluted as he passed and he invariably returned the salute. I heard one of them say as he passed: 'Boys, he's not much for looks, but if we'd had him we wouldn't have been caught in this trap.'" A chorus of agreement greeted this pronouncement. Nor were Old Jack's own men unappreciative of what he had done in sparing infantrymen with adroit artillery tactics. Jeb Stuart and his faithful follower Maj. Heros von Borcke galloped up while Jackson surveyed his spoils, and the hearty congratulations from Stuart pleased him, but when von Borcke added his plaudits, Jackson said: "Ah, this is all very well, Major, but we have yet much hard work before us."[54]

During the afternoon Jackson had all his divisions, save Hill's, cook two days' rations and make ready to march.[55] Lee had named Sharpsburg, Maryland, as the point of reconcentration and had indicated there was no time to lose.

Ruin stared the Army of Northern Virginia squarely in the face. Although Jackson probably did not know it yet, McClellan had obtained a copy of Special Order No. 191 wrapped around some cigars; the copy D. H. Hill received from Lee had fallen from someone's pocket and been found by a Federal soldier. Possession of Lee's dispersal order explained

Little Mac's unwonted speed in marching westward toward Hagerstown and his swift attacks on Confederate units guarding the passes in South Mountain. When Lee discovered that McClellan had a copy of Order 191,[56] the situation had already deteriorated. Heavy columns had assaulted McLaws's rear on the Maryland Heights, and the enemy had engaged large portions of Lee's army on South Mountain during the night of September 14–15. That night it became all too clear that the Confederates could not hold the crest—the army must retreat. And for a few desperate hours Lee had feared he might have to retreat to Virginia in bits and pieces. McLaws's position most concerned the commanding general, for it had been assailed in reverse. Could McLaws break off his battle and escape? If so, where should he go? If Jackson could take Harpers Ferry swiftly, McLaws could march down Maryland Heights, cross the Potomac into the town, and burn the bridges behind him. If not, he would have to try to find a route across the Potomac himself. All these worries came to an end when Lee received the dispatch Jackson sent on the night of the fourteenth. Old Jack thought his objective would be won the next day.

Lee's outlook changed. He could yet remain in Maryland, there would be time to reconcentrate the army without abandoning hope of invasion. Fixing on the little hamlet of Sharpsburg as a rendezvous for the army's stray elements, Lee outlined his situation to President Davis in a dispatch written on the sixteenth.

> *Headquarters,*
> *Sharpsburg, Md., September 16,*
> *1862.*

Mr. President: ... Learning later ... that Crampton's Gap (on the direct road from Fredericktown to Sharpsburg) had been forced, and McLaws' rear thus threatened, and believing from a report from General Jackson that Harper's Ferry would fall next morning, I determined to withdraw Longstreet and D. H. Hill from their positions and retire to the vicinity of Sharpsburg, where the army could be more easily united. Before abandoning the position, indications led me to believe that the enemy was withdrawing, but learning from a prisoner that Sumner's corps (which had not been engaged) was being put in position to relieve their wearied troops, while the most of ours were exhausted by a fatiguing march and a hard conflict, and I feared would be unable to renew the fight successfully in the morning, confirmed me in my determination. Accordingly, the troops were withdrawn, preceded by the trains, without molestation by the enemy, and about daybreak took position in front of this place. The enemy did not pass through the gap until about 8 o'clock of the morning after the battle, and their advance reached a position in front of us about 2 p.m. Before their arrival, I received intelligence from General Jackson that Harper's Ferry had surrendered early in the morning. ...

This victory of the indomitable Jackson and his troops gives us renewed occasion of gratitude to Almighty God for his guidance and protection.

I am, with high respect, your obedient servant,

R. E. Lee,

GENERAL.[57]

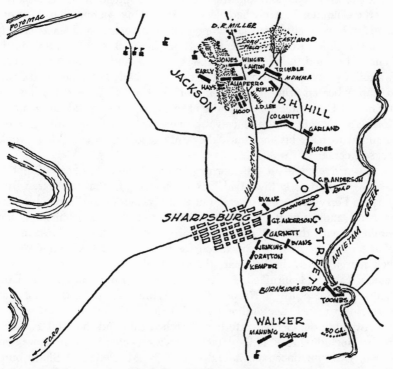

Confederate positions in the Battle of Sharpsburg (after Freeman, R. E. Lee)

Confident this letter was, giving no hint of the brutal odds facing the thin line of 18,000 men stretched along lazy Antietam Creek as it meandered on toward the Potomac. Through the morning of the sixteenth Lee, Longstreet, and D. H. Hill watched the blue host gathering: dust columns came from east and south as swarms of Yankees assembled. Little Mac began the process of concentrating his army—for the first time he planned an attack. Could Lee's thin line on the rolling hills east of Sharpsburg stand off columns which must number at least 60,000, perhaps 80,000, men? If he thought not, Lee's calm demeanor gave no sign.[58] He had ridden along part of his line during the morning, had helped guide some of his last troops into the position from which "we will make our stand." [59]

The ground held by the shadow force had natural advantages. A rolling, fairly open farm country lay around Sharpsburg and a ridge of hills along the eastern side of the town commanded the low ground near Antietam Creek, a mile or more farther east. As Lee deployed his troops along this ridge he found an added advantage in a road from the Potomac to Hagerstown, passing through Sharpsburg on almost a north-south axis and keeping within the Confederate lines along the ridges. Ready communication along the front was assured. But there were certain features of the position calculated to disturb any general intending its defense. In a way the Confederate Army had elected to stand in a spot much like the one in which Lee sought to ensnare Pope in late August, as he maneuvered to catch the Union troops between the Rappahannock and the Rapidan. In front of Lee and to his right ran the Antietam, and behind him, a scant two miles west, the twisting turns of the formidable Potomac stood ready to trap a beaten army. Lee's men were in the "V" formed by the two streams. If Little Mac showed more of his unexpected speed, the Army of Northern Virginia might conceivably have to swim for it. Still, Lee determined to hold his line until the army reconcentrated. When would Jackson come? [60]

He arrived late in the morning, with General Walker.[61] Right to Lee's headquarters in town Old Jack rode, to report that the march from Harpers Ferry had been "severe" but that his division and Lawton's were on hand and coming up. Walker announced that his command, too, would be with the army during the afternoon.[62] Although Jackson and Walker had been deeply concerned for the safety of Lee's force during their march across the Potomac, they were glad to see the commanding general calm and unruffled. He shook hands warmly and congratulated them on the capture of Harpers Ferry. While the two dusty, hot, and worn riders rested, Lee outlined the situation.

Although the Confederate line stretched thin and the total available troops—including A. P. Hill's detached division—numbered no more than 40,000, Lee announced he intended to fight McClellan at Sharpsburg. There were sound reasons for it. The ground offered some defensive possibilities, although Lee would have liked more depth between his lines and the Potomac,[63] and political considerations dictated a battle on Maryland soil. Having vowed to aid in liberating the state, Lee could not bring himself to leave with the humiliation of South Mountain as a farewell. Then, too, the character of McClellan gave an added reason to stay; he had never fought an offensive battle and his inbred caution might offer the opportunity to strike a blow, even in the face of overwhelming Union numbers. Old Jack, listening closely to the reasons for fighting and to Lee's estimate of the military position at Sharpsburg, formed his opinion. If any chance existed of hitting McClellan hard, he was for it—as Lee said, Jackson "emphatically concurred with me." [64] If Brigadier General Walker questioned the decision of Marse Robert and Stonewall, he prudently kept silent.

Tired though they were, Jackson's men marched a little over a mile to the left of the Confederate line and formed near a small Dunkard

Church—a landmark many were to remember to the end of their lives. Jackson carefully reconnoitered the ground his men were to hold. Every advantage of ground and natural cover must be used, for nowhere along the Confederate line of battle would there be any surplus of troops. Lee would have only about 25,000 men until R. H. Anderson, McLaws, and A. P. Hill could arrive.

As matters had developed, Jackson would command the whole of Lee's left; his men would connect with the left elements of Hood's division which, in turn, hinged on D. H. Hill's 3,000, charged with holding the center. On Hill's right a gap yawned in the line, partially covered by guns on high ground. Just north of Sharpsburg Longstreet's brigades took up the line, covered the road to Boonsboro and held, more or less, the Confederate right as it looked down from commanding heights on a crossing of the Antietam, which, after the seventeenth of September, 1862, would be known as Burnside's Bridge.

Since McClellan had obligingly advertised his intention of attacking the Confederate left, Lee had concentrated the larger portion of the army there at the expense of weakening the right. So weak was the right, in fact, that Lee directed General Walker's two brigades to take their stand there when they came up. Supporting this four-mile front of disconnected infantry units were fifty batteries—about 200 guns—which would be outnumbered and outranged by enemy ordnance when the battle started.

Delay was about all the Confederates could hope to do. With an eye to holding ground, Jackson rode along the left. What he saw must have both pleased and worried him. His line of battle would have to form at almost right angles to the main army positions, since his men were to hold the flank from the Hagerstown road to the Potomac. Topographically the lay of land westward from the Pike toward what looked like the distant Potomac bottoms offered some tactical advantages to a defender— but also to an attacking force. Using the Dunkard Church as the point of orientation, Jackson noticed a heavy woods some two hundred yards north—the "West Wood" stretched for some distance westward and protected a cornfield just north of the church grounds. A rolling swale of ground sloped downward in front of the church, broke upward toward the southern edge of the woods and continued east across the Pike to a ridge which dominated the area around the church. The woods and the high ground must be held, since indications were that the enemy would come at the gray lines from the northeast, probably launching their drive from another patch of woods some distance to the north and east—the "East Wood," as it came to be called. To hold the Hagerstown Pike and to connect with Hood's left, Jackson posted his own division with its right on the road and its left in the woods to the west. Jubal Early's brigade deployed to form the left flank element of Jackson's infantry line, and Stuart's cavalry assisted in prolonging the line toward the Potomac. Behind Jackson's division, commanded by Gen. J. R. Jones, Lawton's troops stacked arms and rested near the Dunkard Church. Sporadic artillery firing along Jackson's lines did not seriously hamper deployment and the men got into position swiftly.

Rarely had a more bedraggled and weary battle line been drawn. The forced march from Harpers Ferry had been hot, and dust caked on the sweating faces of the infantry. Green corn and apples had been the ration—and even these were scarce. Straggling had so reduced Jackson's command that the famous old Stonewall Brigade counted only 300 muskets. The total of both Lawton's and Jones's divisions could not have been more than 5,500.[65]

As the bright September sun began to sink, Yankee artillery erupted a volcano of shells along the Confederate left and a Union skirmish line picked its way toward Hood's men. Fighting Joe Hooker had attacked. Hood's men soon were hotly engaged and the high-pitched rattle of musketry could be heard above the cannon. As it grew dark, the battle slowed and then ceased, although artillery growled long after nightfall.

Old Jack had placed his men, had observed the artillery firing on his front and listened to Hood's battle. When at last he concluded that there would be no general assault, he found a large tree with roots which would serve as a pillow, stretched out and was asleep. Soon he was awakened by John Hood with an urgent request. His men, he said, were tired and half-starved; they must have some rest and a chance to cook rations. Lee had no men to put in their place, but had suggested Hood ask Jackson if he could spare a force to take Hood's position in the line. Yes, he could send Lawton's men, but first Hood must promise to support these troops on call. Agreed. At 10 P.M. Hood's jaded boys retired behind the line, as Lawton came up. It was a bad night for sleeping. Nervous picket firing stuttered along the front; an occasional shell crashed behind the lines. Men slept under arms.[66]

One question stood uppermost in Lee's mind that night: Where were the three absent divisions?

The weary army woke at 3 A.M. on the seventeenth—skirmish lines were ablaze. As soon as the gunners could see anything at all, cannon jumped and flamed all along the left of Lee's front. Awake instantly, Jackson went to his embattled command. Artillery in front heaved masses of shells at his men, but a battery he had posted on his left, along with his guns in front, fought back grimly. From beyond the Antietam came the most damaging fire; long-range Federal ordnance raked Jones's and Early's positions in reverse while bluecoated infantry deployed to attack.[67] Hooker, wasting no daylight, had his First Corps in motion.

Almost before anyone could tell what had happened, Harry Hays's and Lawton's brigades were wrecked, Jones's division was mowed down like wheat. Hood must come up! A staff officer galloped madly to find him, panting, "General Lawton sends his compliments with the request that you come at once to his support." "To arms" sounded, and Hood's men dashed for the front, only to find that the front had all but disappeared. Hood saw Lawton, badly wounded, being carried to the rear by litter bearers. Where were his men? Soon Hays could be seen, rallying a tiny group—about forty men—and trying to stem the steady advance of the serried ranks in blue. Hays's "brigade" had no cartridges, but the gallant Harry would stand. Suggesting he go to the rear to regroup, Hood deployed his 2,000 men. Faced with masses so heavy, Hood saw but one thing to do—charge.

On Jones's front the "storm of shell and grape" tore huge gaps in his 1,600 men, but he held the remnants together for an advance. Before he could get it going, a shell exploded over his head and so stunned him that he turned the command over to the competent Brigadier General Starke. The din of battle reached fantastic heights. Citizens in the little hamlet of Shepherdstown, across the Potomac a few miles west, distinctly heard "the incessant explosions of artillery, the shrieking whistles of the shells, and the sharper, deadlier, more thrilling roll of musketry; while every now and then the echo of some charging cheer would come, borne by the wind, and as the human voice pierced that demoniacal clangor we would catch our breath and listen. . . ." [68]

To the men fighting under Starke it seemed, suddenly, as if the "air was alive with shells" [69] and as if the blue infantry covered all the ground to the north. Relentlessly, doggedly, Hooker pushed on.

Watching his command evaporating before his eyes, Jackson, too, noted the "terrific storm of shell, canister, and musketry." [70] Starke still held some organization, and would try to attack; Hood's men had formed a thin gray line and were moving forward through a cornfield now reddened with gore. Appalling news heightened the crisis. Starke had fallen, and Colonel Grisby now commanded a corporal's guard passing for a division. Were there any reserves to throw in? Riding swiftly to the left, Jackson sought the redoubtable Jubal Early, anchoring firm the left with his men and Stuart's. More than half of Lawton's and Hays's brigades were gone, more than a third of Trimble's—every regimental commander save two in those brigades had been killed or wounded. Early must take command of the fragments, he must stem the avalanche! Instantly he went, taking all his brigade save a small force which he left to help Stuart.

As Early moved to his right, the scene greeting his gaze was ghastly. Every Confederate brigade which had stood between his old position on the left and the Hagerstown road had been brushed away—not more than a handful of organized troops faced the Federals. And the enemy appeared to be receiving reinforcements!

Eastward, by the Dunkard Church, Hood's attack developed. Aiming straight for the gap in the Confederate front—a chasm, it appeared, on either side of the Dunkard Church—Hood's men advanced. He got some help. On his right, D. H. Hill's men, shaken but still there, fired into the awesome ranks of Union attackers. On the left Old Jube formed a semi-line almost perpendicular to Hood's. The Federals were marching into a box with Early on their right, Hood in front, and Hill on the left. Confederate bullets cut them down in windrows.

An exciting and crucial moment! Jackson, commanding his field with great calm, sent Sandie Pendleton to Hood with a question: How stood the field? Could anything be done to help? Hood was wading in, fighting lustily, when Pendleton arrived. Barely taking his eyes from his men, he sent back this message: "Tell General Jackson, unless I get reinforcements I must be forced back, but I am going on while I can!" While Sandie retraced his route through a hail of death, Hood went on. The Federals caught in the pocket retired and Hood pushed them back farther.[71] Soon he ran into still hotter fire from Mansfield's XII Corps (formerly Banks's), which had replaced Hooker's in the advance. Finally, outnumbered and almost out of ammunition, Hood's line stalled—he must hold on!

Pendleton raced to Old Jack with Hood's soldierly message. Good, good. But who could be sent to reinforce him? On to General Lee, Pendleton must ride—Lee would have to send more men. Already John Walker had been ordered from right to left, and Lee promised to send McLaws's men, just arrived. Hood, Early, and the heroic fragments under Grigsby and Leroy Stafford were promised help—if they could last long enough. These patched-up forces beat off Mansfield's attack, though they were not aware of it.

When Old Jack heard that Walker's division had been ordered to the left, he sent a staff officer to meet it and to direct Walker in support of Hood. The enemy must be driven from the West Wood, the key to the battlefield. As Walker moved toward the Dunkard Church, Hood retired to refill his cartridge boxes, still waving his colors and showing a bold front. Around 10:30 A.M. Walker and some of McLaws's men reached the front, and found themselves heavily engaged with the fresh Union II Corps under "Daddy" Sumner. The front had steadied somewhat, and Sumner soon slowed, stopped, then retired.[72] When the surge of bluecoats ended, the Confederates were back to their original positions—a point Jackson proudly recorded in his later report of the battle.[73]

Every man had been thrown in now, and if the enemy brought up new hordes there seemed little hope of saving the army. But miraculously the pressure on Jackson eased, the action shifted. The second battle of Sharpsburg began.

Now it was up to D. H. Hill. McClellan had changed the point of attack, throwing fresh columns at the Confederate center, where the line stood weakest. Again the dead strewed the field in staggering numbers, piling up in heaps along what came to be known as the "Bloody Lane." Hill's line broke, all but disappeared. Loath to believe his men would let the army down, Harvey personally rallied a handful and, aided by artillery and the shining courage of the Twenty-seventh North Carolina and, Third Arkansas Regiments, stemmed the assault. Curiously enough, on Hill's front one of the Union divisions seeking to divide him from Jackson's lines had been commanded by Maj. Gen. William Henry French, a man whose memory apparently was long.

So hard and stern were the Federal drives at the center that Lee sought desperately for a way to ease the pressure. A diversion might do it, but where—and, more important, how? Jackson's front had temporarily calmed. Could he lead an attack on the Federal right, the flank which appeared not to touch the Potomac? A little after noon, Jackson, sitting his horse in the rear of McLaws's lines, calmly plucking apples from a tree and munching slowly, talked with General Walker. With one leg casually thrown over the pommel of his saddle, Jackson appeared utterly unaware of a battle in progress. The apple absorbed his attention; he ignored the roar of guns, the flicking of branches, the presence of troops. Between bites, he queried, "Can you spare me a regiment and a battery?" Walker could. Jackson then said that he was trying to scratch together a force of about 5,000 men. Stuart would be put in command of it, and he would try to turn the Union right. Fiercely swinging his foot back into the stirrup, he announced, "We'll drive McClellan into the Potomac." [74]

Nothing came of the scheme. Stuart scouted along with Jackson, and they regretfully concluded that Union artillery thoroughly ruled out any turning movement. Bad news, for the battle had shifted further to Lee's right and by four o'clock it was all but lost.

On Longstreet's extreme right, where scarcely more than a reinforced skirmish line held Burnside's Bridge over the Antietam, the third battle of Sharpsburg had opened. At 3 P.M. waves of bluecoats advanced behind a ripple of skirmishers, moving steadily, battle flags arrayed, up the slopes guarding the southeastern flank of Sharpsburg. D. R. Jones deployed his division, trying to give his 2,460 men every advantage of ground and artillery protection. But against this screen in gray came Gen. Ambrose E. Burnside's IX Army Corps, 13,000 strong.[75] Jones could count on Lilliputian reinforcement. Robert Toombs's brigade, which had been holding the approaches to the bridge, was falling back on the Confederate line near the Hagerstown road south of Sharpsburg. Lee ordered up all the batteries he could find—even from as far away as Jackson's front—in support of Jones. As the blue infantry plodded up the slope, Confederate gunners switched to canister—each bark of a gun sprayed lethal doses of lead into the oncoming ranks. Infantry opened fire. The Yankee wave crested, paused. If only Jones could hold awhile longer!

Down that lonesome, empty road toward Shepherdstown—the road which Lee searched so longingly that afternoon—rose a column of dust. A. P. Hill was coming. If he had known at that moment of Powell Hill's incredible march, even Old Jack might have forgiven him his transgressions. Moving like a raging Mars along his sweating, dust-grimed line, Hill's red battle shirt seemed everywhere. He had learned from Stonewall, admit it or not. Close up, men, close up. Press on! With each roar of battle borne to his ears from afar, Hill's anxiety shortened his patience a little more. This time there was no stickler to tell him to keep his marching schedule—anyone who slowed felt the point of Powell Hill's saber. Forward! And while he fought the heat, the choking dust, and the numbing force of fatigue, the Army of Northern Virginia balanced on the thin edge of catastrophe.

On Jones's front, everything poised for a final decision: it was one of those moments when fate seems to stand off briefly to gaze at its handiwork and choose sides. Hope almost vanished, even in the stanchest and truest of the dogged wraiths in gray. For Marse Robert they had done all they could, but still the enemy lines inched forward. Now they were in the outskirts of the town; soon they would be swarming over the Shepherdstown road, and then. . . .

Batteries careened into position on the right. Direct to General Lee rode Hill, whose men that day proved their right to the *nom de guerre* "The Light Division," proved they belonged to the Army of the Valley. Although Lee had borne the approach of doom with characteristic calm, none could miss the vast relief with which he greeted General Hill.[76] The troops were almost at hand; Lee directed that they go in on the right —there would be no time for rest, even after a punishing pace for seventeen miles.[77] When all Hill's men were in line they would number no more than 3,000, but the added strength at the crucial point ought to turn the tide.

So it did. Burnside, watching the course of his attack, noted carefully the arrival of A. P. Hill [78] and soon felt the effect of a strong counterattack. From the heights to the right of Jones's spent men, a long line of tattered demons poured downhill; then it came, that high-pitched, vibrating Rebel yell. Back went the Union flags, farther back, until they huddled beneath the cover of heavy metal along Antietam. The day was done—and it had not been lost.

With nightfall the firing died away. Darkness screened the macabre, restless battlefield. Men, powder-burned, begrimed into grotesque caricatures, moved drunkenly seeking their companies and their fallen comrades. All around rustled the peculiar movement of a field after the slaughter ceases. The piteous sounds of the wounded—"water, water"— floated in on the warm night breeze.

Thirty miles from the bloody slopes of Sharpsburg, bedridden Dick Ewell thought of the safety of a comrade. Recuperating from a leg amputation, Old Baldy had heard the grim din of the battle. All through the day he grew increasingly restless, in an anguish of fear lest something happen to Stonewall. If he fell, Ewell told his brother, the Confederacy might fall with him—he might be "crazy as a March Hare," but method surely lurked in Old Jack's madness.[79] Ewell's affectionate concern had been shared by many who came in contact with Jackson that day as he recklessly exposed himself commanding his front. But it was a strange day for Deacon Jackson. That day when the God of War reigned furiously along the Potomac, the Lord of Hosts came close to him. As he ranged his thin and desperate line, urging here, encouraging or ordering there, he gave no thought to safety. In a hail of death unprecedented in the memory of the army, Old Jack moved in an aura of invulnerability. Never before in his many battles had he had the feeling that came over him when the skirmishers began to quarrel on the morning of the seventeenth. God would protect him as he rode in the shadow of death, "no harm would befall him." And as he surveyed the carnage on that gruesome field in the evening, still the feeling lingered. Across the leveled stumps of corn lay the Amalekites—and Joshua stood unscathed.[80]

From the foreboding West Wood on the north to the bloodstained slopes south of Sharpsburg, more than 10,000 grayclads lay dead or wounded. Even more than Second Manassas, this had been a battle saved by the "blessing of Providence." Miraculous it was that anyone had lived through the day.

One thing remained to be done. Jackson rode to the field headquarters of General Lee. Assembled there were Old Pete, whose doughty fighting had steadied the right center all day, D. R. Jones, Hood, Early, D. H. and A. P. Hill. Each officer had his own long toll of the dead and the dying—the army stood bleeding and sorely tried. A third of Lee's troops were casualties. Lee listened and pondered. Finally he concluded that he could not launch an offensive the next day, but he was certain that the army could hold its lines. Preparations must be made. The Army of Northern Virginia would present a closed front to Little Mac in the morning; if he had a stomach for fighting, he would get it.[81]

Jackson's camp for the night was an open field near town. All around lights of litter bearers winked as the doctors sought to aid the wounded. Men cooked rations near dead comrades—war had become grim.

Next day both armies faced each other with McClellan massing as if anticipating an attack. One further effort Lee made to turn the Federal right. Jackson and Stuart again advanced to scout, and still the Union guns covered the approach; it would be suicidal to hurl men at the bristling Union cannon. Faithful Jed Hotchkiss made a reconnaissance on the other side of the Potomac, and sent a sketch of the strong enemy lines and pickets to Jackson.[82] Sadly Jackson reported, and sadly Lee abandoned hope of a counterthrust.[83]

Still no movement from the Yankee lines. McClellan waited for reinforcements and sought to contain Lee's army. Although some stragglers had come up during the night, Lee could not afford a waiting game at the odds offered. To Jackson General Lee put the problem, suggested that retreat would be the better part of prudence, and asked Old Jack's opinion. Jackson had seen enough of the Federal positions that day to conclude that further delay might be fatal. The army ought to cross into Virginia. And although Sharpsburg had not been a victory, he told Lee he thought it "was better to have fought in Maryland than to have left it without a struggle." [84] But the army must move now and move fast.

Suddenly the most important man in Jackson's command was Maj. John Harman, the reluctant quartermaster.

17

THE SECOND CORPS

Jackson looked on disapprovingly. A jam of wagons, caissons, guns, and men choked Boteler's Ford on the Potomac. As he sat his horse in the middle of the river and watched the retreat of the army, Stonewall heard an uninterrupted stream of highly original blasphemy scorching the rain-cooled night air. No mistake—Maj. John Harman must be near at hand, "cussing" the wagons and mules across the river. Such language from the incorrigible quartermaster came as no surprise, but it always bothered Old Jack. Try as he might, he could not break the major's habit. Nothing else would move a stubborn mule, Harman asserted, and had more than once proved his point.[1]

No one tried to halt Harman's invective that night of September 18–19, for the safety of the Army of Northern Virginia depended on getting men and equipment over the river before McClellan could launch a pursuit. Lee shared Jackson's watery vantage point, and both generals urged the men to push on, close up. When John Walker's division crossed in the morning of the nineteenth, the division commander greeted Lee cheerfully. Returning the greeting, Lee inquired "what was still behind." Only Walker's ambulances and a single battery. "Thank God," said the commanding general.[2]

The army needed a breathing space and consequently McClellan must be held north of the Potomac. General William N. Pendleton, commanding the reserve artillery, received orders to place batteries along the bluffs guarding the ford and to blow back any Yankee attempt to cross. He would have an infantry force to support his guns. While Pendleton held back the enemy, Lee's spent troops moved slowly toward Martinsburg, camping for the night a few miles beyond the river.[3]

Men fell where they halted, and slept—there would be no battle in the morning; they could rest secure.

Headquarters of what remained of the Army of the Valley were established in a field about four miles south of the river.[4] Sometime after midnight an almost incoherent General Pendleton rushed in with a report that a disaster had occurred along the river. Federals had forced their way over, had brushed aside Pendleton's infantry support—which he had frittered away with incredible incapacity—and had captured every one of the army's reserve guns! No message imaginable could have more thoroughly alarmed Professor Jackson. All the army's guns lost? If true, McClellan could push on swiftly, bring Lee to a stand, and blast him to pieces while the Confederates could fight back with only limited artillery cover. How large was the enemy force taking the guns? Pendleton could not say definitely, but he supposed not large. No matter. Waiting for no orders, asking no advice, Jackson sent instructions to A. P. Hill. The Light Division would march for Boteler's Ford and drive back the Federals already on the Southern side. Even if the guns could not be retaken, the Union beachhead must be eliminated before McClellan had time to consolidate.

While Hill sped his men toward the river, Jackson rode far ahead to reconnoiter. When Hill's men arrived, Old Jack knew what had to be done. Swiftly, tersely, his battle order passed along the line. Harvey Hill rode to Jackson to report his division on hand in reserve, and Old Jack told him quietly: "With the blessing of God they will soon be driven back." Two lines of battle formed in the early daylight and charged into what Powell Hill described as "the most tremendous fire of artillery I ever saw." The Federals tried to turn the Confederate left, it was extended, and the men dashed on. It seemed to their proud commander that each man of the Light Division "felt that the fate of the army was centered in himself." Unaided by a single Southern cannon, the gray infantry soon drove the bluecoats into the Potomac. As the splashing, yelling, floundering men threshed frantically for the Union shore, Hill's men coolly shot them by the dozens. "An appalling scene of the destruction of human life," Jackson noted.[5]

When the shore again rested safely in Confederate hands, examination showed that Pendleton's blunder had been rectified. Instead of losing some forty guns, he had lost only four. Hill's brilliant attack had saved not only the army but also the reserve artillery—but at a cost of 261 casualties.

An obscure little action, Boteler's Ford, or Shepherdstown, became the center of a considerable controversy. D. H. Hill, whose division had arrived in support of A. P. Hill but had not been engaged, contended that Jackson's initiative had saved the day. Lee, Hill maintained, had been so unstrung by Pendleton's midnight message that his only thought had been to form a defensive line with Longstreet's men. Harvey Hill could hardly believe his ears—a line of battle four miles behind the river would not save the artillery and would give McClellan a chance to get his whole army over. And Lee did not plan even that action until morning. "The result," wrote Hill later, "would have been the most disastrous conceivable. . . . I have sometimes thought that the Army of N. Va would almost have ceased to have an organized existence but for this splendid movement." As far as Hill could see, Jackson's swift action, taken without waiting to consult Lee, plus his "genius" in selecting A. P. Hill's relatively fresh division, had saved Lee's army and his reputation.[6]

Ragged, footsore, and incredibly dirty, Jackson's and Longstreet's infantry desperately needed time to rest, to bathe, and to obtain new clothes. Fortunately Little Mac showed no inclination to try another thrust across the Potomac, and it seemed that there would be at least a few weeks of leisure. In this time the Army of Northern Virginia might be refitted and reorganized: stragglers could be rounded up, sick and wounded could be sent back to the ranks from hospitals, various shattered units could be recruited once again. For a few delightful days joyous men splashed and swam in the cool and beautiful Opequon Creek, not far from Martinsburg. Human beings began to emerge from the encrusted dirt and dust of Maryland and Northern Virginia. Battalions of vermin were killed off as the army tried to delouse itself. Something like regular rations helped to boost the wilted spirits of men who had departed from Maryland after a drawn battle. Slowly the army revived, began to look better and show a return of morale. But a tremendous job of reorganization faced Lee and his two "wing" commanders, Jackson and Longstreet.[7]

After a week's stay along the Opequon, Lee took the army ten miles south of Martinsburg to new campsites at Bunker Hill. Here, on the main road from the Potomac to Winchester, a good highway increased the efficiency of supply agencies; more food, clothing, and munitions could reach the army. Lee and his wing commanders devoted much time to improving the commissary and quartermaster operations in the various divisions.[8] As stragglers were rounded up, in response to the none too gentle efforts of strong provost guards,[9] increased amounts of matériel were needed. Jackson noticed with obvious concern that many of his men were without shoes, that the supply of blankets fell far below the number required, and that the increase of manpower from returning stragglers and returning convalescents brought on a shortage of arms. Reporting these deficiencies to General Lee, Jackson firmly requested that every effort be made to supply them; most important in rebuilding the morale of a wearied army were the small things, the things which Old Jack always watched carefully. A good campsite near water, fair clothes, a respectable pair of brogans, a knapsack, and a blanket roll—not important, perhaps, to an officer with a Negro servant, but all that stood between a Johnny Reb and the indignity of poverty.

The general's own military life seemed to be lived in much the same manner as that of his men. His dirty uniform and casual soft hat—which at length replaced his famous old cap—reflected none of the "brass" which some generals loved. His camp equipment could be carried easily in part of a wagon, and even the paraphernalia of Valley District Headquarters seemed invariably pared to a minimum. Because he understood the personal privations of his amazing infantry and lived so much like them, his men developed increasing affection for Old Jack. They adored him in a peculiar way. They feared his wrath, they sweated under his iron discipline, and at times they disliked him intensely for tolerating nothing less than their utmost efforts. But at the same time, they held him in an adoring sort of awe. There was nobody in the army quite like him. He worked his men like fiends, and in return he gave them victory. Around him clung an aura of invincibility which his men shared and in which the whole country stoutly believed.[10] To fight for Old Jack was a mark of distinction, elevating his men a cut above other Confederates, whether the others admitted it or not—which is why, when a wild, joyous shout ran through the camps of the Army of the Valley, the men would exclaim: "Boys, look out! Here's 'Old Jack' or a rabbit!"[11]

Jackson always found that strict discipline did more for the morale of his men than anything else. No sooner were the troops in camp near Bunker Hill than he renewed his usual regimen of hard daily drills. Then, too, while his troops were drilling, they were not getting into the many various types of camp mischief which sometimes appalled regimental and brigade commanders.

While the physical well-being of the men remained uppermost in the mind of Jackson, he fully agreed with General Lee's views on the crippling effect of straggling[12] and sought to prevent it within his own command. Lee suggested strong disciplinary measures, and Jackson put them into effect. Deserters and AWOL's he thought should be shot,[13] although he tempered justice with mercy in cases involving veterans whose records showed previous devotion to duty.[14]

Under his firm hand, morale returned—as it did to the entire army —and in a few weeks ranks were filling well with returnees and conscripts. As long as Major Harman and Major Hawks could work their wonders, Jackson's men would not suffer unduly, although all of Lee's men were beginning to feel the pinch of attrition. From Staunton came some supplies of blankets, shoes, and arms, and with these the rehabilitation of the enlisted men appeared well on the way to completion.

But rehabilitation of the men amounted to only half the problem of reorganization. The campaigns in Virginia and Maryland had shattered the officer corps, had wrecked the command structure. Where were new generals, colonels, and company officers to be found? From both Jackson and Longstreet, Lee asked for recommendations; new generals of all grades, colonels, all ranks, would have to be selected. Jackson pondered the query. His top officers had been mowed down in shocking numbers and he would have to have at least two major generals. Instantly he thought of one who wanted the rank and who had earned it—Isaac R. Trimble. In recommending him, Jackson praised his attack on Manassas Junction in rare terms indeed: "I regard that day's achievement as the most brilliant that has come under my observation during the present war." [15]

One other officer under Old Jack's immediate command had earned promotion—Jubal Early. At Sharpsburg he had assumed division command with aplomb, and had delivered an attack which won Jackson's honest admiration.[16] Cool and determined in battle, Early appeared to have the executive capacity for permanent division leadership.

Outside of his own command Jackson also had a candidate for a major general's stars and wreath. It was unusual that he went outside the confines of his own divisions, but John Hood's steadfast gallantry on the left at Sharpsburg had gained "my admiration." Not telling Hood, of course, Jackson wrote a strong letter supporting his promotion.[17]

To take charge of the weakened but still gallant Stonewall Brigade, Jackson nominated his assistant adjutant general, Maj. Elisha Franklin Paxton. Paxton's conduct under fire while assisting Jackson on many fields convinced Old Jack that any brigade, even the immortal Stonewall, would be well handled in his charge.[18]

Long lists of suggested promotions to fill other vacancies went from Lee to the War Department where action, it was hoped, would be swift. The command structure had to be patched up quickly, else the whole army reorganization would lag.

Most important in the over-all reorganization was a new idea of command which had gradually been evolving. The scheme came partly from Federal experience, partly from Confederate, and partly from the changing nature of war. President Davis, the Adjutant General, and the Secretary of War had at last come to the conclusion that military operations were now so complex as to make the older methods of command obsolete. No longer could isolated generals fight isolated actions with individual brigades or divisions. By October, 1862, it would be impossible to fight a battle with the unit organization in effect during the Seven Days' Battles. The grim efficiency which Lee's charge at Second Manassas illustrated and the tenacious defense of Sharpsburg's heights came only from a businesslike organization of brigades into divisions and of divisions into wings, or "Corps." The wings were commanded by senior major generals, who were able to achieve coordination and unity in the activities of the various divisions. This sort of Corps organization had already been used with good effect in the Union Army. Since war now was a thing of mass fighting machines, run by governmental corporations, the time had come to recognize the change in command structure. Fortunately Congress agreed, and on September 28 Davis wrote Lee:

> Authority has been given to appoint commanders of *corps d'armee*, with the rank of lieutenant-general. You have two officers now commanding several divisions, and may require more. Please send to me, as soon as possible, the names of such as you prefer for lieutenant-general; also those for major-general and brigadier-general to the extent required for the organization of your army.[19]

Happy that Congress was catching up with reality, Lee had no trouble deciding who to name for the rank of lieutenant general. Longstreet without a doubt should be promoted. His steady, dogged improvement in field command and in administration of several divisions showed his inherent competence, and on him Lee increasingly relied. Jackson, too, had been commanding several divisions and had served as commander of a separate army. In the valley he had demonstrated amazing strategic and tactical capacity—facts which appear not to have impressed Lee as much at the time as they did later. He had not done well on the Peninsula, but his conduct of operations against Pope at Cedar Mountain and the magnificent flank march to Manassas Junction followed by the great stand at Groveton stamped Stonewall as a general to rank with the best.

Somewhere in the back of Lee's mind there had apparently been a lingering doubt. When he sent in his recommendations, Lee made no comment about Longstreet other than to recommend him for promotion, but about Jackson he wrote: "My opinion of the merits of General Jackson has been greatly enhanced during this expedition. He is true, honest, and brave; has a single eye to the good of the service, and spares no exertion to accomplish his object."[20] What prompted this caveat? Had Lee felt that Jackson's ambition was as limitless as Dick Taylor believed? Did he think that Jackson did poorly as a subordinate because he longed for an independence which would increase his fame? Whatever the cause of Lee's previous lurking distrust, Jackson's singleminded efficiency during the Second Manassas, Harpers Ferry, and Sharpsburg battles had removed it. Lee could hardly have felt anything but gratitude for the Confederacy's hero who in the face of dispersal of force had salvaged something from the Maryland campaign and saved the Army of Northern Virginia.

Promotions were made swiftly, and as of October 11, 1862, Jackson became a lieutenant general, to rank from the previous day. The new lieutenant generals and the Corps organization were not announced to the army until November 6,[21] and in the meantime Jackson reorganized his own headquarters. James Power Smith became an aide-de-camp; a new chief signal officer appeared on the headquarters list as the general sought to improve the signal service throughout his Corps; and arrangements were made to permit Kyd Douglas to return to his company as its newly elected captain.[22]

An unfortunate episode broke the routine of administration while Jackson's men were at Bunker Hill. A. P. Hill, still smarting under Jackson's charges of neglect of duty, wrote General Lee seeking a court of inquiry. He had, he said, "been treated with injustice and censured and punished at the head of my command." These things should either be explained or dismissed. Never had he been furnished with a statement of how he had neglected his duty, which he thought equally unfair. The letter, of course, went through Jackson's hands. It put him in an embarrassing spot. Hill had done so well after having been restored to command before Harpers Ferry that Jackson had lost much of his distrust of the Light Division's leader. Still, since Hill now made it part of Lee's business, Jackson felt he had to say something about the charges. He did not draw up a formal statement but summarized the episodes of alleged dereliction and concluded by saying that he found his orders much better carried out by Hill's temporary replacement.

Pained at the revival of controversy and at the appearance of it in the open, Lee did his best to mollify A. P. Hill. In an endorsement on Hill's request for a court, Lee said that since Hill could now see from Jackson's remarks why he had been arrested and where Jackson fancied neglect of duty, instances, he added, "which from an officer of his [Hill's] character could not be intentional and I feel assured will never be repeated, I see no advantage to the service in further investigating this matter nor could it without detriment be done at this time." [23]

When Hill read Lee's note he was more insulted than ever—the commanding general appeared to believe Jackson's charges. "If," he wrote Lee, "Genl. Jackson had accorded me the courtesy of asking an explanation of each instance of neglect of duty as it occurred, I think that even he would have been satisfied and the necessity avoided of keeping a black list against me. . . ." If Jackson's charges were true, Hill asserted, then he surely was unfit to command the Light Division, but "if untrue, then censure should be passed upon the officer who abuses his authority to punish, and then sustains his punishment by making loose charges against an officer who has done and is doing his utmost to make his troops efficient." A list of charges and specifications against Stonewall was sent to Lee.[24]

Things had gotten out of hand. Unwilling yet to crack down on

Hill, Jackson took the time to draw up formal charges and specifications, sent them to Army Headquarters, but added a note of caution:

As the object in arresting Gen. Hill, which was to secure his stricter compliance with orders, has been effected, I do not consider further action on my part necessary, and consequently he has not been re-arrested nor furnished with a copy of the charges and specifications. Should Gen. Hill be re-arrested upon this charge of neglect of duty I will send him a copy of the charges and specifications.[25]

In further explanation, Jackson said that no black list had been kept against Hill and that Hill certainly ought to know why he had been arrested —"he had ample opportunity of knowing his neglect of duty." Stung by Hill's language, Jackson's was equally stinging.[26]

Months later Lee gazed at the pile of manuscript on his desk. His two good generals would not be placated. What could be done? To Hill he wrote again, saying that he doubted Jackson had perverted his power of arrest. By January, 1863, the commanding general had forgotten some of the details involved in the countergrievances, but decided that

upon examining the charges ... I am of the opinion that the interests of the service do not require that they should be tried, and have, therefore, returned them to General Jackson with an indorsement to that effect. I hope you will concur with me that their further prosecution is unnecessary, so far as you are concerned, and will be of no advantage to the service.[27]

Powell Hill must have been wearing his red battle shirt when he fired his final epistolary blast in reply to Lee. As the months had passed, he had grown increasingly wrathful against Jackson and wrote that he had never questioned the right of a commanding officer to arrest any officer under him and to release him without filing charges

provided the *party arrested consented thereto.*—Otherwise an engine of tyrrany [sic] is placed in the hands of Commanding Officers, to be exercised at their will, to gratify passions or whims, and against which there is no appeal. In my own case, the Commanding General having returned the charges preferred against me by General Jackson without trial is a rebuke to him, but not as public as was General Jackson's exercise of power toward me. The general must acknowledge that if the charges preferred against me by General Jackson were true, that I do not deserve to command a division in this army; if they are untrue, then General Jackson deserves a rebuke as notorious as the arrest.

What rankled most was Jackson's callous assertion that the arrest had produced the desired effect. "I beg leave," frothed Hill,

to disclaim any credit which General Jackson may have given me for the good results of his punishment, as to my better behaviour thereafter, and that its only effect has been to cause me to preserve every scrap of paper received from corps headquarters, to guard myself against any new eruptions from this slumbering volcano.[28]

So bitter did the trouble between Jackson and Hill become that only the most formal communications passed between them, and when they met—which they both appeared to do their best to avoid—they merely saluted each other stiffly.[29] The staffs of both generals regretted the whole thing exceedingly and hoped that the chill would thaw in time.[30] Hotchkiss summed up the problem: "I hope all may blow by. Gen. Hill is a brave officer but perhaps too quick to resent seeming over-stepping of authority.... General Jackson sincerely intends to do his whole duty."

General Hill seemed never to appreciate the fact that Old Jack did not jump at the chance to press for a court-martial. Lee probably noted this indication of growth on Jackson's part; when the good of the service would not be advanced by indulging his addiction to legal forms, Jackson counseled moderation.

Not everything at Bunker Hill had such an unpleasant air as the altercation with Hill. While Jackson devoted himself to clothing his ragged troops, Jeb Stuart thought of clothing Old Jack. One afternoon in late September Major von Borcke, Stuart's jolly staff assistant, rode to Jackson's headquarters bearing a gift. General Stuart, Von Borcke reported, had been concerned about the loss of buttons on Jackson's coat—the ladies at Martinsburg had taken too great a toll and the garment barely held together.[31] As a remedy, Stuart offered a new and shiny coat, gleaming with brass buttons, just arrived from a Richmond tailor. Old Jack looked at the "buttons and sheeny facings and gold lace," and Von Borcke could scarcely hold back hearty guffaws "at the modest confusion with which the hero of many battles regarded the fine uniform from many points of view, scarcely daring to touch it, and at the quiet way in which, at last, he folded it up carefully, and deposited it in his portmanteau." In a quiet and embarrassed voice Jackson said: "Give Stuart my best thanks, my dear Major—the coat is much too handsome for me, but I shall take the best care of it, and shall prize it highly as a souvenir. And now let us have some dinner."

Von Borcke would not be foiled. Stuart, he said, would demand to know if the coat fitted well. Smiling, Jackson tried it on—an excellent fit. So good did it look and so nice did it feel, that Old Jack wore it out of his tent as he and Von Borcke walked to supper. The staff could scarcely believe their eyes. Jim was bringing a turkey to the table when he first saw the general, and almost dropped the precious bird. Word spread rapidly, and in no time at all "soldiers came running by hundreds to the spot, desirous of seeing their beloved Stonewall in his new attire." A temptation, indeed, the coat would have to be worn sparingly lest the simpler things become too plain.[32] A note of thanks went to Stuart:

> Near Bunker Hill,
> Sept. 30, 1862

General,
  I am much obliged to you for the beautiful coat you have presented to me. Your injunction will be heeded. My lost buttons have been replaced. We learn by experience. When you come near don't forget to call & see me.
  Your Much attached friend,
  T. J. Jackson [33]

Stuart was always glad to visit Jackson, whom he admired and adored. And Old Jack had an affection for Stuart greater than that he felt for anyone else in the army, save possibly Ashby. When that merry jingle which surrounded Stuart wherever he went reached Jackson's quarters, Old Jack would come out and give the glittering cavalryman fond greeting.

After Stuart returned from his dashing second "ride around Mc-Clellan" on October 12, Jackson waited in great excitement for Jeb's report. Old Jack had wanted to go along, just for fun, as a private in the ranks, and had wished Stuart all the best.[34] When the victorious cavalry chief rode to Jackson's tent, he was met some forty yards in front of it by Stonewall, who exclaimed, "How do you do, Pennsylvania!" [35] "Get off and tell us about your trip. They tell me that from the time you crossed the Potomac into Maryland until you got back again you didn't sing a song or crack a joke, but that as soon as you got on Virginia soil you began to whistle 'Home, sweet Home.'" [36] Disclaiming any enemy inconvenience, Stuart doubtless regaled Jackson with the daring exploits of his troopers as they raided into Pennsylvania and went all around Little Mac.

Other examples there were of the affection between the cavalryman and the Professor of Artillery Tactics. Douglas recalled, with high glee, the night that Stuart climbed in Jackson's bed without removing anything save his saber. In the morning he arose first and was outside the tent warming himself by a fire when Old Jack emerged.

"Good morning, General Jackson," Stuart asked bravely, "how are you?"

Stonewall ran a hand through his tousled hair, and in tones of mock severity replied: "General Stuart, I'm always glad to see you here. You might select better hours sometimes, but I'm always glad to have you." Then, rubbing his calves, Jackson added, "But, General, you must not get into my bed with your boots and spurs on and ride me around like a cavalry horse all night!" [37]

Jeb Stuart's adoration of Stonewall was equaled now by that of the whole Confederacy, for by October, 1862, Jackson had become the hero of a nation. Catapulted from the uncomfortable obscurity of garrison duty in the "Old Army," he now ranked as the burning hope of the Southern cause. Anna basked in the warm glow of a country's fervent favor, and when she learned of Thomas's promotion, wrote him suggesting that she might have an article about him prepared for publication so that the Confederate people could learn more of their beloved Stonewall.

Not Thomas but Deacon Jackson replied:

Don't trouble yourself about representations that are made of your husband. These things are earthly and transitory. There are real and glorious blessings, I trust, in reserve for us beyond this life. It is best for us to keep our eyes fixed upon the throne of God and the realities of a more glorious existence beyond the verge of time. It is gratifying to be beloved and to have our conduct approved by our fellow-men, but this is not worthy to be compared with the glory that is in reservation for us in the presence of our glorified Redeemer. . . . I would not relinquish the slightest diminution of that glory for all this world can give. My prayer is that such may ever be the feeling of my heart. It appears to me that it would be better for you not to have anything written about me. Let us follow the teaching of inspiration—'Let another man praise thee, and not thine own mouth: a stranger, and not thine own lips.' I appreciate the loving interest that prompted such a desire in my precious darling.[38]

And because he meant each word of this—every word reflecting the eternal struggle he waged against himself—Anna would not have been surprised to hear about an episode which occurred to Thomas while his men were engaged in tearing up the B&O Railroad in the vicinity of Martinsburg. The perceptive and socially conscious Capt. Charles Blackford, who commanded a cavalry picket guarding the rail wreckers, recorded it:

My picket was stationed at the house of a section foreman, whose young and pretty wife was a great rebel. Her husband, whatever his sympathies, was in the employ of the railroad company and had thought it best to remain inside the Federal lines. She was quite a refined person for one of her position and more educated than might be expected. She was kind to us and delighted above all things in hearing of Lee, Jackson and Stuart, for whom she had the most romantic fascination.

It happened that on the second day there General Jackson and one or two of his staff rode out to inspect the enemy's position from our post. He stood and gazed from his horse through his glass long at the enemy's position, during which time our pretty hostess found out who it was and seemed almost overcome with the double emotion of awe and admiration. She watched him earnestly, and just as she thought he was through and might go off, she ran into the house and brought out her baby, quite a handsome boy of about eighteen months and handing it up to the General asked him to bless it for her. He seemed no more surprised at this strange request than Queen Elizabeth at being asked to touch for the 'King's Evil.' He turned to her with great earnestness and, with a pleasant expression on his stern face, took the child in his arms, held it to his breast, closed his eyes and seemed to be, and I doubt not was, occupied for a minute or two with prayer, during which we took off our hats and the young mother leaned her head over the horse's shoulder as if uniting in the prayer. The scene was very solemn and unusual.

Blackford wished for the artist's gift at that moment, so that he might capture forever Jackson's figure bent on Little Sorrel, the pretty worshiper by his side, his soldiers in threads and patches nearby, while to one side stood the section house, its dingy gray mingling with the Rebel garb. Beyond the little group jutted the grim background of war in the form of twisted track and pyres of crossties. Autumn browns lent weird color to a moment's peace.[39] For the first time Blackford began to understand the man "whom I admired, respected but never loved."

A nation's faith in Stonewall was revealed by the floods of presents which came to his headquarters. Mrs. Graham sent up two sponge cakes from her Winchester oven, along with an invitation to visit the family soon. A Mr. Vilweg, another Winchester citizen, sent Old Jack "an excellent arm-chair for camp use," which prompted him to write Anna: "I wish I could keep it until the close of the war, as I think my *esposa* would enjoy it."[40] Handkerchiefs, gloves, and scarves came in by the dozen, but Jackson seemed most touched by a particular pair of socks. They came from faraway Tennessee and were the gift "of an old lady ...of about eighty years." Finally he had to tell Anna: "Don't send me any more socks, as the kind ladies have given me more than I could probably wear out in two years."[41] One of the most useful of presents was a roll of gray cloth which would make up into a handsome uniform. These showers of gifts prompted Thomas to give thanks where most due: "Our gracious Heavenly Father strikingly manifests his kindness to me by disposing people to bestow presents upon me."[42]

Had he read the newspapers Jackson would have seen even more impressive evidence of his hero status. Column after column in papers the length and breadth of the Confederacy told something of his life story—usually wrong—and gave glimpses of his plain living and honest piety. Nor were his praises confined to the Confederate press alone. The Northern papers lost no love on him, but their fearful speculations on his doings reflected the highest praise. Abroad, Jackson's fame had become a matter of common conversation and his exploits the subject of admiring recitation. His fame transcended that of his cause, and although he was the personal property of every Confederate he was also an international hero.

Fame brought not only presents but also visitors. Colonel Bradley

T. Johnson brought them, and they came well introduced with letters, since they were "three English gentlemen of consequence." Colonel Garnet Wolseley—later field marshal and commander in chief of the British army—and his two companions, Frank Vizetelly of the *Illustrated London News* and Francis C. Lawley of the London *Times,* first called on General Lee and then set out to see the famous Stonewall. Wolseley had come to Canada with some British troops when the *Trent* affair had threatened war with the United States, and now traveled on a leave of absence. The two correspondents were curious in line of duty, but a little beyond the line when visiting Jackson. Not knowing what to expect from the supposed Cromwell, they were pleased to be greeted warmly and with ease by the general, who bade them be seated in front of his tent.

Before they could begin questioning him, Jackson launched into a fond reminiscence of his trip to England. In particular, he said, he had been fascinated with the architecture of Durham Cathedral. Soon the visitors were listening to a learned discourse on the Bishopric of Durham, which betrayed General Jackson as a student of history. Colonel Johnson's surprise could hardly be concealed, and as Jackson "examined and cross-examined the Englishmen in detail about the cathedral and the close and the rights of the bishop," Johnson had to hide a smile. There was no chance to ask Jackson any questions about military affairs; Jackson, whose knowledge of Durham and its bishop was larger than that of his guests, kept them too busy dredging up answers to his piercing queries.

After the interview ended and the visitors were riding away in company with their guide, Johnson spoke up: "Gentlemen, you have disclosed Jackson in a new character to me, and I've been carefully observing him for a year and a half. You have made him exhibit *finesse,* for he did all the talking to keep you from asking too curious or embarrassing questions. He did not want to say anything, so he did all the talking. I never saw anything like it in him before." A hearty laugh came from the newsmen, who admitted that Old Jack had been too much for them.[43]

Underneath the polish and finesse, however, Colonel Wolseley saw a great soldier:

> With him we spent a most pleasant hour, and were agreeably surprised to find him very affable, having been led to expect that he was silent and almost morose. Dressed in his grey uniform, he looks the hero that he is; and his thin compressed lips and calm glance, which meets yours unflinchingly, give evidence of that firmness and decision of character for which he is so famous. He has a broad open forehead, from which the hair is well brushed back; a shapely nose, straight, and rather long; thin colourless cheeks, with only a very small allowance of whisker;

a cleanly-shaved upper lip and chin; and a pair of fine greyish-blue eyes, rather sunken, with overhanging brows, which intensify the keenness of his gaze, but without imparting any fierceness to it. Such are the general characteristics of his face; and I have only to add, that a smile seems always lurking about his mouth when he speaks; and that though his voice partakes slightly of that harshness which Europeans unjustly attribute to all Americans, there is much unmistakable cordiality in his manner: and to us he talked most affectionately of England, and of his brief but enjoyable sojourn there. The religious element seems strongly developed in him; and though his conversation is perfectly free from all puritanical cant, it is evident that he is a person who never loses sight of the fact that there is an omnipresent Deity ever presiding over the minutest occurrences of life, as well as over the most important. Altogether, as one of his soldiers said to me in talking of him, 'he is a glorious fellow!' and, after I left him, I felt that I had at last solved the mystery of the Stonewall Bridge [Brigade], and discovered why it was that it had accomplished such almost miraculous feats. With such a leader men would go anywhere, and face any amount of difficulties; and for myself, I believe that, inspired by the presence of such a man, I should be perfectly insensible to fatigue, and reckon upon success as a moral certainty. Whilst General Lee is regarded in the light of infallible Jove, a man to be reverenced, Jackson is loved and adored with all that childlike and trustful affection which the ancients are said to have lavished upon the particular deity presiding over their affairs. The feeling of the soldiers for General Lee resembles that which Wellington's troops entertained for him—namely, a fixed and unshakable faith in all he did, and a calm confidence of victory when serving under him. But Jackson, like Napoleon, is idolised with that intense fervour which, consisting of mingled personal attachment and devoted loyalty, causes them to meet death for his sake, and bless him when dying.[44]

No finer confirmation of Wolseley's impression could have been found than in Gen. George Pickett's supplication, made in a letter to his wife: "I only pray that God may spare him to us to see us through. If General Lee had Grant's resources he would soon end the war; but Old Jack can do it without resources."[45] Luster indeed had he brought to the name of Jackson, and in so doing fulfilled an old ambition.

No city in the whole Confederacy loved Jackson more wholeheartedly, nor felt more deeply that he was its own particular savior, than doughty, embattled Winchester. In late October when Lee took Longstreet's Corps east of the Blue Ridge, leaving Jackson's behind, headquarters of the old Valley District shifted around to several towns and finally settled in loyal Winchester.[46] The citizens went wild; Stonewall was back. Another wave of presents broke over him, and though he tried to remain aloof, he found it impossible. After all, Winchester, next to Lexington, was home, its people were old friends, and he loved them.

Not long after arriving there, Jackson wrote to tell Anna that "our headquarters are about one hundred yards from Mr. Graham's, in a large white house back of his, and in full view of our last winter's quarters, where my *esposa* used to come up and talk with me. Wouldn't it be nice for you to be here again?" [47] Since the army had long rested in the valley, Winchester's citizens thought Stonewall would be among them for a considerable time. He had been in and out of the city on several occasions, particularly on Sundays, when he attended Dr. Graham's services at the Presbyterian Church. There he seemed to attract embarrassing notice, and would doubtless have been disturbed had he been allowed to read an entry in the diary of one of Winchester's fair ladies. Dated November 16, 1862, the entry read: "Went to the Kent Street church today and heard a beautiful sermon from Mr. Graham. General Jackson was there. He sat quite near where I was. He had on a splendid new uniform, and looked like a soldier. He looked, too, so quiet and modest, and so concerned that every eye was fixed on him." [48]

Reverend Graham invited Jackson to visit the family and threatened dire things if he refused. Busy as he was, Jackson needed no urging. That visit might be the last chance he would have for some time—the army had to move, and move quickly. Lee needed the Second Corps east of the Blue Ridge. For an afternoon, though, all cares of a Corps Commander could be forgotten. Mrs. Graham had tea ready when he strode up the familiar walk on the afternoon of the twenty-first. Home again! Dinnertime found Jackson and the family saying grace together, and, as Mrs. Graham said, Anna's presence "was all that was wanting to complete the pleasure of the evening." [49]

A rare treat had been allowed the Graham children in staying up to play with the general. They climbed all over him, as usual. When she wrote Anna that night of Thomas's visit, Mrs. Graham specifically mentioned the children:

He really seemed overjoyed to see them. I never saw any one who seemed to be more delighted than he was with playing & fondling them ... and they were equally pleased—I have no doubt it was a great recreation to him—he seemed to be living over last winter again & talked a great deal about the hope of getting back to spend the winter with us in that old room.[50]

Only two topics of conversation might have marred the pleasure of the evening. Mrs. Graham seemed completely taken with how handsome he looked and how happy he seemed. Then, too, she commented that certainly he had "adulation enough to spoil him," but he bore it without any show. When he tried to turn the conversation, she found an even more embarrassing topic. Was it true? The whole town had been speculating, and she had suspected since March ... was Anna expecting?

A rumor had been circulating that Anna had already given birth to a son, a "little Stonewall," and some stories had it that the general's staff thought the boy ought "to be brought to camp and committed to their tender mercies."

A very red and much discomfited general squirmed and replied that there seemed to be some truth to the rumors but that no child had yet been born. Yes, Anna was overdue. No, he did not know the reason.[51] He had to admit, though, that a child would be the greatest of God's blessings. As the Grahams knew, both Ellie and Anna had been denied that Providential gift. If, in His mercy, this now should be the time, a humble servant in His army would be forever grateful.

Perhaps, that happy evening, Jackson recounted to the Reverend Graham how good the Lord had been to him in recent months. Not only was Anna with child, but God's bounty had also been showered on the deacon in the form of presents from so many kind people. The crowning glory, though, could be seen in the camps of the army. It had pleased God to "visit my command with the rich outpouring of His Spirit," and a great revival had blazed through the Second Corps. Through the efforts of a remarkably able minister, Reverend Dr. Joseph C. Stiles, unofficial Chaplain General of the Confederate States, tremendous interest in religious matters had developed in the army.

The general had often been seen attending the revival meetings in camp, and along with the battle-hardened veterans, Old Jack had been profoundly moved by many of the sermons. One in particular struck him forcefully and he recorded his reaction in a letter to Anna:

> Dr. Stiles' . . . text was 1st Timothy, chap. ii., 5th and 6th verses. It was a powerful exposition of the Word of God; and when he came to the word "*himself*" he placed an emphasis upon it, and gave it a force which I had never felt before, and I realized that, truly, the sinner who does not, under Gospel privileges, turn to God deserves the agonies of perdition. . . . It is a glorious thing to be a minister of the Gospel of the Prince of Peace. There is no equal position in this world.[52]

He might have added that perhaps the next most exalted position was to command an army sworn to God's cause.

Campaigns in the cause of the Lord had to give way for the present to campaigns of men against one another. Much as he would have liked to, Jackson could not linger in Winchester. To the dismay of the citizens, on November 22 Jackson's men began another march south, toward ground made famous by the old valley army. The columns of the Second Corps marched past the field of Kernstown, and here Old Jack took time for a brief visit. The new men on the staff wanted to know all about it, and as they rode over the ground the general reviewed the action in detail. Much to the liking of young Jimmy Smith, formerly of the Rockbridge Artillery, the stern professor complimented that fine unit in glowing terms for its fight on the rolling hills west of the Valley Pike.[53]

As he looked over that ghostly place, Jackson may have considered how long the war had been since that battle in March, and how far he had come. Eight months before, his command numbered scarcely 6,000 men, with a few batteries and the partisan cavalry under the incomparable Ashby. Now, as he sat the Sorrel and looked down on the long gray line tramping southward, he could count four divisions and twenty-three batteries—in all, some 34,000 men and 98 guns.[54] The tiny Army of the Valley had grown to be the Second Corps of one of the finest fighting armies ever to take the field. It must have been a proud moment.

No time could be lost in reviewing the past, however; the Army of the Potomac appeared belligerent. When Lee moved east with Longstreet's Corps, he had permitted Jackson to remain behind in the Shenandoah, where his well-known proficiency in independent service might be used to threaten the flank of any Yankee thrusts beyond the Blue Ridge and where he could directly oppose an invasion west of the mountains. As McClellan began a concentration on Warrenton for what appeared to be an attack against Longstreet, Lee hoped Jackson could threaten the right flank and rear of the Federals, thus forcing them back to the Potomac. But before McClellan could put his plan of attacking a segment of the Confederate Army into effect—a plan obviously borrowed from his adversary's repertoire—he had been summarily dismissed, and to his place came a bumbling, good-natured nincompoop. Ambrose E. Burnside's sole qualification for command was an ingenuous incompetence, and under his direction the Union advance shifted eastward toward Fredericksburg. At that point, then, Lee could gather his clans. Jackson must move there by the safest route.[55]

He decided not to move too fast, lest he miss a chance to hit some exposed portion of the Federal Army. By November 24 the vanguard of the Corps had crossed Massanutton via Luray Gap, and camped that night near Hawksbill in the Blue Ridge. When morning broke, beautifully clear and cold, Jackson's staff came out of their tents and stood transfixed by the gorgeous view. From the crest of the mountains they could see dark, imposing Massanutton to the west, and south of it the checkered patches of rich Shenandoah farm land. There, stretching in front of their gaze, lay the scene of Old Jack's fabulous Valley Campaign. When they about-faced and peered east, the startlingly blue-green foothills of the Blue Ridge rolled away toward Orange and Madison Court Houses. Surely over that happy land hung no dread of war? But the men of the staff knew that the tranquil colors hid only temporarily Burnside's blue invaders.

If Smith, Pendleton, and the others thought nature's beauties that morning the most lavish they had seen, they were soon surprised. Out of his tent—probably the conical Sibley he so admired [56]—stepped Lt. Gen. T. J. Jackson, resplendent in the coat Stuart had given him. As he walked toward the open-air breakfast table the staff gaped in amazement. Not only did the general have on the dazzling coat, he also sported a new saber! Jackson noted the hushed awe of the staff, halted, blushed, and then broke into a smile. It was a special occasion and merited special trappings. "Young gentlemen," said Old Jack—who invariably thought of his official family as far younger than his advanced thirty-eight years —"young gentlemen, this is no longer the headquarters of the Army of the Valley, but of the Second Corps of the Army of Northern Virginia." The announcement merely confirmed a long-standing suspicion that the Corps marched to join Lee.[57]

Lee's discretionary orders gave Jackson authority to decide on his route and on his timetable after he crossed the mountains. Hoping that a stray part of Burnside's host might wander in his path, Stonewall delayed the march between Madison Court House and Gordonsville through the twenty-fifth, twenty-sixth, and twenty-seventh, and on the twenty-eighth moved close to Orange. Perhaps, in this one instance, considerations not strictly military made him tarry en route. Anna had been given firm instructions not to telegraph her vastly important news—when the baby came she must write him, and the address he gave was Gordonsville.

The letter came.[58] In the strict privacy of his quarters Thomas broke the seal and began to read:

My Own Dear Father,—As my mother's letter has been cut short by my arrival, I think it but justice that I should continue it. I know that you are rejoiced to hear of my coming, and I hope that God has sent me to radiate your pathway through life. I am a very tiny little thing. I weigh only eight and a half pounds, and Aunt Harriet says I am the express image of my darling papa, and so does our kind friend, Mrs. Osborne, and this greatly delights my mother. My aunts both say that I am a little beauty. My hair is dark and long, my eyes are blue, my nose straight just like papa's, and my complexion not all red like most young ladies of my age, but a beautiful blending of the lily and the rose. Now, all this would sound very vain if I were older, but I assure you I have not a particle of feminine vanity, my only desire in life being to nestle in close to my mamma, to feel her soft caressing touch, and to drink in the pearly stream provided by a kind Providence for my support. My mother is very comfortable this morning. She is anxious to have my name decided upon, and hopes you will write and give me a name, with your blessing.... I was born on Sunday, just after the morning services at church, but I believe my aunt wrote you all about the first day of my life, and this being only the second, my history may be comprised in a little space....

Your dear little wee Daughter.[59]

Sister-in-law Harriet Irwin wrote that Anna had given birth to the precious little girl on November 23 at the home of Mrs. D. H. Hill— all were doing fine.

Thomas knew that Anna had been afraid that a daughter would disappoint him, and as soon as he had a brief moment to write, he reassured his *esposa:* "Oh! how thankful I am to our kind Heavenly Father for having spared my precious wife and given us a little daughter! I cannot tell you how gratified I am, nor how much I wish I could be with you and see my two darlings." Lest he sound too indulgent, he entered some words of stern advice: "I expect you are just made up now with that baby. Don't you wish your husband wouldn't claim any part of it, but let you have the sole ownership? Don't you regard it as the most precious little creature in the world? Do not spoil it, and don't let anybody tease it. Don't permit it to have a bad temper." As he wrote, he could not keep to his stern line, and again sounded like a doting daddy: "How I would love to see the darling little thing! Give her many kisses for her father. . . . I am so thankful to our ever-kind Heavenly Father for having so improved my eyes as to enable me to write at night. He continually showers blessings upon me; and that *you* should have been spared, and our darling little daughter given us, fills my heart with overflowing gratitude. If I know my unworthy self, my desire is to live *entirely and unreservedly to God's glory*. Pray, my darling, that I may so live." A final reassurance for Anna: "Give the baby-daughter a shower of kisses from her father, and tell her that he loves her better than all the baby-boys in the world, and more than all the other babies in the world." [60] For a name, Thomas suggested that of his mother, Julia—and so it was.

Fredericksburg, Virginia, was an old and honored city, on the fall line of the Rappahannock. Washington, Monroe, John Paul Jones, Robert E. Lee, and many another famous Virginian had known its genteel hospitality. Not crowded or especially bustling, Fredericksburg nonetheless had an air of being sufficient unto itself. Nature served it well. The town nestled in the river valley, with verdant and productive heights looking protectively down from above. From the spacious streets of the town, the country on the south side of the river spread fanlike to the southeast between the river and the ridge guarding the higher ground toward Guiney's Station, the North Anna and Richmond, some fifty miles away. By the end of November, 1862, Fredericksburg, the heights dominating it, and all the country surrounding were held firm in the grip of a hard winter. As rain and snow lashed the little city, two hostile armies slowly massed on the opposing heights. Years of peace and industrious commerce had abruptly ended; Fredericksburg was a no man's land.

Huddled around their campfires along the heights south of the river —the lesser of the two ridges—Lee's men looked across the Rappahannock at the massive array in blue which Burnside had concentrated along Stafford Heights through the last week of November. Would the Yankee general hurl those hordes across the river and up at the Confederate hills? And if he did, could the bluecoats be hurled back? Easily, if Jackson's Corps were at hand. But when would it come?

Forty miles Jackson rode on November 29, ranging far ahead of his toiling infantry and trains. As the afternoon wore on, he found that the road grew darker, that daylight made feeble headway against the vast stands of timber through which he galloped. The area was new to him, and went by the apt name of the Wilderness. Several roads led through this primeval forest, and he directed his men to follow different ones to relieve traffic congestion. The artillery and wagons were ordered to take a route toward Fredericksburg which passed through the tiny settlement of Chancellorsville, buried deep in the Wilderness. Beyond giving the order to use that route, Jackson paid no attention to the place or the name.

In the evening Jackson found Lee's headquarters, established in a tent near Hamilton's Crossing about three and a half miles southeast of Fredericksburg. Snow covered the ground around GHQ and the cold made the soldier campfires inviting indeed. But General Lee's welcome equaled the campfires in warmth. Jackson found himself ushered into Lee's tent, and seated for supper. The commanding general wanted the Second Corps to go into line behind and to the right of Longstreet's First Corps—in that position Jackson's men could either support Longstreet in a defense of the town or serve as a fluid reserve to protect other Rappahannock crossings farther south. Burnside would hardly be foolish enough to make a grand assault on the virtually impregnable Marye's Heights immediately southwest of the city. He might feint an attack there, while pushing part of his 125,000 men across the river, possibly at Port Royal, almost twenty miles downstream.[61]

On December 1 Jackson's veterans filed into their new positions. He had a right to be proud of them. Despite his unremitting efforts and almost desperate solicitude,[62] many of the men were barefooted still, and the shortage of warm clothing—particularly in a northern Virginia December—was shocking. But never had morale been so high. What they lacked in footgear and in garments, they supplied in spirit.[63]

For his part, despite the effervescence his men showed, Jackson appeared unhappy. In a conversation with brother-in-law D. H. Hill during which he ordered Hill's division to Port Royal, Jackson explained the reasons for his dissatisfaction. The whole position had been badly selected, he thought. "I am opposed to fighting here, *we will whip the enemy, but gain no fruits of victory,*" he said. Where would be the best line of defense? "I have advised the line of the North Anna, but have been over-ruled."[64] Perhaps, when he had protested the line to Lee, the commanding general spared his feelings to the extent of not telling him that the North Anna line had already been considered—indeed advocated—but that reconnaissance showed it to be no stronger than the Rappahannock, and to take the army south some twenty-five miles would expose much valuable food and forage to enemy pillagers.[65]

Once his protest had been lodged, Old Jack forgot his objections and set about making his dispositions in accordance with Lee's plans. But other, less vital irritations appeared to add variety around Second Corps headquarters. Echoes of the A. P. Hill controversy stirred again, and it seemed likely that something serious might emerge from the smoldering embers. Jackson had not relented. Then, too, relations between Lee's and Jackson's staffs became stiff and formal for a while, though this petty problem seemed to raise no serious questions.[66]

Unexpectedly, a routine request for a shift of guns from one unit to another forced the commander of the old valley army to defend his own. Lee innocently started the trouble by writing to Second Corps headquarters recommending that D. H. Hill's division be given a "fair proportion" of Napoleon guns—specifically, four which Hill's men had captured at the battle of Seven Pines. These guns had been assigned to one of Longstreet's batteries, and Lee thought they could be transferred back to Hill easily enough if Jackson would send four replacements to Longstreet. Since he now had 127 guns to Longstreet's 117, Jackson ought to be willing to engage in a fair exchange.[67]

Lee had fallen into error on one vital point. In his letter he asserted that "I observe, from General Pendleton's report, that more of the captured guns are in your corps than in General Longstreet's." Apparently the commanding general not only wished to take away some of the valley army's guns but also felt that Jackson had helped himself to more than his share of the Harpers Ferry prizes. No time could be lost in putting Lee straight.

First it must be made clear that no guns should be taken from the Second Corps to make up a deficiency in Hill's division, especially if the replacement guns were among those originally belonging to the valley troops.

I hope [he wrote Lee] that none of the guns which belonged to the Army of the Valley, before it became part of the Army of Northern Virginia, after the battle of Cedar Run, will be taken from it. If since that time any artillery has improperly come into my command, I trust that it will be taken away, and the person in whose possession it may be found punished, if his conduct requires it. So careful was I to prevent any improper distribution of the artillery and other public property captured at Harper's Ferry, that I issued a written order directing my staff officers to turn over to the proper chiefs of staff of the Army of Northern Virginia all captured stores. . . . General D. H. Hill's artillery wants existed at the time he was assigned to my command, and it is hoped that the artillery which belonged to the Army of the Valley will not be taken to supply his wants.

Hill might belong to the Second Corps, but deep in Old Jack's heart rested a special place for those few thousand ragamuffins who had turned the face of the world toward the Shenandoah Valley. None who came later ever quite belonged—and first in that special place always stood the grim remnants of the Stonewall Brigade.

By now Lee had become accustomed to dealing with the sudden whims of jealous commanders, but probably never before had he had to deal with a case exactly like this one. Never before had he tried to take anything from the Army of the Valley. Perhaps it would be best never to try again.[68]

More and more men crowded Stafford Heights, stretching northwestward past the beautiful home "Chatham" and on to Falmouth. Burnside had assembled a juggernaut, and he seemed about to aim it at Lee's 78,500 men.[69] The Confederates shivered through early December's bitter cold, watched the enemy massing, marching, emplacing batteries, read Lincoln's "claptrap argument for emancipation,"[70] and took no counsel of their fears.

The Confederate high command, charged with defending lower ground, and with having to guard against possible crossings of the Rappahannock downstream, found it necessary to disperse available force. By December 11, Jackson's Corps had become so spread out that it would be difficult indeed to concentrate all his divisions quickly. D. H. Hill had been guarding the river at Port Royal, twenty miles to the right of the main Confederate positions in front of Fredericksburg. Jubal Early, leading Ewell's division with growing ability, had deployed in a horseshoe of the river at Skinker's Neck, about fourteen or fifteen miles southeast. General William B. Taliaferro, whose wound had healed sufficiently to permit his return to command Jackson's division, guarded the Richmond, Fredericksburg & Potomac Railroad near Guiney's Station —almost ten miles to the southeast and slightly behind Longstreet's extreme right flank. Powell Hill's Light Division had gone into camp— somewhat cold and uncomfortable camp—near Yerby's, which put him about two miles behind Longstreet's right.[71]

The high ground in front of Fredericksburg, called Marye's Heights, had been occupied by Longstreet, whose Corps protected almost four miles of front. Stretching from a point opposite Hunter's Island in the Rappahannock on the left, along the high ridge and hills commanding the town, Longstreet's Corps covered some of the falling terrain as far to the right as the little stream called Deep Run. Hood's division formed the far right of Longstreet's front at Hamilton's Crossing.

A cold mist eddied up from the river during the early hours of December 11. The miasma dimmed the moonlight, but even so, at 2 A.M. Confederate pickets caught glimpses of enemy activity opposite the town. Pontoons! Burnside had elected to try it. Bridges were coming across—the move that all had been dreading. Could the crossing at

Fredericksburg be made as costly to the Yankees as had been Burnside's Bridge spanning the Antietam? There seemed every chance. From the hills behind the town boomed two guns, the signal that enemy bridges were building. A brigade of infantry in the city, the fine Mississippi unit under Gen. William Barksdale, defended the Confederate shore, firing into the murky mist, aiming at sounds. The spirited delaying tactics of Barksdale's men stopped Federal operations at the two points where they had been extending pontoons toward the city. Farther downstream, below the point where Deep Run emptied into the river, blue pontoniers had more success, since the ground offered little cover for defenders and the fog hung thick and baffling.

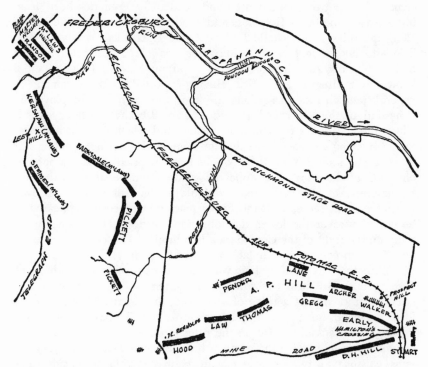

Confederate positions at Fredericksburg, Virginia (Jackson's Corps on the right) (after Freeman, R. E. Lee)

When Barksdale could no longer dispute the crossing, he fell back into the streets, and retired slowly in the face of Union assault columns brought over in boats to secure the bridgeheads. So stoutly did Barksdale's men contest the enemy advance that they were not compelled to abandon Fredericksburg until 7 P.M. By the time the last of the grayclads fell back to Confederate positions on the ridges, final preparations to receive Burnside's attack were well under way.[72]

While the Federals worked feverishly at their bridges, Jackson watched intently. Lee's notification of a serious Federal threat made it necessary to call up Jackson's absent divisions. Orders went to A. P. Hill, who also received similar orders direct from Lee, to strike camp at dawn on the twelfth and to relieve Hood's troops near Hamilton's Crossing. Taliaferro's brigades were to move from Guiney's and take their station behind Hill's lines. D. H. Hill and Early could stay where they were until Burnside's full intentions were developed.

Four A.M. of Friday, December 12, was an extremely cold hour, but Jackson had given orders that the staff must be up and ready for work. When he strode into the eating tent and found that several men were using it as sleeping quarters, he ordered breakfast served outdoors. Uncomfortable, but fed, he mounted and headed for Fredericksburg, leaving word for the tardy Hotchkiss and another of the staff to follow. On, along the ridge which would be held by A. P. Hill as soon as his men filed into line, rode Jackson, leading for Lee's field headquarters on a high hill below and slightly west of imposing Marye's Heights, a hill known ever after as Lee's Hill. Having reported to the commanding general, Jackson rode back along the line to observe Hill's deployment. If he said anything to Powell Hill about a small triangle of boggy woods which bisected Hill's front near its center, and which might offer cover to an attacking spearhead, the division commander did not mention it.[78]

Careful attention to Hill's whole front focused Jackson's interest on the Confederate right. It appeared exposed and possibly "in the air," but assurances that Stuart's troopers would be the flank element removed worries on that score, although heavy masses of bluecoats appeared to be crowding over the lower Rappahannock bridges. Heavy enemy activity on the right of the Confederate line brought Lee over in the afternoon, and in company with Jackson he rode along Hill's positions.

With the exception of that weak bit of boggy wood dividing the high ground, Hill held exceedingly strong terrain. His men were concealed in the edge of a ridge of woodland, and in their front an open field stretched for about a mile down to the Rappahannock. From Prospect—or Jackson's—Hill on the right, both generals could see long columns in blue crossing the pontoon bridges below Deep Run. Wagons, guns, caissons, all types of war machinery in staggering profusion came across with the men. What did the enemy plan to do? Jackson wanted a better look at the Federals and so did Lee. Both of them rode to the right, toward Hamilton's Crossing, where they might get a clearer view along the enemy flank.

Soon the two officers were hailed by the hearty Major von Borcke, of Stuart's staff. Stuart and he, reported the big Prussian, had found a magnificent vantage point close to the Yankees diligently fortifying near Hamilton's Crossing. Careful scrutiny had revealed that the Yankees were strengthening the cover offered by the Richmond Stage Road which ran between the river and the RF&P Railroad, whose track ran right along the base of A. P. Hill's infantry and gun positions.

Jackson and Lee had to see for themselves. There might be danger, cautioned Von Borcke, who appeared to be sorry he had mentioned anything about Stuart's reconnaissance. No matter, he must show them the way. Since they would be close to the enemy and secrecy would be all-important, the large staffs of both generals had to be left behind. That done, the three riders moved out ahead of the Confederate line. Coming to a small barn which offered some cover, the horsemen dismounted and began to inch their way, bent low, along a ditch toward two old gateposts large enough to hide a man standing up. Von Borcke lagged behind, lest his strapping bulk draw fire, and soon Jackson and Lee were sweeping the Federal working parties—not 400 yards away—with their glasses. Their guide had a few bad moments when he thought of what one shell or an enterprising squad of Yankee cavalry might do to the cause of the South. But eventually, to his relief, the two finished their scout and slowly picked their way back to the safety of the barn.[74] Dangerous though the mission had been, it produced valuable information. Federals were concentrating in strength and seemed to be intending a major effort on the front of the Second Corps.

Jackson made one further personal survey of the enemy's left that afternoon. So pleased was he with the results that Hotchkiss, in obvious surprise, reported his whistling as he rode back to Hill's positions.[75]

Now was the time to summon D. H. Hill and Early. Their divisions would be needed on the morrow, for Burnside apparently had grown tired of doing nothing. The two absent units were a good long march away, but if they pushed on through the night, they would be in support of Hill by morning. Headquarters wagons were found near A. P. Hill's bivouac, and as Jackson made ready for evening prayer, the fog and smoke still hung heavy over battered Fredericksburg.

The sun on the morning of December 13 came up "red and fiery," strong enough to melt away the fog soon. Old Jack's staff did not lag this morning. Everyone was up, the wagons packed and sent to the rear. The Old Man's orders for the day showed him in a grim battle mood. All stragglers who refused to go forward were to be shot without ceremony. A man found skulking to the rear for a second time—on the testimony of two witnesses—was also to be shot. Behind the Second Corps, line of battle a curtain of provost guards kept careful watch—Old Jack had found a way to stop straggling! [76] Ranges had been sighted for the Corps artillery. Jackson's stray divisions filed into support positions, Early aiding the right and D. H. Hill in general reserve, a luxury rarely experienced in Lee's army.

The general emerged from his tent. Even in the dismal dawn of that cold day he fairly sparkled. Stuart's coat glinted in the faint light; his cap, a present from Anna, was swathed in braid [77] and gave him a taller, more martial look; his new trousers were immaculate and the gigantic boots shone. Altogether Old Jack looked the very model of a lieutenant general. Accustomed by now to the numbed looks of his staff, Jackson ate, mounted, and rode toward Lee's lookout. As he spurred Little Sorrel —who appeared so impressed with Jackson's looks as to step higher and more lively [78]—the men along the lines gaped at the finery. Old Jack was "dressed up as fine as a Lieutenant or a Quartermaster." [79] "Old Jack will be afraid of his clothes and will not get down to work." [80] One grimy infantryman called out to his comrades: "Come here, boys. Stonewall has drawed his bounty and has bought himself some new clothes." [81]

Impervious to these comments but not completely unaware that they were mixed with loud cheers, the general continued his tour of inspection. With him rode D. H. Hill, whom Jackson wanted to have a good look at the front in case his men were called up. The generals, with an assortment of aides, ran the gauntlet not only of good-natured joking but also of some annoying sharpshooter fire. Apparently oblivious to the whizzing lead, Old Jack paced the sorrel slow. A. P. Hill's deployment, on first glance, looked strong. His right had been anchored by fourteen guns emplaced on Jackson's Hill—where the Corps command post would be during the day—and his first infantry unit on the right was the solid brigade of J. J. Archer, spread from Hamilton's Crossing northwestward to the "boggy wood." Along Archer's line Jackson ran an approving gaze, but when he and Harvey Hill reached the patch of marshy woodland they slowed for a closer look. "The enemy," said Old Jack coldly, "will attack at that point." [82] If Jackson was right, serious trouble might follow, since a gap of perhaps 500 yards broke the Confederate front line at the bog. Archer's brigade did not extend quite to the edge of it and on the other side Jim Lane's brigade failed to touch it. Nor had a connection behind the wooded area been established between these brigades. Lane, who had the good sense to be worried about a break in the front despite the formidable batteries placed to command it, had informed Archer's men of it and had taken pains to be sure that Gen. Maxey Gregg, commanding the second line in support, knew about it also. The division commander's attention had been directed to the weak spot, but A. P. Hill had not acted, apparently feeling that the ground was impassable and that any thrust toward the bog could be blunted by the raking fire of his guns. Jackson, strangely enough, did no more than comment on the point of enemy attack; he made no specific effort, as far as available evidence shows, to see if precautions had been taken to strengthen the line.

Lane's brigade Jackson found slightly advanced on ground which jutted ahead of the Light Division's main line, but it seemed well placed.

Another gap appeared on Lane's left. Pender's brigade did not connect, but this gap had been covered by posting Thomas's brigade behind the break. No need to worry here. A. P. Hill's left was held by Hood's division of the First Corps, and all along Hill's front strong reserves were bivouacked. Although the ground on Jackson's front was not as high or as formidable as on Longstreet's, the density of infantry on a two-mile front made the whole position seem almost impregnable.

Casting no more than a perfunctory look at the rest of his front, Jackson rode for Lee's Hill, where he found the commanding general, Jeb Stuart, and Old Pete. And who was the splendid-looking fellow who had joined them? Embarrassed, Stonewall mumbled something about Stuart's being guilty. Jokes came from all quarters, but Stuart beamed with pride.[83]

From Lee's Hill a fantastic panorama extended along the Rappahannock. Multitudes of bluecoats could be heard all along the Confederate line, but the valley lay shrouded in a clinging white gauze. Above the layer of fog, Union battery positions on Stafford Heights and the camps near Falmouth were coming into view. When the sun burned off the vapor it would be a fine day, and all could guess at the spectacle which would be spread out before them. Old Jack thought the Confederates had better attack. While the fog still offered cover from the Yankee guns, which would not dare fire blind into the valley, there would be an opportunity to drive the Yankee infantry into the river. Stuart heartily agreed, but Lee decided against it. Far better, he thought, to receive attack in a virtually impregnable position and cut the attackers down. When they had been thinned and battered—that would be the time for a counterstroke.[84]

Defensive battle from strength—such strategy and tactics vastly pleased Old Pete and his mood grew expansive. Jackson, as always, became the target for blunt Pete's ponderous wit. By now the outlines of Yankee thousands could be dimly seen on open ground in front of the Second Corps, and Longstreet asked: "Are you not scared by that file of Yankees you have before you down there?"

"Wait till they come a little nearer," came Old Jack's solemn answer, "and they shall either scare me or I'll scare them!"[85]

Mounting, Jackson started to leave, but Longstreet still had one more question: "Jackson, what are you going to do with all those people over there?"

Pausing, Old Jack formed his reply—and when it came it was deadly: "Sir, we will give them the bayonet."[86]

There was no time now for more banter. The enemy was deploying in earnest. Back to his front galloped Jackson, taking station on the hill which gave him a clear view of most of his line and of the Federal left flank as it came forward. On one score he had reason for satisfaction.

Never had his batteries been in better position, emplaced so that they had so commanding a sweep of the field or aimed to do more deadly execution.[87] True, his guns were in a "fixed position" and were exposed to concentrated counter battery fire, but they could take it.

Big Heros von Borcke galloped up with a message from Stuart: The enemy were about to advance against Jackson's lines. The Prussian voiced concern lest the mobs in blue which were forming three lines of battle overwhelm Jackson—could he hold out? "Major," came the reassuring reply, "my men have sometimes failed *to take* a position, but *to defend* one, never! I am glad the Yankees are coming." Von Borcke must ride back to his general with a request to run out his Horse Artillery and try to rake the Yankee left flank.[88]

Calmly Jackson scanned the fields stretching from the railroad to the river. There must be at least 55,000 Union troops out there.[89]

Ten o'clock. Wisps of fog blew away. In three long lines of battle Federal troops stood to arms on the sunlit plain. Jackson could see the glint of countless bayonets, formidable batteries guarding the flanks, standards flapping in the breeze. Backs to the river, faces to the Rebel hills, the ranks began to walk slowly forward. Rarely had the Southern boys seen so impressive an array.[90] They could not conceal their admiration—disciplined and determined the straight blue lines moved with cadenced tread. Franklin's Left Grand Division it was, and it bore its name gallantly.

Two guns—a Blakely rifle and a Napoleon—suddenly careened onto the field from Stuart's sector on the far right. On they went, rocking, bouncing, sluing forward until they reached the junction of the road from Hamilton's Crossing and the Richmond Stage Road, fully half a mile in front of the Confederate lines. Smartly wheeled, the pieces were unlimbered, loaded, and opened fire. Aiming directly into the left elements of Franklin's men, these two foolhardy guns raked the enemy lines so fast and furiously that the advance halted. Gun after gun on the Federal side aimed at the two Rebel pieces. Dirt churned all around the Confederate gunners, bits of shrapnel and grape whizzed around their heads. Load, fire! Swab, load, fire! Major John Pelham, Stuart's gallant horse artillerist, was having a day the likes of which neither army had ever seen. One of his guns—the Blakely rifle—soon was knocked out of action. Calmly, without bothering to slacken the fire from the Napoleon, Pelham ordered the disabled gun to the rear. Redouble the volume from the remaining gun! Furiously four Union batteries flung iron toward the fantastic cannon blocking the advance of a whole division.[91] Pelham's special tactics of firing, then changing position and firing again, baffled all attempts to silence his gun. His rate of fire increased, and so swiftly did he move from position to position that some confused Federal observers thought he had a whole battery in action.[92]

A hail of shell and shot fell around Pelham. Gunners went down, but those remaining stood to their piece without stopping to take a breath. When there were not enough left to serve the gun, Pelham helped load and fire. While the ground leaped under the storm of Federal shell, Pelham kept hammering the Union lines.

From the advanced pickets of his cavalry command, Stuart watched Pelham with excited admiration. Twice he sent messages that Pelham might withdraw, twice came the reply that the artillerist could hold his ground. Finally, when the third message arrived, the major limbered up and galloped from the field. His ammunition was almost exhausted —he could fight no longer anyway.[93] But for close to an hour he had stalled the Federal advance. Lee, watching the brisk little battle, had remarked: "It is glorious to see such courage in one so young." And later that day, when meeting Jackson, the commanding general would say, "You should have a Pelham on each flank." [94]

Now the batteries which had been banging away at Pelham changed objective and blasted Hill's lines along the ridge. Union heavy batteries from way beyond the Rappahannock joined in the bombardment. Splashes of dirt leaped among the waiting Confederates, trees shook and dropped limbs, shellbursts rained death above the men on Jackson's Hill. Gunners tending the fourteen cannon crowding the crest huddled in their revetments; infantry crouched beyond the top of the hill, near a military road cut along the Confederate line. Faster, more fiercely fired the enemy batteries. They were firing for effect and were trying to drive the Confederates out of hiding—trying to make them expose their gun positions.[95] Strict orders kept the Rebel guns silent, and angry and uncomfortable crews had to hang on and bear the hail of death. Finally, at about 11:30,[96] the Federal barrage lifted—Jackson thinking that the enemy probably thought they had destroyed his guns by now—and the blue infantry resumed the slow, almost ceremonious advance. It was as if there were so many men involved in the attack that little speed could be generated. The slow pace added to the drama. Unhurried, in overpowering numbers, the enemy came on.

Range, 1,000 yards. Still the men of George Gordon Meade's superb command marched forward without taking a shot from the Confederate lines. Jackson, slightly concerned about his right, sent some guns there to join with the "gallant Pelham" in crossing fire with the fourteen pieces on Jackson's Hill.[97]

Range, 900 yards. An eerie stillness hung over the Confederate lines. The blue ranks could be clearly seen now, the men with set faces, in desperate earnest, fighting for the Union.

Range, 800 yards. Fire! A sheet of flame, a cloud of smoke, a rocking sensation as the ground heaved under the single explosion of fourteen guns, and then death cut raw holes in the Union lines as men staggered, fell, or reeled under the shock. Bewildered, Meade's troops halted to re-form, took a second salvo right in the face, and wilted. Back they went as Pelham's reinforced guns took them in flank. Beyond range of the killing artillery, the Union lines re-formed again.

During the lull on the right, Jackson could hear the roar of Long-street's guns from Marye's Heights and the ripping sound of musket volleys. The Federals had attacked the bastion in front of Fredericksburg. Slaughter, red and bestial, must be taking place there. Burnside seemed determined to slay the flower of the North along the hills of Fredericksburg. There could be no denying that those boys in blue marched to almost certain death with a cold bravery which, in A. P. Hill's phrase, was "right gallant." [98]

As rows of Yankees fell before Old Pete's hot guns, Jackson's men made ready once more to kill. Anxious to see to the safety of his flank, Jackson ordered the quiet, intense Jimmy Smith to follow, and galloped to the right, ahead of his front line. Dismounting, he began to walk out on the flat ground to the front and left of the Federal advanced battle line. Jimmy followed him, gallant to the end. Old Jack seemed to want a terribly close look at the enemy! Soon both of the graycoated men were far away from help in most exposed country. Bang, zzzzz. A sharpshooter had leaped up from the tall grass not two hundred yards away and was taking careful aim for another try. The first shot had hissed between the general's and Jimmy's heads, and the second might be closer.

Turning to Smith, whom he loved to tease, Jackson beamed and said: "Mr. Smith, had you not better go to the rear? They might shoot you." Smith's reply, if he made one, has been lost to history.[99] Soon Jackson joined him in returning to the protected Southern heights.

No sooner had they reached Jackson's command post than the blue waves again rolled forward. Franklin's men, aided now by Hooker and by a terrible storm of artillery which wreathed the Rebel heights in fire and smoke, aimed grimly for Jackson's lines. Confederate artillery tore at them, blasted men down, hacked holes in the Federal left, and the attack drifted to the right, centering at last on that haven of woodland near the middle of Hill's line which might offer cover from the hideous shellfire.[100]

Now they were within musket range. Sheets of flame danced along the Confederate heights, blue ranks evaporated, but replacements stalked forward to fill the gaps. Volleys gave way to rapid firing at will: bite, ram, fire; bite, ram, fire. Right at the boggy wood the Federals drove. Hill's guns to the right and left tried to turn so that they could take the wood in a cross fire, but they could not come to bear. Streams of bluecoats raced along the ground which Powell Hill had thought to be impassable.

The Yankees were attacking just where Old Jack had said they would. From his vantage point to the right of the bog, Jackson looked for signs of a counterattack. Lee, too, far to the left, looked for some indication that the attack had been halted. Nothing happened. On into the woods streamed hordes of the enemy—a break-through! Archer's left regiments and Lane's right were thrown into confusion as the enemy plunged into the underbrush between the two Confederate brigades. Desperate efforts to change front were made by both brigade commanders, with some success, and they called for help from the second line.

Behind the boggy wood, Gregg's South Carolinians had stacked arms and were lying down for protection against artillery fire. Without warning, a full-blown emergency burst on them. Into the lazing camps of Orr's Rifles, a crack and proud outfit, stormed a wildly cheering, milling melee. Gregg, confused by his deafness, mistook foe for friend and tried to prevent his men from firing on the Yankees—an act of leadership which further demoralized the Confederates—and in so doing he stopped a Minié ball.

Federals were crowding into the gap, trying to widen it and to take Hill's lines in reverse. If they got through the second line. . . .

After the shock of the break-through had passed and the supporting brigades found out what had happened, help began to arrive for Archer and Lane. Various units of Gregg's brigade rallied, and from the rear came Early's division. Shouts of "Here comes old Jubal! Let old Jubal straighten that fence! Jubal's boys are always getting Hill out o' trouble" [101] restored morale and a counterattack began.

Soon, to Jackson's immense relief, a wild, confused mass of bluecoats ran pell-mell out of the boggy wood and headed for the safety of their original line. From the woods behind them came that unearthly Rebel yell, and suddenly a raging gray horde burst through the tangle, formed a hasty line, and rushed in pursuit. Formation quickly lost, the Confederates ran on, apparently trying to carry out Old Jack's desire to drive the enemy into the river. Repeated orders to halt were ignored, but finally Yankee artillery stalled the rush. It was that unstoppable charge which caused Lee to say, as he watched from his hill: "It is well that war is so terrible—we should grow too fond of it!" [102]

Other Federal efforts against Jackson's left had met with some small success, but the only other major attack—aimed at the declivity formed by Deep Run—had been gallantly thrown back and pursued, at the same time that Early's men were "straightening" Hill's "fence." [103] Before 3 P.M. infantry attacks had ended on Jackson's front. His lines continued to take a severe pounding from Union heavy guns, but the Union infantry had spent its strength. Of this, of course, Old Jack could not be certain, and he thought he detected some indications of a renewed effort.

"I waited some time," he reported, "to receive it"; but when nothing happened he determined to try an attack of his own. Something decisive ought to be wrung from so vicious a battle. Orders went to some of his commands: prepare an advance designed to "drive the enemy in the river." [104]

Old Jack had timed his proposed advance carefully; it would jump off late in the evening "so that, if compelled to retire, it would be under the cover of night." Confusion in transmitting orders held up his arrangements, and when some units crept forward in fading twilight the storm of Yankee shell rained so heavy that Jackson called off his attack.[105]

Night mercifully fell on the hideous slaughter pens along the Rappahannock Valley and in front of Fredericksburg. Ambrose Burnside had proved one thing: Union men would march doggedly to death as often as ordered and with greater grandeur each time. Beyond that he had achieved nothing save the death or maiming of over 12,500 men.[106] As the victorious Confederates huddled around their fires or searched for the wounded,[107] they all wondered when Burnside would start on the morrow. As if to accentuate the question a blazing, ghostly light flashed from far up the Rappahannock, faded, and blazed again. Was it an omen that these were called the "Northern lights"? [108]

18

HEADQUARTERS, MOSS NECK

So MANY were dead to so little purpose. If Burnside resumed the destruction of his army the next day—the fourteenth—something decisive might be done. During the night the Confederate lines must be strengthened with entrenchments, fields of fire improved, added batteries brought up to sweep the whole front with increased power.[1] When at last Jackson became convinced that nothing more could be done at the front, he rode wearily back to his field quarters.

Almost at dawn came a messenger. General Maxey Gregg, the gallant South Carolinian, lay on his deathbed and wished to speak with General Jackson. He would go immediately. Jimmy Smith was wakened; he had carried Jackson's concerned regards and sympathy to the wounded general the night before. Together Jackson and Smith rode swiftly.

Gregg was resting at the hospitable Yerby house, and Jackson hastened to his room. Gregg roused, there was something he wanted to say. An endorsement on some paper... he had written it and sent it to Corps headquarters... it may have given General Jackson offense. Gregg's innate courtesy, his never-failing concern lest he hurt others, made him worry. Would Jackson overlook the incident? Old Jack could not remember the offending document; Gregg must not trouble himself about it.

Then, with the human kindness that so many never appreciated, since it usually lay hidden beneath an outer crust of discipline, Stonewall took the dying soldier's hand in his, and in tones of husky warmth said: "The doctors tell me that you have not long to live. Let me ask you to dismiss this matter from your mind and turn your thoughts to God and to the world to which you go." Jackson choked as he spoke, and Gregg, too, was almost overcome with emotion. "I thank you," came the South Carolinian's polite reply. "I thank you very much." [2] A brief farewell, then Stonewall and his aide rode back to the front. Many more gallant men might be dead before night fell. Killing had become so much a part of life that decent time could not be taken to mourn the dead.

But General Burnside did not attack that day. His subordinates, sated with wholesale death, talked him out of renewing the assault. Jackson, Lee, Longstreet, all the Confederate leaders hoped he would try it again. The fourteenth passed; the fifteenth, too, with the Union lines still there, but fronted now with entrenchments. Artillery on both sides occasionally lobbed shells across the lines—nothing more. Dawn of the sixteenth disclosed empty Union trenches; the Yankees had escaped! Burnside had slunk away; the great winter offensive against Richmond had drowned in Northern blood.

Unhappy that nothing more had been done to the enemy, Jackson still hoped that the Federals might try to cross the Rappahannock downstream and could be hit again.

A rumor that a crossing appeared to be shaping up at Port Royal on the sixteenth spurred Old Jack to quick action. Down the road toward the threatened town the Second Corps marched, Jubal Early's men leading the way. When the advance reached the vicinity of Moss Neck a messenger galloped to Jackson with a dispatch from Jeb Stuart. The rumor had been no more than that; no enemy activity had been observed at Port Royal. Immediately Old Jack halted his cold columns. The troops might bivouac, if they could find suitable locations.

Unfortunately the ground at the head of the Corps offered no inviting campsites, the road at that point being "hedged in by dense and well-nigh impenetrable pine thickets." The front of the column would certainly have to countermarch for some distance until more open terrain could be found. Jackson himself started for the rear, but the road was narrow and the way blocked by his infantry. Momentarily he thought he might be able to "flank" the column by taking to the woods, but this proved impossible. Nothing to do but put his head down and start up the road.

No sooner did the high-spirited troops see Old Jack threading his way among them than they began to cheer him madly. The Old Man and his staff, galloping single-file along the little path made by the parting lines of men, were almost deafened by the yelling. The men even cheered the staff, throwing taunts at them as they followed the general: "Close up." "You will get lost." "You will never find him." Away back toward the rear, the men were doubtless saying, as they heard the cheers rolling toward them: "It's Jackson or a rabbit." [3]

Out of the narrow road, Jackson led his entourage to a clearing which seemed to offer some shelter from the cold. Leaves and firewood were abundant. The trouble was that no one in the party had any food. Some of his "young gentlemen" tried to suggest that it might be best for the general to seek hospitality from one of the large homes in the vicinity. Moss Neck, the palatial home of the Corbin family, lay not far distant—doubtless the Corbins would gladly offer lodging for the night. But no, he would camp out. Jimmy Smith and Jed Hotchkiss sulked, and as he grew colder and hungrier, Smith got mad.

A fire close to a large and venerable poplar offered the only consolation, and men stretched in a circle around it, feet toward the flames. A long, disgruntled silence. Then came a query from the general: Did Jimmy Smith have any biscuits in his haversack? No, replied Smith, with malicious pleasure.[4] Silence again. The wind blew "sharp and raw," the fire flickered on the figures wrapped in saddle blankets and overcoats.

Suddenly a great crash roused everyone. The tree which had been a chimney for the fire had burned out and fallen to the ground. Fortunately no one had been hit. Jackson sat up awhile and then admitted being chilly and hungry. And when Capt. Hugh McGuire joined the group around the embers Old Jack soon discovered that here was a man who knew the surrounding country well, having tutored in the neighborhood. Could the captain find some food? Easily, he replied, and mounted. In a short time he returned, having gone to Moss Neck with his request. He had been loaded down with a basket of biscuits and half a ham—a feast! Everybody crowded round and ate heartily.

Feeling much better, Stonewall and the staff stretched out once more. Half an hour passed. Old Jack sat up again and spoke quietly to McGuire. "Captain, let's go to the 'Moss Neck' house." He had an earache, he explained, else he would never have given in to such weakness.[5]

Banging on the huge door of the Corbin home, a staff officer announced that General Jackson and his staff were there "to see if we could be entertained for the night, as it is late to put up tents, and the General is suffering with earache." The door flew open; Stonewall Jackson must come in! He hesitated to inconvenience the family. No inconvenience, the house had ample space—a whole wing could be his for the taking. Ushered to a spacious "chamber," Old Jack soon fell into a luxurious bed.

Waiting for sleep to blot out the earache, Jackson perhaps thought of Anna and daughter Julia. During the morning he had taken time from war to write his dear *esposa* that the enemy had been repulsed "through God's blessing" and that he had been so happy to read in "baby daughter's last letter" that she "no longer saw the doctor's gray whiskers." And he had put into words a thought always with him: "I tell you, I would love to caress her and see her smile. Kiss the little darling for her father. . . ."[6]

War wrought its privations and separations, but Virginian hospitality remained changeless. When Jackson arose to begin the day's duties, he found that a breakfast of sausage, pork steaks, waffles, and muffins, all in bountiful supply, awaited him. Old Jack did his best, but must have been outclassed by the wolfish staff.[7]

Mrs. Roberta Corbin, the gracious hostess, had a request to make of the general. Would he consent to use one of the wings of her spacious residence as his headquarters for the winter? He could see that such an arrangement would hardly discommode the family since the Corbin mansion had innumerable rooms, and its wings offered as much privacy as the general might wish. A well-filled larder would always be at his command.

Thanking Mrs. Corbin for her generous offer, Jackson declined, saying that the house was "too luxurious for a soldier, who should sleep in a tent." Could it have been that Tidewater splendor overawed the mountain man? He would, however, consent to a Spartan compromise. Headquarters, Second Corps, would be established in the yard near the Corbin house. By afternoon of a sunny, warm December 17, Jackson's tents had been set up and work began.[8]

So much had to be done. Entrenchments had to be thrown up from the old Fredericksburg battlefield downriver toward Port Royal,[9] and careful attention had to be given to finding good winter campgrounds for the troops. Serious attention would be devoted to a thorough reorganization of the Corps.

"War," said Stonewall to Hotchkiss, "is the greatest of evils," and it was made worse by the weather around Fredericksburg. Jackson had expected the winter to be cold, but not so brutally cold during late December.[10] The weather doubtless caused the recurrence of the general's earache, which became so bad that after spending about a week under canvas, he broke down and asked Mrs. Corbin if he might use one of the "offices" of the Moss Neck estate as his quarters. Cordial consent led to a shift in Corps headquarters. The office turned out to be almost too palatial for Old Jack's tastes. Standing in front and to the left of the mansion, the small frame building had three rooms, the largest of which had been tastefully decorated with sporting and racing pictures and boasted ample, well-stocked bookshelves on each side of the door. In this room Jackson established himself, with his small cot on one side of the fireplace and his field desk on the other. The small lobby served admirably as a waiting room, and the closet to the left of the main entrance, as well as the small attic, offered more space than Jackson needed. Here he recovered from his long troublesome earache and here, too, he found that his general health greatly improved.[11] The office soon became well known as Old Jack's Headquarters and there he stayed for almost three months—the familiar figure of a guard from the Irish Battalion constantly pacing back and forth in front.[12]

A flurry of excitement ruffled headquarters during the latter part of January. Burnside, stung into an attempt to recoup his losses, tried a flanking movement upriver from Lee's army. But this time he did not come to grips with the gray army; he stalled in the mud. After his lackluster "Mud March," Burnside was slated for early dismissal. When this last Federal attempt oozed to a halt, Lee became convinced that winter would prevent further operations. Now the Army of Northern Virginia could concentrate on preparations for the spring campaign.

Preparations were made in good earnest at headquarters of the Second Corps. First, Jackson undertook to prepare himself. Corps command imposed new and undefined responsibilities. As the commanding general had implied in his report of the battle of Fredericksburg, the new command system had worked well, but Jackson knew it could be improved.[13] In some ways he found the job of Corps commander more difficult than that of army commander. When he alone had directed the operations of the Army of the Valley he had been responsible for strategy, tactics, and logistics—admittedly a large task. But the entire valley army had not been as large as the 30,000-man Second Corps, and now he had the added problem of conforming to the over-all direction of an immediate superior. Lee may have felt, before the Maryland campaign, that Jackson chafed under supervision and that he did not do his best when he could not have credit for independent action. Such an impression was wrong. The simple fact is that Jackson's talent lay not so much in army administration as in fighting. His was not so much the mind of the adjutant as it was that of the strategist.

It seems clear that Jackson recognized his limitations as a subordinate, limitations which were increased because of his strict belief in discipline and the chain of command. Because he did not conceive it to be his duty to argue with General Lee, or to offer advice not specifically requested, he had not shown at his best during the Seven Days' Battles. On the Peninsula he had been in unfamiliar territory, denied Hotchkiss's service, and involved in a complicated battle at a time when he was dead tired. Without his usual means of intelligence—those being reserved to the army commander—and moving almost "in the dark," he had been slow and uninspired.

Detached for a blow at Pope's advanced units, he had begun to regain his self-confidence and his battle poise at Cedar Run. And during the magnificent march behind Pope's army in the Second Manassas campaign, he had not only been himself again, he had manifestly grown as a general. When he fought the battle at Groveton, waiting for Lee and Longstreet, he fulfilled all the expectations raised by the Valley Campaign.

When Lee showed unlimited confidence in Jackson's capacity by detaching his men for the Harpers Ferry expedition, a model partnership began. Thereafter Lee always selected Jackson for detached assignments; he could rely on Stonewall to work out any problems of strategy or tactics which might present themselves. To Jackson, Lee gave broad, discretionary orders, leaving it to his lieutenant to decide on how to do the job.

Still, Jackson realized that as an administrator he needed to improve. He could do what he willed to do. He determined to improve, and he did.

New system appeared at Corps headquarters. With Sandie Pendleton at the head of the staff—and soon promoted to a majority—all work settled into an efficient routine. Jackson clung to an old habit in his new job. Each morning he met his chief supply officers—quartermaster, commissary, medical, ordnance—for a report on the wants and necessities of the men. After they departed with orders, or with promises from the general to assist in efforts to pry deficient items out of Richmond depots, Sandie appeared. Not yet twenty-three, Sandie actually ran headquarters. Possessed of judgment far beyond his years, of tact and manners to beguile the most irritated officer, Sandie smoothed much of Jackson's administrative path. In the morning he brought in two stacks of papers, one consisting of documents coming down from the War Department or Army General Headquarters, the other coming up from division level, destined for Jackson or Lee. Paper work took time, but Pendleton lightened the burden by taking notes on letters which must be written, on orders to be issued, and by discussing with Old Jack what ought to be done with each problem.

Next came reports from the Inspector General of the Corps and from courts-martial feverishly meting out stern military justice in each division and brigade. When these had been read and noted, Jackson issued his instructions for the day to division commanders, gave such special instructions as might be needed to the staff, and then set himself down to write important letters—to General Lee, to the Secretary of War, to Congress, to his clerical friends. He ate with the staff in a dining tent, but never dawdled there. Soon after his frugal meal he returned to headquarters, or rode to inspect his camps.

A few weeks after he settled in at Moss Neck the vexing business of writing reports of the battles from Kernstown to Fredericksburg began; the War Department had grown impatient. When this work started, Jackson devoted part of his afternoon to it, but always ceased work before supper, in time to take a solitary walk in the woods. Good for the digestion, walking helped take his mind off the worries of the day.

In the evening, after supper, Pendleton brought him great sheaves of documents which he had to sign, and he bent over his desk, eyeshade affixed, scrawling "T. J. Jackson" time after time. Sometimes the stack stood so high Old Jack fell asleep in the middle of a signature.[14]

In short order Pendleton and the rest of the staff realized that the Old Man expected complete information on what happened within the Second Corps. Nothing escaped his notice, his approval or rejection. The welfare of the lowliest private in the most obscure company of conscripts he considered his responsibility. Inefficient or indifferent officers, of any grade and assignment, soon found that their dereliction had been noted by the general. Inefficient officers propagated loose discipline, and loose discipline could effectively destroy the army. Perennial concern for discipline, so essential to good morale, focused Jackson's attention always on his provost guards and his courts.

The guards were instructed to screen the rear of the Corps to prevent skulkers or deserters from slipping away, and to check with exceeding care the passes of everyone who sought to leave the campsites.[15] Punishment for desertion or for going AWOL had to be severe, lest the tendency increase in the face of lenient justice. In late January several nasty cases came to Jackson for final decision.

One of his brigade commanders had been accused of cowardice and would have to be court-martialed. Such a charge had never before been leveled at a general under Jackson, and it would not be a pleasant affair.[16] From Gen. E. F. Paxton, commanding the Stonewall Brigade, came a sheaf of papers concerning six enlisted men tried for desertion and condemned by brigade courts. The sentences were severe. One of the unfortunates received six months' hard labor with ball and chain; two were to be flogged (a practice recently reintroduced for the express purpose of dissuading deserters); the remaining three were to be shot.

General Paxton, whose dedication both to duty and to Christ had won the warm admiration of the lieutenant general, forwarded with the court proceedings a recommendation that only one of the men be shot, and that he be chosen by lot. Stonewall read the recommendation, and lost some of his respect for Paxton. Sending the documents on to General Lee, Old Jack added an endorsement:

> With the exception of this application, General Paxton's management of his brigade has given me great satisfaction. One great difficulty in the army results from over lenient Courts and it appears to me that when a Court Martial faithfully discharges its duty that its decisions should be sustained. If this is not done, lax administration of justice and corresponding disregard for law must be the consequence. The Army Regulations define the duty of all who are in service and departures from its provisions lead to disorganization and inefficiency, etc.[17]

Although usually compassionate, General Lee sustained his lieutenant in the decision to shoot the men. President Davis, having final review of the case, granted clemency, a fact Jackson probably noted with cold disdain. Wars were times of harshness: in a war of the Lord mercy must yield to the good of the cause.[18]

With equal sternness Old Jack handled lesser cases. When a lieutenant in the Fifty-eighth Virginia was convicted of stealing chickens and sentenced to dismissal from the service, Jackson approved the sentence but directed that the hapless officer be put in the ranks.[19] Fiercely he read of one instance which involved a captain accused of gambling. The court sentenced the captain to be reprimanded. In a General Order publishing the reprimand to the Corps, Jackson gave his own views on the case, saying that gambling was "wholly inconsistent with the character of a Southern Soldier and subversive of good order and discipline in the Army," and that the captain had failed in his duty of setting an example for his men. A reprimand hardly served to punish the crime.[20]

Severity in dealing with breaches of discipline characterized Jackson's attitude throughout the winter of 1862–1863. So famous did he become for his iron hand that part of the "Jackson was a Cromwell" myth began to grow up during this period. Even Kyd Douglas, now a hardworking captain in the Stonewall Brigade, commented that in disciplinary matters "Jackson was as hard as nails; in the performance of a duty he always was. I never knew him in such a case to temper justice with mercy; his very words were merciless." Jackson kept the record of his clemency as secret as he kept his strategy.[21]

Part of Douglas's opinion was based on Jackson's views concerning leaves of absence. So strictly did he reject most applications that the staff resented it and spread the word of his harshness. They felt that the fact that he took no leave himself was no reason to deny them the privilege. Engineer Capt. James K. Boswell became so desperate to see his sweetheart that when his application came back from the general marked disapproved, he asked Jeb Stuart—sympathetic to heart troubles —for help. Stuart borrowed Boswell's services and sent him on a "mission" to the county in which dwelled his lady fair.[22] Later, when Kyd Douglas mustered the courage to mention, as a hint, that he "had not been out of the army since [he] entered it for a day," the general interrupted with: "Very good. I hope you will be able to say so after the war is over."[23]

One matter of discipline which had been smoldering for months erupted afresh during January. Upon receiving A. P. Hill's request for a hearing on Jackson's charges against him, Lee had, it will be recalled, decided that no good purpose would be served by ordering a court-martial, a view with which Hill violently disagreed. A long, testy correspondence followed, erupting at last into Hill's remark about Jackson's being a "slumbering volcano." There the matter simmered until, in March, Hill forwarded his report of the Cedar Run operations in which he stated his version of the whole series of allegedly slow marches. When Jackson read this report—it had to pass through Corps headquarters—he got mad all over again. Hill virtually accused Jackson of neglecting to do his duty by failing to give proper orders for the march to Cedar Run,[24] and this allegation goaded Old Jack into counteraction.

Various officers who had served on his staff at the time were quizzed about the sequence of events on the several nights before the battle of Cedar Run. What exactly did A. P. Hill say when he received Jackson's messages via the staff? Frank Paxton, who had then been on Jackson's staff, submitted a written account of the one time he took orders to Hill. Stapleton Crutchfield did the same. When he had all the information it seemed possible to collect, Jackson painfully wrote out another draft of his charges and specifications against Hill.[25]

Before Army Headquarters did anything about the Jackson-Hill controversy, which could be so damaging to morale in general, more trouble flared. Powell Hill, a great fighter in battle, had some of Old Jack's rigid dedication to form when in camp. Firmly he believed that an official piece of paper destined for any officer in his division had to pass through his headquarters. No matter if the communication was from the Chief of Ordnance to the ordnance officer of the Light Division and dealt only with the dreary technology of the ordnance service, it must first cross the division commander's desk. Hill, of course, did not have a monopoly on this theory; many officers throughout the army held the same view, but it was an open question. The Adjutant General, absolute arbiter on matters of red tape, had not as yet handed down his ukase.

Knowing full well Hill's penchant for trivia, Jackson apparently set out to ensnare him in the toils of army regulations. Without fanfare, Old Jack wrote Lee's Adjutant General, Gen. R. H. Chilton, in early January to ask what Lee's decision might be on this issue and commented that he had always permitted direct contact between staff departments and his supply officers, as long as copies of documents which might alter his logistical plans came to him. Lee decided in favor of Jackson's practice, and Old Jack remarked that since "such orders are properly so sent by one staff officer to another, without notification being sent to the intermediate Commander, I shall in future insist upon their being obeyed, and will prefer charges and specifications against any commanding officer who shall forbid his staff officer obeying the order when sent direct." [26] There were two virtues to Jackson's position: he now stood firmly on the side of cutting administrative red tape, and he neatly built a trap for the officious Powell Hill. It worked.

The Light Division's leader was congenitally unable to divest himself of the petty correspondence which cascaded over his desk. When he protested the disciplining of one of his officers who, caught in the squeeze of conflicting orders from Jackson and Hill, had decided to obey Hill and not the Corps commander, Jackson's patience ended. Reviewing the situation in a note to Lee on April 23, Jackson made the final break: "When an officer orders in his command such disregard for the orders of his superiors I am of the opinion that he should be relieved from duty with his command, and I respectfully request that Genl. Hill be relieved from duty in my Corps." [27] Now confronted with what appeared an almost insoluble problem of personalities, Lee pondered what to do. Possibly the decision could be delayed until the next campaign—if delay would not wreck the Second Corps. Was Jackson ever going to learn to handle his own subordinates?

Personality problems were not confined to the high brass alone. Such a relatively prosaic enterprise as preparing reports of Jackson's battles stirred up resentment among the younger staff members, a reaction Jackson could hardly have anticipated. The trouble began when he appointed an outsider to help in gathering data and in writing the long, sometimes tedious accounts of campaigning and battling. Reverend Dr. Dabney, whom he would have liked to have back on the staff,[28] still suffered from a disabling illness. In his place came Lt. Col. Charles J. Faulkner, Adjutant General's Department, a man of culture, erudition, diplomacy, and charm. Faulkner, whose selection was probably the result of a suggestion by Col. Alex Boteler,[29] had before the war been United States Ambassador to France and consequently possessed sufficient pedigree to qualify for a respectable job in the army.

Faulkner possessed, too, the literary ability which Old Jack knew to be necessary in making his reports acceptable to the War Department. The whole task of compiling and writing the reports appeared to frighten the general. Those few times he tried to hack his way through a draft battle account, the manuscript bore painful evidence of his fancied awkwardness with a pen. Then too, he had to avoid overstraining his eyes —they were much better but ought not to be used too much at night. So Faulkner seemed the answer to a baffling problem. When the highly touted amanuensis arrived, things began to go wrong.

For one thing, he was older than the rest of the staff and even older than Jackson. He bore his fifty-five years with a *savoir-faire* acquired through years of distinguished service to his state and to his country. His poise irked the "young gentlemen" the more for being unconscious. Another thing marked against him was Stonewall's obvious esteem. Unfortunately Jackson made a mistake regarding Faulkner. Apparently thinking that his seniority and acknowledged accomplishments entitled him to recognition, he decided to appoint Faulkner his Chief of Staff.[30] Although Pendleton received a promotion, which pleased him greatly, this scarcely compensated for the slight of passing over him in selecting a new head of the staff. Pendleton deserved the appointment, and many of his friends resented the Faulkner affair.[31]

Be it said in Faulkner's behalf that he had an exceedingly hard job.

He had never fought with Jackson, knew nothing of his methods and nothing of the battlefields he must describe. Jackson imposed certain rules for writing the reports which increased Faulkner's difficulties. Nothing which could be considered even remotely controversial would be included; only events verified beyond doubt were discussed; no laudatory remarks about the living were permitted, and even some of the tributes to the dead were toned down. When Faulkner complained at Jackson's removing every statement giving the reasons for a certain military move, and told him that later students of his campaigns would be anxious to have such explanations, Old Jack had a ready response. "The men who come after me must act for themselves; and as to the historians who speak of the movements of my command, I do not concern myself greatly as to what they may say." [32] So severe were Old Jack's stipulations that Faulkner commented to Hotchkiss on the general's "Roman simplicity" of style.[33] The general himself would have the final veto, and he read every report coming from Faulkner's pen with painstaking care. Diligently the Chief of Staff went round the camps of the old valley army, seeking out officers and men who could give him information. Hotchkiss's maps proved invaluable aids,[34] but faced with personal hostility on the part of a portion of the pro-Pendleton staff, and tethered closely by the general, it is hardly surprising that Faulkner was eager to finish his task and be gone.[35] Considering the hindrances which dogged his path, Faulkner did reasonably well; [36] Jackson had selected a good man for a difficult job.

Jealousy complicated Jackson's personnel problems in one final instance. The central figures in the case were Gen. William B. Taliaferro and Gen. Isaac R. Trimble. The central issue revolved around who would command Jackson's old division which had, since Cedar Run, been under Taliaferro. When official news came in January, 1863, that Trimble had gained the major general's rank he coveted and would take charge of Jackson's division, Taliaferro sulked. Never had Jackson forgiven him for his part in the Romney protest—he had known it all along, and now there could be no doubt. Passed over for promotion, he must request transfer; it was the only course for a gentleman. His petulance broke out in asserting his division commander's authority, while he still had it, and this brought him into conflict with Gen. Frank Paxton, who could be fairly petulant himself.

Hostilities between the two started over a minor question of military etiquette—whether or not court-martial proceedings should be forwarded through channels and whether the division commander had a right to open a sealed packet of court documents. Taliaferro thought so, Paxton thought not. Paxton stated his opinion in somewhat firm language. Taliaferro sent his adjutant over bedecked in sash and saber, and Paxton found himself arrested for being "very disrespectful." That suited the commander of the Stonewall Brigade. He would be happy to fight it out with Taliaferro, whom he did not, apparently, regard with the warmest affection. "The offense of Genl. Taliaferro, in abusing his power as my superior officer, I think he will find, in the opinion of all disinterested gentlemen, is a much graver offense than any I have committed," [37] declaimed the brigadier. Charges went up to Army Headquarters, but harried General Lee rejected the application for a court-martial. He did, however, support Taliaferro's position rather more than he did Paxton's. It seemed sad that such a minor problem grew to such large proportions and took up the time of so many busy officers.[38]

Vindication in his tilt with Paxton gave Taliaferro the victory he needed to leave Lee's army gracefully. In a manly letter to the commanding general, Taliaferro asked to be relieved of his command and transferred. He reviewed the achievements of his division since he had been in command, praised his men in affectionate terms, and said:

> It is a source of gratification to me to know that on being relieved from the command of the division the duty will devolve on one whose previous services, military education & conspicuous gallantry has been & will be appreciated. Yet I sincerely trust that the Comdg Genl will recognize and appreciate the delicacy of sentiment which influences me to urge that he will not insist that after occupying the position of a Division Commander for so long a time I will be required to assume a subordinate position in the same division.[39]

Lee approved the request and Taliaferro departed the army for duty in the Southeastern states. No comment did Jackson make when Taliaferro went—his opinion can only be inferred from his failure to recommend the division commander for promotion.[40]

Personnel problems appear to be the rock upon which Jackson, the administrator, was broken; but the appearance is deceiving. The instances of trouble were exceptions rather than commonplaces. With most of his subordinates Stonewall maintained the most cordial relations. His primary concern had always been the effectiveness of his command and the welfare of his men. During the winter at Moss Neck he perfected the supply services of the Second Corps, increased drills and parades, prodded the quartermasters into issuing as much clothing as the South could provide, and as a result the morale of his whole command rose higher than ever before.[41]

Beyond maintaining efficiency he cared nothing for personnel matters. He worked hard to get good officers promoted—witness the case of Trimble—and worked equally hard to remove incompetents. Never did he change an opinion formed early in the war that "a single worthless officer can ruin his command," and he meted out promotion or dismissal with cold judgment.[42] His judgment, naturally, sometimes erred, but far more often was he right than wrong, a fact which probably prompted Lee's declaration that "I have great confidence in the recomm[endations] of Genl Jackson."[43]

Worrisome as Corps administration proved to be, Jackson nonetheless enjoyed that winter. Happily the revival which had swept through the command during the valley sojourn late in 1862 had not died out. True, there were some backsliders, but religious interest remained high throughout most of the camps and Jackson found the spiritual climate peculiarly agreeable.

Now that he had something like regular working hours, he could devote more time to religious affairs, and as the weeks passed, he underwent almost total spiritual rebirth, his delight in attending camp services and reading religious books knowing no bounds. "Time," he exclaimed in a letter to Anna, "thus spent is genuine enjoyment."[44] Morning prayers were part of headquarters routine, with Jackson usually leading the staff devotions. Evening prayer meetings were held twice a week, and during the pleasant Sunday afternoons at Moss Neck, the staff would gather to join Old Blue Light in sacred songs. He knew he had no musical ability, but a Christian must do his duty. His toneless voice always could be heard joining in some of the hymns he loved best:

> How happy are they
> Who the Saviour obey!

or:

> 'Tis my happiness below,
> Not to live without the cross.

and a special favorite:

> Show pity, Lord,
> Oh, Lord forgive![45]

Since that winter had been given over to organizing, Jackson determined to organize the chaplains who worked in his Corps. He summed up his idea in a February letter to Colonel Preston, Maggie's husband:

Among the wants of the Church in the Army, is some Minister of such acknowledged superiority and zeal, as under *God* to be the means of giving concert of action. Our Chaplains at least in the same Military organization, encamped in the same neighborhood; should have their meetings, and through *God's* blessing devise successful plans for spiritual conquests. All the other departments of the Army have system, and such system exists in any other Department of the Service, that no one of its officers can neglect his duty without diminishing the efficiency of his branch of the Service.[46]

So should it be with the chaplains.

Sticking by his idea, he finally succeeded in establishing a Chaplains'

Association, which held weekly meetings and worked out strategical and tactical problems posed by the religious needs of the men.[47] With an eye to proper military administration, Jackson sought to have an unofficial Chaplain General appointed for his Corps—a minister with a roving commission who might ride the circuit of the camps, ministering where no chaplain had been. His choice for this assignment was the Reverend Tucker Lacy, an able, industrious, and honest Christian. The Adjutant General was requested to issue an appointment to Lacy, since there were many regiments much in need of religious guidance and Lacy had special qualifications. "A bad selection of a chaplain," in Jackson's view, "may prove a curse instead of a blessing." A query about what denominations should be represented by the field chaplain service brought a typical Jackson reply: "My views are summed up in these few words: Each Christian branch of the Church should send into the army some of its most prominent ministers. . . . I would like to see no questions asked in the army as to what denomination a chaplain belongs; but let the question be, 'Does he preach the Gospel?' " [48]

More and more chaplains came, and to the army they brought a wave of evangelical zeal. The stalwart remnants of the Stonewall Brigade built a log chapel, other units constructed places of worship, prayer meetings increased, and religion loomed large in camp discussions. Much to the delight of the troops and to the satisfaction of the chaplains, Old Jack frequently attended soldiers' services and on at least one occasion led his warriors in a prayer to bless the enemy in everything but the war.[49] The great revival later so famous in the annals of the Confederate Army owed much of its origin to the diligent labors of Deacon Jackson, who overcame inertia in all quarters.[50] His own interest, of course, was not confined to Christian labors in the army. He renewed his campaign against the irreligious practice of carrying the mail on Sunday, arguing that not until the Confederacy overcame its sinful ways could it hope to win ecclesiastical and political freedom. When Jackson heard that Congress had been debating the prohibition of mail shipments on Sunday, he wrote Colonel Boteler urging him to vote for the ban and pointing out that

the punishment of national sins must be confined to this world, as there are no nationalities beyond the grave. . . . God has greatly blessed us, and I trust He will make us that people whose God is the Lord. Let us look to God for an illustration in our history that "righteousness exalteth a nation, but sin is a reproach to any people." [51]

As increasing numbers of soldiers professed religion, the deacon general watched with gratitude. The Lord again was blessing his Corps. And daily Jackson acknowledged manifold blessings to himself. Not only had the Lord been pleased to cause people to give Jackson presents, but also He had been pleased to provide good friends everywhere. The Methodist Home Mission Society gave Jackson a life membership; public subscriptions purchased him a life directorship in the Bible Society of the Confederate States. Great blessings, these, and they showed that the deacon and the general warred successfully on two fronts.[52]

The little office in the Corbin yard became something of a branch Confederate States Post Office. Packages came not only from neighbors but also from remote parts of the South. Various pieces of clothing—handkerchiefs, socks, gloves—must have almost inundated the staff. Larger gifts, too, added to the confusion. Citizens of Augusta County, Virginia (Staunton, the county seat) sent to the Champion of the Valley a "magnificent horse, with an excellent saddle and bridle." In describing the gift to Anna, Thomas exclaimed:

> It is the most complete riding equipment that I have seen. My kind friends went so far as to get patent stirrups, constructed so as to open and throw the foot from the stirrup in the event of the rider being thrown and the foot hung in the stirrups. How kind is God to us! Oh that I were more grateful! [53]

Gifts came even from foreign lands, an indication of celebrity which seemed continually to surprise Stonewall. As a steady stream of English and Continental visitors called at Headquarters, Second Corps, many of them brought parcels from Jackson's admirers in different parts of the world. A particularly lavish English gift brought out a special facet of Jackson's character. In writing his thank-you letter, Old Jack revealed latent talents in diplomacy:

> *Head Quarters 2d Corps*
> *Army of Northern Va.*
> *February 24, 1863*

Mr. W. F. De La Rue,
London.

Dear Sir:
I had the honor of receiving . . . your esteemed favor of 14 November last, accompanied by your present of an English military saddle, with every appurtenance for its complete use, which a liberal and judicious taste could suggest. I take pleasure in advising you of the safe arrival of the box with its contents, and to assure you of my cordial acceptance of your present. I desire especially to return you my thanks for those generous sentiments towards my country which have prompted this testimonial of your friendly consideration.
Very Respectfully Your Obedient Servant,

> *T. J. Jackson*
> LT. GENL.[54]

Despite the shortage of rations in the army and the scavenging the men did in the vicinity of their camps, many people who lived fairly close to Jackson's little office sent him baskets of various delicacies. Not the least of his providers was his gracious hostess, Mrs. Richard Corbin. With her husband (a private in the Virginia cavalry) almost fanatically devoted to Stonewall,[55] she seemed to take the general in as a member of her family, showering as much attention on him as he would permit. So well stocked was the headquarters' larder that in December, 1862, Jackson grew expansive and decided to invite General Lee, Jeb Stuart, and the Reverend Gen. William Pendleton to Christmas dinner. Their staffs, too, were included in the invitation. Poor Jimmy Smith drew the chore of procuring the food and preparing the dinner for the distinguished guests, who all agreed to come.

Having considerable personal interest in the dinner, Smith did himself proud. To a nearby residence he sped, seeking to buy a turkey for the occasion, only to return laden with two turkeys, gifts to Stonewall Jackson. From "somewhere down the river" came a bucket of oysters, and a group of prescient ladies in Staunton sent another turkey, a huge ham, a sumptuous cake, and a bottle of wine. The box containing these tempting viands had its few empty spaces filled with "white biscuit and the best of pickles." Such raw material spurred Jim Lewis to Olympian heights of culinary achievement, and John, the boy who faithfully served Jackson as waiter and general handy man, even put on a white apron in appreciation of the occasion.

The guests came, full military regalia shimmering in the winter sun. General Lee, as always, looked magnificent in his finest uniform, perfectly tailored to his handsome figure. Genial Jeb, spurs and saber jingling, wore his big plumed hat in honor of the repast, and the slightly rumpled Reverend General Pendleton came for the serious business of eating. None of the guests could have been disappointed when they looked upon the epicurean table spread before them.

Pendleton raced through grace and began his systematic attack on the food; others were not slow. Stuart's merry eye wandered round the room as he munched away, then fell on the large cake of butter adorning the middle of the table, resplendent with a print of a gallant rooster upon it. Aha! What, sir, is that? Obviously a fighting cock. As Jackson gazed at the offending dish with mortification, Stuart went on. That display had been put there for a purpose surely—it must be Jackson's coat of arms! The table rocked with laughter, and Old Jack himself smiled. Stuart's humor never failed to please.

General Lee, too, looked round the room. Incredibly good food, excellent cooking, a white-aproned table attendant—high living indeed. Jackson and his staff, mocked the commanding general, were only playing at being soldiers. If they wanted to see how soldiers really lived, they must come to his quarters.

True, said Stuart, adding that all this conspicuous consumption worried him. Look at the pictures spaced around the walls—race horses, gamecocks, a rat terrier. Since Jackson put them there, they must reflect the general's personal taste, and that could only mean one thing: his moral character had gone into a rapid decline! Another laugh, and more good eating. It was a dinner, and a day, to remember.[56]

All the many presents which made headquarters life pleasant imposed added work on Jackson. Not only did he write letters to all who sent him gifts—a courtesy he never forgot—but also he found it necessary to visit the homes of the generous donors who lived fairly close to headquarters. The Corbins, of course, were his frequent hosts, and even more frequently the hosts to his "young gentlemen," since Miss Kate Corbin, Mrs. Richard Corbin's beauteous sister-in-law, became a center of attention.

Aside from the distracting influence of the Corbin household (Sandie finally married Kate) there were other amusing episodes growing out of Jackson's thank-you visits. Once, when paying a social call to Hayfield, the lovely home of the Taylor family located not too far from the Corbins, Stonewall found himself beleaguered by two pretty lasses who wanted to cut off locks of his hair. Young Jimmy Smith expected his general to dissolve in a burst of embarrassment, as the request invariably brought a deep blush. But no, the general had hidden founts of coquetry—he flirted with the girls! As one young lady clung adoringly to his arm, begging for the prize, he said, "Well, you may have a little if you promise not to take any grey hairs." "Oh! General Jackson," the girls cried, "you are a young man, you have no grey hairs." A moment's pause, then Jackson said archly: "Why, don't you know the soldiers call me Old Jack?" [57]

While Jackson took small bits of time every now and then to go visiting himself, by far the greater part of his spare moments were taken up by hordes of admirers visiting him. All found that Stonewall received them "with all his usual affability." He practically wore out his writing hand giving autographs, but never seemed quite to understand why people coveted that scrawled signature.[58] The general displayed none of that Cromwellian grimness ascribed to him. Invariably polite, courteous, he talked easily on a wide variety of subjects, and adroitly avoided military discussions. He was, in fact, a gentleman. One visitor, in particular, would not have recognized her general had he been referred to as anything but a kind, generous, sweet man.

Mrs. Corbin's daughter Janie, a five-year-old darling with golden tresses and sparkling wistful eyes, loved the general dearly. When all the men left the office in the afternoon and he sat back to rest, that was her time to see him. Always he had some little something to strike her fancy. And she could do something he could not: she could cut the Stonewall Brigade out of paper—long lines of stalwart, slightly bow-legged veterans. But the general tried hard, and finally learned to do it pretty well. He knew so many good stories and exciting things, though, that his clumsiness with paper dolls could be forgiven. On some days the two of them would talk and play for hours at a time: Janie sitting on the office floor, tossing her sunny curls out of her eyes so she could look up at General Stonewall, Jackson looking fondly down and telling some delectable tale.

The general found he had serious competition. The whole staff adored little Janie, and they trooped over in droves to pay homage, bringing her whatever little gifts could be found around the poverty-ridden camps of Lee's army. But the general had the vast advantages of proximity and of an inexhaustible storehouse of games and stories.

He won his complete victory when he yielded to the longing gaze which Janie cast at his new and shiny cap. She had always admired it, and one afternoon he asked her what had become of her comb—the hair still tumbled in her eyes. She had lost it. He remembered then her covetous glances at the gold braid on his cap, took out his pocket knife, and cut the band off. After tying it around her flowing curls, he held her cheeks in both hands and said: "Janie, it suits a little girl like you better than it does an old soldier like me." [59]

Janie comforted Jackson a great deal, helped take his mind away from the wearing problems of the army, and filled a longing—a void. Mary Graham, had God spared her, might have looked like Janie and had her trusting, solemn sweetness. And Julia Laura might have her eyes, her brightness, and her warmth. If only Anna could come and bring the baby! Other generals had their wives quartered in some of the big houses near the army; would it be wise to urge Anna to come? [60]

There were several reasons why it seemed imprudent, even though Jackson grew unbearably envious when he saw Mrs. General Longstreet, Mrs. General A. P. Hill, and Mrs. General Robert Rodes riding around the camps, happy in the company of their husbands. Julia had recently had the chicken pox—which had worried Jackson to the extent of per-suading Dr. McGuire to write out detailed methods of treatment for Anna's guidance—and since smallpox appeared in the army during January, it would probably be best not to risk her health. [61]

Jackson grew suddenly more solicitous for Julia's well-being when Janie came down in mid-March with one of the most dread of all scourges, "malignant scarlet fever." She lay abed, while Jackson broke up his headquarters, preparing to return to canvas life and thinking it would be "rather a relief to get where there will be less comfort than in a room, as I hope thereby persons will be prevented from encroaching so much upon my time."[62] Once more, before he departed, he would "encroach" on Mrs. Corbin's time. How fared sweet Janie? Doctors had good news. Janie seemed out of danger.[63] Reassured, Jackson mounted Little Sorrel and rode to a tent near Hamilton's Crossing on the Fredericksburg battlefield. But soon a sad messenger came to General Stonewall's quarters; Janie had grown worse, she had sunk rapidly, and now she was dead. Stonewall wept. Even in the midst of wholesale death, the loss of the innocent struck deep; but Janie had been called to God, who in His wisdom, knew the pure in heart.

Illness threatened to wreak havoc with the whole Confederate cause during March. General Lee lay in bed, seriously ill, and Jackson redoubled his prayers—the loss of "Marse Robert" could well be fatal to the nation.[64] Another death occurred in that doleful month: the gallant Pelham, the dashing, daring, romantic artillerist who had so excited the army when he fought the Union forces alone on the Confederate right at Fredericksburg, was killed in a cavalry action at Kelly's Ford. The army, the country, and especially Jeb Stuart mourned. Jackson knew the depth of Jeb's suffering, and extended his condolences simply: "I deeply regret the loss of Pelham, and am assured that you do too." If it would lighten the usually jovial cavalryman's burden, he should visit Corps headquarters: "I was at your HdQrs . . . but you were absent fighting Yankees as usual . . . I design visiting you soon but dont let any of my designs interfere with your visiting me."[65]

Spring seemed a peculiarly depressing season and the weather accentuated the feeling. Wetter, drearier than usual, northern Virginia became almost a bog.[66] If only Anna could come on a visit, things would brighten immeasurably. Quarters might be a problem, but Jackson felt he could solve it somehow. Would she consent to come if arrangements could be made? Anna would not only consent, she practically insisted.

At the hospitable Yerby house the general found spacious and ready accommodations for wife and child. Anna might come then, if she felt that the trip would not hurt Julia. As soon as things could be settled in North Carolina, she would leave. Waiting proved terribly hard. On April 18, Thomas wrote his truant *esposita*:

> Last night I dreamed that my little wife and I were on opposite sides of a room, in the centre of which was a table, and the little baby started from her mother, making her way along under the table, and finally reached her father. And what do you think she did when she arrived at her destination? She just climbed up on her father and kissed him! And don't you think he was a happy man? But when he awoke he found it all a delusion.[67]

Monday, April 20, 1863, had been wetter than usual around Guiney's Station; the myriad camps stretching in all directions around the army's railhead dripped soddenly. Straight to the station rode the man in the rubber coat, reined up, swung out of the saddle, and strode quickly toward the train. Along the crowded aisles he went, dripping little puddles of water but paying no attention. The cars from Richmond were crowded with returning soldiers, officers, and the usual rear-area hangers-on. Where . . . ? There! The bewhiskered face broke into a beam as he embraced Anna. Then he looked at Julia for the first time. She smiled as she saw his intense look, and soon she too was beaming. He wanted to take her in his arms, but the wet coat might be dangerous. He would wait. As Anna, the baby, and the proud father stepped from the cars, loud cheers greeted them from the nearby troops. Straight ahead to the carriage—it would not do to betray parental emotions here. In the carriage on the way to the Yerbys' the general looked often at Julia and commented on how pretty, how large she was.

At the Yerby house, as soon as the Jackson family gained the privacy of their room, off came the coat, and father Jackson took his "angel" in his arms. In front of a mirror he would take her often after that first meeting, would hold her up and say, "Now, Miss Jackson, look at yourself!" [68] Anna found that she had some difficulty in getting Thomas to take his eyes off Julia long enough to see her, but this dereliction was instantly forgiven.

During the next few days Jackson did his best to be firm with his new daughter, to impose some of his vaunted discipline. He met with some success, but his heart hardly seemed to be in the project. There was too much to be done to bother with a rigid regimen of correction. April 23 would be Julia's five months' birthday, and that day had been appointed for her baptism.

Reverend Tucker Lacy had consented to officiate, and the rite would take place in the Yerby parlor. Jimmy Smith appeared with a special request: he had heard that the baptism was to be private, but he very much wished to attend. Would the general consent? A doting father readily agreed: "Certainly, Mr. Smith, you can go; ask the others to go with you." So came the whole staff, who still resented the fact that they had only recently learned that their leader was a father.[69] A very martial group gathered for the ceremony. Amidst such unaccustomed pomp something went wrong with the logistics of the affair; Mrs. Jackson did not appear on schedule. The general marched out of the room, found his daughter, gathered her up, and returned. Press on! [70] Mr. Lacy knew his business, and performed a handsome service. "Very fine, very fine." [71]

If Anna thought she had been royally received when she visited the army near Manassas, she discovered now that her previous reception had been mild indeed. Groups of officers continually called at the Yerbys' to pay their respects. A lively interest continued throughout the Corps in seeing the general's wife and little Miss Stonewall.[72] "There is," wrote Jed Hotchkiss to his wife, "much importance pertaining to the 'Lieutenant Generaless.'"[73]

Anna's most dazzling moments came when *"General Lee and his staff...* called to see Mrs. Jackson." She had a moment of panic. The name Lee simply overawed her, but she took firm hold of her courage and went to meet the general and his gentlemen. "I was met by a face so kind and *fatherly*, and a greeting so cordial, that I was at once reassured and put at ease... and the call was greatly enjoyed."[74] Her ordeal had not yet ended, though, for on Sunday, the twenty-sixth, she went on display. Anna was to attend church with Thomas, in front of all the other officers, their wives, and several thousand men of the Corps. It was a grand occasion, with Reverend Lacy taking full advantage of his distinguished audience to preach an "earnest and edifying" sermon and to lead the congregation in prayer and song. Before and after the tent service, Anna received the courteous greetings not only of Lee but also of numerous other generals in the Second Corps. That Sunday and that service were more special than she knew.

Sunday afternoon Thomas and Anna spent together with their baby. "His conversation," recalled Anna later, "was more spiritual than I had ever observed before. He seemed to be giving utterance to those religious meditations in which he so much delighted. He never appeared to be in better health than at this time, and I never saw him look so handsome and noble."[75]

On Monday, the twenty-seventh, and Tuesday, the twenty-eighth, Thomas had to leave his ladies for part of the day—military business as usual. He probably did not bother Anna with discussions of his orders for the march, his directions to the division commanders about cooking rations. His regular appearance at headquarters, while his wife and child were visiting him, surprised some of the staff, but he continued a schedule of duty which would be a "pattern for all good soldiers—but one," thought Jed Hotchkiss, "which many of them would be slow to imitate under like circumstances."[76]

When the day's work ended, Thomas galloped to the Yerby house. Not a moment with Julia would be missed. As one lady observed, "The general spent all his leisure time in playing with the baby."[77] That observation, though, lacked complete truth. A happy father, Thomas was also the happy husband, reveling in having Anna near him after so long an absence. Anna had not seen him since Jeb Stuart had presented the new coat, nor since the avalanche of presents had piled up at headquarters. All these he proudly displayed. One morning during her stay, Anna was surprised to see Thomas come riding up to the Yerby house. He had left headquarters just to show her another gift—a fine bay horse named Superior, which must have made Little Sorrel look small and scraggly. Seated on this splendid steed, Jackson spurred and went flying away, showing off his riding prowess to an admiring wife, who saw him as the "impersonation of fearlessness and manly vigor." [78]

So healthy and handsome did Thomas look, so martial in his dress grays, that Anna persuaded him to sit for a photograph at the Yerby house—an exercise he much despised. She thought the resulting picture most soldierly, but felt it did not have his "*home-look.*"

Happy and content were the Jacksons, but the rains were ending, the roads were drying, and Union General Fighting Joe Hooker was beginning to give signs of restlessness. Longstreet's Corps, detached on a food-gathering mission in North Carolina, received stand-by orders: The First Corps might be recalled at any moment. Everything pointed to active campaigning soon. Old Jack knew that the Second Corps had been made as ready for battle as diligent and steadily improving administration could make it and that morale had never been better. The Corps was prepared. So was the Corps commander, although he hoped that for a few more days he could stay with his baby and his darling *esposa.*

A message from Jubal Early's adjutant woke Jackson on the morning of April twenty-ninth. Swinging out of bed, Thomas said calmly: "That looks as if Hooker were crossing." Anna felt the quick chill of dread. Dressed, Thomas hurried down to see Early's adjutant. He was right: Hooker had moved. Back up the familiar, the happy stairs. The spring campaign had started, a battle loomed, and it might be unsafe for Anna and the baby to stay. He would arrange for their safe conduct to Richmond. If he could he would come back to see them off. If not . . . a fervent kiss for Anna, a loving squeeze for Julia . . . and then off to the front without breakfast. [79]

A few days before, when writing one of his chatty family letters to Maggie, Thomas had grown briefly mournful, engulfed in memories, and wrote of "our precious Ellie, and of the blessedness of being with her in heaven." [80]

19

"DUTY IS OURS,

CONSEQUENCES ARE GOD'S"

—JACKSON

CANNON BOOMED along the Rappahannock Valley. Smoke from a man-made storm added clouds to that spring morning of April 29. Straight toward the smoke and the sound rode Jackson. At the front he found that "Jube" Early already had his skirmishers out toward the Richmond Stage Road searching for signs of the enemy. Reports coming to Old Jack were that the Federals had pushed some pontoon bridges across the Rappahannock and were massing along the riverbank. Fighting Joe Hooker meant business. Anna must leave at once.

Scribbling a hasty note explaining why he could not return to see the family off, Thomas added a few tender words for Julia and commended Anna and the baby to the care of Providence. Joseph Morrison, Anna's brother, was asked to see that mother and daughter safely reached the train at Guiney's, but he begged to stay with Jackson, who surely would need all the staff assistance he could get. Very well, Chaplain Lacy might perform the necessary duty. Not long after came the comforting word that the train had departed—the family would soon be in Richmond.[1]

Now that he need not worry about his two darlings, Jackson focused his full attention on the front. Much had to be done. First General Lee must be informed of Hooker's activities. Captain Jimmy Smith rode off to awaken the commanding general and soon Lee appeared. Lee could see nothing definite. He rode to Jackson's point of observation and the two discussed the proper disposition of the gray forces. Jackson listened as General Lee reviewed intelligence reports of enemy activity northwest of Fredericksburg. Information from Stuart and other scouts seemed

455

to show that the Federals were moving upstream, and Lee thought Hooker would throw the main weight of his attack around on the Confederate left flank. What ought to be done?

While the commanding general wrestled with a problem complicated by the absence of Longstreet with Hood's and Pickett's divisions, Jackson carefully prepared his line. Large numbers of the Second Corps were distant from the Fredericksburg positions; they must be brought up as fast as rations could be cooked and wagons harnessed. Joseph Morrison, staying at the post of duty, took out his note pad and wrote down the orders as Jackson drafted them. Generals Raleigh Colston (a brigadier commanding Jackson's division until Trimble could return), A. P. Hill, and Robert Rodes (a brigadier commanding D. H. Hill's division until "Allegheny" Johnson could resume the field) received orders to move toward Fredericksburg.[2] Crutchfield must send up the artillery and enough horses to make mobile the guns already in position along the Fredericksburg line. Speed the operations, for the enemy had crossed the river.[3]

Rumors and pseudo reports flooded Army Headquarters: the enemy was crossing the Rappahannock upstream with large forces; the enemy's main effort would be in front of Fredericksburg. Most of a long and anxious day Lee spent in sifting these conflicting stories but in the afternoon a telegram from Stuart gave concrete information. The cavalry had engaged a large Union force nine miles east of Culpeper—prisoners were from several Federal corps. Doubtless Lee informed his own Corps commander that Hooker had certainly moved upstream with substantial units. Whether that meant the main attack would come from the left still could not be determined. While Lee pondered how best to use his 62,500 men against at least 130,000 bluecoats,[4] Jackson continued to strengthen the entrenchments of the Second Corps.

By evening of the twenty-ninth Lee felt almost certain that Hooker's main blow would fall on the Confederate left, and yet the continued presence of large Federal forces in his immediate front made it impossible to shift the whole army to meet a threat upstream. Lee determined on a compromise: Gen. R. H. Anderson, whose division held the extreme Confederate left, would bring up all his brigades and move westward toward Chancellorsville in the Wilderness. He would keep a sharp eye out for approaching Yankees and contest their advance. Hardly did Anderson need to be told that his was a heavy responsibility—his force on the flank might have the task of holding off a good portion of the Army of the Potomac.[5] He marched that Wednesday evening.

Jackson camped for the night at his old headquarters near Hamilton's Crossing and ordered each of his division commanders to be doubly alert for any Federal actions along the river's edge.[6] Devotions must have been long that evening.

Morning mist shrouded the Rappahannock bottoms on the thirtieth. The sun, though, soon would melt away the film and Federal positions could be observed.[7] Long before dawn broke, Jackson had been up attending to the myriad details of striking his tents and moving Corps headquarters. Now that the campaign had begun he became all soldier; his staff noted the change and conformed to his mood. Staff officers and enlisted men worked swiftly at packing wagons, carrying orders. Just before his own tent came down, Deacon Jackson went in, closing the flap behind him. Faithful Jim Lewis, holding Little Sorrel's reins, motioned to silence the staff workers. "Hush," he said, "the general is praying." Quiet settled over the little clearing in the greening woods. Fifteen minutes passed and then Old Jack came out, gave some final instructions, and rode off. That was the last time he used the tent.[8]

At the front line Jackson joined Lee and the two looked across at Stafford Heights. As he saw the formidable Federal batteries on the ridge, the resting lines of Union troops in front of his Corps, Jackson's fighting blood rose. He wanted to attack, to drive the enemy into the river. The commanding general listened with the respect he always showed toward a Jackson suggestion, but he had to disagree. Virtually the same conditions which had prevented an attack on the evening of December 13 still prevented it. Much better, he thought, to hold the heights and repel a Yankee advance. Jackson looked grimly at the enemy lines—he still wanted to fight. Deferring to his lieutenant's tactical judgment, Lee conceded that "if you think it can be done, I will give orders for it."[9]

A moment's silence. Then: Would General Lee allow him time to make a thorough reconnaissance before he made up his mind? Certainly. Touching the sorrel's side, Jackson rode forward to examine the ground and the Federal positions near the river. Rain ran in rivulets down his rubber coat, drenched the ground, but Old Jack rode along, dismounting now and then, looking always at the enemy. Late in the afternoon he went to Army Headquarters and regretfully admitted that in the face of the formidable Yankee cannon "it would be inexpedient to attack here." Did General Lee have a plan? He did. Quickly Jackson received exciting orders. "Move," said the commanding general, "at dawn tomorrow up to Anderson." So he had made a decision: The real threat would come on the left.

As Lee developed his plan Jackson learned that McLaws's command and the whole Second Corps, excepting one division, would move. The remaining Second Corps division, to be selected by Jackson, would have to hold the Fredericksburg lines with the assistance of Barksdale's famous sharpshooters. Instantly Old Jack named the veteran units of Ewell, now under Jube Early, to defend the heights.[10]

Once again Lee was dividing his army in the face of an enemy attack

—and once again Jackson was happy. The country west of Fredericksburg offered superb possibilities for maneuver. Not only did the vast, virtually impenetrable Wilderness promise to confuse and possibly ensnare a large army, but also the junction of the Rappahannock and Rapidan Rivers might serve to trap Hooker as it had almost trapped Pope months before. The Lord of Hosts might send the blue hordes into that V-shaped angle.... Long prayers, then sleep.

Shortly after midnight on May 1, Old Jack was up and dressed in full and resplendent uniform.[11] Ordering the troops aroused, he prepared to lead the advance. Rodes would be in the van, then A. P. Hill and Colston. No daylight could be wasted: the Second Corps must reach Anderson in time to head off Hooker's march through the Wilderness. Down the Plank Road from Fredericksburg to Orange Court House swung the long line of lean veterans,[12] with the familiar half-crouched figure of Old Jack trotting ahead on Little Sorrel. Press on, men, close up. A nice morning for marching, once the mists cleared, and the men stepped forward briskly. As 8 A.M. approached, Jackson and the leading men in Rodes's column could hear firing from the west.[13]

Shortly Jackson found General Anderson, who had diligently entrenched a line facing west and northwest guarding the Old Turnpike and the Plank Road, which led to Chancellorsville. Jackson knew from one of Hotchkiss's admirable maps that these roads came together at Chancellorsville a little more than four miles ahead.[14] A third, coming into the Old Turnpike on the right, was called the Old Mine Road, since it led from the United States Mine Ford on the Rappahannock, and this, too, Anderson covered.[15] At hand to assist Anderson were three of McLaws's brigades, which meant that six Confederate brigades held the line of works. From all the information which Anderson could collect, the Federals were moving through the Wilderness on Chancellorsville and beyond it toward the fortified road junction. No doubt remained about where the enemy had gone; Anderson had encountered strong units south of the Rapidan and the Rappahannock. Hooker apparently had crossed his army at Germanna and Ely's fords over the Rapidan and had aimed his advance at the left rear of Lee's army.[16]

Anderson had done well with the few troops he had, but as Old Jack looked into the Wilderness he grew impatient. Hooker must be attacked while still in the clogged woodland, where soldiers could see scarcely forty yards ahead. Some of Anderson's men, supported by McLaws, were ordered to go forward on the Old Turnpike. One of Anderson's brigades would lead the way on the Plank Road, which diverged slightly south. The Second Corps would follow on that highway. On the right Old Jack could see that the roads ran too close to the Rappahannock for maneuver, but the Plank Road might offer an opportunity to hit Hooker's flank element as it stumbled through the underbrush. Move, then, swiftly.

By about 11 A.M. on the first day of May Jackson's advance began. McLaws commanded the force moving on the Turnpike. Jackson, with Anderson, directed operations on the Plank Road. The two columns moved cautiously forward, skirmishers well out, probing the woods. Five minutes, ten—the troops were into the woods now, where the sun fought grimly to light the pathways. Fifteen minutes. Suddenly came the sound of musket fire on the Turnpike! McLaws had run into the enemy; skirmish lines were battling. Still Jackson pushed his own column straight ahead, and still it met no resistance. Old Jack's main concern at the moment centered on his flanks. Were there so many Yankees infesting the woods that they would envelop his columns as they pressed along the roads? Shortly came the sharp reports of skirmish firing in front of the gray vanguard. Halt! Skirmishers pushed ahead to "feel out" the Federal position. This time there would be no mistake about a careful scouting of the ground; the woods and dense leaves made a careful look imperative. A blind assault on an unseen line would be madness.

Reports came to Old Jack that a large enemy force could be dimly seen, apparently in the process of deploying for battle. Important intelligence, for it confirmed that Hooker guarded both main roads and was aggressive. Directing McLaws to hold his ground in front of what seemed to be masses of bluecoats, Jackson ordered Alexander's guns forward to shell the Federals as they deployed. A "whiff of grape" as they were trying to keep their organization, straighten their line, and make ready to attack might demoralize them completely. While the experiment with artillery took place, the infantry could rest on the road —all except Stephen D. Ramseur's brigade from Rodes's division, which was en route to Jackson.[17] If guns did not dislodge the enemy, Jackson told McLaws, he would try to flank them and attack from behind.[18]

A courier from Stuart brought a message. Jackson broke the seal of the dispatch and read Jeb's familiar scrawl. The cavalry, said Stuart, after harrowing adventure, had come around Hooker and now stood in position to protect Jackson's left flank. "I will close in on the flank and help all I can when the ball opens," wrote Jeb. Then he added a line for the special attention of the Deacon: "May God grant us victory." All worry about the left flank ceased. Turning the paper over, Jackson wrote in haste: "I trust that God will grant us a great victory. Keep closed on Chancellorsville." [19]

As he urged the skirmish line to heavier work, Jackson was overtaken by General Lee, who had left Fredericksburg in charge of Jube Early with 10,000 men and 45 guns [20] and had ridden toward the front. The two rode together along a cheering line of men as Jackson outlined dispositions and hopes. Lee had no changes to make or advice to impart. Leaving the left to Jackson's capable management, the commanding general rode toward the Confederate right, where the extent of the enemy line had not yet been determined.

Old Jack rode out to Anderson's advanced troops and urged the men to press ahead, to keep the enemy off balance and falling back. Curiously enough, the enemy did fall back, and without stiff fighting. All along the Union line units drew in, retiring readily before Confederate pressure. What did this mean? Could it be that Fighting Joe had had enough of fighting and was drawing his army back across the river? Had his grand strategy failed? Not sure yet, Jackson kept driving his men forward. Joe Morrison, sticking stanchly by the general's side, took out his notebook and penned an order.

> Hdqrs. Second Corps, Army of
> Northern Virginia,
> May 1, 1863—2:30 p. m.

Major-General McLaws,
  Commanding Division:

General: The lieutenant-general commanding directs me to say that he is pressing on up the plank road; also, that you will press on up the turnpike toward Chancellorsville, as the enemy is falling back.

Keep your skirmishers and flanking parties well out, to guard against ambuscade.

Very respectfully, your obedient servant,
  J. G. Morrison,
    ACTING ASSISTANT ADJUTANT-GENERAL.[21]

Taking post with the new lead brigade—Ramseur's—Jackson eagerly watched the strange conflict in the woodland. Confederate skirmishers, followed by a battle line, would go forward; the Federals would fire a volley or so, and fall back. Gradually resistance stiffened, and Ramseur, directing his skirmishers personally, found his brigade hotly engaged. Old Jack kept up with the line. When a particularly dense patch of woods approached—a patch which seemed to offer good cover for a bushwhacking party—Professor Jackson would halt his advance and have the woods soundly shelled. "Press them" became his standard phrase that day.[22]

About midafternoon Anderson sent a brigade to the left along an unfinished railroad cut toward the right rear of Federal units which were making a stand, and the flank move forced the enemy back still farther.[23] Satisfied that Anderson could handle operations in the center, Old Jack galloped off toward the far left. Joe Morrison tagged along.

A road, branching left from the Plank Road, led conveniently along the Confederate line, and Jackson kept to it until he arrived at an iron-

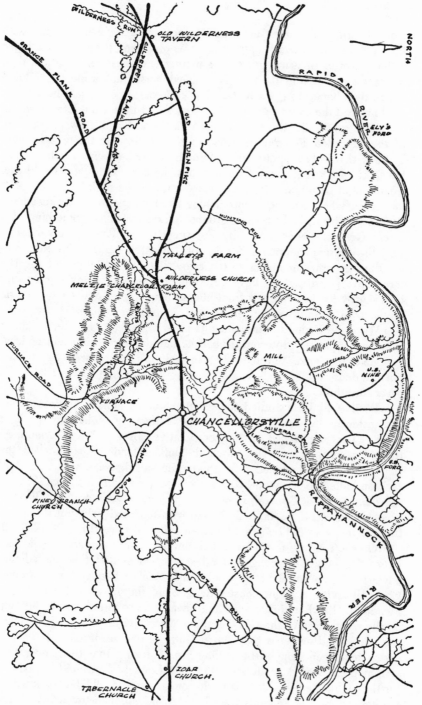

Terrain and roads surrounding Chancellorsville, Virginia

works bearing the name Catharine Furnace. On a slight hill nearby with the First Virginia Cavalry, Jeb Stuart was observing the work of a horse artillery section. A warm greeting, a moment's earnest conversation, then the two generals and their staffs touched horses and rode for a knoll where they hoped to get a better view of Federal positions. Slick, sticky mud marked the trail to the top, but horses had little trouble negotiating the slight grade. On the crest Jackson and Stuart had a sweeping view of the supposed Federal positions to the north, but the woods were so thick that only a spotty idea of roads could be gained. What roads led to Hooker's rear? Stuart pointed out those he knew and could see. There might be others. Old Jack looked hard at the rolling, dense woodland. Somewhere out there, entrenching like beavers, were Hooker's men. Perhaps, as he looked over the ground, Jackson recalled something of a recent General Order issued by Fighting Joe, explaining how he had won the present campaign: "It is with heartfelt satisfaction the commanding general announces to the army that the operations of the last three days [April 27–30] have determined that our enemy must either ingloriously fly, or come out from behind his defenses and give us battle on our own ground, where certain destruction awaits him." [24]

Were the Federal entrenchments as formidable as Hooker claimed? Was he completely protected, or had he blundered to the extent of leaving one of his flanks "in the air"? From Jackson's knoll it was hard to say, but the dense underbrush, while covering a defending force, might also cover an attack.

While Old Jack studied the terrain, Stuart's guns went into action and instantly drew such a hot response of bursting shells that the little band of horsemen raced for the comparative safety of lower ground. As the riders slipped and slid down the hill, a terrific blast rocked the slope, bits of iron whined through the air—a horseman was wounded! Jackson halted to see who had been hit. Major Channing Price, Stuart's Assistant Adjutant General, slumped in his saddle; he would be all right, he said, but soon he fainted. Jackson waited anxiously until satisfied that the major would be cared for, then galloped toward the Plank Road.

On the road he met Powell Hill, and probably Anderson, who had interesting news. A strong Federal stand had stalled the Confederate advance. There could be no doubt that Hooker had gathered around Chancellorsville a mighty host indeed. Send this news to General Lee. Meantime Hill should ride with him toward the sound of serious fighting on the right, close to the Old Turnpike. Near McLaws's front line, Jackson and Hill discovered that Harry Heth, in charge of Hill's three brigades, had been stopped by galling fire. Thinking that further fighting at that point would produce nothing, McLaws had ordered a bivouac for the night. Heth still hoped to do something and Old Jack wanted to see how strong the Federals were here. As he galloped toward the lines, he caught sight of a rider racing toward him. Captain Alexander C. Haskell, the gallant South Carolinian, saluted as he drew rein near Jackson, Hill, and their entourage. "Captain Haskell, what is it?" asked Old Jack. Relieved beyond words to see his "beloved Commander," Haskell answered: "Ride up here, General, and you will see it all." Off to the right of the road the captain went and on to the crest of a little hill. At last, a place from which a good view of partially open ground in the Confederate front could be had. Out came Old Jack's field glass; slowly he moved it from side to side. Spread before the lens were three Yankee battle lines, behind heavy earthworks. As the slouching man on the scrubby sorrel horse took his time about surveying the geography, Federal cannon banged away at the hill. Shells began to heave up clouds of dirt; explosions frightened most of the horses. But Old Jack and Little Sorrel stood serenely unaware that they were the targets. After satisfying himself that he had seen all the terrain visible, Jackson lowered the glass, picked up the sorrel's reins, called Haskell closer, and said, "Hold this position until 9 o'clock tonight, when you will be relieved by General Fitzhugh Lee." Closer, come closer. Old Jack's clipped tones came now in a whisper: "Countersign for the night is, Challenge, Liberty; Reply, Independence." A rare confidence, indeed.[25]

Wheeling, Stonewall galloped along the road toward Catharine Furnace until he reached the point at which the Plank Road crossed his path. Here he halted, and shortly before dark General Lee arrived. Jackson saluted his chief; the two dismounted. An annoying Yankee sharpshooter, aiming at some Confederate cannoneers, forced the two officers to leave the road and seek shelter in the piny woods near the crossroads. A log became a convenient bench. Jackson reported to the commanding general what had happened on the left. He stressed the ease with which the Federals had been shoved back. From what he had seen, he said in his earnest, quiet tones, he felt that something had gone wrong with Fighting Joe's offensive. Either the Confederates were wrong and the move had not been the major Yankee attack, or else Hooker had failed. The more he thought about it, the more convinced he became that "by tomorrow there will not be any of them this side of the river."[26]

Clearly Lee did not agree. He hoped Jackson was right, but he felt sure that Hooker had made his big push here and could hardly give it up without a serious contest. Admittedly, his plans were obscure, but that he would retreat after light contact appeared unlikely. Stubbornly, Stonewall stuck to his idea; Hooker would be gone the next day. As he listened to the reiteration, Lee may have recalled the story of Jackson's conviction the night after Malvern Hill that Little Mac would be gone in the morning. The chances were good that his present prognostication might be less accurate than the earlier one. The commanding general would have to assume the presence of Hooker the next day, and make preparations to meet him. If he still held his lines, he must be attacked, but where, and how? Old Jack listened as Lee summarized his scout on the right; nothing could be done there. The woods were too thick; enemy positions could not be clearly located. How about the immediate front? Old Jack could not say.

Lee suggested a reconnaissance—he would send his engineer friend, Maj. T. M. R. Talcott. Jackson named his alert engineer Capt. James Boswell. The two men were summoned and told to scout the front carefully, estimate enemy infantry and artillery strength, and report their findings. Speed would count.

After the engineers departed, Lee voiced the question which certainly had arisen in Jackson's mind: What if there were no feasible way to get at Hooker in front? Would that mean Fighting Joe's boastful Order No. 47 had been correct—would the Confederates be forced to inglorious flight? Could something be done on the Confederate left? Jackson still felt that the ground to the south and southwest offered possibilities for maneuver. Although he reported the hot fire he had experienced when perched on the knoll near Catharine Furnace, he doubtless felt that this did not necessarily mean Hooker had extended his flank much farther south. He had seen vague outlines of roads, and some of Hotchkiss's sketches showed hints of backways and byways. It might be worth a try, if a route sufficiently screened from the Yankees could be found.

While Jackson and Lee talked, Jeb Stuart rode up, dismounted and joined in the high-level discussions. He was in high glee. Fitzhugh Lee, his daring young lieutenant, had ranged far to the west and returned convinced that Hooker had not anchored his right flank on any natural or artificial barrier. It was, in the parlance of the battlefield, "in the air." Instantly the character of the conference changed.

Attention focused on how to turn the exposed Union right. A secret and comparatively short route must be found. If it were overly long, a day might be wasted and the infantry would be too tired to attack after they reached the enemy's rear. Now the dense and forbidding Wilderness began to seem friendly; it might provide secrecy, particularly since Hooker had dispatched the major portion of his mounted force on a raid toward Richmond and Lee's railroad communications. Stuart stood up, saying that he would go look for a road that fitted the necessities. Jingling merrily, he mounted and thundered away.

Lee and Jackson continued their discussion, and in an hour or so Talcott and Boswell returned with news which now must have been hoped for: an attack in front would be suicidal. Lee peered intently at a map and finally, as if talking to himself, said: "How can we get at those people?" That problem would have to be solved by Lee alone. The loyal Jackson said: "You know best. Show me what to do, and we will try to do it." Of that Lee had not the slightest doubt. But for a while he did not know exactly what to suggest. He studied the map in the flickering candlelight, and finally began to trace a route around the Yankee flank and rear; a pincers attack, to be made by two wings of the army. This meant that some of the army would have to be detached for the flank march. A moment's expectation, then Lee gave the coveted order— Jackson would lead the detached force and would be screened by Stuart with the cavalry! The strategy had been decided and now Jackson must work out the tactics. The compliment supreme!

Never before had Stonewall been offered just such a prize. Now with the infantry he was to duplicate Stuart's "rides around McClellan." With God's blessing he might strike an unparalleled and decisive blow on an unsuspecting enemy host. Smiling broadly, Old Jack rose from the log, saluted General Lee, and said, "My troops will move at 4 o'clock." [27]

The commanding general had one parting thought: If Stonewall still felt Hooker's army would be gone in the morning, he could settle the point by sending a gun or two to the little hill Stuart's artillery had used during the afternoon. A few shells lobbed toward the Federal entrenchments would soon produce an answer. But as Old Jack moved off into the woods seeking a place to sleep, he probably ceased to concern himself with the question of Hooker's morning whereabouts; if General Lee expected the enemy still to be behind their works, there they would be.[28]

A little clearing in the woods invited the spread of a saddle blanket and the repose of a tired soldier. Unbuckling his sword and leaning it against a tree, Jackson stretched out nearby. Headquarters wagons were far behind, and in the rush of events he had forgotten to bring along his blanket roll, so in the chill of the May night he prepared to huddle without covers. Sandie Pendleton, ever watchful for the comfort of Old Jack, quickly offered his overcoat. No, no, Pendleton must keep that for himself. Would the general accept the cape from the greatcoat? Since that would mean an equal division of the garment, Jackson consented. There was something unaccountably bone-chilling about the cold. It was a feeling enhanced by the presence of thousands of mortal enemies in an eerie woodland, waiting for daylight and a chance to kill. The two Confederate officers, good and tried friends, lay down close together and slept.[29]

Quiet hours passed in the Wilderness. Campfires flickered low, vast thousands of men slumbered hard; strength would be needed on the morrow. The ground grew cold and clammy. A cloak was not enough to shut out the chill of the night air and the dankness of the ground. Jackson awoke, and right away knew he had the beginnings of a head cold, possibly a bad one. Getting up, he saw Sandie's huddled figure, went over to the sleeping form, and spread the cape. One cheery oasis appeared in the gloom of the Wilderness. A courier's fire—snapping, crackling twigs—offered tiny but cheerful resistance to the darkness. A cracker box provided a seat, and, wrapped in his old rubber coat, Jackson drew close to the fire and warmed his hands. A word or two with the wakeful courier, then closer to the fire—it might help drive the dampness away and retard the progress of the head cold.

Another hunched form around the fire awoke. Chaplain Lacy came to the blaze and stood rubbing his stiff fingers. "Sit with me," the General said, but Lacy politely declined. Seeing that his reverend friend hesitated to crowd him, Jackson inched toward one end of the box. "Come sit down," he said, "I wish to talk with you." To the surprised chaplain, Old Jack began to talk of army problems, problems not connected with the chaplain service. The enemy, he was saying, lay in heavy force in front; the Confederate right offered no possibilities for decisive action. But Lacy had once preached in this section of country: did he know of usable roads on either Federal flank? Lacy had already reported to General Lee on road conditions and needed no time to think. There were none on the right, he announced, but on the left a maze of small trails and traces led around Chancellorsville to the Old Turnpike.

Out of a pocket came one of Hotchkiss's outline maps and a pencil. "Take this map," commanded Stonewall, "and mark it down for me." Lacy traced a line. Jackson looked and said, "That is too near: it goes within the line of the enemy's pickets. I wish to get around *well* to his rear, without being observed: Do you know no other road?" No, but it seemed altogether probable that some trail did exist which would serve the general's purpose. "Then where can you find this out certainly?" The proprietor of the Catharine Furnace, Col. Charles C. Wellford, ought to know, and his young, intelligent son should make a good guide. "Go," ordered Old Jack, "with Mr. Hotchkiss to the furnace . . . send Mr. Hotchkiss back with the information." Send a guide too. And Hotchkiss must find out one other thing. Professor Jackson woke the engineer, told him to search for the road, and if a road existed, be sure it could be used by artillery.[30]

Off into the black the two men rode. Jackson sat close to the circle of heat. No others stirred until Col. A. L. Long of Lee's staff rose and approached the fire. Good mornings exchanged, the colonel noticed that Jackson looked cold. Soon the general complained of the chill. Long saw some army cooks fixing breakfast not far away, and excused himself and went to procure some coffee for Old Jack. Jackson accepted the steaming tin cup eagerly, and as he sipped, the two chatted in low tones. Conversation was broken off suddenly by a loud clatter. Looking around, the two noticed that Jackson's sword, standing for so long by the tree, had fallen to the ground. Long later remembered it had fallen "without *appar-*

ent cause," and he thought it an ill omen. The colonel retrieved the weapon and gave it to Jackson, who muttered his thanks and buckled it on.[31]

As dawn began to show in the east and the chill of the night began to wear off, General Lee made his way to Jackson's fire.

Greetings were exchanged and Jackson informed the commanding general of dispatching Jed Hotchkiss on his scouting mission. The big question remained: Could the march be made in time to cripple Hooker before he did something himself? With the Army of Northern Virginia divided, and Hooker outnumbering both segments, the Yankee general could attack in the Wilderness or at Fredericksburg. If he pushed General Sedgwick across the Rappahannock against Early, the Confederate rear might fold up and Lee's troops might be caught in a closing pincers. Hooker must be made to stand and wait—but how? The observant Hotchkiss brought an answer.

There was a road! It fitted all the necessities—sufficiently screened and yet not too long. He had made a sketch. Spreading it out on another cracker box, Hotchkiss began to explain the map. The Catharine Furnace road ran on to the southwest, he said, pointing the way as he talked. Finally it ran into the larger north-south Brock Road. Do not turn right, or north into the Brock Road; turn left, and proceed southward for about 600 yards where a dirt trail turns right (west) from the Brock pike. Take this road which soon turns north and follow it until it rejoins the Brock Road near the Orange Plank Road. The Orange road should lead to the rear of the Union right flank, distance eleven or twelve miles. As Hotchkiss talked and pointed Jackson stared at the map with his eyes narrowed —when Hotchkiss explained geography he always listened with complete concentration. At last he appeared satisfied—he understood. The march could be made.

As the topographical engineer finished his report, Lee looked at Stonewall. "General Jackson," came the calm question, "what do you propose to do?" Eyes still glued to the map, Jackson pointed to Hotchkiss's route and said, "Go around here." That had been expected, but now Lee asked the most important question: "What do you propose to make this movement with?" Lee was asking, not telling, and he offered an opportunity which Jackson had been considering for some hours. In his mind Stonewall had arrived at a plan which he put into few words. He would move, he said, "with my whole corps." The attack on the Union rear would not be a small diversionary action designed to draw off some of Hooker's troops so that Lee could attack in front. If the enemy had left his rear unguarded, he had opened the way to a complete, decisive victory for the Confederates. Take advantage of every opportunity, a maxim Jackson had developed in the Valley Campaign. Lee had not expected Jackson's answer, had not thought in terms of a gigantic blow on the

Federal rear. But had he thought more about the nature of his lieutenant he could not have been surprised. Jackson never designed an operation which did not wring the last possible advantage from the situation. Never did he think in small or defensive terms. Assume the offensive and press the enemy with everything at hand. Now was the time to hit Hooker where he least expected the blow. And hit him in such overwhelming force that he could not stem the juggernaut. Audacity; mystery; surprise.

Finally came Lee's next question: "What will you leave me?" Instantly Old Jack had the answer, for he had carefully worked out the whole scheme: "The divisions of Anderson and McLaws." Taking 28,000 men with him, Jackson would leave Lee about 14,000 to face the whole of Hooker's masses. It was just the plan to come from Jackson and just the plan to suit his superior. But could Lee dare the risk with his numbers so few and reinforcements so remote? A long moment passed, a moment upon which hung the fate of the Confederacy, of Lee's army, the reputation of Lee as a commander, and the future of Stonewall Jackson. Lee's decision could not have surprised Jackson, who knew Lee so well that he would follow him anywhere: "Well, go on." Then Lee's pencil began to jot down notes for his final orders. Old Jack departed to make ready.

Jackson had already matured plans for the march: Rodes's division would take the lead, Colston's and Hill's divisions to follow. Every piece of Second Corps artillery would go along. Not only would the enemy be hit with infantry en masse, but Professor Jackson would use his guns to blast a way for the foot soldiers; he had not forgotten the lessons of the Seven Days. Cavalry would screen the front and right of Jackson's columns. Men would march at standard Corps speed—one mile in twenty-five minutes with a ten-minute rest every hour. Division ammunition wagons, ambulances, artillery, all would follow the infantry of each division. Ranks must be kept closed up and provost-marshal troops must follow the columns to bayonet any stragglers. This march would be made efficiently—no chance would be offered for dawdling or delay.[32]

Tangled brush and hidden roads delayed the beginning of the flank march until about 8 A.M., but Old Jack appeared unperturbed. There would be time enough to do the job if the march were not slowed further en route. Down the Furnace road came the veterans under Rodes, followed by the rest of the Corps. After the cavalry and the leading brigade of Colquitt had moved across the Plank Road on the way to Catharine Furnace, Old Jack trotted into the pike, following his van. As he and a small cluster of couriers and staff officers reached the crossroads, they encountered General Lee. Jackson approached, pulled the sorrel up for a brief moment, and spoke quickly to the commanding general. Stonewall, eyes ablaze, pointed ahead. Lee nodded. Spurs to the sorrel, Old Jack trotted on down the road. Lee and Stonewall Jackson had met for the last time.

Old Jack had his battle look about him that warm morning, and though his troops wanted to cheer him they had orders to keep silent; that fierce, glinting light in Stonewall's eye served as a stern reminder. The tattered lines in gray looked at their general, some nodded, some waved, but they kept quiet and kept at the business of walking. Walking proved not as difficult as it had been many times before. The road, still damp from rain, added spring to the step and yielded no dust. And although it had turned warm after a frigid night and water became scarce, the men were in fine spirits. They knew that Old Jack had some big surprise in store for Fighting Joe Hooker; they believed in whatever the surprise might be, and were confident of success. As staff officers rode along the sweating column, the good cheer of the men broke out in taunts and jibes at the hapless horsemen: "Say, here's one of Old Jack's little boys, let him by, boys." "Have a good breakfast this morning, sonny?" "Better hurry up, or you'll catch it for getting behind." "Tell Old Jack we're all a-comin'." "Don't let him begin the fuss till we get thar!" [33] A fine display of superb morale, but most embarrassing to the sensitive young staff officers.

Near the head of his long, twisting line, Jackson soon noted a potential danger point. The Furnace road ran through almost a tunnel of leaves, then suddenly climbed up and over a small hill just before crossing Lewis' Creek near Catharine Furnace. The hill jutted up above the green treetops and was itself bare of cover. Open ground yawned dangerously, south of the Furnace. Men, guns, and wagons would surely come under enemy fire as they rushed over the hill and across the clearing. The men might run quickly to avoid the hail of iron, but what of the wagons and guns? Was there an alternate route available, farther to the south and beyond the enemy's sight? Soon one had been located. A small track skirted the hill and came back into the road about a mile and a half beyond the Furnace. Put the wagon train on that road immediately, double-quick the infantry over the hill and into the cover of the woods. As the men made the climb and started down the other side of the rise a Federal battery began probing for the range, dropping shells around the hill. A trail from the direction of the enemy's lines entered the road close to the Furnace. Old Jack ordered Rodes to station a regiment there to guard against attack. "See that the column is kept closed and that there is no straggling," Old Jack said again and again. "Press forward." Nothing could weaken his determination to gain his objective.

As the men swung easily along the dirt road, Jackson dug spurs into Little Sorrel and galloped on ahead of the infantry. When he pulled even with his old friend Col. Tom Munford and General Rodes, riding as a vanguard with the Second Virginia Cavalry, he reined the sorrel to a walk and began to chat. Munford, long an admirer, understood at once that Old Jack's burst of loquacity came as a result of satisfied excitement—the march must be going according to plan. Raleigh Colston soon rode to the little group of horsemen, and his arrival gave Jackson a special topic of conversation. Speaking with ease in his quiet, half-clipped phrases, Professor Jackson reminisced about the days at VMI when all four had been together: Jackson, Rodes, and Colston on the faculty, and Munford the willing cadet adjutant. Each of the four recalled old classmates or students who now served in the Confederate Army, and the conversation became nostalgic.[34] Finally talk turned to the subject of Hooker and his army. Jackson broke in with a piercing comment on a fundamental Confederate deficiency:

> I hear it said that General Hooker has more men than he can handle. I should like to have half as many more as I have today, and I should hurl him in the river! The trouble with us has always been to have a reserve to throw in at the critical moment to reap the benefit of advantages gained. We have always had to put in all our troops and never had enough at the time most needed.[35]

As the road turned more toward the west and led far around the known Union positions, Jackson showed no concern, his sole emotion being displayed in the flashing blue of his eyes. Always he kept up the "press on, press on," urging his staff to close the column. No word came from the rear to indicate any serious enemy attempt on the wagon trains at the exposed point. The steady tramp of infantry marked off the miles. A progress report must be sent to Lee. In a hastily written dispatch Jackson told the commanding general of success so far, and doubtless expressed the hope that with God's blessing he soon would be in position to strike. A courier thundered along the road sometime in midafternoon, spotted Jackson's bent figure jogging loosely on Little Sorrel, reined up and saluted. A dispatch from General Lee, sir. A moment's pause while the seal was broken, and then Jackson read:

> Head Quarters Plank Road,
> May 2
>
> Lieut. Gen. T. J. Jackson,
>   Commanding Corps:
>
>   General: I have received your note of 10 1/2 to-day. I have given directions to all the commanders to keep a watch for any engagement which may take place in rear of Chancellorsville and to make as strong a demonstration as possible with infantry & Artillery & prevent any troops from being withdrawn in their front. I sent a dispatch to Gen. Stuart a short time since to your care saying that the enemy had reached Trevilians [?] & was tearing up the R. Road Central [sic] there. Force stated from one to four thousand. Everything is quiet in front at present.
>   Very respectfully, your obedient servant,
>
> R. E. Lee
> GENERAL [36]

Very good. General Lee would pin down any possible reinforcements for the Yankee right and rear and he had everything well in hand along the front. Into the Brock Road, a turn left for a short march, then sharp right again along a small dirt trace paralleling the Brock Road; Hotchkiss had been right—the new road not only could be used, but stood far beyond the restricted gaze of Union spyglasses. Northward now, toward the Orange Plank Road.

The hour's rest for lunch had come and gone; the men, still in high spirits, kept at their marching. As they moved closer to the enemy and to a fight, they grew more excited and eager. Not long after the head of the column reentered the Brock Road, Jackson spotted a gray horseman racing toward him. Reining amid loud jingles and creaking leather, the youthful brigadier Fitz Lee saluted in breathless haste. He wanted a private word. "General," gasped the youngster, "if you will ride with me, halting your columns here, out of sight, I will show you the enemy's right, and you will perceive the great advantage of attacking down the old turnpike, instead of the Plank Road, the enemy's lines being taken in reverse. Bring only one courier, as you will be in view from the top of the hill." [37]

Picking a courier and ordering the infantry to halt in the road, Old Jack set off with Lee along a trail running north of and roughly parallel to the Plank Road. Some distance into the heavy underbrush the cavalryman led the way, until at last he brought Jackson out of the Wilderness maze atop a hill. Spread before Old Jack's eyes were the left flank elements of the Army of the Potomac: long lines of men resting, arms stacked, unaware of the nearness of death. Campfires showed where army cooks were at work fixing supper—the men had apparently long since ceased constructing breastworks and gun emplacements. A few scattered cannon pointed toward the south, mute evidence of passing concern for the safety of the flank.

Swiftly Old Jack glanced over the Federal positions and as he looked a fiercer light burned in his eyes—"a brilliant glow," noted Lee, "lighting his sad face." The cavalryman reported on his earlier reconnaissance of the area, describing as much of the terrain as possible. None of this appeared to reach Old Jack, who seemed lost in some intense concentration of his own. Along the Federal line ran his eye: Where was the end? How far in the woods to his left was the extreme flank unit? Clearly the flank was "in the air," but the precise location had to be determined. Could the Second Corps attack along the Plank Road? No. If Jackson's infantry came up the Plank Road to attack they would strike the front of the enemy works at an oblique angle instead of taking them from behind. Young Lee had been right; far better to march to the Old Turnpike and be certain of gaining the Yankee rear than to attack here.

Grimly Old Jack studied the field, lips moving in silent communion. A wave to the courier: "Tell General Rodes to move across the Plank

Road; halt when he gets to the old turnpike, and I will join him there." One last look at the tempting scene, then, without a word to Lee, Jackson pulled the sorrel's head around and started down the hill so lost in thought that Lee feared he might fall off his horse.[38]

Back on the Brock Road, Old Jack snapped orders in tones as sharp as a rifle crack.[39] Detach Paxton with the Stonewall Brigade to guard a crossing of the Plank Road and another which ran northwestward toward the Turnpike: if that crossroads were held, the Confederate right flank would be secure. The left could be guarded by the Second Virginia Cavalry. "Colonel," said Jackson to Tom Munford, "look well to our left and, as we advance, endeavor, if possible, to seize the Ely's Ford Road and hold it and keep me posted on that flank." As Munford prepared to gallop ahead, Jackson called a parting and prophetic exhortation: "The Virginia Military Institute will be heard from today." [40]

On now to the Turnpike—nothing would swerve him from his purpose. The afternoon was half gone and much time would be consumed in deploying to attack, especially in the woodland. The column must be closed, ammunition wagons pushed along, straggling held down. Rodes's men were striding rapidly forward; the time had almost come! Reining up momentarily, Old Jack took out a wrinkled sheet of paper. General Lee, holding against such vastly superior numbers, would want to know how fared the flanking Corps. Resting the paper on the pommel of his saddle, Stonewall wrote:

Near 3 P. M.
May 2d, 1863

General,
 The enemy has made a stand at Chancellor's which is about 2 miles from Chancellorsville. I hope as soon as practicable to attack.
 I trust that an Ever Kind Providence will bless us with great success.
          Respectfully,
            T. J. Jackson
            LT. GENL.

Genl. R. E. Lee
 The leading division is up & the next two appear to be well closed.
              T. J. J.[41]

Through the bright greenery of freshly washed foliage Jackson's gray legions toiled ahead until, at length, the column turned right into the Old Turnpike. No mistake about it now, Old Jack had taken them clear around the Union Army and they were going to plow into Hooker's ample divisions from behind. They had come out of their entrenchments right enough, but not exactly where Fighting Joe had anticipated. Almost straight east now, Rodes led his men and after about a mile the long line of tattered and footsore grayclads halted on a gentle ridge. Four o'clock it was, when the order came to deploy. Form line of battle; skirmish line, go forward! General Rodes drew his line with extreme care. Instructions were given to each brigadier so that as much organization as possible could be kept in the tangled country ahead. The Turnpike divided Rodes's line of battle: Alfred Iverson's brigade on the left of the front line; next on his right, Edward O'Neal; across the road were George Doles's men; and over on the far right, A. H. Colquitt's brigade. Ramseur's fine command constituted the division reserve and took position behind Colquitt to serve as a flank guard.

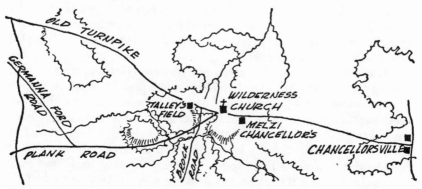

Area of Confederate attack at Chancellorsville (after Freeman, Lee's Lieutenants)

Each brigadier understood Jackson's attack plan. Using the pike as a guide, the whole line would sweep forward at the sound of the charge, aiming for the clearing around Talley's farm—a position which appeared to dominate some of the surrounding country. Next, the assault must concentrate on Melzi Chancellor's farm on the crest of a second, lesser ridge. Should the enemy make a determined fight here, leading Confederate units would take cover while Professor Jackson arranged to rake the position with the Corps artillery. Any pressure on the right of the attacking force could be handled by Ramseur, who must give personal attention to that flank. Above all, Old Jack wanted one thing understood: "Under no . . . circumstances was there to be any pause in the advance."[42]

Behind Rodes the other divisions were formed, until two full lines, each almost a mile and a half long, stretched through the Wilderness on both sides of the pike. Half of a third line began to form, backing up the left. Ten brigades were in position; another, the Stonewall, guarded roads to the right; and two others were still filing into the pike from the Brock Road. Thirteen brigades in all would be on hand for the attack. What had happened to the remaining two? News probably reached Old Jack about 5 P.M. that the two stray units had countermarched earlier in the day to protect the trains against a determined Yankee attack at the exposed hill near Catharine Furnace, but they were now en route to join him.

Through the maze of trees and bushes officers fought to establish their lines, to see that the men were kept together. Deployment under prevailing ground conditions took time, as Old Jack had expected. Thousands of men, guns, wagons, and animals milled around in the forest, as an army made ready to attack. Surely all the noise must have reached the ears of the enemy; but all indications were that the Yankees were preparing to eat supper, blissfully unaware of Stonewall Jackson and his men "who ran on wheels." Artillerists were ordered to bring up their batteries as soon as the infantry cleared the roads and good positions could be found. The limbers and caissons creaked forward. Division wagons must be halted in the rear, and the Corps hospital should be established at a safe distance behind the lines.

Late afternoon now, not much daylight left. Hard to remain calm, waiting for final details to be attended to while precious minutes slipped by, minutes which might mark the difference between victory and defeat. Press right on, men, press on. Old Jack sat Little Sorrel, eyes ablaze now, anxious to be at it. Still through the warm sunlight his officers struggled to deploy their men. The day had been warm and mild. The march had been hard, but not too hard; the men were still fairly fresh, and they were eager to finish the job. A touch on the sorrel's flank and Old Jack trotted forward to the first line. General Rodes was there, surveying his formation, and Jackson drew rein beside him.

Everything had been done to put more men on the Yankee flank than the enemy had in position. Everything had been done to ensure secrecy, and although it seemed that Hooker ought to have some advance notice, secrecy appeared to have been preserved. Everything had been done to make the attack of the Second Corps decisive. Reaching into a pocket beneath his coat, Old Jack took out his watch and gazed at it intently, lips pressed tight together. It was, he saw, 5:15 P.M.

"Are you ready, General Rodes?"

"Yes, sir," came the determined response.

"You can go forward then," Stonewall said, quietly and without visible excitement.

Rodes swept his line with hard blue eyes, nodded his blond head. A bugler straightened, inhaled. Through the sleepy, warm woodland rang the notes. Charge! Other bugles took up the call. Right, left, in the center. A moment of tense silence as the chilling notes floated over the army. Men gripped their rifles, bayonets fixed, and watched the skirmishers dash through the brush. Slowly at first, then with gathering speed, the massive lines moved forward. Faster, until at last the men were running, crashing, tearing through the trees and scrubs. Ahead of them startled deer, rabbits, and other animals fled in terror toward the Union Army. A moment's pause to untangle part of the skirmish line, then on again, faster than before. Out of a belt of woods at last, into relatively open ground, straight at the stacked arms of lazing boys in blue. A feeble scattering of shots, then the enemy ran.

Still that endless, ragged, incredibly tattered streak of gray came on, bearing down on the few Federals who tried to form a line. The Federals were firing a few more shots, trying to get some guns in action, desperately changing front. Forward! Press on, men, press them. Straight at the thin blue line rolled the gray wave. Fiercely now the Rebels charged, and as they saw the Yankees waver they began that eerie, spine-tingling Rebel yell. It floated over the field, died away, and rose again. A mad, headlong rout of the XI United States Army Corps began. No longer was there any doubt about who those wildly screaming, savage skeletons were—Stonewall Jackson's men! Jackson was behind the Union Army, he was in their midst, he was ruining them. Hooker's right and rear melted rapidly away toward Melzi Chancellor's farm. Talley's farm fell quickly to the charging demons.

Some confusion on Colquitt's front slowed the attack on the right, but the men on the left were unstoppable, invincible. Flawlessly officers deployed to meet pockets of resistance, to straighten the line, to re-form beyond rough ground. The charge rolled on, resistless, inexorable. Melzi Chancellor's ridge had been fortified with works facing south and west— those facing south were taken in flank and those facing the onrushing gray horde were stormed with a hair-curling scream, a scream which boded doom for the Army of the Potomac as twilight settled over the tortured Wilderness.[43]

Signs of wreckage could be seen on all sides. Fleeing Federals had flung aside all kinds of equipment; guns were falling into Confederate hands along with dazed groups of prisoners. The impetus of that first wild rush still carried Jackson's men forward. New tactics were evolved on the spot as the front line would rush, fire, and halt to load while the men behind raced ahead for their chance to fire. A solid mass of men came on from the rear, adding to the shattering effect of the waving Rebel flags, ragged flashes of Southern muskets, and the cacophony of cheering, yelling men.

Growing darkness, the disarrangement resulting from the rugged terrain, and stiffening bits of resistance gradually wore down the leading Confederate units. The second line had come forward to blend with the first as the works at Chancellor's were stormed, and so inextricably did the two mix that it became completely impossible to separate them. No attempt was made—they rushed on together toward Chancellorsville and Fighting Joe's headquarters. Another tight maze of woods engulfed the gleeful attackers; black night dropped over them like a shroud, and soon the right elements of the line were ensnared on an unexpected line of abatis. Clearly, all organization had vanished. Rodes reluctantly determined to halt the advance while he regrouped his men.

A courier from Rodes found Old Jack eagerly watching the battle from a spot close to the front.[44] Stonewall appeared inspired by the fighting; never had war so thrilled him. Like a Joshua leading on his "mighty men of valor," [45] he kept close to the front, and the men saw him stop now and then to gaze upward and to raise an arm: Smite them, O Lord! Stretch forth Thine arm! When a fallen figure in gray was seen, Jackson would stop and again raise his arm in that gesture of supplication: Receive Thy servant, Lord God of Hosts. Forward! [46]

It was sad indeed that Rodes had been forced to call a halt, but his request that A. P. Hill's division should come up from reserve to press the advance while the leading brigades caught their breath showed he had the proper spirit. Very good, very good. Order Hill to the front—wherever the front was. Stygian blackness hid the enemy; nothing could be seen of his positions. If only the sun would stand still on Gideon! Then would the Yankees be hurled in the river. Timidly at first, then boldly the moon shone. In the ghostly light the field began to take shape: woods ahead, the turnpike leading straight into the Union lines, here and there a clearing. What about the roads, and where exactly were the main Union works, if, indeed, there were any between the Confederates and Chancellorsville? Closer to the front Old Jack urged Little Sorrel; he must see for himself. Did a usable road lead northeastward behind the main bulk of Hooker's huddled masses? Would it be possible to throw the Second Corps between Hooker and United States Ford, pinning him in a vise to be squeezed by Jackson and by Lee?

Stonewall decided to examine the ground ahead and to look for a road which might answer the purpose taking form in his mind. Powell Hill, doubtless swathed in that fiendish red battle shirt, galloped up to report the rapid deployment of his men. Good, good. "Press them. Cut them off from the United States Ford, Hill. Press them!" [47] Hill spun to rejoin his troops; Old Jack, accompanied by a small cluster of couriers and staff officers, continued ahead.

A sudden, nervously effective cannonade from a massed enemy battery on a hill toward the east raked the road, driving everyone to cover. When Moorman's fine horse artillery—hard worked at the head of the advance through most of the late afternoon—ceased firing, the enemy fire sputtered out. Silence, and in the silvered dimness Hill's men filed into place on either side of the pike. A clatter of hooves, then a courier saluted, saying, "General Jackson, I have a dispatch for you from General Stuart." Old Jack took the envelope, read the dispatch quickly, and looked sharply at the courier, David J. Kyle. "Do you know all of this country?" Yes, sir. "Keep along with me." Straight toward the east on the Orange Plank Road rode Jackson until he reached the vicinity of a well-known local landmark, an old schoolhouse about 2,000 yards west of Chancellorsville.[48] A group of officers encountered here were quizzed about the situation in front. What little they could tell took only a short time and then Old Jack dug Little Sorrel's side, urging him farther ahead. A brief ride —covering about 200 yards—brought Jackson's little caravan to a line of Confederate infantry, formed across the Plank Road. These were A. P. Hill's men, making ready to resume the advance. General Jim Lane approached to say that he had almost completed the deployment and had been looking for General Hill to give the attack order. Would General Jackson give it?

Decisively Old Jack swept his hand toward the enemy lines, saying, "Push right ahead, Lane." The job must be done thoroughly—do not let the enemy get too well set in any position; capitalize on panic; terrorize the Army of the Potomac. The sooner the attack could be resumed, the sooner the end of Hooker would be achieved, and if Hooker were ruined, routed, the wreckage of his command driven into the river, this night's work might win the war! It was late, about 9 P.M., but the hour, the darkness, and the confusion of ground would doubtless demoralize an already shattered enemy more than the victorious Confederates. Staff officers began to report. Captain R. E. Wilbourn had news of Hill's progress in forming the line of attack; Joe Morrison rode up from some duty on another part of the field; James Boswell, the faithful engineer, was near at hand.

The only sure way to find out if a good highway led to the United States Ford Road behind Hooker was to go out to the skirmish line, to make a personal reconnaissance. Wilbourn stuck close by the general, still giving details of Hill's preparations. Soon the little group of riders came to a moonlit clearing. On the right Moorman's battery stood emplaced, protected by a thin curtain of infantry. Off to the left of the open ground two roads dimly could be seen, leading northeast into the woods. Where was the courier, Kyle? Swiftly he galloped to Jackson's side. Those roads on the left, where do they lead? One, said Kyle, the more distant, went to the Bullock farm not quite a mile north of Chancellorsville; the other, closer one, bore the name of Mountain Road and ran roughly parallel to the Plank pike at a distance of possibly a hundred yards and did not extend to Chancellorsville.[49]

If Kyle could be so sure of the way, he should take the lead on the closer road. Move on. This order stirred some concern among the staff. Already the knot of horsemen was far out, possibly in front of the Confederate picket line. One of the staff reined up by Old Jack with a question: "General, don't you think this is the wrong place for you?" In the intense excitement of an unfolding victory, Jackson's judgment failed him. "The danger," he said, "is all over—the enemy is routed!—go back and tell A. P. Hill to press right on!"[50] Eyes straining to see into the murk ahead, body bent forward as he listened with his slightly deaf ear, Old Jack followed Kyle toward the enemy lines. Soon he was beside the courier. After a time he pulled the sorrel up, and in the darkness splotched with shimmering moonlight, he cocked his head slightly. Noises, and not far away. Axes ringing on wood, men commanding other men to fall into line. Not much farther down the Mountain Road lay the Federal works; Old Jack had found the enemy.[51]

A moment's listening, then around came the sorrel's tired head. The little troop started back toward the Confederate positions. As he followed along the old trail, Jackson probably debated the wisdom of a renewed attack in the night against fortifications, but during that whole day perseverance had most distinguished the commander of the Second Corps. Dogged dedication to plan had made the flank march a success, had launched the attack late in the day, and had gained spectacular initial success. That same dedication might accomplish the full object of the turning movement: Hooker still could be blown out of the war. The attack, of course, would go on.

Lost in thought about where to aim his main thrust, how to hold a position behind Hooker once it had been gained, Old Jack trotted along the Mountain Road and soon approached an old frame house not far from the Plank highway.[52] South of the dark pike Confederate pickets were nervously straining for sounds of enemy activity.

From north of the Plank Road came the sound of horses—Federal cavalry? A shot tore the nervous silence of the front, another, then a well-delivered volley. A. P. Hill's voice instantly could be heard above the echoing shots: "Cease firing, cease firing." Little Sorrel for once yielded to panic, bolted and raced madly north toward heavy woods. Pull up, hold control. Reining with one hand and holding his cap on with the other, Jackson finally wheeled his mount back in the direction of the Confederates. Confusion and panic spread among Jackson's little coterie. Joe Morrison, leaping from his frightened horse, ran desperately toward the gray lines yelling, "Cease firing! You are firing into our own men." "Who gave that order?" thundered an unseen officer. "It's a lie! Pour it into them, boys." And before Morrison could reach the colonel commanding a North Carolina regiment, a steady volley from a kneeling line blazed into the night.

Hit! Possibly in several places. The sorrel was running wildly away again. One arm could not be used. Rein in with the other. Branches lashed his face, cutting him, ripping off his cap. A limb almost knocked him from the saddle. With great effort he hauled the sorrel back toward his lines, but could not stop him. A voice came from the darkness, a voice speaking to the horse. Someone had the reins. His right hand had been hit and his left arm hung useless—there might be another wound. The men who were helping? Captain Wilbourn and Lieutenant Wynn, also of the Signal Corps. Wilbourn had said, "They certainly must be our troops," looking toward the place from which the volley had come. Jackson nodded faintly, looking in perplexity toward his lines. Had his own men shot him? "You had better take me down." Finally, after much pain in his left arm, which surely must be broken, the two men got him down from his horse. For a few yards he stumbled along between the two aides, and at length he was stretched out beneath a tree.

Wilbourn competently sent an unidentified bystander to find out what Confederate troops were in front and he sent Wynn careening through the woods to find Dr. Hunter McGuire. Faces, voices, things, all grew dim. Faintly Jackson could feel Wilbourn remove his field glasses and haversack, then tear the sleeve of the rubber coat, the uniform sleeve, and the two shirts on the shattered arm. Tortured pain, swimming reality. Horses; a familiar voice; Powell Hill was here. "I have been trying to make the men cease firing." [53] There he was, kneeling, his sad face strained with worry. "Is the wound painful?" asked Hill, all thoughts of disagreement forgotten.

"Very painful, my arm is broken."

With a gentleness strange in so raging a fighter, Hill took off Jackson's bloody gloves, sword, and belt. Was there no whisky to give the general? He needed stimulant. A small amount from a flask the general fought down, and asked for water, which he drank with obvious relief.[54] Would someone send for a surgeon? Reassuring news—McGuire had been summoned and should be at hand soon. People still fussed over his wounds. Wilbourn and Jimmy Smith, who spurred to Jackson's side as soon as he heard the news, put a tourniquet on the broken arm and the blood began to clot. Wilbourn asked if the general had any other wounds. "Yes," came the calm reply, "in the right hand, but never mind that; it is a mere trifle." [55]

Soon, through the sea of faces, appeared a new one and Jackson heard the practiced tones of a surgeon from Pender's brigade. Making a quick examination, the doctor vetoed an additional tourniquet and debated what next to do. "Is he a skillful surgeon?" in a whisper to Powell Hill. The doctor had a high reputation in his brigade, replied Hill, and anyway all he proposed were the usual precautionary measures. "Very good." One thing had to be decided: Should the general be moved? To leave him where he was might expose him to further wounds or to capture, but to move him might start another hemorrhage. While the urgent question waited for an answer, Powell Hill heard a loud commotion on his front and, expecting an attack, gently gave Jackson's head and shoulders to another, excused himself, and went to command.

No sooner had he reached his line and barked crisp orders to repulse the expected thrust, than he heard a sudden cannonade and felt a jarring blow on his feet. Both boot tops had been cut by a piece of flying shell. No blood welled from his boots, but so painful had been the bruise that he soon found himself unable to walk with any agility. He must yield command. Who served as senior brigadier? That good soldier Robert Rodes, but he had just assumed charge of a division. From brigadier to Corps commander in one day! Such a responsibility would be too much to fasten on Rodes. Finally Hill concluded to turn over command to Rodes temporarily while a messenger sped to Jeb Stuart, presumably the nearest major general, asking him to come and take over.[56] A sad duty—Stuart felt no one could replace the "immortal leader" of the Second Corps, even temporarily [57]—but he came, although he had no previous experience at commanding infantry.

All of the changes in command were not reported to Jackson until much later; he had a wracking battle of pain to fight on his own. All kinds of alarms worried his attendants and soon they were convinced that the Federals were nearby. Jackson heard a shouted report: "The enemy is within fifty yards and is advancing; let us take the General away!" A proposal to pick him up and carry him brought a quick veto from Jackson: "No, if you can help me up, I can walk."

Willbourn and Capt. Benjamin Leigh, of Hill's staff, got on each side of the general and helped him to his feet in the midst of a sudden shelling by Federal guns which ended as swiftly as it began. Would he ever get out of these woods? It was easy to grow despondent. He must take firm grip on himself. If it is God's will . . . No word of unsolicited complaint escaped his tightly pressed lips; the iron self-control was coming back. Leaning heavily on his companions, Jackson stumbled toward Hill's lines. Powell Hill wisely thought the news should be kept from the men. If those thousands of dedicated Rebels should learn that Stonewall—invincible Stonewall—lay maimed and seriously wounded, none could tell what effect it might have on morale.

As the little group drew near Hill's troops the expected questions came: "Who is that?" "Who have you there?" The answer was blurted out hastily: "Only a friend of ours who is wounded." Something did not sit quite right about that answer; too many people attended that one wounded man, too much care and concern for a minor officer. Who was it? Men pressed close, looking hard, growing suspicious. Old Jack gave an order: "When asked," he murmured, "just say it is a Confederate officer." [58] But even that neat equivocation did not solve the problem. One grizzled, powder-stained veteran infiltrated the cordon of attendants and took a look at the bloody figure, reeling along between two aides. "Great God," came the heartbroken cry, "that is General Jackson." No, no, he was told, it looked like Jackson, but was someone else. He nodded slowly, took another piteous look at his cherished leader, and went toward the front.[59]

Visibly the general grew weaker. Litter bearers at last arrived. Two enlisted men took handles, and the devoted Jimmy and Captain Leigh took the other two. Lifting the limp figure to their shoulders, the men started for the rear. Again a flash and roar from the Federal lines, as nervous gunners probed the Rebel woods. Lethal bits of iron and lead hissed through the air; one of the litter bearers jumped, hit in both arms. He fell, and the agile Leigh caught the handle before it dropped too far. The other litter bearer wanted no more of his task; the general had to be laid once again on the ground while someone went in search of more help.

Grape, canister, shells of all kinds whined over Jackson's improvised bed. They crashed into trees, clipped limbs, ricocheted from rocks, and exploded in a hideous pyrotechnic display. To lie there might be quick and certain death. Jackson struggled to rise; he would try again to walk. Gently but firmly Smith, Morrison, and Leigh pushed him down. "Sir, you must lie still; it will cost you your life if you rise!" [60] And as the iron hail increased in volume and ferocity, they spread themselves in a protective shield around three sides of the litter while Wilbourn fought to steady the horses. The four "young gentlemen" would absorb the bits of flying death which struck sparks on flint in the road and caromed upward. That such an act was the last full measure of devotion no one bothered to consider—the wounded man was Stonewall Jackson, the hope of their country. Who would not do the same? [61]

After an endless moment between life and death, the Federal guns lifted the barrage and fired far over the heads of the little band on the road. Jackson at once offered to walk and hung between his loyal aides as they struck off into the woods where he would be safe and where there would be less chance of the troops' finding out he had been wounded. Again his strength appeared to be ebbing and he had to stop. Wilbourn had already gone in search of more whisky. Smith and Morrison hoped he would hurry, for the general desperately needed stimulant. It would be silly, though, to wait for the whisky to come; Jackson must be moved on toward a hospital as fast as possible. Help must be sought from some of the men nearby.

But none of the men wanted to leave the protection of the woods and carry a wounded officer; it was hard work and, with the lobbing shells, dangerous. Man after man was approached and skulked off into the darkness. Captain Leigh resisted the temptation to shout at those men that they were letting Stonewall Jackson die, and kept trying to find one good Samaritan. Finally, in an agony of frustration at the men, at the enemy cannon, and at the roughness of the road, he told the next man he saw. Without a word, without a moment's hesitation, a willing, anxious back leaned into carrying the load. From then on there were any number of helping hands.[62]

Swiftly now, the litter moved behind the lines, moving farther from the scene of danger. On the way Gen. Dorsey Pender stepped up to Jackson, saying: "Ah! General, I am sorry to see you have been wounded. The lines here are so much broken that I fear we will have to fall back." [63]

That phrase, "we will have to fall back," cut through the haze of pain and shock. Fire kindled once again in those cold blue eyes. Up from the litter came that pain-etched face, and Jackson snapped in his old clipped tones: "You must hold your ground, General Pender! You must hold your ground, sir!" [64]

Through the woods for about half a mile the litter bearers picked their way with the general lying conscious, silently fighting pain. Finally, in an even, weak voice he had a question to put to them: Could some stimulant be obtained? Soon, he heard; soon he would have it. Very good. Back to the thin-lipped battle with an unfamiliar foe. Slowly he seemed to adjust to the gentle swinging of the stretcher. It was all right. . . . One of the men stumbled on a root or some sort of vine and pitched forward headfirst. The litter fell heavily on that side; Jackson landed on his shattered arm. A groan—the only one; whiter, thinner grew his lips. Keep hold of himself—fight it. Jimmy Smith sprang to help him. "General," came the anxious question, "are you much hurt?" A moment; then, "No, Mr. Smith; don't trouble yourself about me." [65]

Where were they now? Would they ever get out of the woods and would daylight ever come again? Was he dying? He thought so, several times he thought so. He was ready, if God so willed it, and as he gave himself into the hands of the Lord a great peace came over him. There was no pain, no fighting, no hate—it was the supreme victory.[66]

At long, long last, the little group of struggling bearers came out on a road and saw an ambulance waiting in the moonlight. Confederate ambulances left much to be desired in the way of comfort, but at the moment any shelter, any professional care, even on the almost springless boards of an army ambulance, appeared a magnificent boon. The litter soon was lifted inside, where Jackson saw another figure stretched out in pain. Sad, sad, it was friend Stapleton Crutchfield, trusted Artillery Chief of the Second Corps. He had a badly battered leg and the pain must have been frightful. Jackson instantly worried about him. It was thought best, though, to keep the nature of both men's wounds secret as a means of preventing undue concern. Another, less dangerously wounded officer who had been in the ambulance quickly had given up his place to the Corps commander.

Anna's brother, the dutiful Joe Morrison, climbed in with the general to hold the broken arm. Soon the wheels rumbled and banged on the way to the Corps hospital. Frequent stops were made as the ambulance creaked toward the rear; men passing were asked if they had any "spirits." If they did, they did not admit it. Jackson finally broke down to the extent of complaining about the wound in his right hand; extremely painful, he said, and he would like some whisky. But everything connected with the gruesome journey went wrong. Whisky could not be found; the road was rutted and terribly bumpy; it had been hard to find litter bearers;

Dr. McGuire had not yet appeared—it seemed as if everything conspired to frustrate the frantic efforts of Jackson's staff. The extreme emergency seemed to result in maddening slow motion. Not until the ambulance reached the Reverend Melzi Chancellor's could any "spirits" be found.[67]

Far more welcome than the whisky was the new face which appeared in the gloom of the ambulance. Dr. McGuire had hurried to the Chancellors' house to intercept the general. What a comfort. Always Jackson had been fond of him, had relied on his judgment, had trusted him. He trusted him now. That calm voice came through the haze of pain and weakness: "I hope you are not badly hurt, General." McGuire would expect the truth: "I am badly injured, Doctor; I fear I am dying." McGuire's thin sensitive face showed as little emotion as possible; he made a hasty and necessarily superficial examination. Jackson resumed: "I am glad you have come. I think the wound in my shoulder is still bleeding."

McGuire had already seen the continuing hemorrhage and applied pressure to the artery while he readjusted the tourniquet. The preliminary examination showed Jackson to be in severe shock—skin clammy, face chalk-white, lips tightly compressed into a bloodless line. To all of McGuire's questions and attentions Jackson responded with unfailing courtesy, a courtesy which impressed a doctor who had seen human suffering in many of its most inhuman forms. "He controlled," wrote McGuire later, "by his iron will, all evidence of emotion, and more difficult than this even, he controlled that disposition to restlessness which many of us have observed upon the field of battle, attending great loss of blood." [68] Bleeding had been so severe and had taken such a toll of the general's strength that the doctor decided to give him additional stimulant while, at the same time, administering morphia to ease the wracking pain. Soon Jackson felt so much stronger that the ambulance resumed its jolting way to the Corps hospital, almost four miles away.[69]

All during the ride McGuire sat holding his finger on the artery. As men called out to the ambulance asking whom McGuire attended, he followed Old Jack's order and replied, "A Confederate officer." Once the general reached up with his right hand, pulled McGuire's head down, and whispered, "Is Crutchfield dangerously wounded?" "No, only painfully hurt." "I am glad it is no worse." Soon Crutchfield asked the same question about Stonewall, and when told he had been seriously wounded, the artillerist cried, "O, my God!" Jackson mistook the cry for one of agony and ordered the ambulance halted so that something could be done for Crutchfield.

Not until sometime after 11 P.M. did the ambulance roll up to the field hospital at Wilderness Old Tavern. Quickly Jackson's litter was carried inside a tent already warmed for him by Dr. Harvey Black, the surgeon in charge. More whisky and water were given the general; he dozed and gradually began to revive. After two quiet hours had passed, Dr. McGuire, seconded by Surgeons Black, Walls, and R. T. Coleman, told him that chloroform would be administered preparatory to a careful examination of his wounds. From all indications, said McGuire, the left arm must be amputated: if that proved necessary, should the operation proceed at once? "Yes, certainly; Dr. McGuire, do for me whatever you think best."

The cone-shaped cloth came down over the general's pale face; he breathed deeply. Swiftly the fumes took effect. A vast relief—a vast relief. "What an infinite blessing . . . blessing . . . blessing . . . bless. . . ." Then a soft, enticing wave of unconsciousness swept over him; pain, everything vanished.

Examination of the wounds showed a ball in the back of the right hand, just under the skin. Two metacarpal bones had been fractured. A swift incision removed the ball, and the doctors then concentrated on the broken left arm. "The left arm was then amputated," recorded McGuire, "about two inches below the shoulder, very rapidly, and with slight loss of blood, the ordinary circular operation having been made." [70] After the amputation and after all dressings had been applied, the general began to come out of the anesthetic. Jimmy Smith, who had faithfully held the lights during the operation, watched by the bedside and after about half an hour he roused Jackson and helped him drink a cup of coffee.[71]

Soon—it must have been around 3 or 3:30 A.M.—Dr. McGuire entered the tent with a visitor. Sandie Pendleton—Sandie, who had been far away on urgent army business and who had raced to find McGuire when he first heard of Jackson's wound, fainting from his saddle when he delivered his summons—Sandie came now with an urgent message from Jeb Stuart. McGuire had said he could not disturb Jackson, but the life of the army depended on it. Old Jack brightened at once. "Well, Major," he said in a strong voice, "I am glad to see you; I thought you were killed." Immensely relieved to see his chief in fairly good spirits, Pendleton succinctly sketched what had happened to the Corps since Jackson had left the field. Hill, too, had been disabled; Rodes had turned the command over to Jeb Stuart. And Jeb, willing, eager to carry on for Stonewall, had sent Sandie for any instructions Jackson might want to give. What should Stuart do?

Alert right away, Jackson shot some questions at the major, wanting to know more details. He thought a moment. Everyone in the tent waited for his orders; out in the dark woodland thousands of weary men in gray waited too. That high, intelligent brow creased in deep study, the jaw set in a familiar pose, the lips pursed—a flash in the blue eyes. He almost gave the order—then the moment passed, the fire dimmed, the muscles relaxed. "I don't know," he said with a great sadness, "I can't tell; say to General Stuart he must do what he thinks best." [72] Pendleton looked on this transformation with anguish—Stonewall unable to give a battle order? The wound must be grievous indeed. Back to Stuart rode the disheartened Sandie, and Stuart, too, when he heard how broken was his great and good friend, must have wondered what lay in store for the army resting in the Wilderness. He would do his best, would renew the attack in the morning. Still, could anyone but Stonewall give those gaunt gray men that spark which made them mighty?

After Sandie left his bedside Jackson remained in a talkative mood. His operation interested him and he began to discuss it with Jimmy Smith. Chloroform, he declared, had indeed been a boon, but still he would not like to meet death while under its influence; a man should have a clear mind then. The vapor, he said, had numbed all sensation of pain, and all he could remember was a faint sound of delightful music—"I believe it was the sawing of the bone." [73] To all this Smith listened with manifest politeness though he hated seeing his general so unlike himself. Dr. McGuire wanted the general to sleep, Jimmy Smith reminded: did he not think he should do so? If the doctor—now his superior—so desired, Jackson would try. He slept well.

The sun had risen far by the time Jackson awoke at 9 A.M. on Sunday, May 3. [74] Daylight brought new strength; pain had subsided, the depression of darkness had vanished. He looked bright, took some food, and listened intently to the rolling boom of guns far to the east. The sound appeared to be fading, so the enemy must be in retreat. Stuart was pressing them, pushing right on. Good, good. This interest in things martial, the ability to eat, and the patient's over-all outlook greatly encouraged his doctors. He would get well—all the signs indicated he would get well.

Already he had enough strength to think of official duties. Lieutenant Smith wrote a note to the commanding general informing him of the transfer of command and explaining why this had been necessary. All his staff save Smith, said Jackson, must go to the front and assist General Stuart; the post of duty was to the east. Joseph Morrison must ride for Richmond and tell Anna what had happened. Bring her to the hospital if possible. [75]

Later that morning Jackson complained of pain in his right side, but McGuire's examination showed nothing. A "simple application was recommended, in the belief that the pain would soon disappear." [76] Still suffering from the chest pain, the general received Chaplain Lacy, who burst into the tent with a tactful "Oh, General! what a calamity!" Not at all, not at all—the will of God could never be considered a calamity. Lacy subsided, [77] particularly as Jackson continued with a Christian discussion on how the reasons for loss of his arm would be revealed to him in afterlife. Lacy might understand better than anyone else, though, the great feeling of peace and victory which Jackson had felt when he believed himself to be dying during that ghastly trek from the battlefield. Eagerly he talked of the wound, the pain, and the spiritual catharsis which followed. Eagerly Lacy listened, tucking away bits of conversation to embroider in retelling.[78]

After Lacy left, Kyd Douglas had come from the front, and although not allowed to see Jackson he had brought news, both bad and good. Captain Boswell had been killed in the volley which struck down Jackson, and the bright, the pious, the promising Elisha Franklin Paxton had fallen—another sacrifice to the jinx of commanding the Stonewall Brigade. Sad, so sad—both had been particularly good friends. The cheerful news, though, brought pride to Jackson's eye. He should have seen the charge made that very day by his old brigade; Stuart had made a special appeal, and the Stonewall Brigade had answered with its own especial *élan*. Tears came to those kind blue eyes; the clipped, quiet voice quavered: "It was just like them to do so; just like them. They are a noble body of men." [79]

In the afternoon the tent grew quiet. Then came the sound of a galloping horse, a slowing pace, creaking leather as a man dismounted in front of the tent. A courier, with a message for General Jackson from Army Headquarters. Smith took the dispatch, and Jackson made him read it:

Headquarters, May 3, 1863.

General Thomas J. Jackson,
  Commanding Corps:

General: I have just received your note, informing me that you were wounded. I cannot express my regret at the occurrence. Could I have directed events, I should have chosen for the good of the country to be disabled in your stead.

I congratulate you upon the victory, which is due to your skill and energy.

Very respectfully, your obedient servant,

R. E. Lee,
GENERAL [80]

A long silence in the tent. Jackson turned his face away from Smith—was it from emotion? Were there tears at such high words from Robert Lee? A Christian must never forget his first loyalty: "General Lee is very kind, but he should give the praise to God." Even more pleased Jackson would have been, had he known how choked with emotion was Lee's own voice as he dictated that note,[81] and of a statement Lee would make to a visitor a few days later when talking of his lieutenant: "Such an executive officer the sun never shone on. I have but to show him my design, and I know that if it can be done it will be done. No need for me to send or watch him. Straight as the needle to the pole he advances to the execution of my purpose." [82]

That Sunday afternoon, as Hooker sought feverishly to salvage something from the wreckage of his army and to stand off the linked forces of Lee and Stuart, the commanding general sent word that Jackson must be moved farther to the rear as soon as his condition would permit. Troops would be sent to guard the Corps hospital until the move took place; the enemy must not capture Stonewall.

Jackson had no worries on that score. "If the enemy does come," he told Dr. McGuire, "I am not afraid of them; I have always been kind to their wounded, and I am sure they will be kind to me." [83] He would stay, if Dr. McGuire thought it best. By now he had become convinced that he had been spared by Providence—there were other duties which he must perform. Whatever work God dictated, he would discharge it happily. To make ready for his mission, he would concentrate on getting well. That evening, though, General Lee again sent word to Dr. McGuire that Jackson must be moved, and preparations were made to start the next morning, the fourth of May.

Lee's order to move the general was coupled with one to McGuire: Stay with Jackson, watch over him. Old Jack had refused to permit McGuire to devote his whole attention to one patient, but he could not overrule the orders of his superior. "General Lee," he said with obvious relief, "has always been very kind to me, and I thank him." [84]

Left to Jackson was the choice of a place to recuperate, and he selected—subject to the approval of the family—the home of the Thomas Coleman Chandlers, near Guiney's. He had enjoyed many kindnesses at their hands during the happy months at Moss Neck. Their invitation came immediately. As he looked ahead to the weeks of recovery, Jackson thought of spending some time again in Lexington, amid friends and happy scenes.

The patient slept well during the night of May 3-4, the pain in his side subsided, and he appeared immeasurably stronger. Dr. McGuire thought the journey would not harm him, particularly since the weather promised to be clear and warm.[85] When the ambulance began its trek on the morning of the fourth, Jackson's mental attitude could hardly have been better. Doubtless he learned with satisfaction that Crutchfield, much improved, would ride with him over a route carefully selected by the incomparable Jed Hotchkiss.

Hotchkiss found the shortest way to be the smoothest, and the ambulance rolled through Todd's Tavern, Spotsylvania Court House, and on to Guiney's.[86] Along the road wounded men making their way to the RF&P Railroad sensed that Old Jack rode in the covered vehicle and they cheered him lustily, some shouting that they wished they had been wounded in his place. Had there ever been an army like this before?

The twenty-five-mile ride gave time for much stimulating conversation with Chaplain Lacy, Dr. McGuire, and Jimmy Smith. They talked of all manner of things, of the battle, and finally of the part the Stonewall

Brigade had played in it. The brigade had petitioned the government for official permission to use the special name always. "They are a noble body of patriots," exclaimed Old Jack when told of this; "when this war is ended, the survivors will be proud to say: 'I was a member of the old Stonewall Brigade.' The Government ought certainly to accede to their request, and authorize them to assume this title; for it was fairly earned." A moment's thought and then: "The name Stonewall ought to be attached wholly to the men of the Brigade, and not to me; for it was their steadfast heroism which ... earned it at First Manassas." [87] The conversation then turned to Hooker's plan of battle, and Jackson praised it, saying that the fatal blunder had been made when the Yankee cavalry was sent away. "It was that which enabled me to turn him, without his being aware of it, and to take him by his rear. Had he kept his cavalry with him, his plan would have been a very good one." [88] He talked freely of what he had intended to do at Chancellorsville—there was no chance of his strategy's leaking to the enemy now. He had been aiming to cut Hooker off from United States Ford, to take a strong position, and to receive attack.

In an untypical mood, he warmly praised several of his subordinates for their gallantry and skill at Chancellorsville; it seemed as though he was for the first time relaxing from the tensions of command and enjoying reminiscences of the war. Clear and bright his mind appeared through all the day's talk, and only in the late afternoon did he complain of any discomfort—a slight nausea. Dr. McGuire complied with a request to apply a wet towel to his abdomen, an old familiar remedy.[89]

Welcomed when he arrived at the Chandlers', he brightened immediately upon seeing his friends. They had made ready the little office in the yard of Fairfield, where the general would not be bothered by the numbers of other wounded already in the mansion. The Chandlers were most kind, the office seemed made to order. When carried inside he first saw a small sort of anteroom and noticed two bedchambers behind that; the one on the right would be his. Upstairs were two half-rooms. All around spread a fine lawn, dotted with graceful trees. Instantly at home in these happy surroundings, Jackson found appetite for some bread and tea. Soon he fell asleep. McGuire did not conceal his pleasure at the patient's progress. Good appetite, cheerfulness, and the wounds healing normally—the outlook was bright for a speedy recovery.[90]

When he awoke on Tuesday morning, Jackson could not have missed noticing the hurried activity around Guiney's, although no one told him of a threatened enemy approach. Most of the officers around the station came to bid him farewell and rode off, he supposed, to normal calls of duty. Hotchkiss came to say good-by and found the general cheerful and hopeful of being with his men soon. He should take his best regards to General Lee.[91]

McGuire's examination of the wounds that day pleased Jackson, and he asked how long before he could take the field. That would depend. Jimmy Smith still kept his vigil by the general's side, and to him Jackson addressed a bit of philosophy: "Many would regard [these wounds] as a great misfortune, I regard them as one of the blessings of my life." To this Smith had an old Jackson rejoinder: "All things work together for good to those that love God." "Yes," came the instant response, "that's it, that's it." [92]

The day would have been long had not Smith and Lacy kept close by. Smith, a serious-minded young Presbyterian with a leaning toward the ministry, listened well and contributed much to stimulating theological discussions. But Jackson had a question for him, one that might catch him off guard. "Can you tell me where the Bible gives generals a model for their official reports of battles?" Smith laughed; no, it had never occurred to him to look in the Bible for a lesson in military reporting. "Nevertheless," said Jackson earnestly, "there are such: and excellent models, too. Look, for instance, at the narrative of Joshua's battle with the Amalekites; there you have one. It has clearness, brevity, fairness, modesty; and it traces the victory to its right source, the blessing of God." [93]

On the subject of battles, Jackson soon heard something of how Lee's operations were going against Hooker. The Union general had fortified strong ground north of Chancellorsville, and again awaited attack. "That is bad; very bad," came the short analysis.[94] On the drizzling morning of May 6 Lee learned that Hooker had slipped across the Rappahannock, but of this Jackson apparently received no word.

Still he grew better. No complications, and his interest in theological discussion taxed the knowledge of both Lacy and Smith. Even Dr. McGuire felt the force of Deacon Jackson's Biblical annotations. Did the doctor suppose that any who had been healed by Jesus ever again suffered from the same illness? That the doctor could not say. "Oh for infinite power!" [95] Jimmy Smith retreated before a blistering quiz: "What were the Head-quarters of Christianity after the crucifixion?" Smith thought he had the answer, and began an erudite lecture on Christian centers of influence at Jerusalem, Antioch, Iconium, Rome, Alexandria. General Jackson brought him up sharply: "Why do you say 'centres of influence'? Is not 'Head-quarters' a better term?" The hapless theology student without sufficient military mien supposed it was.[96]

Although he tired toward the end of the day, Jackson's progress continued. Chaplain Lacy, at the behest of Dr. McGuire, went to General Lee and secured the temporary detail of Dr. S. B. Morrison to Jackson's bedside. Morrison, one of Anna's relations and an old friend, would relieve some of the others at their vigil and would give the general wider interests. Lee granted the detail and sent Lacy back to Stonewall with a

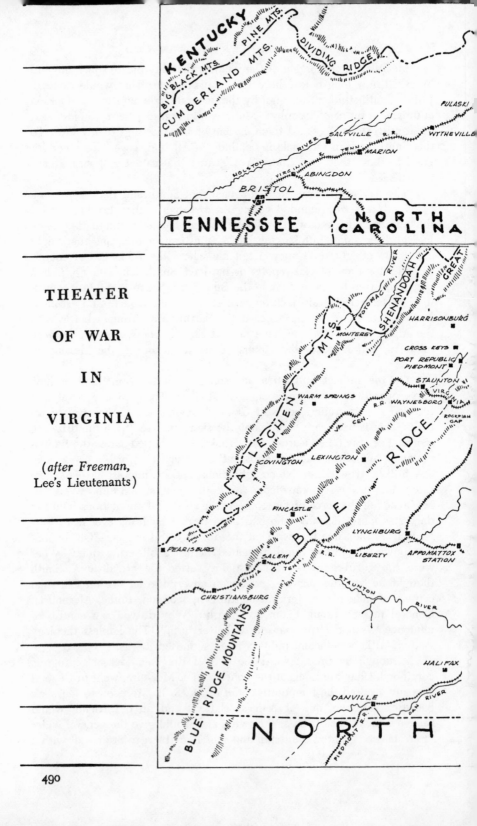

THEATER

OF WAR

IN

VIRGINIA

(*after Freeman,*
Lee's Lieutenants)

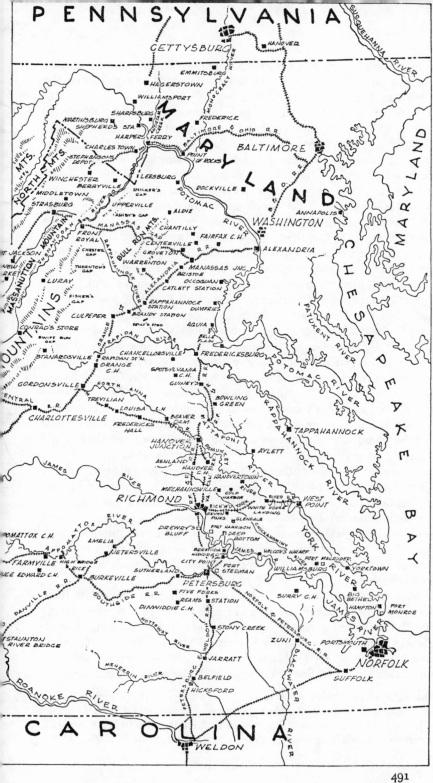

special message: "Give him my affectionate regards, and tell him to make haste and get well, and come back to me as soon as he can. He has lost his left arm; but I have lost my right arm." [97]

Night, May 6, 1863. After a long, wearing day during which his patient showed steady improvement, Dr. McGuire thought it safe to leave Jackson in the affectionate care of Jim Lewis and to stretch out on the sofa for a much-needed rest. Jim sat quietly watching as his beloved general fell asleep. On the sofa the doctor, too, slept soundly.

Thursday, May 7, about 1 A.M. Jackson stirred and awoke, nauseated. Jim was asked to get a wet towel and bathe the stomach; that would help. Jim objected: shouldn't he wake the doctor? Let him sleep, said the general, he needs it. Get the towel. This time the old cure helped not at all. The right side flared again in violent pain while nausea continued. Grimly Jackson set about fighting this now familiar enemy. Jim wanted to wake McGuire. Wait. At dawn Jackson yielded—wake him.

McGuire sprang to Jackson's side, heard his breathing, examined his chest. Pneumonia! The wet cloths had not caused it, but they had not helped.[98] Swiftly the young doctor set about doing all that medical knowledge dictated—cupping, mercury, antimony, and opium—all these were tried. How far had the disease progressed? McGuire had a lurking fear: lung inflammation might have started that night in the Wilderness when the stretcher fell. He discussed it with Jackson, who thought he was right; the fall had been harder than he wanted to admit. But the doctor must not look so concerned, his patient was not afraid. What he willed to do he could do, always remembering that the will of God would prevail.

Treatment proved drastic and it wrought a tragic change. Drugged with morphia and with fever Jackson slipped now into a limbo of lucidity and delirium, sometimes rational, sometimes not. About noon he grew warm and uncomfortable—the doctors had ceased their fussing over him. Could he have a glass of lemonade? That fruit had always tasted so good. A long delay, and then Smith gave him a glass. A sip, and a stern rebuke: "You did not mix this, it is too sweet; take it back." Now he faded again into incoherence.

Someone else in the room? Anna! At last, she had come from Richmond. Her trip had been one long anguished fear, with reports varying from Thomas's certain recovery to his terrible decline. At last, after experiences to shake the will of the bravest soldier, she arrived at Guiney's. There had been no way for her to come before, the enemy had cut communications. When she first saw Thomas on the seventh, she was terrified:

the sight which ... met my eyes was ... appalling, and sent such a thrill of agony and heart-sinking through me as I had never known before! Oh, the fearful change since last I had seen him! It required the strongest effort of which I was capable to maintain my self-control. ... *Now*, his fearful wounds, his mutilated arm, the scratches upon his face, and, above all, the desperate pneumonia, which was flushing his cheeks, oppressing his breathing, and benumbing his senses, wrung my soul with such grief and anguish as it had never before experienced.[99]

Yes, it was Anna. She looked so frightened! "My darling, you must cheer up, and not wear a long face. I love cheerfulness and brightness in a sick-room." What was she saying? . . . Speak more distinctly . . . he missed some of the words. "My darling, you are very much loved." "You are one of the most precious little wives in the world."

Poor Anna, she said she wished she had been the one who was wounded. God knows what is best for us. Did he want to see Julia? . . . Sweet little Julia. "Not yet; wait till I feel better." Other things must be thought of—"Tell Major Hawks to send forward provisions to the men." "Order A. P. Hill to prepare for action. . . . Pass the infantry to the front." [100]

Long hours dragged by. Friday and Saturday blended into a dwindling hope. A great authority on pneumonia had come from Richmond, but the doctors wore increasingly longer faces. Fever raged, but a moment's clarity brought the group of doctors surrounding the bed into focus. "I see from the number of physicians that you think my condition dangerous, but I thank God, if it is His will, that I am ready to go." [101] Anna came to the bedside—it was Saturday night—asking if he wanted her to read from the comforting Psalms. He suffered so much, had to concentrate so hard on fighting pain that it would be hard to listen. Sternly, then, he took hold of himself. A Christian must always remember. . . . "Yes, we must never refuse that. Get the Bible and read them." [102] He listened. Night came on. He grew more tired, he breathed harder. Sing, he asked Anna. Sing the spiritual songs he so loved. Joseph Morrison was there now, steadying Anna, helping her keep her courage as Thomas slowly began a long retreat. They sang one he specially wanted:

> Show pity, Lord; O Lord, forgive;
> Let a repenting rebel live;
> Are not thy mercies large and free?
> May not a sinner trust in thee?
>
> Yet save a trembling sinner, Lord,
> Whose hope, still hov'ring round thy word,
> Would light on some sweet promise there,
> Some sure support against despair.[103]

The tenth of May came on Sunday in 1863. Jackson still fought for life with firm faith and ebbing strength. Anna faced that day a sterner test than any she had known. Dr. Morrison called her from the sickroom. Sadly he told her what she doubtless knew deep in her heart. Medicine had done all it could; Thomas could not live. She had to tell him; he had said that although ready to die at any moment God called, he would prefer a few hours' preparation. She had to tell him.

There was Anna again. She said something . . . he could not understand. The doctors said he would soon be in heaven. Was he willing to go? The clouds cleared, the eye sparkled. Calmly and clearly he said: "Yes, *I prefer it, I prefer it.*" Then, said Anna, he must know that before the day ended . . . could she go on? God must give the strength . . . before the day ended Thomas would be with "the blessed Saviour in his glory." It was Sunday . . . he had always wanted to die on Sunday. "I will be an infinite gainer to be translated."

There were family matters to discuss. He wanted to be buried in Lexington. Anna could go to her father in North Carolina. Suddenly there was Julia in the room. "Little darling! sweet one!" He looked at her for a long, fond moment, and she smiled, a big, broad, happy smile. Another long haze. Anna had come back—it was later in the morning and she had not been sure he had understood before. He would be in heaven before sundown, she was saying. He would comfort her. "Oh no! you are frightened, my child; death is not so near; I may yet get well." [104] It was too much—she wanted so to believe him. Anna broke down, fell on the bed and sobbed. Would Anna call Dr. McGuire? There he was. "Doctor, Anna informs me that you have told her that I am to die to-day; is it so?" Yes. Those blue eyes turned for a moment to the ceiling while the general thought hard. "Very good, very good, it is all right." He had much he wanted to say to Anna, but weakness prevented. Midday came and went. Dr. McGuire offered the wildly breathing figure a glass of brandy and water. Something of that iron will broke through the delirium: "It will only delay my departure, and do no good; I want to preserve my mind, if possible, to the last." [105]

The room quieted down; the short, choking breathing went on, weaker now. Prayers were being said in camp for the general. The army had heard the dread rumor of Jackson's condition. The troops prayed fervently. The army. . . . Order A. P. Hill. . . . Tell Major Hawks. . . . Then he could see the objective . . . at last the great battle was won . . . duty had been done; the consequences were God's . . . it came clear now. "Let us cross over the river, and rest under the shade of the trees." [106]

What river did he think of then—was it the Potomac or was it the Jordan?

NOTES

Chapter 1

1. Roy Bird Cook, *The Family and Early Life of Stonewall Jackson* (3d ed.; Charleston, W. Va., 1948. Cited hereinafter as Cook), chaps. 2 and 4; Mrs. Mary Anna Jackson, *Memoirs of Stonewall Jackson* (Louisville, Ky., 1895. Cited hereinafter as Mrs. Jackson), pp. 10–11.
2. Mrs. Jackson, p. 14; Cook, p. 91 and *ante;* William Couper, *One Hundred Years at V M I* (4 vols.; Richmond, Va., 1939. Cited hereinafter as Couper), III, 174 *n.*
3. Thomas Jackson Arnold, *Early Life and Letters of General Thomas J. Jackson ("Stonewall" Jackson)* (New York, 1916. Cited hereinafter as Arnold), p. 26.
4. Cook, pp. 44–46.
5. Cook, p. 43. See Burke Davis, *They Called Him Stonewall* (New York, 1954), p. 89, where there is some question about the disease.
6. Cook, p. 20.   7. Mrs. Jackson, p. 15.   8. *Ibid.*
9. There is some confusion on this point. Cook, p. 47, says that Thomas and Laura "seemed to have been at Jackson's Mill and then either went with their mother or were sent to the new home." Arnold, p. 27, says that they went with their mother to Fayette County. Mrs. Jackson, p. 16, says that the two boys were given to the care of their father's relations and that Laura stayed wtih her mother. Robert L. Dabney, *Life and Campaigns of Lieut.-Gen. Thomas J. Jackson* (New York, 1866. Cited hereinafter as Dabney), p. 11, implies that all the children were farmed out to relatives. As in most matters of dispute about the early years of Jackson's life, Roy B. Cook's account has been followed as being most trustworthy.
10. There is a possibility that Thomas and Laura stayed on in Fayette County with the Woodsons until their mother's death. See Cook, pp. 21, 47–48. For the family tradition see Arnold, p. 28; Mrs. Jackson; pp. 16, 17; Dabney, pp. 11, 12.
11. This date is in dispute, but so says Cook, pp. 21, 26. Dabney, p. 11, says death occurred on Dec. 4, 1831.
12. Cook, pp. 47, 179; Davis, *op. cit.*, p. 90.   13. Dabney, p. 12; Cook, p. 47.
14. Dabney, p. 13; Cook, p. 19.   15. Arnold, pp. 30–31.
16. Cook, p. 48; Arnold, pp. 29–30; Mrs. Jackson, p. 20, says that this episode involved Warren and not Thomas; but Dabney, pp. 12–13, gives the story with Thomas as the actor. Dabney is the source of the quotation.
17. Dabney, p. 13.   18. Dabney, p. 12; Arnold, p. 31; Cook, p. 48.
19. Letter, West Point, Aug. 2, 1845, in Arnold, p. 71.
20. Arnold, p. 54.   21. Cook, p. 61.   22. Cook, pp. 52–53.
23. *Ibid.*, p. 56.   24. Dabney, p. 19.
25. His legal guardian at this period was his uncle, James Madison Jackson. See Cook, p. 62, for details of Jackson's guardianship.   26. Cook, pp. 56–57.
27. Cook, p. 54; Arnold, pp. 31–34; Mrs. Jackson, pp. 22–24; Davis, *op. cit.*, p. 90; Col. G. F. R. Henderson, *Stonewall Jackson and the American Civil War* (Amer. ed.; New York, 1949. Cited hereinafter as Henderson), pp. 6–7; Dabney, p. 16.
28. Cook, pp. 59–61.   29. *Ibid.*, p. 59.
30. *Ibid.*, p. 62; Davis, *op. cit.*, p. 91.
31. See Thomas Jackson to Laura, Fort Hamilton, N.Y., Mar. 8, 1850 (MS letter in Manuscripts Division, University of Virginia Library).
32. Cook, pp. 67–72; Arnold, pp. 35–37; Mrs. Jackson, pp. 27–29; Dabney, pp. 21–23, 26–28.
33. Cook, pp. 69–70.   34. *Ibid.*, pp. 82–83.   35. *Ibid.*, pp. 85–86.

36. Arnold, p. 332.
37. Cook, pp. 84–85. Other versions of this conversation are in Dabney, p. 31, and Mrs. Jackson, p. 31.
38. There is some confusion about the date of appointment. Hays's letter is dated June 19 and the endorsement on the back by Spencer reads June 18. The Secretary's calendar possibly was behind. For the correspondence relating to Jackson's appointment, see Gibson J. Butcher to Hays, Weston, Va., June 14, 1842; Smith Gibson to Hays, Lewis County, Va., June 14, 1842; Evan Carmack to Hays, "Home," June 14, 1842; two petitions to the Secretary of War, the first undated, signed by Evan Carmack and twelve others; the second dated June 14, 1842, signed by Cummins Jackson, J. M. Bennett, and sixteen others; Samuel L. Hays to Spencer, Washington, June 19, 1842, all in the Army Section, War Records Branch, National Archives, Washington, D.C. See also Cook, pp. 85–89. The well-known story that Hays took Jackson to see the Secretary of War—recounted in Mrs. Jackson, p. 32, Dabney, pp. 31–32, Henderson, p. 9, Davis, *op. cit.,* p. 92 —is refuted by Cook, p. 91, although his evidence is questionable.
39. The date is disputed. See Cook, p. 93; Davis, *op. cit.,* p. 92. Henderson, p. 10, neatly sidesteps the issue.
40. Dabney H. Maury, *Recollections of a Virginian* (New York, 1894), pp. 22–23; Cook, p. 96; Henderson, p. 10; Dabney, p. 32; Mrs. Jackson, p. 34.
41. Mrs. Jackson, p. 34.
42. J. B. James, "Life at West Point One Hundred Years Ago," in *Mississippi Valley Historical Review,* XXXI (1944–1945), 22.
43. Arnold, p. 63.   44. *Ibid.,* p. 74.
45. Henderson, p. 11.   46. Arnold, p. 73.
47. Margaret Junkin Preston, "Personal Reminiscences of Stonewall Jackson," in *Century Magazine,* XXXII (New Series X) (1886), 933. (Hereinafter cited as Preston).
48. Fort Putnam was a Revolutionary relic dear to the hearts of many generations of cadets.
49. Mrs. Jackson, p. 34.   50. Henderson, p. 15.
51. Quoted in Henderson, p. 15.   52. Maury, *op. cit.,* p. 23.
53. Quoted in Mrs. Jackson, p. 33.   54. Mrs. Jackson, pp. 35–36.
55. Letter, West Point, Jan. 28, 1844, in Arnold, p. 64.
56. Letter, West Point, Aug. 2, 1845, in *ibid.,* pp. 71–72.
57. Letter to Laura, West Point, Sept. 8, 1844, in *ibid.,* pp. 66–67.
58. Letter, West Point, Apr. 23, 1846, in *ibid.,* p. 74.
59. Letter to Laura, West Point, Feb. 10, 1845, in *ibid.,* pp. 68–69.
60. James, *op. cit.,* pp. 39–40.

Chapter 2

1. Cook, p. 97.   2. See Cook, pp. 97–98; Arnold, p. 78.
3. Cook, p. 98; Arnold, pp. 78–79. There are slight differences in the quoted conversations in these two sources.
4. Cook, pp. 98, 99; Arnold, p. 79; Thomas to Laura, Point Isabel, Tex., Sept. 25, 1846, in Arnold, pp. 79–81.
5. Couper, I, 231 n.
6. D. H. Hill to R. L. Dabney, Petersburg, Va., July 11[?], 1864, in Robert Lewis Dabney Papers, III, doc. 48, Union Theological Seminary, Richmond, Va. See also D. H. Hill, "The Real Stonewall Jackson," in *Century Magazine,* XLVII (NS XXV) (1893–1894), 624 (hereinafter cited as Hill).
7. Hill to Dabney, Petersburg, Va., July 11[?], 1864, Dabney Papers, III, doc. 48; Hill, p. 624. In Hill's *Century* article Jackson is quoted as saying, "*I should like to be in one battle.*"
8. Henderson, p. 20.   9. Cook, pp. 99–100.
10. Justin H. Smith, *The War with Mexico* (2 vols.; New York, 1919), I, 264.
11. *Ibid.,* I, 265.

12. Robert S. Henry, *Story of the Mexican War* (Indianapolis and New York, 1950), p. 171.
13. This phase of Jackson's Mexican War service is slighted in most accounts. See Henderson, pp. 20–21.
14. Return of the First Artillery, December, 1846; January, 1847 (MS in Army Section, War Records Branch, National Archives). See also Henry, *op. cit.*, p. 258.
15. Thomas to Laura, Vera Cruz, Mar. 20, 1847, in Arnold, p. 84.
16. Return of the First Artillery, February, March, 1847 (MS in Army Section, War Records Branch, National Archives).
17. Henry, *op. cit.*, pp. 263–269; Vandiver, *Ploughshares into Swords: Josiah Gorgas and Confederate Ordnance* (Austin, Tex., 1952), pp. 17–18.
18. Arnold, p. 85. 19. *Ibid.*, pp. 84–86. 20. *Ibid.*, p. 85.
21. *Ibid.*, p. 86. A similar admonition was contained in a letter from Jackson to his uncle Isaac Brake, Mar. 31, 1847, in Cook, pp. 100–101.
22. Jackson to Isaac Brake, Mar. 31, 1847, in Cook, pp. 100–101.
23. Thomas to Laura, Jalapa, Apr. 22, 1847, in Arnold, p. 90.
24. Smith, *op. cit.*, II, 49.
25. Winfield Scott, *Memoirs* (2 vols.; New York, 1864), II, 433.
26. Thomas to Laura, Jalapa, Apr. 22, 1847, in Arnold, p. 89.
27. Scott, *op. cit.*, II, 436.
28. The account of the Battle of Cerro Gordo is based upon Henry, *op. cit.*, chap. 17; Smith, *op. cit.*, II, chap. 23; Scott, *op. cit.*, II, 430–451.
29. See Jackson to Roger Jones, Adjutant General of the Army, Jalapa, Apr. 26, 1846 [1847] (MS in Army Section, War Records Branch, National Archives).
30. See Smith, *op. cit.*, II, 343, showing the organization of the artillery at Vera Cruz. See also Return of the First Artillery, July, 1847, showing that Jackson joined Company G in May, 1847, at Jalapa. See also Henderson, p. 24.
31. Smith, *op. cit.*, II, 361, where the garrison force is given in detail; Thomas to Laura, Jalapa, May 25, 1847, in Arnold, p. 91.
32. Thomas to Laura, Jalapa, May 25, 1847, in Arnold, p. 91.
33. Henderson, pp. 23–24; Arnold, p. 93.
34. Quoted in Henderson, p. 24; also quoted, without the quotes within quotes, in Arnold, p. 93. The quotation must be regarded as suspect because it does not sound like Jackson's later form of speech. Ordinarily he would have avoided using Magruder's name (or that of any other superior officer) in such a familiar manner. This is not to say that nothing of the kind was said, but only to point out that the direct quotation is possibly erroneous.
35. Return of the First Artillery, July, 1847. The exact date of the transfer is not given in the return, but the first indication of a change appears in the July report.
36. Vandiver, *op. cit.*, p. 24.
37. Thomas to Laura, City of Mexico, Oct. 26, 1847, in Arnold, pp. 128–130. For the account of the guerrilla attack see *ibid.*, pp. 94–95.
38. Henderson, p. 27. 39. Scott, *op. cit.*
40. S. Ex. Doc. 1, 30th Cong., 1st sess., pp. 196 ff., Appendix.
41. Henry, *op. cit.*, p. 334.
42. Douglas Southall Freeman, *R. E. Lee: A Biography* (4 vols.; New York, 1934–1935), I, 272.
43. D. H. Hill to R. L. Dabney, Petersburg, Va., July 11 [?], 1864, Dabney Papers, III, doc. 48.
44. Smith, *op. cit.*, II, 403.
45. Thomas to Laura, Mexico City, Oct. 26, 1847, in Arnold, p. 130.
46. Preston, pp. 929–930. The dialogue of this episode varies in several sources. See Henderson, p. 30; Davis, *op. cit.*, p. 104; Mrs. Jackson, p. 43.
47. Thomas to Laura, Mexico City, Oct. 26, 1847, in Arnold, p. 130.
48. D. H. Hill to R. L. Dabney, Petersburg, Va., July 11 [?], 1864, in Dabney Papers, III, doc. 48.
49. Henderson, p. 35.
50. S. Ex. Doc. 1, 30th Cong., 1st sess., pp. 403, 404–405.
51. *Ibid.*, p. 391.

52. Thomas to Laura, Mexico City, Oct. 26, 1847, in Arnold, pp. 128–130.
53. S. Ex. Doc. 1, 30th Cong., 1st sess., pp. 196 ff., Appendix.
54. *Ibid.*, p. 380; Scott, *op. cit.*, II, 519–520.
55. Henderson, p. 36; Dabney, p. 52.
56. Arnold, pp. 135–137.   57. Henry, *op. cit.*, p. 368.   58. Arnold, p. 124.
59. Letter of Mar. 23, 1848, in Arnold, pp. 135–137. See also Preston, p. 933.
60. Arnold, pp. 128–130.   61. Preston, pp. 932–933.
62. *Ibid.*; Mrs. Jackson, p. 46.
63. Letters of Mar. 23, Apr. 10, 1848, in Arnold, pp. 135–136, 137–139.
64. Hill, pp. 624–625.
65. Return of the First Artillery, December, 1847; January, February, March, June, 1848. See also Cook, p. 102.
66. Preston, p. 930; Mrs. Jackson, pp. 47–49; Dabney, pp. 54–59.
67. Dabney, p. 54.
68. Preston, p. 930. See also Henry C. Semple, S.J., "The Spirituality of Stonewall Jackson and Catholic Influences," in *Catholic World*, CXVI (1922–1923), 349–356.
69. Mrs. Jackson, p. 49; Dabney, pp. 45–47; Henderson, pp. 39–40.
70. Thomas to Laura, Feb. 28, 1848, in Arnold, pp. 130–133.

Chapter 3

1. Personal Service File of Thomas J. Jackson, Adjutant General's Records, National Archives. Also Arnold, p. 140.
2. Thomas to Laura, Aug. 26, 1848, in Arnold, pp. 140–141.
3. He was absent on court-martial duty from Aug. 28 to Sept. 14, 1848. Personal Service File, T. J. Jackson.
4. Letter dated Carlisle Barracks, Sept. 5, 1848, in Arnold, p. 142.
5. Dabney, pp. 70–71.
6. Thomas to Laura, Carlisle Barracks, Sept. 5, 1848, in Arnold, pp. 142–143, 143–144, 279 n.
7. Thomas to Laura, Fort Hamilton, N.Y., Jan. 1, 1849, in *ibid.*, p. 144.
8. Letter dated Feb. 1, 1848, in *ibid.*, pp. 147–148.
9. Thomas to Laura, Fort Hamilton, Dec. 3, 1849 (MS in T. J. Jackson Papers, University of Virginia Library).
10. Cook, p. 112.
11. Thomas to Laura, Fort Hamilton, Mar. 1, 1849, in Arnold, pp. 148–149; *ibid.*, chap. 9, *passim*.
12. Thomas to Laura, Fort Hamilton, Apr. 7, 1849, in *ibid.*, pp. 150–151.
13. *Ibid.*   14. *Ibid.*
15. Letter dated Fort Hamilton, July 2, 1849, in *ibid.*, pp. 154–157.
16. *Ibid.*, p. 157.
17. Letters dated Mar. 8, Apr. 1, Aug. 10, 1850, in *ibid.*, pp. 158–160, 160–161, 163–164.
18. Thomas to Laura, Aug. 10, 1850, in *ibid.*, pp. 163–164.
19. Letter dated Jan. 1, 1849, in *ibid.*, p. 144.
20. Letter dated Mar. 1, 1849, in *ibid.*, pp. 148–149.
21. Dabney, p. 60; Mrs. Jackson, p. 50; Cook, p. 109.
22. Letter dated Fort Hamilton, Mar. 8, 1850, in T. J. Jackson Papers, University of Virginia Library.
23. *Ibid.*   24. *Ibid.*
25. See, for example, Thomas to Laura, Fort Hamilton, June 12, 1849, in Arnold, p. 151.
26. Thomas to Laura, Fort Hamilton, July 2, 1849, in *ibid.*, p. 154.
27. Letter in T. J. Jackson Papers, University of Virginia Library.
28. Thomas to Laura, Fort Hamilton, Apr. 1, 1850, in Arnold, pp. 160–161.
29. Thomas to Laura, Fort Hamilton, Dec. 3, 1849, in *ibid.*, p. 157.
30. Thomas to Laura, Aug. 10, 1850, in *ibid.*, pp. 163–164.

31. Maury, *op. cit.*, pp. 61, 62, 71.
32. Thomas to Laura, Fort Hamilton, Feb. 1, 1849, in Arnold, pp. 146–148.
33. Cook, pp. 107–108.   34. Arnold, p. 57; Cook, p. 110.

Chapter 4

1. Oliver O. Howard, *My Life and Experiences Among Our Hostile Indians* (Hartford, Conn., 1907), p. 75; A. J. and K. A. Hanna, *Lake Okeechobee* (Indianapolis and New York, 1948), p. 59.
2. Personal Service File, T. J. Jackson.
3. Return of the First Artillery, November, 1850 (MS in Army Section, War Records Branch, National Archives).
4. Brevet Brig. Gen. Thomas Childs to Lt. Col. W. W. S. Bliss, Headquarters, Western Division, Fort Casey, Fla., Dec. 13, 1850 (MS in Letters Received, Department of the West, Sept.–Dec., 1850; Jan.–Apr., 1851, Records of U.S. Army Commands, Record Group 98, National Archives. Cited hereinafter as West, *NA*).
5. Federal Writer's Project, *Florida: A Guide to the Southernmost State* (New York, 1939 [1955 ptg.]), p. 370.
6. "Annual Return of the Alterations and Casualties Incident to the First Regiment of Artillery ... During the Year 1850" (MS in Army Section, War Records Branch, National Archives).
7. Howard, *op. cit.*, p. 82.
8. Baird to French, Fort Meade, Jan. 17, 1851, West, *NA*.
9. Jackson to French, Fort Meade, Feb. 1, 1851 (MS in Selected Letters Received, Department of Florida, Relating to Majors T. J. Jackson and W. H. French, 1851, Records of the War Department, U.S. Army Commands, National Archives. Microfilms in writer's files. Cited hereinafter as Jackson-French Papers).
10. French to Lt. T. S. Everett, Fort Meade, Feb. 1, 1851, in *ibid.*
11. French to Everett, Fort Meade, Feb. 26, 1851, in *ibid.*
12. Thomas to Laura, Fort Meade, Mar. 1, 1851, in Arnold, pp. 168–170.
13. Hanna and Hanna, *op. cit.*, pp. 60–64.
14. French to Everett, Fort Meade, Feb. 26, 1851, in Jackson-French Papers.
15. French to Everett, Fort Meade, Mar. 18, 1851, in West, *NA*.
16. Everett to French, Fort Brooke, Fla., Jan. 8, 1851, in Jackson-French Papers.
17. Hill, pp. 624–625.
18. French to Capt. J. M. Brannan, Fort Meade, Apr. 16, 1851, in Jackson-French Papers. Brannan was serving as Acting Assistant Adjutant General of the Fifth Military Department, headquarters in New Orleans.
19. Jackson to Everett, Fort Meade, Mar. 23, 1851, in Jackson-French Papers.
20. French to Brannan, Fort Meade, Apr. 14, 1851, in *ibid.*
21. *Ibid.*   22. French to Everett, Fort Meade, Mar. 26, 1851, in *ibid.*
23. Everett to Jackson, Headquarters of the Troops in Florida, Western Division, Tampa Bay, Mar. 29, 1851, in *ibid.*
24. Return of Company E, First Artillery, March, 1851 (MS in Army Section, War Records Branch, National Archives); Jackson to French, Fort Meade, Apr. 15, 1851, in Jackson-French Papers.
25. Thomas to Laura, Fort Meade, Mar. 1, 1851 (MS in Manuscripts Collection, University of Virginia Library). See also Arnold, pp. 168–170.
26. Thomas to Laura, Fort Meade, Mar. 1, 1851, in T. J. Jackson Papers, University of Virginia Library. The version of this letter printed in Arnold, pp. 168–170, leaves doubt as to whether Laura is the subject of the passage quoted. The original manuscript makes it clear that she is.
27. Record of testimony taken by French, Fort Meade, Apr. 13, 1851 (MS in Jackson-French Papers).
28. French to Brannan, Fort Meade, Apr. 14, 1851, in *ibid.*; record of testimony taken by French, Apr. 13, 1851, in *ibid.*
29. Charges and Specifications, n.d., Jackson against French, in *ibid.*

30. Jackson to French, in *ibid.*
31. French to Jackson, Fort Meade, Apr. 15, 1851, in *ibid.*
32. Hill, pp. 624–625.
33. See Jackson to Everett, Fort Meade, Apr. 13, 1851, in Jackson-French Papers, in which Jackson gives his reasons for investigating French's conduct: "On being informed that Capt and Bt Maj. . . . French . . . was guilty of conduct unbecoming an officer and a gentleman, I considered that it was my duty as the next officer in rank to him, to investigate the subject. . . . I was actuated by a sense of duty. . . ."
34. French to Brannan, Fort Meade, Apr. 14, 1851, in *ibid.*
35. Jackson to Brannan, Fort Meade, Apr. 15, 1851, in *ibid.*
36. French to Brannan, Fort Meade, Apr. 14, 1851, in *ibid.*   37. In *ibid.*
38. French to Brannan, Fort Meade, Apr. 17, 1851, in *ibid.*
39. *Ibid.*, and Charges and Specifications enclosed with the letter.
40. French to Brannan, Fort Meade, Apr. 14, 1851, in *ibid.*
41. Jackson to Brannan, Fort Meade, Apr. 21, 1851, in *ibid.*
42. Jackson to Brannan, Fort Meade, Apr. 23, 1851, in *ibid.*
43. French to Jones, Fort Meade, May 21, 1851, in *ibid.*
44. Endorsement on *ibid.*, Aug. 25, 1851.
45. W. W. S. Bliss to French, Headquarters, Western Division, East Pascagoula, Miss., Aug. 9, 1851, in Records of the War Department, Adjutant General's Office, National Archives; Special Orders No. 58, Headquarters, Western Division, Sept. 5, 1851, in *ibid.*
46. Endorsement on French to Conrad, Fort Myers, Mar. 6, 1852, in *ibid.*, dated Mar. 25, 1852.
47. Endorsement by Secretary of War Conrad on *ibid.*, dated Apr. 8, 1852.
48. Smith to Jackson, VMI, Feb. 4, 1851, in Cook, p. 126; Thomas to Laura, Fort Meade, Apr. 2, 1851, in Arnold, pp. 170–172.
49. *Ibid.*
50. French to Roger Jones, Fort Meade, May 21, 1851, in Jackson-French Papers; Return of First Artillery, May, 1851.
51. Cook, p. 116.

Chapter 5

1. Dabney, p. 62.   2. Preston, p. 932.
3. *Ibid.*, and Mrs. Jackson, p. 57, where a difference in italics appears.
4. The interview may have taken place early in 1851, although late 1850 seems likely. See Couper, I, 250.
5. Hill to Dabney, Petersburg, Va., July 11 [?], 1864, in Dabney Papers, III, doc. 48, Union Theological Seminary, Richmond, Va.
6. Couper, I, 234 n.; Mrs. Jackson, p. 56.   7. Arnold, pp. 173–175.
8. Cook, p. 117; Couper, I, 253.   9. Cook, pp. 112–119.
10. See Couper, I, 253–254, quoting the order assigning Jackson to duty.
11. The account of T. T. Munford, titled "How I Came to Know Maj. Thos. J. Jackson," probably written in 1897, is in the Charles E. and George W. Munford Papers, Manuscripts Collection, Duke University Library, Durham, N.C. See a typescript of a similar account by Munford (with some different details) in the Jackson Collection of Col. William Couper, Lexington, Va.
12. Couper, I, 245 n. The Corps of Cadets went into barracks on Sept. 24. See *ibid.*
13. *Ibid.*, pp. 246, 257.
14. Dabney, p. 65; Preston, p. 932; Mrs. Jackson, pp. 81–82, 109–110; Henderson, p. 51.
15. Notes in W. H. C. Bartlett, *Elements of Natural Philosophy—Spherical Astronomy* (New York, 1855) in the VMI Library. This copy belonged to Cadet Thomas B. Robinson, who apparently purchased it in 1856.

16. Charles Marshall Barton to [Joseph M. Barton], VMI, Sept. 28, 1855, in the Jackson Collection of Col. William Couper. Partially printed in Couper, I, 313. Charles Barton served loyally and devotedly under Jackson in the war and lost his life on May 25, 1862.
17. Mrs. Jackson, p. 68. 18. Couper, I, 313.
19. Charles Mason to F. H. Smith, June 16, 1852 (MS in Letters Received, VMI, 1852, doc. no. 184, VMI Correspondence Files).
20. M. Robinson to [F. H. Smith ?], Feb. 3, 1853 (MS in Letters Received, VMI, 1853, doc. 304).
21. Couper, III, 179. Walker is reputed to have challenged Jackson to a duel as a result of this trouble. Jackson declined to fight since it would be un-Christian. See *ibid.*, and Hill, p. 627.
22. Minutes of the Board of Visitors, VMI, 1856, p. 107, in VMI Files. See also Couper, I, 313; and III, 184.
23. *Ibid.*, III, 183. 24. *Ibid.*, I, 263. 25. *Ibid.*
26. Annual Report of Superintendent, June 22, 1857, p. 22, in VMI Files.
27. See Arnold, pp. 212–215; Cook, pp. 133–135; R. E. Lee to Board of Visitors, University of Virginia, West Point, Jan. 26, 1854, in Jackson Papers, Virginia Historical Society, Richmond. Jackson formally applied for the University of Virginia position on Jan. 2, 1854. See Jackson to Board of Visitors, Lexington, Va., Jan. 2, 1854, in Jackson Papers, Virginia Historical Society. The original is in the Manuscripts Collection, University of Virginia Library. See also Jackson to J. J. Allen, Lexington, Dec. 28, 1853, in Manuscripts Collection, University of Virginia Library; D. H. Mahan (one of Jackson's West Point professors) to [F. H. Smith], Mar. 8, 1854, in Letters Received, VMI, 1854, doc. 243; also in Couper, I, 282. Jackson's motives in wanting the Virginia position are obscure. See Arnold, p. 214, where money is listed a possible reason.
28. Thomas to Laura, Lexington, June 12, 1854, in Arnold, p. 212.
29. Mrs. Jackson, p. 82.
30. Minutes of the Board of Visitors, VMI, 1857, p. 138, in VMI Files; Couper, I, 313–314.
31. Couper, III, 187.

Chapter 6

1. Lexington's population in 1850 was 1,105 white and 638 colored. The total population in 1860 was 2,135. See Couper, I, 256 n.
2. Elizabeth Preston Allan, *Life and Letters of Margaret Junkin Preston* (Boston and New York, 1903), pp. 49–50.
3. See "Memoirs of Clem Fishburne" (2 vols.; MS no. 2341, University of Virginia Library), vol. I, pp. 19–21.
4. Preston, p. 927. 5. Mrs. Jackson, p. 71.
6. H. M. White (ed.), *Rev. William S. White, D.D., and His Times: An Autobiography* (Richmond, 1891), p. 139.
7. *Ibid.*
8. Hill to Dabney, Petersburg, Va., July 11 [?], 1864, in Dabney Papers, III, doc. 48, Union Theological Seminary, Richmond, Va.; Dabney, pp. 83–84; Mrs. Jackson, pp. 57–58; Cook, pp. 128–129; Henderson, p. 45; Arnold, pp. 16–19. See Henry Kyd Douglas, *I Rode With Stonewall* (Chapel Hill, 1940. Cited hereinafter as Douglas), p. 373, for an erroneous statement that Jackson's first wife "had led Jackson into the Presbyterian Church before her death."
9. J. W. Wayland, *Stonewall Jackson's Way* (Staunton, Va., 1940), p. 7.
10. Mrs. Jackson, p. 61. 11. Preston, p. 933. 12. Mrs. Jackson, p. 61.
13. Henderson, p. 45.
14. The quotation is in Mrs. Jackson, p. 61, and also in Dabney, p. 91. The two versions differ slightly.

15. Dabney, pp. 91–92; Mrs. Jackson, pp. 61–62. Again there are slight differences in the quoted statement.

16. Dabney, p. 92; Mrs. Jackson, p. 62.   17. Hill, p. 625.

18. Preston, p. 936. Jackson's church slumbers were often ascribed to a drowsiness which all who suffered from dyspepsia seemed to share. It should be noted that in later years Jackson's nephew, Thomas Jackson Arnold, wrote that he was never certain that his uncle actually slept in church. He gave all outward signs of sleep, but always seemed to know something of what had been said during the sermon. Arnold, p. 252.

19. See Wayland, op. cit., pp. 6–7; Cook, picture facing p. 71; Mrs. Jackson, p. 67.

20. Hill to Dabney, Petersburg, Va., July 11 [?], 1864, in Dabney Papers, III, doc. 48; Hill, "The Real Stonewall Jackson," p. 625.

21. Letter dated Lexington, Apr. 15, 1853, in Arnold, pp. 199–200.

22. Letter dated Lexington, Sept. 7, 1852, in ibid., p. 190.

23. Ibid., p. 198.   24. Preston, p. 927.

25. Hill, p. 625; Allan, Margaret Junkin Preston, p. 60.

26. Letter dated Lexington, June 6, 1853, in Manuscripts Collection, University of Virginia Library.

27. Letter dated Lexington, Jan. 10, 1852, in Manuscripts Collection, University of Virginia Library.

28. Letter dated Lexington, Feb. 21, 1852, in Arnold, p. 182.

29. Mrs. Jackson, p. 63.   30. Arnold, pp. 202–203.

31. Hill to Dabney, Petersburg, Va., July 11 [?], 1864, in Dabney Papers, III, doc. 48.

32. Ibid. In speaking of Mrs. Hill's concern about the Jackson-Junkin romance, Hill wrote: "My wife had been very intimate with Miss Eleanor [sic] Junkin & with the match-making propensity of the sex (dont let her or Mrs D[abney] know of this) had been anxious to bring about the union of Maj J & her friend." See also quotation from Mrs. John H. Moore, Memories of a Long Life in Virginia (Staunton, Va., 1920), in Wayland, op. cit., p. 7.

33. See the marriage license, dated Aug. 4, 1853, in Register of Marriages, Rockbridge County, Va., I, 435, in Rockbridge County Court House, Lexington, Va. Jackson's best man was probably young Charles Harrison, fellow resident at the Lexington Hotel. See Cook, pp. 129–132.

34. Letter dated Rockbridge Alum Springs, Aug. 3, 1853, in Arnold, p. 203.

35. Mrs. Jackson, pp. 98–99.

36. See [Margaret Junkin], Silverwood, A Book of Memories (New York, 1856). In a note to Rebecca Glasgow, probably written in 1856, Maggie wrote of Silverwood: "I send you a book to read which I hope will interest you, inasmuch as the author is well known to you. I wrote it to embalm the characters of dear mother, Ellie, and brother Joe. You will recognize the characters, and many of the scenes are from life. Don't let anybody know the authorship; it is a secret." (Allan, Margaret Junkin Preston, pp. 85–86.) A close reading of Silverwood reveals that the character "Zilpha" is meant to portray Ellie and that "Edith" is Maggie's self-characterization.

37. The typescript of this poem is in the T. J. Jackson Papers, Southern Historical Collection, University of North Carolina Library.

38. Preston, pp. 931–932. See also Thomas to Laura, Lexington, Oct. 19, 1853, in Arnold, pp. 205–206.

39. Preston, pp. 931–932.   40. Ibid., pp. 930–931.

41. Letter dated Revere House, Boston, Aug. 18, 1853, in Cook, pp. 118–119.

42. Cook, pp. 131–132.

43. Preston, pp. 934–935; Mrs. Jackson, pp. 72–73, repeats this account.

44. Letter dated Lexington, Oct. 19, 1853, in Arnold, p. 205.

45. See ibid., pp. 205–210.

46. Letter dated Lexington, Feb. 14, 1853 [1854], in Arnold, p. 208.

47. Letter dated Lexington, Mar. 4, 1854, in Manuscripts Collection, University of Virginia Library; Obituary Notice, giving date of Julia Junkin's death as Feb. 23, 1854, in Lexington Gazette, Mar. 2, 1854. See Maggie's touching description of the death scene in Allan, Margaret Junkin Preston, pp. 66–67.

48. Thomas to Laura, Lexington, Mar. 4, 1854, in MSS Collection, University of Virginia Library.
49. Thomas to Laura, Lexington, Apr. 7, 1854, in *ibid.*
50. Allan, *Margaret Junkin Preston*, pp. 66–67.   51. Preston, p. 930.
52. *Ibid.*, 935.
53. Despite the numerous stories to the contrary, a check of the extant records of the Franklin Society does not show that Jackson ever became a member. The records are in the Washington and Lee University Library, Lexington, Va.
54. See Mrs. Jackson, p. 62, where the story of Jackson's joining the Franklin Society is repeated, probably on the evidence of Dabney, p. 72. The story appeared again in Hill, p. 626, and in Davis, *They Called Him Stonewall*, p. 115.
55. Hill, p. 626.
56. See the *Lexington Gazette* for the years 1854–1855. The editor of the paper was a Native American man to the core. Nowhere in the files for these years is Jackson linked with this party.
57. See Couper, I, 276–280; Report of the Superintendent, June 22, 1854, p. 49, in VMI Files; also Lexington *Valley Star*, Apr. 20, May 4, 1854, and *Lexington Gazette*, Apr. 27, 1854.
58. Thomas to Laura, Lexington, May 2, 1854, in Arnold, pp. 211–212.
59. *Lexington Gazette*, June 22, 1854, listing Ellie, Julia, E. D. Junkin, and W. Junkin as arrivals at the Natural Bridge Hotel during the week of June 18.
60. Thomas to Laura, Lexington, July 1, 1854, in Arnold, pp. 217–218, including a rare postscript by Ellie.
61. In *Lexington Gazette*.   62. Mrs. Jackson, p. 83.

Chapter 7

1. Thomas to Maggie, Lexington, Feb. 6, 1855, in Allan, *Margaret Junkin Preston*, pp. 72–73.
2. Thomas to Maggie, [Lexington,] Mar. 1, 1855 (MS in Margaret Junkin Preston Papers, Southern Historical Collection, University of North Carolina Library).
3. Thomas to Maggie, Home, Mar. 10, 1855, in *ibid.*
4. Thomas to Laura, Lexington, Nov. 14, 1854, in Arnold, pp. 219–220.
5. Thomas to Maggie, [Lexington,] Mar. 1, 1855, in Margaret Junkin Preston Papers.
6. Preston, p. 932.
7. Thomas to Mrs. Neale, [Lexington,] Feb. 16, 1855, in Mrs. Jackson, pp. 84–85.
8. D. X. Junkin, *The Reverend George Junkin, D.D., LL.D.: A Historical Biography* (Philadelphia, 1871), p. 503, saying of Ellie that "her babe and she were laid in the same grave."
9. Hill to Dabney, Petersburg, Va., July 11 [?], 1864 in Dabney Papers, III, doc. 48, Union Theological Seminary, Richmond, Va. See also Hill, p. 625.
10. Thomas to Maggie, Home, Mar. 10, 1855, in Margaret Junkin Preston Papers.
11. Mrs. Jackson, p. 85; Allan, *Margaret Junkin Preston*, pp. 72–73.
12. Thomas to Maggie[?], Lexington, Feb. 6, 1855, in Allan, *Margaret Junkin Preston*, pp. 72–73.
13. See Allan, *Margaret Junkin Preston*, pp. 71–72; Preston, pp. 927, 932.
14. Thomas to Maggie, Neale's Island, Wood County, Va., Aug. 16, 1855, in Margaret Junkin Preston Papers.
15. Maggie to Rebecca Glasgow, sometime in 1855, in Allan, *Margaret Junkin Preston*, p. 70.
16. Preston, p. 927.   17. Junkin, *op. cit.*, pp. 503–504.
18. Quoted in Mrs. Jackson, p. 67.   19. Junkin, *op. cit.*, p. 502.
20. Mrs. Jackson, pp. 84–85; Thomas to Maggie, Mar. 1, 1855, in Margaret Junkin Preston Papers.
21. White (ed.), *Rev. William S. White, D.D., Autobiography*, p. 143. In *ibid.*, pp. 157–158, the date for these collections is given as 1856. A slightly different version of this episode appears in Mrs. Jackson, pp. 78–79.

22. So says Mrs. Jackson, p. 77, although there is some doubt about the date. See *Lexington Gazette and Citizen*, Aug. 25, 1876. The school certainly was functioning in May of 1856.
23. *Lexington Gazette and Citizen*, Aug. 25, 1876.
24. Thomas to Maggie, Lexington, May 31, 1856, in Margaret Junkin Preston Papers.
25. See MS "Minutes of Lexington Presbytery," XIV, 101–104 (typescript copy, p. 171) in Washington and Lee University Library; White, *op. cit.*, pp. 157–158.
26. Preston, p. 935.   27. Mrs. Jackson, pp. 114–115.
28. Preston, pp. 935–936. See also George W. Cable, "The Gentler Side of Two Great Southerners," in *Century Magazine*, XLVII (NS XXV) (1893–1894), 293; Mrs. Jackson, pp. 142–143; Dabney, pp. 95–96.
29. In 1852 Jackson claimed and received 160 acres of Mexican War Bounty land, apparently in Iowa. See Bounty Land Files, Can No. 374, Bundle No. 145, National Archives.
30. Letters dated Lexington, Oct. 6, 1855, and June 6, 1856, in Arnold, pp. 231–232, 243–244.
31. Thomas to Laura, July 18, 1856, in *ibid.*, pp. 246–248.
32. See advertisement of the "Lexington Savings Institution," naming Col. F. H. Smith, president; James Compton, Samuel McD. Moore, Prof. J. L. Campbell, Maj. T. J. Jackson, Col. S. McD. Reid, and Andrew Winthrow, directors. *Lexington Gazette*, Feb. 8, 1855. to Jan. 31. 1856.
33. Thomas to Laura, Ship *Asia*, at sea, July 18, 1856. in Arnold, pp. 246–248.
34. Thomas to Laura, Naples, Sept. 9, 1856, in *ibid.*, pp. 248–249; to Laura, Lexington, Oct. 25, 1856, in *ibid.*, pp. 249–250; to J. Jaquelin Smith, Lexington, Apr. 11, 1859, in Cook, pp. 149–151. See also Preston, p. 934.
35. Douglas, p. 233; Dabney, pp. 82–83.
36. Hill to Dabney, Petersburg, Va., July 11 [?], 1864, in Dabney Papers, III, doc. 48.
37. Mrs. Jackson, p. 88. Somewhat different dialogue is given in Dabney, p. 116.
38. Cook, pp. 136–137; MS "Memoirs of Clem Fishburne," I, 101, doc. no. 2341, Manuscripts Collection, University of Virginia Library.
39. "Memoirs of Clem Fishburne," I, 25.   40. Mrs. Jackson, p. 100.
41. Thomas to Laura, Lexington, Dec. 6, 1856, in Arnold, pp. 250–251; *Lexington Gazette*, Nov. 27, 1856.
42. Mrs. Jackson, pp. 75–77; Dabney, pp. 88–89.
43. Letter dated Apr. 25, 1857, in Mrs. Jackson, pp. 101–102.
44. Letter dated May 7, 1857, in *ibid.*, p 102.
45. Letters dated May 16 and June 20, 1857, in *ibid.*, pp. 102–103.
46. MS letter, doc. no. 2341, in Manuscripts Collection, University of Virginia Library.
47. *Ibid.* Laura was invited to the wedding but could not attend. See Arnold, pp. 254–255.
48. "Memoirs of Clem Fishburne," I, 27; Mrs. Jackson, pp. 103–104.
49. Mrs. Jackson, pp. 39. 104–105.
50. Thomas to Laura, Rockbridge Alum Springs, Aug. 11, 1857, in Arnold, pp. 256–257.
51. Mrs. Jackson, p. 105.
52. Mary Anna Jackson, "With Stonewall Jackson in Camp," in *Hearst's Magazine*, XXIV (1913), 386.
53. Couper, I, 324.
54. Allan, *Margaret Junkin Preston*, p. 107; Anna Jackson to Laura, Lexington, Sept. 27, 1857, in Cook, pp. 145–147.
55. Mrs. Jackson, p. 105.   56. *Ibid.*, p. 106.
57. Bought from Dr. Archibald Graham, deed dated Nov. 4, 1858. See Couper, I, 23.
58. Mrs. Jackson, pp. 106–107.   59. Preston, p. 932.
60. Some of Jackson's books are preserved in Battle Abbey, Richmond, Va. A sampling of the collection shows John Gummere, *An Elementary Treatise on Astronomy* [Philadelphia, 1842], heavily annotated in Jackson's hand; Richard Whatley, D.D., *Elements of Logic* (Boston, 1845), heavily annotated; J. G. Spurzheim, M.D., *Education: Its Elementary Principles, Founded on the Nature*

of Man (12th Amer. ed., New York, 1847), not marked; Jacob Abbott, *History of Julius Caesar* (New York, 1849), slightly annotated; Abbott's *Xerxes* and *William the Conqueror* and other lives of great captains; *Instructions for Field Artillery, Horse and Foot* (Baltimore, 1850), compiled by a Board of Artillery Officers, well annotated; *El Nuevo Testamento de Nuestro Señor Jesu-Christo, traducido en Español* (New York, 1851), inscribed "T. J. Jackson from his affectionate Sister. M. J. Christmas, 1853"; George Bush, *The Life of Mohammed* (New York, 1852 [The Family Library, No. 10]), slightly annotated, first 47 pages; Richard Mason, M.D., *The Gentleman's New Pocket Farrier: Comprising a General Description of the Noble and Useful Animal, the Horse; with Modes of Management in All Cases, and Treatment in Disease* (Philadelphia, 1858); John Gibbon, *The Artillerists Manual, Compiled from Various Sources, and Adapted to the Service of the United States* (New York, 1860), slightly annotated. There is also a well-used Latin grammar, 1840 ed., and a slightly used French grammar, English to French. See also Mrs. Jackson, p. 111.

61. Sometimes, toward the end of the term, he had to go back to VMI for an hour's artillery practice.
62. Cook, pp. 147–148, and Jackson Collection of Col. William Couper, Lexington, Va.
63. Mrs. Jackson, pp. 110–111.   64. *Ibid.*, p. 78.   65. *Ibid.*, p. 63.
66. White, *op. cit.*, p. 139.
67. Lyle had probably suffered a stroke and was partially paralyzed in 1856, but recovered sufficiently to be his usual helpful self for years. *Ibid.*, pp. 139–143; Jackson to Thomas Arnold, Lexington, Dec. 1, 1856, in Arnold, p. 302.
68. Mrs. Jackson, p. 72.
69. Thomas to Laura, VMI, Feb. 1, 1853, in Arnold, pp. 194–196.
70. Mrs. Jackson, pp. 71, 72.
71. Thomas to Laura, Lexington, Dec. 19, 1857, in Arnold, pp. 257–258.
72. *Ibid.*, pp. 264–265.
73. Thomas to Laura, New York, Aug. 18, 1858, in *ibid.*, pp. 265–266.
74. R. H. Catlett to Col. F. H. Smith, VMI, Sept. 8, 1858, in Letters Sent, VMI, 1858, doc. no. 93, VMI Files; Couper, I, 338.
75. Jackson to Rufus Barringer, Lexington, May 1, 1858, in Manuscripts Collection, University of Virginia Library; to Laura, Lexington, Mar. 1, May 22, 1858, in Arnold, pp. 261–262; Mrs. Jackson, p. 111; Jackson to his niece, Anna Grace Arnold, Lexington, June 7, 1858, in Arnold, pp. 263–264.
76. Mrs. Jackson, pp. 114–119.   77. Arnold, pp. 298–308.
78. Mrs. Jackson, p. 120.   79. Preston, p. 933.
80. Letter dated Lexington, Oct. 23, 1858, in Arnold, pp. 266–267.
81. See Jackson to Thomas Arnold, Lexington, Sept. 13, 1859, in Arnold, pp. 303–304; to Laura, Lexington, Oct. 23, 1858; Feb. 19, May 9, 1859, in *ibid.*, pp. 266–273.
82. Letter dated Lexington, May 9, 1859, in *ibid.*, p. 269.
83. Thomas to Laura, White Sulphur Springs, Aug. 13, 1859, in Cook, pp. 151–152; to Laura, Lexington, Aug. 27, 1859, in Arnold, pp. 273–274.
84. For the whole account of Jackson's part in the John Brown episode, see Couper, II, 1–21; Mrs. Jackson, pp. 129–132; *Richmond Daily Dispatch*, Dec. 5, 1859, where the cadet uniforms are described; *Lexington Gazette*, Oct. 27–Dec. 2[?], 1859.
85. Mrs. Jackson, p. 132.
86. Letter dated Lexington, Jan. 21, 1860, in *ibid.*, p. 132.
87. Extracts from notes for an address, written in the hand of Thomas T. Munford, probably sometime in the 1880s, in the Jackson Collection of Col. William Couper, Lexington, Va.; Arnold, p. 327
88. Letters dated Lexington, Feb. 8, Mar. 8, 1858, in Arnold, pp. 258–261.
89. Thomas to Laura, Lexington, June 30, 1860, in *ibid.*, pp. 282–283.
90. Cook, pp. 152–153; Mrs. Jackson, pp. 133–135.
91. Mrs. Jackson, p. 139.

92. Letter dated Lexington, Jan. 26, 1861, in Arnold, pp. 293–294; Thomas to Laura, Lexington, Feb. 2, 1861, in Cook, p. 154.
93. *Lexington Gazette*, Nov. 29, 1860.
94. Dabney, pp. 153–154; Mrs. Jackson, pp. 140–141.
95. See Mrs. Jackson, p. 142.   96. In Arnold, pp. 291–292.
97. Jennings C. Wise, *The Long Arm of Lee* (2 vols.; Lynchburg, Va., 1915), I, 63, 64; Cook, pp. 152–153.
98. Letter dated Lexington, Jan. 23, 1861 (MS in the Century Collection in the New York Public Library). This curious letter may not be in Jackson's hand, but other contents indicate it is probably genuine.
99. Mrs. Jackson, pp. 136–139.
100. Letter dated Lexington, Apr. 6, 1861, in Arnold, pp. 295–297.
101. See Couper, II, 81–82.   102. *Ibid.*, p. 86.
103. See *ibid.*, p. 89 and *n.*; Junkin, *op. cit.*, pp. 524–526.
104. Cook, p. 154.   105. Couper, II, 91.   106. *Ibid.*, p. 92.
107. Mrs. Jackson, pp. 144–146.   108. Couper, II, 95–97 and *n.*
109. *Ibid.*, pp. 96–97; Thomas T. Munford, "How I Came to Know Maj. Thos. J. Jackson" (MS in the Charles E. and G. W. Munford Papers, Duke University Library).

Chapter 8

1. See Couper, II, 98–99 and *n.*, giving the time of arrival at Staunton as ten o'clock on the night of April 21.
2. Mrs. Jackson, p. 148.   3. See the *Richmond Enquirer*, Apr. 23, 27, 1861.
4. Mrs. Jackson, p. 148; Dabney, p. 183.
5. See Thomas to Laura, Fort Meade, Fla., Mar. 1, 1851, in *Arnold*, pp. 168–170. On the matter of Jackson's commission, see Couper, II, 111; Cook, pp. 156–157; Dabney, pp. 183–185; Mrs. Jackson, p. 150.
6. This episode is in dispute. The accounts in Mrs. Jackson, p. 150, and in Cook, pp. 156–157, disagree, and that in Henderson, p. 86, is at variance with the other two. The account in the text is an attempt to reconcile all versions in a sequence of plausible events.
7. *War of the Rebellion: A Compilation of the Official Records of the Union and Confederate Armies* (70 vols. in 127 and index; Washington, 1880–1901. Cited hereinafter as *OR*), ser. I, II, 785, 786.
8. Couper, II, 111–112.   9. Mrs. Jackson, p. 151.
10. Quoted in Couper, II, 112 and *n.*
11. Special Orders No. 7, Headquarters, Virginia Forces, Richmond, Apr. 28, 1861, in *OR*, I, II, 787; Couper, II, 112; John D. Imboden, "Jackson at Harper's Ferry in 1861," in R. U. Johnson and C. C. Buel (eds.), *Battles and Leaders of the Civil War* (4 vols.; New York, 1887–1888. Cited hereinafter as *B&L*), I, 120.
12. Imboden, *op. cit.*, in *B&L*, I, 121; *OR*, I, II, 793–794.
13. Mrs. Jackson, pp. 151–152.
14. Douglas Southall Freeman, *Lee's Lieutenants: A Study in Command* (3 vols.; New York, 1942–1944. Cited hereinafter as Freeman, *LL*), I, 10.
15. *OR*, I, II, 806–807.
16. Jackson to Lee, Harpers Ferry, May 6, 1861, in *ibid.*, pp. 809–810.
17. Jackson to Lee, May 7, 1861, in *ibid.*, p. 814.   18. *Ibid.*, p. 833.
19. Imboden, in his article "Jackson at Harper's Ferry in 1861," *B&L*, I, 123–124, appears to confuse this early altercation with a later, more famous, instance of Ashby's dissatisfaction. It is possible that Imboden had completely mistimed the episode. Freeman, in *LL*, I, 10–11, gives no credence to the Imboden story.
20. *OR*, I, II, 809–810, 814–815, 822, 823–825.
21. *Ibid.*, pp. 832–833, 836, 863; Douglas, p. 6; Imboden, *op. cit.*, in *B&L*, I, 122–123.
22. *OR*, I, II, 836.   23. See Lee to Jackson, May 9, 1861, in *ibid.*, p. 822.

24. *Ibid.*, p. 825.   25. *Ibid.*, p. 836.   26. *Ibid.*, pp. 814–815.
27. *Ibid.*, pp. 832–833.   28. *Ibid.*, p. 822.   29. *Ibid.*, pp. 832–833.
30. *Ibid.*, p. 822.   31. Imboden, *op. cit.*, in B&L, I, 122.
32. *OR*, I, II, 806, 832. For Little Sorrel, see Mrs. Jackson, pp. 170–173.
33. *OR*, I, II, 840.   34. *Ibid.*, pp. 863–864.   35. Mrs. Jackson, p. 158.
36. Freeman, *LL*, I, 12; *OR*, I, II, 871–872.   37. *OR*, I, II, 877.
38. Mrs. Jackson, pp. 157–158.   39. *OR*, I, II, 849.
40. *Ibid.*, p. 810.   41. Mrs. Jackson, p. 168.
42. Strength return, June 30, 1861, *OR*, I, II, 187; Clement A. Evans (ed.), *Confederate Military History* (12 vols.; Atlanta, 1899), III, 71.
43. See indorsement on Col. J. W. Allen to Jackson, June 7, 1861 (MS no. JO 392, Joseph E. Johnston Collection, Henry E. Huntington Library, San Marino, California).
44. Mrs. Jackson, p. 159.   45. *Ibid.*
46. "Memorandum in relation to Harper's Ferry," *OR*, I, II, 881.
47. *Ibid.*, p. 924.   48. Mrs. Jackson, pp. 160–161.
49. Joseph E. Johnston, *Narrative of Military Operations Directed During the Late War Between the States* (New York, 1874), pp. 23, 24.
50. *OR*, I, II, 934, 937.   51. Mrs. Jackson, p. 162.
52. W. H. C. Whiting to Jackson, Winchester, Va., June 19, 1861 (MS in T. J. Jackson Papers, Virginia Historical Society).
53. See Mrs. Jackson, p. 168.   54. *Ibid.*, p. 163.
55. Whiting to Jackson, Headquarters, Army of the Shenandoah, 5 A.M., June 23, 1861 (MS in T. J. Jackson Papers, Virginia Historical Society).
56. Mrs. Jackson, p. 163.   57. *OR*, I, II, 717, 729–730.
58. See Mrs. Jackson, p. 165, and also Jackson's report of the action in *OR*, I, II, 185–186.
59. *OR*, I, II, 160.   60. Mrs. Jackson, p. 166.   61. Johnston, *op. cit.*, p. 30.
62. Mrs. Jackson, p. 167.   63. Cook, pp. 157–159; Arnold, pp. 333–334.
64. *OR*, I, II, 185.   65. Cook, p. 159; Mrs. Jackson, p. 166.
66. *OR*, I, II, 963; Cook, p. 159.   67. *OR*, I, II, 967.
68. Mrs. Jackson, p. 169.   69. *OR*, I, II, 973–974.
70. Johnston, *op. cit.*, p. 21.
71. *OR*, I, II, 478; Johnston, *op. cit.*, p. 33, reporting that Beauregard also sent an appeal to Johnston for aid.
72. Freeman, *LL*, I, 58–59; *OR*, I, II, 187.   73. See *OR*, I, II, 163–172.
74. Johnston, *op. cit.*, p. 35.
75. See "Memoirs of Clem Fishburne," I, 141 (MS no. 2341, Manuscripts Collection, University of Virginia Library); John O. Casler, *Four Years in the Stonewall Brigade* (Girard, Kans., 1906; Marietta, Ga., 1951. The 1951 edition is used throughout and is cited hereinafter as Casler), p. 21.
76. There is some confusion about the time. Jackson, in Mrs. Jackson, p. 175, put the arrival at the river at "about dark," and in Fishburne's "Memoirs," I, 141, the time is also listed as "about dark." Johnston, in his *Narrative*, p. 37, placed the time much earlier. Jackson's account is in a letter to Anna and is accepted as accurate.
77. Wayland, *Stonewall Jackson's Way*, pp. 33, 34. This account does violence to the romantic story which is recounted in James Ryder Randall's famous poem, "The Lone Sentry":

> 'Twas in the dying of the day
>   The darkness grew so still,
> The drowsy pipe of evening birds
>   Was hushed upon the hill.
> Athwart the shadows of the vale
>   Slumbered the men of might—
> And one lone sentry paced his rounds,
>   To watch the camp that night.

The "lone sentry," of course, was Jackson. The story has often been told of his standing guard at Paris that night as the men slept. Henderson, p. 101, accepts the story as does Davis, *op. cit.*, p. 145, doubtless taking it from Dabney, p. 212, and from a letter of Jackson to Anna, in Mrs. Jackson, pp. 175–176. In this letter, which seems strangely out of character all the way through, Jackson comments on the night's stay in Paris: "I mean the troops slept, as my men were so exhausted that I let them sleep while I kept watch myself." Manifestly this quotation can be read several ways. Read one way, it sounds as though Jackson alone guarded the bivouac; and yet, this is not what he said. He said that he kept watch himself—this does not exclude the possibility of others' helping him. Nothing like the lone sentry episode is recalled in Fishburne's "Memoirs," I, 141–143, and he was in Paris during the night of July 18–19, 1861. Many years later Hill, p. 624, discounted this whole affair. He found it touching but "monstrously absurd, and reflects but little credit on Jackson as a soldier. . . ." Hill could not see how as careful a general as Jackson would permit one man to stand sentry for a whole brigade.

78. The time is in dispute. Jackson, in Mrs. Jackson, p. 177, puts the arrival at "about six o'clock." Johnston, in his *Narrative*, p. 37, said Jackson's men reached Piedmont "before eight o'clock Friday morning." Seven o'clock is offered as a reconciliation. It possibly should be set later, since three miles an hour is moderately rapid marching speed, and sunrise came fairly close to 5 A.M.

79. Casler, p. 22.

80. *Ibid.*; Mrs. Jackson, p. 177; Robert C. Black, III, *The Railroads of the Confederacy* (Chapel Hill, N.C., 1952), pp. 61, 62; Johnston, *op. cit.*, pp. 36, 37.

81. Fishburne, "Memoirs," II, i.

82. OR, I, II, 441. See also Freeman, *LL*, I, 48, pointing out the errors in this description.

83. The main sources used in constructing the account of the battle of First Manassas, in addition to the reports of leading generals printed in the OR, are: Freeman, *LL*, I, chap. 5; T. Harry Williams, *P. G. T. Beauregard: Napoleon in Gray* (Baton Rouge, La., 1955), chap. 5; Johnston, *Narrative*, chap. 2; Joseph M. Hanson, *Bull Run Remembers . . .* (Manassas, Va., 1953), pp. 1–28; Robert M. Johnston, *Bull Run, Its Strategy and Tactics* (Boston, 1913), chaps. 6–10 (the most exhaustive single study of the battle). Other sources are cited in subsequent notes.

84. OR, I, II, 569.

85. Jackson probably recalled his two regiments. See Casler, p. 25.

86. OR, I, II, 985.

87. Freeman, *LL*, I, 82 and Appendix V. For Beauregard's movements see Beauregard, "The First Battle of Bull Run," in *B&L*, I, 210.

88. Henderson, p. 113.

89. These batteries were Battery I, 1st U.S. Artillery, Capt. J. B. Ricketts; and Battery D, 2d U.S. Artillery, Capt. Charles Griffin. See Freeman, *LL*, I, 68.

90. "Memoirs," II, ix.   91. Hanson, *op. cit.*, p. 18.

92. Freeman, *LL*, I, 68 and *n.*, discusses the question of timing these two charges.

93. Henderson, p. 114.

94. A. C. Cummings to Gen. J. E. Johnston, Abingdon, Va., Dec. 27, 1870, in Johnston Papers, William and Mary College Library.

95. Mrs. Jackson, p. 178.   96. OR, I, II, 500.

Chapter 9

1. Mrs. Jackson, pp. 179–180.

2. Letter dated July 28, 1861, in Cook, pp. 160–162.

3. OR, I, II, 482; Henderson, p. 120.

4. Caution must be used in recounting this episode. One of the persistent stories about Jackson after the battle of Manassas is that during the dressing of his wound he remarked, "Give me 10,000 men and I will take Washington City tomorrow" (Hunter H. McGuire, *The Confederate Cause and Conduct in the War*

Between the States [Richmond, 1907], p. 197). The story apparently first was printed in Dabney, p. 227, probably on the authority of Dr. Hunter McGuire. A slightly different version, giving the number of troops needed as 5,000, appeared in E. P. Alexander, *Military Memoirs of a Confederate* (New York, 1907), p. 42. Alexander asserted that Jackson addressed his remark to President Davis, a recent arrival to the field. Something of the sort may have been said by Jackson—although ordinarily he would not have been given to such boasting—since the fire of battle was still in him and he knew clearly the need for pursuit. See also Henderson, p. 117, and Davis, *They Called Him Stonewall*, p. 152.

5. Mrs. Jackson, pp. 181–182.   6. Casler, pp. 49–50; Mrs. Jackson, p. 185.

7. Jackson to Maj. T. G. Rhett, Headquarters, 1st Brigade, Camp Harman, Aug. 27, 1861 (MS in J. E. Johnston Papers, Henry E. Huntington Library, San Marino, California).   8. Mrs. Jackson, p. 183.   9. *Ibid.*, p. 170.

10. *Ibid.*, p. 184.   11. *Ibid.*, p. 185.

12. *Ibid.*, p. 190; Mary Anna Jackson, "With Stonewall Jackson in Camp," in *Hearst's Magazine*, XXIV (1913), 390.

13. Fishburne, "Memoirs," July 25, 1861, II, 15.

14. Douglas, p. 11; Mrs. Jackson, p. 191.

15. Richardson to Jackson, Richmond, Oct. 14, 1861, in T. J. Jackson Papers, Virginia Historical Society, Richmond.

16. Jackson to Richardson and Gen. T. S. Haymond, Committee, Centreville, Va., Oct. 22, 1861, doc. no. 22070, Virginia State Library, Archives Division, Richmond.   17. Mrs. Jackson, p. 192.

18. Minutes of the Board of Visitors, VMI, 1861, p. 32, in VMI Files; Couper, II, 135.

19. See, for instance, the *Lexington Gazette*, Aug. 16, 1861, where an admiring article is printed on "Gen. Thomas J. Jackson's Brigade." Col. William Gilham was appointed to fill Jackson's chair at VMI until the end of the war. Couper, II, 135.

20. Mrs. Jackson, pp. 193–194.   21. Douglas, p. 14.

22. John W. Daniel to "Dear Sister," Centreville, Oct. 31, 1861 (MS in Daniel Papers, Manuscripts Collection, University of Virginia Library).

23. Mrs. Jackson, p. 195.   24. *Ibid.*, pp. 198–199.   25. *Ibid.*, p. 199.

26. *Ibid.*, p. 195.   27. Douglas, p. 14.   28. *OR*, I, v, 913.

29. MS in T. J. Jackson Papers, Virginia Historical Society, Richmond; also printed in *OR*, I, v, 909. There are slight textual differences.

30. *OR*, I, v, 942–943.   31. *Ibid.*, p. 926.   32. *Ibid.*, p. 936.

33. Fishburne, *op. cit.*, II, 21.

34. MS Journal of Robert G. H. Kean, pt. I, entry of May 11, 1863, in Manuscripts Collection, University of Virginia Library.

35. Douglas, p. 15.

36. The time is not specifically indicated, but since Jackson reported that he arrived at Winchester in the evening of Nov. 4, having left Manassas "by the first train of cars," the farewell meeting must have taken place sometime in the early morning. See Douglas, p. 16, and *OR*, I, v, 937. It is possible, of course, that the meeting occurred on Nov. 3, but all accounts agree on the fourth. See Henderson, p. 126; Dabney, p. 248.

37. This speech is reported in all the standard works (Dabney, pp. 248–249; Mrs. Jackson, pp. 200–202; Henderson, pp. 126–127) and they all disagree on the exact wording. Douglas, pp. 16–17, recorded the speech as he heard it, and his account seems the most reliable. See Douglas, pp. 361–362, for a discussion of the various versions of the address.

38. Mrs. Jackson, p. 200.   39. *OR*, I, v, 937.

40. *Ibid.*, pp. 389, 937, 942–943.   41. *Ibid.*, pp. 938, 940, 946.

42. *Ibid.*, p. 946.   43. *Ibid.*, p. 944.

44. Cornelia McDonald, *A Diary with Reminiscences of the War and Refugee Life in the Shenandoah Valley, 1860–1865* (annotated and supplemented by Hunter McDonald; Nashville, 1934), p. 37; Casler, pp. 59–61.

45. Mrs. Jackson, p. 215.   46. Henderson, p. 132.   47. *OR*, I, v, 965–966.

48. Mrs. Jackson, p. 218.

49. *OR*, I, v, 966–969; Freeman, *LL*, I, 122.   50. *OR*, I, v, 983–984.
51. See *ibid.*, pp. 975 and 966.   52. Douglas, p. 19.   53. Mrs. Jackson, p. 205.
54. *Ibid.*, pp. 209–210.   55. *Ibid.*, pp. 210–211.
56. J. T. L. Preston to Maggie, Winchester, Dec. 5, 1861, in Allan, *Margaret Junkin Preston*, pp. 122–123.
57. *OR*, I, v, 389, 989; Taliaferro to [?] Conrad, Gloucester Court House, Va., July 11, 1877, in W. B. Taliaferro Papers, Box 12, William and Mary College Library.
58. Maj. M. G. Harman to the Quartermaster General, Staunton, Nov. 2 [22], 1861 (MS in Confederate Records, chap. V, vol. 2, p. 252, National Archives).
59. Jackson to L. B. Northrop, Winchester, Dec. 13, 1861 (MS in Letters Sent, Valley District, Box 8, Jed Hotchkiss Papers, Manuscripts Division, Library of Congress).
60. Mrs. Jackson, pp. 208–209. See also Dabney, p. 250.
61. See, for example, Jackson to Capt. Baylor, Dec. 28, 1861 (MS in Box 8, Hotchkiss Papers, LC).
62. Letter dated Dec. 24, 1861, in *ibid.*
63. Jackson to Lt. Col. M. G. Harman, Dec. 24, 1861, in *ibid.*
64. Jackson to Ashby, Dec. 27, 28, 1861; in *ibid.*
65. Jackson to Ashby, Dec. 25, 27, 1861; in *ibid.*
66. This is conjecture. It is known that Jackson wanted Johnson's men to join him and that he did not get them at this time. See Mrs. Jackson, p. 217. For Preston's letter, see Allan, *Margaret Junkin Preston*, pp. 127–128.
67. *OR*, I, v, 1005.   68. *Ibid.*, pp. 1003, 1005–1006.
69. Circular, Dec. 31, 1861, in Box 8, Hotchkiss Papers, LC.   70. *Ibid.*
71. General Orders No. 68, Valley District, Dec. 31, 1861, in *ibid.*
72. For information on how the troops had been entertained by townspeople, see Cornelia McDonald, *Diary*, pp. 37, 38.
73. Mrs. Jackson, p. 488.   74. Douglas, p. 20.
75. *OR*, I, v, 390. Henderson, p. 144, put the number at 9,000. William Allan, in his excellent study "Jackson's Valley Campaign," *Southern Historical Society Papers* XLIII (NS V) (1920), 125, put Jackson's strength at "some eight or nine thousand." Dabney, p. 264, and Mrs. Jackson, p. 223, accept 8,500 as the number—and this is the estimate made by Jackson in his report of the expedition.
76. Allan, "Valley Campaign," p. 126. Henderson, p. 144, listed the objectives of Jackson's expedition as follows: "By dispersing these detachments [at Bath and Hancock] he would prevent strong support being sent to Romney; by cutting the telegraph along the railroad he would sever the communication between Banks at Frederick and Rosecrans in West Virginia, and compel Kelly either to evacuate Romney or fight him single-handed. To deal with his enemy in detail, to crush his detachments in succession, and with superior force, such was the essence of his plan."
77. Sam R. Watkins, *"Co. Aytch"* (ed. with an Introduction by Bell I. Wiley; Jackson, Tenn., 1952), p. 57.
78. Casler, p. 63, for the shoulder-to-the-wheel episode.
79. Fishburne, *op. cit.*, II, 33.   80. *OR*, I, v, 1039.
81. See Jackson to Benjamin, Jan. 20, 1862, in *ibid.*; to J. E. Johnston, Jan. 21, 1862, in *ibid.*, pp. 1039–1040; Allan, "Valley Campaign," pp. 133–134. See also Jackson to Maj. T. G. Rhett, Winchester, Jan. 28, 1862, and to Benjamin, Jan. 29, 1862, in Box 8, Hotchkiss Papers, LC.
82. W. B. Taliaferro to [?] Conrad, Gloucester Court House, Va., July 11, 1877, Taliaferro Papers, Box 12, William and Mary College Library.
83. *OR*, I, v, 394.   84. *Ibid.*, p. 1033.
85. Couper, II, 138, for Gilham's return to VMI on Jan. 16, 1862. The charges are mentioned in Freeman, *LL*, I, 127 and *n*. A damaged copy of these charges is in the T. J. Jackson Papers, Southern Historical Collection, University of North Carolina Library. They appear to have been drawn up almost immediately after Gilham's abortive advance against Sir John's Run Depot, Jan. 4, 1862. He was accused of failing to attack the enemy when he overtook them in retreat, and also of failing to report to Jackson his reasons for not attacking.

86. Jackson to Dr. W. F. Carrington, Winchester, Jan. 28, 1862, in Box 8, Hotchkiss Papers, LC.
87. *OR*, I, v, 1044.
88. Fanny B. Graham to Mrs. Jackson, Winchester, Apr. 3, Aug. 9, Oct. 13, Nov. 21, 1862; June 20, Sept. 2, Dec. 31, 1863; Mrs. Jackson to Mrs. Graham, Cottage Home, N.C., Oct. 6, 1862; July 20, 1863 (MSS in Rare Book Collections, The Library, The University of Texas, Austin). See also Mrs. Jackson, pp. 212–216.
89. Mrs. Jackson, p. 212.   90. *Ibid.*, p. 490. See also *ibid.*, pp. 485–507.
91. *OR*, I, v, 1053.   92. *Ibid.*   93. Freeman, *LL*, I, 126–127.
94. Mrs. Jackson, p. 493.   95. *Ibid.*, p. 496; *OR*, I, v, 1040–1041, 1046–1047.
96. Taliaferro to [?] Conrad, Gloucester Court House, Va., July 11, 1877, in Taliaferro Papers. It should be noted here that although Benjamin issued the order and has often been blamed for making the decision to recall Loring, he was simply carrying out Davis's instructions. See R. D. Meade, "The Relations Between Judah P. Benjamin and Jefferson Davis," in *Journal of Southern History*, V (1939), 473.
97. *OR*, I, v, 1059–1060.   98. *Ibid.*, p. 1062.   99. *Ibid.*, p. 1053.
100. Freeman, *LL*, I, 128.   101. *Douglas*, pp. 25–26, letter of Feb. 2, 1862.
102. *OR*, I, v, 1062–1063. For Jackson on the reasons for his resignation, see his letter to Reverend Dr. Francis McFarland, Winchester, Feb. 11, 1862, in VMI Library, Lexington. For examples of letters to him protesting his resignation, see McFarland to Jackson, Mint Spring, Augusta County, Va., Feb. 5, 1862; John T. Harris to Jackson, Harrisonburg, Va., Feb. 6, 1862; Jonathan M. Bennett to Jackson, Richmond, Feb. 7, 1862, all in T. J. Jackson Papers, Virginia Historical Society, Richmond.
103. Douglas, pp. 26–27.
104. See MS letters of Maj. John A. Harman to his brother, Feb. 2, 3, 6, 9, 1861. Harman's letters are in Box 14, Hotchkiss Papers, LC, and will be cited hereinafter as Harman Papers.
105. Allan, "Valley Campaign," pp. 140–145; *OR*, I, v, 1093.
106. Fanny B. Graham to Mrs. Jackson, Winchester, Oct. 13, 1862 (MS in Rare Book Collections, The Library, The University of Texas).
107. *OR*, I, v, 1092.

Chapter 10

1. Freeman, *LL*, I, 305. It will be remembered that Jackson had lost Loring's command, plus some troops furloughed after reenlistment.
2. *OR*, I, v, 1088, 1095.   3. *Ibid.*, p. 1095.   4. Freeman, *LL*, I, 306.
5. *OR*, I, v, 1095.   6. Freeman, *LL*, I, 306.
7. J. A. Harman to his brother, Winchester, Mar. 6, 10, 1862; in Harman Papers.
8. L. L. Montague, "Subsistence of the Army of the Valley," in *Military Affairs*, XII (1948), 228.
9. See Henderson, p. 173.
10. *Ibid.*, pp. 173–174; Freeman, *LL*, I, 306; Mrs. Jackson, p. 241.
11. Mrs. Jackson, pp. 241–242; Henderson, pp. 174–175, quoting Dr. H. H. McGuire; Freeman, *LL*, I, 306.
12. *OR*, I, xii, pt. 3, p. 835; Jackson to A. C. Myers, Hawkinsville, Va., Mar. 19, 1862, in Box 8, Hotchkiss Papers, LC.
13. James Cooper Nisbet, *Four Years on the Firing Line* (Chattanooga, Tenn., n.d.), pp. 59–60.
14. Freeman, *LL*, I, 307; Montague, *op. cit.*, p. 227.
15. Douglas, pp. 35–36.   16. *OR*, I, xii, pt. 3, p. 835.
17. 11,000 men and 27 guns. See Henderson, p. 175.   18. *Ibid.*, pp. 178, 179.
19. Johnston to Jackson, Headquarters, Department of Northern Virginia, Mar. 19, 1862, in T. J. Jackson Papers, Virginia Historical Society, Richmond.
20. *OR*, I xii, pt. 3, p. 835.

21. John H. Worsham, *One of Jackson's Foot Cavalry* (New York, 1912. Cited hereinafter as Worsham), p. 66; Freeman, *LL*, I, 312.

22. Manuscript Journal of Jedediah Hotchkiss, Mar. 22, 1862, in Box 68, Hotchkiss Papers, LC. Cited hereinafter as Hotchkiss Journ.

23. *Ibid.*, Mar. 23, 1862.   24. See *ibid.*, and Worsham, p. 66.

25. Mrs. Jackson, p. 249.

26. *Ibid.*, pp. 246–247; Henderson, p. 185; Freeman, *LL*, I, 315–316.

27. See Casler's remark, p. 68, that "after the fight was over it was a mystery to us why General Jackson would evacuate Winchester and fall back fifty miles, and then turn around with a smaller force than he left Winchester with and go back and attack such a large force, with no chance of success."

28. Henderson, pp. 188–189.   29. *OR*, I, xii, pt. 3, p. 836.

30. *Ibid.*, pt. 1, p. 384. Jackson believed that the Federal losses greatly exceeded his own. See *ibid.*, pp. 380, 383.

31. Hotchkiss Journ., Mar. 26, 1862.

32. Freeman, *LL*, I, 322 and *n*.

33. See Worsham, p. 71; Casler, p. 69; Hotchkiss Journ., Mar. 24–Apr. 17, 1862.

34. *OR*, I, xii, pt. 1, p. 383.   35. Henderson, p. 193.

36. General Orders No. 34, Valley District, Apr. 1, 1862, in Jackson's MS Order Book, Box 8, Hotchkiss Papers, LC.

37. Douglas, p. 38. See Freeman, *LL*, I, 317–318, and R. B. Garnett Court-martial Papers, Confederate Museum, Richmond, Va. These papers cover the whole proceedings in considerable detail. Garnett never received a final verdict on the charges and, with his arrest suspended by order of the Adjutant General, died while commanding a brigade at Gettysburg.

38. Freeman, *LL*, I, 325–327.   39. *Ibid.*, p. 326.   40. Casler, p. 73.

41. Letter dated Apr. 14, 1862, near Mount Jackson, Va. (MS in Box 8, Hotchkiss Papers, LC); quoted in Freeman, *LL*, I, 327.

42. Letter dated Strasburg, Mar. 5[15?], 1862, in William Porcher Miles Papers, Southern Historical Collection, University of North Carolina Library.

43. See Freeman, *LL*, I, 327; Taliaferro to [?] Conrad, Gloucester Court House, Va., July 11, 1877, in Taliaferro Papers, Box 12, William and Mary College Library.

44. Freeman, *LL*, I, 323–324; *OR*, I, xii, pt. 3, p. 880.

45. Douglas, p. 83.   46. See, for instance, *OR*, I, xii, pt. 3, pp. 840–841.

47. This perceptive description is that of William C. Kean, member of the Rockbridge Artillery, and is contained in a letter to his niece, "Dear Sukey," from a camp near New Market, Apr. 11, 1862 (MS in the Civil War Letters of W. C. Kean, 1861–1863, item no. 4185, Manuscripts Collection, University of Virginia Library).

48. Douglas, p. 41. Accounts of this episode vary a good deal. The version in the text is based on the Hotchkiss Journ., Apr. 17, 1862. See also Freeman, *LL*, I, 338–339.

49. W. H. Taylor to Jackson, Richmond, Apr. 16, 1862, in T. J. Jackson Papers, Virginia Historical Society, Richmond.

50. Hotchkiss Journ., Apr. 24, 1862; J. A. Harman to his brother [Camp Swift Run Gap?], Apr. 25, 1862, in Harman Papers; Freeman, *LL*, I, 338.

51. Freeman, *LL*, I, 338, stated that eight companies were assigned to the First and Third Brigades, implying that the remainder were regimented and that part of the total was to be used by Ashby in the advance guard. The version here given is based upon the citations in the preceding note.

52. So said Hotchkiss in his Journal, Apr. 24, 1862. But there appears to be some conflict of evidence on this point. See Freeman, *LL*, I, 339 and *n*. 79.

53. Hotchkiss Journ., Apr. 24, 1862.

54. Harman to his brother, Apr. 25, 26, 1862, in Harman Papers.

55. Letter dated Staunton, May 6, 1862, in Alexander Robinson Boteler Papers, Duke University Library.

56. See Jackson to W. H. Taylor, Staunton, May 5, 1862, in Box 8, Hotchkiss Papers, LC, printed in *OR*, I, xii, pt. 3, p. 880.

57. R. L. Dabney (for Jackson) to Ashby, Apr. 25, 1862, in Box 8, Hotchkiss Papers, LC.
58. Casler, p. 70.
59. See Freeman, LL, I, 323; Hotchkiss Journ., Apr. 2, 1862; Hotchkiss to his wife, near New Market, Apr. 14, 1862, in Box 3, Hotchkiss Papers, LC; Jackson to Lee, near Mount Jackson, Apr. 15, 1862, in *ibid.*, Box 8.
60. Jackson to Maj. A. W. Harman, Conrad's Store, Apr. 21, 1862, in Box 8, Hotchkiss Papers, LC.
61. General Orders No. [?], Headquarters, Valley District, Apr. 17, 1862, in Confederate Records, chap. II, vol. 7, p. 2, National Archives; Sandie Pendleton to Brigade Commanders, Apr. 16, 1862, in Box 8, Hotchkiss Papers, LC.
62. Douglas, pp. 27–28.
63. OR, I, XII, pt. 3, pp. 844–845.
64. OR, I, XII, pt. 1, p. 384; James M. Matthews (ed.), *Statutes at Large of the Confederate States of America* (Richmond, 1862), 1st Cong., Res. 7 (p. 54).
65. Letter dated near Mount Jackson, Mar. 29, 1862, typescript copy in Dabney Papers, III, documents 1–67, Union Theological Seminary, Richmond, Va.
66. *Ibid.*
67. See, for an example of growing logistical problems, Capt. H. M. Bell to [J. A. Harman ?], Staunton, Apr. 2, 1862, in Harman Papers.
68. Mrs. Jackson, p. 248.   69. Letter dated Mar. 29, 1862. See footnote 65.
70. Hotchkiss to his wife, Camp at Rude's, near New Market, Apr. 14, 1862, in Box 3, Hotchkiss Papers, LC.
71. Every three days new units were sent to Ashby. See Sandie Pendleton to Col. J. A. Campbell, Apr. 10, 13; to Gen. C. S. Winder, Apr. 10, 13, 1862, in Box 8, Hotchkiss Papers, LC.
72. Freeman, LL, I, 330.   73. *Ibid.*, pp. 329 and *n.* 38, 330.
74. Harman to his brother [?], Apr. 20, 1862, in Harman Papers.
75. Hotchkiss Journ., Apr. 19, 1862.   76. *Ibid.*, Apr. 20, 1862; Casler, p. 74.
77. OR, I, XII, pt. 3, p. 875. The same letter, dated Apr. 29, is in the T. J. Jackson Papers, Virginia Historical Society, Richmond.

Chapter 11

1. Hotchkiss Journ., Apr. 18, 1862.   2. Douglas, p. 42 ff.
3. For the exchange of letters dealing with a junction of Jackson's and Ewell's forces, see OR, I, XII, pt. 3, pp. 845–850, 852–855, 857, 858, 860–861, 864, 868–872.
4. It seems probable that the message Douglas took to Ewell is the one printed in *ibid.*, p. 858, dated Apr. 18, 1862, despite the fact that it is marked as received on Apr. 19 at 1 P.M. The message read: "Circumstances have so changed since Mr. Boswell left that I will be prevented from joining you at Fisher's Gap. You will therefore come on the direct road to this point via Stanardsville."
5. See Freeman, Lee, II, 30–37.   6. OR, I, XII, pt. 3, p. 866.
7. See Henderson, p. 210.   8. OR, I, XII, pt. 3, p. 871.   9. *Ibid.*, p. 872.
10. J. A. Harman to his brother, Swift Run Gap, Apr. 29, 1862, in Harman Papers.
11. See Freeman, LL, I, 345 and *n.*
12. Dabney to Taliaferro, Headquarters, Valley District, Apr. 30, 1862, in Confederate Records, chap. II, vol. 7, pp. 7–8, National Archives.
13. Hotchkiss Journ., May 1, 1862.   14. Allan, "Valley Campaign," p. 181.
15. Hotchkiss Journ., May 3, 1862.
16. Henderson, pp. 217–218, stated definitely that morale declined.
17. OR, I, XII, pt. 3, pp. 126, 129, 132, 136–137.   18. See *ibid.*, pp. 124–150.
19. See Harman to his brother, Swift Run Gap, Apr. 23, 27, 29, 1862; in Harman Papers.
20. Memoranda from the Diary of J. Addison Waddell, Apr. 11–May 4, 1862, in Box 16, Hotchkiss Papers, LC.

21. *OR*, I, xii, pt. 3, p. 878.   22. *Ibid.*, p. 879.   23. *Ibid.*, p. 881.
24. *Ibid.*, pp. 881–882.
25. Percy G. Hamlin (ed.), *The Making of a Soldier: Letters of General R. S. Ewell* (Richmond, 1935), p. 108. Letter of May 13, 1862.
26. Jackson's report, in *OR*, I, xii, pt. 1, p. 470.
27. Allan, "Valley Campaign," p. 177.
28. See Henderson, pp. 224–229, for a complete account of the battle. Jackson's report of the battle is in *OR*, I, xii, pt. 1, pp. 47–73.
29. Mrs. Jackson, pp. 254–255.
30. Allan, "Valley Campaign," p. 192; Hotchkiss Journ., May 10, 11, 1862.
31. In Box 8, Hotchkiss Papers, LC.
32. This story was told by E. M. Alfriend, in "Recollections of Stonewall Jackson," *Lippincott's Monthly Magazine*, LXIX (Jan.–June, 1902), pp. 583–584. There are some inaccuracies in detail which mar the article as a whole, but the story of the Sunday meeting has so much of Jackson in it that it deserves repeating.
33. Circular, Headquarters, Army Valley District, Camp on Road, May 13, 1862, in Confederate Records, chap. II, vol. 7, pp. 9–11, National Archives.
34. General Orders No. 46, Headquarters, Valley District, May 13 [15?], 1862, in Box 8, Hotchkiss Papers, LC.
35. *OR*, I, xii, pt. 3, pp. 888–889.   36. *Ibid.*, p. 891.
37. *Ibid.*, pp. 892–893.
38. General Orders No. [?], Headquarters, Valley District, Lebanon Springs, May 15, 1862, in Confederate Records, chap. II, vol. 7, p. 13, National Archives.
39. *OR*, I, xii, pt. 3, p. 888.   40. *Ibid.*, pp. 894–895.
41. Mrs. Jackson, p. 258; Hotchkiss Journ.
42. *Southern Historical Society Papers*, VII (1879), 527; Freeman, *LL*, I, 357, 364–365.
43. *OR*, I, xii, pt. 3, p. 897.
44. Freeman, *LL*, I, 363; Dabney to Taliaferro, Headquarters, Valley District, May 15, 1862, in Confederate Records, chap. II, vol. 7, pp. 13–14, National Archives.
45. Casler, p. 76.
46. Freeman, *LL*, I, 366. Richard Taylor, *Destruction and Reconstruction* (ed. by Richard B. Harwell; New York, 1955. Cited hereinafter as Taylor), p. 88. Taylor said the march was made on the twenty-first.
47. Taylor, pp. 50–51.   48. *Ibid.*, p. 37.   49. *Ibid.*, pp. 52–53.
50. *Ibid.*, p. 53.
51. *OR*, I, xii, pt. 3, pp. 896–897; Freeman, *LL*, I, 367–368; Freeman, *Lee*, II, 55–57. Note how Freeman altered his account of these important events as first given in *Lee*. See *LL*, I, 371 n.
52. *OR*, I, xii, pt. 3, pp. 897, 898.
53. See Freeman, *LL*, I, 371, and *Lee*, II, 57. Johnston's intention had not been to suspend the attack on Banks. In two dispatches dated May 18 he told both Jackson and Ewell that their objective remained "the prevention of the junction of Genl Banks' troops with those of Genl McDowell," and that the attack should be abandoned only if it "be now too late to prevent that by attacking." He added that "I cannot provide for modifications of the case—But, having full confidence in the judgment & courage of Both the division Commanders, rely upon them to conform to circumstances, without fear for the result." His definite statement that "the whole question is, whether or not General Jackson & yourself [Ewell] are too late to attack Banks—If so the march eastward should be made—If not (supposing your strength sufficient) the attack," shows Johnston to have been as anxious as anyone to strike a successful blow. See Johnston to Jackson, near Richmond, May 18, 1862; to Ewell and Jackson, May 18, 1862, 2 P.M., in T. J. Jackson Papers, Virginia Historical Society, Richmond. Freeman, *LL*, I, 371 n., considered it possible that these dispatches might have reached Jackson by the evening of the twentieth, but thought it improbable. If they did arrive on the twentieth, they of course removed all doubt as to the permissibility of attacking.
54. Taylor, p. 53; Hotchkiss Journ., May 21, 1862.   55. Taylor, p. 53.

56. Mrs. Jackson, p. 257.
57. Harman to his brother, May 22, 1862, in Harman Papers; Dabney, p. 364.
58. See Freeman's fine account of the strategic considerations which absorbed Jackson on May 23 in *LL*, I, 376.
59. *Ibid.*, p. 377.
60. Randolph H. McKim, *A Soldier's Recollections* (New York, 1910), pp. 96–98.
61. Douglas, pp. 51–52. This account sounds a bit exaggerated. Taylor, pp. 53–54, reported inaccurate information from La Belle. See her own *Belle Boyd in Camp and Prison* (2 vols.; London, 1865), I, 129–136.
62. Diary of Lucy R. Buck, May 23, 1862, p. 58, quoted in Freeman, *LL*, I, 378–379.
63. This particular dialogue is pieced together from Dabney, pp. 365–366, and Freeman, *LL*, I, 380. The account of the battle of Front Royal is based upon Jackson's report, *OR*, I, XII, pt. 1, pp. 701–727; Freeman, *LL*, I, 377–381; Dabney, pp. 364–367; Henderson, pp. 242–246; Allan, "Valley Campaign," pp. 205–212.
64. *OR*, I, XII, pt. 1, pp. 702, 725; Freeman, *LL*, I, 380–381; Dabney, pp. 367–368.

Chapter 12

1. Lincoln to McClellan, Washington, May 24, 1862, 4 P.M., in Roy P. Basler (ed.), *Collected Works of Abraham Lincoln* (8 vols.; New Brunswick, N.J., 1953–1955), V, 232.
2. See his interesting and thoroughly erroneous summary of the valley situation, dated May 22, in *OR*, I, XII, pt. 1, pp. 524–525.
3. *Ibid.*, p. 526.
4. So Banks reported to Stanton on May 24 in a dispatch received at the War Department at 7:05 A.M., in *ibid.*
5. *Ibid.*   6. *Ibid.*, p. 527.   7. *Ibid.*   8. *Ibid.*   9. *Ibid.*, p. 528.
10. Taylor, p. 58.
11. See Freeman, *LL*, I, 735–739, where a discussion of the confusing problem of Jackson's route is given in detail.
12. Casualties numbered 904 killed, wounded, and missing on the Union side, out of a total of about 1,063. See *ibid.*, pp. 381–382.
13. *OR*, I, XII, pt. 1, p. 703.   14. *Ibid.*, p. 704.   15. *Ibid.*   16. *Ibid.*
17. Douglas, p. 55.   18. *Ibid.*, p. 56; Dabney, pp. 374–375.
19. Taylor, p. 60.   20. *Ibid.*   21. *Ibid.*, pp. 60–61.
22. Mrs. Jackson, p. 243.   23. Taylor, p. 61.
24. See Freeman, *LL*, I, 393–394, quoting J. B. Avirett, *The Memoirs of General Turner Ashby and His Compeers* (Baltimore, 1867), pp. 196–197; Douglas, p. 57, gave slightly different dialogue.
25. *OR*, I, XII, pt. 1, p. 736.
26. Freeman, *LL*, I, 396–398; *OR*, I, XII, pt 1, pp. 705, 736–737.
27. *OR*, I, XII, pt. 1, p. 755; Dabney, p. 378; Freeman, *LL*, I, 399.
28. Douglas, p. 58. Freeman, *LL*, I, 400, discounted Douglas's rendition of the dialogue. Taylor, p. 61, said that Jackson directed him to attack the ridge held by the Federals.
29. Taylor, pp. 62–63.   30. Worsham, p. 87.   31. *OR*, I, XII, pt. 1, p. 705.
32. Douglas, p. 59.   33. *OR*, I, XII, pt. 1, p. 706.
34. Mrs. Jackson, p. 265; Cornelia McDonald, *Diary*, p. 68; Dabney, p. 380.
35. Dabney, p. 381.   36. *OR*, I, XII, pt. 1, p. 706.
37. Hotchkiss Journ., May 25, 1862; Dabney, p. 381.   38. Taylor, p. 65.
39. The timing is in doubt. See Freeman, *LL*, I, 402, 404; *OR*, I, XII, pt. 1, p. 706; Allan, "Valley Campaign," p. 232; Dabney, p. 383; Henderson, pp. 261–262.
40. Henderson, p. 262.   41. *OR*, I, XII, pt. 1, p. 707.
42. See Freeman, *LL*, I, 404–405; Dabney, p. 382. Pendleton's account of his strange encounter is in *OR*, I, XII, pt. 1, pp. 709–710.
43. Allan, "Valley Campaign," p. 233; Freeman, *LL*, I, 407; *OR*, I, XII, pt. 1, pp. 708, 719–724.

44. McDonald, *Diary,* p. 163.
45. Fanny B. Graham to Mrs. Jackson, Winchester, Aug. 9, 1862, in Rare Book Collections, The Library, The University of Texas.
46. *OR,* I, xII, pt. 1, p. 707.
47. In Jackson's MS Letter Book, Box 8, Hotchkiss Papers, LC; Mrs. Jackson, pp. 263–264.
48. General Orders No. 54, Headquarters, Valley District, May 27, 1862, in Box 8, Hotchkiss Papers, LC.
49. *OR,* I, xII, pt. 3, p. 900.
50. *Ibid.* There were ample uniforms ready for issue to Jackson's army in Staunton as soon as active campaigning ceased. See Waddell Diary, May 28, 1862, in Box 16, Hotchkiss Papers, LC.
51. General Orders No. 54, Headquarters, Valley District, *ibid.,* in Box 8.
52. Freeman, *LL,* I, 407, where it is pointed out that these casualties represented 31 to 34 per cent of Banks's total strength. See also Allan, "Valley Campaign," pp. 233 and *n.,* 234 and *n.;* Harman to his brother, Winchester, May 25, 1862, in Harman Papers.
53. *OR,* I, xII, pt. 3, pp. 219–220.   54. *Ibid.,* pp. 220–221.
55. *Ibid.,* p. 221.
56. Dispatch dated May 24, 1862, 7¼ P.M., in Basler, *op. cit.,* V, 231.
57. *OR,* I, xII, pt. 1, p. 644.   58. *Ibid.*   59. *Ibid.,* p. 645.
60. *Ibid.,* pt. 3, p. 228; Basler, *op. cit.,* V, 234–245.
61. Basler, *op. cit.,* 235–236.   62. *Ibid.,* 236–237.
63. J. A. Harman to his brother, Winchester, May 27, 1862, in Harman Papers.
64. Allan, "Valley Campaign," pp. 243–244.   65. *OR,* I, xII, pt. 1, p. 707.
66. Allan, "Valley Campaign," p. 244.   67. Douglas, p. 66.
68. Freeman, *LL,* I, 413; Hotchkiss Journ., May 30, 1862.
69. Boteler was assigned to Jackson's staff as Volunteer Aide-de-Camp by General Orders No. [?], May 30, 1862, copy in Polk-Brown-Ewell Papers, Southern Historical Collection, University of North Carolina Library.
70. Boteler, in *Southern Historical Society Papers,* XL (1915), pp. 164, 165.
71. *OR,* I, xII, pt. 3, p. 267.   72. Freeman, *LL,* I, 410 *n.*
73. Hotchkiss Journ., May 30, 1862.
74. *Ibid.* The story is also told in Freeman, *LL,* I, 417.
75. Harman to his brother, Winchester, May 31, 1862, in Harman Papers.
76. Boteler, in *Southern Historical Society Papers,* XL (1915), p. 168.
77. Hotchkiss Journ., May 31, 1862.   78. See Harman Papers, May–June, 1862.
79. *OR,* I, xII, pt. 1, p. 647.   80. Basler, *op. cit.,* V, 254.
81. Harman to his brother, Winchester, May 31, 1862, in Harman Papers.
82. McDonald, *Diary,* p. 71.   83. Freeman, *LL,* I, 419.
84. *Ibid.;* Hotchkiss Journ., May 31, 1862; Douglas, p. 69.
85. Hotchkiss Journ., June 1, 1862.
86. H. K. Douglas to Ewell, Headquarters, Valley District, May 31, 1862, in Polk-Brown-Ewell Papers.
87. *OR,* I, xII, pt. 1, p. 708.   88. See Basler, *op. cit.,* V, 232–233, 252.
89. Taylor, p. 67.   90. Allan, "Valley Campaign," pp. 250–251.
91. Hotchkiss Journ., June 1, 1862.
92. *Ibid.;* Taylor, pp. 67–68; Allan, "Valley Campaign," p. 252; *OR,* I, xII, pt. 1, p. 708.
93. Taylor, pp. 69–70.   94. *Ibid.,* p. 72.   95. *OR,* I, xII, pt. 1, p. 14.
96. McKim, *A Soldier's Recollections,* pp. 107–108.
97. Freeman, *LL,* I, 422; Taylor, p. 74.   98. *OR,* I, xII, pt. 1, p. 711.
99. Douglas, p. 71.   100. Taylor, pp. 77–78; Hotchkiss Journ., June 2, 1862.
101. Douglas, pp. 73–74.   102. Dabney, p. 397.
103. Freeman, *LL,* I, 425.   104. Hotchkiss Journ., June 4, 1862.
105. See Freeman, *LL,* I, 429 and *n.,* for discussion of troubles encountered in burning the Conrad's Store bridge.
106. *OR,* I, xII, pt. 1, p. 712.   107. *Ibid.,* pt. 3, p. 906.
108. Harman to his brother, June 4, 5, 1862, in Harman Papers.

109. Harman to his brother, June 6, 8, 1862; in *ibid.*
110. Letter dated June 5, in *ibid.*
111. Fishburne, "Memoirs," II, 67, 69 (doc. no. 2341, Manuscripts Collection, University of Virginia Library).
112. Harman to his brother, June 6, 1862, in Harman Papers; Parole of John A. Harman, Apr. 20, 1865, in Personal Service File of John A. Harman, Confederate Adjutant General's Records, National Archives.
113. Taylor, pp. 69–70.
114. Hotchkiss Journ., June 6, 1862; Douglas, p. 78. For an excellent review of Jackson's situation in the valley, see Freeman, *LL*, I, 428–429.
115. *OR*, I, XII, pt. 3, p. 905.
116. Apparently Jackson had outlined something like this plan to Boteler, who had passed it on to Davis. The President made a cryptic reference to Front Royal in his letter to Jackson on June 4. Lee knew a little about Jackson's desire to attack Shields and push on to Front Royal. See *OR*, I, XII, pt. 3, pp. 905–906.
117. *Ibid.*, p. 907.
118. Taylor, pp. 23, 79; Douglas, p. 79; Freeman, *LL*, I, 432.
119. Douglas, p. 79.
120. See Dabney, pp. 399, 400; Freeman, *LL*, I, 432–433; Henderson, p. 275. There is some disagreement among the various sources about where Ashby was hit—whether in the heart, breast, or body. There is also some small dispute as to whether he was shot by his own men who mistook him for a Federal soldier. See Hotchkiss Journ., June 6, 1862; also, Notes by Jed Hotchkiss in *Life of Stonewall Jackson*, by a Virginian (this volume, with Hotchkiss's notes, is in the Manuscripts Collection, University of Virginia Library). On p. 65 of the book Ashby's death is mentioned and on the top of this page is the notation: "Gen. Ashby was [no?] doubt killed [?] by [?] our [?] own men. I carefully examined his wounds after death, & from the position he was in when shot they beyond all question came from our Infantry. H. McG[uire]." Hotchkiss asked various people who knew or had served with Jackson to add notes to this volume, so the McGuire notation is probably genuine.
121. *OR*, I, XII, pt. 1, p. 712.
122. Freeman, *LL*, I, 434, quoting Avirett, *op. cit.*, p. 226.
123. Douglas, p. 77.   124. *OR*, I, XII, pt. 3, p. 907.
125. See the summary of these considerations in Freeman, *LL*, I, 435–437; Dabney, pp. 407–409.
126. Hotchkiss Journ., June 7, 1862; map in Freeman, *LL*, I, 436.
127. *OR*, I, XII, pt. 1, pp. 712–713; Freeman, *LL*, I, 438.
128. *OR*, I, XII, pt. 3, pp. 907–908.   129. *Ibid.*
130. Dabney in Memoranda for Col. Henderson, May 7, 1896, in Box 13, Hotchkiss Papers, LC.
131. The time is disputed. See Freeman, *LL*, I, 439 and *n.*; Douglas, p. 85; Hotchkiss Journ., June 8, 1862.
132. Dabney's account, Maj. J. McD. Carrington's account, Crutchfield's statement, all in Dabney, Memoranda for Col. Henderson, in Hotchkiss Papers.
133. This episode has been twisted into various forms by retelling. John Esten Cooke seems to have been the authority for original embroidery which gave rise to the story that Jackson impersonated a Federal officer on the Port Republic side of the bridge and ordered the Union guns to limber up and depart. Douglas's memory of the event failed him sadly and he added to the facts (Douglas, p. 85). Dabney avoided the pitfalls of the story entirely (Dabney, p. 412).
134. *OR*, I, XII, pt. 1, pp. 712–713.   135. Taylor, pp. 81–82.
136. Dabney, pp. 414–415.   137. *OR*, I, XII, pt. 1, p. 784.
138. Hotchkiss Journ., Apr. 4, 1863. See also Freeman, *LL*, I, 448.
139. Dabney, pp. 420–421.   140. *Ibid.*, p. 421.
141. Imboden, "Stonewall Jackson in the Shenandoah," in *B&L*, II, 293.
142. Douglas, p. 89.   143. *OR*, I, XII, pt. 1, p. 740; Freeman, *LL*, I, 450.

144. OR, I, XII, pt. 1, p. 740; Allan, "Valley Campaign," pp. 279–280; Freeman, LL, I, 450–451.
145. OR, I, XII, pt. 1, p. 798.
146. The location of his bivouac is conjectured from the somewhat ambiguous language in Taylor, p. 83.
147. Ibid., p. 84; Hotchkiss Journ., June 9, 1862.   148. Taylor, p. 84.
149. OR, I, XII, pt. 1, p. 741; Freeman, LL, I, 455–456.
150. OR, I, XII, pt. 1, p. 715.   151. Douglas, p. 91.   152. Taylor, p. 86.
153. OR, I, XII, pt. 1, pp. 732, 742.   154. Ibid., p. 716.
155. Ibid., pp. 690, 697.
156. Some wagons, 450 prisoners, a gun and about 800 muskets were taken during the pursuit.

Chapter 13

1. Freeman, Lee, II, 83.   2. OR, I, XII, pt. 3, pp. 906–907.
3. Ibid., p. 906.   4. Freeman, Lee, II, 83 and n.
5. See ibid., and Henderson, p. 271.
6. Lee had suggested to Davis on June 5 that troops from the Deep South be sent to Jackson for an invasion of Maryland and Pennsylvania—a move which might, in Lee's view, "change the character of the war." A question which Davis would have to help answer was whether or not the states from which Jackson's reinforcements would have to come would part with them. See Freeman (ed.), Lee's Dispatches (New York, 1915), pp. 5–6.
7. Freeman, Lee, II, 94; LL, I, 465, 466.   8. OR, I, XI, pt. 3, p. 594.
9. Quoted in Freeman, LL, I, 467.   10. OR, I, XI, pt. 3, pp. 589–590.
11. Hotchkiss Journ., June 12, 13, 1862.
12. See map in Allan, "Valley Campaign," facing p. 256.
13. See J. A. Harman to his brother, June 12, 13, 14, 16, 1862, in Harman Papers; Hotchkiss Journ., June 13, 14, 15, 1862; General Orders No. 58, Headquarters, Army of the Valley, June 13, 1862, in Box 8, Hotchkiss Papers, LC.
14. Hotchkiss Journ., June 15, 1862.   15. Mrs. Jackson, pp. 283–284.
16. OR, I, XII, pt. 3, p. 913.
17. Harman to his brother, June 13, 19, 1862, in Harman Papers.
18. See Allan, "Valley Campaign," pp. 292–293; OR, I, XII, pt. 3, pp. 912, 914; Henderson, p. 298.
19. OR, I, XII, pt. 3, p. 914.
20. Imboden, "Stonewall Jackson in the Shenandoah," in B&L, II, 296–297.
21. Douglas, p. 96.
22. See James L. Nichols, "Confederate Map Supply," in Military Engineer, XLVI (Jan.–Feb., 1954), 32.
23. Taylor, p. 89.   24. Ibid., p. 90.   25. Ibid., p. 91.
26. Arnold, p. 169.
27. Richmond Examiner, June 17, 1862, cited in Freeman, Lee, II, 86.
28. Freeman, Lee, II, 101.   29. Hotchkiss Journ., June 17, 1862.
30. Ibid., June 18, 1862; Freeman, LL, I, 469.
31. Hotchkiss Journ., June 18, 1862.
32. C. M. Blackford, III (ed.), Letters from Lee's Army (New York, 1947. Cited hereinafter as Blackford), pp. 84–85.
33. Hotchkiss Journ., June 19, 1862; Freeman, Lee's Dispatches, p. 8.
34. Black, Railroads of the Confederacy, p. 180.
35. Harman to his brother, June 19, 1862, in Harman Papers.
36. Freeman, LL, I, 470; D. H. Hill, "Lee's Attack North of the Chickahominy," in B&L, II, 348.
37. Ibid., pp. 348–349.
38. Hunter H. McGuire to Jed Hotchkiss, Richmond, Mar. 30, 1896, in Hotchkiss Papers, LC. Cited hereinafter as McGuire Papers.
39. Freeman, LL, I, 466 and n.; Black, op. cit., p. 179.   40. Douglas, p. 98.

41. Henderson, p. 301.
42. So stated Freeman, in *Lee*, II, 108, but he avoided the time in recounting the episode in *LL*, I, 492 and *n*. Henderson, p. 301, put the time at 1 A.M. Harman, in an account of the incident given to Hotchkiss in April, 1863, said Jackson left Fredericks Hall "at about midnight . . ." (Hotchkiss Journ., Apr. 15, 1862).
43. This was probably Charles Harris. See Freeman, *Lee*, II, 108 *n.*, although it is not made clear in *LL*, I, 492.
44. Hill, "Lee's Attack North of the Chickahominy," p. 350.
45. Douglas, p. 99. The dialogue is probably doctored by several retellings, but this delicious story is typical of many which circulated after Jackson's ride to Richmond. See Henderson, p. 301; Dabney, p. 435.
46. J. B. Jones, *A Rebel War Clerk's Diary at the Confederate States Capital* (ed. by Howard Swiggett, 2 vols.; New York, 1935. Cited hereinafter as *RWCD*), I, 128 *n*. The Dabb House conference is hard to reconstruct, since the evidence is scant and confused. The account in the text is based on Freeman, *Lee*, II, 109–112; *LL*, I, 494–498; Hill, "Lee's Attack North of the Chickahominy," pp. 347–348; James Longstreet, *From Manassas to Appomattox* (Philadelphia, 1896), pp. 120–122.
47. Hunter McGuire to Hotchkiss, Mar. 30, 1896, in McGuire Papers.
48. Freeman, *LL*, I, 499.   49. See *ibid.*, pp. 500–501 *n*.
50. Freeman, *Lee*, II, 116.
51. *The Civil War Diary of General Josiah Gorgas* (ed. by Frank E. Vandiver; University, Ala., 1947), p. 7.
52. McGuire to Hotchkiss, Mar. 30, 1896, in McGuire Papers; Freeman, *LL*, I, 503–504.
53. Freeman, *LL*, I, 504, quoting Dabney memorandum in Hotchkiss Papers.
54. *OR*, I, XI, pt. 1, p. 49.   55. Freeman, *LL*, I, 505; Dabney, p. 440.
56. See Dabney to Hotchkiss, Victoria, Tex., Apr. 22, 1896, in Box 13, Hotchkiss Papers, LC.
57. Whiting's division was stirring at 3 A.M. (*OR*, I, XI, pt. 2, p. 562), but the army's advance did not begin until much later. See Freeman, *LL*, I, 508.
58. Jackson had ordered Hotchkiss to stay in the valley and to work on maps. Hotchkiss Journ., June 24, 25, 26, 1862.
59. Douglas, p. 101.   60. *RWCD*, I, 128 *n*.
61. See Douglas, p. 115; Dabney to Hotchkiss, Victoria, Tex., Apr. 22, 1896, in Box 13, Hotchkiss Papers, LC.
62. *OR*, I, XI, pt. 2, p. 614.
63. Jed Hotchkiss, "Incidents Relating to the Life of Gen. Jackson," entry no. 9 (MS in Manuscripts Collection, University of Virginia Library).
64. *OR*, I, XI, pt. 2, p. 553; Dabney, p. 442; Freeman, *Lee*, II, 137, map.
65. Robert Stiles, *Four Years under Marse Robert* (New York, 1903. Cited hereinafter as Stiles), p. 98.
66. Freeman, *Lee*, II, 140–141.   67. Dabney, pp. 443, 444.
68. Worsham, p. 99.   69. *OR*, I, XI, pt. 2, p. 553; Freeman, *LL*, I, 527.
70. Freeman, *LL*, I, 528–529.   71. Freeman, *Lee*, II, 148.
72. Worsham, p. 99.   73. *OR*, I, XI, pt. 1, p. 56.
74. Freeman, *Lee*, II, 153.   75. *Ibid.*, pp. 153–154.
76. John B. Hood, *Advance and Retreat* (New Orleans, 1880), pp. 25–26.
77. Freeman, *Lee*, II, 154. Curiously enough, this conversation between Lee and Hood is recounted as taking place between A. P. Hill and Hood in Freeman, *LL*, I, 532.
78. Freeman, *Lee*, II, 155.   79. *OR*, I, XI, pt. 2, p. 615.
80. Douglas, p. 102.
81. Dabney, p. 456, said Jackson used little artillery. See Jackson's report in *OR*, I, XI, pt. 2, p. 556, and Douglas, p. 104.
82. J. B. Hubbell (ed.), "The War Diary of John Esten Cooke," in *Journal of Southern History*, VII (1941), 532.
83. Hood, *op. cit.*, p. 28; Dabney, p. 454.

84. Dabney to Hotchkiss, Apr. 22, 1896, in Box 13, Hotchkiss Papers, LC.
85. It is probable that Jackson sent word of the time he would cross the river to Magruder at about 3 P.M. See Jackson to Stuart, Grapevine Bridge, June 29, 1862, 2:50 P.M., doc. SA 30, in J. E. B. Stuart Collection, Huntington Library, San Marino, Calif.
86. Dabney to Hotchkiss, Apr. 22, 1896, in Box 13, Hotchkiss Papers, LC.
87. R. H. Chilton to Stuart, Hd. Qrs., Charles City Road, June 29, 1862, doc. SA 71 in Stuart Collection, Huntington Library.
88. OR, I, XI, pt. 2, p. 675. There is much confusion over Jackson's activities during June 29. Freeman, in LL, I, 562–563 and n., discussed the myriad problems posed by trying to fix the general's movements and to time them with accuracy. There is, for instance, the testimony of Dabney that Lee and Jackson met after Jackson crossed the Grapevine Bridge and the supposition is that during this meeting Lee outlined Old Jack's "other important duty." Freeman could not credit the story of the meeting, and it seems probable that it was Stuart's message and not a meeting with the commanding general which gave Jackson his new orders. The Stuart dispatch has curiously escaped notice. Its great importance in explaining Jackson's delay at the Grapevine Bridge can hardly be exaggerated. Had Freeman known of this dispatch he doubtless would have recast his narrative as written in LL, I, 562–563. The reconstruction of events in the text is conjectured, but appears logical.
89. Freeman, LL, I, 554, 568; Lee, II, 194; Mrs. Jackson, p. 297; Dabney, p. 461.
90. OR, I, XI, pt. 2, p. 665.   91. Ibid.
92. See Stiles, pp. 97–99; Freeman, LL, I, 569–570.
93. Mrs. Jackson, p. 297.
94. Dabney, pp. 464–465; OR, I, XI, pt. 2, p. 561; Freeman, LL, I, 573–574.
95. OR, I, XI, pt. 2, p. 556.
96. See Jennings C. Wise, The Long Arm of Lee, I, 219.
97. This was Jackson's explanation in his official report of the White Oak affair, in OR, I, XI, pt. 2, p. 557. See also Dabney, pp. 465–466.
98. Dabney, p. 466.   99. OR, I, XI, pt. 2, p. 557.
100. Dabney to Hotchkiss, Apr. 22, 1896, in Box 13, Hotchkiss Papers, LC.
101. See OR, I, XI, pt. 2, p. 810.   102. See Freeman, LL, I, 577.
103. Charles Marshall, An Aide-de-Camp of Lee (ed. by Maj. Gen. Sir Frederick Maurice; Boston, 1927), p. 111.
104. Hunter McGuire, in Henderson, p. 380.
105. See the testimony of Hampton, in Marshall, op. cit., pp. 111–112 (the writer is indebted to Mr. William B. Ruggles of The Dallas Morning News for this reference); Hampton, in Alexander, Military Memoirs of a Confederate, pp. 149–151.
106. Douglas, p. 107.
107. Dabney, pp. 466–467; Dabney to Hotchkiss, Apr. 22, 1896, in Box 13, Hotchkiss Papers, LC.
108. OR, I, XI, pt. 2, pp. 56, 77–78.   109. Henderson, p. 382.
110. Stories of what was wrong with Jackson at the White Oak bridge are legion. The various versions are presented in: Henderson, pp. 379–383; Dabney, pp. 464–468; Freeman, Lee, II, 194–199 and LL, I, 571–580, 656–659. D. H. Hill, in "McClellan's Change of Base and Malvern Hill," B&L, II, 389–390, voiced the theory that "pity for his own corps, worn out by long exhausting marches, and reduced in numbers by its numerous sanguinary battles" led Jackson to give his men a day's rest. Considering Jackson's quick decision to attack at Gaines' Mill and his subsequent action at Malvern, this theory is patently absurd and ascribes to him actions which were totally out of character. Some of the most severe criticism leveled at Jackson for his dilatoriness is that of Alexander, Military Memoirs of a Confederate, pp. 143–153.
111. See Worsham, p. 103.   112. Dabney, pp. 468–469.
113. Hill, "McClellan's Change . . . ," p. 391; Freeman, LL, I, 590.
114. Dabney, p. 469.   115. Freeman, Lee, I, 202.

116. So said Freeman, *LL*, I, 592; but Jackson, in his report, identified the intermediate brigade as Taylor's (*OR*, I, xi, pt. 2, p. 557).
117. *OR*, I, xi, pt. 2, p. 566.   118. Hill, "McClellan's Change . . . ," p. 392.
119. *OR*, I, xi, pt. 2, p. 574.   120. Douglas, pp. 108, 109.
121. Doc. SA 32, in Stuart Collection, Huntington Library.
122. The sequence of events is in doubt, but the note to Stuart could have been the one mentioned in Douglas, p. 108.
123. *OR*, I, xi, pt. 2, p. 558.   124. *Ibid.*, p. 559; Freeman, *LL*, I, 603.
125. *OR*, I, xi, pt. 2, p. 558.   126. Douglas, p. 109.
127. Dabney to Hotchkiss, Victoria, Tex., May 7, 1896, in Box 13, Hotchkiss Papers, LC.

Chapter 14

1. R. L. Dabney to Hotchkiss, Victoria, Tex., May 7, 1896, in Box 13, Hotchkiss Papers, LC; the conference is described in Freeman, *Lee*, II, 222–224. See also Henderson, pp. 391–392.
2. See Freeman, *Lee*, II, 226; Henderson, p. 393.
3. Dabney in Memoranda for Col. Henderson, May 7, 1896, in Box 13, Hotchkiss Papers, LC. See the version of this story in Douglas, pp. 111–112, in which Douglas casts himself in Dabney's role.
4. See R. E. Lee to Mrs. Jackson, Lexington, Va., Jan. 25, 1866, typescript in Dabney Papers, III, docs. 1–67, Union Theological Seminary, Richmond, Va.; Freeman, *Lee*, II, 227–229.
5. *OR*, I, xii, pt. 3, pp. 473–474.
6. General Orders Nos. 5 and 7, Headquarters, Army of Virginia, Washington, July 18, 10 [?], 1862, in *ibid.*, pt. 2, pp. 50, 51.
7. Worsham, p. 104.   8. Mrs. Jackson, p. 302.
9. See Douglas, pp. 113–123; Mrs. Jackson, p. 302.   10. Douglas, p. 113.
11. Boteler, in *Southern Historical Society Papers*, XL (1915), 180–181.
12. Freeman, *Lee*, II, 265.   13. *OR*, I, xi, pt. 2, pp. 494, 495.
14. *Ibid.*, xii, pt. 3, p. 915.   15. See Henderson, p. 399; Freeman, *LL*, II, 23.
16. See Charles W. Turner, "The Virginia Central Railroad at War," in *Journal of Southern History*, XII (1946), 529; *OR*, I, xii, pt. 3, pp. 915–916.
17. Jackson to Rev. Dr. Francis McFarland, July 31, 1862 (MS in VMI Library, Lexington, Va.).
18. Mrs. Jackson, p. 304. Jackson wrote Anna that "it was with tearful eyes that I consented to our separation," and to Dabney he said: "My prayer is that you may soon be restored and at your post." (Letter dated July 24, 1862, in Dabney Papers, III, docs. 1–67, Union Theological Seminary, Richmond, Va.)
19. Blackford, pp. 85–86.
20. *Ibid.*, pp. 87–88. Versions of this delightful story appear in Douglas, p. 118, and Mrs. Jackson, p. 302, where the language is much watered down.
21. Douglas, p. 122.   22. *Ibid.*, pp. 120–121.
23. Hotchkiss Journ., July 19, 20, 1862.
24. *Ibid.*, July 20, 1862; A. S. Pendleton to Brig. Gen. Beverley Robertson, July 12, 1862, in Box 8, Hotchkiss Papers, LC.
25. Hotchkiss Journ., July 24, 1862.
26. Mrs. Jackson, pp. 308–309; Dabney, pp. 489–490.   27. Mrs. Jackson, p. 309.
28. Hotchkiss Journ., July 20, Aug. 3, 1862; Blackford, p. 97.
29. Letter dated July 22, 1862, in Allan, *Margaret Junkin Preston*, pp. 151–152.
30. Mrs. Jackson, p. 310.
31. Jackson to Rev. Dr. Francis McFarland, July 31, 1862 (MS in VMI Library, Lexington, Va.).
32. See Casler, pp. 101–102; Freeman, *LL*, II, 3–4.
33. Freeman, *LL*, II, 5, 6; *Lee's Dispatches*, 42, 43.

34. Jackson to Chilton, Headquarters, Valley District, July 28, 1862, in Box 8, Hotchkiss Papers, LC.
35. So it would appear from Hotchkiss's Journal, July 29, 1862. Lee's letter is in *OR*, I, XII, pt. 3, pp. 918–919.
36. See Stuart to Jackson, July 19, 1862, in Stuart Papers, Confederate Museum, Richmond, Va. In this letter Stuart asked: "Did you receive the volume of Napoleon & His Maxims I sent you through Gen. Ch. S. Winder's orderly?" Jackson acknowledged the gift in a letter of July 25. See Doc. SA 33, Stuart Collection, Huntington Library.
37. Hotchkiss Journ., Aug. 6, 1862.
38. Freeman, *LL*, II, 8, 9. See also R. B. Garnett MSS, Confederate Museum, Richmond, Va.
39. McHenry Howard, *Recollections of a Maryland Staff Officer* (Baltimore, 1914), pp. 162–163.
40. Hotchkiss Journ., Aug. 7, 1862.
41. *OR*, I, XII, pt. 3, p. 926.
42. *Ibid.*, pt. 2, p. 182.   43. *Ibid.*, pp. 214–215, 216–217.
44. Hotchkiss Journ., Aug. 8, 1862; Henderson, p. 405.
45. G. W. Cable, "The Gentler Side of Two Great Southerners," *Century Magazine*, XLVII (1893–1894), 293.
46. *OR*, I, XII, pt. 2, p. 181.   47. See Mrs. Jackson, p. 288.
48. Hotchkiss Journ., Aug. 9, 1862. Henderson, p. 407, put the time at "shortly before noon."
49. *OR*, I, XII, pt. 2, p. 182.   50. Henderson, p. 408.
51. Douglas, p. 123; *OR*, I, XII, pt. 2, p. 227.
52. *OR*, I, XII, pt. 2, p. 189; Freeman, *LL*, II, 33–34.
53. *OR*, I, XII, pt. 2, p. 183.
54. Blackford, 105. Another version of the dialogue is in Dabney, p. 501. See also Hotchkiss Journ., Aug. 9, 1862.
55. Blackford, pp. 104–105.   56. Douglas, p. 124.
57. Comprehensive accounts of the battle of Cedar Mountain are contained in Henderson, chap. 15, pp. 396–420; Freeman, *LL*, II, chap. 2, pp. 16–51; Dabney, chap. 15, pp. 486–508. Jackson's report of the action, and the reports of his subordinate commanders, are contained in *OR*, I, XII, pt. 2, pp. 180–239. These reports constitute the best source on the battle and are indispensable.
58. *OR*, I, XII, pt. 2, p. 216.   59. Mrs. Jackson, p. 312; Dabney, p. 503.
60. Hotchkiss Journ., Aug. 10, 1862; Dabney, p. 504. Some 5,000 small arms fell into Confederate hands.
61. Jackson to Stuart, near Gordonsville, Aug. 7, 1862, doc. SA 34, in Stuart Collection, Huntington Library. Freeman, in *LL*, II, 42 and *n.*, noted Stuart's arrival at Jackson's headquarters and also the fact that Jackson, in his report, commented that Stuart was making an "inspection." Freeman pointed out that from the evidence in the *OR* the reasons for Stuart's visit to Jackson were obscure, although he suggested the possibility that Jackson sent for him. The Stuart letter quoted in the text establishes clearly the fact that Stuart came to make an inspection and also came on Jackson's invitation.
62. *OR*, I, XII, pt. 2, p. 184.   63. Hotchkiss Journ., Aug. 10, 1862.
64. Dabney, pp. 505–506.   65. *OR*, I, XII, pt. 2, p. 183.   66. *Ibid.*, p. 185.
67. Hotchkiss Journ., Aug. 12, 13, 1862.
68. *Ibid.*, Aug. 13, 1862; Freeman, *Lee*, II, 272.   69. Douglas, p. 129.
70. H. E. Gourdin to Robert N. Gourdin, Hagerstown, Md., Sept. 15, 1862, in Robert N. Gourdin Papers, Duke University Library.
71. Longstreet, in *B&L*, II, 405.
72. General Orders No. 86, Aug. 13, 1862, in Box 8, Hotchkiss Papers, LC.
73. Hotchkiss Journ., Aug. 14, 1862.
74. Freeman (ed.), *Lee's Dispatches*, p. 48.
75. Jackson to Lee, near Gordonsville, July 25, 1862, 5:50 A.M., in T. J. Jackson Papers, Duke University Library. The letter read, in part: "I have the greatest

abundance of it [transportation], and on the march to Richmond reduced the amount of Company transportation to one 4 horse wagon for every 100 rank & file present & for duty. . . . This allowance is enough for a summer campaign."

76. John N. Shealy to Jennie Shealy, July 16, 1862, in John N. Shealy Collection, Archives Collection, Louisiana State University.
77. Freeman, *Lee*, II, 280; Henderson, p. 424, fixed Pope's strength at 52,500.
78. The plan is admirably explained in Freeman, *Lee*, II, 273–288.
79. *Ibid.*, pp. 285–286.   80. See Blackford, p. 113.   81. *Ibid.*
82. Freeman, *LL*, II, 63.   83. *OR*, I, xii, pt. 2, p. 649.
84. Hotchkiss Journ., Aug. 20, 1862.   85. *Ibid.*, Aug. 19, 1862.
86. *Ibid.*   87. *Ibid.*, Aug. 21, 1862.   88. Douglas, p. 129.
89. *OR*, I, xii, pt. 2, p. 642.   90. *Ibid.*, p. 719.
91. Referred to in some reports as Fauquier White Sulphur Springs.
92. *OR*, I, xii, pt. 2, p. 706; Freeman, *LL*, II, 73–78.
93. This whole affair is covered in Freeman, *LL*, II, 73–78, and in *OR*, I, xii, pt. 2, pp. 642, 705–707.
94. Freeman, *LL*, II, 81–85; *Lee*, II, 300–301 and *n.*; *OR*, I, xii, pt. 2, pp. 553–554, 642–643. See Douglas, pp. 132–133, for his version of this conference, which is probably confused.

Chapter 15

1. *OR*, I, xii, pt. 2, p. 678; Casler, p. 106.   2. Mrs. Jackson, p. 317.
3. Dabney, p. 517.   4. *OR*, I, xii, pt. 2, p. 747.   5. *Ibid.*, pp. 733–734.
6. See the review of the strategic situation in Henderson, pp. 438–441.
7. *OR*, I, xii, pt. 2, pp. 643, 670.   8. *Ibid.*, p. 643.   9. *Ibid.*, p. 723.
10. Casler, pp. 107–108.   11. *OR*, I, xii, pt. 2, p. 643.
12. Worsham, pp. 120–121.   13. Taliaferro, in Mrs. Jackson, p. 523.
14. *OR*, I, xii, pt. 2, p. 644.   15. Worsham, p. 121.
16. C. G. Chamberlayne (ed.), *Ham Chamberlayne, Virginian* (Richmond, 1932), p. 100; Henderson, p. 440.
17. Douglas, p. 136.   18. *OR*, I, xii, pt. 2, pp. 644, 723; Freeman, *LL*, II, 96.
19. Casler, p. 108.
20. See *OR*, I, xii, pt. 2, p. 656; Freeman, *LL*, II, 106 and *n.*
21. *OR*, I, xii, pt. 2, p. 645.
22. *Ibid.*, pp. 645, 656–657; Freeman, *LL*, II, 107–108.
23. *OR*, I, xii, pt. 2, p. 657.
24. *Ibid.*, pp. 645, 657; Freeman, *LL*, II, 111–112.
25. Freeman, *LL*, II, 111.   26. *OR*, I, xii, pt. 2, p. 646.
27. Douglas, p. 138.   28. *OR*, I, xii, pt. 2, pp. 556, 646, 671.
29. Douglas, p. 138.   30. *Ibid.*, pp. 137–138.
31. Chamberlayne, *op. cit.*, p. 101.
32. Freeman, *LL*, II, 118; *OR*, I, xii, pt. 2, p. 672.
33. McGuire in Allan, *Margaret Junkin Preston*, pp. 149–150.
34. Jackson to Maggie, Bunker Hill, Va., n.d., in *ibid.*, p. 152.
35. McGuire in *ibid.*, pp. 149–150. Another version of this conversation is given in Dabney, p. 531. Dabney's version has been widely copied, but since McGuire himself is the source for the dialogue quoted in the text—even though he wrote in 1897—his words are accepted. Verisimilitude is added by the wealth of detail which McGuire included in his account.
36. Edward A. Moore, *The Story of a Cannoneer under Stonewall Jackson* (Lynchburg, Va., 1910), p. 121.
37. The time is variously stated by participants as anywhere from 2 to 4 P.M. See Freeman, *LL*, II, 123 n.; *OR*, I, xii, pt. 2, pp. 413, 557, 647, 671.
38. See *Confederate Veteran*, XXII (1914), 231.
39. *OR*, I, xii, pt. 2, p. 563.   40. Henderson, p. 477.
41. The last three paragraphs are paraphrased from Douglas's touching account of this incident in Douglas, p. 142.

Chapter 16

1. J. N. Shealy to Jennie Shealy, Richmond, Va., Sept. 2, 1862, in J. N. Shealy Collection, Archives Collection, Louisiana State University.
2. Hotchkiss Journ., Aug. 31, 1862; *OR*, I, xii, pt. 2, p. 647; Freeman, *Lee*, II, 338.
3. Mrs. Jackson, p. 327; Dabney, p. 540.
4. "Minutes of Lexington Presbytery," Sept. 6, 1862, XIV, 344–345 (typescript page 246) (MS in Washington and Lee University Library).
5. The battle of Chantilly, or Ox Hill, is treated in full in Henderson, pp. 480–481; Freeman, *Lee*, II, 341; *LL*, II, 130–134.
6. Freeman superbly surveys Lee's dilemma in *Lee*, II, 342, 350–355.
7. For a complete review of the strategical and political considerations leading to Lee's decision, see Freeman, *Lee*, II, 350–355, where the pertinent sources are cited.
8. Alexander, *Military Memoirs of a Confederate*, p. 219; Freeman, *LL*, II, 146; *Lee*, II, 344.
9. *OR*, I, xix, pt. 2, pp. 590–591.
10. Longstreet, *Manassas to Appomattox*, p. 199.
11. Hotchkiss Journ., Sept. 5, 1862; Freeman, *LL*, II, 147–148.
12. "Reminiscences of Berry Greenwood Benson, C.S.A.," I, 113, typescript in Southern Historical Collection, University of North Carolina Library. It is possible that this statement of Jackson's was made a few days earlier, but since Gregg is known to have taken umbrage at something Jackson said on the morning of Sept. 4, the dialogue is included at this point in the text. (See Freeman, *LL*, II, 148.)
13. Charges against Gen. Hill, Oct. 4, 1862 (MS in T. J. Jackson Papers, Southern Historical Collection, University of North Carolina Library); Freeman, *LL*, II, 148 and *n*.
14. Hotchkiss Journ., Sept. 4, 1862.   15. *Ibid.*, Sept. 5.
16. *Ibid.*; Worsham, p. 137.
17. [John Esten Cooke] *The Life of Stonewall Jackson*, by a Virginian (Richmond, 1866), p. 308.
18. Hotchkiss Journ., Sept. 5, 6, 1862; Douglas, p. 148.
19. Freeman, *Lee*, II, 340.   20. *OR*, I, xix, pt. 2, p. 592; Douglas, p. 148.
21. Hotchkiss Journ., Sept. 6, 1862.
22. Freeman, *LL*, II, 154; G. Moxley Sorrel, *Recollections of a Confederate Staff Officer* (2d ed.; New York, 1917), p. 104.
23. Douglas, p. 149.   24. *Ibid.*   25. *Ibid.*
26. Paxton to Hill, Sept. 7, 1862, in Box 8, Hotchkiss Papers, LC.
27. Douglas, pp. 149–150.   28. Mrs. Jackson, p. 332.
29. *OR*, I, xix, pt. 2, pp. 601–602.   30. Dabney, p. 546.
31. *OR*, I, xix, pt. 2, p. 602; Freeman, *LL*, II, 159.   32. See *B&L*, II, 606.
33. *OR*, I, xi, pt. 1, p. 89.
34. H. E. Gourdin to Robert N. Gourdin, Hagerstown, Md., Sept. 15, 1862, in Robert N. Gourdin Papers, Duke University Library.
35. *OR*, I, xix, pt. 2, pp. 603–604.
36. Douglas, pp. 151–154, 158; Hotchkiss Journ., Sept. 10, 1862; *OR*, I, xix, pt. 2, p. 604.
37. Hotchkiss Journ., Sept. 11, 1862; Douglas, p. 155; Freeman, *LL*, II, 165.
38. From the "Texas Bible."   39. See Freeman, *LL*, II, 165.
40. Most of the account of the march from Frederick is rewritten from Douglas, pp. 150–158.
41. Hotchkiss Journ., Sept. 12, 1862.   42. *OR*, I, xix, pt. 1, p. 953.
43. Hotchkiss Journ., Sept. 13, 1862.
44. *OR*, I, xix, pt. 1, p. 953; Freeman, *LL*, II, 194. McLaws had four guns in battery by 2 P.M. on the fourteenth. (Wise, *Long Arm of Lee*, I, 289.)
45. *OR*, I, xix, pt. 1, p. 958.   46. *Ibid.*, pt. 2, p. 607.

47. *Ibid.*, pt. 1, p. 959.   48. *Ibid.*, p. 951.
49. Douglas, p. 162; *OR*, I, xix, pt. 1, p. 980.   50. *Ibid.*, p. 528.
51. *Ibid.*, 951.   52. Mrs. Jackson, p. 338.
53. D. X. Junkin, *Rev. Geo. Junkin*, pp. 552–553. The timing of this meeting is conjectured from internal evidence in Junkin's account.
54. Douglas, p. 163; Heros von Borcke, *Memoirs of the Confederate War for Independence* (2 vols.; London, 1866), I, 221–222.
55. *OR*, I, xix, pt. 1, p. 1007.
56. Lee probably found out about McClellan's windfall during the night of Sept. 13–14. See Freeman, *LL*, II, 173–174.
57. *OR*, I, xix, pt. 1, pp. 140–141.   58. See *B&L*, II, 675.
59. Freeman, *Lee*, II, 378.
60. See the survey of Lee's situation in *ibid.*, chap. 26.
61. Lee fixed the time of arrival as "early on the 16th" (*OR*, I, xix, pt. 1, p. 148), and Jackson said he reached Sharpsburg "on the morning of the 16th" (*ibid.*, p. 955). Gen. John G. Walker put the time at "a little past the hour of noon on the 16th" (*B&L*, II, 675).
62. *OR*, I, xix, pt. 1, p. 955.   63. Freeman, *LL*, II, 203.
64. Lee to R. L. Dabney, Lexington, Va., Jan. 25, 1866, in Dabney Papers, III, docs. 1–67, Union Theological Seminary, Richmond, Va.
65. Henderson, p. 519.
66. *OR*, I, xix, pt. 1, p. 955; Hood, *Advance and Retreat*, p. 42.
67. *OR*, I, xix, pt. 1, p. 956.   68. See *B&L*, II, 690–691.
69. Worsham, p. 144.   70. *OR*, I, xix, pt. 1, p. 956.
71. Freeman, *LL*, II, 208–209, citing Susan P. Lee, *Memoirs of W. N. Pendleton* (Philadelphia, 1893), p. 216.
72. Freeman, *LL*, II, 209–210; *B&L*, II, 677–678.
73. *OR*, I, xix, pt. 1, p. 956.   74. See *B&L*, II, 679–680.
75. Freeman, *LL*, II, 217; Henderson, p. 526.
76. Freeman, in *LL*, II, 222, chronicles a tradition that Lee embraced Hill with vast emotion as they met.
77. *OR*, I, xix, pt. 1, p. 981.   78. *Ibid.*, p. 420.
79. See *Southern Historical Society Papers*, XX (1892), 30.
80. D. H. Hill to R. L. Dabney, Petersburg, Va., June 7, 1863, in Dabney Papers, III, doc. 47.
81. Freeman, *Lee*, II, 403–404.   82. Hotchkiss Journ., Sept. 18, 1862.
83. *OR*, I, xix, pt. 1, p. 820; Von Borcke, *Memoirs*, I, 237–238; Henderson, pp. 542–543.
84. Lee to Mrs. Jackson, Lexington, Va., Jan. 25, 1866, in Dabney Papers, III, docs. 1–67.

Chapter 17

1. Douglas, p. 180; Hotchkiss Journ., Sept. 18, 1862; *B&L*, I, 238.
2. *B&L*, II, 682.   3. Hotchkiss Journ., Sept. 19, 1862.
4. Lee to R. L. Dabney, Lexington, Va., Jan. 25, 1866, in Dabney Papers, III, docs. 1–67, Union Theological Seminary, Richmond, Va.
5. *OR*, I, xix, pt. 1, pp. 957, 982.
6. D. H. Hill to Dabney, Petersburg, Va., July 19, 1864, in Dabney Papers, III, doc. 49; Dabney, Memoranda for Col. Henderson, May 7, 1896, in Box 13, Hotchkiss Papers, LC. In 1866 General Lee, having read Dabney's account of the Shepherdstown affair, based on Hill's testimony, wrote the statement Dabney published—in somewhat altered form—in Dabney, pp. 577–578 (see *supra*, note 4). These accounts present an interesting conflict of evidence. Hill's presence on the field, plus his having seen and talked with Lee shortly after Pendleton's despairing report, seems to lend credence to his statement. It should be pointed out, however, that after Jackson's death Hill developed a strong case of hero worship for his late brother-in-law and conceivably remembered

the events of Sept. 19 as more creditable to Jackson than they actually may have been.

7. Hotchkiss Journ., Sept. 21, 22, 24, 1862; Freeman, *Lee*, II, 415–420.
8. See Jackson's AAG to Capt. A. M. Garber, Oct. 6, 1862, in Box 8, Hotchkiss Papers, LC.
9. *OR*, I, XIX, pt. 2, pp. 613, 614; Harman to the Quartermaster General, Sept. 27, 1862, in Confederate Records, chap. V, vol. 5, p. 247, National Archives.
10. *RWCD*, I, 154.
11. Henderson, p. 555. Many versions of this story are extant. The text gives a composite of several.
12. *OR*, I, XIX, pt. 2, pp. 618–619.
13. See, for some idea of his views, General Orders No. 93, Sept. 5, 1862, in Box 8, Hotchkiss Papers, LC.
14. General Orders No. 99, Oct. 7, 1862, in *ibid*.
15. Jackson to Gen. Samuel Cooper, Sept. 22, 1862, in *ibid*.
16. *OR*, I, XIX, pt. 1, p. 956.   17. Hood, *Advance and Retreat*, pp. 45–46.
18. Freeman, *LL*, II, 264–265.
19. *OR*, I, XIX, pt. 2, pp. 633–634; see also James M. Matthews (ed.), *Statutes at Large of the Confederate States of America* (Richmond, 1862), 1st Cong., 2d sess., chap. 3, authorizing the rank of lieutenant general. Act approved Sept. 18, 1862. Also *ibid*., chap. 26.
20. *OR*, I, XIX, pt. 2, p. 643.
21. *Ibid*., pp. 698–699: Commission, in T. J. Jackson Papers, Virginia Historical Society, Richmond, Va.
22. General Orders No. 95, 116, 120, Sept. 22, Oct. 29, Nov. 11, 1862, in Box 8, Hotchkiss Papers, LC.
23. Freeman, *LL*, II, 244.
24. See A. P. Hill to R. H. Chilton, Headquarters, Light Division, Sept. 22, 30, 1862, in Light Division Letter Book, Confederate Army Manuscripts, Manuscripts Division, New York Public Library; also, *OR*, I, XIX, pt. 2, pp. 729–731.
25. Jackson to Chilton, Oct. 3, 1862, in Box 8, Hotchkiss Papers, LC.
26. *OR*, I, XIX, pt. 2, pp. 729–733.   27. *Ibid*., p. 732.
28. Hill to Chilton, Jan. 29, 1863, in Light Division Letter Book, Confederate Army Manuscripts, Manuscripts Division, New York Public Library. See also *OR*, I, XIX, pt. 2, pp. 732–733.
29. Jed Hotchkiss, "Incidents Relating to the Life of Gen. Jackson," entry no. 1 (MS in Manuscripts Collection, University of Virginia Library).
30. Hotchkiss Journ., Oct. 7, 1862.
31. James P. Smith, "With Stonewall Jackson in the Army of Northern Virginia," in *Southern Historical Society Papers*, XLIII (NS V) (1920), 21, 22. Cited hereinafter as Smith.
32. Von Borcke, *Memoirs*, I, 295–297.
33. Doc. SA 36, Stuart Collection, Huntington Library, San Marino, Calif.
34. Cooke, *Jackson*, p. 335.   35. Blackford, p. 128.   36. Douglas, p. 192.
37. *Ibid*., p. 196.   38. Mrs. Jackson, pp. 349–350.
39. Blackford, pp. 130–131.   40. Mrs. Jackson, pp. 347, 349.
41. *Ibid*., pp. 349–350.   42. *Ibid*., p. 351.   43. *Ibid*., pp. 529–531.
44. Wolseley, "A Month's Visit to the Confederate Headquarters," in *Blackwood's Edinburgh Magazine*, XCIII (1863), 21.
45. A. C. Inman (ed.), *Soldier of the South: Gen. Pickett's War Letters to His Wife* (Boston and New York, 1928), pp. 27–28.
46. See Hotchkiss Journ., Oct. 25, Nov. 19, 1862. Jackson officially moved his headquarters to Winchester on Nov. 19.
47. Mrs. Jackson, p. 352.   48. Cornelia McDonald, *Diary*, p. 105.
49. Fanny Graham to Anna, Nov. 21, 1862, in Rare Book Collections, The Library, The University of Texas. Also in Mrs. Jackson, p. 358. There are textual differences between the manuscript and printed versions.

50. *Ibid.*
51. That such a conversation took place seems probable from the contents of Fanny Graham to Anna, Oct. 13, Nov. 21, 1862, in Rare Book Collections, The Library, The University of Texas.
52. Mrs. Jackson, p. 348.   53. Smith, p. 24.
54. Alexander, *Military Memoirs of a Confederate,* p. 280; Freeman, *Lee,* II, 436.
55. For a careful review of the military situation in October and early November, 1862, leading to Jackson's march toward Fredericksburg, see Freeman, *Lee,* II, chap. 29.
56. Mrs. Jackson, p. 351.   57. Smith, p. 24.   58. Douglas, p. 203.
59. Mrs. Jackson, pp. 360–361.   60. *Ibid.,* pp. 360–363.
61. The tactical considerations are given in detail in Freeman, *Lee,* II, 438.
62. Mrs. Jackson, p. 351.
63. See Freeman, *Lee,* II, 439, citing John Gallatin Paxton (ed.), *Elisha Franklin Paxton Memoir and Memorials* (Washington, 1907), p. 73.
64. Hill to Dabney, Petersburg, Va., July 21, 1864, in Dabney Papers, III, doc. 50, Union Theological Seminary, Richmond, Va.
65. Freeman, *Lee,* II, 430.   66. *Ibid.,* p. 489.   67. *OR,* I, xxi, 1043–1044.
68. *Ibid.,* p. 1044.   69. *Ibid.,* p. 1057.
70. Hotchkiss Journ., Dec. 5, 1862. For weather conditions during early December Hotchkiss's Journal is an admirable source.
71. The description of Jackson's divisional locations is based on the map in Freeman, *Lee,* II, 449.
72. Barksdale's gallant delaying action is thoroughly covered in *ibid.,* pp. 444–448 and in *LL,* II, 335–338.
73. Hotchkiss Journ., Dec. 12, 1862.   74. Von Borcke, *Memoirs,* II, 109–110.
75. Hotchkiss Journ., Dec. 12, 1862.   76. *OR,* I, xxi, 641.
77. Smith, p. 29.   78. Douglas, p. 205.   79. *Ibid.*
80. See Freeman, *LL,* II, 346.   81. Douglas, p. 205.
82. Hill to Dabney, Petersburg, Va., July 21, 1864, in Dabney Papers, III, doc. 50. Dabney used this letter as the source for his version of the incident in Dabney, p. 610.
83. Freeman, *Lee,* II, 454; *LL,* II, 347.
84. Von Borcke, *Memoirs,* II, 114; Freeman, *Lee,* II, 454.
85. Frank Moore (ed.), *The Rebellion Record* (12 vols.; New York, 1862–1871), VI, 110. Another version of this dialogue is given in Dabney, p. 611.
86. Sorrel, *Recollections of a Confederate Staff Officer,* p. 138. See also Freeman, *Lee,* II, 454 n., and *LL,* II, 348, where the account varies according to the sources used.
87. *OR,* I, xxi, 636–639.   88. Von Borcke, *Memoirs,* II, 117.
89. *OR,* I, xxi, 631.   90. See *B&L,* III, 139.   91. *OR,* I, xxi, 553.
92. *Ibid.,* p. 511.   93. Freeman, *LL,* II, 350.
94. See Freeman, *Lee,* II, 457 and n.   95. *OR,* I, xxi, 631.
96. The time is difficult to fix precisely, since Jackson said the renewal of the advance started at 11 A.M., after Pelham held up the march for an hour (*OR,* I, xxi, 631). A. P. Hill agreed that Pelham slowed the attack for an hour, but said that after Pelham withdrew, Federal batteries shelled his lines "for an hour or more." This seems to fix the time at about noon (*ibid.,* pp. 645–646). The hour stated in the text is an attempt to reconcile the various accounts.
97. *Ibid.,* p. 639.   98. *Ibid.,* p. 646.   99. Mrs. Jackson, p. 369.
100. *OR,* I, xxi, 632, 646.   101. See *B&L,* III, 140.
102. Freeman, *Lee,* II, 462; *OR,* I, xxi, 646–647.
103. See Freeman, *Lee,* II, 462.   104. Hood, *Advance and Retreat,* p. 50.
105. See Jubal A. Early, *Autobiographical Sketch and Narrative of the War Between the States* (Philadelphia and London, 1912), pp. 177–178; Freeman, *LL,* II, 369–373.
106. Henderson, p. 590.

107. Confederate casualties, killed, wounded, and captured, were estimated at 4,201, of which 2,682 were in Jackson's Corps. *OR*, I, xxi, 567.
108. Hotchkiss Journ., Dec. 14, 1862.

Chapter 18

1. Freeman, *Lee*, II, 468.   2. See Smith, p. 34.
3. Hotchkiss Journ., Dec. 16, 1862.   4. Smith, p. 36.
5. *Ibid.*; Hotchkiss Journ., Dec. 16, 1862; Mrs. Roberta Cary Kinsolving, "Stonewall Jackson in Winter Quarters," in *Confederate Veteran*, XX (1912), 25; Freeman, *LL*, II, 495–496.
6. Mrs. Jackson, p. 372.   7. Mrs. Kinsolving, *op. cit.*, p. 25.
8. *Ibid.*; Smith, p. 37; Douglas, p. 307.   9. Hotchkiss Journ., Dec. 22, 1862.
10. *Ibid.*, Dec. 21, 1862.   11. Mrs. Jackson, p. 398.   12. Smith, p. 39.
13. *OR*, I, xxi, 556.   14. Smith, pp. 39–40.
15. See, for example, General Orders No. 3, Headquarters, 2 Corps, January 17, 1863, in Box 8, Hotchkiss Papers, LC.
16. Hotchkiss Journ., Feb. 27, Apr. 1, 1863.   17. Douglas, p. 213.
18. For another instance of Jackson's views on desertion, see Jackson to Brig. Gen. R. H. Chilton, Jan. 21, 1863, in Box 8, Hotchkiss Papers, LC.
19. General Orders No. 10, Headquarters, 2 Corps, Feb. 12, 1863, in *ibid.*
20. General Orders No. 16, Mar. 5, 1863, in *ibid.*   21. Douglas, p. 214.
22. For indications of Jackson's furlough policy, see Mrs. Jackson, pp. 374, 401; General Orders No. 15, Mar. 4, 1863, in Box 8, Hotchkiss Papers, LC.
23. Douglas, p. 217.   24. *OR*, I, xii, pt. 2, pp. 214–216.
25. Freeman, *LL*, II, 511–512.
26. Jackson to Brig. Gen. R. H. Chilton, Jan. 2, 1863, in Box 8, Hotchkiss Papers, LC; Freeman, *LL*, II, 512.
27. Freeman, *LL*, II, 514.
28. See Jackson to Dabney, Headquarters, 2 Corps, Jan. 15, 1862 [1863], in Dabney Papers, III, docs. 1–67, Union Theological Seminary, Richmond, Va.
29. Freeman, *LL*, II, 501 n.
30. See Hotchkiss Journ., Jan. 19, 1863; Douglas, p. 210.
31. Douglas was particularly bitter. See Douglas, pp. 210–211.
32. Henderson, pp. 627–628.
33. Hotchkiss Journ., Mar. 29, 1863; Hotchkiss to his wife, camp near Hamilton's Crossing, Apr. 2, 1863, in Box 3, Hotchkiss Papers, LC.
34. *Ibid.*   35. *OR*, I, xix, pt. 1, p. 952.   36. Henderson, pp. 627–628.
37. Freeman, *LL*, II, 505, citing Paxton, *Elisha Franklin Paxton Memoir and Memorials*, pp. 83–84.
38. Lee to Jackson, Headquarters, Army of Northern Virginia, Jan. 12, 1863, in Taliaferro Papers, Box 1, William and Mary College Library.
39. Taliaferro to Brig. Gen. R. H. Chilton, Headquarters, Jackson's Division, Jan. 30, 1863, in *ibid.*
40. Happily Taliaferro took no ill will toward Jackson with him. Years later, in recalling his service with Stonewall, Taliaferro wrote that "our relations . . . were most friendly," and it was a source of pride to him that Old Jack had selected him to lead "Jackson's Division" for so many months. See Taliaferro to [?] Conrad, Gloucester Court House, Va., July 11, 1877, in *ibid.*, Box 12.
41. Smith, p. 40.
42. Jackson to William Porcher Miles, Strasburg, Va., Mar. 5, 1862, in W. P. Miles Papers, Southern Historical Collection, University of North Carolina Library; to Samuel Cooper, Feb. 11, 1863, in Box 8, Hotchkiss Papers, LC, recommending Col. Bradley T. Johnson for promotion to brigadier general; to Samuel Cooper, Feb. 10, 1863, in *ibid.*, recommending Brig. Gen. Edward Johnson for promotion to major general, saying Johnson "was with me at the Battle of McDowell, where he so distinguished himself as to make me very desirous of securing his services as one of my Division Commanders"; to Samuel Cooper,

Apr. 14, 1863, in *ibid.*, recommending Col. Stapleton Crutchfield's promotion to brigadier general in glowing terms; General Orders No. 22, Headquarters, 2 Corps, Mar. 25, 1863, in *ibid.*, directing officers to study the tactics not only of their present grade but also those of the next higher.

43. Endorsement on Jackson to Cooper, Apr. 14, 1863, in Personal Service File, Stapleton Crutchfield.
44. Mrs. Jackson, pp. 394–395, 401.   45. *Ibid.*, pp. 406, 453.
46. Letter dated Feb. 23, 1863, in Margaret Junkin Preston Papers, Southern Historical Collection, University of North Carolina Library.
47. Dabney, pp. 650–651.   48. Mrs. Jackson, pp. 384, 385.
49. Hotchkiss Journ., Mar. 29, 1863.   50. Dabney, p. 656.
51. Mrs. Jackson, pp. 389–390. Jackson's quotation is one he doubtless remembered seeing on the wall of the chapel at West Point.
52. For a full development of Jackson's religious experience during the months at Moss Neck, see Dabney, pp. 640–656; also Journal of Maggie Preston, entry for Mar. 11, 1863, in Allan, *Margaret Junkin Preston*, pp. 160–161, in which Maggie wrote: "Had a note yesterday from Gen. Jackson . . . hardly anything else in it than earnest breathings after heavenly peace and rest. He surely is a most devoted Christian." See Receipts, Bible Society of the Confederate States, July 22, Aug. 6, 1862, typescript copies furnished the writer by Dr. Fannie E. Ratchford, Rare Book Collections, The Library, The University of Texas.
53. Mrs. Jackson, pp. 398–399.
54. MS in Confederate Memorial Hall, New Orleans, La.
55. See Henderson, p. 630.
56. Mrs. Jackson, p. 379; Smith, pp. 37–38; Douglas, p. 209.
57. Jed Hotchkiss, "Incidents Relating to the Life of Gen. Jackson," entry no. 14 (MS in Manuscripts Collection, University of Virginia Library). There are several versions of this story. See Hotchkiss Journ., Apr. 14, 1863.
58. See Heros von Borcke, *Memoirs*, II, 178–179, for an amusing instance of autographing by Jackson.
59. Mrs. Kinsolving, *op. cit.*, p. 26; Mrs. Jackson, p. 408; Douglas, p. 214.
60. Mrs. Jackson, pp. 397–398.
61. *Ibid.*, p. 397; Dabney, p. 640.   62. Mrs. Jackson, p. 404.
63. *Ibid.*, p. 396.
64. Hotchkiss to his wife, Apr. 2, 1863, in Box 3, Hotchkiss Papers, LC.
65. Jackson to Stuart, Mar. 25, 1863, doc. SA 41, in Stuart Collection, Huntington Library, San Marino, California.
66. Hotchkiss to his wife, Apr. 24, 1863, in Box 3, Hotchkiss Papers, LC.
67. Mrs. Jackson, p. 407.   68. *Ibid.*, p. 409.   69. Douglas, p. 203.
70. Mrs. Jackson, pp. 410–411.
71. Hotchkiss to his wife, Apr. 24, 1863, in Box 3, Hotchkiss Papers, LC.
72. Douglas, p. 217.
73. Letter dated Apr. 24, 1863, in Box 3, Hotchkiss Papers, LC.
74. Mrs. Jackson, p. 412.   75. *Ibid.*, p. 411.
76. Hotchkiss to his wife, Apr. 24, 1863, in Box 3, Hotchkiss Papers, LC.
77. Mrs. Jackson, p. 413.   78. *Ibid.*   79. Mrs. Jackson, pp. 415–416.
80. Journal of Maggie Preston, entry of May 12, 1863, in Allan, *Margaret Junkin Preston*, pp. 164–165.

Chapter 19

1. Mrs. Jackson, pp. 416–417.
2. Circulars to Colston, Hill, and Rodes, Apr. 29, 1863, in Box 8, Hotchkiss Papers, LC.
3. Jackson to Crutchfield, Apr. 29, 1863, in *ibid.*
4. Freeman, *Lee*, II, 506.   5. *OR*, I, xxv, pt. 2, pp. 759–760.
6. Jackson to Colston, Apr. 29, 1863, in Box 8, Hotchkiss Papers, LC.
7. Hotchkiss Journ., Apr. 30, 1863.   8. Dabney, pp. 666–667.

9. See Freeman, *LL*, II, 527.
10. See Special Orders No. 121, Headquarters, Army of Northern Virginia, Apr. 30, 1863, in *OR*, I, xxv, pt. 2, p. 762.
11. Freeman, *LL*, II, 528.   12. *OR*, I, xxv, pt. 1, p. 939.
13. *Ibid.*, pp. 939–940.   14. Hotchkiss Journ., Apr. 30, 1863.
15. See Map 10, in John Bigelow, *The Campaign of Chancellorsville* (New Haven, Conn., 1910).
16. *OR*, I, xxv, pt. 1, pp. 849–850.   17. *Ibid.*, p. 940.   18. *Ibid.*, p. 825.
19. *Southern Historical Society Papers*, XI (1883), 137–138.
20. Freeman, *Lee*, II, 517.   21. *OR*, I, xxv, pt. 2, p. 764.
22. Freeman, *LL*, II, 534.   23. *OR*, I, xxv, pt. 1, p. 850.
24. General Orders No. 47, Headquarters, Army of the Potomac, Apr. 30, 1863, in *ibid.*, p. 171.
25. Louise Haskell Daly, *Alexander Cheves Haskell: The Portrait of a Man* (Norwood, Mass., 1934), pp. 99–101.
26. T. M. R. Talcott, "General Lee's Strategy at the Battle of Chancellorsville," in *Southern Historical Society Papers*, XXXIV (1906), 17. See also, Freeman, *LL*, II, 538. The time of the first Lee-Jackson conference was about 7 P.M.
27. For this whole sequence see Freeman, *Lee*, II, 519–521, 584–589, and *LL*, II, 538–541. In these accounts the basic sources are cited and the problem of timing is carefully worked out. Considerable misunderstanding arose after the war concerning the details of this conference. Many Confederates believed, including Gen. D. H. Hill, and Jackson's biographer, R. L. Dabney, that Lee favored a frontal assault against Hooker's main positions. Lee himself denied this in a letter to Mrs. Jackson, Jan. 25, 1866 (Dabney Papers, III, docs. 1–67, Union Theological Seminary, Richmond, Virginia), and D. S. Freeman in his exhaustive reconstruction of the conference demolished this thesis. See *Lee*, II, 584–589 and Appendix II.
28. Freeman, *LL*, II, 541.
29. A romantic version of this episode was given in Dabney, p. 675, where Jackson is represented as waiting until Sandie fell asleep to spread the cape over him. Freeman, in *LL*, II, 542 n. destroys the myth. See also A. L. Long, *Memoirs of Robert E. Lee* (New York, 1886), p. 258, where Jackson is described as "the first to rise from the bivouac . . . ," indicating that he spread the cape only after he awoke from his own slumbers.
30. Henderson, p. 665; Dabney, pp. 675–676.
31. The early-morning scene is described in Dabney, pp. 675–676; Henderson, p. 665; Long, *op. cit.*, p. 258; Freeman, *Lee*, II, 522, and *LL*, II, 543–544.
32. See *OR*, I, xxv, pt. 2, p. 719; Henderson, p. 665; Freeman, *LL*, II, 548.
33. *B&L*, III, 205–206.
34. Hunter H. McGuire, *The Confederate Cause and Conduct in the War Between the States*, p. 214; Couper, II, 171 ff.
35. See Memorandum of T. T. Munford, Munford Papers, Duke University Library. Also quoted in Freeman, *LL*, II, 551.
36. Doc. SA 136, Jeb Stuart Collection, Huntington Library, San Marino, Calif. Jackson's dispatch to Lee has not been found but the content may be conjectured from Lee's reply.
37. Freeman, *LL*, II, 552.   38. *Ibid.*, pp. 319–320.
39. McGuire, *op. cit.*, p. 200.   40. Couper, II, 170–173; Freeman, *LL*, II, 554.
41. *B&L*, III, 206.   42. *OR*, I, xxv, pt. 1, pp. 940–941.
43. *B&L*, III, 208; *OR*, I, xxv, pt. 1, pp. 915–916, 940–942, 984–985, 1004–1005, for various reports of officers leading the Confederate attack.
44. *OR*, I, xxv, pt. 1, p. 941.   45. See Joshua, i, 14.
46. Curious as this story may sound, it comes on the good authority of Capt. R. E. Wilbourn of the Signal Corps, who stayed close to Jackson during the later part of the charge. Wilbourn's account is used in Freeman, *LL*, II, 561 ff. The full narrative is in *Southern Historical Society Papers*, VI (1878), 266–275, and a partial quotation appears in Cooke, *Jackson* (ed. of 1876), 416 n.

47. Clement A. Evans (ed.), *Confederate Military History*, III, 385.
48. See map in Freeman, *LL*, II, 566; *Confederate Veteran*, IV (1896), 308.
49. See Freeman, *LL*, II, 564–565. 50. Cooke, *op. cit.*, pp. 419–420.
51. *Confederate Veteran*, IV (1896), 308.
52. The description of Jackson's position at this time is necessarily vague since the various accounts conflict in describing the house. See Cooke, *op. cit.*, p. 420; *Confederate Veteran*, IV (1896), 308. The building was probably the Van Wert house. See Freeman, *LL*, II, 567 and n.
53. Hotchkiss Journ., May 2, 1863; *The Land We Love*, I (1866), 181–182.
54. Cooke, *op. cit.*, p. 423.
55. Dabney, p. 693; Wilbourn to Jubal Early, n.d., in Early, *Autobiographical Sketch*, 216 n.
56. *OR*, I, xxv, pt. 1, pp. 942–943, giving Rodes's statement on the summoning of Stuart. See *ibid.*, pp. 885–886, for A. P. Hill's account. Stuart described the receipt of orders to take command in *ibid.*, p. 887.
57. *Ibid.*, p. 886.
58. Wilbourn in *Southern Historical Society Papers*, VI (1878), 270.
59. *Ibid.* 60. Dabney, p. 689. 61. *Ibid.*; *B&L*, III, 212.
62. Wilbourn, *op. cit.*, p. 263. 63. Cooke, *op. cit.*, p. 427. 64. *Ibid.*
65. Dabney, p. 691; *B&L*, III, 212
66. Dabney, p. 708, where the long flight of rhetoric must be viewed with skepticism.
67. See Freeman, *LL*, II, 577 n., where the conflict of testimony about when whisky was procured is reviewed.
68. McGuire, *op. cit.*, pp. 220–221. 69. *Ibid.*, p. 221; Freeman, *LL*, II, 578.
70. McGuire, *op. cit.*, p. 222. See also Capt. C. B. Camerer, Med. Corps, U.S.N., "The Last Days of 'Stonewall' Jackson," in *Military Surgeon*, LXXVIII (1936), 138.
71. Dabney, p. 695; McGuire, *op. cit.*, p. 222. 72. *Ibid.*, p. 223.
73. Dabney, p. 696. 74. Hotchkiss Journ., May 3, 1863.
75. Dabney, p. 707; Mrs. Jackson, p. 436; Hotchkiss Journ., May 3, 1863.
76. McGuire, *op. cit.*, p. 223; Camerer, *op. cit.*, p. 140.
77. Dabney, p. 707.
78. *Ibid.*, p. 708; Freeman, *LL*, II, 600 and n., 601 and n.
79. Dabney, p. 709. 80. *OR*, I, xxv, pt. 2, 769.
81. *B&L*, II, 214; Freeman, *Lee*, II, 542–543. 82. Henderson, p. 699.
83. McGuire, *op. cit.*, p. 224. 84. *Ibid.*
85. Hotchkiss Journ., May 4, 1863. 86. *Ibid.*
87. Dabney, pp. 712–713. The quotations are transposed from third to first person.
88. *Ibid.*, p. 713.
89. McGuire, *op. cit.*, p. 225; Dabney, p. 712, where the timing of the towel incident does not agree. See Freeman, *LL*, II, 639.
90. McGuire, *op. cit.*, p. 225. 91. Hotchkiss Journ., May 5, 1863.
92. McGuire, *op. cit.*, p. 226.
93. Dabney, pp. 714–715. It should be pointed out that the sequence of conversations during this week cannot be fixed exactly.
94. *Ibid.*, p. 715. 95. *Ibid.*, p. 720. 96. *Ibid.* 97. *Ibid.*, p. 716.
98. McGuire, *op. cit.*, p. 226. 99. Mrs. Jackson, pp. 450–451.
100. *Ibid.*, p. 452. 101. McGuire, *op. cit.*, p. 227.
102. Mrs. Jackson, p. 452. 103. *Ibid.*, p. 453; Freeman, *LL*, II, 677.
104. McGuire, *op. cit.*, p. 228; Mrs. Jackson, pp. 455–456.
105. McGuire, *op. cit.*, p. 228.
106. Mrs. Jackson, pp. 450–457; McGuire, *op. cit.*, pp. 225–229. See also Freeman, *LL*, II, 669–682.

BIBLIOGRAPHY

A full listing of sources dealing with the personal and military life of Stonewall Jackson would require far more space than is available, and for that reason the present bibliography is restricted to the works cited in the footnotes.

Manuscripts

Confederate Museum, Richmond, Va.:
R. B. Garnett Papers (this collection is valuable for information on Garnett's court-martial).
Col. William Couper, Lexington, Va.:
Colonel Couper's monumental collection of data on the life of Stonewall Jackson served as a main source, and the usefulness of his note files cannot be overestimated.
Duke University Library (Manuscripts Collection):
Alexander Robinson Boteler Papers (there are some scattered letters in this collection dealing with Jackson).
Robert Newman Gourdin Papers (a few pertinent letters).
Frederick William Mackey Holliday Papers.
Thomas Jonathan Jackson Papers (a small, but extremely helpful file of letters and documents).
Robert Edward Lee Papers.
Charles Ellis and George Wythe Munford Papers (contains one highly informative manuscript by Thomas T. Munford).
Robert A. Stiles Papers.
Henry E. Huntington Library, San Marino, Calif.:
Joseph E. Johnston Collection (a rather extensive and helpful collection, containing several important Jackson letters).
James E. B. Stuart Collection (contains several vital Jackson documents).
Library of Congress, Washington, D.C.:
John A. Harman Papers (a small collection of letters in the Hotchkiss manuscripts).
Jedediah Hotchkiss Papers. (The most important manuscript source dealing with Jackson's military career. Included are voluminous notes taken by Hotchkiss preparatory to writing a life of Jackson, myriad memoranda for Col. G. F. R. Henderson written by many former Confederates who had fought under Jackson, scattered maps and sketches done by Hotchkiss [the Library of Congress has a special collection of Hotchkiss's maps], and the manuscript diary of Hotchkiss—an indispensable source for all phases of Jackson's military operations.)
J. Addison Waddell, diary (in the Hotchkiss manuscripts).
Department of Archives, Louisiana State University, Baton Rouge:
John N. Shealy Collection (a small file of letters illustrative of an enlisted man's impressions of Jackson).
National Archives, Washington, D.C.:
Confederate Records:
Correspondence of the Quartermaster General (Chapter IV).
Adjutant General's Records, personal service files of Stapleton Crutchfield, John A. Harman, T. J. Jackson.
United States Adjutant General's Records (in the Army Section, War Records Branch).
Mexican War Bounty Land Files.
United States War Department, Records of United States Army Commands, Department of the West (Record Group No. 98).

Department of Florida, Selected Letters Received relating to Maj. Thomas J.
Jackson and Maj. W. H. French, 1851 (microfilm in writer's possession).

Records of the First United States Artillery (in Army Section, War Records
Branch).

Correspondence of the United States Secretary of War, 1842–1852.

New York Public Library (Manuscripts Division), New York City:

Century Collection.

Confederate Army Manuscripts (contains the letter book of A. P. Hill's Light Division).

University of North Carolina Library, Southern Historical Collection, Chapel Hill, N.C.:

Edward Porter Alexander Papers.

J. Howard Beckenbaugh Collection of H. K. Douglas Papers (a few important
Douglas letters, dealing with Jackson's campaigns).

Berry Greenwood Benson Papers.

J. L. Campbell Papers.

Charles W. Dabney Papers.

Clement Daniel Fishburne Collection (contains a copy of Fishburne's manuscript
"Memoirs").

William Montgomery Gardner Papers.

Thomas Jonathan Jackson Papers (a valuable group of letters to and from Jackson).

Robert Edward Lee Papers.

Lafayette McLaws Papers.

William Porcher Miles Papers (a few important letters from Jackson).

Polk-Brown-Ewell Collection (scattered documents of importance in dealing with
Jackson's military operations).

Margaret Junkin Preston Papers (an extremely valuable group of letters and documents concerning Maggie and her relationship with Jackson).

Southern Education Papers.

John George Walker Papers.

Rockbridge County, Virginia, Clerk's Office, Lexington:

Register of Marriages, Rockbridge County.

Rare Books Collections, The University of Texas Library, Austin:

Mary Anna Jackson Letters (correspondence with Mrs. Fanny Graham, Winchester,
Va.; an illuminating file).

Union Theological Seminary, Richmond, Va.:

Robert L. Dabney Papers. (In this extensive collection of Reverend Dabney's papers
are to be found several important letters from Maj. Gen. D. H. Hill, giving his
impressions of Jackson. Much of the material which they contain was not used by
Dabney in his biography of Jackson. This collection of Hill letters is, in some
ways, the most important source on certain phases of Jackson's life in Lexington.)

Virginia Historical Society, Richmond:

Thomas J. Jackson Papers (an invaluable collection of letters, official orders, documents, and memoranda covering much of Jackson's military career).

Virginia Military Institute, Lexington:

Thomas J. Jackson Papers (a few Jackson letters, of some importance, are in the
VMI Library).

Letters Received, 1852–1861 (the Superintendent's correspondence files for these
years contain several letters from Jackson and many concerning his activities as
a member of the staff).

Virginia State Library, Richmond:

Thomas J. Jackson Collection (this collection is very small, and disappointing in
content).

University of Virginia Library (Manuscripts Collection), Charlottesville:

Clement Daniel Fishburne Papers. (Here is to be found the original of Fishburne's
manuscript "Memoirs" in two volumes. Certain portions of the Fishburne collection are unfortunately closed at present.)

John W. Daniel Papers.

Jedediah Hotchkiss Papers (some letters, memoranda, and notes in this collection are of particular interest, especially those written by Hunter H. McGuire and Sandie Pendleton).

Thomas Jonathan Jackson Papers. (The originals of many of Jackson's letters to his sister Laura are to be found here. The collection of correspondence is not complete, but is nonetheless vital. A comparison with the printed letters to Laura in Arnold's *Early Life and Letters* shows significant deletions in the printed version.)

Robert G. H. Kean, Manuscript Journal.

William C. Kean Papers.

Washington and Lee University Library, Lexington, Va.:

Records of the Franklin Society of Lexington.

"Minutes of Lexington Presbytery" (manuscript and typescript copies are available and contain several important references to Jackson).

William and Mary College Library, Williamsburg, Va.:

Joseph E. Johnston Papers. (These papers are particularly important in dealing with the beginning of Jackson's Confederate military career and shed some light on the opening of the Valley Campaign. Many of the letters have been printed in the *Official Records*.)

William B. Taliaferro Papers. (A large and fascinating collection, containing a number of letters and documents illustrative of Taliaferro's relations with his superior officer, Jackson. Much material is to be found here on the John Brown raid and on Jackson's Romney, Virginia, expedition.)

Newspapers

Lexington Gazette (Lexington, Va.), 1851–1861.
Lexington *Valley Star*, scattered issues, 1852–1856.
Lexington Gazette and Citizen, Aug. 25, 1876.
Richmond *Dispatch* (Richmond, Va.), Dec., 1859–Dec., 1860.
Richmond *Enquirer*, Apr. 23, 27, 1861.

Printed Sources

Alexander, Edward Porter. *Military Memoirs of a Confederate*. New York, 1907.

Alfriend, E. M. "Recollections of Stonewall Jackson," *Lippincott's Monthly Magazine*, LXIX (Jan.–June, 1902), 582–588.

Arnold, Thomas Jackson. *Early Life and Letters of General Thomas J. Jackson ("Stonewall" Jackson)*. New York, 1916.

Basler, Roy P. (ed.). *Collected Works of Abraham Lincoln*. 8 vols. New Brunswick, N.J., 1953–1955.

Blackford, Charles M., III (ed.). *Letters from Lee's Army*. New York, 1947.

Borcke, Heros von. *Memoirs of the Confederate War for Independence*. 2 vols. London, 1866.

Boyd, Belle. *Belle Boyd in Camp and Prison*. 2 vols. London, 1865.

Casler, John O. *Four Years in the Stonewall Brigade*. Girard, Kans., 1906; Marietta, Ga., 1951.

Chamberlayne, C. G. (ed.). *Ham Chamberlayne, Virginian*. Richmond, 1932.

Douglas, Henry Kyd. *I Rode with Stonewall*. Chapel Hill, 1940.

Early, Jubal A. *Autobiographical Sketch and Narrative of the War Between the States*. Philadelphia and London, 1912.

Freeman, Douglas Southall (ed.). *Lee's Dispatches; Unpublished Letters of General Robert E. Lee, C.S.A., to Jefferson Davis and the War Department of the Confederate States of America, 1862–65*. New York, 1915.

Hamlin, Percy G. (ed.). *The Making of a Soldier: Letters of General R. S. Ewell*. Richmond, 1935.

Hill, Daniel Harvey. "The Real Stonewall Jackson," *Century*, XLVII (New Series XXV) (1893–1894), 623–681.

Hood, John B. *Advance and Retreat*. New Orleans, 1880.

Howard, McHenry. *Recollections of a Maryland Staff Officer*. Baltimore, 1914.

Howard, Oliver Otis. *My Life and Experiences among Our Hostile Indians*. Hartford, Conn., 1907.

Hubbell, J. B. (ed.). "The War Diary of John Esten Cooke," *Journal of Southern History*, VII (1941), 526–540.

Inman, A. C. (ed.). *Soldier of the South: Gen. Pickett's War Letters to His Wife.* Boston and New York, 1928.

Jackson, Mrs. Mary Anna. *Memoirs of Stonewall Jackson.* Louisville, Ky., 1895.

————. "With Stonewall Jackson in Camp," *Hearst's Magazine*, XXIV (1913), 386–394.

Johnson, R. U., and C. C. Buel (eds.). *Battles and Leaders of the Civil War.* 4 vols. New York, 1887–1888.

Johnston, Joseph E. *Narrative of Military Operations Directed during the Late War Between the States.* New York, 1874.

Jones, J. B. *A Rebel War Clerk's Diary at the Confederate States Capital.* Edited by Howard Swiggett. 2 vols. New York, 1935.

[Junkin, Margaret.] *Silverwood, A Book of Memories.* New York, 1856.

Kinsolving, Mrs. Roberta Cary. "Stonewall Jackson in Winter Quarters," *Confederate Veteran*, XX (1912), 24–26.

Long, A. L. *Memoirs of Robert E. Lee.* New York, 1886.

Longstreet, James. *From Manassas to Appomattox.* Philadelphia, 1896.

McDonald, Cornelia. *A Diary with Reminiscences of the War and Refugee Life in the Shenandoah Valley, 1860–1865.* Annotated and Supplemented by Hunter McDonald. Nashville, 1934.

McGuire, Hunter H. *The Confederate Cause and Conduct in the War Between the States.* Richmond, 1907.

McKim, Randolph H. *A Soldier's Recollections.* New York, 1910.

Marshall, Charles. *An Aide-de-Camp of Lee.* Edited by Maj. Gen. Sir Frederick Maurice. Boston, 1927.

Matthews, James M. (ed.), *Statutes at Large of the Confederate States of America.* Richmond, 1862.

Maury, Dabney H. *Recollections of a Virginian.* New York, 1894.

Moore, Edward A. *The Story of a Cannoneer under Stonewall Jackson.* Lynchburg, Va., 1910.

Moore, Frank (ed.). *The Rebellion Record.* 12 vols. New York, 1862–1871.

Nisbet, James Cooper. *Four Years on the Firing Line.* Chattanooga, Tenn., n.d.

Preston, Margaret Junkin. "Personal Reminiscences of Stonewall Jackson," *Century*, XXXII (New Series X) (1886), 927–936.

Scott, Winfield. *Memoirs.* 2 vols. New York, 1864.

Senate [U. S.] *Executive Document* 1, 30th Cong., 1st sess. And Appendix.

Smith, James Power. "With Stonewall Jackson," *Southern Historical Society Papers*, XLIII (New Series V) (1920), 1–110.

Sorrel, G. Moxley. *Recollections of a Confederate Staff Officer.* 2d ed. New York, 1917.

Stiles, Robert. *Four Years under Marse Robert.* New York, 1903.

Taylor, Richard. *Destruction and Reconstruction.* Edited by Richard B. Harwell. New York, 1955.

Vandiver, Frank E. (ed.). *The Civil War Diary of General Josiah Gorgas.* University, Ala., 1947.

War of the Rebellion: A Compilation of the Official Records of the Union and Confederate Armies. 70 vols. in 127 and index. Washington, D.C., 1880–1901.

Watkins, Sam R. *"Co. Aytch."* Edited with an Introduction by Bell I. Wiley. Jackson, Tenn., 1952.

White, H. M. (ed.). *Rev. William S. White, D.D., and His Times. An Autobiography.* Richmond, 1891.

Wolseley, Col. Garnet. "A Month's Visit to the Confederate Headquarters," *Blackwood's Edinburgh Magazine*, XCIII (1863), 1–29.

Worsham, John H. *One of Jackson's Foot Cavalry.* New York, 1912.

Secondary Works

Allan, Elizabeth Preston. *Life and Letters of Margaret Junkin Preston.* Boston and New York, 1903.

Allan, William. "Jackson's Valley Campaign," *Southern Historical Society Papers*, XLIII (New Series V) (1920), 113–294.

Bartlett, W. H. C. *Elements of Natural Philosophy—Spherical Astronomy*. New York, 1855.

Bigelow, John. *The Campaign of Chancellorsville*. New Haven, 1910.

Black, Robert C., III. *The Railroads of the Confederacy*. Chapel Hill, 1952.

Cable, George W. "The Gentler Side of Two Great Southerners," *Century*, XLVII (New Series XXV) (1893–1894), 292–294.

Camerer, Capt. C. B. "The Last Days of 'Stonewall' Jackson," *Military Surgeon*, LXXVIII (1936), 135–140.

Cook, Roy Bird. *The Family and Early Life of Stonewall Jackson*. 3d ed. Charleston, W.Va., 1948.

[Cooke, John Esten.] *The Life of Stonewall Jackson*, by a Virginian. Richmond, 1863.

Couper, William. *One Hundred Years at V.M.I.* 4 vols. Richmond, 1939.

Dabney, Robert L. *Life and Campaigns of Lieut.-Gen. Thomas J. Jackson*. New York, 1866.

Daly, Louise Haskell. *Alexander Cheves Haskell: The Portrait of a Man*. Norwood, Mass., 1934.

Davis, Burke. *They Called Him Stonewall*. New York, 1954.

Evans, Clement A. (ed.). *Confederate Military History*. 12 vols. Atlanta, 1899.

Florida: A Guide to the Southernmost State. Federal Writer's Project, WPA. New York, 1939 [1955 printing].

Freeman, Douglas Southall. *Lee's Lieutenants: A Study in Command*. 3 vols. New York, 1942–1944.

———. *R. E. Lee: A Biography*. 4 vols. New York, 1934–1935.

Hanna, A. J., and K. A. Hanna. *Lake Okeechobee*. Indianapolis and New York, 1948.

Hanson, Joseph Mills. *Bull Run Remembers: The History, Traditions and Landmarks of the Manassas (Bull Run) Campaigns before Washington, 1861–1862*. Manassas, Va., 1953.

Henderson, Col. G. F. R. *Stonewall Jackson and the American Civil War*. Authorized American Edition. New York, 1949.

Henry, Robert S. *The Story of the Mexican War*. Indianapolis and New York, 1950.

James, J. B. "Life at West Point One Hundred Years Ago," *Mississippi Valley Historical Review*, XXXI (1944–1945), 21–40.

Johnston, Robert M. *Bull Run, Its Strategy and Tactics*. Boston, 1913.

Junkin, D. X. *The Reverend George Junkin, D.D., LL.D. A Historical Biography*. Philadelphia, 1871.

Meade, Robert D. "The Relations Between Judah P. Benjamin and Jefferson Davis," *Journal of Southern History*, V (1939), 468–478.

Montague, Ludwell L. "Subsistence of the Army of the Valley," *Military Affairs*, XII (1948), 226–231.

Nichols, James L., "Confederate Map Supply," *Military Engineer*, XLVI (Jan.–Feb., 1954), 28–32.

Semple, Henry C., S.J. "The Spirituality of Stonewall Jackson and Catholic Influences," *Catholic World*, CXVI (1922–1923), 349–356.

Smith, Justin H. *The War with Mexico*. 2 vols. New York, 1919.

Talcott, T. M. R. "General Lee's Strategy at the Battle of Chancellorsville," *Southern Historical Society Papers*, XXXIV (1906), 1–27.

Turner, Charles W. "The Virginia Central Railroad at War, 1861–1865," *Journal of Southern History*, XII (1946), 510–533.

Vandiver, Frank E. *Ploughshares into Swords: Josiah Gorgas and Confederate Ordnance*. Austin, Tex., 1952.

Wayland, John W. *Stonewall Jackson's Way: Route, Method, Achievement*. Staunton, Va., 1940.

Williams, T. Harry. *P. G. T. Beauregard: Napoleon in Gray*. Baton Rouge, La., 1955.

Wise, Jennings C. *The Long Arm of Lee; or, The History of the Artillery of the Army of Northern Virginia; with a Brief Account of the Confederate Bureau of Ordnance*. 2 vols. Lynchburg, Va., 1915.

INDEX

Adjutant General, USA, **226**
Alabama, 218
Alaman, Don Lucas, 42
Alburtis's battery, CSA, 162
Aldie Gap, 362
Alexander, Gen. Edward P., CSA, 159, 459
Alexandria, Va., 356, 359, 362
Allegheny Mountains, 174, 178, 180, 209, 220, 247, 258
Allen, Israel, 267–268
Allen, Judge J. J., 81
Allen, Col. James W., CSA, 151, 162
American Party, 103
Ampudia, Gen. Pedro de (Mexican Army), 39
Amissville, Va., 354
Amy, Jackson's Negro cook, 110, 120
Anderson, Gen. Richard H., CSA, 393, 456–458, 461–462, 468
Ann-Smith Academy, Lexington, Va., 84
Ansaldo, Mexico, 35
Ansted, Va., 4
Antietam Creek, 391–394, 398, 423
Anton Lizardo, Mexico, 23
Appomattox Court House, Va., 1
Aquia Creek, 357
Archer, Gen. J. J., CSA, **426**, 431
Arkansas, USS, 23, 45
Arkansas, Third Infantry Regiment, 397
Army of Northern Virginia, 346, 353, 381, 389–401, 403, 421, 437, 450, 467; reorganized after Sharpsburg campaign, 405–409
Army of the Northwest (CS), 178, 180–182, 184, 186, 193
Army of the Potomac (CS), 174, 177
Army of the Potomac (US), 417, 454, 456, 471, 475, 477
Army of the Shenandoah (CS), 146, 148, 152–164
Army of the Valley (CS), 181, 190, 198–199, 201, 211–212, 223, 225, 227, 231–234, 240–244, 247–263, 266, 268–269, 271, 273, 281, 283, 286, 290, 292, 295, 298–303, 324, 329–330, 338, 340–341, 345–346, 348, 353–358, 364, 375, 378, 381, 398, 402, 404, 417–418, 421–422, 437; marches vs. Shields, 204; reaction to disciplining of Turner Ashby, 216; affected by conscription, 217
Army of Virginia (US), 326, 347, 349, 357
Arnold, Anna Grace (niece of Jackson), 52–53
Arnold, Jonathan, 47, 53, 121, 130; religious views, 94
Arnold, Laura Jackson (sister of Jackson), 2–6, 9, 14, 17–18, 19, 24, 26, 30–31, 36, 41–42, 45–54, 64, 70, 73, 91, 96, 106, 111,

120–121, 129–130, 143, 290; religious problems, 92–94, 101, 127; health, 93; children of, 100; interest in Ellie, 100; receives Jacksons at home, 103–104; visits Lexington, 123
Arnold, Thomas Jackson, 19, 47, 100, 121–123
Ashby, Gen. Turner, CSA, 138–139, 185, 196, 200, 203–207, 211, 214–216, 219, 225, 227–228, 238–244, 248, 253–254, 262, 265–273, 279, 302, 334–335, 343; description of, 215
Ashby's Gap, 154–155
Ashland, Va., 286, 296, 298–301, 321, 332
Atalaya, Mexico, 27–28
Avery, A. C., 130
Avery, Susan Morrison, 130, 169
Ayotla, Mexico, 32–33

Baird, Lt. Absalom, 58–59, 66, 68–69
Ball's Bluff, Va., 375
Ball's Ford, 158
Baltimore, Md., 115, 262, 377
Baltimore and Ohio Railroad, 138, 140, 142, 148, 180–181, 185, 189, 191, 233, 411–412
Banks, Gen. Nathaniel P., USA, 188, 196, 198, 200, 203, 208, 215, 219–220, 223–224, 226–228, 230–231, 233–238, 240, 245–247, 250, 258–260, 264, 285, 293, 346, 396; in Battle of Winchester, 250–253; retreats from Winchester, 253–255; reasons for retreat, 257; in Battle of Cedar Mountain, 339–345
Barksdale, Gen. William, CSA, 422, 457
Barnett's Ford, 337
Barney, Dr. Lowry, 73, 97–98
Bartlett, Capt. Joseph L., CSA, 384
Bartlett, W. H. C., 81
Bartonsville, Va., 207–208
Bartow, Col. Francis S., CSA, 160
Bath, Va., 185–186, 188–189
Baxter, Capt. George, 243
Baxter, Rev. George, 84
Baylor, Col. W. S. H., 370, 372
Beauregard, Gen. P. G. T., CSA, 27, 144, 152–164, 165–167, 170, 172, 174
Beaver Dam, Va., 298–300, 315
Beaver Dam Creek, 296, 302–303, 307, 309
Bee, Gen. Barnard E., CSA, 16, 39, 150, 160, 165; gives Jackson sobriquet of "Stonewall," 161; killed, 161
Belen *garita*, 36, 39
Belgium, 111
Benjamin, Judah P., 178–182, 185, 189–190; assigns Jackson to command Shenandoah Valley, 173–175; troubles over Jackson's resignation, 192–195

Bennett, Jonathan M., 12–13, 135, 152, 166
Berlin, Va., 140
Berryville, Va., 260
Bethesda Church, 303, 305
Beverly, Va., 46–48, 94, 100, 103–104, 121, 127, 143, 179
Beverly Ford, 349
Bible Society of the Confederate States, The, Jackson a director of, 447
Big Spring, Va., 151
Black, Dr. Harvey, CSA, 483–484
Blackburn, Cadet Thomas, 103
Blackburn's Ford, 156, 158, 362
Blackford, Capt. Charles M., CSA, 341–342, 347–348, 351, 411–412
"Bloody Lane," 397
Blue Ridge Mountains, 139, 154, 174, 196, 198, 203, 209, 217, 221, 223, 225, 227, 235, 239–240, 247, 271, 274, 280, 286, 290–291, 333, 335, 414–415, 417
Boatswain's Swamp, 306
Boggs, Gen., CSA, 190
Bolivar Heights, 139, 384, 389
Bonham, Gen. Milledge L., CSA, 158–160
Boonsboro, Md., 380, 382, 393
Boston, Mass., 98
Boswell, Capt. James K., CSA, 218, 354, 440, 464, 477, 486
Boteler, Alexander R., 199, 216, 261–263, 272, 284, 285, 328–329, 442, 446; persuades Jackson to withdraw resignation, 194–195
Boteler's Ford, 401–403
Bottom's Bridge, 310
Botts, Archie, 19
Botts, Col. Lawson, CSA, 365
Bowlegs, Billy, 56
Boyd, Belle, 241
Brake, Isaac (Jackson's uncle), 5–6
Brake, William, 5
Branch, Gen. Lawrence O'B., CSA, 236–237, 301–302, 342, 375
Brandy Station, Va., 222
Brannan, Capt. J. M., USA, 68
Brattleboro, Vt., 127
Bravo, Gen. Nicolas (Mexican Army), 37
Breckinridge, John C., 128
Bristoe Station, Va., 356–357, 360–361
Brock Road, 467, 471–473
Brockenbrough, Judge, 103
Brockenbrough's battery, CSA, 162
Brown, John, 124–126, 136
Brown Hotel, New York City, 19
Brown's Gap, 225–228, 271, 274, 278, 283, 285
Bruning, Corp., 66
Buckton, Va., 243
Buena Vista, Mexico, 24
Buffalo Gap, 227

537

Bull Run, 156–164, 166, 169, 359, 362, 371–372
Bull Run Mountains, 156, 355
Bullock farm, 477
Bunker Hill, Va., 147–148, 153, 196, 403–404, 407, 409–410
Burks, Col. Jesse, CSA, 205, 212-213
Burnside, Gen. Ambrose E., USA, 160, 364, 397–398, 417, 419–420, 422, 424–425, 433–434, 437; in Battle of Fredericksburg, 426–432
Burnside's Bridge, 393, 397, 423
Butcher, Gibson J., 12

California, 55
Campbell, Col. John A., CSA, 251
Canada, 54, 97–98, 413
Carlisle, John S., 47–48, 73
Carlisle Barracks, Pa., 46, 48, 54, 336
Carpenter, Capt. Joseph, CSA, 280, 359, 387
Carson, Gen., CSA, 189
Casler, Pvt. John, describes plunder at Manassas Junction, 358–359
Catharine Furnace, 462, 464, 466–469, 473
Catholic Church, 31, 44
Catlett's Station, 351
Cedar Mountain, 406, 437, 443
Cedar Mountain, Battle of, 339–345, 421, 440–441
Cedarville, Va., 243, 247
Centreville, Va., 152, 156, 158, 167, 169, 175, 362, 374
Cerro Gordo, Mexico, 27–29, 31, 57
Chambersburg, Pa., 381
Chamberlayne, Ham, 368
Chancellor, Melzi, farm, 472–473, 475, 483
Chancellorsville, Va., 420, 456, 458, 461–462, 466, 470, 476–477, 488–489
Chancellorsville, Battle of, 458–489
Chandler, Mr. and Mrs. Thomas E., 487–488
Chantilly, Battle of (Ox Hill), 373
Chapultepec, Battle of, 36–38
Charles City road, 310
Charles Town, Va., 124–126, 153, 260–263
Charlottesville, Va., 291
Chesapeake and Ohio Canal, 138, 140, 182–183
Chesterfield, Lord, 43
Chew, Col. Robert P., CSA, 203
Chickahominy River, 286, 296, 298–299, 301, 304, 306–307, 309–312, 327, 332
Chihuahua, state of, 22
Childs, Bvt. Col. Thomas, USA, 30
Chilton, Gen. R. H., CSA, 312, 441
Churubusco, Mexico, 32–36, 57
Clark's Mountain, 347–348
Clarksburg, Va., 2–6, 46
Clay, Henry, 55

Coahuila, state of, 21
Cocke, Col. Philip St. G., CSA, 158–160
Cocke, Thomas L., 115
Cofre de Perote, 29
Cold Harbor, Va., 298, 304–307
Coleman, Dr. R. T., CSA, 484
Colquitt, Gen. A. H., CSA, 468, 473, 475
Colston, Gen. Raleigh, CSA, 456, 458, 468, 470
Columbia Bridge, 267, 269
Compromise of 1850, 123
Congress, Confederate, 217, 406, 438
Congress, Republic of Mexico, 21–22
Conner, Col. Z. T., CSA, 262–263
Conrad, C. M., US Secretary of War, 69–70
Conrad, Peter, 47
Conrad's Store, Va., 209, 220–221, 223–226, 269, 274–275
Conscription, Confederate, 216–217
Contreras, Battle of (Padierna), 36, 57
Cooper, Gen. Samuel, CSA, 147, 152–153, 175, 178, 182, 194, 213, 223, 405
Corbin, Janie, 449–451
Corbin, Miss Kate, 449
Corbin, Mr. and Mrs. Richard, 435–436, 447–451
Cortes, Hernando, 26, 32
Cottage Home, N.C., 94, 113, 115
Couch, Gen. Darius N., USA, 16
Cox, W. H., 79
Crittenden House, 339–341
Cromwell, Oliver, 202, 289, 413, 440, 449
Cross Keys, Va., 270, 275, 284
Cross Keys, Battle of, 277
Crown Point, N.Y., 54
Crutchfield, Col. Stapleton, CSA, 242–243, 248, 280, 314–315, 319, 441, 456, 482–483, 487; thinks Jackson mad, 260
Culpeper Court House, Va., 153, 221–222, 224, 228, 336–340, 342–343, 456
Cumberland, Md., 180
Cummings, Col. A. C., CSA, 162–163, 214
Cutshaw's battery, CSA, 251
Cyrus (one of Jackson's slaves), 120

Dabb House, 294–298
Dabney, Rev. Maj. Robert L., 231, 235, 239, 256, 275, 277, 287, 291–293, 299–301, 311–312, 319, 322, 324–325, 442; joins Jackson's staff, 218; characterized, 293; on Jackson in the White Oak Swamp, 315; resigns from staff, 330
Dam No. 5, 182–183
Darbytown road, 310
Darksville, Va., 151, 153
Davidson College (N.C.), 94, 112, 114–115
Davis, Jefferson, 144, 147, 179,

185, 194, 234, 238, 261, 285, 296, 309, 323–324, 328–330, 335, 374, 390–391, 405–406, 439; on pursuit of Federals after First Manassas, 166–167; and assignment of Jackson to Shenandoah Valley, 173–175; and Jackson's resignation, 193; praises Jackson's Valley Campaign, 272
Davis, Col. Joseph, CSA, 323
Deep Run, 422–424, 431
De La Rue, W. F., 447
Dispatch Station, Va., 309, 312
Doles, Gen. George, CSA, 473
Doubleday, Gen. Abner, USA, 364–365
Douglas, Henry Kyd, 176, 182, 202, 215, 260, 308, 319, 321, 327–328, 332, 340, 367–368, 377–378, 381–383, 387–389, 407, 410, 440, 486; first meeting with Jackson, 171; as messenger to Ewell, 221–222; meets Belle Boyd, 241; converses with Jackson about ladies of Winchester, 249; on Sir Percy Wyndham, 272
Douglas, Mrs., 377
Dranesville, Va., 374
Dred Scott Decision, 123
Dublin Station, Va., 182
Dunkard Church (Sharpsburg), 392–396
Dunkards, as conscientious objectors, 203
Durham, England, 413

Early, Gen. Jubal A., CSA, 158, 164, 172, 339, 341, 344, 350–352, 366, 368, 393–396, 399, 405, 424–425, 431, 434, 454–455, 457, 459, 467; praised by Jackson, 351
Echols, Col. John, CSA, 162
Edmiston, Matthew, 12
Eleventh Army Corps, USA, 475
Eleventh US Infantry, 37, 41
Elk Run Valley, 223–224
Ellerson's Mills, 307
El Penon, in Mexico City defenses, 32–33
Ely's Ford, 458, 472
Elzey, Gen. Arnold, CSA, 248, 277
Emma (one of Jackson's slaves), 120
England, 111, 374, 413–414
Episcopal Church, 52, 86–87
Europe, 70, 73, 111–112
Evans, Gen. N. G., CSA, 160
Evelington Heights, 325
Ewell, Gen. Richard Stoddert, CSA, 158, 219, 224, 226, 231, 233–234, 237–240, 242–243, 245–248, 250, 255, 264–266, 270, 272–273, 275, 286, 301–303, 306–308, 310, 312, 321–322, 329, 336–342, 344, 350–351, 353, 355–356, 360–362, 364–365, 457; ordered to join Jackson's army, 221–222; dyspeptic, 223; marches to join Jackson, 223; worries at Jackson's absence, 228–229; thinks

Jackson an "old fool," 235; decides to stay with Jackson, 235–236; in attack on Banks, 236–237; in Battle of Winchester, 252; in Battle of Cross Keys, 277; in Battle of Port Republic, 278–283; irked by Jackson's secrecy, 289, 292; evaluation of, 360–361; wounded at Groveton, 365; fears for Jackson's safety at Sharpsburg, 399
Ewing, Rev. and Mrs. D. B., 333

Fairfax Court House, Va., 167
Falling Waters, action at, 149–152, 383
Falmouth, Va., 422, 427
Faulkner, Col. Charles J., CSA, 442–443
First Artillery, US, 20, 23–24, 26, 30–31, 41, 45, 48, 55–70
First US Infantry, 24
Fishburne, Clement D., 162; best man at Jackson's second wedding, 114–115; describes Jackson's wedding preparations, 115
Fishburne, Junius, 114
Fisher's Gap, 209, 223
Florida, 56–70, 73, 86, 261, 336
Flournoy, Col. Thomas, CSA, 243, 254
Floyd, Gen. John B., CSA, 181–182
"Foot cavalry," 232–233, 337
Forge Bridge, 312
Forno, Gen. Henry, CSA, 339, 350, 368
Fort Brooke, Fla., 57
Fort Casey, Fla., 57
Fort Columbus, N.Y., 20, 45, 57
Fort Donelson, 197
Fort Hamilton, N.Y., 20, 47–49, 52, 55
Fort Henry, 197
Fort Meade, Fla., 57–70, 72
Fort Ontario, 54
Fort Putnam, 16
Fort (Castle) San Juan de Ulúa, 23–24
Fort Sumter, 164
Fort Ticonderoga, 54
Fort Washington, N.Y., 86
Fourteenth US Infantry, 37, 41
Fourth Artillery, US, 24
France, 111, 374, 442
Franklin, Gen. William B., USA, 160, 314–315, 317, 428, 430
Franklin, Va., 231, 258
Franklin Society, Lexington, Va., 102–103
Frayser's Farm, 316–317
Frederick, Md., 361, 376–379, 381, 390
Fredericks Hall, Va., 291, 293–294, 300
Fredericksburg, Va., 223–224, 226, 233–235, 257, 288, 292, 349, 352, 357, 417, 419–420, 422–427, 430, 432, 436, 438, 451, 455–458, 467
Fredericksburg, Battle of, 422–432
Fremont, Gen. John C., USA,

229–231, 233, 237, 245–246, 258–259, 261, 263–266, 268–269, 271–272, 274–275, 277–278, 280–284, 287–288, 294, 346
French, Gen. William H., USA, 56–70, 72, 316, 397
French, Mrs. William H., 61, 66–67
Front Royal, Va., 209, 224, 239–240, 245–248, 254, 257, 262–264, 272, 353
Front Royal, Battle of, 239–244, 346
Fry, Birket, 14
Fugitive Slave Act (1850), 123
Fulkerson, Col. Sam, CSA, 204–207, 212–213, 250, 308
Funsten, Maj. O. R., CSA, 215

Gaines' Mill, 304–309, 312, 314
Gainesville, Va., 356, 362, 364
Gardner, Gen. Frank, CSA, 16
Garibaldi, Giuseppe, 272
Garnett, Gen. Richard B., CSA, 179, 188–189, 211–213; court martial proceedings, 333, 336
Garnett, Col. T. S., CSA, 341
Gauley Bridge, Va., 5
Geary, Gen. John W., USA, 259
Georgia, 286, 289
Georgia, Twelfth Infantry Regiment, 262–263, 341
George (one of Jackson's slaves), 120, 170
Germanna Ford, 458
Germany, 111
Gibbon, Gen. John, USA, 364–365
Gibraltar, 318, 325
Gilham, Col. William, CSA, 74–76, 84, 125, 172, 190
Gordonsville, Va., 228–229, 292–293, 329–330, 334, 336, 345, 418
Gorgas, Col. Josiah, CSA, 300
Governor's Island, N.Y., 45
Grafton, Va., 180
Graham, Rev. and Mrs. James, 183–184, 186, 191, 196, 199–200, 205–207, 255–256, 412, 415–416
Grant, Gen. U. S., USA, 1, 16, 414
Grapevine Bridge, 309–311, 329
Green Spring Depot, 181
Gregg, Gen. Maxey, CSA, 368, 375, 426, 431, 433–434
Griffin's battery, USA, 162
Grigsby, Col. A. J., CSA, 365, 395–396
Groveton, Va., 362, 364–366, 406, 437
Guiney's Station, Va., 419, 422, 452, 487–488, 492
Gulf of Mexico, 29

Hagerstown, Md., 379, 381, 390, 392–393, 395, 397
Halltown, Va., 260, 386
Hamilton's Crossing, 420, 422, 424, 426, 428, 451, 456
Hampton, Gen. Wade, CSA, 160, 316

Hancock, Gen. Winfield Scott, USA, 16
Hancock, Md., 188
Hannum, Frank, 78
Hanover, Va., 300
Hardee, Gen. William J., CSA, 140
Harman, Maj. John A., CSA, 142, 150, 167–168, 184, 199, 216, 219–220, 224–226, 236, 239, 247, 249–250, 255, 257, 263, 269–270, 279, 288, 291–293, 299, 346, 400–401, 404; characterized, 270
Harman, Messrs., & Co., 125
Harper, Col. Kenton, CSA, 136–137, 149–151, 162
Harpers Ferry, Va., 124, 135–146, 153, 177, 189, 204, 245, 253–254, 260, 262, 264, 379–380, 383–390, 392, 394, 406, 421, 438
Harris, John T., 129
Harris, Nathaniel, 293
Harrisonburg, Va., 209, 220–221, 223, 225, 227–229, 234, 236, 246–247, 258, 265, 267, 269–270, 272, 274
Harrison's Landing, 324–325, 327
Haskell, Capt. Alexander C., CSA, 463
Hawkinsville, Va., 267
Hawks, Maj. Wells J., CSA, 184–185, 199, 247, 262, 387, 404, 493, 494
Hawksbill, Va., 417
Hay Market, Va., 356
Hays, Gen. Harry T., CSA, 336, 356, 394–395
Hays, Samuel L., 12–13
Hebert, Gen. Paul O., CSA, 41
Heintzelman, Gen. S. P., USA, 160
Henderson, N.Y., 73
Henry, Judith, 161
Henry House, 160–163, 314, 362, 371
Herman Lodge, AF & AM (Clarksburg, Va.), 3
Heth, Gen. Harry, CSA, 462
Hetty (Anna Jackson's nurse), 120
High Meadows, scene of Lee-Jackson conference, 294–298
Hill, Gen. Ambrose Powell, CSA, 14, 149, 294, 298, 302–304, 306–307, 309–311, 317–318, 335, 338, 340–342, 346, 348, 351, 353, 355, 359–360, 362, 366–368, 373, 375, 383–384, 386–389, 392–393, 398–399, 402–403, 420, 422, 424–427, 430–431, 450, 456, 458, 462–463, 468, 476–480, 493, 494; description of, 295; joins Jackson's army, 336; troubles with Jackson over lax discipline, 375, 377, 382, 407–409, 440–442; wounded, 479–480
Hill, Mrs. A. P., 450
Hill, Gen. Daniel Harvey, CSA, 21, 29, 39, 81, 84–87, 90–91, 94–96, 106–107, 112, 114–115, 196, 198, 294, 298, 302–306, 308, 313, 315, 317–321, 374,

376, 380–381, 389–391, 393, 396–397, 399, 402–403, 419–422, 424–426, 456; recommends Jackson for professorship at VMI, 72–73; description of, 295

Hill, Isabella (Mrs. D. H.), 84–86, 90, 94–95, 112

Holmes, Gen. Theophilus H., CSA, 174, 310–311, 329

Hood, Gen. John B., CSA, 289, 293, 301, 307, 393–396, 399, 405, 422, 427, 456

Hooker, Gen. Joseph, USA, 394–396, 430, 454–456, 458–459, 462; in Battle of Chancellorsville, 458–489

Hot Springs, Va., 47–48

Hotchkiss, Jedediah, 208, 234, 258–259, 262–264, 267–270, 274, 281, 287, 289–291, 301, 311, 332, 337, 345–346, 377, 399, 409, 424–425, 435–437, 443–453, 458, 464, 466–467, 471, 487–488; characterized, 218–219

House Mountain, 83

Huger, Gen. Benjamin, CSA, 139, 296, 298, 310–311, 314, 318

Hundley's Corner, 302, 315

Hunter, Gen. David, USA, 160

Illustrated London News, 413

Imboden, Col. John D., CSA, 137, 161–162, 279, 288–289

Indian Territory, 56

Indiana, 364–365

Irwin, Mrs. Harriet, 418–419

Italy, 111

Iverson, Gen. Alfred, CSA, 473

Jackson, Alfred, 184

Jackson, Andrew, 15

Jackson, Anna (Mrs. T. J.), 94–96, 112–123, 127, 130, 132, 136, 142–147, 149, 151–152, 164–173, 177–178, 186, 191, 193–196, 205, 218, 239, 256, 287, 313, 327–328, 333, 353, 372, 378, 388, 411–412, 426, 435, 445, 450, 455, 485, 489; description of, 116; pregnant, 415–416; birth of daughter, 418–419; visits Jackson at Yerby's, near Fredericksburg, 451–454; meets Gen. Lee, 453; on first seeing Jackson at Guiney's, 492–493; at Jackson's bedside, 492–494

Jackson, Cummins (T. J. Jackson's uncle), 5–14, 17, 19, 55, 72; description of, 6–7

Jackson, Elinor Junkin ("Ellie"), 84, 90–96, 98–104, 108, 112, 115, 131, 369, 416, 454; description of, 96; described by T. J. Jackson, 98; pregnant, 103; dies in childbirth, 104

Jackson, Elizabeth (sister of T. J. Jackson), 2–3

Jackson, Capt. George, 12

Jackson, Jonathan (father of T. J. Jackson), 2–3

Jackson, Mrs. Julia (mother of T. J. Jackson, later Mrs. B. B. Woodson), 2–5, 7, 44, 101

Jackson, Julia Laura (daughter of T. J. Jackson), 418–419, 435, 450–455, 493

Jackson, Mary Anna (*see* Jackson, Anna)

Jackson, Mary Graham (daughter of T. J. Jackson), 120, 384, 450

Jackson, Gen. Thomas Jonathan, CSA, birth, 2; lives with grandmother, 4; lives with Uncle Cummins Jackson, 5; love of home, 6–7; boyhood amusements, 8; slow learner, 8–9; on trip to Mississippi River, 9; engineering assistant for Turnpike Company, 9–10; as schoolteacher, 10; considers entering ministry, 10; wants higher education, 10; as constable, 10–12; appointed cadet, USMA, 12–13; in Washington, D.C., in quest of final appointment, 13; on entering West Point, 14; class standing at West Point, 15; study habits at West Point, 15–17; and exact justice, 16; impression on others, 16; on career after West Point, 17–18; personal maxims of, 17–18; graduated from West Point, 18; wants assignment to artillery, 18; travels to Mexico, 20; anecdote about, in Mexico, 21; in Vera Cruz expedition, 23–26; in Battle of Cerro Gordo, 29–30; promoted to second lieutenant, 30; studies Spanish, 30–31; attached to Magruder's battery, 31; skirmishes with guerrillas, 31–32; commended for action at Padierna, 35; cited for gallantry, 36; in Battle of Churubusco, 36; promoted to first lieutenant and brevet captain, 36; in Battle of Chapultepec, 36–39; promoted to brevet major, 40–41; feelings in battle, 41; personal life in Mexico City, 41–43; and Catholic Church, 44; and strategical and tactical lessons of Mexican war, 44; in New Orleans, 45; homesick, 45–46; visits Laura, 46–48; fond of his nephew, 47; accused of horse stealing, 47–48; assignments during 1849, 48; weight, 48, 50; eating habits, 49–50; frequents health resorts, 50–51; baptized, 51–52; on ill health as Divine punishment, 51–53; on New York City, 53–54; reading taste, 53, 55; and recreation, 54; court-martial duty, 54–55; at West Point, 54–55; favors Compromise of 1850, 55; on death of Cummins Jackson, 55; studies Napoleon's campaigns, 55; ordered to Florida, 55–57; contrasted with W. H. French, 57–58; duties in Flor-

ida, 57–70; on official prerogatives, 60–63; troubles with W. H. French, 60–70; religious study in Florida, 64; candidacy for position at VMI, 70; reasons for accepting VMI professorship, 70–72; how selected for VMI position, 72–73; reports for duty at VMI, 73–74; in command of VMI cadet corps, 74–75; and discipline, 75–76, 78–79; quarters at VMI, 76; duties at VMI, 76–77; study routine at VMI, 77; cadet opinion of, 78–82; criticized as teacher, 80–81; fears losing job, 80–81; seeks position at U. of Va., 81; wants teaching investigated by board, 81; in Lexington society, 84–86; no musical talent, 85, 109–110; joins Presbyterian Church, 86–87; principles of, command respect, 87–88; attitude toward Christian duty, 88–89; handsome, 89; sleeps in church, 89; and the ladies, 89–90; loves Ellie Junkin, 90–91; on own appearance, 91; woos Ellie, 91–95; lovers' quarrel, 95; on Mary Anna Morrison, 95; married to Ellie, 95–96; takes Maggie along on honeymoon, 97–98; on Battle of the Plains of Abraham, 97–98; on sanctity of Sabbath, 98; on Ellie, 98; social life, 99–100; and Laura's religion, 101; character influenced by Ellie, 102; public speaker, 102–103; a Democrat, 103; grief after Ellie's death, 105–110; fond of Maggie, 108; collects for Bible Society, 109; his Sunday school for Negroes, 109–110; owns slaves, 110, 120; a bank director, 111; and slavery controversy, 111; investments, 111; European tour, 111–112; visits Mary Anna Morrison in North Carolina, 113; love letters, 113–114; on Sunday mails, 114, 152, 446; marriage to Mary Anna Morrison, 114–116; buys house in Lexington, 117–118; his library, 118; daily routine (1857–1861), 117–119; farm near Lexington, 118; Deacon of Presbyterian Church, 119; birth and death of daughter, 120; playfulness at home, 121; tutors nephew, 122–124; describes hanging of John Brown, 125–126; on state of Union after Brown's death, 126–128; votes for Breckinridge, 128; eager to preserve Union, 128–129; proposes united peace prayers, 129; preparations for war, 129–130; saddened at departure of Dr. Junkin, 130; addresses cadets on when to "draw the sword," 130–131; commands cadets on march to Richmond, 131–134; on R. E. Lee, 134; on Winfield

Scott, 134; in Virginia Engineer Corps, 134–135; transferred to line and sent to command Harpers Ferry, 135–136; problems at Harpers Ferry, 137–138; drills men, 138, 140; fortifies Harpers Ferry, 139; nicknamed "Old Jack," 140; tactics at Harpers Ferry, 140–141; rebuked for invading Maryland, 141; buys Little Sorrel, 142; on holding northwestern Virginia, 143; relieved of Harpers Ferry command, 143–145; as brigade commander, 145–146; on Stonewall Brigade, 145, 164; attacks B & O railroad, 148; in action at Falling Waters, Va., 149–151; on Jeb Stuart, 151; promoted to brigadier general, 151–152; en route to Manassas, 154–155; praised by Beauregard, 164; church contribution after Manassas, 167; on morale, 170; requests leave from VMI for duration of war, 170–171; promoted to major general, PACS, 173; assigned to command Valley District, 174–175; initial problems faced in Shenandoah Valley, 175–179; farewell to Stonewall Brigade, 175–177; Stonewall Brigade sent him, 178–179; organizes Valley Army, 179; attacks Dam No. 5, 182; Anna visits him in Winchester, 183–196; his staff (1861–1862), 184–185; and whisky on Romney march, 187; prefers charges vs. William Gilham, 190; tenders resignation because of interference by Secretary of War, 192; results of his offer to resign, 192–195; withdraws resignation, 195; prefers charges vs. W. W. Loring, 195; offensive-defensive, 198; on importance of Shenandoah Valley, 199; on councils of war, 199–200; abandons Winchester, 200–201; routine in the field, 201–202; nicknamed "Old Blue Light," 202; and conscientious objectors, 203; on Sunday fighting, 204–205, 250; anecdote of geography of Shenandoah Valley, 208–209; prefers charges vs. R. B. Garnett, 211–212; on Gen. Taliaferro, 212–213; on ingredients of generalship, 213; personnel problems, 213–214; on Turner Ashby, 214–216; reorganizes army, 211–219; needs reinforcements, 219–223, 261; security measures on march, 227–228; nicknamed "Fool Tom," 228; issues historic marching orders, 232–233; praises VMI cadets, 233; and lemons, 237, 266, 308; on Richard Taylor's brigade, 237; homesickness, 239, 287; dubbed the "wagon hunter," 248–249,

250, 264; on pillaging by Ashby's men, 248; eager to capture enemy property, 248–249; on ladies of Winchester, 249; reasons for hard marching, 250, 256; needs cavalry, 253–254; visits in Winchester, 255–256; uses engineering in defense, 259; matures as field commander, 261; dines at Maj. Hawks's, 262; on why he did not drink, 263; and bravery of Tom Strother, 266, 270–271; anecdote of inquisitive private, 267–268; restricted opportunity, 272; praised by President Davis, 272; meets Sir Percy Wyndham, 272–273; estimate of Turner Ashby, 273; on reasons for Shields's failure to advance, 277; advocates offensive, 285; ordered to Richmond, 285–290; relaxes, 286; anecdote of his troops concerning, 291; on Hood's attack at Gaines' Mill, 309; on McClellan's intentions after Malvern, 322; confers with Lee after Malvern, 323–324; reconnoiters Harrison's Landing with Lee, 325; advocates offensive beyond Potomac, 328–329; opinion of Lee—willing to "follow him blindfolded," 329; detached to attack Pope, 329–332; considered a Roundhead, 331; anecdote of the oat field, 331–332; hears "Dixie" played, 332; prayers described, 333; distrusts Gen. Beverley Robertson, 335; use of spies, 336; "partnership" with Lee begins, 337; respected by Federals, 342, 389; urged to go to rear during action, 342; asks aid of Jeb Stuart, 343; on death of Gen. C. S. Winder, 344; reconnoiters Pope's position near Clark's Mountain, 347; as Wing Commander, 348; concern for Early at Warrenton Springs, 350–351; on quality of his troops, 355; on death of Willy Preston, 369; and wounded soldier at Second Manassas, 371; receives prayers of Lexington Presbytery, 373; on value of celerity, 375; troubles with A. P. Hill, 375, 377, 382, 407–409, 440–442; crosses into Maryland, 376; almost captured, 382; surrenders to admirers, 383–384; sees D. X. Junkin at Harpers Ferry, 388–389; recommendations for promotion, 405; development as commander, 406; promoted to lieutenant general, 406–407; and his staff, 377, 407; receives new coat from Jeb Stuart, 409–410; visits in Winchester, 414–417; as commander of Second Corps, ANV, 415–432; marches to Fredericksburg, 416–420; on birth of his daughter, Julia, 418–419; alter-

cation with Lee over artillery, 421–422; on quality of his troops, 428; establishes headquarters at Moss Neck, 435–454; evaluation of, as general, 437–438; daily routine at Moss Neck, 438; model partnership with Lee, 438; prepares reports of battles, 438, 442–443; personnel problems, 440–445; on historians, 443; enjoys hymns, 445, 491; establishes Chaplains' Association in his corps, 445–446; diplomacy of, 447; affection for Janie Corbin, 448–451; visits around Moss Neck, 449; leaves Moss Neck, 451; brings family to Yerby's, 451–454; sees daughter for first time, 452; photographed at Yerby's, 454; thinks of being with Ellie in heaven, 454; meets Lee for last time, 468; on Confederate military weakness, 470; last dispatch to Lee, 472; excitement in battle, 476; wounded at Chancellorsville, 478–483; arm amputated, 484; in corps hospital, 484–487; praised by Lee for victory at Chancellorsville, 486; moved to Guiney's Station, 487–488; on Hooker's strategy at Chancellorsville, 488; last days, 488–494

BATTLES:
Troop strength and casualties, 138, 140, 151, 166, 176, 178, 188, 195–198, 204, 208, 215, 219–220, 223, 229–230, 236, 239, 243, 254, 265, 277, 282, 285, 299, 308, 321, 330, 336, 340, 344, 362, 365–366, 368–369, 394, 397–398, 402, 417, 437, 468

Cedar Mountain, 337–345; evaluation of conduct of battle, 344–345; congratulated by Lee, 345

Chancellorsville, 458–488; first day, 458–465; tactics, 458–478; first conference with Lee, 463–465; second day, 465–484; detached on flank march, 465–467; second conference with Lee, 467–468; decides to attack with whole corps, 467–468; flank march, 468–473; attacks, 474–476; strategy, 488

Chantilly (Ox Hill), 373

Fredericksburg, 420–432; on Confederate positions, 420; reconnoiters front with Lee, 425; reconnoiters his own front, 426; advocates attack, 427; tactics, 428–432; advocates attack, 457

Harpers Ferry Expedition, 380–392; operations against town, 384–387; tactical use of artillery, 384–387; use of semaphore signals, 384–387; demands unconditional surrender, 387; prisoners and captured stores, 388

Kernstown, 204–208; moves against Gen. Shields, 204;

strategy, 204–205; strategic results of battle, 208; evaluation of Jackson as commander after battle, 211; receives thanks of Confederate Congress for, 217
First Manassas, 158–164; first position at, 158; moves to Confederate left, 159–160; in position on Henry House hill, 159–161; receives sobriquet of "Stonewall," 161; use of artillery, 161–164; tactics, 161–164; wounded, 161, 164; attacks, 163–164; eager to pursue, 166–167; evaluation of, in campaign of First Manassas, 173–174
Second Manassas, 353–371; ordered to march behind Pope, 352; march to Manassas, 353–358; strategy, 357, 361–362; in Groveton action, 364–366; in battle of Second Manassas, 366–371; tactics, 366–371
Romney Expedition, 180–190; submits plan for, 180–181; preparations for, 181–186; march to Romney, 186–190; tactics, 188; delays encountered, 188–189; unpopular with troops, 189; plans to hold Romney, 189–190; evaluation of tactical dispositions, 195–196
Seven Days' Battles, 290–322; en route to Richmond, 290–301; rides to conference with Lee, 293–294; in conference with Lee, 294–298; slow progress to opening battle, 298–300; element of surprise, 300–301; begins attack, 301–302; overcautious, 302–303; confers with Lee, 304; in battle of Gaines' Mill, 305–309; delay at Grapevine Bridge, 310–312; at White Oak Swamp, 314–317; delay at White Oak Swamp, 316–317; in battle of Malvern Hill, 318–322; ordered to rear by Lee at Malvern, 319; physical fatigue during Seven Days, 299–301, 312–313, 315–317, 321, 327
Sharpsburg (Antietam), 392–400; reconnoiters his front, 393–394; considers diversionary attack, 397–399; feels invulnerable, protected by Providence, 399; on advisability of fighting at Sharpsburg, 400
Shepherdstown (Boteler's Ford), 402–403
Valley Campaign, 219–284; plans attack on Banks, 219–220; concentrates against Milroy, 220; three plans of attack in Shenandoah Valley, 223–224; moves against Milroy, 225–227; battle of McDowell, 227–230; pursues Milroy, 230–231; congratulates troops, 231; on Federal rear guard tactics, 231; marches against Banks, 232–233; evaluation of Banks's intentions, 233–234; decision to attack Front Royal, 237–238; moves against Front Royal, 238; strategy, 239–240; tactics, 239–244; directs cavalry charge, 243–244; strategy after Front Royal, 246–247; pursues Banks to Winchester, 247–251; battle of Winchester, 250–253; chastises Taylor for swearing, 252; cheers victory, 253; pursues Banks, 253–255; forces change in Federal plans, 257–283; advances to threaten Harpers Ferry, 260; prepares to retreat, 260–262; begins retreat up valley, 262; arrests officer for debacle at Front Royal, 262–263; abandons Winchester, 264–265; reaches Strasburg, 265; estimate of situation at Strasburg, 265–266; halts Fremont's advance, 265–266; eludes Lincoln's trap, 266; retreats from Strasburg, 267; strategic considerations, 268–270; reasons for moving on Port Republic, 270; strategic and tactical importance of position at Port Republic, 271; care of wagon train, 274; barely escapes capture, 275–276; at battle of Cross Keys, 277; reasons for attacking Shields, 277–278; proposes time schedule, 278; supervises construction of temporary bridge over South River, 278–279; strategic considerations at Port Republic, 278–279; fights battle of Port Republic, 279–283; tactics, 279–283; fails to reconnoiter, 280; tactics changed to exclude attack on Fremont, 281; victory at God's hands, 282, 284; strategic results of Valley Campaign, 284
DESCRIPTIONS OF: 331, 413–414
as a boy, 5; on entering West Point, 13–14; in 1848, 45; in Florida, 57–58; on arrival at VMI, 74–75; in Lexington, 85; in 1853, 94; dressing for wedding, 115; in early 1862, 202; at beginning of Seven Days' Battles, 295
FAME: 1, 171, 290, 327, 376, 383, 411–415, 447–448
HEALTH: 7, 9, 17, 26, 46, 48–55, 59, 64, 66, 73–74, 76–77, 85–86, 112, 119–120, 122–123, 127, 138, 149, 152, 250, 327, 453
HUMOR: 202–203, 267–268, 449
MILITARY ADMINISTRATION: 149, 167–172, 185, 190–191, 199, 201–203, 256–257, 335–336, 404–405, 437–444
MILITARY CHARACTERISTICS:
aggressiveness, 148–149, 179–180, 207, 219–220, 235, 261, 467–468
attention to needs of troops, 167–168, 201, 403–404, 439
audacity, 196, 268–270, 280, 354
bravery, 38, 161–162, 320
concern for stores and trains, 219–220, 225, 265–267, 343–344, 357–361
conserves manpower, 200, 205
criteria for promotion, 212–213
dedication to duty, 168–169, 171, 440
determination, 144, 206–207, 251–252, 267, 290, 367–368, 385, 469–470, 478
discipline, 171–172, 179, 185, 211–212, 216–217, 236, 333–335, 348–349, 404, 439–440
energy, 144, 181, 188
logistics, 199, 236, 293
personal leadership in battle, 207, 249, 341–342, 414
popular with his troops, 404, 434
pursuit of defeated foe, 164, 230, 234, 243–244, 253–254, 342
reconnoiters, 160–161, 185, 251, 311
secrecy, 146, 184, 219–220, 224, 226–227, 238–239, 247, 250, 256, 262, 269, 279, 288–289, 291–294, 337, 362
Spartan life in field, 404
speed of marching, 232–233, 354, 374–375
straggling, measures against, 237, 256, 425
strategy, 179–181, 223–224, 257–259, 268–270, 288
subordination, 167
surprise, 240–247, 260
tactics, 190, 205–207, 223, 242–243, 251–253, 306–309, 314–316, 339–345, 420
PERSONAL CHARACTERISTICS:
ambition, 25, 58, 64, 289–290, 334
anger, 324–325
concentration, 16–17
determination, 13–15, 17, 72
discretion, 25
excited in battle, 281
finesse, 413–414
honesty, 7–8, 12, 79, 86
humility, 30, 78–79
modesty, 166, 411
seriousness, 86
shyness, 7–8, 85, 377, 383–384, 415
stamina, 248–250
RELIGIOUS NATURE: 10, 30, 43–44, 51–53, 87–89, 93–94, 99, 102, 105–110, 118, 171–173, 178, 190, 202, 213, 218, 223, 231–232, 234–235, 246, 255, 272–273, 277, 279, 286–287, 301, 305, 313, 333–334, 344, 369, 378, 386, 388, 399, 411, 416, 445–447, 459, 482, 485–486, 489
Jackson, Warren, 2, 4, 9–10, 101
Jackson, Col. William L., CSA, 290–291
Jackson's (Prospect) Hill, 424, 426, 429

Jackson's Mill, Va., 5–7, 9, 19
Jalapa, Mexico, 26, 29–31
James River, 307, 310, 329, 346
Jeffersonton, Va., 352, 354
John (Jackson's handy man), 448
Johnson, Col. Bradley T., CSA, 412–413
Johnson, Gen. Edward, CSA, 185, 190, 220, 224–230, 264, 456
Johnson, Samuel, 290
Johnston, Gen. Albert Sidney, CSA, 197
Johnston, Gen. Joseph E., CSA, 143–167, 169–170, 172, 174–176, 178–181, 189–190, 193–196, 198, 204, 208, 211–213, 219, 226, 235, 237–238, 262, 272, 284; description of, 143
Jomini, 140, 288
Jones, Gen. David Rumple, CSA, 16, 158–159, 312, 397–399
Jones, Gen. J. R., CSA, 386, 394–395
Jones, John Paul, 419
Jones, Roger, Adjt. Gen., USA, 69
Jones, Gen. Sam, CSA, 172
Jones, Gen. William E. ("Grumble"), CSA, 343
Joshua, 489
Julia (nurse in household of Maj. W. H. French), 64–67
Junkin, David X., 388–389
Junkin, Rev. Dr. George, 84, 95, 100, 102, 104, 107, 388; his impression of Jackson, 91–92; marries Ellie and Jackson, 96; on Jackson's religious nature, 99, 108; resigns as President of Washington College, 131
Junkin, George, 382, 388–389; on Jackson's staff, 184
Junkin, Julia (Ellie's mother), 100–101
Junkin, Julia (Ellie's sister), 103

Kanawha River, 181
Kansas, 103, 111, 124
Kate Hunter, army transport, 57
Kearny, Gen. Phil, USA, 373
Kelley, Gen. Benjamin F., USA, 180, 188
Kelly's Ford, Va., 451
Kemper House, 275
Kenly, Col. John R., USA, 242–244
Kentucky, 197
Kernstown, Va., 200, 218, 237, 333, 336, 365, 416, 438; battle of, 204–207, 217
Kerr, Maggie, 86
Kester, Conrad, 7–8
Keyes, Gen. E. D., USA, 160
King, Gen. Rufus, USA, 364–365
Kyle, David J., 476–477

Lacy, Rev. Dr. Drury, 115
Lacy, Rev. Tucker, 446, 452–453, 455, 466, 485–487, 489
Lafayette College, 91
Laidley, Theodore T. S., 72
Lake Chalco, 32–33
Lake Texcoco, 32–33
Lake Tohopekaliga, 59, 60
Lake Xochimilco, 32–33

Lander, Gen. Frederick W., USA, 191, 196
Lane, Gen. James, CSA, 426, 431, 477
Law, Col. Evander M., CSA, 289
Lawley, Francis C., 413
Lawton, Gen. Alexander R., CSA, 285–286, 289, 292–293, 301, 307–308, 350, 365–366, 373, 383, 386, 394–395
Lebanon Springs, Va., 234
Lee, Edwin, 149
Lee, Gen. Fitzhugh, CSA, 347, 464, 471–472
Lee, Gen. Richard Henry ("Light Horse Harry"), 134
Lee, Gen. Robert E., CSA, 1, 13, 27–28, 34–35, 37, 81, 124, 134, 136, 138–139, 141, 143–145, 147, 152, 179, 181–182, 215, 220, 223–224, 228, 233–234, 238, 260, 273–274, 284–288, 290–291, 293, 319, 323–325, 328–331, 337, 344–349, 352, 354, 357, 360, 362, 366, 369, 371–374, 376–381, 384, 387–390, 392–409, 411, 413–414, 417–432, 434, 437, 439–442, 444, 448–451, 453, 455–489; on Jackson, 284; conference on strategy at High Meadows, 294–298; Seven Days' Battles, 300–322; confers with Jackson, 304; orders Jackson to stay at Grapevine Bridge, 312; on A. P. Hill, 335; "partnership" with Jackson begins, 337; on the "indomitable Jackson," 391; model relationship with Jackson, 438; meets Jackson for last time, 468; on Jackson as executive officer, 486; on losing his "right arm," 489, 492; description of, 295
Lee, Col. Stephen D., CSA, 370
Lee's Hill, 424, 426–427
Leesburg, Va., 198, 259, 374
Leigh, Capt. Benjamin, CSA, 480–481
Letcher, Gov. John (Va.), 131, 134–136, 144, 172, 192–195, 330
Letterman, Jonathan, 66, 69
Lewis, Gen., 225, 275
Lewis, Jim (Jackson's personal servant), 230, 293, 303, 321, 325, 338–339, 348, 353, 368–369, 382, 409, 448, 457, 492
Lewis, Julia, 86
Lewis, William, 86
Lewis's Ford, 158
"Lewiston," 225, 275, 277, 279–280, 282
Lexington, Va., 70–132, 146, 167, 170–172, 192, 202, 208, 218, 313, 338, 373, 389, 414, 487, 494; description of, 83–84; social life in, 83–86; feels tension of secession crisis, 127–132
Lexington Presbytery, 110, 373
Liberty Mills, Va., 336
Lightburn, Joe, 10
Lincoln, Abraham, 128, 245–246, 257–266, 326, 378, 422
"Literary Fund" of Virginia, 10

Little Sorrel, 142, 176–177, 186, 189, 200–201, 206–207, 226, 231–232, 242, 249, 252–253, 265, 331, 341, 348, 351, 375, 383, 412, 417, 426, 451, 454, 457–458, 463, 470, 472, 474, 476–479
Lobos, Island of, 23
Logistics, 23, 25, 236, 447
London Times, 413
Long, Col. A. L., CSA, 466–467
Longbridge road, 310
Longstreet, Gen. James, CSA, 16, 158–159, 172, 294, 298, 302–304, 306–307, 310–311, 314, 316–318, 320, 323–325, 330, 345–346, 348–349, 354, 357, 366, 369–370, 374, 376–377, 380–381, 390–391, 399, 403, 405–406, 417, 420–422, 427, 430, 434, 437, 450, 454, 456; opinion of Jackson and his men, 298, 345–346; description of, 295
Longstreet, Mrs. James, 450
Loring, Gen. William W., CSA, 178, 180–182, 184, 186, 188–190, 193, 195–196, 204, 212
Los Reyes, Mexico, 32
Loudoun Heights, 139, 262, 380, 384–387
Louisa Court House, 332
Louisiana "Tigers," 242, 247, 272, 303, 308
Luray, Va., 209, 219, 238–239
Luray Gap, 238, 417
Luray Valley, 209, 236, 239, 249, 263, 269
Lyle, John B., 84, 85–87, 119

McCally, Dr. James, 3
McCann's Run, Va., 8
McClellan, Gen. George B., USA, 16, 54, 72, 180, 197, 203, 226, 257–285, 290–292, 294–296, 298–322, 324–325, 328, 337, 346, 349, 352, 357, 362, 378, 380, 389–392, 394–403, 410, 417, 465
McDonald, Col. Angus W., CSA, 176
McDowell, Gen. Irvin, USA, 155–164, 226, 245, 257–261, 264, 288, 292, 326
McDowell, Gov. James, 84, 89
McDowell, Mrs. James, 84
McDowell, Va., 232–233
McDowell, Battle of, 229–230
McFarland, Rev. Dr. Francis, 172
McGaheysville, Va., 221, 227
McGuire, Capt. Hugh, CSA, 435
McGuire, Dr. Hunter H., 190–191, 200–201, 207, 368–369, 371, 450, 479, 483–485, 487–489, 492, 494; characterized, 218
McLaws, Gen. Lafayette, CSA, 374, 380, 384–387, 390, 393, 396–397, 457–459, 461–462, 468
McLean's Ford, 158
Madison Court House, Va., 209, 222, 339, 417–418
Magruder, Gen. John B., CSA, 31, 34–41, 43, 296, 298, 310–314, 317–318, 320–321

Malvern Hill, 317–321, 323–324, 337, 463
Manassas, Va., 292
Manassas, First Battle of, 155–169, 171, 201, 371, 488
Manassas, Second Battle of, 366–371, 399, 405–406, 437
Manassas Gap, 209
Manassas Gap Railroad, 155, 163, 209, 259, 355
Manassas Junction, 136, 152, 209, 356–362
Marion, Francis, 10
Martinsburg, Va., 139–140, 148–149, 151–152, 189, 253–254, 257, 260, 383, 402–403, 409, 411
Marye's Heights, 420, 422, 424, 430
Maryland, 141, 240–244, 257, 285, 328, 346, 353, 373–400, 403–404, 406, 437
Maryland, First Infantry Regiment (CS), 240–244
Maryland, First Infantry Regiment (US), 240–244
Maryland Heights, 139, 141, 260, 380, 384–385, 389–390
Mason, Cadet, 79
Mason, Capt. C. R., CSA, 311
Mason, James M., 145
Massanutton Mountain, 209, 224, 236, 238–239, 265, 267, 269, 284, 286, 292, 301, 417
Massie, Capt. J. W., 130
Maury, Gen. Dabney H., CSA, 14, 16–17, 19, 54–55
Meade, Gen. George Gordon, USA, 429–430
Mechanicsville, Va., 298, 303–304, 331
Mechum River Station, Va., 209, 225–226, 228–229, 272, 290–291
Meem, Gen., CSA, 189–190
Meem's Bottom, 268
Methodist Home Mission Society, gives life membership to Jackson, 447
Mexicalcingo, Mexico, 32
Mexican War, 19–44, 61, 80, 92, 134, 374
Mexico, 18–19, 45, 57, 72, 88
Mexico City, 22–23, 25–26, 29–30, 32–40, 48, 243
Miami University, 91
Middletown, Md., 381
Middletown, Va., 245–248, 256
Miles, Col. Dixon S., USA, 387
Miles, William P., 213
Millwood, Va., 154
Milroy, Gen. Robert H., USA, 220, 226, 228–231, 235, 237
Mississippi, 423
Mississippi River, 9, 20
Mitchell's Ford, 158
Mixcoac, Mexico, 36
Molino del Rey, 36–37
Monongahela River, 2, 7
Monroe, James, 419
Monterey, Mexico, 20, 22
Monterey, Va., 180
Montreal, Canada, 54, 97
Moorefield, Va., 258, 264
Moorman's battery, CSA, 476–477

Morrison, Eugenia (Anna Jackson's sister), 94–95, 112–113, 120
Morrison, Joseph, 377–378, 388, 455–456, 461, 477–478, 481–482, 485, 493
Morrison, Rev. Robert Hall, 94, 113, 115
Morrison, Mrs. Robert Hall, 113
Morrison, Dr. S. B., 489, 493
Morrison, William, 115
Mosby, Col. John S., CSA, 336
Moss Neck, Va., 434–436, 487
Mount Crawford, Va., 267
Mount Jackson, Va., 199, 201, 203, 209, 236, 267–268
Mount Meridian, Va., 274, 287
Mount Solon, Va., 235
Mountain road, 477–478
Munford, Col. Thomas T., CSA, 74–76, 78, 314–316, 335, 356, 469–470, 472
Myers, Capt. G. W., 275

Napoleon, 18, 55, 166, 181, 189, 199, 201, 259, 288, 414
National Palace (Mexico City), 42
National Road, Mexico, 23, 25, 27–28
Natural Bridge, Va., 83, 103
Neale, Alfred (uncle of Jackson), 9
Neale, Mrs. Alfred, 106, 126
Neale, Thomas (grandfather of Jackson), 2
Nebraska, 103
Neff, Col. John, CSA, 251–252, 365
Negro Sunday School (Lexington), 109–110, 119, 167, 338
Negroes, 110, 120, 311, 404
New Bridge, 310
New Jersey, 359
New Market, Va., 209, 219, 223–224, 228, 233, 236, 238, 265, 267–268
New Mexico, 197
New Orleans, La., 20, 45, 65, 68, 91
New York, 19, 49, 73, 97, 115, 120
New York Mercury, 202–203
Newtown, Va., 200, 207–208, 248–249, 266
Niagara Falls, 54, 97, 115–116
North Anna River, 419–420
North Carolina, 130, 285, 356, 451, 454, 478, 494
North Carolina, Twenty-seventh Infantry Regiment, 397
Northampton, Mass., 127
Northrop, Col. Lucius B., CSA, 184–185
Nottingham, the Misses, 84
Numbers (of troops), 32, 35, 39–40, 138, 140, 145, 148, 153, 156, 158, 160, 172, 180–181, 198, 204, 207, 219–220, 227, 229, 236, 245–246, 255, 257, 260–261, 265, 280, 284, 299–300, 302, 307, 309, 313, 329, 340, 344, 346–347, 359, 366, 374, 379, 388, 391–393, 397, 399, 420, 422, 428, 432, 456, 459, 468

Occoquan River, 156
Ohio River, 9, 20, 179, 181
Old Turnpike, 458–459, 462, 466, 471–473, 476
O'Neal, Gen. Edward, CSA, 473
Opequon Creek, 148, 403
Orange and Alexandria Railroad, 351, 355–356
Orange Court House, Va., 329, 337–338, 343, 417–418, 458
Orizaba, 29
Orlean, Va., 354
Orr's Rifles, 431
Osborne, Mrs., 418

Padierna, 34–36
Palo Alto, Tex., 23
Pamunkey River, 286, 296
Paris, France, 111–112
Paris, Va., 154–155
Parkersburg, Va., 2, 5, 9, 180
Parkersburg & Staunton Turnpike Co., 9
Parrott, Capt. Robert P., 129
Patterson, Gen. Robert, USA, 23, 29, 147–150, 152, 153
Patton, Col. J. M., CSA, 268, 278
Paxton, Gen. Elisha Franklin, CSA, 377–378, 405, 439, 441, 443–444, 472, 486
Peace River, 57
Peaked Mountain, 270
Pedregal, the, 33–35
Pelham, Maj. John, CSA, 428–430, 451
Pender, Gen. W. Dorsey, CSA, 386–387, 427, 479, 481–482
Pendleton, Alexander ("Sandie"), 149, 178, 184, 202–203, 254–255, 267, 319, 330–331, 347–348, 396, 417, 438–439, 442–443, 449, 465, 484–485; believes Jackson's secrecy indicates he's "crazy," 279; characterized, 218
Pendleton, Gen. William Nelson, CSA, 150–151, 162, 319, 401–403, 421, 448–449
Pennsylvania, 46, 153, 273, 285, 379, 410
Perote, Mexico, 30–31
Philadelphia, Pa., 105, 115–116
Pickett, Gen. George Edward, CSA, 16, 456; faith in Jackson, 414
Piedmont, Va., 155
Pierce, Gen. Franklin, USA, 32, 43
Pikes, 217
Pillow, Gen. Gideon J., USA, 28, 33–35, 37, 40–41
Pittsburgh, Pa., 20
Plains of Abraham, Battle of, 97–98
Plan del Rio, Mexico, 27
Plank Road, 458–459, 461–463, 467–468, 470–472, 476–478
Plattsburg, N.Y. 54
Poague, Col. W. T., CSA, 251, 276, 359, 387
Poindexter farm, 318–320, 323
Point Isabel, Tex., 20–23
Point of Rocks, Va., 140, 147
Polk, James K. (President of US), 21–22

Pope, Gen. John, USA, 326–327, 329–330, 332, 335–338, 343, 345–352, 354, 357, 361–362, 365–373, 378, 406, 437, 458

Port Republic, Va., 224–225, 227, 268–272, 274–283, 286, 288, 310, 339

Port Royal, Va., 420, 422, 434, 436

Porter, Gen. Fitz-John, USA, 16, 160, 306–309

"Portici" House, 163

Potomac River, 135, 138–140, 147, 156, 179–181, 188–189, 196, 238, 253–254, 260–262, 284, 345, 355, 373, 375–376, 379–380, 383–384, 386, 390–393, 397, 399–403, 410, 417

Powhite Creek, 304, 306

Presbyterian Church, Lexington, Va., 84, 86–87

Preston, Col. J. F., CSA, 151, 162

Preston, Col. J. T. L., CSA, 84, 116, 130–131, 137, 144, 178, 184–185, 203, 233, 334, 369, 445

Preston, Margaret Junkin ("Maggie"), 84, 91, 97–99, 105–108, 112–113, 116–117, 131, 203, 273, 369, 454; on Jackson's character, 87, 92; description of, 96

Preston, Will, 369, 372

Price, Maj. Channing, CSA, 462

Puebla, Mexico, 31–32

Pughtown, Va., 186–187

Quebec, Canada, 54, 97–98

Quitman, Gen. John A., USA, 33, 37, 39

Railroads as military transportation, 133, 136, 155, 163, 293, 330

Ramseur, Gen. Stephen D., CSA, 459, 461, 473

Randall, James R., 507

Randolph, Gen. George W., CSA, 405

Rapidan River, 219, 292, 338, 347, 392, 458

Rappahannock River, 347, 349–350, 353–354, 356–357, 361, 392, 419–420, 422, 424, 427, 429, 432, 434, 455–458, 467, 489

Ratchford, Dr. Fannie E., 529

Ray, Robert P., 8

Reid, Cadet Legh W., 81–82

Republican party, 127

Richardson, Col. I. B., USA, 158

Richardson, Gen. William H., 80, 170–171

Richmond, Va., 3, 47–48, 73, 83, 115, 124, 133–134, 136–138, 140–144, 152, 174, 184–185, 193, 195, 199, 204, 212, 217–219, 225–226, 228, 230, 234–235, 238, 258–259, 261, 263, 271–274, 284–285, 287, 291–296, 298–300, 309, 326–327, 329–330, 333, 346, 379, 409, 419, 434, 438, 452, 455, 464, 485, 493

Richmond, Fredericksburg and Potomac Railroad, 425, 487

Richmond Stage Road, 424, 428, 455

Ricketts's battery, USA, 162

Rio, Martinez del, 42

Rio Grande, 22

Roanoke, Va., 83

Roanoke Island, 197

Robertson, Gen. Beverley H., CSA, 335, 338, 343

Robinson, James, 161

Robinson, "Uncle," 5

Rockbridge Alum Springs, Va., 76, 83, 116

Rockbridge Artillery, CSA, 162, 369, 416–417

Rockfish Gap, 227, 290

"Rockingham Rebellion," 217

Rodes, Gen. Robert E., CSA, 450, 456, 458–459, 468–476, 480, 484

Rodes, Mrs. Robert E., 450

Romney, Va., 149, 178, 180–181, 186–193, 195, 199, 201, 226, 237, 240, 261, 324, 365, 443

Rosecrans, Gen. William S., USA, 16, 72, 179

"Round Hill Water Cure," 127

Rude's Hill, 212, 215, 218

Ruffin, Edmund, 125

Ruggles, William B., 520

St. John's Church, Richmond, 109

Salem, Va., 355

Saltillo, Mexico, 21–23

San Agustin, Mexico, 33–34

San Antonio, hacienda, 33–35

San Cosmé garita, 36, 39–40

Santa Anna, Gen. Antonio Lopez de, 22, 24–28, 32, 34–38

Saratoga, N.Y., 115

Savage Station, Va., 311, 313

Saxton, Gen. Rufus, USA, 260–261, 264

Schenck, Gen. Robert C., USA, 229–230

Scotland, 111

Scott, Gen. Winfield, USA, 22–29, 31–40, 69, 134; praises Jackson, 40–41; lessons learned from his campaigns, 44

Second Artillery (US), 58

Second Cavalry (US), 124

Second Corps, ANV, 415–418, 420–422, 425, 427, 434, 436–442, 444, 446–447, 451, 453–454, 456–458, 461, 467–469, 471–472, 474, 476, 478, 480, 482–484, 486–487; artillery in, 421, 425, 428, 468, 473

Second US Infantry, 24

Secretary of War, CSA, 214, 218

Sedgwick, Gen. John, USA, 467

Seminole Indians, 56–59, 63

Seven Pines, Battle of, 421

Seventh US Infantry, 24

Seymour, Truman, 16

Shakespeare, William, 43

Sharpsburg, Md., 381, 383, 389–394, 399–400, 405–406

Sharpsburg, Battle of, 394–400

Shealy, Pvt. Noah, CSA, 372

Shenandoah River, 135, 154, 209, 221, 224, 238–240, 267–269, 271, 274–275, 277, 380, 386

Shepherdstown, Va., 140–141, 188, 398, 402–403

Sherman, Gen. William T., USA, 160

Shields, Gen. James, USA, 28–29, 196, 203, 205–207, 235, 238, 260, 262–265, 267, 269, 271–272, 274–275, 277–278, 280–281, 284, 287, 294, 346; in Battle of Port Republic, 277–283

Sierra Madre, 21

Silverwood, A Book of Memories (by Margaret Junkin), 108

Sitlington's Hill, 229

Skinker's Neck, Va., 422

Slaughter's Mountain (see Cedar Mountain)

Smead, Col. Abner, CSA, 262

Smith, Gen. E. K., CSA, 16, 155, 163–164, 172

Smith, Col. Francis H., 70, 72–73, 80, 84, 103, 111, 120, 125–126, 130–131, 233

Smith, Gen. Gustavus W., CSA, 72, 172

Smith, Capt. James P., CSA, 407, 416–417, 430, 433–435, 448–449, 452, 455, 479–482, 484–489, 492

Smith, Gen. Persifor F., USA, 23–24, 34–35, 37

Smithfield, Va., 196

South Carolina, 128, 316, 368

South Mountain, 379, 381, 386, 390, 392

Spencer, John C., US Secretary of War, 13

Sperryville, Va., 209, 224

Spotsylvania Court House, Va., 487

Stafford, Col. Leroy A., CSA, 396

Stafford Heights, 419, 422, 427, 457

Stanardsville, Va., 221–222

Stannard's battery, CSA, 162

Stanton, Edwin M., 246, 257

Starke, Gen. William E., CSA, 365–366, 369–370, 373, 383, 395

Staunton, Va., 125, 133, 180–182, 184–185, 217, 219–220, 223–224, 226–229, 233, 236, 264, 269, 271, 286, 288–290, 404, 447–448

Steuart, Gen. George H. ("Maryland"), CSA, 247, 255, 277

Stevens, Gen. I. I., USA, 373

Stewart, Gen. Alexander P., CSA, 72

Stiles, Rev. Joseph C., 416

Stone Bridge, 158–160, 362, 364, 371

Stoneman, Gen. George, USA, 16

Stonewall Brigade, 145, 147–151, 154–164, 167–168, 170, 172, 175–179, 182, 188–190, 201, 204–207, 211–212, 216, 225, 248, 251–253, 263–267, 279–283, 287–289, 301, 308, 342, 344, 358, 364–365, 372, 386, 394, 404–405, 414, 422, 439–440, 444, 446, 450, 472, 486; praised by Jackson, 164, 166, 486–488

Strange, John B., 80
Strasburg, Va., 178, 183, 199–201, 203–204, 209, 219, 235, 238–240, 245–247, 257, 260–267, 271
Strother, Tom, bravery of, 266, 270–271
Stuart, Gen. J. E. B., CSA, 138–139, 149, 151, 153, 155, 162–163, 172, 290, 298, 302, 309, 312, 319–320, 324–325, 336, 343, 347, 349, 351–352, 356, 358, 360, 369, 377, 389, 394–399, 409–411, 418, 424–429, 434, 440, 448–449, 451, 453, 455–456, 459, 464–465, 480, 484–487
Sudley Springs Ford, 362, 366, 372
Sumner, Gen. E. V., USA, 390, 396
Superior (one of Jackson's horses), 454
Susquehanna River, 261
Swift Run Gap, 217, 219, 221, 223–224, 227–228, 232–233
Switzerland, 111

Talbott, Col. John, 8
Talcott, Col. T. M. R., CSA, 464
Taliaferro, Gen. William B., CSA, 125, 184–185, 189, 193, 212–213, 215, 236, 276–277, 279, 282, 341–342, 353, 355, 359–360, 362, 364–365, 443–444
Talley's farm, 473, 475
Talleyrand, 52
Tampa, Fla., 57, 67
Tampico, Mexico, 23
Taylor, Capt. Francis, 20, 29–30, 43–44, 46, 48, 51–52, 57
Taylor, Gen. George, USA, 21, 73, 359
Taylor, Gen. Richard, CSA, 222, 236–237, 239, 241–242, 246–254, 265–267, 270–271, 276–277, 280–283, 286, 289–290, 301, 320, 330, 356, 406
Taylor, Zachary, 20–24
Taylor's Hotel, Winchester, Va., 183
Tennessee, 197
Tepeyahualco, Mexico, 31
Texas, 73, 308–309
Thermopylae, 139, 144
Third US Infantry, 24
Thomas, Gen. E. L., CSA, 427
Thomas, Gen. George H., USA, 54
Thornton's Gap, 209
Thoroughfare Gap, 355–357, 362, 366
Tobler, Mrs., 42
Todd's Tavern, Va., 487
Toombs, Gen. Robert, CSA, 172, 397
Tower, Lt. Zealous B., USA, 27
Traveller (Lee's war horse), 376
Trent affair, 413
Trimble, Gen. Isaac R., CSA, 277–278, 282, 303, 308, 318, 321, 339, 349–350, 357–358, 364, 368, 443–444, 456; praised

by Jackson and recommended for promotion, 405
Trist, Nicholas, 36
Trousdale, Col. William, USA, 37, 40–41
Turner, Nat, insurrectionary slave, 124
Turner's Gap, 381
Twelfth Army Corps, US, 396
Twiggs, Gen. David E., USA, 23–24, 26–30, 32–35, 69–70
Tygart Valley, Va., 47
Tyler, Gen. Daniel, USA, 160
Tyler, Gen. E. B., USA, 280–283

Unger's Store, Va., 186, 188–189
Union Mills Ford, 158
US Army, 19, 21, 33, 36, 39–40, 56–70, 72
US Military Academy, 6, 12–19, 44, 52, 54, 73, 75, 77, 81, 97, 261, 295
United States Mine Ford, 458, 476–477, 488
University of Virginia, 81, 103
Utterbach, farmer, 167–170

Valencia, Gen. (Mexican Army), 34–35
Van Dorn, Gen. Earl, CSA, 172
Vera Cruz, Mexico, 23–26, 28–29, 45
Vera Cruz, state of, 29
Vilweg, Mr., 412
Virginia, 2, 9, 12; reaction to John Brown's raid, 124–125; divided opinion in, on secession, 128–131; secedes from Union, 131; in Confederacy, 145
Virginia, First Cavalry Regiment, 462
Virginia, Second Cavalry Regiment, 314–315, 469–472
Virginia, Second Infantry Regiment, 365
Virginia, Fourth Infantry Regiment, 371
Virginia, Seventh Cavalry Regiment, 343
Virginia, Tenth Infantry Regiment, 375
Virginia, Twenty-first Infantry Regiment, 365
Virginia, Twenty-seventh Infantry Regiment, 365
Virginia, Thirty-third Infantry Regiment, 365
Virginia, Fifty-eighth Infantry Regiment, 440
Virginia and Tennessee Railroad, 181–182
Virginia Central Railroad, 209, 225, 271–272, 292–293, 299–301, 333, 470
Virginia Commission for Public Defense, 129
Virginia Military Institute, 70–71, 74–82, 84, 90, 104, 111, 118, 120, 122, 125–127, 129–134, 167, 170–171, 190, 192, 227, 233, 470, 472
Virginia State Convention, 135
Vizetelly, Frank, 413

von Borcke, Maj. Heros, CSA, 409–410, 424–425, 428

Walker, James A., 79–80
Walker, Gen. John G., CSA, 374, 379–380, 384–387, 392–393, 396–397, 401
Walls, Dr., CSA, 484
Walnut Grove Church, 303–305
War Department, CSA, 178, 182, 273, 405, 438
War Department, USA, 20–21, 47, 55, 245
Wardensville, Va., 264–266
Warm Springs, Va., 76, 83, 228–229
Warrenton, Va., 153, 224, 356, 362, 364, 366
Warrenton Springs, 350
Washington, George, 131, 419
Washington, John A., 144
Washington, D.C., 56, 124–125, 140, 158, 166, 180, 182, 245, 257, 259, 262, 291–292, 296, 326, 352, 354–357, 373
Washington College, Lexington, Va., 72, 81, 84, 86, 90, 99, 104, 114, 131, 162, 167
Waterloo, Battle of, 111–112
Waterloo Bridge, 350
Waynesboro, Va., 269, 290
Webster, Daniel, 55
Weems, Parson, 10
Wellford, Col. Charles C., 466
Wellington, Duke of, 414
West View, Va., 226
Weston, Va., 7, 11–12, 14, 19–20
Weyer's Cave, 286, 289
Wheat, Maj. Roberdeau C., CSA, 242, 272, 303, 308
White, Miss B., 241
White, Hugh, 373
White, Gen. Julius, USA, 387–388
White, Sylvanus, 20
White, Rev. Dr. W. S., 84, 87–89, 110, 119, 129, 132, 167, 172–173, 334, 373
White Hall, Va., 228
White House, Va., 296, 304, 307, 309
White House Bridge, 267, 269
White Oak Swamp, 310, 313–314, 316–318, 329
White Oak Swamp Bridge, 313–317, 329
White Plains, Va., 355
White's Ford, 375
Whiting, Gen. W. H. C., CSA, 285–286, 288–290, 292–293, 301, 303, 305–307, 317–319
Wilbourn, Capt. R. E., CSA, 477–481
Wilcox, Gen. Cadmus M., CSA, 16, 19
Wilderness (Va.), 420, 456, 458, 464–467, 471, 473, 475
Wilderness Old Tavern, 483
Willcox, Gen. O. B., USA, 160
Williams, Capt., 126
Williamsburg road, 310
Williamson's, 268
Williamsport, 147–148, 181, 189, 253, 260, 264, 383
Willis, Lt. Edward, CSA, 276

Willis Church, 317–319, 324
Winchester, Va., 136, 143, 147–
148, 152–154, 175, 178–180,
182–193, 195–201, 204, 208,
215, 224, 227, 233, 242, 246–
252, 256–257, 260–262, 264–
265, 285, 333, 346, 359, 403,
412–416
Winder, Gen. Charles S., CSA,
212, 215–216, 248, 249, 251–
253, 262, 264–267, 276–282,
287–290, 300, 306–308, 334,

336–337, 339, 341–342, 344,
365; description of, 212
Wisconsin, 364–365
Wisconsin Iron Brigade, 364–365
Wise, Gov. Henry A., 124–125
Wolfe, Gen. James, 98
Wolseley, Col. Garnet, 413–414
Woodson, Capt. Blake B., 4–5
Woodson, Wirt (half-brother of
Jackson), 4, 9, 111
Woodstock, Va., 196, 265, 267
Worsham, John, 360–361

Worth, Gen. William J., USA,
21–24, 26, 30, 33, 37–40, 374
Wyndham, Sir Percy, 272
Wynn, Lt., CSA, 478–479

Yellow fever, 25–26
Yerby House, 422, 451–454
York River Railroad, 296, 298,
304, 309, 313

Zacharias, Rev. Dr., 378